W. W. AFFELDT

THE CHANGING CURRICULUM

and the

ELEMENTARY TEACHER

G. WESLEY SOWARDS
Stanford University

MARY-MARGARET SCOBEY
San Francisco State College

THE CHANGING CURRICULUM
and the
ELEMENTARY TEACHER

Wadsworth Publishing Company, Inc.
San Francisco

PREFACE

In the present atmosphere of educational reappraisal and re-examination, the authors realize that elementary school curriculum must change. They firmly believe, however, that only an educational *profession* can provide the informed leadership necessary to guide such change. This book is designed to improve the professional skills and insights of the elementary school educators who plan and execute curriculum.

The book has four parts. Each represents one area of understanding that can serve to increase the professional abilities of elementary school teachers. Part One describes the elementary school from three positions: as we know it today, as we view it in terms of its unique history, and as it appears in light of the purposes that guide its efforts.

Part Two presents the foundations upon which curriculum decisions are based. It also analyzes the various ways that school curriculum has been designed. Part Two closes with a discussion of school organization and staffing in terms of curriculum facilitation.

Part Three devotes a chapter to each of the major programs within the elementary school curriculum: receptive communication, expressive communication, the use of numbers, the social area, the natural environment, esthetics and creativity, physical and mental health. Part Four focuses upon the classroom teacher's role as the implementor of curriculum. Particular attention is given to achieving educational objectives by effectively utilizing time, space, materials, and evaluation procedures.

v

To acquaint the reader thoroughly with the nature of educational changes, the authors discuss in each of the four parts many moot questions now being raised about elementary curriculum. They take positions on many of them, encourage the reader to do the same, and make numerous suggestions for discussion and thought. It is hoped that in this way the reader will understand the "why" of much that elementary school educators are doing or are urged to do.

Special appreciation is expressed to Professors Alice Miel, John Goodlad, and Clarence Hunnicutt for their careful reading of the manuscript, wholly or in part, and for their helpful suggestions for its improvement. The authors are indebted also to the several authors, publishers, and school districts who granted permission to quote from their publications.

Recognition is given, too, to the many unnamed colleagues and students with whom the authors have had rich associations over the past decade and who have contributed greatly, though perhaps unknowingly, to this book.

G. W. S.
M-M. S.

Stanford, California

CONTENTS

THE CHANGING CURRICULUM

and the

ELEMENTARY TEACHER

PART 1

ELEMENTARY SCHOOL EDUCATION

1

THE ELEMENTARY SCHOOL:
AN INTRODUCTION

The elementary school has long been the foundation of the public school system in our country. Once the idea of a free, tax-supported school system began to take form in this country the intent was clearly to develop an educational facility that would offer quality education for all. Historically, a free or public school had been synonymous with a charity school, associated with pauperism; such an institution tried to develop only the barest of literacy skills among the masses of the people. Families of any status and means sent their children to private schools and paid tuition fees. This sort of divided school effort, so typical of Europe in the seventeenth century, was not compatible with the more democratic system—social, political, and economic—that had begun to develop in the New World. Instead, it was felt necessary to develop a truly "common" school—"common" not meaning ordinary, or not equal in quality to the private school—but meaning that the school would be open to all people, no matter their station in life. The program of education it would offer was to be equal to that found in any private school, and well-suited to the aspirations and ideals of a proud and ambitious citizenry.

Many of our forefathers believed that such a school experience in childhood held the promise of providing a seed-bed in which the loftiest of the ideas concerning equality and liberty expressed in the Declaration of Independence, and guarded by the Constitution, would be most likely to take root. The public school experience was envisioned by many as providing the sort of educational "cement" needed to hold this young country together at the outset and to insure its future in the years ahead.

Samuel Lewis, the first superintendent of instruction in Ohio, wrote in 1836:

> Take fifty lads in a neighborhood, including rich and poor—send them in childhood to the same school—let them join in the same sports, read and spell in the same classes, until their different circumstances fix their business for life; some go to the field, some to the mechanics shop, some to merchandise: one becomes eminent at the bar, another in the pulpit: some become wealthy; the majority live on with a mere competency—a few are reduced to beggary! But, let the most eloquent orator, that ever mounted a western stump, attempt to prejudice the minds of one part against the other—and so far from succeeding, the poorest of the whole would consider himself insulted.[1]

To a great extent, we have succeeded in realizing this vision in the public elementary school system. In 1958, some twenty-nine million children between the ages of five and thirteen were enrolled in schools.[2] These children come to the school from families representative of all social and economic strata in our society. The situation suggested in the quotation above is still accepted as a desirable goal in our society. The elementary school has truly become a "common" school as it has contributed to the realization of this vision.

In spite of the very strong support for a free public school system as the proper answer to America's educational needs, the right of the private school to exist has never been deeply questioned. The supporters of the public school idea have felt that a quality school program, free and tax supported, could and would win the acceptance of the people, but parents should retain the right to choose the private school over the public school if they so desired. The enrollment figures cited above represent about 90 per cent of the total possible enrollment at these ages. About 15.6 per cent of the number of children in elementary school are attending private schools.[3] It would appear that the challenge extended to the public school system over the years has been adequately met. The support the public has given to the system is related to the belief, in our society, that the welfare of our democracy rests, in no small way, on the people's knowing, trusting, and accepting each other in order to solve common problems through cooperation. The public elementary school is seen by the vast majority of our people as the proper educational milieu in which to begin such accomplishments.

---

[1] Educational Policies Commission, *Public Education and the Future of America* (Washington, D.C.: National Education Association, 1955), p. 18.

[2] U.S. Bureau of the Census, *Statistical Abstract of the United States: 1959* (Eightieth edition; Washington, D.C.: 1959), Table 128, p. 104.

[3] *Ibid.*, Table 133, p. 106.

DEFINING THE ELEMENTARY SCHOOL

The elementary school is actually many things in one. What sort of composite definition would point out the many perspectives in which this institution must be seen to be understood? The following discussion outlines several of these perspectives.

An Institution for Formal Education

Education has been provided for all human groups in the past and is in the present, whatever the level of civilization existing in any particular group. The elementary school is an institution for formal education, but the school, as a social invention, has not always existed.

Some education has always taken place, and still takes place, in the informal setting of day-to-day living. Defining education as the modification of behavior, we can see that many living experiences educate. We learn to eat, or to run, or to greet people properly, with a minimum of instruction. Such factors as the family living experience, the community experience, the neighborhood play experience, and motion pictures and television all present models, both good and bad, of all aspects of living to us, and we in turn shape our behavior from these models. We set a purpose (or accept one), have experiences and reflect on them, correct and practice as the situation permits, and finally generalize our responses to future situations.

The first step toward formalizing education occurs when the parents or grandparents accept certain responsibilities for the education of their children with consciousness of purpose. They purposefully involve the young in certain experiences for the learning that will result. Thus, the mother may enlist the help of the daughter in certain tasks that girls typically perform in a given society; the father may teach the typically male tasks to his son. Further elements of formalization are added when certain people, elders perhaps, or highly skilled craftsmen, or hunters, or warriors, are asked to accept some responsibilities for teaching the young outside their immediate family groups. The cultural anthropologist has helped us to recognize the fairly intricate and exact systems of education that exist in some societies that, from the outside, appear to be almost totally without such structures. These systems reflect certain characteristics of formal education—that is, of conscious, goal-directed efforts to modify the behavior of the young.

The establishment of a school is usually thought of as the ultimate in formal education. The presence of such an institution in a society is evidence that people have made a free and open choice to develop to the fullest the children of the coming generation. The school is usually

established whenever the culture developed by a particular society puts educational demands on the young that are too great to be left to chance, and too complex for the family or other community persons to assume. Certain tasks of education are delegated to the school. It is usually housed in a special place, with a limited group of people selected and prepared to function as teachers.

This is one vantage point from which to view the elementary school— as an institution for formal education. The elementary school exists so that certain factors of chance are minimized in the education of our children. It is supported by society and receives its authority from society. In turn, the school is responsible to society. Its efforts are clearly goal-directed; its charge is to modify the behavior of the young in very specific directions: children are helped to learn to read, to use our number system, to know about our past history, and so on. Both the completely informal sort of education that comes from day-to-day living, and the more systematic efforts to instruct that stem from parents, church, and other community groups, continue to have an effect on children; but the school is seen as the great formal force in the education of the child.

A Part of a Continuous School Education

Direct attention to the elementary school sometimes leads to the conclusion, unfortunately, that the elementary school is an independent entity, rather than simply one phase of a continuous school program. This idea may have developed originally because many communities once had only elementary schools. When the secondary school was reoriented in the tradition of the common school and made more readily available in communities, it was often developed with little or no concern for or attention to the already existing elementary school program. Further division of the secondary school into junior and senior high schools contributed, in many instances, to the isolation of each segment. And, of course, the development of the kindergarten, first as a private and later as a public organization but always as a *preschool* experience, led to detachment and autonomy at the beginning levels. This whole formal school experience—extending as it does now in most communities from kindergarten through the twelfth year of school—must be seen as one continuing effort to assist children toward the general objectives of the educative effort, although there is a place for uniqueness and individuality within any one segment of the total effort.

An Administrative Unit

Most elementary schools are now organized as six-year units, encompassing the first six grades of school. Many schools include a kinder-

garten as a regular part of the elementary school program, extending the unit over seven years. Other school units include the seventh and eighth grades, too, making the school a nine-year institution. Some school districts encompass only the elementary school years; in others, the elementary school units are part of a larger district that includes the secondary school. The latter are often spoken of as unified, centralized, or consolidated school districts.

As an administrative unit, the elementary school is usually headed by a school principal, who is the educational leader of his particular school. Depending on the size of the school and the policy of the school district, he may attend to the duties of the principalship full-time, or he may be called upon to teach a class in addition to his duties as principal. Each classroom is typically handled by one classroom teacher, who guides and directs the learning experiences for one group of pupils. The services of certain specialists in music, art, or physical education, who work either with teachers or directly with students to reinforce these particular areas of the program, are available to many schools. Other specialists such as psychologists, speech therapists, school nurses or doctors, counselors and the like may work full- or part-time in a school. A full-time school secretary or clerk, a custodian for the care of the building and grounds, and, if a large hot lunch program is operated in the school, a dietician and one or more cooks may all be employed. Together, such a faculty and staff are responsible for the operation of an elementary school.

A Community or Neighborhood Institution

For a number of reasons the elementary school is seen as a neighborhood institution. Social scientists have used the attendance boundaries— the geographical and social area from which a school draws its student group—of the individual elementary school as an operational definition for neighborhood. As such, the school is close to the people. The elementary school is that part of the total educational system to which children first come, and to which parents must entrust their children for the first sustained significant experiences outside of the family group. These years are the beginnings of a long school experience, and because a good beginning is so often linked with a satisfactory ending, parents are probably more interested in this part of their children's school experience than in any other. Thus, they are more likely to visit school during these years, and to be active in parent associations of various kinds. Parents are younger themselves, of course, when their children are in elementary school, and they are more likely to assist on field trips or help serve noon lunches than when they are older. Also, children of these ages will accept a kind of parent involvement at school

and in their school affairs—an involvement that is more or less taboo when they reach adolescence and attempt to establish their independence in so many ways.

These are years, too, when child and parent share certain special occasions through school activities. Halloween, a children's holiday certainly, becomes a family holiday through a school-centered and parent-school sponsored Halloween carnival. Similar affairs, linked to other holidays, result in similar appropriate projects. These activities bring parents to school and make the school a focus of neighborhood activity.

Parent association meetings often provide the stimulus for meetings on matters other than school affairs; when these meetings are held in the school building, the facility functions as a neighborhood center. In those places where several neighborhoods are brought together in one elementary school district and in some rural areas, the elementary school functions as a community center for various family gatherings. The multipurpose room of many newer elementary schools is in part a reflection of the value of the school as a neighborhood center.

All of these situations suggest why the elementary school is such a strong neighborhood or local community institution. It is close to the people, it involves a most precious possession of parents, and it is flexible enough to meet a diversified set of neighborhood and community needs.

A Community of Children

In a very real sense the elementary school is a community of children. Children speak of *their* school, of *their* teacher, of *their* principal. The elementary school provides time, place, and purpose for them to leave the family circle and proceed, more or less, on their own. It provides a testing ground for intellectual power, for physical skill, for social competence, and for emotional stability. In all of these areas of human development, the child is challenged by the school community. Of course, the whole institution is designed to help him to succeed, but in the final analysis he must do the succeeding.

Various types of human competence and personality emerge in this child's community: the social leaders, who seem to get along well with their peers and whom the larger group is willing to follow; the political leaders, who seem to be particularly interested in and adept at meeting some of the problems of individual and group control so essential in this "community"; the athletes, and the "best dressed," and the "bores"; and so on. Sociometric studies have called our attention to the *stars,* the very popular children, and the *isolates,* those children who seem to be without supporting friends. Strong likes and dislikes, and

the existence of forceful cliques at the upper age levels, are parts of this child society.

The power of this community of children is felt more than once by the teacher unable to influence the behavior of a child whose position is strong in his society; it is felt by the teacher who tries desperately to develop the allegiance and support of certain children for more acceptable ways of behaving or studying because he is aware of the influence they exert as models in their child community. A study done by Cunningham some years ago, focused on understanding the group behavior of boys and girls in the school community, illustrates well the importance of seeing the elementary school as a community of children.[4]

A Curriculum Unit

The elementary school is primarily a curriculum unit. It is in most instances the child's first attempt to learn quite purposefully outside the family. A few children may have attended nursery school or Sunday School prior to entering the elementary school, but the instructional program at that level is less formal and aimed at restricted purposes.

As a curriculum unit, the elementary school is primarily responsible for developing certain common learnings in our child population; the learnings sought and the educational experiences provided in the elementary school are for all children. There is little or no election of studies, except when offered through a system of clubs that meet at regular times, or through some variations in programming in the seventh and eighth grades when they are a part of the elementary school. Thus, *all* children are expected to be helped to learn to read, to write, and to spell, to understand our number system, and to be involved in social studies and science learning activities, and so on.

This does not mean that identical learning experiences are appropriate for all children. The elementary school curriculum must consider differences in individual ability and motivation while it is still responsible for the accomplishment of stated learning objectives by all children to the limits of their individual ability to learn or to perform. The major focus of this book is, of course, on the elementary school as a curriculum unit. However, it is not necessary to deal extensively with curriculum at this point. The chapters that follow are an attempt to develop understanding of the elementary school curriculum, with a predisposition to approach the task of planning curriculum in a particular way, at both school and classroom levels.

---

[4] Ruth Cunningham and others, *Understanding Group Behavior of Boys and Girls* (New York: Bureau of Publications, Teachers College, Columbia University, 1952).

DEVELOPING PERSPECTIVE
ON ELEMENTARY EDUCATION

In addition to the several perspectives discussed above, the modern elementary school must be seen in an historical perspective in order to understand it fully. Its history is rarely known, since the school is so much taken for granted. The history of the elementary school in this country is one of a struggle for form and integrity through the years, from its roots in Colonial America to its growth as an institution in America today.

This struggle for form and integrity in the democratic, public approach to education has resulted in at least the following distinguishing characteristics:

1. Civil control of schools and the educational system.
2. Compulsory education, compulsory provision of schools, and compulsory attendance.
3. Financial support from public funds, rather than from tuition payments, for a system of schools.
4. Useful school curricula, indicating that the school program is indigenous to and at the service of the society that sanctions and supports it.

The importance of the characteristics above is difficult to grasp, in either their historical significance or their relevance to the present course of development of public education. This attempt to add an element of historical perspective will, we hope, add meaning to these statements. We must understand, in some detail, that the elementary school operates out of a long educational inheritance.

REFERENCES

Baxter, Bernice, Gertrude Lewis, and Gertrude Cross. *The Role of Elementary Education*. Boston: D. C. Heath and Company, 1952.
> The elementary school as a neighborhood institution is discussed in Chapter 11.

Campbell, R. F., and J. A. Ramseyer. *The Dynamics of School-Community Relations*. Boston: Allyn and Bacon, 1955.
> As the title suggests, the reader is enabled to see the school-community relationship; Chapter 5 is especially helpful.

Caswell, Hollis L., and Arthur W. Foshay. *Education in the Elementary School* (Third edition). New York: American Book Company, 1957.
> Chapter 3 offers a useful statement on the characteristics of a good elementary school.

Department of Elementary School Principals. *Community Living and the Elementary School* (Twenty-fourth Yearbook). Washington, D.C.: National Education Association, 1945.
> Points up the relationship of the elementary school to the community, as suggested by the title.

Educational Policies Commission. *Education for All American Children.* Washington, D.C.: National Education Association, 1948.
> A most provocative statement on the kind of elementary school needed by America's children as envisioned at the time.

Herrick, Virgil E., and others. *The Elementary School.* Englewood Cliffs, New Jersey: Prentice-Hall, Inc., 1956.
> Chapter 1 presents some generalizations about the elementary school of today.

Otto, Henry J., Hazel Floyd, and Margaret Rouse. *Principles of Elementary Education* (Revised edition). New York: Rinehart and Company, Inc., 1955.
> Chapter 1 offers some very useful "word visits" to a number of modern elementary schools; Chapter 16 has some helpful material of an introductory nature.

Ragan, William B. *Modern Elementary Curriculum* (Revised edition). New York: Holt, Rinehart and Winston, Inc., 1960.
> Part Five of this book contains some material that adds to the definition of the elementary school attempted here.

Shane, Harold G. (editor). *The American Elementary School* (Thirteenth Yearbook of the John Dewey Society). New York: Harper & Brothers, 1953.
> The expanded role of the elementary school in our society is very well discussed in Chapter 14 of this yearbook.

2

ELEMENTARY SCHOOL EDUCATION: AN HISTORICAL OVERVIEW

It is difficult to know just how best to approach such a large historical task in the space available here. The authors have chosen to present a brief, century-by-century discussion of the history of the elementary school, although the subject deserves more than the single chapter here devoted to it. For a fuller discussion, the reader can turn to the works from which the authors have drawn heavily for the material in this chapter.[1]

IN THE 1600's

Early Laws

Partially as an expression of values brought from Europe, partially as an assurance that purposes for coming to this new land would be realized, and partially as an action borne of necessity in this new land, the New England Colonies, led by Massachusetts, early enacted legislation for the education of children. In 1642, the colonial government of Massachusetts passed a law requiring town officials to compel parents to

---

[1] Freeman Butts, *A Cultural History of Education* (New York: McGraw-Hill Book Company, Inc., 1947); Newton Edwards and Herman Richey, *The School in the American Social Order* (Boston: Houghton Mifflin Company, 1947); Edward Reisner, *The Evolution of the Common School* (New York: The Macmillan Company, 1930).

14

provide elementary instruction for their children. This law did not establish schools in Massachusetts, nor did it require the towns to establish schools, but it did demand that parents provide instruction themselves or employ tutors and schoolmasters to instruct their children. The law stipulated the minimum instructional program : instruction was required in reading, in certain capital laws, in catechism ; and it was necessary for a child to be apprenticed in a trade. The law gave town officials certain powers over the family in the matter of education; the right to levy fines and to compel apprenticeship were among those powers.

Five years later, in 1647, another law was passed in Massachusetts that went even further in establishing the authority of the state in the field of education. This law required each town of fifty families to provide an elementary school teacher, and each town of one hundred families to establish a Latin grammar school. Thus, to the compulsory instruction of children was added the compulsory establishment of schools. Still missing, and it was many years before it came, was a law making school attendance compulsory. Parents still had the choice of instructing their children themselves or of using the schools.

At least three motives apparently were basic to the passage of these laws requiring universal education. One was, obviously, a religious motive : children were to be taught to read so that they might understand and accept the religious base upon which these New England colonies were founded. A second motive was political : all children would be taught to read and understand the capital laws of the colonies. The third was clearly economic : all children were to be taught a vocation. This was, in part, an attempt to meet a growing need for skilled workmen in the colonies, and in part an attempt to keep a large pauper class, which would be a burden on society, from developing in the New World.

Historians disagree as to the true significance of these laws for the future development of education in America. Cubberley, for instance, saw them as providing the very "cornerstone of our American state school systems."[2] Others, however, saw these laws more as an attempt to impose the Puritan creed on all children and to help to maintain the status quo in the social system.

It must be remembered that democracy was not yet the order of the day, so that these decisions were not made to promote the interests of democracy, as were many of the laws of later years, although it is clear that a measure of humanitarianism and a recognition of the importance of education for the young were reflected in these acts.

---

[2] Ellwood P. Cubberley, *The History of Education* (Boston: Houghton Mifflin Company, 1920), p. 366.

The Dame School in New England

The elementary schools, or perhaps more accurately, the schools for children, that were provided in New England at this time were essentially the *dame school* and the *writing school* that had been known in England. In the dame schools, some women in the community would gather a few children into their homes for instruction. They would teach the children the ABC's and the beginnings of reading while they went about their usual chores. This approach was brought to New England, where the curriculum evidently went beyond the ABC's and reading, to include some spelling and certain moral and religious precepts. Some schools attempted to teach writing and arithmetic, but as a rule these subjects were reserved for the more advanced town schools. The dame school experience marked the end of formal education for most girls at this time, and their program might be broadened, therefore, to include sewing and knitting. Boys, once they could handle words of two or three syllables, could go on to the town reading and writing school. Small had this to say about the dame school:

> The dame school was a necessity of the times. Boys were not generally admitted to the master's school until they could 'stand up and read words of two syllables and keep their places'; girls were not admitted at all. The teaching of the simple rudiments was made a family, not a public matter. . . . The floor was scoured to whiteness and covered with the finest sand. Here instruction in arithmetic was oral, Miss Betty making the figures on the sanded floor with her rod, . . . and her pupils, with their square pieces of birch bark and bits of charcoal, copying the sums she gave them. . . . The children, having walked long distances, were made very comfortable at the long recess, as their dinners were many times frozen, and sometimes their food required cooking. Miss Betty was devoted in her care for them in preparing their frugal repast. Apples were roasted and nuts were cracked in profusion, and then with their old fashioned games they had an enjoyable time.[3]

The Elementary School in New England

In New England, the public elementary schools taught reading and writing, and some of them included arithmetic in their curriculum. In England, writing and reading had been taught in separate institutions, but this separation was the exception in the colonies. With the sort of beginning in reading the child received in the dame school, he went on to the public town school, continuing his reading instruction and adding

---

[3] W. H. Small, *Early New England Schools* (Boston: Ginn and Company, 1914), pp. 162–164, as quoted in Henry J. Otto, *Elementary School Organization and Administration* (New York: Appleton-Century-Crofts, Inc., 1954), pp. 1–2.

to it with writing and, perhaps, arithmetic. From this sort of beginning the typical elementary school, devoted to "the three R's," took shape in this country.

One teacher, of course, handled the instruction for all children. The educational system was financed almost exclusively from tuition fees paid by parents, although such fees were often waived for the children of poor families who could not afford to pay. The school might be housed in the teacher's home, in the church, in the town meetinghouse, or in any available building.

Most of what has been described here was true for all of the colonies. However, certain differences in the Southern and Middle colonies must be noted.

In the Southern Colonies

In the Southern Colonies, a pattern of aristocracy dominated life, and education was no exception; schooling was a private affair. Parents who were financially capable made provision for the education of their children. Unlike New England, the Southern Colonies looked upon free education as charity education, for the poor only. However, the church was influential in education in the South, also, so that the aims of education and the content of the curriculum were much the same as they were in New England.

In the tidewater areas of the South, the pattern of social class was not conducive to the development of widespread educational opportunity; in the Southern back-country, the harsh conditions of life retarded such development there. Some schools were provided in the more populated communities in this back-country, but not as extensively as in New England. Still, the very conditions of life in this back-country eventually developed one of the most potent voices for education in the South— Thomas Jefferson.

In the Middle Colonies

The Middle Colonies in the 1600's were sparsely populated, with many diverse religious and civil groups; there was no unified demand for education and schools. Too, these colonies were in great part commercial ventures, and the companies involved were more concerned about goals other than universal education. State and civil control over schools was secondary to private and religious control. The curriculum was usually limited to instruction in reading, writing, and some very simple arithmetic, with emphasis throughout on religion.

Paul Monroe points out the Dutch influence—then prevalent in the Middle Colonies—on American education in the following comment:

The significant fact in regard to this system of parish schools is the marked contrast which it offers to the villages or towns where English customs prevailed. In all of these Dutch settlements a community school existed as one essential part of the structure of society and of the local system of government. While church and town government co-operated, these were essentially town schools supported as a town charge. . . . Undoubtedly the tradition represented by these state-church or parish schools, and the actual working system which they presented were a leading factor in the establishment of the first system of public schools created after the Revolution.[4]

Under English control, however, these Dutch schools became parochial schools, and the English tried to establish a similar sort of institution, tied to the Anglican Church. The attempt was not extremely successful, however, and educational systems generally continued to develop slowly.

IN THE 1700's

Public Interest in Education

The church continued to exercise great control over the schools in the colonies during the 1700's. The Puritan Church was the driving force behind education in the New England Colonies; in New York and the South, the Church of England attempted to increase educational opportunities. Denominational control of education was seen as consistent with religious freedom. At the same time there was evidence in the early 1700's that the close identification of schooling with religion contributed somewhat to a general decline in public interest in education. Forces were already at work moving America toward democracy, and churchmen found their leadership challenged by a growing group of merchants and farmers. At about the turn of the century, the right to vote had been separated from church membership, and involvement in the affairs of towns had widened accordingly. The connection of compulsory education with the rise of the common man was not, however, as clear in the minds of the populace as was its connection to religion and the church. Therefore, compulsory education was not exacted as strenuously from the people through state legislation now as earlier.

Beginnings of the Local School District

The growing dispersion of population, with its accompanying decentralization in social, political, and economic arrangements, was one cause of the decreased public interest in education. This dispersion eventually

---

[4] Paul Monroe, *Founding of the American Public School System* (New York: The Macmillan Company, 1940), p. 82.

developed into a potent force for individualism and localism in American life, which in turn resulted in some fundamental shifts in educational policy and arrangements. Early New England towns covered areas of from twenty to forty square miles, but they were always village-centered. As population increased and families moved out into previously unsettled parts of the town, small communities developed that had a general tendency to want "their own" in matters of government and religion; soon they began to insist on having their own schools. The law required, and they were helping to support, a town school. But it was so often difficult, if not impossible, for their children to get to the town school that they questioned this arrangement. A first compromise saw the development of a "moving" town school, with elementary education brought to the various smaller settlements in the town for a few weeks or months out of the year, with its stay in any one community largely dependent on the amount of taxes paid into the town treasury. The "moving" school did not prove to be satisfactory, however, and soon these groups of families voted to keep their quota of the town school taxes in their own village, and to hire a schoolmaster and operate their own school, as illustrated in the following excerpt from the records of an early New England town:

> We, the subscribers, living very remote from any district where we might be convenient to a school for our children, do humbly petition that the town would vote us off as a district and grant that the money which we pay towards maintaining a school in this town may be laid out for schooling in the said district as near the center as may be convenient. . . . Voted the above request be complied with during the town's pleasure.[5]

Finally, a Massachusetts law of 1789 recognized the local school district and gave it full legal autonomy, with complete authority over its own schools. The local district could build buildings, hire teachers, control the curriculum, set the length of the school term, and tax for the support of the school system. Other states followed suit, and the supremacy of the state over the local community in educational matters was altered. This local district system was probably quite democratic and well-fitted to frontier life. It brought the elementary school very close to the people, and "the little red schoolhouse" moved West with them. The system separated the operation of schools from the general municipal administration; this separation still characterizes American public education. It also helped to increase the use of town money in support of schools, and to decrease the portion of the cost borne directly by parents

---

[5] Small, *op. cit.*, p. 73.

through the payment of tuition fees, and that portion from philanthropic sources. In fact, early public school funds were shared with private and religious schools. This local control of schools attracted both the rational and emotional support of the people. The strong interest in village schools often blinded the people to the shortcomings of such an extreme policy of local determinism in education. A number of state constitutions written during the Revolutionary period did mention education, foreshadowing a contest yet to come. The struggle to re-establish state supremacy in school affairs was bitter in the 1800's. A role for the national government in education was not explicitly stated in the new national Constitution, and federal participation in education is still looked upon with skepticism in our society.

Curriculum

During this period, the elementary school began to be the typical beginning school experience for children, combining in this single institution that which the dame school and the reading and writing schools had provided separately before. The elementary school was concerned primarily with teaching children reading and writing, and eventually with teaching the fundamentals of arithmetic. Religion was still a prime concern in the schools at the beginning of the century, and almost all of the reading material used in the schools dealt with religious matters. A good example of the concern with religion is the *New England Primer*, a reading book used almost universally in the elementary school during the 1700's. Butts's description of the content of this reader is most revealing:

> It commonly contained the alphabet in capital and small letters; lists of syllables; and lists of words emphasizing moral concepts, for example, abusing, bewitching, confounded, drunkenness, faculty, godliness, impudent, everlasting, fidelity, glorifying, and humility. Then came the famous woodcuts illustrating the letters of the alphabet and accompanied by religious and moralistic rhymes, many of them reflecting the gloomy outlook of Puritanism. The reading material followed, usually under such headings as "The Dutiful Child's Promises" and "An Alphabet of Lessons for Youth," and including the Lord's Prayer, the Apostles' Creed, the Ten Commandments, the names of the books of the Old and New Testaments for memorizing, religious verses and stories, and finally the Westminster Catechism.[6]

Later in the 1700's, in response to the mood of the times, revised editions of this *New England Primer* included patriotic sentiments and a good deal of secular material. From the work of Butts, note the following:

---

[6] Butts, *op. cit.*, p. 373.

For example, the early rhyme describing the letter K and expressing loyalty to the king of England had read, "Our King the Good, No man of blood." After the Revolution, patriotism became the motif: "Kings should be good, Not men of blood," "The British King, Lost states thirteen," or "Queens and Kings, Are gaudy things." Other changes reflected patriotic and nationalist sentiments; "Whales in the sea, God's voice obey" became "Great Washington brave, His country did save." . . . practical values of learning to read began to replace its use in reading the Bible. For example, the *New England Primer* exhorted pupils in the following manner: He who ne'er learns his A.B.C. Forever will a blockhead be. But he who learns his letters fair Shall have a coach to take the air.[7]

Even the arithmetic taught in most of the town elementary schools after about 1725 was related to religious training, since the learning of numerals was considered preparation "for the ready finding of any Chapter, Psalm, and Verse in the Bible." It was at a later time that different ends were sought through arithmetic instruction. Spelling, related to the instruction in reading, came to be a regular part of the elementary school curriculum about the middle of the century. History, geography, and science as such were not included in the program.

One teacher handled the teaching in an elementary school, and the individual method of instruction was used. Pupils were called up, one by one, for recitation, and a poor performance was very likely to result in the use of "the rod" as a spur to learning. Class methods of instruction were not prevalent until the next century.

A most interesting description of an elementary school program in the period after the Revolution is cited by Edwards and Richey:

> The schoolhouse chimney was of stone, and the fireplace was six feet wide and four deep. The flue was so ample and so perpendicular that the rain, sleet, and snow fell directly to the hearth. In winter the battle for life with green fizzling fuel, which was brought in lengths and cut up by the scholars, was a stern one. Not unfrequently the wood, gushing with sap as it was, chanced to let the fire go out, and as there was no living without fire, the school was dismissed, whereat all the scholars rejoiced.
>
> I was about six years old when I first went to school. My teacher was "Aunt Delight," a maiden lady of fifty, short and bent, of sallow complexion and solemn aspect. We were all seated upon benches made of slabs—boards having the exterior or rounded part of the log on one side. As they were useless for other purposes, they were converted into school benches, the rounded part down. They had each four supports, consisting of straddling wooden legs set into auger holes.
>
> The children were called up one by one to Aunt Delight, who sat on a low chair, and required each, as a preliminary, "to make his manners,"

---

[7] *Ibid.*

which consisted of a small, sudden nod. She then placed the spelling-book before the pupil, and with a pen-knife pointed, one by one, to the letters of the alphabet, saying, "What's that?"

I believe I achieved the alphabet that summer. Two years later I went to the winter school at the same place kept by Lewis Olmstead—a man who made a business of ploughing, mowing, carting manure, etc., in the summer, and of teaching school in the winter. He was a celebrity in ciphering, and Squire Seymour declared that he was the greatest "arithmeticker" in Fairfield County. There was not a grammar, a geography, or a history of any kind in the school. Reading, writing, and arithmetic were the only things taught, and these very indifferently —not wholly from the stupidity of the teacher, but because he had forty scholars, and the custom of the age required no more than he performed.[8]

Thus was the typical elementary school of the latter 1700's. The requirements for elementary school teachers were to be able to teach reading, writing, and simple arithmetic. Certificates to teach were issued only to those who clearly were religious persons, of ''sober and good conversation,'' with the minister usually being the person authorized to issue the certificate. Ministers were usually expected to supervise both school and teacher to see that the school adhered to its expected role. Certain groups of prominent citizens often augmented the supervision that the clergymen were asked to carry out.

In the Middle and Southern Colonies

The New England Colonies were still setting the pace in education during the 1700's. Development of schools was slow in the Middle Colonies, with a tendency to keep education free of state control or support. Education at private expense and under private control was characteristic of the Southern Colonies, and was consistent with the Southern social order. The nearest approach to a public school system found in the South before the Revolution was the elementary schools maintained by the Society for the Propagation of the Gospel in Foreign Parts. These were charity schools whose chief purpose was religious training, but who also provided instruction in reading, writing, and simple arithmetic.

In the last years of the eighteenth century, two Southern gentlemen spoke out for education. One was Thomas Jefferson, who in 1779, just a few days after being elected governor of Virginia, presented a plan to the state assembly for a program of education to be conceived and operated at the state level. His plan envisioned a structure for education that extended through the college level, beginning with a three-year elementary school experience for all children in the state, free of tuition. Though

---

[8] Edwards and Richey, *op. cit.*, pp. 116–117.

his plan was not accepted it suggested a direction in which education must move.

The other man to speak out for education was George Washington. In his Farewell Address of 1796 he said:

> Promote, then, as an object of primary importance institutions for the general diffusion of knowledge. In proportion as the structure of government gives force to public opinion, it is essential that public opinion should be enlightened.[9]

Thus the stage was set for important developments in the next century.

IN THE 1800's

Mustering Support for Public Education

The 1800's made important contributions generally to the development of a public school system in the United States, and specifically to the reform and reorganization of elementary school education. Progress was slow and laborious, however, for there were many who did not support the idea of a free public school system. Various churches feared it, and the wealthy were generally skeptical about it, but a growing feeling for the enormity of the job that this young nation faced led inevitably toward the development of free education. The argument that the fortunes of a democratic society depended upon a free and equal opportunity for education for all was a strong and convincing one. There was emerging evidence that the growth of our economy was closely related to the extension of educational opportunities. The kind of democracy that developed after the Revolution and during the Jacksonian era supported the idea of public control of education, but our educational history presented some very complex and difficult problems that would have to be resolved. Chief among these problems were the following: (1) the religious domination over education would have to be lifted if the public school was to unite people along the lines of democracy, rather than divide them along the lines of religion; (2) the major responsibility for the support and control of education had to be re-established at the state level rather than at the local level in order to insure adequate schools for all of the children in a given state; (3) there had to be general agreement that a public school system had to be truly free to all children, and therefore supported financially by general taxation. In retrospect these problems may not seem to be the monumental obstacles that they actually

---

[9] *Ibid.*, p. 237.

were, but their solution took the major part of many men's time and energy for the greater part of the nineteenth century. Cubberley comments as follows on this:

> For this work or propaganda hundreds of School Societies, Lyceums, and Educational Organizations were organized; many conventions were held, and resolutions favoring state schools were adopted; many "Letters" and "Addresses to the Public" were written and published; public-spirited citizens traveled over the country, making addresses to the people explaining the advantages of free state schools; many public-spirited men gave the best years of their lives to the state-school propaganda; and many governors sent communications on the subject to legislatures not yet convinced as to the desirability of state action. At each meeting of the legislatures for years a deluge of resolutions, memorials, and petitions for and against free schools met the members.[10]

These were the years when men like James Carter, Horace Mann, and Henry Barnard, all New Englanders, focused attention again on their part of the country for progress in public education. Men of the Middle states, too, worked hard toward the acceptance of public schools. Gains were made in the South, but at a much slower pace and against great resistance. Here the conflict was not only one of a superior-subordinate social system among white planters and growers and white tenant farmers, but also one of the Negro situation, always difficult and especially acute after the Civil War. The West embraced the idea of public schools and public education almost from the outset, and progress in that part of the new nation was relatively rapid and effective. Slowly but surely these problems were faced and opposition was overtaken. The idea that free education was good for everybody came increasingly to be accepted.

The distinctive pattern of American public schools was truly taking form in the 1800's. The European system, a two-track affair that tended to perpetuate separate schools for upper and lower social classes, was rejected. The idea that everyone should go as far as his talents would permit was being accepted. The school system was increasingly tax-supported and secular in its control. Another essential ingredient to the realization of basic purposes was added through the idea of compulsory school attendance. The first law requiring school attendance was set down by Massachusetts in 1852, and most other states had taken a similar step by 1900. (Only the South lagged in this respect, since no Southern state had such a law on the books at that time.) The school, as we know it, was beginning to take shape.

---

[10] Ellwood P. Cubberley, *Public Education in the United States* (Revised edition; Boston: Houghton Mifflin Company, 1934), p. 167.

Developing Elementary School Education

The elementary school felt the full impact of the increasing use of the public schools. The enrollment in the elementary school increased dramatically, and its organization, its procedures, its curriculum, and even its purposes for being were re-examined and revised.

Purposes of elementary school education. At the beginning of the nineteenth century, the aims of primary school curriculum were much the same as they had been earlier: to develop literacy and sound moral character. An adequate elementary school program at this time was outlined in a *Code of Regulations* issued by a Connecticut Association for the Improvement of Common Schools. As quoted in Edwards and Richey, the code in part had this to say about the program:

> In the morning, the Bible may be delivered to the head of each class, and by them to the scholars capable of reading decently or looking over. This reading with some short remarks, or questions, with the morning prayer, may occupy the *first half hour.* The second, may be employed in hearing the morning lessons, while the younger classes are preparing to spell and read. The third in attention to the writers. The fourth in hearing the under classes read and spell. The fifth in looking over and assisting the writers and cipherers. The sixth in hearing the under classes spell and read the second time; and receiving and depositing pens, writing and reading books. . . .
>
> In the afternoon one half hour may be employed in spelling together, repeating grammar, rules of arithmetic, and useful tables, with a clear, and full, but soft voice, while the instructor prepares pens, writing books, &c. The second and third half hours in hearing the under classes and assisting the writers and cypherers. The fourth in hearing the upper classes read. The fifth to hearing the under classes read, and spell the second time. The sixth in receiving and depositing the books, &c. as above.[11]

As the century progressed, purposes other than the development of literacy and moral character began to be felt in the elementary school program. Citizenship education became a larger concern, and the growing commercial and industrial activity in the various states made the development of commercial and industrial skills a necessity among workers. Thus, certain social and practical individual aims slowly emerged as the century unfolded.

An expanded curriculum. From about 1825 to the end of the Civil War in 1865 the elementary school curriculum expanded considerably. The primary purpose of the school remained that of developing literacy among children, and the curriculum comprised work in reading, writing,

---

[11] Edwards and Richey, *op. cit.,* p. 388.

spelling, and eventually the rules of grammar, rhetoric, and composition. Arithmetic was next in importance because of its practical application in daily affairs and because of its value to straight thinking and mental discipline. Next in importance was a social studies program restricted to some study of history and geography. Massachusetts passed laws late in the 1820's requiring that geography be studied in elementary schools; Vermont passed similar legislation with respect to American history about this same time. Later in the nineteenth century the study of government was added to social studies. A program in science, or nature study, began to take form late in the 1800's, and drawing, music, and physical education were given some very limited attention. The earliest instruction in science was restricted to the object study approach, becoming much more nature study oriented by the end of the century. Drawing was first quite formal or draftsman-like and only later did freehand drawing become popular. Music was mostly singing and choral work. Physical education was offered in only a few places, and not until the latter part of the century. None of these latter subjects was very widely developed at the end of the 1800's.

New organization and methods. With the growth of public education came a swelling elementary school enrollment. The one-room school, with a single teacher responsible for the work of a highly varied age group on an almost individual basis, began to feel the pressures. Two developments resulted from the increased enrollment, which still characterize elementary school education today: (1) the elementary school became a graded school, with children of the same age grouped together for instruction; and (2) practices and procedures were developed that would allow a single teacher to work with a class group rather than with individuals. By the end of the Civil War there were usually two elementary schools in a community—a Primary School, comprising grades one through four, and a Grammar School, comprising grades five through eight. By the end of the century the most common unit was an eight-year, graded elementary school, in which teachers were using methods that enabled them to work with large numbers of children at the same time.

Beginnings of teacher preparation. The combination of an expanded curriculum, the graded school, and the class method of instruction necessitated a new kind of specialization in American elementary education. The normal school was developed to give the rudiments of professional preparation to elementary school teachers. The normal school usually admitted students directly from elementary school graduation, and as late as 1900 the most common requirement for admission was only two years of high school work. The course of study in the normal school usually covered two years, with focus on the elementary school subjects and special emphasis on a given grade level for each candidate. There was

some work in philosophy, psychology, and history of education, and a laboratory experience of some sort was usually provided, similar to present-day observation and student teaching programs.

European influences. All during these years certain voices from Europe had great effect on education in America. The work of three Europeans, namely Pestalozzi, Froebel, and Herbart, received the most attention. Pestalozzi's ideas on both the content and method of elementary education were evident. His concern for the practical in education was appealing, and his ideas on a psychological rather than a singularly logical approach to organized subject matter appealed to many. Froebel, a student of Pestalozzi, was primarily concerned with preschool children and established the kindergarten in Germany; by 1900 there were some 4,500 kindergartens, mostly private, operating in the United States. Herbart developed a science of teaching through "the five formal steps" that was widely accepted as the basic approach for planning and executing a lesson. The influence of the work of these men is still identifiable in today's elementary school.

Emerging American educational theory. It was inevitable that a young nation with a distinctly new concept of public education should eventually develop an educational theory unique and indigenous to the American scene. By the close of the nineteenth century this development was beginning to take form. Two voices in particular were beginning to make themselves heard. One was that of G. Stanley Hall, a teacher and researcher at Johns Hopkins University, who investigated much and wrote a great deal on the psychological aspects of the educative process. He turned the attention of elementary educators from a single concern for subject matter to the need for the careful study of child development. His ideas were often controversial, but his influence was no less significant.

The other voice was that of John Dewey, probably the most influential thinker and writer on education that America has produced, whose ideas have stimulated supporters and critics alike to reach for a better quality school experience for children. However, it was not until the 1900's that Dewey began to speak out on educational matters, and to demonstrate to society his conception of sound elementary education.

FROM 1900–1950

Social Changes and Education

The rapid changes that occurred in American life generally from 1900 to 1950 made their impact on American education as a whole, and on elementary education specifically. The consistent movement toward

political, economic, and social reforms and changes prompted educational change. The shift of our economy from an agrarian base to an industrial one put new educational demands on the schools, and our increased national productivity made it possible to finance education more adequately than ever before. Early in the century it became evident that a deeper interest in children and youth was developing, along with a greater desire to meet certain responsibilities toward them. All of these changes took place within the larger framework of World War I, the "roaring" twenties, the Great Depression, World War II, and the continuing era of the Cold War.

This was the setting in which newer philosophies of education, increased knowledge of child growth and development and learning, altered statements of the proper aims of education, and newer conceptions of the curriculum took form—all of which had a greater effect on elementary education than on any other segment of the school system.

Legislation and Education

By 1918 every state in the Union had passed legislation making school attendance compulsory for some stipulated period of time.[12] The legal authority of the state with respect to the schools was now well established; boards and departments of education operated at the state level in all states.

A law passed by the state of Oregon in 1922 led to the clarification of the rights of the state with respect to private and parochial schools that had continued to exist and to operate in many communities as the public school system had grown. The law required children and youth between certain ages to attend a public school. An appeal to the United States Supreme Court resulted in a ruling that the law was unconstitutional, reaffirmed the right of the states to require education, but held that the states could not require parents to use the public school system. It was decided that the state was within its rights to inspect and to supervise all schools, public and private, to see that they were meeting minimum acceptable standards for education, but the right of private and religious schools to exist alongside public schools was guaranteed.

Traditions Challenged

The development of an educational philosophy and curriculum theory that was distinctly American was accelerated in the 1900's. As the twentieth century opened, a subject matter program embracing language, arithmetic, social studies (history, geography, and civics), some science

---

[12] Butts, *op. cit.*, p. 624.

G

or nature study, and a small measure of music, art, and physical education was usual in elementary schools. Some schools offered instruction in the manual and domestic arts in the upper grades, but not on an extensive scale. Great differences existed, of course, between the programs of schools in the growing urban centers and of those in rural America. The typical elementary school found in the United States at the turn of the century is vividly described by Reisner as follows:

> The effect of all the factors surrounding the graded school of the generation following the Civil War was to develop a school machine. In contrast with the school conditions of a generation preceding there was a great deal more material included in the graded course of instruction, but the quality of teaching and learning was improved hardly at all. From the lowest grade to the highest the pupils followed an endless succession of book assignments which they learned out of hand to reproduce on call. The chief end of pupils was to master skills and learn facts as directed by a teacher who in turn was under the automatic control of a printed course of study, a set of textbooks, and the necessity of preparing her class to pass certain examinations on the contents of a specific number of printed pages. From the standpoint of discipline the physical cruelties of the earlier day had to a large degree disappeared, but the control exercised over the pupils was at least negative. The business of the school being what it was, any movement, any conversation, any communication, were out of order. The spirit of control was military and repressive, not constructive and cooperative. Long rows of seats, military evolutions of classes, stated appearances for recitations, with the rest of the school time devoted to narrowly prescribed exercises, had for their moral equivalent being quiet, industrious at assigned tasks, and submissive to the rule of the drill-sergeant in skirts who unflinchingly governed her little kingdom of learn-by-heart-and-recite-by-rote.[13]

This was the traditional elementary school of which John Dewey was so critical. Dewey could not accept this approach to education; he thought its content and its methodology were inconsistent with a growing democracy. His own words best express this point:

> The traditional scheme is, in essence, one of imposition from above and from outside. It imposes adult standards, subject matter, and methods upon those who are only growing slowly toward maturity. The gap is so great that the required subject matter, the methods of learning and of behaving are foreign to the existing capacities of the young. They are beyond the reach of the experience the young learners already possess. Consequently, they must be imposed, even though good teachers will use devices of art to cover up the imposition so as to relieve it of obviously brutal features. . . . Moreover that which is taught is thought of as essentially static. It is taught as a finished product, with

---

[13] Reisner, *op. cit.*, pp. 427–428.

little regard either to the ways in which it was originally built up or to changes that will surely occur in the future. It is to a large extent the cultural product of societies that assumed the future would be much like the past, and yet it is used as educational food in a society where change is the rule, not the exception.[14]

Dewey saw the school as a fundamental method of social progress and reform, and he saw in America a great challenge to link school and society in a way yet unrealized. His conception was bold, it was new, and it was provocative. He wrote and operated a laboratory school at the University of Chicago at the beginning of the century, and continued his writing and teaching at Columbia University after 1904. Because of his ideas, it was not long before a different approach to the education of children was being talked about, written about, and experimented with in a few private schools. This new approach came to be called Progressive Education, and with it was ushered in one of the most controversial and exciting periods in the history of the elementary school. Here was a conception of education that put the experiences of learners, rather than organized subject matter, in the center of the educative process. Dewey's ideas were supported indirectly by the research in psychology of Robert Thorndike at Columbia University, whose findings questioned the rationale basic to much of the methodology and content of the then typical elementary school program. (This "educational revolution" is discussed further in a later chapter on curriculum patterns [see Chapter 7]. It is sufficient here to put this development in its proper chronological place.) This child-centered approach to curriculum development was challenged in the 1930's by a group of educators who contended that the educational process was basically a social one, and that progressive education, as it had developed and was being practiced, did not give sufficient attention to the problems of society. (This approach, too, is discussed in detail in Chapter 7.) Together, these two opposing ideas are still basic to the most fundamental issues in modern theory of elementary school education.

Attempts to Individualize Instruction

A growing awareness of individual differences led to considerable efforts in the early 1900's to individualize instruction within a grade group. For example, the Winnetka plan of the 1920's instituted an arrangement whereby a certain number of projects or units in each subject were assigned to each grade level, but a student was allowed to work his way through at his own rate so long as he mastered the subject matter. The XYZ plan, another approach to this problem of individual differ-

---

[14] John Dewey, *Experience and Education* (New York: The Macmillan Company, 1938), pp. 4–5.

ences, attempted to use intelligence tests to divide students into grade groups of similar aptitude and ability. Thus, the bright were not to be held back by the slow, the slow were not to be discouraged and frustrated by the bright, and the curriculum was to be adjusted to the varied needs of these different groups of students. In these and similar ways elementary educators tried to individualize instruction within the traditional framework of the graded school and the class method of instruction. This concern with the individual is, of course, still very much with us.

Trends in Enrollment

The elementary school continued to be typically an eight-grade unit during the first half of the century, but the development of the junior high school in the larger urban areas made the elementary school a six-year unit. Enrollment in elementary schools reached a high of about 24,000,000 in 1930. The low birth rate and the lower immigration rates of the depression years caused enrollment slowly to decline to about 20,000,000 in 1938.[15] Before this reduction in elementary school population could have much effect on elementary education, however, the unprecedented high birth rate of World War II brought a number of specific problems to elementary education. With some 4,000,000 births per year since World War II have come real problems of shortages of teachers and classrooms with double and triple shifts in many elementary schools, while children attend school for half-day sessions only.

Growth of Early Childhood Education

The provision of a free school experience for children younger than first graders was widely discussed in the early 1900's, and the establishment of nursery schools and kindergartens was accelerated, largely through a strong assist from the federal government during the 1930's. Attention was again focused on the nursery school in the early 1940's, when great numbers of men and women were drawn into military service or industry, and family life was disrupted accordingly. The White House Conference on Children in a Democracy, held in 1940, recommended the public support of nursery schools.

By 1940 some 625,000 children were enrolled in public kindergartens, and another 40,000 were attending private ones.[16] The development of both the kindergarten and the nursery school was largely due to the division of mothers' time between jobs in industry and child-rearing at home, coupled with the importance that child specialists attached to organized educational opportunities for all children in their early years.

---

[15] Butts, *op. cit.*, p. 630.
[16] *Ibid.*, p. 629.

Early childhood education is now a very evident part of elementary school education.

IN THE LAST HALF OF THE TWENTIETH CENTURY

Continuing Growth of Elementary Education

We find ourselves in the last half of the twentieth century with more children being taught by more teachers in the elementary school than ever before. The most recent enrollment figures indicate 29,000,000 children are being taught by over 1,000,000 teachers.[17] Most of the problems of earlier times, such as adequate school finance, religion and public schools, lay participation in school affairs, professional preparation of teachers, equalized educational opportunity, a defensible elementary school curriculum—even the matter of the proper aims and unique function of the elementary school—are still with us.

Desegregation and Elementary Education

It was in 1954 that the United States Supreme Court handed down its decision against segregated school systems in America, ruling that the maintenance of separate but equal facilities for different racial groups was unconstitutional. This decision posed, and continues to pose, a most complex problem in elementary education, especially in the southern part of the United States. Desires to conform to the law of the land are countered by equally strong desires to maintain an educational system separating Negro and White, which is no longer possible. The extension of equal civil rights into the area of education has caused struggles over schools in many places. Various laws have been passed, and are being tested in the courts, that seek ways to circumvent the Supreme Court decision. Some of these go so far as to close the public schools when certain conditions develop in a community or state. While the constitutionality of these laws is being determined, and the larger social problem resolved, the schools are having to operate under great stress and tension. It is difficult to assess at this time just how long the present troubled situation will continue, or to prophesy the form in which public elementary education in the South will emerge from this struggle.

The Cold War and Improved Schools

The latter years of the Cold War have ushered in a new area of concern: the effectiveness of American school systems. It seems clear that the struggle between democracy and communism in the years ahead will be

---

[17] U.S. Bureau of the Census, *Statistical Abstract of the United States: 1959* (Eightieth edition; Washington, D.C.: 1959), Table 144, p. 113.

in great part an educational struggle. In the general re-examination of our society that is currently taking place, education has increasingly come to be a central concern. Its importance is more clearly sensed and its improvement more consistently urged. The key to the future, in the minds both of interested laymen and of professional educators, centers on increased equality of educational opportunity. This is a challenge to which the elementary school must respond.

Debates over Modern Elementary Education

We have come a long way, as this historical sketch has tried to show, in elementary school education, but there is still much to do. At successive points in our history there has been some severe criticism of the quality of education offered in our public school system. The elementary school, as a part of that system, has been the subject of many recent arguments and debates. The intent of most of these has been to offer quite honest, constructive criticism to the end of insuring a dynamic, up-to-date school program. Some of the staunchest supporters of the public school concept have participated in these arguments. The challenge to the educator is to provide the sort of educational leadership and program that will allay the fears and doubts of the public as the school is operated.

Communication between school and community is fundamental. Human beings have a tendency to recall past periods in history, including educational history, more gloriously than the facts would support. The temptation, often, when problems seem great and our response to them inadequate, is to recall some former "golden age of learning" in which all children achieved in a superior way, and in which human frailties were nonexistent. For instance, consider the following reaction to our efforts in the elementary schools of the United States:

> When we were mere boys, boys had to do a little work in school. They were not coaxed; they were hammered. Spelling, writing and arithmetic were not electives; and you had to learn. In these more fortunate times, elementary education has become in many places a sort of vaudeville show. The child must be kept amused and learns what he pleases. Many sage teachers scorn the old-fashioned rudiments; and it seems to be regarded as between a misfortune and a crime for a child to learn to read and spell by the old methods.[18]

Undoubtedly you have heard or read statements similar to this one. Interestingly, the quotation is from a 1902 copy of the *New York Sun*. Reference to the time "when we were boys" would place the elementary school situation described in the 1870's.

---

[18] Harold C. Hand, quoted in "Answering the Critics of the School Program," National Education Association Convention, St. Louis, Missouri, July 2, 1959, pp. 17–18 (mimeo).

Undoubtedly, there will always be statements forthcoming similar to this one. In the meantime, the hope would be that greatly increased educational research would lead to ever more efficient efforts to educate, and that the combination of the two would enable both the elementary educator and the public to view such reactions with the perspective and insight appropriate. As noted earlier, it is entirely within the rights and duties of citizenship for the public to be watchful of its created social institutions. The essence of educational leadership might be seen as an effort to help the public in its assessment, to demonstrate a kind of professional competency and integrity in the process that evokes public confidence.

We look forward to an important and exciting future for the public elementary school. Some few years ago a noted elementary educator referred to this part of our school system as "the doughty elementary school," and went on to detail the progress and achievements of the elementary school in spite of inadequate financing, worn out and overtaxed school plants, unprecedented increases in enrollments, and an acute shortage of qualified teaching personnel, circumstances all born of a succession of events encompassing the depression of the thirties, the hot war of the forties, and the cold war of the fifties.[19] His comments seem to be entirely appropriate; truly this is a "doughty" institution. It is cast in such a tradition, and we are confident that it will continue to be true to that tradition. That great problems demanding great solutions are faced in elementary education only adds to the motivation to succeed. Education, and the elementary school, must rise to the occasion, and this means that *people* must rise to the occasion. In human achievement there is simply no substitute for human energy. Thus, those who would become elementary school educators can look back on a job well done, and ahead to even greater and more compelling reasons for improving on that positive history.

REFERENCES

Beck, Robert H., Walter W. Cook, and Nolan C. Kearney. *Curriculum in the Modern Elementary School.* Englewood Cliffs, New Jersey: Prentice-Hall, Inc., 1953.

> The historical background of the elementary school curriculum is dealt with in Chapter 1.

Butts, R. Freeman, and Lawrence Cremin. *A History of Education in American Culture.* New York: Holt, Rinehart and Winston, Inc., 1953.

> Although this book deals with the whole of American education, those parts that deal directly with elementary education are very helpful and can be selected easily.

---

[19] Fred P. Barnes, in a speech to the elementary teachers in Kansas City, Missouri, 1953.

Caswell, Hollis L., and Arthur W. Foshay. *Education in the Elementary School* (Third edition). New York: American Book Company, 1957.

> A most useful and succinct statement on the historical development of the elementary school is found in Chapter 2.

Cremin, Lawrence A. *The American Common School: An Historic Conception.* New York: Bureau of Publications, Teachers College, Columbia University, 1951.

> This statement contributes historical perspective to the American commitment to the common school from an early time.

Cremin, Lawrence A. "What Happened to Progressive Education?" *Teachers College Record* 61:23–29. October 1959.

> An interpretation of the rise and decline of the progressive education movement in American education, a movement largely restricted to elementary education.

Good, H. G. *A History of American Education* (Revised edition). New York: The Macmillan Company, 1956.

> Particular attention is given to the development of American education in the twentieth century.

Herrick, Virgil E., and others. *The Elementary School.* Englewood Cliffs, New Jersey: Prentice-Hall, Inc., 1956.

> Chapter 2 traces the evolution of the elementary school in this country.

Ragan, William B. *Modern Elementary Curriculum* (Revised edition). New York: Holt, Rinehart and Winston, Inc., 1960.

> Chapter 1 deals with the changing elementary curriculum in the historical background of the elementary school.

Reisner, Edward H. *The Evolution of the Common School.* New York: The Macmillan Company, 1935.

> This is undoubtedly the major historical statement on the development of the elementary school.

Russell, John D., and C. H. Judd. *The American Educational System.* Boston: Houghton Mifflin Company, 1940.

> Chapters 2 and 12 have particular relevance to the development of the elementary school as we know it.

Edwards, Newton, and Herman Richey. *The School in the American Social Order.* Boston: Houghton Mifflin Company, 1947.

> A most provocatively written statement on the history of education in the United States, with outstanding sections devoted to the elementary school.

3

EDUCATIONAL OBJECTIVES: DIRECTION FOR THE ELEMENTARY SCHOOL

Elementary school education, as a formal effort to educate, is a goal-oriented task. The efforts of the school are turned toward a stated set of objectives, which determine the curriculum. These organized statements of objectives provide society's answer to a most fundamental question: namely, "What does it mean to be educated, in this place, at this time?" The history of elementary school education shows that at a time when citizenship was directly related to church membership, which in turn was based in great part on the ability to read the Bible for oneself, the definition of "educated" was narrow, and the almost single objective of elementary education was to teach children to read. As commerce grew and business activity increased, the ability to write and to work with numbers were educational goals added to the elementary school curriculum. Later, as a result of the Revolutionary War and the great task of establishing the future security of the nation, sound citizenship became a characteristic of the educated person, and the elementary school curriculum included history, geography, and civics. As statements of educational objectives have broadened over the years, so has the curriculum.

EDUCATIONAL OBJECTIVES ROOTED IN SOCIETY

Educational Goals and National Policy

It is clear that educational objectives are indigenous to the society in which the educational effort is to take place and inherent in the way of

life most acceptable to that society. Implicit in statements of educational goals is national social policy. The statements function as standards against which the development of individual and group behavior can be checked. Statements of educational objectives are statements of an ideal; they indicate the most desirable direction for human behavior to take in our society. As such, they are to be approximated by each learner to the limit of his individual capacity for development. Attempts to introduce into educational objectives acceptable achievement criteria to which all are to be held are, in all probability, unprofitable. Such criteria usually indicate a level of accomplishment beyond the reach of some and not lofty enough for others. Although there is a general desired level of accomplishment for all goals, sufficient to insure satisfactory individual and social efficiency, actual accomplishment depends on the individual, and achievement criteria must be accordingly flexible.

Educational Goals and Social Change

History demonstrates that educational purposes change from time to time as social circumstances change, and as outlook on life changes accordingly. What it means to be educated is, as noted earlier, contingent on a specific place and time. The temptation to search for an eternal and universal formula for education is great, but human experience has shown the fallacy in such a quest. New situations demand new responses; new situations and responses reveal new educational goals and tasks.

It is probably one of the disasters of human existence that this element of change has not been recognized and accepted as it should be. We seem to educate too often for yesterday's world. There are undoubtedly many contributing factors to this. We fear the new in many areas of life, and are reluctant to seek new behaviors in the schools, even when the old ones no longer serve our purposes. Often we are simply slow in recognizing that circumstances have changed. When change is rapid, as it has been for the past several decades, the task of interpreting exactly what has happened, and what is likely to happen, becomes more difficult. During periods of rapid change, goals are less likely to be carefully reviewed and revised. It is not suggested here that the purposes for which we educate must change on a year-by-year basis, of course. But, over broader sweeps of time, change is inevitable, as new developments in society suggest new goals and present a new foundation from which to pursue old goals. Recognition of this inevitability can help us to avoid the error of the "saber-tooth curriculum," in which tiger-scaring was taught long after there were no saber-tooth tigers to scare.[1]

---

[1] Harold Benjamin, *Saber-Tooth Curriculum* (New York: McGraw-Hill Book Company, Inc., 1939).

Educational Goals: a Public Decision

It must be borne in mind that decisions about the purposes the public school system will pursue in the United States are to be made by the general public. The authority, legally and morally, rests with the people, as does the responsibility. History shows, again, the way our people have shaped and formed educational policy over the years. The legal framework in which decisions concerning school are made focuses the task of setting goals at the local community, county, and state levels. Educational decisions continue to be made outside the normal channels of municipal and civil government, a separation over local school district autonomy that started very early in our history continuing to set the pattern. As is true in political affairs, it is necessary to resort to representative systems in bringing the voice of the public to bear on this matter. Boards of education, composed of laymen, operate at all levels— local community, county, and state. They attempt to reflect in their decisions the will of the people they represent. In order to broaden the base of participation when crucial decisions are to be made, these boards often utilize lay advisory councils, thus bringing a greater number of people directly into the decision-making process. Such lay councils are without legal authority to act except in an advisory way; the ultimate responsibility for action still resides in the elected or appointed board of education.

There have also been efforts to spell out educational objectives, in an advisory way, at the national level, usually outside the government, although sometimes sponsored by the government. An outstanding example of this sort of leadership is the Educational Policies Commission, founded in the mid-1930's, and composed of top level lay and professional persons, who accept the responsibility to speak out on important educational matters in the United States. Their report on educational objectives is discussed at some length later in this chapter. An example of another sort of activity at the national level is that of the 1955 White House Conference on Education, sponsored by the national government in cooperation with many lay national agencies. One part of the conference report was a list of objectives to which, the participants felt, the schools of the nation should be committed. The list carries no official weight in educational matters, but it is helpful in indicating the extent of agreement nationally on educational purposes.

In the matter of determining educational goals, the authority of the professional educator is limited to the persuasiveness of his leadership. His educational arguments may influence public opinion in any direction, so he must try to help the public make informed decisions that will bear close scrutiny. But he is limited, legally and morally, in the degree

to which he can affect the decision of the public. Once the public has decided, he is bound to be guided by this decision. He may continue to express a minority opinion in an attempt to sway the majority to another decision, but he must wait for public sanction and approval before acting.

Educational Goals and Professional Autonomy

As the school refines and interprets the educational objectives determined by the public into ongoing school programs, the authority and responsibility begin to shift to the educators. So that general goals can be translated into specific goals, and so that decisions can be made as to where in the total system certain objectives will be developed most fully, and so that purposes can be determined for various age and grade levels, the public, realizing that these tasks demand a professional competence the general public does not possess, extends a measure of autonomy to the education profession. Despite this autonomy, however, the public educator should keep laymen informed of his plans, so that they may check the school's interpretation of general objectives. In the final analysis, the professional educator is responsible to the public for his program, and he will be judged to have acted wisely or unwisely in terms of the purposes that society has asked him to try to accomplish.

This partnership between the public and the profession can be diagrammed in the table on the following page.

The public identified in this chart may be operating at either the local community, county, or state levels. The profession cited includes teachers, principals, and special staff, as well as the superintendent of schools, and they, too, may be functioning at any of these three levels of educational government. In some instances, the public can be a national one, and national professional organizations often speak out for the profession.

CURRICULUM AS A MEANS TO OBJECTIVES

Generally, we can define *curriculum* as a series of educational situations through which goals and objectives are sought, but for our purposes we must have and use in this book a specific definition of the term.

Older Definitions of Curriculum

When the instructional program of the school first became an object of study and research, it became important to develop definitions for the term "curriculum." Those developed reflected the points of view of various specialists at that time. First efforts usually defined the curriculum as subject matter presented for study, or as the content of in-

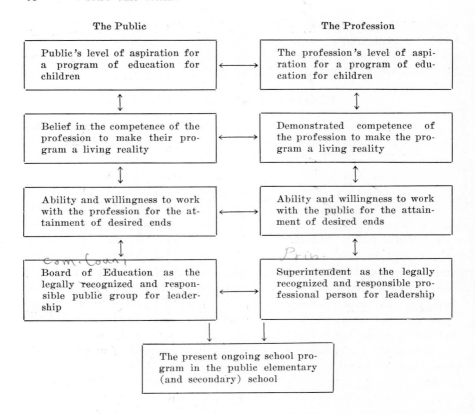

The Public   The Profession

Public's level of aspiration for a program of education for children

The profession's level of aspiration for a program of education for children

Belief in the competence of the profession to make their program a living reality

Demonstrated competence of the profession to make the program a living reality

Ability and willingness to work with the profession for the attainment of desired ends

Ability and willingness to work with the public for the attainment of desired ends

Board of Education as the legally recognized and responsible public group for leadership

Superintendent as the legally recognized and responsible professional person for leadership

The present ongoing school program in the public elementary (and secondary) school

struction, without reference to instructional ways or means, or some similar subject matter-oriented expressions. Such definitions persisted for some time, but gave way under the weight of newer philosophies of education, increased evidence concerning child growth and development and learning, and broader conceptions of the school experience.

Present Definitions of Curriculum

Undoubtedly, one of the most often used definitions of curriculum at the present time is one that suggests that the curriculum consists of all of the experiences that children (and youth) have under the guidance and direction of the school. This definition reflects, obviously, a much broader conception of schooling than was reflected in the older definitions. This one makes a place for classroom experiences, playground experiences, and all-school experiences in the curriculum. It also suggests a much broader conception of content than did the earlier definitions.

Some specialists define the curriculum in slightly different terms, often

in an attempt to reflect a particular position held concerning the role of the school in society, or a basic position with respect to individual pupil development. For instance, in a recent book dealing with elementary education a definition used by Hopkins is quoted as follows:

> The curriculum represents those learnings each child selects, accepts, and incorporates into himself to act with, on, and upon, in subsequent experiences.[2]

This definition emphasizes the individual nature of "becoming educated," and shows how, in the final analysis, the school is at the mercy of the learner himself, who literally makes his own curriculum. While it cannot be denied that children always have the option to accept or reject learnings that the school puts before them, we do not find this definition very helpful in making decisions about instructional programs.

Smith, Stanley, and Shores have defined the curriculum as "a sequence of potential experiences . . . set up in the school for the purpose of disciplining children and youth in group ways of thinking and acting."[3] In this instance, the social role of education is emphasized, and individual development is clearly related to the welfare of the larger group. It calls attention to responsibilities that the school must accept and follow through for the sake of society. Granting the important social role of the school's efforts to educate, many people are skeptical of this sort of definition; they feel that it may suggest a form of indoctrination rather than education.

Our Definition of Curriculum

The definition of curriculum most acceptable to us, and the one we have in mind consistently in this book as the term is used, is one we believe is of more help to the elementary school educator concerned with making curriculum decisions at the system, individual school, or classroom level than are those usually used. Our definition is as follows:

> The elementary (or secondary) school curriculum consists of those experiences that the school consciously and purposefully provides for children (and youth) in light of the accepted purposes of the school, using these experiences, also, as the major source of data upon which to base the evaluation of individual and group progress toward these purposes.

---

[2] L. Thomas Hopkins, *Interaction: The Democratic Process* (Boston: D. C. Heath and Company, 1941), p. 39 f., cited by Harold G. Shane and Wilbur A. Yanch, *Creative School Administration* (New York: Holt, Rinehart and Winston, Inc., 1954), p. 223.

[3] B. O. Smith, W. O. Stanley, and J. H. Shores, *Fundamentals of Curriculum Development* (Revised edition; Yonkers-on-Hudson: World Book Company, 1957), p. 3.

We consider this definition to be more helpful for several reasons: (1) it emphasizes the elements of consciousness and purposefulness in planning school experiences; (2) it directs attention to the relationship of the curriculum to the purposes that the school is seeking to fulfill; and (3) it focuses attention on the fact that the same experiences provided for educative purposes are the major source of data available to the school for the evaluation of its efforts. Granted, the school can seek and obtain some evidence of its success from parent-derived information, but in the main it must find the measure of the effectiveness of a particular experience from data derived of that experience.

We feel that this definition of curriculum helps to delimit the general phenomenon of "becoming educated" in a way that is helpful to the school and the teacher. Although the presence and effectiveness, for education, of experiences outside the school is recognized, the elementary school is asked to attempt particular learnings, related to particular goals. If the school is to be successful, and if it is to justify its procedures, it must be very clear about the nature of school curriculum.

STATEMENTS OF EDUCATIONAL OBJECTIVES

Levels of Statements of Purpose

Statements of purposes are directed at a particular level of the educational system; the direction influences the style and refinement of the statements in most instances. Since their purpose is to give direction to planning at a *level*, we should examine statements prepared for use at various levels in order to grasp the total job to be done.

Some statements of objectives are developed in such a way as to give direction to the total effort to educate in a particular society. These statements are most often referred to as statements of over-all goals and objectives. As good as many of these statements are, they are not as explicit as they must be. Several additional steps are necessary when one considers the way in which the individual school must ultimately deal with the matter of objectives. Such an over-all statement of objectives is presented here; it should be read with an awareness of what goals are included, and of the style in which they are expressed.

Purposes of Education in American Democracy

The most useful general statement of educational objectives in the past few decades is the 1938 document of the Educational Policies Commission, entitled *The Purposes of Education in American Democracy*,[4] a

---

[4] Educational Policies Commission, *The Purposes of Education in American Democracy* (Washington, D.C.: National Education Association, 1938), p. 157.

product of laymen and professional educators working together. We present it here for consideration because we believe it is a set of purposes to which the public school system in the United States can commit itself. Also, it is an excellent example of the way such statements should be expressed if they are to be useful in guiding educational efforts.

The report identified four major groups of educational objectives:

1. The objectives of self-realization—which deal with the individual as he becomes an educated person.
2. The objectives of human relationships—which deal with the individual as a member of the family and the community.
3. The objectives of economic efficiency—which deal with the individual as a producer and consumer.
4. The objectives of civic responsibility—which deal with the individual as a practicing citizen.

Each of these areas is, of course, related to the others, and the total of them all gives a full answer to the question of what it means to be an educated person. Obviously, the total task cannot be accomplished by the school alone. The report itself speaks of these subdivisions as "vantage points from which to study the purposes of education." And, in the words of the report, ". . . the school is only one of the many educational influences in these various fields of human life. Its responsibility extends to all of these areas, but in some areas the weight of education rests on the schools more exclusively than in others."[5] It might be said that one of the pressing educational concerns of our time is the proper distribution of this total job among the various groups and institutions concerned.

But, let us move on to the statement of purposes itself. The goals that the EPC report set down under each of the major groups of purposes are reproduced here in full.[6]

The Objectives of Self-Realization

The Inquiring Mind. The educated person has an appetite for learning.
Speech. The educated person can speak the mother tongue clearly.
Reading. The educated person reads the mother tongue efficiently.
Writing. The educated person writes the mother tongue effectively.
Number. The educated person solves his problems of counting and calculating.
Sight and Hearing. The educated person is skilled in listening and observing.
Health Knowledge. The educated person understands the basic facts concerning health and disease.
Health Habits. The educated person protects his own health and that of his dependents.

---

[5] Educational Policies Commission, *op. cit.*, pp. 47–48.
[6] Educational Policies Commission, *op. cit.*, pp. 50, 72, 90, and 108.

Public Health. The educated person works to improve the health of the community.

Recreation. The educated person is participant and spectator in many sports and other pastimes.

Intellectual Interest. The educated person has mental resources for the use of leisure.

Esthetic Interests. The educated person appreciates beauty.

Character. The educated person gives responsible direction to his own life.

The Objectives of Human Relationship

Respect for Humanity. The educated person puts human relationships first.

Friendships. The educated person enjoys a rich, sincere, and varied social life.

Cooperation. The educated person can work and play with others.

Courtesy. The educated person observes the amenities of social behavior.

Appreciation of the Home. The educated person appreciates the family as a social institution.

Conservation of the Home. The educated person conserves family ideals.

Homemaking. The educated person is skilled in homemaking.

Democracy in the Home. The educated person maintains democratic family relationships.

The Objectives of Economic Efficiency

Work. The educated producer knows the satisfaction of good workmanship.

Occupational Information. The educated producer understands the requirements and opportunities for various jobs.

Occupational Choice. The educated producer has selected his occupation.

Occupational Efficiency. The educated producer succeeds in his chosen vocation.

Occupational Adjustment. The educated producer maintains and improves his efficiency.

Occupational Appreciation. The educated producer appreciates the social value of his work.

Personal Economics. The educated consumer plans the economics of his own life.

Consumer Judgment. The educated consumer develops standards for guiding his expenditures.

Efficiency in Buying. The educated consumer is an informed and skillful buyer.

Consumer Protection. The educated consumer takes appropriate measures to safeguard his interests.

The Objectives of Civic Responsibility

Social Justice. The educated citizen is sensitive to the disparities of human circumstance.

Social Activity. The educated citizen acts to correct unsatisfactory conditions.

Social Understanding. The educated citizen seeks to understand social structures and social processes.

Critical Judgment. The educated citizen has defenses against propaganda.

Tolerance. The educated citizen respects honest differences of opinion.

Conservation. The educated citizen has a regard for the nation's resources.

Social Applications of Science. The educated citizen measures scientific advance by its contribution to the general welfare.

World Citizenship. The educated citizen is a cooperating member of the world community.

Law Observance. The educated citizen respects the law.

Economic Literacy. The educated citizen is economically literate.

Political Citizenship. The educated citizen accepts his civic duties.

Devotion to Democracy. The educated citizen acts upon an unswerving loyalty to democratic ideals.

Despite the usefulness of this statement of purposes, additional steps are necessary if the school is to receive the proper guidance and direction. Each purpose must be defined more extensively to assist the school in deciding what it will and will not do in its curriculum. A goal such as ''reads the mother tongue effectively'' calls for an extensive definition of ''reading effectively.'' A goal such as ''appreciates beauty'' calls for similar deliberate amplification. The whole list must be extensively developed so that what the school ultimately does is defensible in terms of our values, and of present social circumstances, as our people see them.

Once the list of over-all goals is developed to the point that their intent is explicitly stated and understood, decisions have to be made as to which goals will be sought at which levels of the school system. Making these decisions necessitates combining the social priority of each goal with our knowledge of human development, so that efforts to educate take place at the proper time in the total sequence. Let us consider an example of such a statement for elementary school education.

Objectives of Elementary Education

A most comprehensive study was undertaken a few years ago to ascertain the present objectives of elementary school education in the United States. This study attempted to identify the objectives that the elementary school was most often asked to seek in its curriculum; it also attempted to test the reasonableness of the job that was being asked of the elementary school. In other words, the study focused attention on those objectives out of the general, over-all statements that were most often presented to the elementary school. The results of this study were

made available to elementary school educators in 1953. The following recommended objectives were identified at that time as being most often allocated to the elementary school, and were expressed thus in the report:

> 1. *Physical Development, Health, and Body Care.*
> Physical development, health, and body care is a broad category as compared with the narrow conception of physiology and hygiene which it has replaced in the elementary school curriculum. Today it involves both health and safety. It includes individual health and the elementary aspects of public health. It includes physical education, personal grooming, safety, sportsmanship, and an understanding of growth and maturation. . . .
>
> 2. *Individual Social and Emotional Development.*
> This category includes material that is commonly associated with mental health, emotional stability, and the growth of personality [with] emphasis on such goals as understanding oneself and evaluating oneself. . . . In this area there is more difficulty in pointing out basic knowledge and skills than is true in some others, since the area itself is so much one of attitudes and interests. . . .
>
> 3. *Ethical Behavior, Standards, Values.*
> Ethical behavior, standards and values are related to the observance of the moral law and the civil law. This area includes the observance of much that gains validity from the customs and mores of the culture. It involves sportsmanship, kindliness, helpfulness, and the problems involved in living in a society with other people. It is concerned with the integrity and honesty of people. . . .
>
> 4. *Social Relations.*
> This . . . is devoted to the individual as a person in his personal-social relations with others, when he has to consider the needs, interests, motives, convictions, and ideals of others with whom he associates in home, community, and place of work. . . .
>
> 5. *The Social World.*
> This . . . considers the child in a somewhat broader social setting than does . . . social relations. Here we set the goals for the child in terms of the structure and the institutions of our culture. The behavior of the child is considered in relation to community, state, and nation. Geography in its relation to man is in this background. Civics, elementary economics, government, and the traditional American way of life come in this area. . . .
>
> 6. *The Physical World (The Natural Environment).*
> In this . . . attention is centered on an enlarged concept of science, and reference is made to many aspects of the child's environment. Physical science problems, as well as the science that deals with plants and animals, are emphasized. Also stressed are learning to think scientifically and the use of *methods of science* in solving problems in science and problems in everyday living. Emphasis is on thinking that associates facts and relates them in various ways to form generalizations. . . .

7. *Esthetic Development.*

In this . . . emphasis is placed on esthetic appreciation and expression. Though the primary emphasis here is on art, music, and the crafts, . . . many types of artistic and creative endeavor are mentioned. The moral, the intellectual, and the emotional aspects of esthetic development are all included. . . .

8. *Communication.*

This . . . covers the wide variety of means by which man communicates with man. It emphasizes the mechanical and skills aspects of reading, writing, composition, correct usage, spelling, punctuation, speaking, and listening. It includes the use of the library and of references of various kinds. It includes group skills, such as conducting and participating in meetings. It stresses the various constructive uses to which communication skills must be put, if their mastery is to be of value. . . .

9. *Quantitative Relationships.*

Here we find arithmetic and the elementary aspects of algebra and geometry. Here children are introduced to a great variety of measures by which man describes in quantities the things he finds in his world. This involves the ability to analyze and solve problems on the basis of the particular problem, the information needed to solve it, and how to get the information. Emphasis is placed on giving the child an understanding of how our number system works and why, so that he will have greater competence in using numbers. Since mathematics is the language of quantity, it could be included as another means of communication, but it is so important and specialized that it is considered separately.[7]

Together, the report of the Educational Policies Commission and the Kearney report provide a useful base for the study and discussion of the objectives of education generally, and of elementary education specifically. In the main, other statements of purpose that might have been quoted here are very much like these. Some differences may exist among school systems, but they would more than likely be differences of emphasis and priority in objectives rather than of inclusiveness and kind.

Objectives at the Classroom Level

Goals of elementary education must also be expressed in terms of school years: Which learnings will be attempted in the first year? Which in the second year? These goals must be expressed in such a way as to give to the classroom teacher the sort of direction that will enable him to develop an instructional program for the year so that he may contribute effectively to the over-all effort.

Some school systems publish, for the use of teacher, child, and parent, compact little brochures that outline in general the goals to be sought

---

[7] Nolan C. Kearney, *Elementary School Objectives* (New York: Russell Sage Foundation, 1953), pp. 52–113.

at each grade level. The schools in Palo Alto, California, recently developed such brochures, which include in part statements such as the following:

Under a title "What We Teach in the First Grade," we find these statements under arithmetic:

> So that your child will begin to understand the part that numbers will play in his life, he will receive instructions in:
> Number relationships by manipulating objects
> Reading and writing numbers from 1 to 100
> Recognition of number words up to six
> Counting by 2's, 10's
> Addition and subtraction
> Using ordinal numbers from first to sixth
> Making simple measurements
> Naming days of the week and months of the year
> Awareness of time by use of the clock (hour and half hour)
> The value of money—penny, nickel and dime
> Estimating size, distance and quantity
> Tens as a basis of our number system

Under *Social Studies* we find:

> To understand the immediate environment and the child's relationship to it, these experiences are provided:
> A study of the home
> A study of the school
> A study of the neighborhood

> Through these experiences, your child will begin to be aware of:
> His responsibility in the group
> The democratic process
> The need for rules
> Problems and their solution[8]

The brochure for use at the fifth grade level has this to say:

> Arithmetic—Program of instruction will include:
> Review of combinations and the basic processes
> Multiplication and division through 12
> Computation with two place multipliers and divisors
> Reading and using Roman numerals through D and M
> Reading and using numbers through millions
> Reading and using the ruler
> Addition and subtraction of measures: linear, time, liquid, dry and weight
> Addition and subtraction of decimals and whole numbers

---

[8] Palo Alto Unified School District, *What We Teach in the First Grade* (Palo Alto, California: Office of the Assistant Superintendent, October 1958).

Adding and subtracting of like and unlike fractions
Reading and constructing graphs
Constructing maps to scale
Computing area and perimeter of rectangle
Using simple formulae

And, under *Social Studies*, we find:

Major emphasis is placed on understanding American heritage and citizenship:
The Colonial Period
The Westward Movement to Modern Times
At this level, a further emphasis is placed on geographical relationships, conservation, place location, and map skills.[9]

Objectives and Programs in the Curriculum

Usually, in the process of moving from a general statement of educational goals to the specific statement of classroom-level goals, the educator finds it advantageous to translate purposes into operational *programs*. Certain goals together call for a program in the language arts, others a program in arithmetic and mathematics, others a program in social studies, science, or art. Inclusive statements of objectives can be developed for programs, which can be stated as goals for the school or for any grade level therein. Now, it does not follow that the curriculum must, of necessity, be organized on a program-by-program basis, but any curricular scheme must take account of these program goals. (See Chapter 9 for further comment on this matter.) But, it is a step that is useful and necessary as the school attempts to translate the goals it is to seek into the familiar subject matter categories of the organized cultural heritage, and to see ways of relating this heritage appropriately to the objectives being sought.

This discussion on levels of goal setting can be summarized in the diagram on the following page.

Priority Among Objectives

All elementary school systems base their programs on some concept of function, which may vary from district to district, and to a degree from school to school in the same district. Where differences are found among various school systems in emphasis and priority among objectives, they are most often due to differing concepts of the function of the elementary school program. Some schools accept as their primary function the development of the basic skills of language and arithmetic; others, the development of proper citizenship. Still others seem to define

[9] Palo Alto Unified School District, *What We Teach in the Fifth Grade* (Palo Alto, California: Office of the Assistant Superintendent, September 1959).

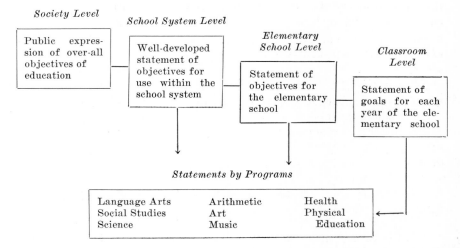

their function in an almost therapeutic way, vowing to help children adjust to themselves and to others, meeting personal needs and solving problems in the process. Each of these schools gives priority to the objectives that best fulfill its concept of function. Almost the only responsibility that the elementary school in the United States has not been asked to accept in any direct way is that of helping learners to make professional and vocational choices and of helping them to prepare accordingly. We have taken the position in our school system that the period of childhood finds the pupil too young, too unsure of his own abilities and interests, and of the possible choices, to pursue in any direct way the objectives of economic efficiency cited in the EPC report.

Breadth of Elementary School Educational Objectives

The reports given above clearly present a very broad set of objectives for the elementary school. They call for efforts to help children to develop intellectually, socially, physically, and emotionally. They recognize, too, that the development of understandings and insights, of loyalties and values, of attitudes and appreciations, and of skills and abilities are legitimate and necessary purposes. Furthermore, the statements reflect the inevitable dual responsibilities of the school both to the individual and to the society of which he is a part. Together, they outline a broad and varied job to be done, demanding a broad and varied curriculum in the elementary school.

This breadth of responsibility presents one of the persistent problems facing elementary school education. On one hand, many people feel that the school is being asked to try to accomplish too much, often in areas

that are properly the work of other social institutions and agencies. On the other hand, living and growing up in our time makes greater demands on the individual than at any time in our history, and it is extremely difficult to cut the educational effort. People seem to want the school to accept very broad responsibilities in the interests of improved child education. There are indications of developments in the elementary school that may help to resolve this problem in the years ahead.

One such development is that of reaffirming in some instances, and re-establishing in others, the idea that the top priority in an elementary school program must go to the intellectual development of children. This development does not mean that the elementary school will not actively seek to help children in their physical, social, and emotional development. It does suggest that the distribution of effort, as well as the degree to which the elementary school will accept responsibilities in these various areas of human development, may shift a bit.

Another development along these same lines is that of re-examining, community by community, the degree to which certain of the school's tasks can be shared with other community institutions and agencies, such as the family group and the church. This development, too, may help to redistribute the efforts of the school more advantageously for children, and in the long run it may increase the effectiveness of the total educational enterprise. However, this complex task is not accomplished either easily or quickly.

These comments must not be construed to mean a cutback in the elementary school curriculum to some of the more restricted sets of purposes of earlier times. Rather, they are meant to suggest that the elementary school, like any social institution, has limitations on what it can do. New arrangements for learning, improved instructional materials, better prepared teachers, and more adequately financed school systems, all hold promise of increased efficiency and are to be weighed accordingly in this re-examination. The most disastrous result of any such reappraisal of the elementary school would be the conclusion that an educational effort "good enough" at some past time is sufficient for the present.

Research done by one of the authors over the past several years has shed some light on these developments. Various community groups, both lay and professional, were asked to list in order of importance the goals the elementary school curriculum should pursue. They were asked to delete, before their attempt to rank the most important goals, any goals that the elementary school should not pursue at all; in almost no instance was any goal on the list deleted. Most people felt that the school should accept very broad responsibilities; however, their ranking did indicate a realization that some of the objectives sought were more

completely the school's responsibility than were others. The composite list is presented below by groups of purposes, rather than by individual rank order.

> First priority purposes:
>> To help children to develop understanding and skill in the area of English language arts (reading, writing, speaking, spelling, listening).
>> To help children to develop understanding and skill in arithmetic.
>> To help chi'dren to become socially competent and secure—adequate in their relationships to others.
>> To help children to develop their powers of reflective thinking, of problem solving, and of reason.
>
> Second priority purposes:
>> To help children to become aware of and to understand the social environment and increasingly to comprehend and appreciate our way of life and that of others.
>> To help children to become aware of and to understand the natural environment and increasingly to comprehend science as a force in modern life and technology as the fruit of scientific endeavor.
>> To help children to understand and be committed to the basic values of democracy and to evaluate their behavior according to these values.
>
> Third priority purposes:
>> To help children to live healthfully and to develop the understandings and habits basic to the maintenance of health, both physical and mental.
>> To help children to become aware of the esthetic aspects of our culture (art and music), to appreciate and participate in them; to release their own creative abilities.

Content Goals and Process Goals

A further examination of the statements of objectives cited in this chapter, including the list immediately above, will reveal at least two categories of objectives, namely content goals and process goals. This is to say that certain objectives, if they are to be realized, demand that the child have direct experience with particular subject matter. Other objectives make it mandatory that the child have direct experiences with certain processes of learning, of problem solving, of creating, and so on. To illustrate: a child cannot learn history, or science, or language without coming into contact with subject matter from these areas, be that subject matter contained in a book, a movie, or a chart. Neither can he learn to solve problems, develop responsibility, show initiative, or realize his creative potential unless he has direct experiences with these processes and in situations which call upon him to be responsible and to initiate action.

However, a single learning experience can contribute to the realization of both content and process goals. For children to develop problem solving skills, there must be a problem to solve. A science learning enterprise may present just such a needed problem and in the process the child learns a good bit of the subject matter of science. In a sense, then, it is meaningless to give a higher (or lower) priority to a goal such as "helping children to become better problem solvers" than to one such as "increasing understanding and insight into the social and natural environment." In a very real way the processes become a part of content; the student learns ways of working as well as subject matter. In the give and take of the classroom some of the suggested priorities found here are difficult to identify.

BEHAVIORAL STATEMENTS OF PURPOSE

Earlier in this chapter we noted that the style in which purposes are expressed affects their usefulness to the school. By *usefulness* we mean the degree to which the statements can be readily translated into educational programs. Past experience has shown that statements of purpose are most useful when they are expressed in terms of human behaviors. Efforts to express objectives have often in the past simply resulted in a list of high-sounding generalities, difficult or impossible to follow in providing an educational program. However, if educational goals are expressed according to a definition of education as "a change in or a modification of human behavior," or in *behavioral* terms, these statements become considerably clearer.

The clarity of statements of objectives is crucial at two points in the educative process: (1) at the outset of curriculum planning, when the school chooses among a number of possible alternatives, the final choice is made in great part in direct relation to the clarity with which the school understands its task; (2) at the time of evaluation, when the school decides whether it has been successful with its pupils in making progress toward particular goals. Behavioral statements more clearly indicate both the source and type of evidence that must be collected and interpreted before growth and achievement can be appraised. As a rule, purposes that cannot be expressed in behavioral terms are not purposes that the school experience can consciously try to accomplish.

Stating Goals Behaviorally

One of the reasons for citing the Educational Policies Commission report on purposes is that it expresses goals in behavioral terms. However, even with this advantage at the outset, the school must know much

more about certain of these purposes before it can use them with assurance as a source of curricular direction. The school must usually develop each of these statements further by processing these general goals not only into elementary and secondary school goals, but further into classroom level and program goals as previously discussed. Goals such as "has an appetite for learning," or "appreciates beauty," or "conserves family ideals" must be developed more precisely into the behaviors that define them and that are evidence of their accomplishment. The behavioral definition of goals insures that the school clearly understands the charge society has extended to it. Once developed, these behavioral statements are of great help to the school and to the teacher as the curriculum is planned and learning experiences are provided. Let us consider together some examples of attempts to state objectives behaviorally in the interests of clarity.

Illustrations of Behavioral Statements of Objectives

To decide what we must do to accomplish a goal such as, for example, "to develop a sense of personal responsibility in children," we must define for ourselves what responsible behavior is in our society, and even more specifically, what responsible child behavior is. Since we are planning a school curriculum, our definition of responsible child behavior will be expressed chiefly in terms of living, working, and playing at school, so that the statement of purpose will be meaningful to the elementary school and the teacher as he plans the school experience. The statement developed can also be used with the public as a check on the school's understanding of the way that traits like "responsible behavior" are defined in the wider society.

For this goal, the following statement might be the result:

> The educated child demonstrates a developing sense of responsibility in all aspects of living. A responsible child:
> a. finishes schoolwork assigned to him for completion;
> b. returns to the classroom equipment that he has taken out for use on the playground;
> c. remembers to bring things from home to school, and vice versa, when the situation demands it of him;
> d. carries through on "classroom helper" assignments without constant reminders from the teacher; etc.

A much longer list could be developed, obviously, but this should be sufficient to illustrate a behavioral statement. The above statement suggests some of the things in which the children will have to become involved in order to become responsible; it also points to sources of

data that the teacher can use to evaluate the development of a given child's responsibility.

Or, suppose the purpose to be sought is the universal one of teaching children to read. Again, the school is more sure of its objective and the teacher is better served by a behavioral statement of this goal. The following statement might be used:

> The educated child reads the mother tongue effectively. Such a child:
> a. discusses with understanding the content of the printed page;
> b. reads with understanding both silently and aloud;
> c. applies various word attack skills to new words;
> d. chooses to read at times when he has a free choice of activities; etc.

The teacher is more likely to know what to do in the classroom to help children to become effective readers if this is the sort of statement he has to guide his efforts. He will be much more sensitive to evidence of a child's progress toward this goal. Such a statement is useful, too, in helping to check with the public the school's understanding of the goal.

EDUCATIONAL OBJECTIVES AND CURRICULUM FUNCTIONS

There is one other important insight to be developed concerning educational objectives as they affect curriculum development: the function, or proper responsibility, of the school curriculum. The discussion that follows here will clarify the concept of function in terms of general and special education.

General and Special Education

The translation of educational goals into actual curricular experiences is divided functionally into *general education* and *special education*. By general education is meant those learning experiences designed to insure that certain understandings, values, loyalties, attitudes, and skills are developed in every child born into our society. They are considered to be minimum essentials for anybody who is to live efficiently and effectively among us as a good and proper citizen. Special education, on the other hand, refers to learning experiences that are designed to insure the development of particular understandings, values, attitudes, and skills that must be developed by persons seeking to fill specific positions in the society. The term usually connotes preparation for a particular profession or vocation. Perhaps the relationship of these

two terms to the development of curriculum can best be explained by means of an analogy from physics.

When a wheel is in motion, there are two opposing forces, centrifugal and centripetal, that insure the form of the wheel by counteracting one another. Centrifugal force is directed outward from the center of the wheel, giving it a tendency to spin apart; the wheel does not spin apart because of the equal and opposite centripetal force, the direction of which is toward the center.

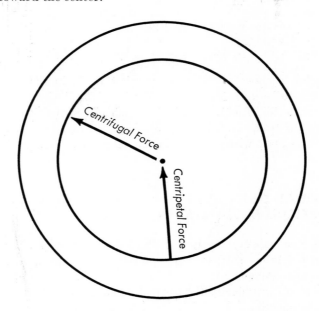

PHYSICAL FORCES ON A FIELD

Applied to society and education, the elements of this analogy are easily identified: we can substitute society for the wheel, special education for centrifugal force, and general education for centripetal force. If the specializations demanded by our culture and personal interests of the individuals in our society were not counteracted by equally strong common interests and values, as developed through general education, the "wheel" of society would spin apart. Thus, through the functional division of the educational effort, the many specialties demanded by the society are provided for, individual interests are served, and at the same time the social system is held together around a common core of values and interests.

The relationship of this functional division to elementary school curriculum becomes clearer if we return to the list of educational ob-

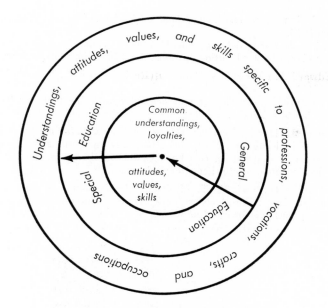

DUAL ROLE OF EDUCATION

jectives for elementary education. This statement, obviously, directs the elementary school to contribute almost exclusively to general education. We do not expect young children to make vocational or professional choices, so there is no need for special education at this level. General education extends beyond the elementary school, of course, and the elementary school does plan for some learnings outside of general education; it is sufficient here to understand the two broad and contrasting functions of general and special education.

REFERENCES

Caswell, Hollis L., and Arthur W. Foshay. *Education in the Elementary School* (Third edition). New York: American Book Company, 1957.
> Educational aims are discussed thoroughly in Chapter 4, with special concern for their role in elementary education.

Educational Policies Commission. *The Purposes of Education in American Democracy.* Washington, D.C.: National Education Association, 1938.
> A provocative analysis of factors that influence educational objectives, a review of important statements on aims over the years, and a statement of objectives consistent with our basic values.

Herrick, Virgil E., and others. *The Elementary School.* Englewood Cliffs, New Jersey: Prentice-Hall, Inc., 1956.
> Chapter 4 deals comprehensively with educational objectives, with attention to the individual- and society-centered aspects.

Kearney, Nolan C. *Elementary School Objectives*. New York: Russell Sage Foundation, 1953.

> Attempts a complete statement of most commonly accepted objectives for elementary education, presented as behavioral definitions.

Krug, Edward A. *Curriculum Planning* (Revised edition). New York: Harper & Brothers, 1957.

> The author deals clearly and helpfully with the matter of objectives in Chapters 2 and 3.

Otto, Henry J., Hazel Floyd, and Margaret Rouse. *Principles of Elementary Education* (Revised edition). New York: Rinehart and Company, 1955.

> The early chapters in this book center on the purposes for which we organize and operate elementary schools.

Shane, Harold G., and E. T. McSwain. *Evaluation and the Elementary Curriculum* (Revised edition). New York: Henry Holt and Company, 1958.

> These authors devote Chapter 2 to the central importance of clear statements of objectives to guide our work with children.

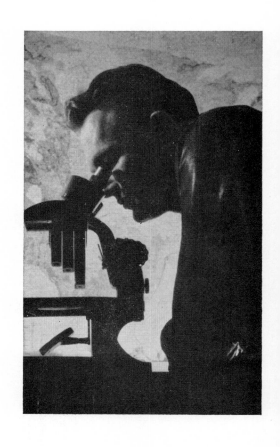

PART 2

DEVELOPING ELEMENTARY SCHOOL CURRICULUM

4

CURRICULUM PLANNING:
AN INTRODUCTION

A great deal of careful and deliberate planning must take place, obviously, if the elementary school is to accomplish its assigned portion of the school's total responsibility for education. The statements of objectives discussed in the preceding chapter must be studied carefully and understood thoroughly by school personnel. *Curriculum planning* is the analysis of these objectives and the designing of educational experiences that lead to their accomplishment. The focus of this endeavor is on the means by which these educational ends may be satisfactorily achieved. The chapters in Part 2 of this book are designed to develop an understanding of this task of curriculum planning. Curriculum is, of course, the very heart of the educational enterprise; it is around this center that schools, classrooms, and teachers are provided.

Let us consider again the definition of curriculum used in this book. The term was defined as follows:

> The elementary (or secondary) school curriculum consists of those experiences that the school consciously and purposefully provides for children (and youth) in light of the accepted purposes of the school, using these experiences, also, as the major source of data upon which to base the evaluation of individual and group progress toward these purposes.

This statement is intended to suggest the deliberateness and the thoughtfulness basic to curriculum planning. It is felt that this definition is consistent, too, with the position taken here with respect to the school as a social institution. In our view, schools are provided in order

to minimize the element of chance in education, so that certain educational objectives will be consciously and purposefully pursued in a situation designed specifically for this pursuit.

PARTICIPANTS IN CURRICULUM PLANNING

There is, in the minds of the people, usually some confusion as to the individuals and groups who actually participate in curriculum planning. A long list of individuals and groups who influence curriculum planning in the interests of better education can be identified. These "participants" include both lay and professional persons and groups, operating at all levels in society, through a variety of channels of communication. Most often their influence is in direct ratio to the powers of persuasion they can muster as they approach boards of education, school administrators, and teachers. Sometimes they are sufficiently persuasive to have their wishes formalized into educational laws that require the schools to include certain programs in their curricula and to give fixed amounts of time to each program or subject.

A recent book dealing with the sociology of the school identified the following as a list of forces that influenced and affected the curriculum of the public schools:

State legislative action	Teacher training programs
Federal working relationships	Textbooks
Local boards of education	Special interest groups
The force of tradition	(religious, patriotic, civic, indus-
Subject matter specialists	trial, etc.)
Teacher associations	Parents
Material resources for working	Students
Regional accrediting associations	School administrators
College entrance regulations	Teachers[1]

In this list one finds recognition of the influence, in shaping the curriculum, of lay persons and groups, scholarly groups interested in public education, government, and the personnel who actually staff our public school system. Obviously, some of these influences are more directly felt in the elementary school than are others, although all influencing factors are felt to some extent from kindergarten through high school, since it is in the very nature of public education to be influenced by its supporting "publics."

---

[1] M. W. Rodehaver, W. B. Axtell, and R. E. Gross, *The Sociology of the School* (New York: Thomas Y. Crowell Company, 1957), pp. 188–196.

A Demand for Professional Competence

At the same time, within curriculum planning there is a professional task to be done, calling for professional skill and competence. Developing plans and providing situations in which the educative process can best flourish is the *sine qua non* of the education profession. Determining broad educational policy, as noted earlier, calls for a most extensive kind of societal participation. Designing the curriculum of the school is best accomplished by persons—school administrators, teachers, and various other educational specialists—prepared to do just that. These are the people who must provide the leadership and the know-how in this endeavor, and these are the people who must execute the plans in the school and classroom.

That school personnel need and want the advice and counsel of other groups is inevitable. Scholars of various fields of human knowledge and lay persons from certain specialized fields of work have much to contribute, and schools situated so that they can conveniently call on these people for assistance are fortunate. This need is evident in the many recent attempts to utilize scientists drawn from local research and industrial groups, and other such persons from other fields, as lay advisors to boards of education and to school groups in specialized matters of curriculum evaluation and revision. Parents, who legitimately want to be close to the school experiences of their children, are helpful participants in determining certain curriculum policies. For instance, the relation of homework to curriculum planning requires a decision that might well be helped by parental participation. But, in the final analysis, it is the responsibility of school personnel to provide sound leadership in the task of curriculum planning.

The matter of differentiating professional responsibility from general

Determining the purposes of education	Determining the best means of accomplishing agreed-upon purposes	Assessing and evaluating the achievement of agreed-upon purposes
Demands the widest possible participation from society, including school people.	Responsibility of school personnel, with lay assistance as sought by school people.	School personnel responsible for continuing systematic evaluation and accounting to society. Also, informal evaluation by society as it meets the up-coming generation.

public responsibility is summarized in the table shown. Since curriculum planning, when seen in this way, is a professional task, it seems

appropriate for society to extend a considerable measure of autonomy to the education profession, as it has to other professions, in order that an important task may be more efficiently accomplished. This view does suggest, too, that this autonomy has its roots in the general public, that there is a close working relationship between the professional and the layman in school affairs, and that the professional is ultimately responsible to the wider society for the results of his work. This autonomy in no way suggests that the profession is usurping the powers of the public; rather it is squarely meeting the responsibility the public extends.

CURRICULUM DEVELOPMENT AND INSTRUCTIONAL IMPROVEMENT

In the discussion thus far, both curriculum development and instructional improvement have been referred to under the inclusive term *curriculum planning;* there is, however, an important difference in focus between these two aspects of curriculum planning, a difference that must be understood before they are dealt with in the chapters that follow.

Curriculum Development

The term *curriculum development* refers to the constant assessment of the adequacy of the curriculum offered by the elementary school. This assessment goes beyond the evaluation of the school's accomplishment of its assigned goals; it focuses, instead, thoughtfully and deliberately on the question of whether the school is pursuing the *proper* goals: Is the curriculum to which the elementary school is presently committed an adequate one? This question implies that there is a ''frontier'' of thought and concern in elementary education, that there is a need for a continuous assessment of the current curriculum. Present evidences of this need are found in the deliberations taking place over the degree to which foreign language instruction should be a part of the elementary school curriculum, or in the concern to reassess elementary school science education with the possibility of drastic reorientation.

Instructional Improvement

The term *instructional improvement* refers to the attempts to increase the effectiveness of instruction. It focuses on the degree to which children are actually learning to read, to work with numbers, to understand the general social environment, and so on. Many of the services furnished by a school system to help teachers, a great deal of faculty meeting time, and a great part of the in-service study program of a school system are concerned with instructional improvement. Decisions may lead to the purchase of additional varieties of instructional equipment, to the adoption of

new printed materials, to the replacement of outmoded school furniture, or to some other action that it is felt will lead to improved instruction. Whatever the result, these efforts are put forth to help the school do the best job it can do with the presently accepted curriculum.

APPROACHING THE TASK OF CURRICULUM PLANNING

Planning the curriculum requires some sort of structure or over-all working concept in order to see the exact nature of the job to be done and to get that job accomplished. This task can be viewed as the effort to give considered responses to a number of relatively explicit questions that the educator must answer as he plans the curriculum, whether he is a system-wide representative on the superintendent's staff or a teacher developing a classroom program.

Two important matters have already been decided: whether to have schools, and what educational objectives schools should pursue. Curriculum planning requires answers to the following questions:[2]

To accomplish these objectives—

What shall we teach?	The selection of subject matter.
How shall we teach?	The determination of method.
When shall we teach?	Grade placement and continuity.
How shall we organize for teaching?	Over-all curriculum design.
How shall we know how well we have taught?	Evaluation techniques and procedures.
How shall we improve all of our efforts?	Research and development in curriculum planning.

Curriculum is planned as these questions are answered. They must all be answered in some way, or the total job of curriculum planning will not be accomplished.

Over the years, of course, many answers have been given to each of these questions, and particular sets of answers have been so intimately associated one with the other that curriculum patterns, or theories of curriculum planning, have been presented, practiced, analyzed, and argued in educational circles. The most common patterns are discussed in Chapter 7. It is enough at this point to note that systematic and consistent sets of answers to the above questions have been formulated in a way that provides some theoretical models for curriculum planning. Of course, the adequacy of any one of these models must stand the test of professional study and school practice. Let us turn briefly to the way answers to these questions are developed.

---

[2] Adapted in part from ideas developed in a paper by Arno A. Bellack, Teachers College, Columbia University.

THE FOUNDATIONS OF EDUCATION AND CURRICULUM PLANNING

Faced with the task outlined here, educators have had to seek answers that would lead to a curriculum that would be effective in accomplishing educational purposes. The task has been one of identifying those areas of human knowledge that seemed to hold the promise of fact and of hypothesis, out of which would develop practices and procedures for curriculum planning.

Identifying the Foundations of Education

Attention directed to this matter has made it increasingly evident that sound education and defensible curricula depend on an understanding of at least three areas of knowledge:

1. the present and emerging social scene;
2. the values sought by society;
3. the human organism, its growth, development, and learning processes.

These three areas of human knowledge are the sources of the facts, concepts, generalizations, and hypotheses that lead to sound answers to problems in curriculum planning. These areas are typically referred to in the profession as the *Foundations*. More specifically they are as follows:

The Social Foundations of Education

Those areas of human knowledge about society, culture, and man. Together they yield information on cultural transmission and change, and on the current and emerging social scene.

The Philosophical Foundations of Education

That area of human thought about our basic values and beliefs, which helps us to be more explicit about our most desired way of life. It presents the educator with a normative picture of life, that is, life as it ought to be and not necessarily as it is or is becoming.

The Biopsychological Foundations of Education

Those areas of human knowledge about human growth and development, which help the educator to understand the processes of learning and socialization.

Together, these foundations form a kind of triangle of human knowledge and belief against which choices may be cast and decisions weighed to insure as far as possible that curriculum objectives, content, and processes are sound and defensible. The chart on the following page illustrates the dynamics of this triangle:

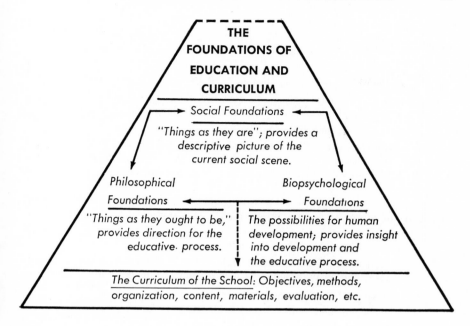

It must be remembered that curriculum decisions do not flow automatically from these foundation areas. These foundations do furnish the educator with facts and concepts, with principles and generalizations, with hunches and hypotheses as to the most appropriate answers to the wide variety of questions inherent in curriculum planning. But the information they furnish must be put into a frame of reference useful in curriculum work. Much of the information in each of these areas is not produced with the school curriculum primarily in mind. For instance, the studies by sociologists on class in American society were not undertaken in the interests of improved curriculum, but the findings have been useful in helping the school to understand better some of the problems it faces in planning a curriculum for all of the children in our society. If these data are to be used in school affairs, educators must reflect on them in terms of their most effective uses.

Using the Foundations in Curriculum Planning

Insights into the foundations have bearing both on decisions about over-all curriculum patterns and on decisions about any one learning program in the curriculum. For instance, suppose that attention is focused on the teaching of reading in the elementary school curriculum. We find:

In the social foundations:

> ample evidence that this skill is of great importance in our culture; insight into the various kinds of reading individuals are asked to undertake.

In the philosophical foundations:

> ample support for the fact that self-realization in our society means that people ought to be able to read the language.

In the biopsychological foundations:

> evidence concerning individual differences in verbal ability; insight into the best time to introduce children to reading; many ideas as to procedures and materials to use in teaching reading.

Or, to take a more complex situation, if a decision is faced concerning the study of minority groups in our nation, we find:

In the philosophical foundations:

> clear suggestions as to the rights of minority groups in our democracy, and clear direction as to how they should be treated.

In the social foundations:

> confusing and contradictory evidence as to how minority groups are actually treated in our society, and varied opinion as to how they should be treated.

In the biopsychological foundations:

> evidence concerning the degree to which instruction may influence attitudes; data on the nature of prejudice; information on stereotyping, and so on.

While these foundation areas are not always brought into such sharp focus in curriculum planning, they are as central to the decision-making as the above illustrations suggest. The next two chapters are devoted to a systematic discussion of each of the foundations. In the first of these chapters, attention is given to society, culture, and values as guides to curriculum planning in light of present and emerging social circumstances. This discussion is followed in the second chapter by a similar discussion of the child and the learning process as guides to curriculum development.

REFERENCES

Alcorn, Marvin D., and James M. Linley (editors). *Issues in Curriculum Development.* Yonkers-on-Hudson: World Book Company, 1959.

> A selection of interesting statements on curriculum, its determination and operation, and the general direction in which curriculum planning is moving.

Caswell, Hollis L., and Arthur W. Foshay. *Education in the Elementary School* (Third edition). New York: American Book Company, 1957.
> Chapter 1, dealing with the major issues and problems in elementary education, is relevant to the discussion here.

Goodlad, John I. "Illustrative Programs and Procedures in Elementary Schools," in *The Integration of Educational Experiences* (Fifty-seventh Yearbook, Part III). National Society for the Study of Education. Chicago: University of Chicago Press, 1957.
> Describes and analyzes five approaches to the integration of learning experiences that relate to curriculum planning.

Hanna, Paul R. "Society–Child–Curriculum," in Clarence W. Hunnicutt (editor), *Education—2000 A.D.* Syracuse: Syracuse University Press, 1956.
> This chapter deals with the relation of curriculum to the child on one hand and to society on the other.

Lee, J. Murray, and Dorris May Lee. *The Child and His Curriculum* (Third edition). New York: Appleton-Century-Crofts, Inc., 1960.
> Chapters 1 and 6 in this most recent revision of an outstanding book contain material relevant to planning the curriculum.

Miel, Alice. *Changing the Curriculum*. New York: Appleton-Century-Crofts, Inc., 1946.
> A most provocative discussion of the processes of curriculum change.

Shane, Harold G. (editor). *The American Elementary School* (Thirteenth Yearbook of the John Dewey Society). New York: Harper & Brothers, 1953.
> Chapter 6, which deals with changing interpretations of the elementary curriculum, contains material helpful for understanding the forces that affect curriculum planning.

Spears, Harold. *The Teacher and Curriculum Planning*. Englewood Cliffs, New Jersey: Prentice-Hall, Inc., 1951.
> Develops a number of principles related to curriculum planning, including the meaning of the curriculum and the foundations of education in relation to curriculum planning.

5

SOCIETY, CULTURE, AND VALUES: GUIDES FOR CURRICULUM

Because the elementary school is a creation of society, it is influenced by the dynamics of society. Tasks of cultural transmission and cultural improvement root the elementary school curriculum directly in present social circumstances. The elementary educator must be a student of society and of culture; he must know things as they are and as they are becoming. Only by an astute and insightful assessment of present social circumstances can he be assured that the school curriculum does not teach for a time and a world no longer existent. Too, he must go beyond descriptive data and concern himself with the more crucial and difficult question of things as they ought to be. He must clearly understand the values to which our society is committed; he must be sensitive to areas of agreement and of conflict therein; he must be aware of change that may be taking place with respect to particular values. As noted earlier, the current social scene—things as they are—sets the task for our educative efforts. Values—our beliefs about things as they ought to be— set the direction for the educational task. The knowledge and insight called for here must be possessed by the educator if he is to discharge his responsibilities to society as he should. Let us look more closely at the realities of our time, at what is and at what ought to be, and their use as guides to curriculum development. Obviously in the space available here the discussion cannot be complete, but salient characteristics can be noted.

THE CONTINUING SCIENTIFIC
AND TECHNOLOGICAL REVOLUTION

Nothing is more characteristic of our time than its scientific-techno-logical orientation. Since the beginning of the Industrial Revolution that started about the middle of the eighteenth century, we have harnessed mechanical power to do man's work and have designed machines for the production and distribution of goods at an ever increasing rate. While industrialization has taken place in many parts of the world, the United States has set the pace. The American mind has been most inventive and the American worker very industrious. This country has developed a productive capacity such as the world has never known; it provides goods for the people in an abundance never before approached in any society. Central to this abundance is the research laboratory, which has become, in a sense, a new kind of frontier in America. New knowl-edge is uncovered at a breathtaking pace; change is the watchword of the day; new products, some revolutionary in impact and meaning, are made available constantly.

But, let us be more explicit about some of the changes this scientific-technological revolution has contributed to our society. Space here will permit only a partial listing of the major inventions and developments, but the reader should consider the general impact these changes have had on our way of life, the revisions and the innovations in our culture, the new opportunities and the improved possibilities for living, and the social problems and social dislocations that many of these revolutionary developments have brought in their wake.

Some Contributions of Science and Technology

Any list of the major contributions of science and technology in the twentieth century would have to include the following developments:

> The modern motor vehicle—the family car, the passenger bus, the commercial truck.
> Modern railroad transportation—both the long distance systems that crisscross our country, and the rapid transit systems so vital in our metropolitan centers.
> The airplane—especially jet-propelled aircraft, whose commercial use has revolutionized travel, and whose military use has reformed the art of warfare.
> The dial telephone system.
> Modern telegraphy.
> Radio and television—basic tools for entertainment, information, and commercial purposes.
> Food processing—dehydrated, canned, and frozen foods for the health and convenience of the American family.

Labor-saving devices—such as the automatic clothes washer and dryer, the automatic dishwasher, refrigerators and deep freeze units for the use of the housewife.

Automation and the automatic factory, following earlier successes with mass production and assembly-line techniques.

Man-made fibers, such as Orlon and Dacron, to supplement animal and plant fibers in a variety of products.

Plastics—a supplement to available metallic ores and other natural resources.

Mechanized farming, improved hybrid seed and fertilizers, and better bred livestock.

Greatly improved medicine, with new immunizations and antibiotics, advanced surgical techniques, increased insight into mental disorders, and so on.

The release and harnessing of atomic energy.

Continued experimentation with solar power.

Rockets and missiles—the beginnings of explorations in outer space.

This list could be extended, of course, but it does suggests the great productivity of our science and technology.

Not evident in this list is the great impact of these inventions on our culture. The development of whole new industries, the establishment of new occupations and areas of specialization, the increased demand for raw materials and natural resources, the need for highways, airports, and skyways, the development of regulations and laws of many kinds, the need for systems of licensing and insurance, the expansion of traffic control forces and facilities both on the ground and in the air, the changed nature of warfare, the ease and intimacy with which commercial and governmental business is carried on both nationally and internationally, the great increase in tourism and in people who actually know "what's on the other side of the mountain"—all of these changes and more have been the result of this scientific and technological revolution. It has brought manifold opportunities, increased national wealth, improved standard of living, and complex social problems.

On the subject of this rapid progress, David Sarnoff, Chairman of the Board of the Radio Corporation of America, wrote as follows:

> The dominant physical fact in the next quarter-century will be technological progress unprecedented in kind and in volume. In relation to the total history of the human race, the last hundred years have been no more than a split second. Yet they have compassed more technological achievement than the millennia that preceded. . . .
>
> It is not a case of continued increase . . . but of continued acceleration of increase. We need only project the curve into the future to realize that we are merely on the threshold of the technological age.[1]

---

[1] David Sarnoff, "The Fabulous Future," *Fortune*, January 1955, pp. 82–83, 114–118.

This statement is full of promise for the future, yet we cannot help wondering, in light of past experience, whether we will be ready and able to assimilate change into our culture at the pace promised.

Science, Technology, and Elementary School Curriculum

To apply technological progress as a guide to curriculum planning in the elementary school, we must answer a number of questions similar to those listed below:

> What kind of experience with science will enable children to capture its essence as a force and enable them to explore interest and aptitude in science?
>
> To what extent should our developing technology itself be an object of study?
>
> What sort of educational experience is the best preparation for the promise of the future?
>
> Can children be helped early to grasp the concept of change controlled and directed by man, of a future shaped by man, rather than man at the mercy of the future?

THE ERA OF "BIGNESS" IN INDUSTRY, BUSINESS, AGRICULTURE, AND GOVERNMENT

Along with this revolution in science and technology have come many changes in political, social, and economic arrangements. Not the least of these is the emergence of "bigness" as a characteristic of our industry and business, of our agriculture, and even of our government.

The Development of Bigness in Industry and Business

Modern factories, with their demand for large buildings and grounds and expensive machinery, represent large investments of capital that are beyond the fiscal capacities of individuals. Still, mass production and assembly-line operations in the processes of production demand large industrial plants. Thus, we have seen the development of "big business" and the large corporation in America. With this shift to bigness has come a kind of specialization in our industry, with a great measure of interdependence, indicating that the welfare of the whole depends on the welfare of its parts. A rise or cutback in demand for particular goods is felt all along the industrial line. A slump in automobile sales may curtail steel production in a given year; or a work-stoppage in the steel industry may slow up automobile production drastically.

There are still some small businesses in our country, and the federal government does make some attempts to support and stimulate these

enterprises, but fewer people are in business for themselves. Most men now sell their skill and competence on the labor market; they work for someone else. Many people buy into the huge industrial enterprise through the purchase of stock in various companies, but this kind of holding accounts for a small portion of the total investment, and the control exerted by any one individual is smaller still. These developments are true of systems of distribution as well as of production; goods are moved from factory to store and are made available to the public through large merchandising systems. Volume is the goal sought in both production and distribution enterprises.

The Development of Bigness in Agriculture

Volume seems to be the key to success in agriculture, too, in the modern world. To replace the small family farmer of earlier years has come the large landholder, controlling hundreds or thousands of acres of land. Owning and farming land and raising stock is still a good business investment in the United States, but it takes considerable capital to operate in the way that modern agriculture seems to dictate. The large acreage demanded for success, along with the heavy financial investment necessary for buildings and equipment, contributes to this development most directly. Those who want to live on the land are increasingly living on somebody else's land, working it often as their own, and sharing the profits with the owner on a landlord–tenant-farmer basis. The federal government does have programs that attempt to help and support the small family farmer, but, although some feel that the family farmer need not disappear from the American scene, it seems that agriculture, like other industries, is increasingly shifting to a volume production base, and will be operated in ways comparable to mass production in industry.

The Development of Modern Advertising

With the significant increase in our ability to produce a great volume and variety of goods and products has come the development of modern advertising to develop "wants" on the part of the consumer. That is, high volume production calls for high volume sales; and high volume sales calls for a buying public, a public that wants to purchase new goods and replace old ones in ever increasing quantities. Our newspapers, our magazines, radio, television, our roadsides and our building-sides constantly remind us to buy this, look at that, or try some new product. People are repeatedly admonished to look like this, smell like that, eat thus, or dress in this style, and so on. Mass production demands

the mass market, and the mass market calls for a certain kind of mass-mindedness in buying habits. Purchasing appetites are whetted and markets are created; and yearly campaigns are designed to capture a certain portion of this market for a given company's product.

Through it all the consumer must maintain some measure of personal identification of his wants and needs, some criteria to use in making decisions about purchases, and some defenses against the subtleties of much of modern advertising. The consumer is protected by certain state and national laws related to the grading and classification of products, to the ingredients and materials that may or may not be used in certain commodities, and so on. Similarly, there are active state and federal commissions that play a "watchdog" role in these matters. Still, in the final analysis it is the individual consumer, as a person or as a family unit, that must make buying decisions.

The Development of Bigness in Government

Even a cursory examination of the American scene enables us to observe the great growth that has taken place in government at all levels, especially at the national level, and the increased participation of government in all aspects of American life. To many this development seems only natural; they reason that along with big business must come big government. To others this development appears to be a direct contradiction to the earlier climate of opinion that saw the best government as the least government, which did for the people only those things they could not do as well for themselves, and felt that these things were few indeed. The first group simply accepts the fact that there are now many more things the government can do for the people better than they can do for themselves. The degree to which government should participate in various aspects of life in America is a lively national issue; our major political parties are in great part characterized by their different positions on this matter.

But, in spite of historical positions and present diverse opinions, the degree to which government participates and regulates in areas of the economy, public health, housing, law enforcement, communication, transportation, and so on, has increased tremendously. Most recently the debate has centered on the degree to which the national government should increase its participation in the area of education. Note that the development of atomic energy has been largely a federal project and not one of private enterprise. The federal government operates many financial institutions and programs that affect the economy. The national government cooperates with state and local governments in the construction of highways, airports, bridges, and dams. Later comments in

this chapter on social security, unemployment insurance, minimum wage laws, and the like, further illustrate this point.

Representing and safeguarding the activities of our nation at the international level has increased government activity, too. The maintenance of a large military force, the consummation of collective systems of security with other nations, the determination of international trade arrangements and agreements, the provision of assistance to underdeveloped nations, the participation of our country in the United Nations—all add responsibilities to government and expand government in the process. The civil service force has grown tremendously as government has expanded: there was a 54 per cent increase in government workers from 1940 to 1950, until at present about one out of every ten persons in the labor force is employed by some unit of local, state, or national government.[2]

Still, our experiment with a republican form of government continues to be successful. Government, in spite of its expanding size and growing power, is still responsive to the will of the people. Our major political parties relinquish the reins of government at any and all levels (without hesitation) when they are defeated in an election. Always, these elected public servants are ultimately accountable for their record at the polls.

That public debate will continue on this matter of "bigness" in government seems to be inevitable and to the good. Within this debate are found some of the dynamics that will help us to steer a wise course in this matter. But, in light of the actions of government at the time of the Great Depression, and the responsibilities of government in the years after World War II, the future seems to suggest a slow but inevitable increase in the activities of government, alone or with private enterprise, in an attempt to capture more of the good life for all of our people.

Bigness and the Elementary School Curriculum

Again, for elementary school education, this development raises questions concerning the curriculum, such as:

> Is this shift to bigness an important concept for children to meet early in their lives?
>
> Are there particular attitudes, understandings, or skills that enable one to live more efficiently and happily with "bigness"?
>
> Are there particular learnings implied in the area of consumer education?
>
> To what extent should the growth of government be an object of study in the curriculum?

---

[2] M. W. Rodehaver, W. B. Axtell, and R. E. Gross, *The Sociology of the School* (New York: Thomas Y. Crowell Company, 1957), p. 43.

CHANGES IN ECONOMIC ARRANGEMENTS

The very fundamental changes that have taken place in science and technology, and the accompanying shift toward "bigness" in industry, agriculture, and government, have brought equally fundamental changes in both the actual economic arrangements in our society and the general attitude of our people toward the economy.

The Emergence of Labor and Management

As business has grown, employer-employee relationships have become less the primary, or face-to-face, relationships of former days and more the secondary, or group-to-group, relationships of organized effort. The worker is now most often a member of a labor union, and is represented by labor leaders when bargaining for the length of the work day or week, hourly wage rates, length of vacation periods, retirement pay, and other factors of significance to the working man. The modern corporation has developed a new type of executive to represent it in these negotiations. Thus, personnel management and labor leadership are now full-time jobs for many persons. Bargaining sessions between labor and management are almost yearly occurrences, with one group of participants holding the power of access to plant and machines, and the other the power of worker supply. The outcomes of these labor-management bargaining efforts are so important to our national economy that federal legislation has been passed in an attempt to regulate the process, and federal officials are often participants in the more crucial of these bargaining campaigns.

Occupational Shifts in the Economy

An economy as vast as the American one creates millions of jobs and makes heavy demands on manpower. Many years ago, of course, a major shift in occupational structure took place when people left the farm to seek their livelihood in the factory. Since that day our large industrial plant has kept workers of diverse kinds busy in increasing numbers. This occupational growth has not been without occupational strife, however. Often the invention of new machines and processes in established industries has caused serious job dislocations. Job and skill obsolescence have been and continue to be realities of modern industry, and workers find it necessary literally to "re-tool" themselves at times if they are to continue to be employable.

Automation is the latest of these basic developments to face the American labor force. Arguments and counter-arguments are raised that prom-

ise more and better jobs, or fewer and harder-to-get jobs, in a world of automation. At least two developments seem to be likely: the already identifiable shift of people out of the direct lines of production into service classified occupations will undoubtedly continue; and the demand for unskilled labor, falling since 1900, will continue to fall. The jobs developing in the new industries call for a considerable level of technical skill.

This discussion on the occupational structure would not be complete without some reference to the increasing tendency for women to fill jobs of various kinds. That the great majority of our female population will hold a job at some time in their lives, and that a significant number of them are destined to work for a number of years, is indicated in all the studies done recently on this matter. What this development may mean, in any general way, for life in America, remains to be seen.

Efforts Toward Economic Security

In light of the depression of the 1930's and the continual shifts and changes in the economy, a number of steps have been taken to provide a measure of economic security to our people. Ours is a system in which the power and the willingness of the people to purchase must be ever present. To help to insure this, legislation of various kinds has been enacted. We now have laws stipulating minimum hourly wages. We have systems of unemployment insurance to protect the worker when he is off the job. Savings that people deposit with most of our financial institutions are now protected by federal insurance systems. A program of federal social security provides persons with a basic income after retirement from active employment. In addition to these state and federal government programs, private systems of various kinds operate to supplement these economic measures. Especially is this true in the area of health, where private insurance systems are used by many to guard against the economic crises that may come to a family in times of sickness or injury. With improved medical care has come higher medical costs. In fact, a major national issue focuses on whether we should have a federal government-sponsored system of health insurance for our people, too.

Credit

Credit, as an economic phenomenon, has become a dominant factor in our economy. It operates at all levels from individual and family purchasing to business and industry, and at all levels of government. Buying-on-time has become so much the way in which people purchase expensive products, in which housing is financed, in which industry

expands its capital investment, in which communities build water systems and schools, and in which the state and federal governments themselves underwrite many of their programs through bonds sales, that extensive systems of control have had to be developed. There are restrictions on the size of down payments and total length of contracts for family purchases; at the other extreme there is a limit on the size of the debt the national government may accumulate. In our economy, credit is a centrally important concept, and we must learn to live with it.

Wages, Prices, and Taxes

Individual and family income is higher today than it has ever been in our history, and economists promise steady increases in the years ahead. Per capita income, as an index of economic growth, has risen from $1,059 in 1943[3] to about $2,057 in 1958.[4] We have been, and continue to be, a wealthy nation. However, the forces of inflation in the years since World War II have worked to reduce the purchasing power of the American dollar to a new low. Figuring 1947–49 as a base period for the value of the dollar, it would in 1958 buy only $.81 worth of goods and services, but in 1935 it would have bought $1.70 worth.[5]

In addition, the American public carries an extremely heavy tax burden. The developing world situation makes it impossible or unwise to reduce taxation from the heavy levels of the World War II years. Big government means big taxes, and the people do not question the right and necessity for government at all levels to tax. That they are ready to pay their just and full share is evident from the small number of delinquent taxpayers in any given fiscal year. Still, there are efforts to realize some tax relief.

Economic Arrangements and the
Elementary School Curriculum

As a guide to curriculum planning, these economic realities bring to mind such questions as:

> Should economics become an object of more serious and deliberate study in the elementary school?
>
> To what extent should children study the development of organized labor?

---

[3] *The World Almanac and Book of Facts*, 1950, p. 707.
[4] *The World Almanac and Book of Facts*, 1960, p. 752.
[5] U.S. Bureau of the Census, *Statistical Abstract of the United States: 1959* (Eightieth edition; Washington, D.C.: 1959), Table 429, p. 333.

To children just growing up in a society, do such things as occupational change have any real meaning or relevance to elementary school experiences?

Should a direct effort be made to acquaint children with the welfare legislation of the past half century?

Can children be helped to grasp the relationship between our scientific-technological revolution and changing economic arrangements?

DEVELOPMENTS IN THE SOCIAL SPHERE

From the earliest days it has been accepted that the United States would work to avoid a social system that marked people at birth and, in the process, indicated their destiny in society. To this end we have tried hard to maintain a high degree of flexibility and fluidity in our social system. The current scene indicates that we continue to maintain this flexibility with a degree of success, although great problems remain.

Social Mobility

There are two kinds of social mobility that our society has traditionally tried to maintain: *horizontal mobility,* or the degree to which people are free and encouraged to better their lot in life by changing employers, by changing their place of residence and moving to another part of the country, by changing their vocation itself, and so on; and *vertical mobility,* or the degree to which a person has the opportunity to move, not just horizontally, but vertically, or upward, in the social and economic scheme. Custom grants that a man and his family will be free to seek out for themselves the best that life has to offer them. As our science and technology have developed, as our industry and business have grown, as there has been a greater demand for professional services, as government has become larger—the possibility for people to move upward in this scheme of things has been ever present, and young people have been admonished to do just this. While the phrase "there is always room at the top" calls for some qualification in its application, it does in great measure describe the past and current state of affairs. The person with ability or talent, and with the motivation to develop that ability or talent through education, finds himself in a social system that encourages and facilitates this upward mobility. It has been and continues to be important for this characteristic of mobility to remain a part of the American social scene. It provides great encouragement, and inspires a deep faith in the future on the part of our younger generations. And, it works against the "freezing" of individuals and families into preordered niches in the general social scheme.

Social Class

To the contrary of many general observations and comments about our democratic society, we do have social classes in the United States. Every major study that has focused on this problem has documented this characteristic beyond the shadow of a doubt.[6] The term *social class* refers to the division of society into groups of individuals, the level of each group determined by criteria of wealth, education, or other common characteristics. Most American communities have at least their upper and lower social classes; the larger communities, with more complex social systems generally, have social subclasses. These latter groups are often identified by the use of such terms as "upper upper and lower upper," or "upper middle and lower middle," and "upper lower and lower lower." Many factors contribute to the assignment of persons into a given social class: such things as income, occupation, racial and ethnic background, religion, education, and place of residence are among them. The race factor is such a strong determinant in this matter that some have said that a caste system, as well as a social class system, operates to some degree in the United States.[7]

Although social class is less obvious now than formerly, it is likely to be a continuing part of the American scene. It is as much a product of cultural complexity as of conscious societal choice. Americans are not particularly class conscious, but they are concerned to a great extent with their position in the social scheme. Thus, they will merely tolerate some situations and actively encourage others that seem to be basically contradictory. Generally speaking, most Americans identify themselves with the "great middle class." As an example of the complexity of this matter of social class, the school is encouraged to orient itself to the values of this great majority group, and at the same time admonished for such a biased and restricted value orientation.

The Demand for Equality

An unmistakable characteristic of the current social scene is the increasing insistence of certain minority groups for social and political equality in our society. This is often headlined as the issue over "civil rights" in our country. Persons of minority religious, ethnic, and par-

---

[6] See Granville Hicks, *Small Town* (New York: The Macmillan Company, 1947); R. S. Lynd and H. M. Lynd, *Middletown* (New York: Harcourt, Brace and Company, 1929); R. S. Lynd and H. M. Lynd, *Middletown in Transition* (New York: Harcourt, Brace and Company, 1937); James West, *Plainville, U.S.A.* (New York: Columbia University Press, 1945); and John Dollard, *Caste and Class in a Southern Town* (New Haven: Yale University Press, 1931).

[7] Dollard, *op. cit.*

ticularly racial groups are pressing for a greater measure of equality to go along with the freedom society has extended to them. This demand for equality reaches out to job opportunities, housing, voting rights, and the use of public and private services generally. The crisis that has been precipitated in education in the South over this issue is a well-known example of this demand.

A look at the past indicates that there has been progress in extending a greater measure of equality to all minority groups in recent years. Various forces are removing or reducing the obstacles to complete civil rights for all of our people. That the United States must work toward a successful solution to this problem is imperative for the welfare of our national society, and it is fundamental to any world leadership our country is to exercise among peoples of diverse racial and religious groups. The position of the moral force in our society in this problem area is clear, but the realities of tradition, custom, fear, and ignorance loom as formidable forces for the status quo in many situations.

> What sort of promise for the future should the school extend to children in line with our open and flexible social system?
> In what ways does social class affect the curriculum of the school?
> What should the school do about social class lines as it provides school experiences for children?

THE AMERICAN FAMILY

Let us consider briefly the position and the status of the American family. It is still the basic unit of social organization in our society, and is fundamental to our way of life. The growing complexities of our culture have made their impact on the family, of course. Adjustments have been necessary, and sometimes difficult. At the present time the family gives every evidence of continuing in its priority role in our society, and shows signs of growing in security and certainty in that role.

From Producer Unit to Consumer Unit

The American family has been a consumer unit for many years now. The industrial revolution made it clear that the family would be better off if the husband became a wage earner and then purchased, rather than produced for his own family, the goods and services his family needed. Even in the farm family, few vestiges of family production are still evident. They, too, find it better to consume, in the main, the products of others.

This shift from producer unit to consumer unit has had some far-reaching implications for the life of the family. Children and youth no

longer enjoy the opportunity to contribute directly to the family welfare. We continually search for a constructive role in society for our young people while they are growing up. We want them to feel a sense of personal worth, and to be able to feel responsibility of a kind that was more easily provided when the family was considerably more "on its own." The wife, too, is often tempted into the labor market to increase the family income and to enable the family to consume even more. The decision to have the wife stay at home with living adjusted to a smaller income, or to work away from home with a larger income, has had to be made by many American families.

Adjusting to Varied Working Patterns

Developments in business and industry have made necessary certain adjustments in family living, too. Some families have had to learn to adjust their pattern of living to a husband who works at night. Changes in the locations of businesses, industries, and housing areas have led to widespread commuting practices. Father leaves the house early in the morning for an hour or longer trip to his place of employment and does not return until early evening. Thus, mother is left to be the head of the family during most of the waking hours of the children. This development is further complicated by the practice, with improved rapid transportation, of many husbands to be away from home frequently on business trips to far-away places. This practice adds to the responsibilities the wife must accept for running the household generally as well as for raising the children. Through it all the American family seems to retain enough flexibility to make needed adjustments and to continue to operate with satisfaction.

Establishment of Families

Perhaps the best evidence of the vitality of the American family is the increased rate at which families are being established in our society. More people than ever before are getting married, and at a younger age. The birth rate of the past few years indicates that these people bear children along a pattern of about three per family. This trend is quite the reverse of that of the depression era, with its low marriage and birth rates. These new families seek houses, rather than apartments, to live in, and their demand has resulted in the many large suburban housing developments of the post-World War II years. These families are, in the process, living in ways in which the social development of children is often facilitated, apart from the school, to a much greater extent. Certainly, this great increase in marriages suggests that the American family is "here to stay."

Dissolution of Families

There continues to be a high number of families dissolved each year in divorce actions; very often, there are children involved. Some people point to information that suggests a slow but identifiable decrease in the number of broken homes, and as more and more communities establish family counseling agencies it may well be that many of these separations can be avoided.

Fortunately, improvements in modern medicine work to the advantage of the stability of family life. Maternal mortality rates at the time of childbirth are greatly reduced; better general medical care, as it increases life expectancies, increases the number of years that both husband and wife can be expected to remain in the family circle. These medical advances help to keep the family together for a longer period of time.

Increased Leisure Time

Every technological, economic, and social change since 1900 has brought increased leisure time to the American people. Since machines do more of what men were doing formerly, in industry and in the home, families in our society have more time for themselves than ever before. And, in spite of the urgency of the present social, political, and economic situation—so often described as calling for greater sacrifices from the American people—the realities of the situation suggest that the future holds the promise of shorter work days and weeks, more labor-saving devices, and greatly increased leisure time for all.

What our people will do with this time raises another kind of question. There are those who, because of the experience of the past, do not see a very encouraging use of such time in the future. They fear that it will be frittered away in pursuits that will not work to the best interests of the people. On the brighter side, some point to the vast and rapidly developing ''do-it-yourself'' movement, to the increasing numbers of community playhouse groups and of amateur photographers and painters, and to increased circulation rates in libraries as an indication of the constructive way in which our people can and will use their leisure time. Not to be overlooked is the vastly growing number of people who travel in our own country and abroad. This great increase in leisure time may well prove to be a most significant development.

> Is the American family an important object for study in the elementary school?
> Is there *the* American family, or are there *many* American families?
> Can the school experience help answer the need for a place in which

children can accept responsibility and contribute directly to an important undertaking?

Can the school experience help children to accept varied family patterns?

What is the elementary school's responsibility toward the use of leisure time?

MASS MEDIA OF COMMUNICATION

Related to this great increase in leisure time is the availability and extensive use of mass media of communication in our society. The ease with which people can read a newspaper, magazine, or paperback, or listen to the radio, view television, or attend a motion picture is the result of both more time and freer access, and the evidence indicates that our people are involved a great deal of the time with mass media of communication. This development holds the promise of increasing awareness and understanding over a wide range of subjects, to an extent not possible in earlier times. People can keep abreast of current happenings more efficiently, can be more fully informed, and certainly more easily entertained. In these ways, this development is all to the good, but, as with most elements of progress, there are points at which it must be carefully evaluated. People need standards and skills for consuming these media. For instance, the use of large news wire services increases the effectiveness of the small newspaper tremendously, but it brings also a heavy degree of standardization to news reporting. The ease with which radio and television can inform and entertain is a modern miracle, but the cost of operating large networks concentrates these channels of communication in the hands of a few people, for whom the responsibility for integrity, comprehensiveness, and objectivity in all matters is heavy. Codes of ethics protect the public, of course, and certain government organizations police these media to a degree in the interests of the general welfare, but the people, too, have to be discriminating consumers who demand quality in modern radio and television operations. Similar comments might well be made concerning the models of life presented by many of our movies and paperbacks. Selections made must be enlightened ones; we need some criteria for choice lest we fail to realize the wonderful possibilities of modern communication media simply by taking anything that is offered, leading to the mistaken notion on the part of producers and writers that this is what the public wants.

What understandings do children need concerning the development and growth of mass communication media?

How can children be helped to learn to consume mass media of communication in an enlightened way?

ORGANIZED RELIGION IN AMERICA

The church continues to be a strong moral force on the American scene; its influence extends beyond its regular members to reach others in innumerable ways. As a source of moral sanctions, and as a set of ideas about life and living, religion has proved to be a powerful complementary force to democracy. Certainly the United States can be described as a religious nation, and our people as a whole consider religion to be an important part of our culture. Still the majority of our people are not churchgoers; their attendance is spasmodic and often geared to special religious seasons. Some two out of every five of our people have no direct affiliation with any church.

The church has had to face many problems in our emerging industrial society. It has had to become a religious force oriented to life as people are having to live it. Its program has had to expand in ingenious ways in order to capture and hold the interest of young people and adults alike. It has had to learn to live with an age of science, and to compete for time in a world heavily dominated by other activities that capture the attention of most people and make demands on their time.

Still, the record shows that religion remains, and probably grows, as a force in our society. Establishing some sort of satisfactory religious commitment is a major concern of a great many of our people. Religious prejudice seems to be diminishing, with the ready acceptance of Judaism, Catholicism, and various branches of Protestantism, in most of our communities. There are indications that the freedom of religion guaranteed by our Bill of Rights is more secure today than ever before.

Of course, there are those who feel that man is quickly outliving his need for organized religion, and that the church as we have known it will cease to have a necessary function to perform in society, but these are opinions of an extreme minority. The number of churches in many American communities that are prospering and contributing meaningfully to the lives of hundreds of thousands of Americans indicate that this idea should not be taken seriously. An America without a strong and active church is difficult to contemplate, for religion has much to offer to a society built on the tenets of democracy and permeated with concerns for the individual and for the welfare of all.

> Is the role of organized religion in American life, as a focus for school study, in conflict with the basic separation of church and state in our society?
>
> Should children in the elementary school be helped to understand organized religion as a force in American society?

DEVELOPMENTS IN POPULATION

The phrase *population trends* is more often than not written as *population explosion* in recent years. The human family is increasing in numbers at an unprecedented rate, in our own country and in many other parts of the world. A recent report of a national study commission carried the following dramatic statement:

> The extent of the "spurt" can be measured in startling figures. An hour from now there will be over 5,000 more members of the human family. By this time tomorrow, the world's population will have increased by about 125,000 people. That means 45,000,000 more within a year. Since 1920 the world's population has expanded by close to 50 percent, and if current rates are continued, the population of the earth will double before the year 2000.[8]

Other national and international groups have recently spoken out in similar terms calling attention to this phenomenon. Many informed persons feel that one of man's greatest challenges, if not his greatest, lies in this problem of the numbers of people that must be clothed, fed, housed, educated, kept well, given jobs, and so on. These total increases are coming from two complementary developments. On the one hand we have higher birth rates and lower infant mortality rates. On the other hand we have greatly increased life expectancy in much of the world. Owing to better living conditions and greatly improved medical practices people are simply living much longer than in former years. When the Roman Empire was at its height, a man expected to live about thirty years. In the most advanced Western countries today a man expects to live about seventy years. Together these developments add up to increased population, and bring with them some particular and unique social and economic problems. Let us consider the matter briefly, first in the United States, and then in international dimensions.

Population in the United States

On the basis of the low birth rate of the depression "thirties," population experts were estimating then that by 1960 the population of the United States would level off. They felt that we were already close to our maximum, and that the future would find us having to adjust socially and economically to an ultimately declining population.[9] It is true that the growth noted in the 1940 census was the lowest we had ever known,

---

[8] From a draft report of the Commission on the Social Studies of the National Council for the Social Studies, presented in San Francisco, November 1958.

[9] Based on a bulletin of the Metropolitan Life Insurance Company, *Statistical Bulletin* 32, October 1950.

but the unforeseen developments of the 1940–50 decade upset the long range predictions and estimates. The combined impact of a major war and economic prosperity resulted in a much higher marriage rate and a concomitantly higher birth rate. In 1950 the population of the U.S. stood at 150,697,361, a gain of 14.5 per cent over the figure reported in the 1940 census, while in this same period the number of families established in our country increased by some 25 per cent. And, while the large family of earlier days seems to have disappeared from the American scene, a pattern of expectation for three children in a family seems to be a growing trend. Between 1940 and 1950 the infant mortality rate in the U.S. was reduced by 40 per cent, so that in 1948, 968 children out of every 1,000 born were destined to live. At the present time our child population under the age of five accounts for a larger proportion of our total population than at any time since 1920; more than one out of ten fall into this group.

At the older age levels similar gains have been registered through increased life expectancies. Population data indicate that, while the total population doubled from 1900 to 1950, the number of those 65 years of age and over quadrupled. Estimates are that their number will double again by 1980.[10]

Assuming that present conditions prevail, and present trends continue, it now seems obvious that we shall still grow for some years to come, and that our total population should exceed the 200 million mark before the turn of the century.

The Rural–Urban Situation. The people of the United States continue to be on the move. Shifts from South to North and from East to West characterize our major migrations, accompanied by a shift from rural to urban areas. By the definition of urban used in the 1950 census, the United States is now considered to be more than two-thirds urban. Actually, a great part of this urban group inhabits the fringe areas around our large cities. People move out of the city or from the rural areas into this fringe area, seeking better employment opportunities and improved family living generally. Some of these areas become vast patterns of interlocking communities, comprising millions of people, and forming what is coming to be referred to as the metropolitan area. With these newer patterns of population concentration come a whole host of political, social, and economic problems to which new, creative solutions must be applied. These population areas cross county lines, and often state lines as well; many of our political institutions, general cultural patterns, and educational systems, too, have not yet caught up with this new kind of metropolitan center.

---

[10] U.S. Bureau of the Census, *U.S. Census of the Population: 1950*, Vol. II, Characteristics of the Populations (Washington, D.C.: 1950).

Population at the World Level

At the world level much the same sort of developments in population are taking place, but the problem is much more acute and critical in some parts of the world than in others. For instance, Asia, with about one-fifth of the land area of the earth, already has more than half the world's population, and the population in Asian countries is increasing at a far more rapid rate than in countries of the West. The birth rate is very high in these countries, and advances in medicine are slowly decreasing their infant mortality rate and increasing their life expectancy. Of the Asian countries with population problems, only Japan seems in recent years to be achieving some sort of control over the problem. In Japan we find the birth rate actually diminishing slightly, and the future holds promise of a stable population in the years ahead for this industrialized island nation.

The realities of this situation indicate that the most explosive developments in population are coming actually in many of the most underdeveloped areas of the world, in those countries that are among the least able to care for a rapidly growing human group. The countries discussed later as now emerging from the yoke of colonialism, with intense desires for a strong, independent nation state, whose inhabitants demand that they be able to share more reasonably and humanely in the general advances in living found elsewhere, are almost invariably the countries faced with the most severe population problems. At a time when major increases in productive capacity are needed if these countries are to improve the living standard of their present population, the population is multiplying at such a rate that their ability to produce goods and provide services is taxed beyond all realistic possibilities. The tensions that inevitably build up in these situations are obvious, and the "explosions" that occur at times are understandable. It is for these reasons that aid to underdeveloped countries takes on dimensions of urgency and priority in the world today.

> To what extent should the elementary school sensitize children to the problems of expanding populations?
>
> In what ways, if any, does population mobility affect curriculum planning?

THE QUEST FOR PEACE

Interdependence: the Emergence of a World Community

Without a doubt, one of the major realities of our time is the intense desire of our people, and of the great majority of the peoples of the world,

to live in peace. History has been too often interrupted by the ravages of war, and the consequences of war make it increasingly difficult to define the fruits of victory. Unmistakably, many of man's most treasured rights have been successfully defended on the battlefield, but experience suggests that there must be a more efficient, less costly way to protect and safeguard the rights of individuals and of nations than by resorting to war. In fact, man has recently been so successful in inventing and improving weapons of war that nations must consider more seriously than ever before the futility of armed conflicts. The power of destruction of modern weapons is sufficient to destroy the whole of man's painfully and laboriously developed civilization if this power is unleashed on an extensive scale.

At the same time, one of the most fundamental by-products of our achievements in science and technology has been the reduction in time and space barriers between people. Our coasts have become closer together; business in the United States is conducted increasingly on a national level; and more and more of our people have been able to travel easily and comfortably throughout our own country, getting better acquainted with each other and with our land.

But the most dramatic results of this aspect of technological advance have been at the international level. In our time, the world has truly become a small neighborhood. Communication around the world is instantaneous, and the speed and efficiency of modern jet-propelled airplanes means that a trip around the world would take about two days.[11] Modern means of communication and transportation have literally transformed the conduct of human affairs, from the daily life of the individual to the conduct of business and the diplomatic relations between nations.

The economy is already a world-wide, interdependent one. Raw materials have had to be sought and bought all over the world, as have certain finished goods. National boundaries have long been transcended in economic matters: an international tension, a lapsed trade agreement, a raised or lowered tariff, a closed source of supply of raw material, or a closed market for finished goods is quickly felt in many places. The current social scene shows many attempts to realize the international dimensions of the world's economy more efficiently for all concerned.

These advances in communication and transportation are also bringing the peoples of the world, themselves, into more intimate contact with each other. The exchange of ideas and information, and the actual exchange of people, is ever easier. Being able to watch foreign movies, to see performances by foreign dancers and musicians, to play host to for-

---

[11] *The World Almanac and Book of Facts*, 1960, p. 785.

eign visitors and missions of various kinds, or to tour in foreign countries adds to the opportunities for the exchange of cultural achievement between peoples. There is much more chance for understanding to develop—but there is every opportunity for misunderstanding to develop, too, as we find ourselves actually living together for the first time. As we search for similarities, we must recognize and respect differences. The order is large, but the stakes are high and we must learn to inhabit this planet peacefully. World peace is an item of highest priority in contemporary affairs. It is a continuing sobering thought that the same airplanes that bring statesmen and tourists can bring soldiers; that cargoes of consumer goods can become cargoes of armaments; and that the resources brought to ease the pain and suffering of a natural disaster might have to be utilized for aid to victims of man-made disasters.

Shifts in World Power Centers

To form some sort of workable world community organization we must recognize the significance of the shift that has taken place in the power centers of the world. Since 1900 the political, economic, and military centers of power have shifted from Western Europe to both the East and the West. This shift has been especially evident in the years since the end of World War II. The United States and the Soviet Union stand as the strongest powers in the world today. They exert world leadership and influence significantly the course of events throughout the entire world. They are the centers of power and the rallying points for those nations who think much the same as they do. The United States is most commonly referred to as the leader of the free world, while the Soviet Union is the leader of the Communist bloc of nations. The family of nations is rather distinctly divided into three groups around these great powers. One group is committed to follow the leadership of the United States, the other to follow the leadership of Russia, and the third group attempts to be a neutral or uncommitted bloc, giving allegiance to neither East nor West in the struggle for world domination, while trying to establish communication and relations with both.

Any significant relaxation of tensions in the world today, and any real settlement of basic world problems, depends on the establishment of understanding and cooperation between the United States and the Soviet Union. To establish this cooperation is most difficult since no two nations on earth stem from such different historical backgrounds and are committed to such contrasting systems of values as these two. In the meantime, this is the era of new kinds of international alliances; of the cold war, of summit meetings, and of an intense and increasing competition between the United States and Russia in all fields of human

endeavor as they strive to influence the minds and energies of men in particular directions.

The Dissolution of Colonialism

A development of fundamental proportions that has been increasing at an accelerated pace since World War II is the dissolution of the former great colonial empires held by certain nations of Western Europe for many years. A rising tide of nationalism, and a growing conviction throughout the world that nations and peoples should be allowed to guide and direct their own destinies, has led to the granting of independence peacefully in some situations and to the seizing of independence by force in others. The momentum of this desire is not to be denied, and colonialism looks to be a thing of the past. The peoples of these former colonial areas want not only independence for their countries, but they want also to share more equitably and realistically in the comforts of this world. Disease, poverty, ignorance, and hunger are national characteristics they want to shed. However, these countries are not yet ready or able to achieve their goals on their own; they need help from the outside. In fact, they need desperately the help of the very white man by whom they have so recently been dominated. They must industrialize in whatever ways are reasonable and possible with their natural resources, and to do this they need not only technical assistance, but also financial help. The two most likely sources for both kinds of help are the two great powers already mentioned. They have the surpluses of both technical personnel and money needed to help. But, these newly independent nations are wary lest they lose their recently won right of national determination in their acceptance of proffered aid. It is in the meeting of this problem that some move West, others move East, and still others try fiercely to remain neutral. It is in this situation that the United States points to the promise of progress without the sacrifice of personal freedom, while Russia suggests the need for drastic and rigid state controls over human and natural resources as the way to progress, pointing to her own achievements in the relatively short space of less than fifty years to underscore her point. Thus do the nations of Southeast Asia, the Middle East, and Africa ponder the future, while the great underdeveloped countries of India and Communist China pursue their choices to their eventual conclusion.

An Attempt at International Regulation

At the end of World War II the world was more ready than ever before to try to rise to the challenge of international regulation to safeguard the future welfare of the family of nations. An organization was

needed that could speak with some authority in matters of international disputes and that could help to combine the energies of nations for the solution of world problems. With the memory of the ill-fated League of Nations still alive, the United States took the lead in the immediate postwar years to establish the United Nations. Through allegiance to its founding charter, and through the workings of its General Assembly and affiliated special agencies, the member nations hoped that some sort of secure future might be built for the world on the ashes of this most disastrous of all wars. The strength of this international regulatory body, it was hoped, would do a great deal to preserve the peace, for such an organization held the promise of international arbitration and co-operation in the peaceful solution of the world's problems.

To this end, the United Nations was organized in 1945, its permanent home completed in New York City in 1952. More than ninety nations of the world now maintain active membership. Already it has had to face many complex situations throughout the world. Its record over these past years may be somewhat controversial, but, in light of the tense situation in which it has had to operate, its efforts are to be viewed with considerable admiration. Essentially, its purpose was to preserve the peace, but events have proved that peace has never really come. The UN has taken military action to stabilize areas of conflict in certain instances; it has attacked some of the world's major health problems with success; and it works continually on problems of education through-out the world. The UN has brought about cooperative efforts in scientific endeavor; it assists in the economic development of underdeveloped areas; and it stands generally as a significant moral force in the world for international justice, freedom, and peace. It is still a young organi-zation, and what the future holds for it is difficult to assess. However, in its short history it has displayed a kind of determination and courage that must be admired. While the United Nations Organization, as it is now composed and operates, may not be the final answer to regulation in the world community, its contributions cannot be denied and its pres-ence gives all the world some encouragement.

The Quest for Peace and the Elementary School Curriculum

Herein lies another challenge for the elementary school curriculum. What sort of contribution can the elementary school years make to this earnestly sought peace in the world? For instance:

How can the elementary school curriculum contribute to international understanding?

Should there be more "culture" units, or studies of foreign peoples, in the elementary school social studies program?

Is a more dynamic kind of "human" geography, focused on man in his physical environment, a fundamental for today's children?

Should the work of the United Nations, and its subsidiary organizations, be studied by children in the elementary school years?

Should Russia as a nation, and communism as an ideology, be given more attention in the elementary school?

What is suggested or demanded in the area of foreign language study by these realities, and how does this bear on the elementary school years?

VALUES AND CURRICULUM PLANNING

Thus far in this chapter consideration has been given to the current social scene in a descriptive sense. An attempt has been made to indicate "what is" without much attention to the countering matter of "what ought to be." Expressions of satisfaction or dissatisfaction with the current situation are reflections of the degree to which life has developed, or is developing, in a direction consistent with life as we feel that it should be lived. Attention to this dimension of society is attention to our deep-seated beliefs about it, or, in more formal language, to our *value system*. This is the backdrop against which we may view the current social scene and conclude from what we see whether the situation is good or bad, right or wrong, consistent or contradictory, progressing or regressing. The way in which values set the direction for many curriculum decisions is fundamental for the elementary educator to grasp. They influence the selection of instructional goals, of content and subject matter, of methodology, and of evaluation data. Let us look more closely at the values of our society.

Our Basic Cultural Values

Our social system is called a democracy, and central to this ideology are the basic values around which our lives develop. Though listed differently by various writers, the following tenets capture the very heart of this value system:

1. Respect for the individual human personality.
2. Cooperative effort in the peaceful solution of common problems.
3. Great reliance on reason and reflective thinking.
4. Deep faith in the future; in the ability of man to control and to shape his destiny.

These values suggest that within our society the individual is extended both the opportunity and the responsibility for making a great many per-

sonal decisions about a great many things. A statement published some years ago under the title *When Men Are Free* calls attention to the basic premises, or assumptions, about the individual and about life generally in the United States. It lists the following as basic social and political beliefs in our society.

Under basic social beliefs:

> Every person is of importance as an individual; his well-being is vital in itself.
>
> All persons should have maximum freedom, consistent with the general welfare, to develop as they desire.
>
> All persons should be considered as individuals and judged on their merit; their differences should be respected, their rights safeguarded.
>
> All persons should possess equal rights and liberties.
>
> The rights of any person should not be exercised so as to interfere with the rights of others.
>
> The action of any individual or group must not endanger the welfare of the people or threaten the security of the nation.
>
> Both competition and cooperation among individuals and groups are indispensable to the process of democracy.

Under basic political beliefs:

> Men have the ability to govern themselves.
>
> All power belongs to and comes from the people.
>
> Public officials are responsible to the people.
>
> The people have the right to reform, alter, or totally change their government by lawful means when they so desire.
>
> Government has a responsibility to promote the general welfare.
>
> Government should be by law duly adopted, and not by the whim of any man.
>
> The church and the state should be separate.

This statement goes on to indicate necessary *goals in the economic sphere* that are consistent with these social and political beliefs:

> An increasing national productivity, made possible by technological development, that will lower the cost of goods and raise the standard of living.
>
> The elimination of deep and prolonged depression.
>
> The freest possible economic competition consistent with the general welfare.
>
> Opportunity for full development.
>
> Full employment under safe and healthful working conditions.
>
> Fair pay.
>
> Sufficient food, clothing, housing, and medical care.
>
> Social Security—protection against the basic hazards of existence such as old age, sickness, accident, and unemployment.

The opportunity to enjoy life—no one should be so hard pressed to earn the necessities of life that he cannot take part in "the pursuit of happiness."

And, because our nation has relations with other countries of the world, there are *premises that guide our foreign relations*, too:

The people influence the making and carrying out of foreign policy. We are a politically independent nation, and we want to remain independent.

We are a nation in which the individual is allowed a large degree of freedom; we desire to retain unimpaired our individual rights and liberties; we believe that a large degree of individual freedom everywhere in the world offers the best hope of lasting peace.

We are a peaceful people and we work to rid the world of war and the threat of war.

We are a friendly people with no traditional enemies, and we want to have friendly relations with all people.

We believe that all the peoples of the world are entitled to freedom to develop in their own way.

Through the United Nations we hope to play an active and constructive part in the world community.

We favor the free and uncensored flow of ideas and information throughout the world.[12]

These values and assumptions about life have been emerging in the Western world for a long time. The development of Christianity and the acceptance of its moral sanctions for more than 1500 years in Western civilization directly supported the emergence of such an ideology. The Magna Charta of 1215 in England gave early indication in Anglo-Saxon history of the shape of things to come.

The first settlers did not come to these shores to establish a democratic nation, even though many of them did seek a measure of freedom, especially in religion, that had been denied to them in other countries. However, values consistent with democracy were implicit in documents as early as the Mayflower Compact of 1620, and the general situation in the New World was peculiarly fitted to the ideals of democracy. An examination of documents such as the Declaration of Independence, our national Constitution, and the Bill of Rights indicates clearly the way in which the values of democracy grew and developed in the United States, were accepted as being basic to life as we wanted to live it, and were to be protected by social institutions and laws that would help to give expression to these values in the daily affairs of men.

The American people are deeply committed to the values presented

---

[12] Citizenship Education Project, *When Men Are Free* (Boston: Houghton Mifflin Company, 1954).

here. Many have fought and died in defense of these ideas. They remain central to our future development as a nation, and they are the great moral force that guides our nation in its leadership role in the free world and in the larger community of nations.

The Cruciality of Values in Curriculum Planning

Undoubtedly, the central importance of the role that values must play in curriculum planning is clear. When the elementary educator tries to "breathe life" into the educational objectives, he surveys the current and emerging social scene as an influence on curriculum development, and he would be rather helpless without strong values to cast against the decisions necessary to the process. Values provide the compass by which the educational process may be steered; they provide a sense of direction basic to any such conscious and direct attempt to influence human behavior as the operation of a formal and institutionalized school system. The school is a social institution—indeed a social instrument— by which each generation attempts to insure that its way of life will continue, with increasing improvement, and along an ever more clearly marked course.

Democracy and Freedom on the Defensive?

There are those students of our society who indicate a real concern for the ability of our freedoms, as we have known them, to survive in our culture and in the world as it is developing. They call attention to the forces in a highly industrialized society such as ours that tend to restrict freedom of personal choice and personal determination in many aspects of life. They point to the increasing complexity of most of the public problems and issues that the common man is expected to understand and on which he is to express an opinion with his ballot at election time. These students of society contemplate the long struggle that seems to be inevitable with the communist world—in their view, a totalitarian system that can determine and revise policies and programs without recourse to its public constituents—and feel that the general direction in which things are moving will make it increasingly difficult to practice democracy and to operate free, democratic social institutions.

Certainly, these values cannot be taken for granted, nor will our democratic institutions take care of themselves. If we want democracy, if we want to keep our free institutions, we must work determinedly to protect them from all sorts of incursions, planned and unplanned. The history of the human race generally, and our national history specifically, indicates that no more worthwhile task can be assumed by any group of

people than that implied here. One of the basic tenets of our ideology—
"deep and abiding faith in the future, and in man's ability to control
and direct his destiny"—becomes tremendously important in our time.

Conflicts in Values and Beliefs

In spite of the clarity with which values and beliefs can be stated, and
in spite of the generally determined commitment of our people to these
values and beliefs, there are areas of confusion and debate concerning
them. As the conditions in which our basic values and beliefs must find
their expression change, there is some shifting in the general climate
of opinion with respect to particular aspects of life, and some change
in our basic beliefs themselves. In the wake of such change comes a
measure of uncertainty and confusion.

Individualism and groupism. Life in early America, especially on the
frontier, called for a kind of rugged individualism that came to be
highly valued in our society. A man had to look out for himself to a very
great extent, and had to be strong-willed and determined about most
things in life. Eventual developments in our society cast doubt on the
value of this extreme individualism and caused us to value more highly
the person who was cooperative, who thought, generally, of the other
fellow, often first. Some students of American society have indicated
that, in our urgency to correct some of the faults of rugged individualism,
we have tended to "over-correct," so to speak, and to become too "other-
directed" in the way we make decisions about many things in life. They
have called for a greater sense of personal direction to be restored, with
a re-evaluation and a reinterpretation of individualism in our modern
civilization.[13] Thus, there is a great deal of uncertainty about individualism and groupism. We continue to seek the proper interpretation
of both of these phenomena in a way consistent with present social circumstances.

Work days and work weeks. Similarly, one can find confusion in the
minds of many people over what constitutes a "good and honest day's
work" in this latter half of the twentieth century. Born of an early
history that saw most people toil from sunup till sundown much of the
year, we put great value on hard work; a hard worker could always hold
his head up high and walk with confidence among his fellow men. Now,
with the increasing use of automation, and the ability of the machine to

---

[13] David Riesman, in his books *The Lonely Crowd* (New Haven: Yale University
Press, 1950), *Faces in the Crowd* (New Haven: Yale University Press, 1952), and
Individualism Reconsidered (Glencoe, Ill.: Free Press, 1954), has attempted to deal
with this sort of development in American society. The term *other-directed* as used in
this reference has come from his writings.

produce in quantities unheard of in an earlier day, organized labor groups seek shorter work days and shorter work weeks. The thirty-hour, four-day week is talked of as the emerging pattern of work in modern industry. This development has resulted in confusion about our values of work; we are not sure whether this increased leisure is the just result of the toil and inventiveness of former years, or the first evidence of an increasingly indulgent society on its way to becoming dangerously soft. Progress in one sphere, namely advancing technology, seems to run afoul of long-held beliefs in another. We seem certain that hard work is basic to success, and we are hard pushed to redefine success for ourselves in a way that is consistent both with modern industry and with values and beliefs of long standing.

Internationalism and isolationism. Let us turn for a few moments to the field of international relations and our long-term welfare. For years we pursued a firm policy of isolationism in international affairs. We were bordered by two very wide oceans, and we had been cautioned by our first President to avoid entangling alliances of various kinds. We sought to steer a course that would keep us detached from the rest of the world in as many ways as possible. However, the subsequent course of history has made it increasingly evident that to continue to pursue this policy was both impossible and unwise. Our welfare began increasingly to depend on the role that we played in world affairs, and isolationism began to give way to an emerging internationalism after World War I and especially since World War II. Still, there is some conflict over this course of events; there are those who would urge the United States to try to build our foreign policy again in a way more consistent with our formerly highly valued isolationism. While it seems rather clear that this will not happen, we do have continuing debate as to the kind of internationalism we should pursue, the sort of world leadership we should exert, and the degree to which we should become internationally involved on any continuing basis. There has indeed been a change—at the level of basic values and beliefs—in the general climate of opinion among our people.

Values and Beliefs Change in a Dynamic Situation

That values and beliefs do change is evident in the history of our country. That they change slowly is equally evident, and undoubtedly there is a kind of positive stability that accrues to society as a result of this slow change. These deep-seated values and beliefs are powerful guides to human behavior. When human experience has shown that commitment to particular values leads to reasonable and effective social arrangements in the main, any change must be weighed with extreme care and caution. On the other hand, a social group invites trouble when it holds

stubbornly and blindly to an outmoded value or belief after experience has clearly indicated that, in light of the social arrangements that it sustains, it needs to be reviewed and revised to be consistent with present circumstances. Thus, although basic values tend to persist, there is also a degree of tentativeness about them.

A democracy, of course, guards itself against this kind of disaster in part by tolerating, and in fact encouraging, a plurality of values at one time. That is, there is a dominant value pattern to which the great majority of the people give allegiance. At the same time, minority groups are given encouragement and protection to advance other statements of belief and to try to convince the majority that some change in values is in order. Thus, these peripheral minority group values may ultimately, as they are tested in experience by more and more people, move into a position of dominance and capture the allegiance of the majority of the people. A certain amount of stress and strain accompanies both the entrance of a new value into the system and the withdrawal of an old one from it. But, our democracy is supposed to maintain enough flexibility for change in all areas of life that adjustments can be made with a minimum of conflict and tension.

CULTURAL LAG

The picture painted here of the present social scene, including the values we apply to social circumstances, can be summarized in a meaningful way by introducing the concept of cultural lag in relation to these data. It may prove helpful to relate all of the various elements in this discussion and to introduce a kind of perspective to the situation that will help in interpreting these phenomena.

The Development of Culture

Sociologists and anthropologists have helped us to understand in recent years the development of culture with a clarity not possible before. One way of picturing this process is by reference to a *cultural pyramid*.[14] In such a pyramid the base is made up of the tools that a human group develops when placed in a given natural environment, with particular human needs to satisfy. Then, layer by layer, the cultural pyramid builds on this base, through the development of techniques and processes of production, to social, political, and economic arrangements, through an emerging and powerful climate of opinion concerning many aspects of life, to a final capstone of values, which then permeate the total pyramid

---

[14] Modified from I. James Quillan and Lavone A. Hanna, *Education for Social Competence* (Chicago: Scott, Foresman and Company, 1948), p. 81.

and regulate human behavior in the society. This cultural pyramid can be diagrammed as shown. While the pyramid develops from the bottom up, once values have been stated and agreed upon they are applied from the top down to test the desirability of the particular elements of the culture.

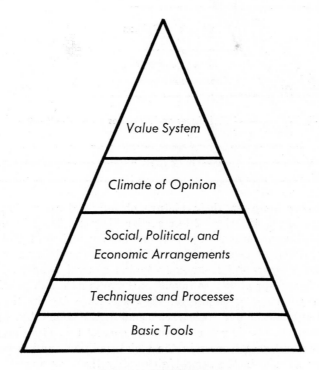

CULTURAL PYRAMID

The Concept of Cultural Lag

The social scientists call attention to the fact that it is possible for the elements of this pyramid to lose their original proportion. When this happens the society involved faces the task of restoring to the pyramid its former shape. Of course, this sort of cultural adjustment takes place continuously to some extent; the critical point is reached only when a great imbalance develops and continues for an extended period of time.

Many students of our society and culture feel that the greatest challenge of our time is to restore a greater balance to our own cultural pyramid. They feel that the material base of our culture so far outweighs its other elements that there is a severe cultural lag, which must be re-

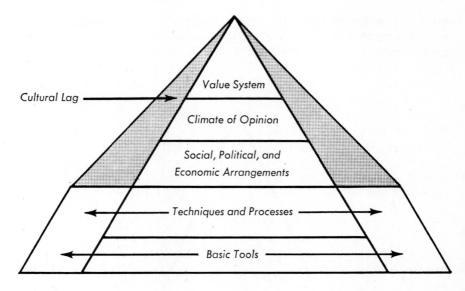

solved. We can diagram their picture of our culture at the present time with some modification of our earlier diagram. They interpret the current social scene as one in which our ability to invent tools and to develop industrial processes has far outdistanced our ability to cope with the fruits of science and technology to the general benefit of society. They see a *lag* in our ability to invent in the area of social, political, and economic arrangements. Similarly, they see some lag in the general climate of opinion in our society concerning life generally, and some inadequacies in our basic value system. To correct this situation calls for inventiveness and creativeness in the social, political, and economic aspects of our culture in the same high quality that has operated in our science and technology. It calls for the development of a more favorable climate of opinion concerning change in certain of our social, political, and economic arrangements—so that we seek and demand more effective arrangements in these aspects of our civilization, just as we do in its more material dimensions. However, the new "gadget" is much more enthusiastically received, and we are much more willing to give it a try, than we are to accept and try a new idea in other areas of living.

We are so appreciative of the freedoms in our society, and we are so satisfied with most of our way of life, that there is a great reluctance to encourage change. However, there is a growing awareness that change is demanded in certain of our social, political, and economic arrangements if we are to realize more completely the values we so dearly cherish. This chapter endeavored to develop in the reader some sensitivity to this demand for change, and to indicate both the impressive progress we have

made as a nation and the high level of the civilization we enjoy, and the kind of progress we still seek in keeping with the values to which we give allegiance.

The Emerging Cruciality of Education

Change is the watchword of our social, political, and economic life— and the pace with which it has come, and promises to come in the future, has been phenomenal. Education is fundamental to the maintenance of progress already made and to the continuation of progress in all aspects of life. Some are beginning to refer to education as "human resources development," which must concern itself with child and youth education, the education of young adults, and the continuing education of older adults. Ours is a time when there is no end to "becoming educated." New insights, new perspectives, new behaviors, changed attitudes are called for again and again. Voters are asked to cast their ballots on extremely complex social, political, and economic matters. As a necessary investment to insure the future, a greater part of our national income is going to have to go to the educational enterprise. To do otherwise is simply not going to be "good business."

This educational urgency is not yet a sharp public issue in the United States in any general sense. There are persons who see it clearly, and they are working to develop this awareness in others. Public debate over the reasonableness of present approaches to the financing of education, over the adequacy of the curriculum, and over teacher education may help to develop greater sensitivity. It is encouraging that our major political parties are beginning to face the problem of education in a more realistic way than formerly. Economists are beginning to ponder some of the "unknowns" in accounting for the growth of our economy, and many find themselves pushed to dealing with the human resources development factor in a new way. The competition for world supremacy between the United States and the U.S.S.R. is openly described now as being as much a contest over educational capabilities and achievements as over any other aspect of life. Activities at the international level aimed at assisting the growth of underdeveloped nations have education and educational enterprises at their very center. Unless the human resource is developed, the development of natural resources is ultimately and inevitably thwarted.

REFERENCES

Allen, Frederick Lewis. *The Big Change.* New York: Harper & Brothers, 1952.

> Deals with the major changes that took place in American life from about 1900 to 1950, presented in a most readable style.

American Association of School Administrators. *Educating for American Citizenship.* Washington, D.C.: National Education Association, 1954.

> The impact of social change, especially of technological advances, on education is treated in Chapter 2. An attempt is made to point out the ideals and values basic to our way of life in Chapter 3.

Beauchamp, George A. *Planning the Elementary School Curriculum.* Boston: Allyn and Bacon, Inc., 1956.

> The relationship between culture, changing social circumstances, and the school program is discussed in Chapter 5.

Brookover, Wilbur B. *A Sociology of Education.* New York: American Book Company, 1956.

> A good general statement on the sociology of education, with Parts I and V addressed directly to the relationship between the wider society and the program of the school.

Childs, John L. *American Pragmatism and Education.* New York: Henry Holt and Company, 1956.

> A very readable discussion of pragmatism as it operates in American society, with particular attention to its relation to points of view about education.

Green, Arnold W. *Sociology: An Analysis of Life in a Modern Society.* New York: McGraw-Hill Book Company, 1957.

> An extremely useful book for the student of education; it covers comprehensively such basic social concerns as social mobility, the family, and social stratification.

Havighurst, Robert J., and Bernice L. Neugarten. *Society and Education.* Boston: Allyn and Bacon, Inc., 1957.

> An excellent interpretation of the relationships between school, society, and culture.

Patterson, Frank (editor). *Citizenship and a Free Society: Education for the Future* (Thirtieth Yearbook of the National Council for the Social Studies). Washington, D.C.: The Council, 1960.

> A provocative statement dealing with citizenship education cast against a careful analysis of what the period 1960–1980 seems to hold for the United States in its domestic and international life.

Rodehaver, Myles W., William B. Axtell, and Richard E. Gross. *The Sociology of the School.* New York: Thomas Y. Crowell Company, 1957.

> A most readable textbook that helps the student of education to interpret the school sociologically and to apply sociology to educational concerns.

Stanley, William O., and others. *Social Foundations of Education.* New York: The Dryden Press, 1956.

> An excellent book that brings the social foundations to bear on problems and issues of present-day education. Chapter 2 is especially relevant to social change and curriculum planning.

Whyte, William H., Jr. *The Organization Man.* New York: Doubleday and Company, 1957.

> A critical analysis of the major trends in American life with obvious relevance to many matters faced in education today.

6

CHILD GROWTH AND DEVELOPMENT: GUIDES FOR CURRICULUM

If we wish to plan curriculum for the elementary school, and to design instructional situations in the classroom aimed at the accomplishment of educational purposes, we must have knowledge of the growth and development of children. Especially must we understand the learning process and how we may most expertly plan for its activation. All of the relevant cues available from the biopsychological foundations of education must be used to help us decide when and how to teach given subjects most effectively. Our goal is a design for learning that will make an effective contribution to living for these children now and that will provide a sound base for future learning and living as they grow on toward adulthood. We can be somewhat more sure of the answers we accept to the questions implied above if we make use of the increasing body of knowledge available from these biopsychological fields. From the early efforts of William James to the present, the psychologist has learned much about children and about learning; coupled with information from human biology, these fields offer a considerable body of facts, concepts, and generalizations that provide a basis for wise decisions about elementary curriculum development. Increasingly, too, the fields of sociology and anthropology are being used to help us to understand child development more completely, and some reference will be made to both in this chapter.

KINDS OF EVIDENCE AVAILABLE

Generally speaking, there are two kinds of evidence available for the elementary educator to use in his attempts to understand child growth and development. One of these we refer to as descriptive information, and the other we shall call interpretive information.

Descriptive Information

From human biology and child psychology we have much descriptive information about children. Babies are measured and weighed at birth, records are kept of the appearance of the first tooth and the taking of the first step. Such careful observations of the physical growth of children cover the years from birth through adolescence. Such attempts to study children also include descriptions of social and personal behavior; thus, we describe in children stages of egocentrism, or of negativism, or of boy-girl segregation, and so on.

Gesell and Ilg have made available a great deal of information on children, presented in the form of *age profiles*. These age profiles are attempts to describe the most typical behavior of children at various age levels. Great care is taken to point out in these materials that the findings are *not* rigid norms or models for child behavior. Rather, they simply illustrate the kinds of behavior that tend to occur at given age levels. Each child has his own individual pattern of development, it is noted, and profiles such as these may help us to interpret that individuality. The following material on the nine-year-old is taken from the writings of Gesell and Ilg as an illustration of these data.

> 1. Motor Characteristics
> Bodily Activity
> Nine both works and plays hard. He is more skillful in his motor performances and he likes to display his skill. His timing is also under better control. He now shows great interest in competitive sports such as baseball.
> Boys are quick to assume an active fighting posture and they strike out at each other and wrestle. They frequently "let off steam" or make a wild rush toward something.
> Nine is apt to overdo. He has difficulty calming down after recess or after a strenuous game. He is apt to ride his bicycle too far or to mow the lawn until he is exhausted.
>
> 3. Emotional Expression
> Nine is finally becoming what his parents have been striving for. He deserves and receives outright compliments such as "He takes more responsibility." "He is both more independent and more dependable." "He is easier to get on with." "He can be trusted." "He obeys well. ..." Nine is a loyal and devoted friend. He can always be sought by his friends for protection and is upset when his friends are brow-

beaten. He is prone to admire members of his own sex, either of his own age or often a few years older. This is the beginning of hero worship.

8. School Life

Teachers report that fourth is a difficult grade to teach. The teacher needs to realize that Nine is an individualist, that he has rather positive likes and dislikes. Nine wants to be independent of his teacher, but in his dealing with her he wants her to be reasonable and resents any decisions that he considers are unfair. The teacher soon recognizes that she delays in helping him until he really needs her. Nine is actually more related to his subjects than to his teachers. Dislike of a teacher may be linked to a dislike of a subject, especially if the child has more than one teacher. He may even blame the teacher for a lowered grade.

9. Ethical Sense

Nine is, as a rule, responsive to any demand put upon him, if he has heard it. His hearing may be related to his absorption in what he is doing, but it also may be related to his interest in and willingness to do the task required. His response often has the quality of a rapid flash. If he acts upon it immediately, he "clicks" in the demanded direction. But if he delays, he is apt to forget and then needs to be reminded. He takes reminding with good grace. Nine's intentions are often higher than his acts. . . . The rudiments of a conscience are developing in Nine. This does not, however, mean that Nine never blames or alibis. He might even blame his difficulties on his piano lessons. If he is in a tight spot, he is capable of making quite plausible excuses. He would often alibi if permitted but he can be held to the evidence of the truth.[1]

Studying this considerable body of information about children, we are undoubtedly more sensible about our general expectations for them. When decisions must be made with regard to individual children, or particular groups of children, these data can be interpreted, to some extent, in terms of "normal," "retarded," or "accelerated" development. Since many of the descriptive studies have been carried on over long periods of time, they yield developmental data, too. Such longitudinal information helps us to see development as a sequence of behavior changes and contributes to our understanding of total development accordingly.[2]

Interpretive Information

Obviously, there are reasons for wanting to be able to explain, rather than simply describe, child behavior. It is important, for instance, to know whether or not we should accept the idea of "normal," as derived

---

[1] Arnold Gesell and Frances Ilg, *The Child from Five to Ten* (New York: Harper & Brothers, 1946), pp. 197–211.

[2] For an example of outstanding work in accumulating longitudinal data of this nature, see W. C. Olson and B. O. Hughes, "Growth of the Child as a Whole," *Child Behavior and Development*, edited by Barker, Kounin, and Wright (New York: McGraw-Hill Book Company, 1943).

from the descriptive information in child development, as being inevitable, or simply most common. Must children do the things we see them doing? Must they go through the phases of development they do? These are important questions, especially to the educator. To answer them calls for information different in kind from the descriptive data mentioned above. The urgency of such questions has redirected a part of the research effort of psychologists, and has had a great deal to do with the increasing utilization of knowledge from sociology and anthropology in the study of child development. It is increasingly clear that, to throw light on such questions, behavior must be related to the particular society in which a child is born, and to the culture developed by that society. Together, culture and society encourage the development of certain human potentialities and discourage or prohibit others. It becomes important, from this point of view, to try to determine what others do to and for the child that may contribute to and explain in part his behavior. Socialization, as a process by which the child learns the ways of his society, and through which he is able to take his place successfully as a child, then as a youth, and eventually as an adult in that society, becomes an important process for the educator to understand. Thus, interpretive information is taking its place alongside descriptive information to help us to explain and deal with the growth and development of children.[3]

UNDERSTANDING HUMAN NATURE

The phrase "you can't change human nature" is often repeated when an explanation is needed to account for some bit of behavior, usually of a questionable kind, when other explanations seem to be inadequate. The phrase is surrounded with a kind of "inevitableness" with respect to the capabilities of the human organism to become something different. It seems to suggest real limitations on the way in which the course of human development may be guided and influenced. This is an important matter for the elementary educator to study and to understand. He needs to understand "human nature" if he is to deal with it successfully in the school situation. If it does limit the degree to which change may take place in the course of human development, or if there is no such thing as an already set and changeless human nature, the educator must know it. The importance of such insight for the school is obvious.

Concepts of Human Nature

A number of interpretations concerning human nature have been expressed over the years, each having unique explanations for the course

---

[3] For a more complete discussion of socialization, see William E. Martin and Celia B. Stendler, *Child Development* (New York: Harcourt, Brace and Company, 1953).

of human development, and each carrying clear suggestions for the way in which an enterprise like elementary school education should be conceived. Let us consider these briefly, with the child in mind.

An inborn behavior expectation. One interpretation of human nature suggests that there is an inborn tendency in the child to behave in certain ways. This enables one to expect all children to demonstrate a rather universal pattern of behavior. To the degree that this expected pattern of human nature is in agreement with the goals sought by the social group into which the child is born, every effort is to be made to encourage and allow the child to develop in a way consistent with human nature. If the inborn set of expectations is at variance with the desires of the social group, specific steps must be taken to try to redirect or to transform this inner pattern in a way that makes it more consistent with the goals sought by the group. An early writing by William James illustrates this principle well. In his essay ''The Moral Equivalent of War'' he writes, ''Our ancestors have bred pugnacity into our bone and marrow, and thousands of years of peace won't breed it out of us.''[4] In this particular essay he goes on to indicate that he does believe that society might be able to put this aggressive, militant tendency to constructive uses. He felt that by a direct attempt to redirect this ''pugnacity,'' man might be convinced to declare war on certain social problems and to be satisfied to conquer them, rather than actually to go to war on the battlefield against other men. In this writing is reflected one conception of human nature.

The general point of view concerning children in early colonial America was similar to the above concept. The child was seen as being by nature evil and bad, and great effort had to be expended to correct this basic fault. Without strong measures to correct the child's basic human nature, his ''feet would not tread the path of righteousness.''

More positively, Rousseau, a Frenchman interested in the education of children, wrote in *Emile: On Education* somewhat differently concerning human nature.[5] He too felt that the basic nature of the child was predetermined. In his view, however, this inborn ''nature'' was quite positively oriented; the tendency of the child was to be and to do good. He felt that society must allow this already fixed pattern to unfold and to develop; to interfere with this development was, in all probability, to thwart the goodness that would otherwise be manifest in the behavior of the child.

These points of view concerning human nature, and concerning children, are no longer readily accepted by informed people. We see children as being by nature neither good nor bad, evil nor righteous. The presence

---

[4] William James, ''The Moral Equivalent of War,'' in *Memories and Studies* (New York: Longmans, Green and Company).

[5] Jean-Jacques Rousseau, *Emile: On Education*, translated by William H. Payne (New York: D. Appleton and Company, 1898).

of basic drives in children has been documented by psychological and physiological research, as has the operation of acquired drives in human behavior. But, the evidence does not support the concept of human nature described above.

An "empty" human nature. In opposition to the above, a point of view was expounded by some to the effect that there was a basic "emptiness" to human nature, especially in the younger years. Proponents of this conception of human nature held that there was little or nothing at all that could be expected of the child. Children were born "empty" and "blank," and the family and school faced the task literally of "filling them up" with knowledge, motives, skills, and so on. From this point of view, what the child becomes is almost completely dependent on factors in his surrounding environment.

Among other things, it is evident that the school experience would play an important role in determining what children would become, that this conception of human nature would encourage a highly directive school program. Both the possibility and the responsibility to determine the course of human development that follows from these ideas seems to call for a kind of "strong" elementary school experience. However, the basic error in this view of human nature detracts from the contribution the school might make. The basic premise of "human emptiness" results in some faulty thinking with respect to the later "filling in" process, because the evidence that has been accumulated does not support the idea of the young child as a blank tablet simply waiting to be written upon.

A "full of possibilities" human nature. The conception of human nature that seems to be most supportable by the evidence from human biology and psychology starts from a basic assumption of "fullness" rather than of "emptiness." The child is seen as being full of potentialities for eventual development. All children do not possess the same potentialities, but all children do possess certain resources that can be developed. These possibilities for development are sorted out, to a great extent, by the society into which the child has been born. Those resources considered to be "good" for the individual and society are nurtured; those considered to be "bad" for the individual or society are not. What is good or bad is culturally determined. The value system in the society, and the conception of the good life held by the group, will determine the way in which such choices for development are made. This way of viewing human nature holds that what the individual eventually becomes depends both on internal personal resources and on external environmental forces. An educative effort is a combination of identifying for and with the child that which he is potentially able to do or to become, and of shaping this potentiality in ways and directions that are in the interests of the individual and of society.

This last point of view concerning human nature is accepted here. It holds that human nature is best conceived as a combination of the potentialities in a given child and factors in the environment of that child. It accepts the child as being educable; it supports the idea of the establishment of schools; it makes a place for goal-directed education. The elementary school educator is asked to view his role as being one of helping in the release of the potentialities of children and of guiding and directing this released potential toward educational objectives that are adjudged to be to the best interests of the child and his society. Considerable insight is demanded, obviously, into child growth and development so that the elementary school can be as effective as possible in meeting its responsibilities.

Heredity, Environment, and Human Nature

This brief discussion on human nature would not be complete without some reference to the factors of heredity and environment. The relationship of these factors has been studied widely by educational psychologists, since it is central to the whole school enterprise. Efforts have been made to determine whether or not one of these conditions was more important and more powerful than the other in setting the eventual course of human development. The evidence gathered enables us to draw certain conclusions with considerable assurance.

Insofar as physical characteristics are concerned, heredity pretty much sets the pattern of development. An individual is destined to have brown hair, or blue eyes, or fair skin; there is little that can be done about this. Similarly, he will be tall, short, or medium in height despite personal preferences. True, environmental factors such as diet may determine the degree to which a person realizes his inherited physical potential in certain ways, but this sort of influence is generally quite limited.

Also, that which we call intelligence, or those collective mental powers a child possesses in some pattern and amount that enable him to learn in various ways, seems to be primarily determined by heredity, and the differences in intelligence we find among children are in the main inherited. As is true of physical characteristics, there are some indications that the particular environment makes it possible for children to use a greater or lesser degree of this inherited potentiality, and environmental changes can improve or reduce the level of intellectual functioning; but there is no indication that an actual change can be made in intellectual potential itself. Intelligence seems to be fixed. Thus, the elementary school must view its operation as one in which intellectual differences among children are recognized and accepted, and must be dealt with accordingly. The school experience is not going to erase these very real

differences, but it can try to provide an environment in which various amounts and kinds of intelligence can function most effectively.

Human personality, defined as a composite of the beliefs, the basic values, the accepted goals, and the controlling emotions of an individual which collectively determine his adjustment to his environment, is highly susceptible to the environment in which it is formed. What a person becomes in these terms is very much dependent on the situation in which he finds himself. Again, there is evidence that heredity influences the development of personality. If a person inherits one physique rather than another, or one set of facial features rather than another, or one kind of energy system rather than another, he may be more likely to view life in a particular way, to participate in one sort of activity rather than another, and to adjust to the environment accordingly. But an individual need not do certain things in certain ways; his heredity *may influence* but *will not determine* his personality.

Thus, it seems clear that what a child is ultimately to become is the result of both hereditary and environmental factors. Nature provides both possibilities for and limitations on the development of individual children. The environment may help or thwart the realization of inherited potentialities, but it does, in and of itself, contribute in significant ways to what a child ultimately becomes. The environment may and does supply values that people will live by; goals that people will want to achieve; attitudes to be held toward other persons and things; symbol systems to be used in communication; and so on. The informed elementary school educator understands the heredity-environment relationship as it is involved in the school's efforts to educate.

MATURATION AND HUMAN LEARNING

The idea of maturation is an important one to clarify early in this discussion. The term *maturation* is usually used to refer to those aspects of development that are the product of innate growth processes, changes in the child that are not susceptible to direct teaching. They take place "from the inside out" so to speak. A child can do certain things successfully and efficiently only after certain kinds of maturation have taken place. Particular structural development is necessary before a child can sit, or stand, or walk, for instance. At least two provocative problems for investigation have arisen from interest in maturation.

Inborn Action Patterns

One area for investigation has concerned itself with the degree to which action patterns of human behavior are inborn, to emerge as nerves,

glands, and muscles grow and mature over the years. Lower forms of animal life seem to rely heavily on this sort of thing: dogs seem to chase cats "naturally," or by instinct; the way in which a bird knows to construct a nest, or a kitten knows to play with a mouse, and so on, are similarly explained. A search for these same kinds of inborn predispositions to action in the human has revealed very little. Evidently, only a very small amount of human behavior is a product of maturation alone; learning is a part of almost all of human behavior. The human being literally learns his way through life. However, it is clear that maturation is a necessary factor in much that we learn.

Maturation and Learning Possibilities

A second problem for investigation that has captured the attention of a good many psychologists has been the degree to which outside influences might speed up the development of behaviors that seem to be highly dependent upon maturation for achievement. Most of these studies have been done with very young children, at a time when the neural system has had little opportunity for certain kinds of development. Usually they have been timed to take place as children were approaching the point of emergence of certain types of behavior. Some children have been given instruction and some have not in an attempt to see whether or not such instruction would speed up or increase the efficiency with which certain things could be done.

For instance, one study dealt with two groups of children in a nursery school setting, and involved the skills of buttoning, cutting with scissors, and climbing. One group was given twelve weeks of practice; then the other was given four days of practice. Prior to the beginning of the experiment there were no reliable pertinent differences between the two groups. After the extended practice for one group and the short period of practice for the other, both groups were still approximately the same. The researcher concluded that factors other than specific training contributed to the development of these three skills.[6]

Other studies of a similar nature have been conducted, focused on a variety of things, and the results have all been similar. They show rather conclusively that an innate process that renders the organism neurally ready for a given learning is a part of human development.

These studies indicate, too, that certain environmental conditions are necessary if a child is to learn those things that he is maturationally "ripe" to learn. That is, the environment must either challenge or

---

[6] J. R. Hilgard, "Learning and Maturation in Preschool Children," *Journal of Genetic Psychology*, 41:31–56, 1932.

assist and encourage the child to make a given response. Especially as children grow older it is increasingly difficult to separate the maturational base from the environmental influences in many learnings.

The Concept of Readiness

The concept of readiness has been widely applied in school curriculum planning in light of this sort of evidence. We speak of a "most teachable time," meaning a time at which the child can learn most efficiently, using the least amount of instructional time while achieving the most lasting results. Thanks to the studies on maturation we know that success with a given learning may be dependent in great part on this inner ripening.

Of course, our understanding of readiness goes beyond the matter of maturation alone. We know that it is also dependent on such factors as intelligence, motivation, and experiential background in a great many instances. When decisions are made to deal with the here and now in the beginning years of the elementary school social studies program, or to use concrete quantitative situations in beginning arithmetic, or to utilize experience charts in reading, or to make first explorations in science in the immediate natural environment, an attempt is being made to plan the curriculum with an eye to the readiness of children in order to profit from it. We know some of the difficulties that young children have with time and space concepts, and we have some knowledge of what is demanded in order to work in the abstract and to deal with the symbolization found in number systems and in language. Combining the evidence on maturation with the other factors that are a part of "being ready" helps the school to provide for certain learnings in the curriculum at times when they are most likely to be handled successfully by the majority of children. The individuality of growth patterns, to be discussed later, will always make it necessary to allow some flexibility in any such planned expectancies, of course. Different children show readiness for specific learnings at different times; therefore it is necessary to allow for the gradual development of concepts over a period of time, although many children can successfully handle a given learning at about the same time.

It should be noted that in the concept of readiness there is more than passivity on the part of the school and the teacher. While the maturational process cannot be speeded up, the school can help to insure that other factors of readiness are given some attention. For instance, the school can take steps to broaden the experiential background of children in line with certain learning tasks that are anticipated for them. The school can provide a rich and stimulating learning environment that

will act as a positive stimulant to the developing child, and that will help to insure that the most teachable moment for a given child or group of children does not pass by unnoticed and unchallenged. Probably as many complications may result from letting the time go by when a child could have and should have accomplished certain learnings while the school continues to "wait," as when the school unwisely attempts to teach too soon, only to have to teach again.

The Idea of Developmental Tasks

In his studies on human development, Havighurst calls attention to the fact that the individual must learn the *developmental tasks* of life. He defines the term as follows:

> A developmental task is a task which arises at or about a certain period in the life of the individual, successful achievement of which leads to his happiness and to success with later tasks, while failure leads to unhappiness in the individual, disapproval by the society, and difficulty with later tasks.[7]

He goes on to call attention to the source of origin of developmental tasks. Some developmental tasks, such as learning to stand erect and later to walk, arise mainly from maturation. Others come from the culture into which the child has been born. Such basic and primary human drives and needs as satisfying one's hunger or eliminating body wastes the child must learn to satisfy in culturally approved ways. The culture will ask that the child learn to read, and to compute with numbers, and so on. A third source for developmental tasks is the person himself. As the concept of self begins to take form, embodying in it the personal values and aspirations of the individual, it becomes a powerful determiner of developmental tasks in its own right. A child may drive himself very hard to perfect physical skills, to learn to play a musical instrument, or to know a lot about the natural environment, if he decides that such knowledge is important and consistent with personal goals.

Examples of Developmental Tasks

Havighurst identifies developmental tasks from the period of infancy through old age. Here we will call attention, by way of illustration, only to those tasks of infancy, and early childhood, and middle childhood. For infancy and early childhood he lists:

1. Learning to walk.
2. Learning to take solid foods.

[7] Robert J. Havighurst, *Human Development and Education* (New York: Longmans, Green and Company, 1953), p. 2.

3. Learning to talk.
4. Learning to control the elimination of body wastes.
5. Learning sex differences and sexual modesty.
6. Achieving physiological stability.
7. Forming simple concepts of social and physical reality.
8. Learning to relate oneself emotionally to parents, siblings, and other people.
9. Learning to distinguish right and wrong and developing a conscience.

In each instance the biological and maturational basis, the cultural basis, and the personal and psychological basis for the task is identified by Havighurst.[8] For middle childhood (from about six to twelve years of age) he lists:

1. Learning physical skills necessary for ordinary games.
2. Building wholesome attitudes toward oneself as a growing organism.
3. Learning to get along with age-mates.
4. Learning an appropriate masculine or feminine social role.
5. Developing fundamental skills in reading, writing, and calculating.
6. Developing concepts necessary for everyday living.
7. Developing conscience, morality, and a scale of values.
8. Achieving personal independence.
9. Developing attitudes toward social groups and institutions.

In an introductory statement to these tasks of middle childhood we find the following:

> Middle childhood . . . is characterized by three great outward pushes. There is the thrust of the child out of the home and into the peer group, the physical thrust into the world of games and work requiring neuro-muscular skills, and the mental thrust into the world of adult concepts, logic, symbolism, and communication. By the end of middle childhood the individual has worked out his particular style and his level in all three areas. At the beginning of this period he is all possibilities, waiting to be realized through the unfolding powers of his body and mind and through the lessons his society will teach him.[9]

Using the Concept of Developmental Tasks

At least two purposes are clear for the use of the developmental tasks concept. First, identification of the tasks is useful in helping us to determine the validity of our educational purposes, and in stating them in a useful way. One can see the elementary school, for instance, as an institutionalized effort to help children with certain of the developmental tasks of middle childhood.

---

[8] *Ibid.*, Chapter 2.
[9] *Ibid.*, Chapter 4.

Second, the concept can be useful in helping us to time our educational efforts. In this way it is related to the concept of readiness. In this regard Havighurst speaks of "the most teachable moment," and defines this as that point at which the body is ripe (maturation), society requires (cultural demands), and the self is ready (personal motivation) for certain learnings. In agreement with the evidence on readiness, he concludes that efforts to teach certain things are largely wasted if they come too soon, and bring unnecessary and detrimental concern if they come too late. A careful study of human development in its cultural setting can go far to assure that teaching takes place at the most opportune time.

THE MEANING OF INTELLIGENCE

It has been noted here that the human individual literally learns his way through life. The ability to learn is of basic importance in determining the uniqueness of the human being in the animal kingdom. We refer to this ability as intelligence. This ability is quite obvious in the achievements of man, but it is nonetheless difficult to define in an acceptable way. For our purposes we shall say that the term *intelligence* refers to whatever pattern and degree of aptitude and abilities a child possesses that makes it possible for him to learn new things readily, to grasp new facts, to develop concepts, and to derive generalizations from experience. Particularly does it make it possible for the child to begin to work in the abstract, and to begin to use man's invented systems of symbolization as found in language and mathematics.

Measuring Intelligence

In conjunction with the earlier discussion in this chapter on heredity, mention was made of the fact that basic intelligence is inherited, and that it varies among individuals. Knowing this, and wanting to make some predictions as to the success that certain children would have with learning tasks, psychologists have put a great deal of effort into the search for ways to measure the intelligence of children. We have intelligence tests, designed to be given to individual children and to groups of children. We attempt to express with numbers a ratio called the I.Q. or intelligence quotient that represents the degree of intelligence a given child seems to demonstrate on the test. This ratio is largely a matter of drawing inferences about his intelligence. We have no way as yet to measure directly his basic intellectual power. Our tests, in the main, ask questions about situations that, it is felt, all children will have had similar opportunity to experience or know about. We infer, from the

number of right and wrong answers given, the intelligence level of the child involved. A high number of correct answers leads to an inference of high intelligence; a low number of correct answers to an inference of low intelligence. The strategic role of a common background of experience in the children being tested is obvious. The literature on intelligence is filled with the problems of inferring accurately about the intelligence of children who have been deprived of opportunities to experience in the way the test assumes they should have, or have simply lived in a cultural setting different from that in which the test was based.[10]

Also, it must be assumed that the child has put forth his best effort in the test, that he feels well and is functioning at his highest, that a positive rapport that facilitated the test situation was established between the testor and the child, and so on. It must be assumed that this was an optimum effort all the way around.

It should be clear from what has been said so far that measuring intelligence has proved to be a difficult and intricate task.

Identifying Several "Intelligences"

To further complicate this matter, research since 1940 has increasingly called attention to the presence of a "bundle" of rather specific intelligences in the human organism rather than just the presence of a general amount of intellectual power. It had long been obvious that the results of intelligence tests such as the Stanford-Binet led most accurately to predictions of success or lack of success with such verbal tasks as reading. The scores on such a test were less helpful in predicting success with other areas of the curriculum like arithmetic, or social studies, or science, and were even less helpful in predicting success in areas like handwriting, or spelling, or certain manual tasks. The inaccuracy of these predictions led to the conclusion that tests such as the Stanford-Binet tested primarily for verbal intelligence, or for the power to handle highly verbal tasks. And it led other researchers to conclude that there must be other intelligences that could be identified and tested for as well. The result of this research has been the development of intelligence tests that yield multiple scores. These tests indicate divisions between verbal and nonverbal intelligence, and then attempt to point out or infer the degree to which certain types of verbal and nonverbal power exist in a given child. Scores are available for such items as reasoning ability, memory, spatial sense, manual dexterity, and the like.

The development of these tests has been an important contribution to

---

[10] See, for example, Lee J. Cronbach, *Essentials of Psychological Testing* (Second edition; New York: Harper & Brothers, 1960).

our thinking about intelligence. No longer do we think of all children simply as having a particular amount of general intelligence; we identify and accept different types of intelligence—literally different types of potentiality. We do not expect all children to accomplish the same things in all aspects of the curriculum, because we are able to appreciate these differences for what they are. Also, we can realize the inevitable results of an elementary school program that is almost exclusively a verbal or reading experience. Certain kinds of intelligence may remain undiscovered and undeveloped. A moment's reflection on all that is implied in the offhand comment "it takes all kinds" leads to the conclusion that in uncovering the phenomenon of multiple intelligences we have uncovered one of the real strengths of the human race.

The Constancy of the I.Q.

A most tantalizing aspect of increased knowledge about intelligence has been whether or not the basic intelligence of people might somehow be improved. Early investigations of distribution of intelligence in the general population indicated that the range of ability approximated the statistically derived "bell-shaped" curve. Efforts to search for ways of

DISTRIBUTION OF INTELLIGENCE IN THE POPULATION[11]

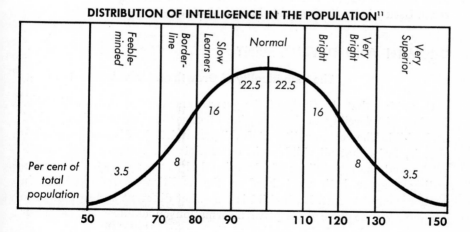

raising the basic intelligence of the lower part of this distribution have been to no avail. This basic element, or power, seems to be rather well-fixed by heredity, and cannot be improved upon. Some psychologists have challenged this conclusion, and have supported their challenge by noting

---

[11] R. Murray Thomas, *Judging Student Progress* (New York: Longmans, Green and Company, 1954), p. 102.

that the scores of certain children have increased on intelligence tests taken over intervals of time. Some children do make different scores at different times—either higher or lower—but there is no evidence that this change reflects a basic change in the amount of intelligence they possess. Rather, such fluctuations seem to indicate either that the environment in which the child has been operating enables him to use more or less of his intellectual power, or that some shift in concept of self has caused the child to use more or less of his inherent intellectual power. But, the evidence supports the idea that the I.Q. is relatively constant, that there are very real limits on what certain children can accomplish, and that no particular method of teaching or use of materials will do more than enable a child to use to the maximum what power he does possess. Obviously, standards of expectation will have to be set with these differences in ability clearly in mind.

In spite of the intricacies in testing for intelligence, and the measured skepticism with which the results of our tests must be used, such tests still provide essential and useful information for the classroom teacher. They furnish clues as to the reasonable expectations for individual children and for a class group as a whole. They indicate the nature of methods and materials that may work best with particular pupils. They help the teacher to assess the effectiveness of his work in the classroom. Used wisely, they provide invaluable data.

GROWTH AND DEVELOPMENT

The Individuality of Growth and Development

One thing that the study of the growth and development of children has brought forcibly to the attention of educators is the uniqueness of each child. The commonality of developmental tasks discussed earlier— that is, tasks that all children in our society must successfully accomplish—and the expressions of educational objectives presented in a preceding chapter both meet head-on the realities of individuality in their accomplishment. Each child is somewhat different and unique unto himself. We do have descriptive information on children on the basis of which we have built profiles of "seven-ness," "eight-ness," "ten-ness," and so on, to help us to anticipate what a group of third graders, fourth graders, or sixth graders will be like. These profiles also enable us to build a certain sense of expectancy for individual children in the group, too, but it must be remembered that these profiles are built on the basis of information gathered from a very large group of children, and that they report the most general tendencies found in this large group, be it a matter of physical, intellectual, emotional, or social de-

velopment. It is safe to assume that many children differ from the general profile in several ways.

There is some evidence to suggest a "going togetherness" with respect to an individual child's pattern of growth and development, too. That is, on the average, a child with superior mental ability will be well above average in physical development, emotional stability, and social competence. But we know from experience that a teacher must assess each child individually. That is, some children with superior mental ability are immature physically, or emotionally unstable, or socially inadequate. The focus of study must be on the individual child when a situation as intimate as the classroom one is being contemplated. It is this sort of thinking that underlies the declaration often heard that "there is no such thing as an average child." Such a creature exists only in statistical data.

Inter- and Intra-Individual Differences. In psychological terms, both inter- and intra-individual differences (*inter-:* between or among separate objects; *intra-:* within one object) must be understood and dealt with when working with children. Inter-individual differences we see all around us. Probably nothing brings this fact home to the elementary school teacher more than the first day of each new school year, especially in the lower grades. As he watches his class approach the room for the first time it is a veritable display of individuality and individual differences. Many children will be walking quietly and easily to the room, some of the youngest with their mothers. A few will come in great confidence, with bold strides that practically exude personal security. Some will appear to be being "pulled" almost every step of the way, and a few of the youngest will be being forced along by their mothers. Some cross the threshold into the classroom with little hesitancy, and proceed to walk around the new room in an inspectorial manner. Others enter bashfully, take the first chair or desk they come to, and give only fleeting and guarded glances around the room. One child will give his name to the teacher with ease; another is barely able to admit to having one. The physical differences of height, weight, facial features, body build, and the like, are even more obvious, of course. It is at such a time as this that the phenomenon of inter-individual differences among children is a living reality for the teacher. Any anticipated "one way" of teaching the group quickly melts away. It is at these times that the teacher yearns for the intimate insight into each and every child that is possessed by the parent, and it is at these times, of course, that the parent hopes earnestly that the teacher will be able to know and understand his child.

Intra-individual differences are not as quickly evident to the teacher, but studies of children document them very clearly, and a few weeks' work in the classroom will make them clearer to the teacher. Intra-

individual differences are the differences evident in the uneven and irregular profile of an individual child's characteristics and abilities. John may begin to be superior in reading, average in arithmetic, and poor in spelling. He may be socially mature, emotionally stable, but underdeveloped physically. Similar varied patterns begin to be evident for most of the children in the class. The child who is strong or weak "across the board" is the exception; the more likely pattern is one of "hills and valleys" in total developmental pattern. Intra-individual differences further accentuate a child's individuality and make additional demands on the teacher to recognize them in his work.

A wide range of abilities and characteristics within each class and a variation of abilities and aptitudes within each child must be anticipated and planned for in the school's curriculum. On the basis of the evidence, it is extremely difficult to think that all children profit from the same teaching procedures and from identical learning materials. The establishment of single, restricted, acceptable levels of accomplishment for all children would appear to be untenable. The levels will be too low for some and too high for others, and probably not very useful for any. It must be remembered, too, that the effects of the school experience on a group of children over the years tend to spread and increase the range of differences found initially, say, in the first grade. The school experience does not act as a leveling influence. All children will make some gains, but the faster learners will gain more proportionately than the slower learners, with the result that the distance from "top to bottom" becomes ever greater.

The Continuity of Growth and Development

Studies of human development have established the principle that growth is continuous. A great deal is said of the way in which growth persists from birth, on through childhood and youth, to adulthood. Many books that deal with human development carry charts of growth curves showing the continuous progress of some aspect of growth, such as height or weight. Typically, these charted curves are very smooth, arching upward in a steady climb; they are indeed continuous. But often it is not noted emphatically enough that these smooth curves of growth have been derived from data on very large samplings of children or youth, and that they have been smoothed out statistically in the process of constructing them. This statistical "smoothing out" leads too often to erroneous conclusions about the nature of continuity in growth and development.

The growth curve for any individual child will still show the tendency for continuous development in keeping with the principles stated in child development literature. But, a curve plotted for the height or

weight of an individual child will not be the smooth curve we are so used to seeing in books. Rather, it will show periods of rapid increases in height or weight and periods of leveling off, and may actually show periods during which weight was lost rather than gained. This pattern of rapid rate of growth, steady climb periods, times of no measurable growth, and even periods of regression seems to be more consistent with the evidence for any particular child. There is some evidence to suggest that intellectual development may follow a similar pattern. Some children may push ahead intellectually for a time, only to level off while they "live with" and consolidate their new understandings and skills for awhile. Then they will go ahead with their learning again, sometimes at a more rapid pace than before. A child progresses for a time, then tends to slow up the process while he assimilates what has been learned, builds up a new supply of mental energy, and proceeds on his learning way again.

Extremes of variation in rate of growth probably account for our observable "early and late bloomers," as we often call certain children. For some reason they maintain a consistent climb in development for a long period of time. The "early bloomer" climbs at a rapid rate, the "late bloomer" at a much slower rate. The pattern for both may and often does alter at some point. The precocious child, however, does not in the end seem to live up to his early promise, and the slower child does much better eventually than anybody thought he would. This variation in rate of growth is part of the reason why we are reluctant to label children in school too soon and too rigidly as either slow or fast learners. We are better off to hold such conclusions merely tentative for some time.

It is this kind of insight into the matter of continuity in growth and development that has led to the idea that each child has his own personal "timetable" for development, and there is little that anyone can do to alter it. We can try to understand it, and we can try to arrange an educational environment in school that extends to children a continuing challenge in keeping with this "timetable." Fortunately, the patterns for a sufficient number of children of a given chronological age are similar enough that they can be worked with as a classroom group. Teachers can anticipate that the majority of their pupils will have reached developmental stages that will fall within a relatively narrow range. Still there will be some who will be outside this range altogether, and they will have to be accepted accordingly.

The Interrelatedness of Human Development

There is evidence to indicate that the various aspects of growth—the physical, the emotional, the intellectual, and the social—are interre-

lated. This phenomenon has been obscured to some extent by the tendency for research on children to be focused on some one aspect of this total process. But, increasingly, investigators have called attention to a certain "oneness" about development and to the interdependent nature of growth processes. As this principle has emerged in the literature on child development, it has given rise to the concept of "the whole child" in elementary school education. This concept is misunderstood in many ways, and, in certain instances, overworked. The misunderstanding is evident in comments often heard like "the child never came to school in parts anyway—he always arrived whole," suggesting that nobody should get *too* excited about such an obvious truth. The overworked idea is evident in the singlemindedness with which some defend almost any practice with the idea that "after all, we are concerned about the whole child." This concept should be seen simply as an attempt to recognize the organismic nature of growth and development, and to insure an insightful and sensitive approach to planning for learning.

If this idea can be accepted, it helps to explain a good many problems that arise in the school and classroom, and it suggests approaches to coping with them. John, physically strong and seldom ill, is likely to do better intellectual work with seemingly the same basic ability as Bill, who has a recurrent pattern of illnesses. Accepting the interrelatedness of development, one is not so likely to demand more intellectual output from Bill as he is to see what can be done to take care of Bill's physical difficulties. A significant increase in effort and achievement on the part of Alice is more readily understood when it is realized that she has at last been accepted socially into the group and is finding opportunities to develop needed friendships. A drop in the zest with which Tom approaches his schoolwork and in the results of his efforts to learn may be related to the tragic loss of the dog he raised from puppyhood and accepted for the past three years as "a boy's best friend."

In the same vein, this sort of insight will cause a teacher to be concerned about the assignment of arithmetic work too difficult for a given child because it may contribute to a negative attitude toward the whole field of mathematics that will be hard to overcome in future instruction. Similarly, an elementary school may view its grading system in part on the basis of the ideas about competition that children who are unable to make a top grade in a highly comparative grading system may form, and on the basis of the concern over the way in which the emerging concept of self may be influenced in the process. Both may determine the energy and enthusiasm with which learning tasks in school will be approached.

It is very difficult to ignore this principle of interrelatedness in cur-

riculum planning in the elementary school. Grasping its significance can improve the school's effectiveness with children.

THE LEARNING PROCESS

A clear understanding of the learning process is, of course, prerequisite to planning for effective school experiences for children. It must be noted at the outset that we do not know nearly as much as we would like to know about learning, how it takes place in the human organism, and the conditions under which learning ability can be most fully utilized. Psychologists, human biologists, and neurologists are constantly probing for increased insight into learning and into the nervous system, and their work holds the promise of increasing our effectiveness with children over the years ahead.

In the meantime theories have been expounded and tested, with the result that there is considerable evidence of agreement on the current state of our knowledge about learning. That is, there are a number of things about learning to which most psychologists would agree. It is from this base of agreement that we work most effectively in the school.[12]

A Description of the Learning Process

Most psychologists and educators would accept a description of the learning process somewhat like the following:

1. *A child* (with given capacities, experiential background, and particular growth stage) *is motivated* (either intrinsically or extrinsically) *to seek a given goal.*
2. *Progress toward the goal is slowed or stopped* (the child lacks skill or knowledge needed to reach the goal, or does not see the relevance of present skill or knowledge to the goal) *and the child is faced with a problem.*
3. *As the child reflects on and explores the problem* (using the provisional try, varying degrees of insight, and varying types of teacher assistance) *he sees a solution in line with the sought goal.*
4. *The child refines and perfects his response* (through practice, through study, through discussion with others, particularly the teacher) *and his skill and insight are improved.*
5. *The response or solution becomes the child's* (by continued repetition in actual and contrived situations at school, and in life away from school).

The basic ideas upon which the over-all curriculum is planned, as well as the actions taken by the classroom teacher in providing instruction

---

[12] See Donald Snygg, ''Some Recent Texts in Educational Psychology,'' *Psychological Bulletin*, November 1955, pp. 510–517.

for his group, are designed to implement the above process in a vital way. Let us take a closer look at various aspects of it, calling attention to additional data related to learning.

The Goal-Seeking Nature of Learning

The above description calls attention first to the goal-seeking element in learning. It is necessary for the child to recognize and accept a given goal as a desired one and one worth working to attain if learning is to take place. The child must want to reach the goal before he will invest time and energy in trying to reach it. Somehow, it must be of value to him; it must appear to be personally vital. The pattern of acceptance in any given classroom group will undoubtedly differ from child to child. For instance:

> Child A accepts the goal readily because it means the opportunity to know more about something already recognized and accepted by him as being quite important.
>
> Child B is ready to seek the goal because it appears to him to be an opportunity to do something or to become acquainted with something new.
>
> Child C is ready to try to reach the goal because he sees in the accomplishment of it the opportunity to gain needed status in the group.
>
> Child D is motivated to strive for the goal as a way of gaining favor with the teacher.
>
> Child E will work willingly toward the goal because he relates its accomplishment to a means of satifying the aspirations which he feels that his parents have set for him.

This list could be extended, of course, but it will serve to call attention to the fact that some kind of motivation is necessary before very much effort and energy will be expended by any child. Studies of children have made it quite evident that the human organism is a goal-seeking one. Children are curious; they reach out for new experiences and new knowledge. To that extent, nature is on the side of society in the learning enterprise. In addition, we know that children reach out more enthusiastically and with greater effort under some circumstances than others, and that the results of learning will vary accordingly.

Motivation and the Learning Process

Psychologists have studied motivation, and have contributed significant insights that can be used in the school situation. In general, they cite two broad categories for motivation that must be recognized in planning for learning to take place: intrinsic motivation and extrinsic motivation.

Intrinsic motivation. We can say that the motivation to learn is intrinsic when there is a close relationship between the task to be learned and the goal of the learner, or for our purposes, between the teacher's goal in the classroom and the goal of the elementary school child. A child who has decided for himself that books contain exciting stories and information that he wants and needs will have little difficulty in accepting the teacher's goal of extending and refining his reading skills. Similarly, a child who finds his natural surroundings of interest will readily accept the teacher's goal of probing the natural environment for answers as to the causes of day and night, the seasonal cycle, the differences in local rock formations, or the habits of local wildlife. In attaining the teacher's goal, the child attains his goal, and vice versa. Under such conditions learning is more likely to be enthusiastically approached, energetically carried out, and comprehensive and meaningful in outcome.

Extrinsic motivation. In contrast, extrinsic motivation is defined as that which is present in the learning situation when the task to be learned, or the teacher's goal, bears no close or necessary relationship to the learner's goal. In such a situation, a child may accept the task of refining his reading skills as necessary because he wants to move on to the next grade with his friends. Or, he may work hard to understand certain aspects of the natural environment for the favor he will gain with his teacher as a result, or for the grade that he feels he will surely get on his grade card. Learning does take place under these conditions, but it is likely to be less meaningful, less comprehensive, and less effective generally.

Obviously, the school and the teacher want children to be intrinsically motivated in all learning situations. This wish is very difficult to attain, however, and is seldom realized for an entire group. More likely, any given learning task will hold elements of intrinsic motivation for some of the group and will have to be extrinsically motivated to some extent for the others. The teacher must be aware of this probability and must plan for it accordingly.

The most desirable direction for the school to take is to try constantly to reduce extrinsic motivation in a learning situation and to increase the intrinsic elements. This direction is best followed when it is based on the premise that all children are motivated to learn and that they want to strive to accomplish the tasks set by the school. The teacher can then bring elements of extrinsic motivation to bear only with those children who seem to need it and only to the degree necessary to initiate their learning, hoping to be able to reduce or eliminate such motivation as the learning situation develops. The reverse of this premise is the assumption that children will not want to learn what the school asks of them; the school and teacher will have to develop an elaborate system

of rewards and punishments that includes gold and silver stars, weekly honor rolls, detention after school, heavy homework assignments, and the like. Such devices become so important in many situations that they become the goal for which the child is striving and direct the major attention and energy of the learner away from the primary task. Too often these situations develop in such a way as to demand more extrinsic devices, rather than fewer, as the teacher tries to develop his classroom instructional program. Extreme uses of extrinsic motivational devices are to be guarded against.

The Development of Interests and Purposes

It must be remembered that the kinds of interests and purposes cited here in relation to the learning process are products of learning themselves. A child is not born with just so many interests and a given number of purposes; rather, as he grows, experiences, and learns he develops interests and accepts purposes. A part of the task of the school, with its goal-directed program of instruction, is to help children develop new interests and to accept new purposes. This task can and must be dealt with directly. Children do not readily see and accept all of the ramifications of a given school activity that the teacher does, or that the wider society does. Nor have they had enough experiences to have developed all of the interests and purposes that they can and must develop.

Psychologically, this task can be related to the continuing efforts of the human organism to maintain a state of equilibrium. The child likes to feel relaxed and secure; he seeks a feeling of contentment and adjustment to his surroundings, both material and ideational. Whenever the child is stimulated to act by some outside force, the general tendency is to try to accomplish that which will restore to him his former feeling of stability and contentment. At times the image of the self that begins to take shape in conjunction with seeking for adjustment motivates the child to ever more adequate and comprehensive approaches to life. The level of aspiration the child sets for himself makes him ever ready to take on the opportunity for a new learning experience. This tendency can and often does work in reverse, too. The self concept built out of a number of unsuccessful or only partially successful attempts to cope with certain learning tasks operates to cause the child to put forth only the very minimum of effort, just enough to restore the feeling of balance necessary for security even though the result is a continuing image of an inadequate self.

Some psychologists say that the task of the school can be seen as an organized effort to provide the child with a variety of situations that

may be temporarily disturbing, and that may bring feelings of discontent to the child as his desired feeling of stability and balance is upset temporarily. However, in the long run, and with the help of the school and the teacher, stability and balance are restored, and the child is more contented with himself and with life than he would otherwise have been. This means an effort on the part of the school to *lead,* sensibly and reasonably, the child who is developing a wholesome self concept and who is moving in a direction that seems to insure continuing personal happiness and social acceptability. It means a similar concerted effort to try to change the emerging self concept for some children when it is detracting from their happiness and efficiency now, and promises to detract even more in the years ahead.

This means that the elementary school must provide a stimulating and challenging environment for children. Processes and procedures that will make it possible for new interests to appear and for new purposes to emerge must be used in the school and classroom. The classroom situation must be "pleasantly disconcerting." It must be conducted in a way that will assure the child that he is progressing satisfactorily in meeting the many learnings society expects him to meet, and that he has already accomplished many of the tasks. At the same time the idea must be kept before him that present skill and knowledge levels can and must be improved, and that there is much more to be known and to be done that is appealing, attractive, and important.

THE USE AND TRANSFER OF LEARNINGS

In the earlier description of the totality of the learning process it was said that, once a child has accepted the presence of a problem and the desirability of solving it, he will explore the problem area until he is able to see a solution in line with the sought goal. This exploring suggests that learning is an active process and that the child is a "participating" learner. It usually means that the child has become sensitive to, or has been helped to see, the relevance of certain already possessed skill or knowledge to the sought goal, and begins to sense the way in which his present skill or knowledge level must be extended if the goal is to be attained. He will attain his goal partly on his own and partly with the help of the teacher. Again, modern psychology is helpful in assisting the school and the teacher to understand the way in which help may be extended at this point in the learning process. Psychologists speak of this point of learning as the problem of transfer of learning: the matter of trying to insure that what is learned at one time in one situation will be helpful in meeting another situation at another time.

Discrediting the Theory of Mental Discipline

Evidence accumulated has successfully discredited one of the early solutions to this problem, namely that of the theory of mental discipline. This theory attempted a relatively simple explanation of the task outlined above. It was built on an analogy between mind and muscle. It could be demonstrated that particular physical exercises increased the power and strength of given muscles in the human body. The strengthened muscle, when put to a later unanticipated test of strength, would be possessed of sufficient power to meet the challenge successfully. Thus, exercises taken at one time to provide added strength in a muscle made available increased muscle power when it was demanded by the situation.

A similar line of reasoning was advanced for the development of intellectual power. The mind was described as consisting of several separate faculties that were related to such intellectual tasks as reasoning, remembering, and the like. Then an attempt was made to identify those subjects that, in their "toughness," would strengthen the various separate faculties, thus providing the mental power necessary to meet more difficult mental tasks in the future. Research on the learning process and on the development of latent mental power has discredited this theory, however. The simple mind-muscle analogy just doesn't seem to hold. The study of a given "tough" subject does not seem to contribute in any general way to the learner's ability to reason, or solve problems, or remember, or perform any mental task. We have not been able to identify particular subjects that discipline the mind in the way that this theory envisioned. Though still argued and debated to some extent, it has been apparent to most psychologists and educators that there was much more to the problem of transfer of training than this point of view recognized.

Present Ideas on Transfer of Training

From research in the area of learning have come some ideas that seem to explain more fully the presence or absence of transfer in learning, and to suggest ideas that the school and the teacher must bear in mind if transfer from one school situation to another and from school to out-of-school situations is to be facilitated. Let us see what is indicated for curriculum planning and for teaching.

Understanding general principles. Starting with the early work of Judd,[13] there has been a persistent line of inquiry that indicates that the mastery of general principles is essential to the transfer of learning. The

---

[13] C. H. Judd, "The Relations of Special Training to General Intelligence," *Educational Review*, 36:28–42, 1908.

results of experimentation in this area show that the learner operates more successfully in facing a new problem, or in a new situation, when he has reached generalizations about earlier problems he has met or earlier situations in which he has found himself. If these results are accepted, and they are difficult to deny, then the school curriculum must emphasize meaning in its approach to learning. As often as possible an inductive approach that will lead toward the stating of generalizations should be taken in the classroom, and a search should be made for inter-relationships among ideas and processes.

The presence of identical elements. Thorndike's early ideas on the necessity for the presence of identical elements in the situation from which transfer is to be made to the new situation are still valid.[14] There must be some similarity between the learnings to be transferred and the task toward which the transfer is aimed. Developing speed and agility in running the base paths in baseball has some transfer potential to other games in which running is important. Learning certain visual and phonetic skills for word analysis in reading is helpful in spelling. Understanding the ideas inherent in the four fundamental processes in arithmetic with whole numbers is helpful in learning to handle these operations with fractions. In a sense, the search for a principle or generalization in a situation, as mentioned above, is a search for an application of a kind of identical element. The principle erected out of one situation is found to be applicable in another.

Teaching for transfer. Like almost everything else in the school situation, if transfer possibilities are to be realized the curriculum must be planned with their realization in mind and teachers must consciously teach for them. Implicit in the earlier point on general principles is a call for an organization of subject matter and a methodology that will facilitate the making of generalizations. The school should strive to arrange the sequence of the curriculum in such a way as to support transfer of learning. It should support a methodology that encourages pupil initiative and rewards efforts to apply already developed learnings to new situations. Children should be oriented to expect to seek and find ways of utilizing their learnings in new situations, either totally or with some adaptations and extensions. This approach to teaching helps children to learn, in addition to generalizations formed at any particular time, a *way* of learning itself, the importance of which is clearly indicated by the evidence of the research on transfer.

Generalizations cannot be given to children "ready-made" and be very

---

[14] E. L. Thorndike, *Educational Psychology*, Vol. II, "Psychology of Learning" (New York: Teachers College, Columbia University, 1914).

meaningful for them. Meaningful generalizations are arrived at out of experience. The curriculum can be designed, and the teacher can approach his work in the classroom, in such a way as to support and facilitate the development of generalizations. Questions like ''Think back to our study of early New England. Will anything we learned then help you now?'' or ''Let's take a look at these problems we have been doing. Can you see a rule that we might state that would help us when we meet such problems again?'' are indicative of the kinds of questions a teacher might ask who is actively working to build generalizations and to encourage the kind of mental set on the part of pupils that transfer seems to demand.

It must be remembered that the matter of individual differences will have to be recognized and dealt with in the area of transfer, too. Differences in age, general maturity, intelligence, will make for differences in the ability of children to see and to utilize transfer of training opportunities. Young children will need simpler and more concrete experiences out of which to begin to arrive at generalizations for themselves. Slow learning children will need to have such arrangements continued for them beyond the beginning years of school. It is likely that these slow learners never will be able to derive or apply some generalizations that others will find extremely useful in meeting new situations. But all should be helped to generalize to the extent possible; it is important for all. The ease and efficiency with which bright children will be able to learn to do this will account for a great deal of the ease with which they will learn new things and the efficiency with which they will apply their learnings to situations in and out of school.

REMEMBERING AND FORGETTING

A final point in the description of the way in which learning seems to take place makes reference to the way in which the new learning, be it a matter of skill or understanding, is refined and becomes the child's own. It is implied that the learning must persist over a long period of time. It is assumed that the child will remember what he has learned and that the learning will be his for future use. This matter is related, of course, to what was said above about transfer.

At the same time, we know that children do forget a great deal of what is supposedly learned at some time. This forgetting is evident in situations wherein children seem to be without a response where an earlier learning would be appropriate and correct; the difficulties involved are often a matter of recall, and the school must reteach, in many instances, what has already been taught. The central importance of this remembering-for-

getting process has attracted considerable study and experimentation, out of which some conclusions can be derived that are related to ''more'' remembering and ''less'' forgetting.

Meaningful, Well-Organized Material

In great part, the very nature of the material that is to be learned has a great deal to do with one's ability to recall it once it has been learned. If the material to be learned is highly meaningful it is more likely to be remembered. If the material is organized in such a way as to relate, rather than isolate, the various elements and details that make up the whole, it will be remembered over a longer period of time. Memorizing a list of the capitals of the various states in the United States is not accomplished with high efficiency if each element in the total learning task is detached and isolated. We are all aware of the way that children and teacher will try to introduce some structure into such a situation by arranging the list in some way so that initial letters of capitals group themselves into words or rhymes and the like to facilitate retention. The same difficulty occurs in trying to remember lists of major agricultural products when such learning has not been accompanied by some study of climate, terrain, soil, and similar information that can be used to suggest the possible products that might come from a given locale.

What has been said here supports directly what was indicated earlier in the discussion on transfer. When material learned is meaningful and understood, and when the learner is made more aware of the total setting surrounding the learning being attempted, it will be remembered longer and recalled more easily, as well as transferred more readily.[15]

Efficient Methodology

Retention is related to the way in which the material has been learned, and therefore, to the way in which the teacher teaches; the methods of teaching and learning are important. A general approach to teaching that emphasizes meaningfulness and understanding will aid retention. The whole must be dealt with as well as the parts; an inductive process must be implemented as much as possible that will lead to the stating of principles and the making of generalizations. Interest in something tends to support memory and recall; the teacher who attempts to capitalize on expressed interests of children in a learning task, or to work directly toward the development of interest in the learning to be attempted, will be helping to insure a higher degree of remembering. In

---

[15] For a good discussion, see R. A. Davis and C. C. Moore, ''Methods of Measuring Retention,'' *Journal of General Psychology*, 12:144–155, 1935.

general, it can be said that the same sort of methodology that supports transfer of learning supports memory and recall.

Repetition and Review

It is evident, too, that material that must be retained over a long period of time must be repeated often in many varied situations. This is sometimes referred to by psychologists as *overlearning,* and experimental evidence shows that overlearning sustains retention.

The school curriculum must make provision for the repetition, review, practice, and use of learning that is implied here. That is, these repetitions must be planned for; they must not be left to chance. True, some of the things that are learned in school are so much a part of what one learns and experiences outside of school that the living situation itself provides for a great deal of review and practice. In activities such as learning to run well, to express oneself orally, or to get along with agemates, practice and review are natural. But, to a very great extent, the learnings sought in school will call for school-provided opportunities for repetition.

In many instances this opportunity for practice and repetition is taken care of in the teacher's general approach to guiding and directing the learning process. For instance, social studies and science experiences can call again and again for study and research skills to be used, for considerable discussion and exchange of ideas, for reading and writing about pertinent material, for using maps and charts, and so on.

In other instances, the school curriculum will have to provide for direct practice, or drill situations, to refine initial learning and support subsequent retention. There is some confusion on this point, with a tendency in some quarters to frown on any mention of drill experiences. But, the evidence is again rather clear that, following initial learning, repetitive practice or drill is helpful and necessary. Its helpfulness is increased in proportion to the degree to which initial learning was understood, the degree to which the children have been helped to recognize their lacks and weaknesses and to relate the practice sessions to them, and the extent to which the drill provided is tailored to the individual needs of the learners involved. This sort of awareness should surround practice on arithmetic processes, on spelling, on handwriting, and so on.

REFERENCES

Beauchamp, George A. *Planning the Elementary School Curriculum.* Boston: Allyn and Bacon, Inc., 1956.
    Chapters 6 and 7 deal specifically with the influence of child develop-

ment and of our understanding of the learning process on curriculum planning.

Beck, R. H., W. W. Cook, and N. C. Kearney. *Curriculum in the Modern Elementary School.* Englewood Cliffs, New Jersey: Prentice-Hall, Inc., 1953.
> The matter of psychological understandings is applied to curriculum planning in Chapters 2, 3, and 4.

Cantor, Nathaniel. *The Teaching-Learning Process.* New York: The Dryden Press, 1953.
> Although the entire book deals with the learning process and its implications for teaching, Chapter 12 addresses itself directly to the principles of learning.

Coladarci, Arthur P. *Educational Psychology: A Book of Readings.* New York: The Dryden Press, 1956.
> An excellent selection of psychological readings related to many of the concerns in education.

D'Evelyn, Katherine. *Meeting Children's Emotional Needs.* Englewood Cliffs, New Jersey: Prentice-Hall, Inc., 1957.
> Gives emphasis to the importance of the teacher-child relationship within the larger concern of meeting adequately the emotional needs of children.

Hurlock, Elizabeth. *Child Development.* Third edition. New York: McGraw-Hill Book Company, 1956.
> One of the most useful and comprehensive statements concerning the growth and development of children.

Lee, J. Murray, and Dorris May Lee. *The Child and His Development.* New York: Appleton-Century-Crofts, Inc., 1958.
> Stresses those principles of human development that have the most significance for teaching, and attempts to make their utilization understandable.

Martin, William E., and Celia B. Stendler. *Child Behavior and Development* (Revised edition). New York: Harcourt, Brace and Company, Inc., 1959.
> A revised and enlarged edition of the authors' earlier work, *Child Development,* an outstanding statement that treats its subject from the standpoint of socialization, and utilizes material from anthropology and sociology to supplement the material from psychology.

McDonald, Frederick J. *Educational Psychology.* San Francisco: Wadsworth Publishing Company, Inc., 1959.
> This most provocative book puts the teacher in the role of decision-maker and relates a wide fund of psychological material to the improvement of the decisions made.

Olson, Willard C. *Child Development* (Second edition). Boston: D. C. Heath and Company, 1959.
> This second edition brings up-to-date one of the most valued and insightful books we have had on the growth and variation of individual human beings.

Prescott, Daniel A. *The Child in the Educative Process.* New York: McGraw-Hill Book Company, Inc., 1957.
> An excellent statement carrying views on child development and offering

ideas on how teachers can develop the skill and knowledge necessary to understand their pupils as individuals.

Rasey, Marie I., and J. W. Menge. *What We Learn from Children.* New York: Harper & Brothers, 1956.
    Utilizes case histories to help the teacher comprehend child growth and learning.

Redl, Fritz, and William W. Wattenberg. *Mental Hygiene in Teaching* (Second edition). New York: Harcourt, Brace and Company, 1959.
    A revision of a pioneer book that relates mental hygiene to teaching and attempts to point the way for the school to foster sound mental health in its contacts with children.

Rogers, Dorothy. *Mental Hygiene in Elementary Education.* Boston: Houghton Mifflin Company, 1957.
    A very fine statement concerning sound principles of mental hygiene in relation to elementary school education.

Russell, David H. *Children's Thinking.* Boston: Ginn and Company, 1956.
    A very complete bringing-together of the past fifty years of research and reflection on children's thinking, with insightful analyses and interpretations.

7

GENERAL CURRICULUM
PATTERNS: DESIGNING
THE CURRICULUM

The actual planning of the elementary school curriculum calls both for general decisions about the over-all approach to be taken in selecting subject matter, determining methodology, and answering related questions, and for more detailed decisions about the various programs of instruction within the curriculum. This latter task is, of course, heavily influenced by the decisions about the former. When a particular choice is made in approaching curriculum as a whole, a choice is being made for its parts, too. Here we would like to consider the choices available to the elementary educator as he faces the over-all job of curriculum planning. Discussion of the separate programs of instruction in the curriculum is presented in Part 3.

IDENTIFYING CURRICULUM PATTERNS

Earlier, mention was made of the identifiable curriculum patterns in elementary education, which represent the different points of view that are taken in curriculum planning. These patterns are relatively closed and consistent systems of thought concerning the job to be done, and stand as conceptual models, or theories, for the study and use of those persons who actually operate schools. There are those who question the use of such models, pointing to the fact that elementary schools, in practice, actually do not follow any *one* of them, and that they are therefore "removed" from schools as they are. We cannot accept this

line of reasoning. One seldom moves from the level of theory to practice in the "pure" sense of the implied relationship. However, a consideration of various curriculum models, seen as different internally consistent sets of answers to the kinds of questions noted in Chapter 4, can make us aware of the points at which truly critical decisions must be made in curriculum planning. At the same time they call attention to the ways in which these decisions might be and have been made in elementary school education.

Other educators, while accepting this reasoning, question the usefulness of such analyses for the teacher, especially for the beginning teacher. Again, we disagree. All curricular actions taken by schools are predicated on some concept of theory, and this concept includes certainly the actions of teachers—both as a faculty group deliberating the nature of the total elementary school program, and as individual persons developing a classroom program. Teachers make judgments concerning "what subject matter is of the most worth" and "what circumstances provoke the most learning" on the basis of some accepted theories of knowledge and learning. This relationship between theory and practice, in our view, should be consciously perceived in order to insure more enlightened judgments. The fact that all teachers operate on the basis of some accepted theory needs to be recognized and dealt with in the interests of improved professional service.

Four Basic Curriculum Patterns

Over the years four major identifiable curriculum patterns have emerged in educational literature. These four curriculum models are sufficiently different, one from the other, to call for study and choice in elementary education. They are referred to as:

1. The separate subjects curriculum
2. The activity (or child-centered, emergent, or experience) curriculum
3. The broad fields curriculum
4. The core or integrative-core curriculum

These curriculum models provide answers to critical questions in curriculum planning that will insure the school's accomplishment of its educational responsibilities. That some differences of opinion exist as to the exact responsibility of the school accounts for some of the differences in these expressed points of view. This is further related to differences in interpretations of the way in which learning takes place, in the role of the teacher, and so on. These positions and counterpositions will be noted in the discussion in this chapter.[1]

---

[1] Harold Rugg, *Foundations for American Education* (Yonkers-on-Hudson: World Book Company, 1947), pp. 700–708; B. O. Smith, W. O. Stanley, and J. H. Shores,

Curriculum Patterns and Cultural Change

An awareness of the relationship between cultural happenings on the one hand and the emergence of curriculum points of view on the other is important at the outset. Large and important social forces are at work that inspire and support new ways of viewing the school and its curriculum; changes are also suggested by the direct study of learning processes, of maturation, of social class, and the like. Therefore, there is a chronology involved in discussing these basic curriculum patterns that is related to cultural developments, as well as to expanding knowledge. This will be pointed out as appropriate in the analyses here. The chart is included on page 142 to help to indicate this chronology, and this cultural relationship, in anticipation of the later discussion. Let us consider each of these curriculum patterns in terms of their most distinguishing characteristics.

THE SEPARATE SUBJECT CURRICULUM[2]

Developing the curriculum in terms of *separate subjects* has been in the past, and continues to be now in a modified form, the most widely used general pattern for curriculum planning. Therefore, it has the strong force of tradition on its side, and is known to many generations of people. Let us take a close look at the ideas inherent in it.

Subjects as Organizing Centers

One of the most obvious characteristics of this curriculum pattern is its use of separate areas of subject matter and skill as the organizing centers for instruction in the school. Instruction is planned and given by subjects; the scope or breadth of the curriculum is the number of subjects to be taught. Each is allotted time during which the focus of instruction is on that particular subject, be it arithmetic, handwriting, history, or reading. Varying amounts of time are allotted to different subjects on the basis of two criteria: (1) a consideration of which subjects are most important to the child's education; and (2) studies of the best length of time for instruction in a certain area, such as spelling or reading, with attention to the maturity level of children,

---

Fundamentals of Curriculum Development (Revised edition; Yonkers-on-Hudson: World Book Company, 1957), pp. 225–228; F. Stratemeyer and others, *Developing a Curriculum for Modern Living* (New York: Bureau of Publications, Teachers College, Columbia University, 1957), Chapter 4.

[2] Henry J. Otto, ''Comparison of Selected Organization and Administrative Practices in 286 Public Elementary Schools and Forty-six Campus Demonstration Schools,'' *Journal of Educational Research*, October 1947, pp. 81–87; Smith, Stanley, and Shores, *op. cit.*, Chapters 10 and 11.

A CULTURAL–CURRICULUM TIME LINE

1700	1800	1900	1910	1920	1930	1940	1950	1960	1970	1980
	End of Colonial America; founding of independent nation	Expanding westward; saving the Union; reconstruction	General growth and consolidation; World War I	Roaring Twenties	Depression	World War II; the Cold War	UN–Korean action; more Cold War			
	Separate subjects curriculum pattern									
			Ideas emerge for the activity curriculum theory	Period of widest use of the activity theory		Continues to be in evidence and to influence practice ——————→				
				Broad fields curriculum ideas emerge		Continues to be in evidence and to influence practice ——————→				
				Core curriculum ideas emerge	Period of widest use of core theory	Continues to be in evidence and to influence practice ——————→				

their attention span, and so on. Organization by subjects and instruction within the separate boundaries of subject matter are basic to this curriculum pattern.

A Classroom Program Developed on the Basis
of the Separate Subject Curriculum Pattern

9:00–9:10	Opening exercises
9:10–10:10	Reading (3 groups; 20 min. each)
10:10–10:20	Recess
10:20–11:00	Arithmetic
11:00–11:10	Recess
11:10–11:40	History
11:40–12:00	Spelling
12:00–1:00	Noon lunch and play
1:00–1:30	Geography
1:30–2:00	Science
2:00–2:20	Physical education
2:20–2:50	Language study (including handwriting)
2:50–3:10	Music (on Monday, Wednesday, Friday)
3:10–3:30	Health (on Monday, Wednesday, Friday)
2:50–3:30	Art (on Tuesday and Thursday)
	Dismissal

The Role of Organized Subject Matter

From this point of view, the *sine qua non* of education is the study of organized subject matter. In it we find the refined and categorized collective experience of the human race; this is the cultural heritage. Certainly no more adequate definition for being educated, from this point of view, can be advanced than becoming extremely well-informed concerning the cultural heritage. The function of the school is to pass on the cultural heritage. It is held that this is the only way in which the culture can be maintained, and certainly the culture can not be used in meeting current problems, or improved in the future, unless it is first known as thoroughly as possible. Therefore, the mastery of subject matter becomes a very important end in itself. Similarly, the teaching of such skills as reading, handwriting, spelling, and arithmetic computation is approached directly in the curriculum from the beginning.

Grade-Placement and Continuity

Of course, organized subject matter must be allotted year by year for study in the elementary school, if this pattern is to be followed. All subject matter cannot be studied; the bulk would simply be too great. Therefore, the selection of subject matter of most worth from each content area looms as an important task. This selection is best made,

obviously, by experts from each area of study. These decisions should be made by people who have specialized in a given subject, who know it extremely well, and who can readily be accepted as authorities in their respective fields.

Once the general content has been selected, decisions are necessary for arranging this subject matter over the elementary school years and for allocating certain amounts of it to particular grade levels for study. In this process, at least two sorts of forces are at play. Each area of subject matter has an internal structure or logic, which is a primary factor in determining the way it should be studied in school, and which in turn determines the curriculum sequence; chronology is centrally important in history, arithmetic is developed along a scheme of prerequisite learning of simple to complex processes, total vocabulary is identified in reading and then "controlled" grade by grade, and so on. Along with this there have been certain scientific inquiries aimed at identifying the optimum chronological or mental age for meeting certain subject matter learnings, and these have some influence on the points at which certain content is assigned for study.

The Predetermined Nature of the Curriculum

From what has been said thus far, another obvious characteristic of this pattern of curriculum planning emerges clearly. This is a pattern in which the curriculum is rather completely predetermined for the child. The subject matter to be studied has been selected by experts; it has been arranged sequentially and assigned grade by grade in the school; the subjects that will be included in the curriculum have been decided. Thus, when a child comes to the school in any given year, his teacher knows with great preciseness what he is going to study and when he is going to study it. It has all been planned.

Learning and the Role of the Teacher

This subject approach to curriculum tends to result in a teaching-learning relationship in which "teacher shows and tells and explains" and the "child listens and watches and remembers." The teacher must be a well-informed person who understands that which he is supposed to teach, and his teaching procedures and methods are heavily influenced by his showing, telling, and explaining role. The child is a more passive participant in the learning situation. His job is too often restricted to listening carefully, watching closely, and trying to remember and reproduce as much as possible of what he has heard or read and of what has been demonstrated to him.

Textbooks and Other Instructional Materials

In this particular approach to curriculum planning, the textbook is the major instructional tool, along with workbooks for spelling, guidebooks in handwriting, and so on. The heavy use of such materials is quite consistent with and supportive of all of the characteristics discussed thus far. Experts can make available the most valuable content in a given subject by preparing textbooks to be used in the classroom. Furthermore, the subject matter in textbooks, singly and in series, can be carefully arranged in light of both the difficulty and the logic of the subject involved, to insure proper sequence. It can be designed to serve directly as an "assistant" to the teacher as he shows, tells, and explains. All of this supports the predetermined nature of this plan. And, in the textbook, the child has a source of reference and review as he attempts to remember and to reproduce. Many teachers will use other audio-visual aids in the classroom, of course, but the textbook is the primary instructional tool.

Evaluation of Learning

The major focus in evaluation is on the degree to which a child has understood, remembers, and can reproduce or repeat the subject matter or skill learnings that have been attempted. Most of the evaluation procedures employ paper and pencil, and the child is asked periodically to give written evidence of the fact that he is learning. There is a heavy premium put on memory, of course, and in certain situations speed also becomes a component in the evaluation procedure.

A Critique of the Separate Subject Curriculum

This is a most widely used and an often debated approach to curriculum planning. It is supported by many different persons for a variety of reasons. Some see in this point of view real assurance that the cultural heritage will be known by children, that it will be used to the maximum in the education of the young, and that none of it will be missed. Others support it because the "logical" elements in it appeal to them. The curriculum can be planned carefully, subject matter arranged year by year with great care, well ahead of the actual instructional situation. Still others are attracted to the conception of the role of the teacher and the place assigned to the learner in the classroom enterprise. A description of this relationship seems to "make sense." And so it goes.

But, this approach to curriculum planning has had many sharp critics, too. A variety of weaknesses have been identified by many school persons. Let us consider the most important of these here.

Too fragmented a learning arrangement. A great deal of criticism has been directed at the high degree of fragmentation in learning that this plan brings about. Every subject has its time and place, each quite separate and distinct from the other. The critics point out that clear relationships exist between many of the various branches of human knowledge, that cause and effect relationships exist between geographic location and culture, and that these connections are important for children to make if learning is to serve the individual as well as it might. They see in this separate subject arrangement an approach to learning that works against this very thing. They see it as a way of experiencing learning which makes it very difficult for the ''twain'' ever to meet in the child's learning.

Too passive a learning experience. Others have taken the position that the passive role assigned to the child and the showing, telling, and explaining role assigned to the teacher in the classroom simply do not agree with the evidence in learning. Here the child is seen as an active, goal-seeking organism, with personal interests, curiosities, and concerns, who needs to be an active participant in teaching-learning enterprises. This view suggests that the showing, telling, and explaining of the teacher should be held to a very minimum, so as not to interfere with the child's efforts to learn. And, to assign the child to a sitting and listening role in the main seems to go against the learning process as it is coming to be understood, as well as the basic nature of childhood itself. Furthermore, this particular approach to the teaching-learning enterprise puts the child in the position of always dealing with the end-products of knowledge, and largely ignores the processes by which knowledge is accumulated and by which people learn. Thus, he has little occasion for finding things out for himself, and little opportunity to learn the processes of problem solving.

Too logical and predetermined. The logical arrangement of subject matter and the predetermined plan for learning have met with criticism, too. The general feeling expressed is that this plan introduces unnecessary and unwise elements of fixity and order into the curriculum. The argument is supported by evidence from the psychology of learning to the effect that, for learning purposes, a logical order of content is not always the best order. Instead, a psychological order of subject matter, or the development of a way through to a given learning goal which is the result of teacher-pupil interaction and planning, is often called for. It is felt that the internal systems of logic identifiable in the various separate subjects do not have to be followed as stringently in curriculum planning as this point of view suggests. And, to predetermine the school experience in such a complete and comprehensive way keeps both teachers and pupils from capitalizing on the developing

situation around them in the interests of reaching educational objectives.

Too verbal an experience. Criticism has been leveled, too, at the extent to which this approach to curriculum planning tends to restrict the school experience to a verbal one. Armed with evidence from learning theory, child development, and intelligence studies, critics have noted some limitations on both the effectiveness and reasonableness of such an approach to children's learning. They feel that children need a variety of learning experiences, in addition to highly verbal ones, if learning is to be meaningful and lasting, and they see little reason to expect such variety in this particular curriculum model.

Too limited evaluation efforts. Lastly, there are those who indicate that the concept of evaluation in this curriculum pattern is quite limited, and that the evidence collected to reveal the accomplishment of learning is meager. They question the heavy reliance on paper and pencil devices that this point of view seems to make necessary. They point out that many other sources of evidence of learning are largely ignored, that there is a tendency to disregard educational objectives in areas other than intellectual development in this curriculum point of view.

These critical evaluations motivated two other developments in curriculum theory. One of these developments was the emergence on the educational scene of a truly revolutionary set of ideas concerning curriculum planning—the activity curriculum. The other was an attempt to modify and improve on the separate subject pattern; these efforts led to the broad fields approach to curriculum planning.

THE ACTIVITY CURRICULUM[3]

You will recall from the earlier chapter on the history of elementary school education that the closing years of the nineteenth century saw the emergence of some very different and revolutionary ideas concerning the role of the school in society and the nature of the school experience itself. The schools operated by John Dewey at the University of Chicago and J. L. Merriam at the University of Missouri in the opening years of the twentieth century were the forerunners of the activity curriculum theory.

The 1920's saw this new view of curriculum planning studied widely,

---

[3] Smith, Stanley, and Shores, *op. cit.*, Chapters 12 and 13; Rugg, *op. cit.*, Chapter 17; Ellsworth Collings, *An Experiment with a Project Curriculum* (New York: The Macmillan Company, 1923); Arthur T. Jersild and others, "An Evaluation of Aspects of the Activity Program in the New York City Elementary Schools," *Journal of Experimental Education*, December 1939, pp. 166–207; National Society for the Study of Education, *The Activity Movement*, Thirty-third Yearbook, Part II (Bloomington, Illinois: Public School Publishing Company, 1934): Harold Rugg and Ann Shumaker, *The Child-Centered School* (Yonkers-on-Hudson: World Book Company, 1928).

practiced in a particular group of private schools, and utilized to some extent in the public schools of the United States. This was the era of progressive education, of the Progressive Education Association, and of revolutionary thought in curriculum. Out of this has come a very clearly identifiable point of view in curriculum planning. It is variously known as the experience curriculum, the child-centered, emergent curriculum, or the *activity curriculum.*

Activities and Impulses as Organizing Centers

In contrast to the separate subject curriculum, the activity approach substitutes activities and impulses of children as the organizing centers of the curriculum in place of subjects. For instance, Dewey's early school tried to use four child impulses—the social impulse, the constructive impulse, the impulse to investigate and experiment, and the expressive or artistic impulse—as the centers around which learning experiences would be organized. Merriam's school replaced subjects with four categories of activities: observation, play, stories, and handwork. Within these impulse or activity areas, the expressed interests and concerns of children determine in the greatest measure the selection of content for study. This point of view is child-centered in its orientation, and not subject-centered. It makes a major place for the interests of children. The general feeling expressed in this set of ideas is that the most meaningful content for study is a matter of determining the points at which children, in growing up and probing their culture as they do, have come across things that concern them, things that they are interested in, and things that they want to know more about.

A Classroom Program Developed on the Basis
of the Activity Curriculum Pattern[4]

9:00	The time for the opening of school is fixed.
12:00–1:00	The time for the noon lunch period is fixed.
3:30	The time for the closing of the school day is fixed. Times for recess are not fixed; they are planned for daily.

9:00–9:30	Opening exercises and teacher-pupil planning for the use of time during the remainder of the day in terms of jobs to be done.
9:30–12:00 and 1:00–3:30	The time in the morning and the afternoon blocks available for instruction would be allotted daily and weekly in light of the current activities of the class, remaining flexible in light of unanticipated developments. The

---

[4] Based on material from J. L. Merriam, *Child Life and the Curriculum* (Yonkers-on-Hudson: World Book Company, 1920).

time would be divided on some basis each day between:

Observation—the study of the physical and cultural environment; includes material from the fields of science and social studies.

Play—seen as a major phase of child life; as a source of fun.

Stories—stories, including music, poetry, and pictures.

Handwork—construction activities in which children engage.

The Role of Organized Subject Matter

From the standpoint of the activity curriculum, the proper role of organized subject matter is as a learning resource. When a person, or for our purposes a child, attempts to satisfy an interest or concern, or to follow through in some problem situation only to find that his response is inadequate or incomplete in some degree, he has the cultural heritage, or organized subject matter, to go to for help. Thus, rather than starting out in the elementary school to cover subject matter as an end in itself, the child would be helped to become aware of organized subject matter and to be able to use it as the resource suggested here. It is felt that, due to the wide variety of interests children will express and the varied questions they will raise, a great deal of the cultural heritage will be studied, but it will be met in the resource context from the beginning. Direct teaching of such skills as reading and arithmetic computation will be related to an emerging realization on the part of the child that there are important skills he must develop.

Grade-Placement and Continuity

Again in contrast to the subject-centered curriculum, there would be no logical analysis of content to be covered nor would there be any specific assignment of material to particular grade levels. The internal logic of the various subject matter and skill areas would not be followed in the curriculum, but instead a psychological ordering of content would take its place. That is, history would be developed in a given learning enterprise around the interests of children in certain historical matters, and those interests might depart greatly from the chronology of a given historical period. Similarly, in arithmetic there would be an attempt to teach children the arithmetic they need in relation to certain quantitative aspects of the developing learning enterprise, rather than to follow some plan of step-by-step sequence in arithmetic. In reading, the logic of the controlled vocabulary would be displaced by an experience approach, which taught children to read the words that would be involved in what they were doing.

The Emergent Nature of the Curriculum

Another major characteristic of the activity curriculum is the fact that it is not determined in advance, but emerges from week to week and month to month over the school year. This accounts for the reference to this point of view at times as the child-centered, emergent theory of curriculum planning. Since the teacher, operating from this position, has a primary commitment to work with the expressed interests and concerns of the children in his class, it is not possible to predetermine the curriculum to any great extent. While the teacher may anticipate that the class will be interested in and want to study some particular thing, and plan for it accordingly, he would be bound to give this up in favor of something else when an actual contact with the class indicates a different sort of concern. Furthermore, the commitment is to the interests of each child, and to the degree that there is a spread of interests in the group the teacher is asked to develop learning enterprises around these varied interests. In other words, common learning experiences call for common interests. It is quite clear that the curriculum, from the standpoint of activity theory, cannot be preplanned.

Learning and the Role of the Teacher

In the area of methodology, the position is taken that the learning situation in the classroom ought to approach a problem-solving situation as much as possible. The starting point for good problem-solving oriented learning is present in the commitment to work with the expressed interests and concerns of children. The first step in such a learning sequence is concerned with the recognition and acceptance of some goal to be sought, and this is carefully done. Intrinsic motivation should be considered. The teacher is to fill the role of guide and facilitator in helping to implement the children's learning. He is to tell and show and explain very sparingly, and only in an effort to "prime" the children's efforts to learn, to supply needed information when this seems to be the only sensible way to supply it, or to demonstrate something that is vital to the problem-solving sequence as it is developing. There is to be a great deal of discussion between the teacher and the class throughout the total learning sequence, including the original determination of important interests and concerns. In fact, the idea of teacher-pupil planning is very central to the activity curriculum. The child is brought into the learning enterprise as an active, participating co-worker. He is expected to demonstrate initiative and responsibility in relation to his own learning, and certainly should not expect simply to sit and be told. It is deemed important that he "learn how to learn."

Textbooks and Other Instructional Materials

The typical textbook is not the important tool in the activity curriculum that it is in the subject curriculum. Children still need to be able to make use of many printed materials as an aid to their learning. But, the kind of materials that are most useful are those that are designed more expressly to be used as a resource in learning, rather than as a total learning experience in and of itself, as is the case with many textbooks. This use of textbooks is consistent with the resource role assigned to organized subject matter in this curriculum pattern. Needed in the classroom, too, is a wide range of printed materials, broad enough to be of some assistance to the wide variety of interests and concerns that are assumed to be operating the class group. Additionally, this approach to curriculum planning accepts the idea that children learn in many ways other than by reading printed materials. A wide selection of audio-visual aids to instruction must be available. A classroom in a school following the activity curriculum is equipped with tools and a great variety of art media. Access to realia and artifacts of various kinds that can be utilized in certain learning units is important. Children are experiencing dramatic play as another useful tool for learning in certain settings, too. Also, the teacher is more likely to find it necessary to prepare some instructional materials himself, since children may develop interests and concerns that lead them far afield from the usual printed materials available at a given grade level, or from topics that are typically treated in school textbooks. Also, the heavy commitment to individualized instruction often makes it necessary for the teacher to prepare materials for individual children, since their concerns and needs may vary from those needs that are anticipated in the commercially prepared materials.

Evaluation of Learning

The evaluation effort made in the activity curriculum is necessarily very broad. Being committed heavily to the total development of the child, that is, his social, emotional, and physical well-being as well as his intellectual development, the instructor attempts to collect evidence in terms of the child's total progress. To do this calls for the use of a wide variety of techniques and procedures in addition to paper and pencil devices. Interest inventories, attitude scales, sociometric techniques, simple projective instruments, and many other devices will be used in accomplishing the evaluation task. Teachers will also collect evidence by observational and conversational approaches and attempt to analyze this sort of information. The intimate association with children in the classroom and on the playground is used accordingly.

A Critique of the Activity Curriculum

The activity curriculum is undoubtedly the most provocative and controversial point of view that has been advanced in curriculum planning. It has been argued in educational circles since its early development, and the public has a tendency to blame any lacks in the results of education on the use of these ideas in developing the curriculum. As a theory, it was developed at a time when it seemed that the dynamic sort of society that was emerging in the United States, with a basic commitment to democracy, called for a kind of education that was itself more dynamic and democratic. In the minds of those who developed these ideas was a concept of the role of the school in society different from that which had long existed. They felt that the typical school situation was too far removed from society and life as it was being lived, and they hoped to bridge this gap with a different type of school experience. Also, they were rather sure that the emerging information on child growth and development and learning called for ways of organizing and teaching that were not found in the subject-centered school and classroom. During the 1920's a great number of private schools were operated on the basis of these ideas in curriculum, and to some extent these ideas found their way into the public schools. But, from the outset the activity curriculum had its outspoken and militant critics. On the one hand, of course, subject-centered advocates saw in this curriculum approach nothing but chaos and superficiality in learning. It struck at the very heart of all that they held to be important. On the other hand, another group of persons who were interested in moving the school curriculum away from a simple subject-centered structure took exception to the activity curriculum for other reasons.

A misunderstood concept of interest. These latter critics of the activity curriculum felt, among other things, that the theory as it developed placed too great a reliance on the present interests and concerns of children. While they did not deny the fact that interest was an important ingredient in learning, they felt that this theory tended to be extreme, and in error in part, in its concept of child interests. The critics took the position that interests are learned, just as so much of human behavior is learned, and that the school ought to be as much a developer of new interests and concerns as a follower of already existing ones. To use the existing interests and concerns of children as the major determiners of the curriculum seemed to be an extreme step. Rather, the position was taken that the school experience is as responsible for helping children to probe their culture systematically as it is for helping them to understand those aspects of the culture that they have happened to experience.

A lack of social consciousness. Along with the above came the criticism

that the activity curriculum was so committed to the interests and concerns of the individual that it overlooked the interests and concerns of society. The activity curriculum is strong on psychological insights but without a real sociological foundation. These critics felt that the welfare of the individual is inextricably involved in the welfare of the larger social group, and that the school has an obligation to help children to become aware of, and predisposed to consider, the larger social setting in which they live as well as their own individual concerns. The social unrest during the Coolidge administration and the Great Depression of 1929 and the early 1930's gave added support to this idea.

A need for a curriculum framework. The emergent nature of the activity curriculum was also a most debatable aspect of it. As educators considered this, and as they analyzed some of the general patterns of experience that were developing in the school lives of children in progressive schools, many began to doubt the usefulness of the activity curriculum. On the one hand, they saw what they considered to be evidences of some very trivial activities under the banner of child interest. On the other hand, they saw what they considered to be indefensible repetitions and omissions in experience. They felt that until some sort of general framework was established in a school and some agreements were reached as to the general focus of experiences from year to year, this situation would not be corrected. These ideas, naturally, were in basic conflict with the activity point of view.

Too passive a role for the teacher. Questions were also raised over the role of the teacher in the activity curriculum. There were many who felt that the role assigned to the teacher in the theory, or at least the interpretations of this role that were seen in practice, made the teacher too passive a participant in the learning enterprise. It was their impression that teacher-pupil planning was very often simply pupil planning. It appeared that teachers were hesitant to take an active part in much of the classroom program, and were vague and undecided on the limits that the activity curriculum placed on their role. The critics felt, generally, that the teacher could and should play a more decisive role in the classroom, and that such a role could be a most positive one and still be far removed from complete direction, or autocratic control. In fact, there were many who felt that the very teachers who pointed with pride to the fact that they were not influencing decisions in the classroom in any decisive way were often exercising a kind of subtle and unconscious persuasiveness that was exerting considerable control over the situation.

Such were the most important criticisms of the activity curriculum. It was out of these criticisms in great part that a point of view in cur-

riculum began to develop that was neither subject-centered nor child-centered, but society-centered. Most commonly this point of view is referred to as the core curriculum. But, before we consider that particular pattern, let us return to the subject-centered advocates again, for a look at the broad fields curriculum pattern.

THE BROAD FIELDS CURRICULUM[5]

Supporters of the subject-centered approach to curriculum planning have not been insensitive to many of the criticisms that were leveled at the separate subjects curriculum pattern. As a result, there were efforts in the 1920's and 30's to make some revisions in that pattern that would meet many of the most serious criticisms. Out of these efforts has come a curriculum model referred to as the *broad fields curriculum*.

Broad Fields as Organizing Centers

Many educators who were followers of a subject matter approach to curriculum planning realized that the criticism concerning the high degree of fragmentation in this approach was not without some foundation. As the responsibilities of the school had grown and as programs of study had multiplied, the list of subjects that children were being asked to study in the elementary school approached the ridiculous. In order to get them all in, the day was indeed a series of short, separate periods of time, each devoted to one of these many areas of learning.

To meet this situation, some educators began to organize subject matter into broad fields. In these instances, content from highly related but separate subjects in the curriculum were combined into one broad field of study. As an example, the separate subjects of history, geography, and civics were grouped together into one broad field known as the social studies. The lines that had formerly separated them in the curriculum were removed. and the resulting arrangement was referred to as a fused course. The broad field still remained as an organized field of knowledge, but the resulting structure provided a broader organization of subject matter, permitting more latitude in instruction. Thus, we have seen the emergence of general science, general arithmetic, social studies, and language arts as broad fields utilized as organizing centers for the curriculum in many elementary schools.

---

[5] Smith, Stanley, and Shores, *op. cit.*, pp. 255–262; Rugg, *op. cit.*, pp. 708–714; Henry Harap, ''A Survey of Courses of Study Published in the Last Two Years,'' *Journal of Educational Research*, May 1935, pp. 641–656; Otto, *op. cit.*; J. Wayne Wrightstone, *Appraisal of Newer Elementary School Practices* (New York: Bureau of Publications, Teachers College, Columbia University, 1935).

A Classroom Program Developed on the Basis
of the Broad Fields Curriculum Pattern

9:00–9:10	Opening exercises
9:10–10:10	Reading (3 groups; 20 min. each)
10:10–10:20	Recess
10:20–11:20	Social studies
11:20–11:30	Recess
11:30–12:00	Language arts (in addition to the above *Reading*)
12:00–1:00	Noon lunch and play
1:00–1:50	Arithmetic
1:50–2:10	Physical education
2:10–3:00	General science and health
3:00–3:30	Music and art (on alternate days)
	Dismissal

The Role of Organized Subject Matter

The role of organized subject matter remains much the same in the broad fields pattern of curriculum as in the separate subjects pattern. The intent remains the same, to "pass on" selected portions of the cultural heritage. Instruction still takes place within these broad fields of subject matter. Some of the relationships between separate areas of subject matter are more readily grasped, of course. For instance, when the United States is studied in a way that relates its geography, its history, and its government in one learning unit, certain relationships that might be obscured by a separate subject organization come to light.

The Predetermined Nature of the Curriculum

The broad fields curriculum pattern still retains the characteristics of preplanning and predetermination that were found in the separate subjects approach to curriculum planning. Sequences are still laid out in advance, assignments of subject matter are still made grade by grade, and the child comes to school with his curriculum already completely determined for him.

Learning and the Role of the Teacher

The basic methodology in the broad fields curriculum is, again, not unlike that of the separate subjects curriculum. The teacher is still committed to a showing and telling and explaining role; the child is committed in the main to a sitting, listening, watching, and remembering role. With the program fixed, and the subject matter of most worth already selected, a more dynamic methodology seems to be unnecessary.

Textbooks and Other Instructional Materials

The textbook is the major instructional tool necessary in the broad fields curriculum. The development of broad fields of study, and fused course organization, has put new demands on the writers and publishers of these materials. For instance, the development of series of textbooks for use in the elementary school social studies or science program in this broad fields setting has called for something new in the materials area. The separate subjects curriculum uses separate history, geography, and civics books, of course. For the broad fields curriculum, content from all three of these areas must be skillfully woven into one textbook series. Similar tasks must be accomplished in the area of science. In the broad field of the language arts, separate materials are retained for reading, spelling, handwriting, and oral and written expression. While certain kinds of flexibility have been developed in the time arrangements for language teaching, and a certain relatedness is practiced in much language arts teaching, the combining of the subject matter into a single textbook is not deemed appropriate in the language area. Of course, many audio-visual aids are used in the broad fields pattern to help the teacher to show, tell, and explain.

Evaluation in the Broad Fields Curriculum

The general approach to evaluation does not change radically in the broad fields curriculum from what it was in the separate subject pattern. Priority goes to techniques and procedures that will give evidence of subject matter achievement, and paper and pencil devices are relied upon rather heavily. There is some greater possibility to test for certain cause-effect relationships, due to the fused nature of the programs of study, in addition to more simple recall tasks, if the teacher is prone to do so.

A Critique of the Broad Fields Curriculum

The attempts at reorganizing the content from certain highly related separate subject areas into broad fields of study have been partially successful in meeting the criticisms of the extreme fragmentation of the separate subjects approach. There seems to be no doubt that this broad fields organization should help the child to become aware of some of the important relationships between the various areas of human knowledge.

Concerns over the arrangement of content. Some subject specialists have attacked the idea of the broad fields arrangement because they feel that the child gets so little knowledge about any one field of study as to

cause concern. They argue that not enough history, or geography, or civics, for instance, can be put into a social studies course. Also, certain specialists feel that to destroy the internal logic that is unique to each of the areas, and to attempt to replace it with some sort of manufactured internal structure, is not defensible. They argue that an experience with the logic—that is, with the internal structuring of subject matter that is unique to a given area of knowledge—is as important a learning experience as to meet the content of the area itself.

A high level of generalizations. There are those, too, who doubt that the tendency to deal with generalizations in a broad field arrangement will help the child grasp the meaningfulness of these generalizations. They know how difficult it is to develop meaningful generalizations with children, and they know the great number of different experiences necessary for the emergence of generalizations. As a result they fear a tendency in the broad fields organization to deal too quickly in the classroom at the level of principle or generalization as a way of covering more content. They wonder whether there isn't a real danger of the learning experience becoming mere verbalization, largely void of real meaning for the child.

At the same time, there is much evidence that this is one of the preferred ways of organizing the curriculum in the elementary school. An examination of courses of study and curriculum guides at the present time will reflect this tendency quite clearly. It seems to be a way of reducing the unacceptable features of the separate subject curriculum pattern, while still retaining many of the major characteristics of subject-centered planning which appeal to many school people, and to much of the public.

THE CORE CURRICULUM[6]

The core curriculum began to take form in the late 1920's. It would be a mistake to picture this pattern as an attempt to evoke a compromise between the two subject matter approaches and the activity curriculum. It was born more of a feeling of urgency among some educators that the

---

[6] Smith, Stanley, and Shores, *op. cit.*, Chapters 14 and 15; Rugg, *op. cit.*, Chapter 18 and pp. 714–716; Oric L. Frederick and Lucille J. Farquear, "Areas of Human Activity," *Journal of Educational Research*, May 1937, pp. 672–679; Virginia State Board of Education, *Tentative Course of Study for Virginia Elementary Schools, Grades 1–7*, Bulletin Vol. XIX, No. 5 (Richmond, Virginia: The Board, 1937); Santa Barbara County, California, *Santa Barbara County Curriculum Guide for Teachers in Elementary Schools*, Vol. II (Santa Barbara, California: Schauer Printing Studio; 1940); Santa Barbara County, California, *Santa Barbara County Program of Curriculum Development*, Vol. VII (Santa Barbara, California: Schauer Printing Studio, 1942); Roland C. Faunce and Nelson Bossing, *The Core Curriculum* (Englewood Cliffs, New Jersey: Prentice-Hall, Inc., 1951).

school's maximum contribution as an agency of society was not being realized. This point of view toward curriculum planning developed initially in the same period as the Great Depression with its myriad social problems and issues. While the core protagonists did not close their eyes to psychology, they were adamant in their insistence that the philosophical and social foundations of education also be used in arriving at a defensible over-all pattern of curriculum. Only by so doing, they felt, could the school become an effective instrument for furthering democracy.

Basic Human Activities as Organizing Centers

As a curriculum model, the core position rejects both the ideas of using subjects or broad fields and of using children's interests and impulses as organizing centers. Rather, it takes the position that the "basic human activities," sometimes referred to as "areas of living," should be used as the centers around which curriculum is planned and instruction takes place. These areas of basic human activities are variously identified by anthropologists and sociologists as they study life in a variety of human groups. A typical and widely used list of these would be as follows:

1. Protecting and conserving life, resources, and property.
2. Producing, distributing, and consuming goods and services.
3. Transporting people and goods.
4. Communicating ideas and feelings.
5. Providing education.
6. Providing recreation.
7. Organizing and governing.
8. Expressing spiritual and esthetic impulses.
9. Creating new tools and techniques.[7]

As social scientists study and analyze the way life was carried on in the past and is conducted in the present all over the world, it is their conclusion that all human groups have had to devise some manner of dealing with these basic human activities. Although the particular arrangement might have been different from one society to another, some arrangement had been made. For example, some groups were governed by the oldest men, some by the oldest women, others by the warriors, and still others by chosen representatives, but all human groups have to make some arrangement for organizing and governing themselves. Similar evidence is available for all of the other areas of activity.

The core curriculum uses these areas of basic human activities as the

---

[7] From a projection of an integrative-core curriculum prepared by Paul R. Hanna, School of Education, Stanford University.

organizing centers for the curriculum. It is felt that subjects themselves are too abstract and categorical, and that the impulses or interests of children are too vague and elusive. It is felt that the use of basic human activities introduces the kind of order that closely resembles life as it is being lived. The use of these activities as the scope of the curriculum should help to relate school to society.

A Classroom Program Developed on the Basis of the Core Curriculum Pattern

9:00–9:10	Opening exercises
9:10–9:30	A look ahead at the day's work; some final teacher-pupil planning
9:30–10:30	These two hours are given over to a large learning unit, often referred to as the unit of work. Typically, this will be social studies and/or science oriented. At times it may develop into two distinct studies, one in social studies and one in science.
(10:30–10:45 Recess)	
10:45–11:45	
11:45–12:00	Clean-up; getting ready for the noon recess period
12:00–1:00	Noon lunch and play
1:00–2:00	Direct attention to language and arithmetic skills, individually or in groups as appropriate
2:00–2:30	Physical education
2:30–3:20	Esthetic experiences of various kinds (music, art, dance, poetry, etc. Perhaps club meetings once a week)
3:20–3:30	Clean-up; get ready for dismissal; perhaps some look back at the day and a brief anticipation of tomorrow
	Dismissal

A Central Role for Values

Values, and our value system, are central to this point of view toward curriculum development. It is felt that human behavior of all kinds is basically determined and steered by a commitment to values. Further, the proponents of this core position feel that the progress the United States has been able to make is largely due to allegiance to democratic values, and that the problems we face are, in most instances, to be finally solved by the application of values. At the same time, those who originally conceived this core curriculum model recognized the confusion and inconsistency in our value system and the need for resolving it. Therefore, one finds in much of the writing on the core curriculum a heavy and obvious commitment to bring values more consciously into the school curriculum, and to push more school studies to the question of "what ought to be," rather than leaving them at the descriptive stage of "what is."

The Role of Organized Subject Matter

The core curriculum is basically committed to the idea that organized subject matter is best viewed in school as a resource to which one goes with problems, concerns, and questions. It obviously rejects the concept of subject matter as an end in itself, which characterizes most of the thinking about curriculum from the subject-centered position. It is closer to agreement with the position taken in the activity theory. There is no denying the relevance of much of the organized cultural heritage to these basic human activities. In fact, a little thought will easily connect many of our organized disciplines to these areas, as economics and the production, distribution, and consumption of goods and services. But the starting point is to be an area of activity, not a subject. The core approach to curriculum planning would also wait for certain evidences of readiness before beginning direct instruction in skill areas like reading and arithmetic.

Grade-Placement and Continuity

The questions of grade-placement and continuity are answered in core theory by a combination of psychological and sociological information. Psychologically, it is felt that the child will best understand, and will accomplish more meaningful learning, if in the early years of the elementary school the focus of attention is on life close to the child. Therefore, the basic human activities are studied in situations that are near and intimate, such as the home, the neighborhood, the school, and the local community. In the intermediate grades it is felt that the child can begin to understand and study places and people farther removed from him, and the focus of attention swings to the state, to the nation, to a foreign country, to another continent. Some core theorists have used the generic term *community* in relation to continuity, and see the matter of sequence as the act of focusing on ever larger "communities of men" sequentially in the elementary curriculum. Others feel that a job well done within the confines of the local community through about grade three should mean that any other community group, large or small, near or far, can be studied with profit in any of the intermediate years.

A General Framework for Curriculum

The core approach to curriculum planning utilizes a broad and general preplanned framework. It cannot accept either the completely predetermined structure of the subject-centered patterns, or the completely emergent concept found in the activity curriculum. The core pattern takes the position that some advanced planning is necessary in a school.

Only in this way can assurances be given that the experience will be truly a cumulative one, free of unnecessary repetitions and unwise omissions. And only in this way can society be assured of consistent social direction in the school experience. Thus, a framework would be developed that might focus primary attention on the basic human activities within some given community of men at a particular grade level. Beyond this, the teacher is to be left free to develop the learning experience in the most efficient way he sees. He is to keep "within the playing field" but to be as creative and imaginative as possible in the development of the learning enterprise itself.

Learning and the Role of the Teacher

Core theory asks that the teaching-learning situation be developed consistent with available information on child growth and development and learning. Insights into problem solving are to be applied in a major way in teaching procedures and processes. There is to be a great deal of teacher-pupil planning as learning units are developed in the classroom. Insights into readiness, individual differences, motivation, and so on, are to be applied in the instructional program. The child is to be an active participant in the learning he is to accomplish, helping to plan for it, helping to guide and direct it, and helping to evaluate programs. The teacher shows, and tells, and explains only when necessary in the interests of improved problem solving. At the same time, the teacher must play a *decisive* role in the classroom, working actively to support the education process.

Textbooks and Other Instructional Materials

There is a clear recognition in this position that children learn in a variety of ways, and that a variety of instructional materials and resources must be available. Printed materials are considered important, but they should be used preferably within the resource and reference idea. Additionally, a wide array of audio-visual aids, a careful utilization of community resources of people and places, opportunities to construct and to process with raw materials, and the use of dramatic play as a material-technique would be central in the development of learning units.

Evaluation of Learning

The approach to evaluation taken in the core pattern is broad and comprehensive. This approach recognizes important purposes in addition to intellectual developments, and calls for the collection and interpreta-

tion of a wide range of information accordingly. Paper and pencil devices will be used, but along with many other instruments and techniques, such as attitude scales, interest inventories, sociometric devices, simple projective instruments, and the like. Teacher judgment, based on careful observations and intimate associations with pupils, counts heavily, too. Attempts to assess progress and development are focused on the group as a group, as well as on each individual.

A Critique of the Core Curriculum

In our attempts to evaluate the core curriculum pattern for the elementary school we must keep in mind the fact that it was first developed as an innovation in secondary school education, and only later was it applied to the elementary school. Thus, a concept of curriculum that, at the secondary level, was to influence only a part of the school day and week has been applied in a much more comprehensive way at the elementary school level. Of course, the core curriculum has had its outspoken critics.

Poor substitute for subjects. Persons with continuing commitments to subject-centered structures have seen this pattern simply as a poor substitute for the well-organized and easily identifiable subject and broad field patterns. They feel that both the child and the teacher will perform more efficiently by utilizing a subjects or broad fields over-all pattern.

Too logical and mechanical. Those educators with heavy allegiance to the activity curriculum see in the core position an attempt to introduce an undesirable kind of preplanning and fixity into the elementary school curriculum again. They perceive the arrangements by which grade emphases are determined and questions of continuity are resolved as being extremely mechanical and logical. Some of them have criticized the core pattern for being unduly sympathetic with a kind of "cultural determinism" in human development. Generally, they seem to take the position that many of the dynamic aspects of the educative process and the nurturing of individual uniqueness and creativeness are reduced unduly in the interests of the demands of society.

A questionable role for the school. There are those who cannot support the core position because of the implied role for the school in the society with which it is identified. In its formative years, the core pattern was associated with social reconstructionist ideas in education. That is, many felt that the school was going to have to play a much more vital role in *leading* in social reconstruction instead of simply *following*. The suggestion was not an "educational revolution" as some have interpreted it, but it did mean that the value dimension in society should become a matter for conscious attention in school, that studies ought to deal with

central values in our culture, and that value change and value conflict had to be recognized in school studies. This approach meant that a good many highly controversial problems and issues would find their way into the classroom, but the early core protagonists felt that only in this way could the school help to equip the upcoming generation with the kinds of insights and understandings, and predispositions to action, that were demanded by the times.

Of course, for the school experience to be conceived in such a way has always been debatable in American society. Many feel that the school should remain more aloof from this kind of social argument, and "tread water," so to speak, while the larger society struggles with important and vital matters. Such a concept becomes even more controversial when it is applied to the elementary school and to children at these ages. This is a time, in the view of many, to build basic skills of literacy, and to begin to build socially useful concepts and generalizations of many kinds. But it is not the time to focus on complex and controversial situations in society. Of course, as the core concept has been applied to the elementary school, the extremes of this concept have been tempered. The central importance of values and of our value system has not been discarded, but the focus of attention is on helping children to be aware of our values, to understand them, and to be able to identify them in practice. In the process the children may become aware of inconsistencies and a lack of completeness in application of these values, but this is not a major focus of study at this level.

WHAT PATTERN FOR THE ELEMENTARY SCHOOL CURRICULUM?

At the outset, it was suggested that some educators questioned the value of reviewing these various curriculum patterns because elementary schools, in practice, do not follow any one of them completely. Some reflection on schools you have visited and know rather well will undoubtedly confirm this point. However, general tendencies are identifiable, and they do influence the curriculum more in one direction than in another. This tendency to "lean" in one way or the other at certain crucial points in curriculum planning is testimony to the fact that choices do have to be made and are made every day in elementary schools and classrooms across our country.

It would not be wise for us to impose our answers to these crucial questions on the users of this book in any final sense. At the same time, we would be derelict in our responsibilities if we did not share with our readers our thinking on many of these crucial points and alert them to the fact that the position taken here is influenced accordingly.

Let us move to a consideration of factors that seem to us to be among the most central of those that must be dealt with in planning the elementary school curriculum.

The Age and General Maturity of Children

Certainly the general maturity level of children during the period from about five or six to twelve or fourteen years must be considered in making decisions about a general approach to curriculum in the elementary school. Even this range is too great to consider as a whole. Young children in the kindergarten and primary grades differ greatly from older children in the intermediate grades, and the young adolescent of grades seven and eight differs from both. Thus, when consideration is given to "freedom" in learning, one must know the age of the children to be so "freed." The extent and nature of guidance and assistance from which the six-year-old will profit will be different from that which is most appropriate for the eleven-year-old. When one attempts to take a position on those aspects of the curriculum that are most important for children in the "fundamentals for living" sense, the answer must inevitably extend to the age of the children to be involved and their place in the elementary school years. One may well give a different answer for a second grader than for a fifth grader, or for a seventh grader.

The Nature of the Learning Involved

It seems clear, too, that the nature of the specific learnings, or areas of learning, to be considered will influence the basic ideas that will be brought to bear in curriculum planning. For instance, if the discussion centers on the responsibilities of the elementary school to develop understanding and skill with the number system, one's thinking may go in the direction of a rather carefully planned sequence of learnings starting in the kindergarten and extending on through the elementary school, with a great amount of detail predetermined at each grade level. It may be decided that the school will have to contrive a good many quantitative situations to insure that children meet the wide variety of number situations that are considered important.

However, if the discussion centers on science, the particular detail in the science curriculum may be less important than the assurance that children truly have an opportunity to experience the processes of science. Only a general sort of planning may be considered necessary in the interests of balance and comprehensiveness. It may be felt that contrived situations will have to be used only sparingly and in support of natural situations.

It follows from this that the position one may take on the question of preplanned or emergent curriculum is more a question of degree and is highly specific to the area of learning under study. The arithmetic curriculum may be much more extensively preplanned than the science curriculum, though the latter will also demand a careful kind of preplanning.

The Function of the Elementary School

The function of the elementary school will influence partly the curriculum ideas to which one may feel these school years are most wisely committed. Earlier in this book it was noted that, generally, efforts to educate could be divided between areas of general and special education, with the elementary school heavily involved with the former. This question of function is important enough to be presented here in a more refined way.

In this analysis, a concept of curriculum functions first developed by Featherstone in conjunction with secondary education will be used, with applications to the elementary school curriculum.[8] He identified four separate and distinct curriculum functions, which, in his view, the school was called upon to accept and plan for in light of the guiding purposes of the school. Using the term *function* in the sense of "the proper action [of schools]" or "the special purpose [of schools]," he listed the following functions and felt that curriculum plans would have to be made accordingly:

1. The integrative function
2. The exploratory function
3. The specialization function
4. The supplementation function

Let us consider briefly the definition of each of these.

The integrative function. The integrative function refers to the responsibilities the school accepts for the development of common loyalties, attitudes, values, understandings, skills, and abilities of all kinds in the general population. Those sought are defended in statements of educational objectives as the minimum of learning that every person should possess for his own welfare and for the welfare of society. The integrative function is highly related to general education and to the program of common learnings sometimes discussed in educational litera-

---

[8] William B. Featherstone, *A Functional Curriculum for Youth* (New York: American Book Company, 1950). Professor Featherstone's untimely death in 1951 terminated what promised to be a most illustrious career in the field of secondary school curriculum. We are especially indebted to him for the work referred to here.

ture. It is one of the legitimate functions of the school curriculum to develop programs to accomplish this "core" learning task.

The exploratory function. By exploratory function, reference is made to those aspects of the school curriculum designed to give students an opportunity to explore on the one hand their own abilities, aptitudes, and interests in one or more lines of human endeavor. On the other hand, these experiences are to acquaint the student with the professional and vocational opportunities for work in the wider society. The intent is to help students to find a certain pattern of ability, interests, and opportunity that might lead to lifetime occupational choices. Programs developed to aid in this function would usually be general courses in science, business, shop, or the like. Student interest is the primary prerequisite for enrollment, and courses include observational and limited participatory possibilities in the general work-a-day world to insure that pupils receive more than a classroom "feel" for any given line of endeavor.

The specialization function. The development of curriculum offerings to meet this specialization function follows rather logically from the above discussion. It is deemed fitting and proper that the curriculum provide opportunities for pupils to specialize as occupational choices begin to be firm and certain prerequisite learning experiences are recognized by the student. This function helps to fulfill the educational objectives of economic efficiency, which suggest that the school ought to help youth to make decisions about, and then prepare for, some "producer" role in society. In course work so offered, demonstrated ability is a requirement along with personal interest. The operating standards in various areas of specialization begin to be the standards of expectancy that students must show some promise of fulfilling. Thus, a pupil interested in engineering, and, therefore, in mathematics, would need to demonstrate the ability to handle advanced mathematics if he were to enroll in such a course. This would be the pattern in all such choices. Again, it is felt that the objectives to which the school is committed demand offerings that meet this function.

The supplementation function. The supplementation function embraces more services than courses. This term refers to those special programs and service agencies operated by the school to help students to succeed in their educational and personal adjustment, and thereby to equalize educational opportunity to a greater extent for them. Speech therapists, reading clinics, psychological services, and the like are provided. A likely candidate for these services is any student who gives promise of being helped by them. Lately, there has been an increased effort to provide special arrangements for superior learners, too, as a supplement to their educational diet, and as a way of extending increased equality of op-

portunity to them. Thus, students who give evidence of being able to go far beyond the level of achievement and performance of the great majority are helped to do so in any of several ways.

Implicit in these defined functions is insight into a dimension of educational planning that is not always grasped. Thus a relationship between the curriculum planned at any one level of the school system and the functions to be provided for begins to reveal itself.

The Elementary School Curriculum and Functions

On the basis of the above definitions, we submit that the primary function of the elementary school curriculum is the *integrative* one. Reflection and observation indicate that the kinds of learning goals sought in this function are usually started in the elementary school, and a great deal of time is given to them. For instance, teaching children to read, write, and spell the English language, to understand and become skillful with the number system, to grasp a feeling for their national heritage, and to develop some systematic understanding of democracy are all parts of this function and are at the very heart of the elementary school curriculum. (Of course, these learnings are continued beyond the elementary school years.)

While there is nothing akin to the *exploratory* program of the junior high school at this level, there are some exploratory opportunities identifiable in the elementary school curriculum. Often, in the progress of social studies or science units, or music and art experiences, for instance, children are presented with situations that lend themselves to exploration. Probably this exploration is more in the direction of *information* about the work of the world than in the direction of personal opportunities to participate in the work. But, students may observe scientists in laboratories, or carpenters building houses, or airplane mechanics servicing aircraft, or musicians entertaining. In the process they develop some personal preferences as to what they might like to do "when they grow up." Sometimes, club programs centered around interests rather than grade levels verge on this exploratory function, and the limited opportunities for elective studies in some eight-year elementary schools are related to this function.

Our desire to be more "preventive" than "curative" if at all possible makes a place for the *supplementation function* in the elementary school curriculum. The advantages in trying to work with very young children to correct certain deficiencies have been proved, and various programs in speech therapy and the like operate at the elementary school level. Guidance services for personal adjustment as well as educational adjustment are growing in the elementary school. Special efforts to work with

both slow and fast learners are increasingly evident. All of these efforts are consistent with the objectives sought for children in school.

The only function defined above that we do not find in the elementary school curriculum is that of *specialization*. As mentioned earlier, we are committed to the idea that childhood is not the proper time to press for a professional or vocational choice, and we do not encourage children to do so. Although interests developed in the elementary school and through the elementary school curriculum may, in retrospect, be interpreted as early specialization choices, this interpretation is hindsight and not the result of purposeful planning.

What has been said here is shown in the chart. Together, the chart and the discussion should help one to grasp in still another way the individuality and uniqueness of the elementary school, this time in terms of curriculum functions. This discussion should help, too, to underscore the idea presented earlier that what goes on in the elementary school is in fact part of a continuing school curriculum, extending from the first year of school to the last. The figures used for the percentages of total time and effort at various levels of the school system should not be taken as precisely and definitely as the chart suggests, but the divisions shown are supportable to a great degree and are not far from what one could identify in most school systems in the United States. What has been set down here will, of course, vary for individual pupils. Some will know quite early where they want to "specialize" and will follow through; others will not have made such a choice at the time of high school graduation but will still be exploring both themselves and the world of work.

It should be evident that the particular function that the elementary school is asked to accomplish should have a great deal to do with the kind of curriculum pattern that is developed. It may be that some one of the possible ways of approaching the curriculum at this level gives more promise of meeting this functional responsibility than another. This is a decision that every elementary school system must make.

Responsibilities to the Individual and to Society

The matter of the responsibility of the school to the individual on the one hand, and to society on the other, is a persisting dilemma in educational planning. At the same time, the answer seems obvious. Certainly the school has responsibilities to both. It must help each individual to realize to the fullest his unique potentialities, and it must make certain that the progress and problems of society are also given attention. The complexity is due to the fact that one is inextricably involved with the other. That is, there is not likely to be full self-realization in other than a healthy vigorous society; and there is not likely to be a healthy

POSSIBLE CURRICULUM DISTRIBUTION BY FUNCTIONS—EXPRESSED IN PERCENTAGE OF TIME

*This would vary greatly; some students would not be involved at all, while a few would spend a much greater amount of time in special programs and with special services.

vigorous society without individuals who have developed their full potential. The two go hand in hand. Therefore, it would seem that a curriculum pattern must be conceived on a ''child in society'' basis.

Content and Process in Curriculum

Let us consider, too, the supposed conflict between content and process in curriculum planning, whether it is more important to learn subject matter, or to ''learn to learn'' in the sense of developing self-propelling individuals. Again, this seems to be a false dilemma. Both are important. It seems to be imperative that children learn something in school, and it seems quite plausible to say that some things are more important to learn than are others. At the same time, it is clearly evident that all things cannot be studied and learned in school, even all of the important things —and with change being such a characteristic of our time, it is indicated that what is most important now may change to some extent in the future. Both of these considerations support the idea that while in school children need to be helped to develop a *way* of learning, as well as to learn the important subjects they are studying at school. For example, if a foreign culture is studied, a part of the outcome should be skills that children can apply in studying any foreign culture. We, then, accept the idea that the school's responsibility is to teach children to think—about particular things. Both the elements of content and process must find a place in an acceptable curriculum pattern, in our view. In fact, it was pointed out in Chapter 3 that process is actually a part of content.

The Role of Organized Subject Matter

The role of organized subject matter in the elementary school is another issue that must be faced as curriculum plans are developed. On the one hand, it may be seen as an end in itself to be pursued directly; on the other, as a resource to which one goes for help and assistance of various kinds. In the main, it is in this latter sense, certainly, that we apply the cultural heritage in our daily lives. The question becomes one of the best way to prepare for this sort of use. We are of the opinion that, in order to do this as efficiently as possible, learners must use organized subject matter as a resource and must also, in the process, study its organization directly. To use organized subjects as such as the organizing centers in the curriculum of the elementary school is to start with too highly an abstracted and refined sort of cultural heritage. Children and teachers need more freedom in developing broad learning enterprises to accomplish best many of the purposes of elementary school education. Together they need a chance to ''discover'' the organized cultural herit-

age, the system of subject matter areas that are a part of it, and the most efficient way to use it. This process of discovery and understanding, accompanied by increased maturity and additional learning purposes, may well progress to the point that, in the seventh and eighth grades of school, pupils need both direct experiences with separate aspects of the organized cultural heritage, and opportunities to use and apply this heritage to general problems and questions. It does seem that those proponents of curriculum patterns who have taken the position that organized subject matter is best used as a resource in school learning were on the right track for elementary school curriculum planning, but their attention to the complexities of accomplishing this has been rather limited. Not enough attention has been given to the matter of determining how much one must really know about organized subject matter, collectively and as individual areas of human knowledge, in order to use it efficiently as a resource. Children, for instance, need to learn some history, they need to learn what an historical question is like, and they need to learn what the subject of history is all about—all from the starting point of "using organized historical subject matter" as a resource in learning. For young children to become aware of the fact that to know about the past is to know history is a significant beginning. For children in the intermediate grades to be acutely aware of the fact that the problems and questions they are concerned with at a particular time in a learning unit are historical questions, and that help with these problems will come most directly from an area of organized subject matter called history, shows a most mature insight on their part. This cumulative understanding of what is involved in using organized subject matter as a resource, along with the skills necessary to use it thus, must find its way into the curriculum.

From what has been said already, and from what follows in this book, it is evident that a great deal of our thinking about curriculum for the elementary school is heavily influenced by the core curriculum pattern. We find much in this point of view that we feel can be wisely applied to the development of the elementary school curriculum. At the same time, influences from the other sets of ideas will be evident. In great part attention will be directed to elementary school curriculum as it seems to be developing in the United States, with no attempt to restrict the discussion.

REFERENCES

Beauchamp, George A. *Planning the Elementary School Curriculum.* Boston: Allyn and Bacon, 1956.
> Different ways of designing the elementary school curriculum are discussed in Chapter 2 of this book.

Caswell, Hollis L., and Arthur W. Foshay. *Education in the Elementary School* (Third edition). New York: American Book Company, 1957.
> A very meaningful statement on curriculum organization is found in Chapter 10 of this book.

Klausmeier, Herbert J., and others. *Teaching in the Elementary School.* New York: Harper & Brothers, 1956.
> Various types of curriculum organization are discussed in Chapter 4.

Lee, J. Murray, and Dorris M. Lee. *The Child and His Curriculum* (Third edition). New York: Appleton-Century-Crofts, 1960.
> This edition of a most valuable book contains in Part I many cues for designing the curriculum in the elementary school.

Ragan, William B. *Modern Elementary Curriculum* (Revised edition). New York: Holt-Dryden, 1960.
> Chapter 5 is directed to a discussion of curriculum organization, covering various ways that this task is approached.

Saylor, J. Galen, and William M. Alexander, *Curriculum Planning.* New York: Rinehart and Company, 1954.
> The question of a most desirable framework for organizing the curriculum is discussed in Chapters 8, 9, and 10.

Smith, B. O., W. O. Stanley, and J. H. Shores. *Fundamentals of Curriculum Development* (Revised edition). Yonkers-on-Hudson: World Book Company, 1957.
> One of the most complete analyses of various approaches to curriculum planning is found in Part IV of this book.

Stratemeyer, Florence B., and others. *Developing a Curriculum for Modern Living.* New York: Teachers College, Columbia University, 1957.
> Various proposals for curriculum organization are reviewed and discussed in Chapter 4.

Taba, Hilda. "General Techniques of Curriculum Planning," in *Curriculum Reconstruction* (Forty-fourth Yearbook, Part I, National Society for the Study of Education). Chicago: University of Chicago Press, 1945.
> The problem of curriculum organization is discussed in a most insightful way in Chapter V of this yearbook.

8

ORGANIZING AND STAFFING THE SCHOOL: FACILITATING THE CURRICULUM

The school organization question is highly related to the matter of curriculum planning. An elementary school must be organized and operated in such a way as to support and to facilitate accepted ideas in curriculum development. The nature of the educational experience desired for children should determine, not be determined by, the way the school is organized and staffed. To some extent this procedure has been followed over the years in elementary schools. Various aspects of the operation of schools have changed with changes in educational insight. But, in some very important ways, change has been exceedingly slow, to the detriment of the education of children. First among these obstacles is the way in which the graded school concept has continued to dominate the organizational scene. Related to this concept are problems of grouping children for instruction and of regulating their progress. Caught up in these problems are questions over the best way to staff the school, the particular problems associated with fast and slow learning children, the individualization of instruction, and related matters. It is our purpose to explore and analyze these concerns in this chapter, trying to see them in their relation to curriculum development.

THE GRADED ELEMENTARY SCHOOL

Undoubtedly, no aspect of present-day elementary school education is more at variance with the sort of experience it is felt a child should have during the first six to eight years of school than is the concept of the graded school, in all of its ramifications. As a basic system of organizing the elementary school, this arrangement into grades had taken form in the United States by the middle of the nineteenth century. Meyer writes, ''Classifying pupils in accordance with their years and their scholastic accomplishment, and arranging them in grades, each with its own master, had become familiar enough in the cities by the forties.''[1] The opening of the Grammar School in Quincy, Massachusetts, in 1848 is often heralded as the opening of the first really graded school in the United States.

> The essential features consisted, first, in giving a separate room to each teacher; second, in grouping a sufficient number of these rooms in the same building to accommodate pupils enough for a good classification; third, in the provision of an assembly hall spacious enough to seat all the pupils accommodated in the building.[2]

Factors such as the establishment of a heavily attended public school system, the emergence of textbooks in graded series, and the way in which teachers were prepared to teach combined to make this development at that time both logical and inevitable.

Over the years this basic organizational scheme has persisted and flourished. It is indeed difficult at the present time to find an elementary school system in the United States that is not graded. As this has happened, curricular thinking has more often than not become subservient to the graded scheme, rather than the reverse. The general developmental pattern of children, too, is supposed to fit this plan. For instance, note the kind of curriculum plan and the conception of child growth and development implicit in the following description of the graded school structure.

A Description of the Graded Structure

Basic to the graded structure is the division of subject matter and skill learnings of various programs, such as reading, arithmetic, or social studies, into blocks of material that can be allocated to each grade level.

---

[1] Adolphe E. Meyer, *An Educational History of the American People* (New York: McGraw-Hill Book Company, 1957), p. 126.

[2] John D. Philbrick, *City School Systems in the United States* (Washington, D.C.: U.S. Government Printing Office, 1885), p. 158.

A logical process in the main, this division results in the identification of content as "third grade work" or "fifth grade work." A part of this packaging process is the decision that the amount of subject matter allotted to a given grade is roughly comparable to what a child at a particular age is able to accomplish. When a child is thought to be succeeding with the work load so determined, he is said to be working "at grade level." A child who is not succeeding would, obviously, be spoken of as working "below grade level"; and a child exceeding the assigned work in some way is said to be "above grade level." To work at "grade level" is to be meeting multiple sets of standards for minimum acceptable achievement that have been decided on, grade by grade and learning area by learning area, with the labels "below" and "above" carrying the obvious connotation.

A View of Children

Implicit in this scheme is a point of view toward children. Grade groups are brought together on the basis of age. First, the assumption is made that children are, in the main, all alike at various chronological age levels. Thus, they should be ready and able to profit from the work of a given grade. To the extent that they are not alike, there seems to be an assumption that the school experience will, in itself, tend to make them so. Second, this conception of individual differences between children is extended to the matter of intra-individual differences, too. The graded structure must, and does, assume a kind of evenness in all areas of development that should find children working at just about grade level in all of the various programs of study.

A Concept of School Progress

In operation, then, children are to come to the school at about age six for entrance into first grade, ready to accomplish whatever has been decided is first grade work. Successful attainment of the agreed-upon minimum standard for achievement in first grade leads to promotion to the second grade for the next year, and this process continues through six, seven, or eight years of school, depending on the system in which the school is organized. It is assumed, of course, that these standards have been set at points that should be reachable by almost every child. That some children may be able to exceed these fixed levels of achievement is realized, and, depending on the degree to which it appears that they are able to do so, some modifications in the plan will be made. They will either be given extra work during the year, with care not to encroach on the next teacher's work in the process, or "double promoted"

at the end of the year so that they skip the next grade and move along accordingly. Too, it is realized that some children, because of the lack of either application or ability, will not reach the minimum acceptable standard by the end of the school year. They will simply be retained, or "failed" as we often say, and asked to repeat the work of the grade again next year, assuming that the second time over the material will result in learning gains. And, of course, this possibility of being held back is considered to provide a constant source of motivation to spur children to apply themselves diligently to their schoolwork.

The trouble with this whole picture is simply that practically none of it is valid or defensible. In the light of greatly increased evidence on children, especially in the area of individual differences, on learning, especially in the area of motivation, and on the relation of organized subject matter to curriculum organization, the whole structure is open to question. But, let us take a systematic look at the contradictory situation in which the elementary school finds itself.

INDIVIDUAL DIFFERENCES

The study of children has provided some rather conclusive evidence concerning their individual differences. We have discussed this matter to some extent in an earlier chapter, but not in direct relationship to school organization. In contrast to the expectations inherent in the graded school idea, children come to school in the first instance very different, one from the other, in physical, social, and emotional development—and in intellectual development, too. These differences are not only evident between children, but within a given child. This is particularly true in the area of intellectual development, where the particular construct or profile of aptitudes and abilities possessed by the child will lead to a varied pattern of achievement in school, with "peaks" in some areas and "valleys" in others.

In this connection, Goodlad and Anderson present some provocative generalizations derived from selected elementary school data on the ability and achievement of children. The particular evidence they analyzed, and there is no reason to believe that their data were unique, gave support to the following generalizations:

1. Children entering the first grade differ in mental age by approximately four full years.
2. The achievement range begins to approximate the range in intellectual readiness to learn soon after first-grade children are exposed to reasonably normal school instruction.
3. Individual children's achievement patterns differ markedly from learning area to learning area.

4. The initial spread among pupils in intellectual readiness to learn (as determined by the M.A. factor)[3] grows still greater as children advance through their second year in school.
5. The spread in achievement in the various subject areas also grows greater, closely approximating the spread in mental age.
6. By the time children complete the fourth grade, the range in readiness to learn (as suggested by the M.A.) and in most areas of achievement is approximately the same as the number designating the grade level.[4]

It is this kind of evidence, when met in the school and classroom, that brings anxious moments to the teacher and frustrating moments to the child. It is this kind of evidence that makes the graded school concept so difficult to "live with" in today's elementary schools.

EXPEDITING PUPIL PROGRESS THROUGH SCHOOL

Direct attention to the "promotion-nonpromotion" aspect of the graded school concept reveals, again, considerable evidence that contradicts the basic rationale upon which it is based. However, an examination of educational writings and extensive opportunities to discuss the matter with teachers point to certain major arguments in support of the idea of holding children back when they have not met a certain agreed-upon standard of achievement for a particular school year:

1. To repeat the work of a given year in school will result in greater achievement on the part of the child the second time. Repetition will insure his being ready to cope successfully with the work of the next grade and to meet the expectations of the teacher at that level, and will eliminate the necessity of lowering the standards in the next grade to the level of his inability.
2. The greater achievement during the repeated year will result in greater feelings of confidence and security on the part of the child, erasing for the most part the discouragement and frustration that comes from not being able to do the work of the grade.
3. Together, these will combine to the advantage of the child in estab-

---

[3] M.A. (mental age) is one way of expressing the mental growth of children. By converting scores from intelligence tests to M.A. scores one gets an indication of the level of mental maturity that the child has reached. That is, a ten-year-old may have a mental age of twelve years, a level beyond his chronological age, or one of eight years, a level below his chronological age. M.A. may be divided by C.A. (chronological age) to determine an I.Q. (intelligence quotient) score. The I.Q. indicates rate of mental growth and relative brightness. For a more complete discussion see: Arden M. Frandsen, *How Children Learn* (New York: McGraw-Hill Book Company, 1957), pp. 361–365.

[4] John Goodlad and Robert Anderson, *The Nongraded Elementary School* (New York: Harcourt, Brace and Company, 1959), Chapter 1.

lishing friendships and close associations with other pupils in the class, contributing in the process to a more positive state of social and emotional adjustment.

A great deal of evidence has been gathered over the years that relates to each of these points, and in every instance it either completely destroys or throws grave doubts on the arguments implied above. Let us consider some of this information.

Nonpromotion and Subsequent Achievement

The studies that have been made in the area of nonpromotion and school achievement all indicate essentially the same thing, and their conclusions are in direct contradiction to the arguments above. These investigations all point to much the same conclusions:

1. Children do not learn more by repeating a grade in the elementary school.
2. Children often learn less, that is, they show actual regression, after repeating the work of a given grade level.
3. Promoted low achievers generally do better in school than do their nonpromoted counterparts.[5]

In this same connection, the evidence that has been gathered does not lend support to the argument that the presence of these low achievers in the next higher grade operates to lower, generally, the work standards and the achievement in that grade. In fact, the data suggest, instead, that achievement is generally lower in the upper grades in districts that practice a high rate of nonpromotion and is higher in those districts that have a high rate of promotion.[6] In light of the evidence, then, it is difficult to reach any other general conclusion than that, insofar as achievement is concerned, the low-achieving child is more likely to do better work in school if he is promoted than if he is retained. All of

---

[5] See the following for a more extensive analysis of individual studies: Charles H. Keyes, *Progress Through the Grades of City Schools* (New York: Bureau of Publications, Teachers College, Columbia University, 1911); Vivian Klene and Ernest Branson, "Trial Promotion Versus Failure," *Educational Research Bulletin*, Los Angeles City Schools, January 1929; Grace Arthur, "A Study of the Achievement of Sixty Grade 1 Repeaters as Compared with That of Nonrepeaters of the Same Mental Age," *Journal of Experimental Education*, December 1936; Carleton M. Saunders, *Promotion or Failure for the Elementary School Pupil?* (New York: Bureau of Publications, Teachers College, Columbia University, 1941); William H. Coffield, "A Longitudinal Study of the Effects of Nonpromotion on Educational Achievement in the Elementary School," unpublished doctoral dissertation, State University of Iowa, 1954.

[6] Walter W. Cook, *Grouping and Promotion in the Elementary Schools*, Series on Individualization of Instruction No. 2 (Minneapolis: University of Minnesota Press, 1941).

these studies were able to point to children who actually did show some achievement gains in the repeated year, but these were highly individual situations. The usual thing was to find no gain in achievement, supporting the old axiom of "when in doubt—promote" if one has the achievement welfare of a child in mind.

Nonpromotion and the Self Concept

The second of the above generalizations suggests that low achievers, when allowed to repeat the work of a given grade, come out of the experience with greater feelings of confidence in themselves, with a more secure feeling generally, and with an improved attitude toward the school experience and learning. Here, again, there is some evidence to throw doubt on this conclusion. One of the best analyses of the studies that have been done in this area is reported by Caswell and Foshay. Contrary to the above generalization, they concluded that the studies found more evidence of emotional depression and discouragement among the nonpromoted. Furthermore, they found that these studies indicated a sense of skepticism on the part of such pupils in their own ability, and a tendency to expect to fail in future school situations, too. Also, the general attitude toward school of pupils who are not promoted was found to deteriorate, with many of them seeking the first opportunity to withdraw from school permanently.[7]

These findings are consistent with the evidence generally reported by recent researchers in the areas of motivation, level of aspiration, and the self concept. Failure does not seem to inspire future success in any general way, nor does it seem to help one to develop a realistic sense of one's own potentialities and limitations. Rather, discouragement, an unreal level of aspiration, and a tendency toward aggression are more likely to follow.[8] Thus, though more research evidence is needed on this point, it is difficult to support the idea that nonpromotion results in any general strengthening of character, or that it contributes positively to the mental health of the pupils involved.

Nonpromotion and Personal Associations

The last of the above generalizations suggested that the nonpromoted pupil, as a result of being retained and thus more successful in school, would find himself better able to establish friendships in his new class

---

[7] Hollis Caswell and Arthur Foshay, *Education in the Elementary School* (Third edition; New York: American Book Company, 1957), pp. 387–394.

[8] Kurt Lewin and others, "Level of Aspiration," in *Personality and the Behavior Disorders*, edited by J. McV. Hunt (New York: Ronald Press Company, 1944), Vol. I, Chapter 10.

group, and his social competency would increase. Again, let us take a brief look at some of the evidence that has been made available on this point.

One of the most complete studies on this matter was done by Sandin. Exploring this phenomenon of personal-social adjustment in connection with nonpromoted children compared with promoted ones, he found that:

1. Children retained more frequently preferred to find their friends among pupils from grades above their own.
2. The majority of retained students did not find ready social approval or acceptance among those regularly promoted.
3. Children retained were rated by other children more often as being unfriendly, cruel, and having a tendency to bully other pupils.
4. Retained children did not really "feel good" toward themselves and found it difficult to "feel good" toward others.[9]

Goodlad, too, has reported a study relevant to this matter. He equated a group of nonpromoted first graders with a group of children who were promoted to the second grade. Studying these children carefully over one school year, he concluded that the nonpromoted children, rejected by many of their peers at the beginning of the year, were even more rejected by the end. The promoted group, however, while starting the year in a sort of "neutral" position in their class, grew consistently in acceptance over the year to a level of normal expectancy. Again in agreement with other studies, he found the nonpromoted group consistently lacking in feelings of adequacy and rating themselves unliked and unwanted by their classmates. The promoted group felt better about themselves generally. One sort of concern was reported, however, in conjunction with their behavior. They did, evidently, feel some pressures to succeed, which caused them to resort to cheating more often in their schoolwork than did the other group.[10] In light of these kinds of findings, it is difficult to support the idea of gains in the area of personal associations through the practice of nonpromotion.

THE ALLOCATION OF SUBJECT MATTER TO GRADES

Little discussion is needed here to throw some doubts on the particular way in which subject matter is allotted to various grade levels by following, in a strict sense, the graded school concept. In the preceding

---

[9] Adolph Sandin, *Social and Emotional Adjustments of Regularly Promoted and Nonpromoted Pupils*, Child Development Monographs No. 32 (New York: Bureau of Publications, Teachers College, Columbia University, 1944).

[10] John I. Goodlad, "Some Effects of Promotion and Nonpromotion on the Social and Personal Adjustment of Children," unpublished doctoral dissertation, University of Chicago, 1949.

chapter on curriculum patterns, considerable discussion was given to the changed way of viewing organized subject matter in the elementary school experience. As experience with a psychological ordering of content has thrown new light on this matter, the assignment of material to grade levels by logical processes alone is increasingly questioned. No one would doubt that in an area such as arithmetic there are kinds of sequences to be dealt with in facing the problem of continuity in the curriculum, or that some arithmetic processes are actually more difficult than others. But, apart from a general framework for making year by year "expectancy" decisions, it is not possible to identify "third grade" or "fourth grade" arithmetic. The same is true of other subject matter areas. Along with this questioning has come a grave reluctance to say, with any real assurance, that children should achieve just so much as third, or fourth, or fifth graders. In some areas, such as social studies or science, it is very difficult to agree on criteria against which any such all-pervading decision could be made. And, in areas such as arithmetic or reading, it is quite apparent that, in any group in any given year, there are many different "acceptable levels of achievement" that depend more on children than on logic.

It would appear, then, that (1) in the face of the obvious differences between pupils and the variable pattern within a given child, and (2) in light of the lack of evidence to support gains in achievement, renewed self-confidence, or more adequate social relations when children are retained for failing to reach minimum acceptable standards of achievement, and (3) in light of the flexibility, in the allocation of subject matter and skill learning to grade levels, that seems to be called for in the elementary school, we must conclude that the burden of proof is on those who would seek to retain the graded school concept in elementary education. Some fundamental revisions and modifications are called for, which may lead eventually to a completely different way of organizing the elementary school.

PAST EFFORTS TO MEET THIS PROBLEM

Attempts to Individualize Instruction

Of course, the mechanical graded school concept was difficult to utilize in yesterday's elementary schools, too. By the beginning of the 1900's there had been some inspired attempts to find ways of improving it. References in the literature to the Pueblo plan, the Cambridge plan, the Elizabeth plan, and others give evidence of these efforts. Basically, they all aimed at a greater individualization of instruction for children.[11]

---

[11] Henry J. Otto, *Elementary School Organization and Administration* (New York: Appleton-Century-Crofts, Inc., 1954), pp. 22–24.

In the early 1900's, Burk presented some ideas at the San Francisco State Teachers College which were later given more extensive development and use in the schools of Winnetka, Illinois. There, under the name *the Winnetka Plan*, a real effort was made to develop a program that would make possible the adaptation of instruction to the abilities of individual pupils. The curriculum, and the school day, were divided into two parts concerned with "common essentials" and "group and creative activities." Each child spent half of each morning and afternoon working individually on common essentials, completing a series of units in each of them at his own pace. The remainder of his school time was spent in group and creative activities. Children were grouped into grade rooms on the basis of age and social maturity in the main, and the individual nature of the work in the common essentials made the moving of pupils from one group to another quite simple. Similarly, promotion as such was an insignificant matter; progress was much more individual. This plan, along with a similar McDade plan in Chicago and a somewhat similar Dalton plan of Massachusetts, had considerable influence during the 1920's and early 1930's on attempts to deal realistically with the graded school.[12] All of these plans were efforts to approach rather mechanically a very complex problem, and were felt by many to be lacking accordingly. At the same time, the intent behind these plans is defensible, and their contribution to our understanding of the problem has been great. The educators involved with these plans have developed greater insights into the complexities of their goal, too, and have made changes accordingly over the years. Otto recognizes these changes when he says, in commenting on the Winnetka plan:

> ... [I]t is only natural that changes would have been made from time to time, many of which did not get into the published literature. . . . The former mechanical aspects of individualization have given way to individualization through small classes, study of the individual child, increased guidance by the teacher, and the so-called developmental approach.[13]

Efforts to Employ Ability Grouping

Beginning in the 1920's efforts were made to solve the dilemma of individual differences by keeping the grade structure but by dividing children of a given grade into groups according to ability. To discuss this grouping calls for some understanding of two terms, *heterogeneous* and *homogeneous,* as applied to grouping into classroom units. *Heterogeneous* refers to the degree to which a group of children is best charac-

---

[12] *Ibid.*, pp. 141–148.
[13] *Ibid.*, p. 145.

terized by differences of age, ability, interest, industry, past experience, physical size, and so on. *Homogeneous* refers to the degree to which the children in a given group are like each other, again in terms of one or more factors as those listed above. The idea in ability grouping is to bring together children of similar potential, as demonstrated on intelligence tests or in actual achievement, to form relatively homogeneous classroom groups. This grouping usually results in the determination of top, middle, and low groups, each consisting of children who show high, average, or low degrees of brightness or achievement.

This approach to grouping has been, and continues to be, used in some form in a great many school districts. Its acceptability has been argued on both philosophical and psychological grounds. Sociologists and philosophers have pointed to possible consequences, such as the kinds of cleavages in society that such an arrangement might nurture at a very early age, and have questioned the advisability of resorting to this kind of grouping in a democratic society. Psychologists have pointed to the difficulties in deciding on *the* criterion to use. The selection of any single criterion, of course, introduces elements of heterogeneity into the group in terms of other criteria. If you choose to use hair color, you get a variety of sizes, shapes, eye color, etc. If you choose reading achievement, you get a variety of performances in arithmetic, spelling, and other areas in the same group. Indications are that the variability in achievement is about 83 per cent as great in grades that can operate with three grade-level ability groups as in unselected ones, and about 93 per cent as great in grades with two such ability groups as in unselected ones.[14] Thus, ability grouping has been found to be a difficult way to erase differences to any great extent. In light of both kinds of arguments, homogeneous grouping has been a controversial practice in elementary schools. Philosophically and psychologically it has been questionable; when such controversy is coupled with the fact that most elementary schools have too small an enrollment to consider seriously such a practice, homogeneous grouping remains often argued and sometimes tried.

MODIFICATIONS WITHIN THE GRADED SCHOOL STRUCTURE

At the present time, of course, the graded school is almost the only organizational structure utilized in elementary education. Most schools for children consist of six grades, with increasing numbers including a kindergarten and many including the seventh and eighth grades. To

---

14 *Ibid.*, p. 202.

ask a child about his school progress is to receive an answer in terms of the grade that he is in. To speak with a teacher about his work is to discuss the grade that he teaches. One way to differentiate the elementary school years from the secondary school years is to refer to "the grade school."

The most typical practice for bringing grade groups together remains that of assigning children of like chronological ages into grade levels. Thus, the "sixes" are in first grade, the "eights" in third grade, and the "elevens" in sixth grade. With school entry dates being fixed in terms of "all children must be six years old no later than December first of their first grade year," or some similar entry formula, there is a small range in age within each class, but the central tendency is very much toward one particular age level. One might say that these groups tend toward homogeneity in chronological age, and are quite heterogeneous in other factors.

Working within these kinds of arrangements, there have been a good many attempts to face the dilemma involved, and to create practices, procedures, and policies that might resolve this dilemma to some extent in the interests of improved child education.

A Less Rigid Assignment of Subject Matter

One evident characteristic of today's elementary school program is a less rigid assignment of subject matter to particular grade levels. In the light of increased insight into the nature of organized subject matter, its probable best use in the elementary school years, and curriculum plans that reflect the conclusions reached concerning these matters, there is less tendency to be adamant about "second" or "fourth" grade work as such. Newer curricular arrangements for bringing children into some systematic contact with their society and its culture have broken away from stringent commitments to the internal logic in certain content areas, as noted in the preceding chapter. The result is that the determination of work for given grade levels is a little more flexible, and decisions are made with consideration of more factors than the subject matter itself. A similar shift is noted in a skill area such as arithmetic. While certain general expectancies are set down in terms of grade levels, there is usually an accompanying expression of policy that notes that some children will not yet be working "at this level" and others will be ready to go considerably beyond these agreed-upon points of progress. The policy anticipates a number of different acceptable definitions for working "at grade level" in arithmetic, recognizing differences among the children in the class group. A similar situation has developed in the area of reading. Thus, there are at present more

flexible and much broader definitions for allocating subject matter to a particular grade level.

Greater Insight Applied to the Formation of Grade Groups

Working within the general policy of grouping children of like ages together at each of the grade levels, a great deal more insight is reflected both in the original assignment of a child to a grade group and in the way the teacher works with such a group once it is formed. It is quite obvious that one reason for organizing children into grade groups is simply to divide the large group of pupils that comes to school into smaller groups that will fit into reasonably sized classrooms and that can be managed and taught with efficiency by the teacher. Were this all there was to it, a process of dividing a large group of eight-year-olds alphabetically into two or three equal-sized groups or of putting all of their names into a hat and drawing them out until the groups were formed might suffice. In an earlier day this was often common practice. But, increased insight into both the objectives sought in the elementary school and the nature of childhood has brought a different kind of deliberateness to this sort of decision.

The group and educational objectives. As the objectives of elementary education have been more carefully studied and more clearly understood, fewer persons see the group of children that must be worked with simply as an obstacle to individual instruction. Instead, they realize that many of the purposes that guide the elementary school effort call for opportunities to live and work with others in the school setting. In other words, were it possible to provide each child with a tutor and to ''school him'' as an individual, some of the most important understandings, attitudes, and skills that the elementary school tries to develop with children would not be reached. Therefore, the potential for learning that resides within the group situation is more clearly recognized for what it is.

The group and individual welfare. Along with the above has come a better understanding of the social nature of children, too. It has been made increasingly clear that children crave and seek associations with other children, and that they are indeed socially inclined. They seek the friendship and companionship of other children with similar interests, with similar desires for active play, with common purposes that are important, and so on. On this count, too, the presence of the group situation in the elementary school can be viewed more positively. It is consistent with the social nature of children. With this insight comes a need for knowing the children to be so grouped as well as possible

as individuals, so that these children may find themselves ultimately in a group that will satisfy their desires for companionship, that will give them a feeling of belonging, and in which they may establish some satisfying and happy working relationships.[15]

The elementary school has moved far beyond the alphabetical or "names in the hat" approach to forming classroom groups. Now one finds care and thoughtfulness applied in deciding which fourth grade group will be the best for Johnnie or Mary. The search for the best working situation has influenced policy in the direction of smaller classes. Most elementary school systems would prefer to have their grade groups composed of about twenty-five children, if possible. There is a greater opportunity for the teacher to know his class members as individual children if the number can be held at about this point, and he can work for the general welfare of each pupil just that much more efficiently. Still, a class of twenty-five provides ample opportunity for large and small group experiences needed by the children, without robbing them of the individualized teaching that they must have at times.

In elementary schools that are large enough to have more than one classroom group at a given grade level, a number of individual traits ranging over inferred ability, actual achievement, apparent social maturity and personal adjustment are considered in the forming of grade groups. There is a tendency to try to spread the varying degrees of each of these traits that will be found in, let us say, the eight-year-old group throughout the two or more classroom groups that are to be formed. Thus, each teacher works with a group of children similar to that of each of the other teachers at that grade level.

Of course, in small elementary schools, with just enough "eights" or "tens" to form one classroom group, this grouping is neither possible nor necessary. It must be remembered, too, that a good many children still attend one-teacher schools, where any given grade group will range from one to perhaps four or five children at most. In 1959 it was reported that some 400,000 children, or 1.1 per cent of all children enrolled in public schools, and some 2 per cent of all classroom teachers were still in one-teacher schools, with most of them at the elementary school level. In such situations, grouping becomes a very different problem.[16]

For a number of years the necessity and the desirability to work with many smaller subgroups within the larger classroom group has been established practice in the elementary school. To work with all of the

---

[15] In this connection see Ruth Cunningham and others, *Understanding Group Behavior of Boys and Girls* (New York: Bureau of Publications, Teachers College, Columbia University, 1951).

[16] Research Division of the National Education Association, "Little Red Schoolhouse," NEA *Research Bulletin*, February 1960, p. 3.

children at one time is in many instances undesirable. Participation on the part of each child is too limited. The teacher's opportunity for individual assessment and assistance is too difficult.

The growing awareness and acceptance of differences in children is reflected here, too, as note is taken of the extent of the range of differences in the class group *among* individuals and *within* individuals. Thus, if more than one group is to be formed in reading, or arithmetic, or spelling, it is considered to be good practice to bring together in these groups children with similar achievement levels and with similar learning problems. By so doing the teacher will be better able to make the best use of the pupil's time while he is working with the group. Also, the necessity of forming these subgroups according to specific learnings has been realized, too. Johnnie may be ready to work with one group of children in reading, with another in arithmetic, and with still another in spelling, because of his profile of intra-individual differences.

Small group work in the classroom. The same possibilities that are found in the total class group for the realization of certain understandings and skill learnings considered to be important in our society are to be found in the small group within the classroom, too. The teacher will often form small subgroups in the class whose direct task will be to produce something for themselves or for the larger group, such as a mural, a wall map, or a research report, that is helpful in some learning enterprise. The teacher sees this small group experience, however, as a vehicle and a setting for learnings far beyond those involved in the specific product at hand. This is a setting in which children may learn to lead and to follow, to reach consensus and to compromise, to contribute and to receive. As Burr, Harding, and Jacobs put it, "through group work children not only get important work done; they also learn the meaning of shared roles of leadership; the responsibility inherent in freedom; the necessity of critical thinking in the solution of problems; and the need for the continuous evaluation both of the products of group action and of the processes employed."[17] The insights that are available to the elementary teacher concerning the dynamics of the classroom group through the application of sociometric techniques lead to a much greater sense of security on the part of the teacher when small groups are to be formed. Sociometry (see Chapter 20 for description of the instruments) has given us an awareness of the centers of power, the presence of cliques, the plight of the isolate, and the general fluidity of the group structure so that they can be studied and utilized toward

---

[17] James B. Burr, Lowry Harding, and Leland Jacobs, *Student Teaching in the Elementary School* (Second edition; New York: Appleton-Century-Crofts, Inc., 1958), p. 150.

desirable ends. Teachers know, for instance, that groups formed on a basis of friendship and assigned a given task in the classroom may produce better results than groups formed on other bases. They know that if certain isolated children are to be helped to find their way into the group they will have to be assigned to small groups for participation. These isolates should be assigned to groups where there are children desired by them as friends, to provide them with an opportunity to be recognized and seen by these children, perhaps in a different light. In this way the study of group processes and group dynamics is most helpful to the elementary school teacher.

Of late there has been a renewed interest in developing procedures that will more nearly result in individualized instruction, rather than small group work, in certain of the skill areas of the curriculum, particularly reading. These procedures are discussed in Chapter 10, which deals with reading, and again in Chapter 19, which deals with the use of time.

Multiple Textbooks for Teaching

The textbooks that are made available for use in the elementary school continue to be produced in graded series. That is, books are published for use in first, or third, or fourth grade arithmetic; or in second or fifth grade science. In toto, each series covers all of the grades of the elementary school. In light of what has been discussed here thus far with reference both to the difficulties that elementary educators have with the graded school structure and to the modifications in practice that are being made to "live with" this structure, it is apparent that teachers have had to take certain liberties with the graded textbook series.

In the main, teachers have tried to use multiple text teaching in almost all areas in the elementary school. If you were to ask a teacher what readers, or arithmetic books, or spellers he was using in his class he would probably indicate that he was using several prepared for use at various grade levels. Thus, if he was a fourth grade teacher he would probably have at least third, fourth, and fifth grade books in use in his classroom in each of these areas. This use of textbooks is consistent with the recognition of different achievement levels among children, regardless of grade level, and the acceptance of work being done at varying grade levels in the same classroom group.

Similarly, and in keeping with the less rigid assignment of particular items of subject matter to particular grade levels, this same teacher might well have science or social studies books for the fourth grade from more than one textbook series as well as some books in science from grade

levels just above and below the fourth grade. By so supplying the classroom it is felt that a richer opportunity for using organized subject
matter is provided and that more questions and concerns relating to
learning units that are developed may be successfully followed through.[18]

Thus, the concept of "multiple text" teaching takes its place alongside "multiple group" teaching as a procedure for helping to remove
some of the obstacles to learning inherent in the graded school structure.

More Enlightened Promotion Policies

There have been significant modifications in policy relating to the
regulation of children's grade progress through the elementary school.
The way in which the kind of evidence cited earlier in this chapter has
weakened the generalizations that were once used so widely to justify
promotion and retention has been a major cause of these modifications.
The concept of minimum grade standards is gradually being replaced
by a point of view that recognizes the relationship between objectives
to be accomplished and the individual ability of children to accomplish
them. The unevenness of development within any one child and the
irregularity of individual growth curves over the years of childhood
have given support to this idea. Also, the fact that the elementary
school program is responsible for contributing to growth in areas in
addition to intellectual development has made its impact on decisions
to promote or to retain. Such decisions are now much more likely to be
made in light of all the needs of a given child and not merely of any
single area of development.

The general result of these combined factors has been a greatly reduced incidence of retention in the elementary school, and when such a
decision is to be considered it will be on the basis of a careful study of
the individual child concerned, rather than on the basis of generalizations about children. In the place of the earlier noted general statements
have come others more like:

1. The slow learning child will achieve just as much, and probably
   more, by being promoted with his group.
2. The range of differences with which the first grade teacher must deal
   will increase, rather than decrease, for other teachers over the succeeding years.
3. To retain a child unwisely is to take great risks with his general personal and social welfare.

---

[18] For an interesting study that relates to the degree of agreement among standard textbook series in science in the assignment of material to grade levels, see M. O.
Pella, "Development of Concepts in Elementary Science," *Science Education*, October 1949, pp. 269–272.

4. It is up to the school to provide the kinds of situations, year by year, from which all children can profit, rather than to force children to conform to a highly rigid and preconceived set of expectations.

Based supposedly on the evidence indicated in this chapter, and in light of general statements as those listed immediately above, some elementary schools have adopted a policy for regulating pupil progress referred to variously as social promotion or automatic promotion. This policy, we feel, cannot be defended except in the most general terms as an argument against a rigid and single-minded promotion-nonpromotion policy. It would appear that in too many cases the use of terms like "automatic" in relation to school progress causes school personnel to become too resigned about the placement of children in grade and classroom groups. The end result is often a kind of laxity about the whole affair, which does not always work to the best interests of the children involved. True, the evidence may well be interpreted as suggesting a "when in doubt—promote" position. But, a policy that calls for a careful examination of all evidence at hand and a reasoned decision about the placement of a child for the coming school year is preferred. No more important decision is made concerning a child's school experience, really, than his assignment to the group in which he will do the major portion of his living and working for a whole school year.

This decision has both its vertical dimension in terms of the next level of work, and its horizontal dimension related to which of our third, or fourth, or fifth year groups is best suited to the total educational needs of a given child. Such a careful assessment will, at times, indicate children who should be "held back," so to speak, in light of a general pattern of immaturity, little achievement, lack of belongingness, unhappiness in school, and so on. Similarly, there will be some children for whom the data might suggest a decision in the opposite direction, and steps may be taken to accelerate them in some way in their placement in school. Certainly this procedure is something other than "automatic." What is sought is a policy that will facilitate a concept of "continuous progress" for the child over a broad front of educational tasks.

TOWARD A NONGRADED ELEMENTARY SCHOOL

Reflection on the many points reviewed here leads inevitably to the conclusion that a kind of nongraded elementary school would serve both the child and the society better in the accomplishment of important educational objectives. In such a school, grade levels, grade barriers, promotion, nonpromotion, third grade work, and so on, would be irrelevant and unused terms and concepts. The differences among children and

within children would be recognized for what they are from the day the child first enters the elementary school. That some children would need more time to accomplish certain learnings would be accepted in light of different degrees of ability, and this same insight would be used to set reasonable long-term learning expectancies for various children. As the school system is now organized, it would be possible for some children to accomplish the work typically expected during the period of childhood in less than six or seven years, while others could take an extra year in doing it. The irregularities and the unevenness in children's learning profiles would be seen as quite normal, and particular children would be working at various achievement and skill levels in the several areas of the curriculum. A great deal of flexibility in the assignment of children to working groups would characterize such a school, and a good deal of interage grouping would be practiced. Careful records would be kept on the progress of each child, and he would be held to standards of work that were reasonable and defensible in terms of his own ability. One may ask, of course, whether or not this is likely to happen in elementary school education. This is hard to say. Such basic changes in structure do not come easily and to attempt such a shift is a most complex undertaking, although there is an identifiable trend toward this goal of modified policies and procedures, and there are some school districts that have moved quite close to the goal suggested here.

The Presence of Nongraded Schools

Two educators, Goodlad and Anderson, have been extremely interested in the development of the nongraded elementary school. This interest has led them to search out, to the best of their ability, those communities in the United States where such units were in operation. Using a definition for *nongraded* as "a school where the grade labels ('first grade,' 'second grade,' 'third grade,' etc.) have been entirely removed from a minimum of two grade levels," they found, in the 1957–58 school year, nearly fifty communities in the United States in which nongraded programs of some sort were identifiable, involving hundreds of individual elementary schools. They found, in addition, nearly thirty other communities studying the idea of the nongraded school. Most of the units they identified were operating at the primary level, with some extending through the entire elementary school.[19] Though this number is a small percentage of the total number of elementary school districts in the United States, it does mean that the nongraded arrangement does exist and is being tested in practice.

---

[19] Goodlad and Anderson, *op. cit.,* p. 55.

The Use of Interage Grouping

While tradition and custom combine to cast doubt on the use of interage grouping in the elementary school, there have long been those who have argued for its use along with same-age practices. Such persons point to neighborhood play groups, interage friendship patterns, and the family circle itself to support their arguments. Lane and Beauchamp have called for the establishment of class groups that would cut across grade and age lines in the interests of improved education. It is their feeling that such an arrangement more truly represents the kind of situations in which most of us usually find ourselves and which condone and nurture various levels of maturity.[20]

The recent report from Torrance, California, of an experiment with seven "multigraded" and "multiaged" class groups lends support to these ideas. In this experiment primary classes were made up of first, second, and third graders, while intermediate classes were composed of fourth, fifth, and sixth graders. As a child moves through the elementary school, under these arrangements, he would be a member of the youngest portion of a group one year, the middle age group the second year, and the oldest age group in the third year. The reports from this project thus far indicate that the children in these multigrade and age classes achieved more and made better social and personal adjustments to school and to each other than did their counterparts in matched but uniform age and grade groups.[21]

It is to be hoped that this experimentation continues, and that similar efforts are undertaken in other places. The extent to which nongraded schools and interage grouping practices will be utilized in the near future is problematical. But, they are being thought about, written about, and tested in experience at the present time. It would appear that there is a great unrealized potential in interage grouping in the elementary school.

SPECIAL CONCERNS OVER FAST-LEARNING CHILDREN

A great deal of concern has been expressed in the past few years over fast-learning children. While this concern creates a complex situa-

---

20 Howard Lane and Mary Beauchamp, *Human Relations in Teaching* (Englewood Cliffs, New Jersey: Prentice-Hall, Inc., 1955), pp. 298–303.

21 Walter Rehwoldt and Warren Hamilton, "An Analysis of Some of the Effects of Interage and Intergrade Grouping in an Elementary School," unpublished doctoral dissertation, University of Southern California, Los Angeles, 1957. See also Warren Hamilton and Walter Rehwoldt, "By Their Differences They Learn," *The National Elementary Principal*, December 1951, p. 29.

tion involving curriculum, it is also a matter related to organizational and staffing arrangements in the elementary school. It is now rather widely accepted that *equality of educational opportunity* is something different from *identical educational experience,* and learning arrangements are being evaluated with this difference in mind. To find a workable and defensible solution to this matter confronts the elementary school with a complex problem. We would like to discuss some of the organizational aspects of this problem at this point.

The Concept of Enrichment

The concept most widely endorsed in elementary education at the present time, and most widely followed in practice, is known as *enrichment.* The general idea in enrichment is to place fast-learning children in classroom groups with average and slow-learning children alike. It is felt that, if classes are kept small, the teacher can provide the necessary qualitative differences in the learning tasks for all of these different children, including the more gifted ones. In addition, it is felt that the general dynamics at work in such a group will be to the benefit of all concerned. The fast learners will provide a kind of model and source of inspiration for those for whom learning is more difficult. At the same time, the fast-learning children will grow in personal insight concerning their ability, the differences in ability among people, and the basic humanity common to all. The more verbally gifted will become aware of other types of giftedness and will grow in appreciation for the contribution of others to the welfare of society. At the same time, the average and slow, too, will develop a more realistic conception of their abilities and of the kind of contribution they can make to the general welfare of the classroom group now and to the wider society at a later time. In all, this kind of living and learning together is seen as making a very positive contribution to understandings and skills that are essential to a furtherance of democracy and to a general cohesiveness in our society.

Of late many observers have raised questions concerning the classroom teacher's ability to provide this enrichment and the degree to which the fast-learning child is really being challenged in the elementary school.

The Idea of Acceleration

One approach that the elementary school has taken at times, and some would have this practice become more common, is simply to accelerate the fast-learning child in his progress through the grades. When a child gives certain evidences of superior ability and achievement, along with advanced social and personal adjustment during the school year,

he would be sent ahead to the next grade immediately. If the decision on placement is held until the end of the year, he would be promoted directly from the third grade to the fifth, for instance. This acceleration has been practiced sparingly in recent years, owing to the influence of at least two causes: (1) very often superior mental ability is not accompanied by advanced stages of maturity in other areas of development, and it appears to be unwise to put such a child ahead with more socially and personally mature children; and (2) this practice appears to be too mechanical and automatic a solution to a complex problem. So often, the feeling is that once the school agrees to the acceleration it has no further responsibility for providing anything extra for the gifted child. Thus, nothing about the school situation changes appreciably except the fact that the child has now been advanced to another grade level and is one year closer to finishing the elementary school. Actually, a great many gifted children will already be far beyond much of the work of this more advanced grade level, which was supposed, in and of itself, to provide the qualitative difference needed in the child's learning diet. Acceleration alone is not usually sufficient.

It should be noted that studies that have been made to follow selected accelerated children through their school experience do not find the great personal harm coming to these children that some elementary educators feel will inevitably result.[22] In light of these data and the seeming urgency of the problem, it is quite likely that the elementary school will experiment with pupil acceleration more extensively in the years ahead. However, such experimentation will in no way provide a very complete or satisfactory solution to the problem of providing the best possible school experience for the fast-learning child.

The Idea of Segregation

One other idea can be employed, of course, in the interests of fast-learning children. They may be separated from average and slow learners for all or a part of their elementary school experience and study and work together. This has been supported and argued against on both sociological-philosophical and psychological grounds.

The socio-philosophical supporters of such an idea point to the necessity for a society like ours, in which leadership in all areas must come from the peer group, to identify and nurture high ability of all kinds from an early age. They feel that, so long as society is kept fluid and

---

[22] See for instance, Lewis M. Terman and others, *Genetic Studies of Genius*, Vol. IV, *The Gifted Child Grows Up* (Stanford, California: Stanford University Press, 1947) and Vol. V, *The Gifted Group at Mid-Life* (Stanford, California: Stanford University Press, 1959).

mobile, and so long as the opportunities for talent to be identified and developed are widespread, the development of an intellectual and talented elite, so to speak, is not to be feared in our society but is to be sought openly. They reason, further, that to promote this development will call for some kind and degree of special educational arrangements for fast-learning and talented children. Those opposed to the idea turn these same arguments in a different direction. They, too, are cognizant of the necessity for leaders to emerge from the peer group, but they want to be sure that these leaders have had some experience with and opportunity to know those whom they are to lead. They argue that a great deal of successful leadership stems from having intimate knowledge of and being known and respected by the group that one is to lead. They see leadership in a democracy as something that the group bestows on an individual, rather than the other way around. Thus, they are more hesitant about supporting plans that include the separation of superior learners from the rest of the group.

Psychologists are concerned, too, about the difficulties involved in identifying children in the elementary school years, especially the early years, who are truly consistently superior performers. They note the presence of "late bloomers" on the one hand, and of "early faders" on the other. Many psychologists feel that children will undoubtedly display characteristics that will support tentative conclusions about their giftedness, but it may take all of the early school years to provide the basis for a reliable assessment of potential. Also related to plans for separating gifted children from the others for special educational experiences is the fact that giftedness is not always a general thing. In fact, rarely is it so; rather, it is very often quite specific with an individual child. Thus, while he may be superior in one or more areas, he may not be in all. Plans for segregated experiences must also cope with this phenomenon.

At the same time, there is some reason to believe that the development of all of a child's potential calls for an educational setting from the outset that provides for continuous challenge, for a situation that "stretches" the child in the best sense of the term. Some children provide such situations for themselves in their hobbies and free-time activities outside of school—but many do not and cannot. If this development calls for a school experience that is partially or completely separate from other children, so the argument goes, such an experience must be made available.

Present Attempts to Solve the Problem

In the meantime, elementary school systems do have fast-learning children in classrooms, children capable of superior performances in

many areas of human endeavor, and they are searching for the best way to handle them. In the process, all of the approaches discussed here are being used separately and together, and their consequences for the children involved are being weighed.

Uses of cluster grouping. In an attempt to simplify some of the complex aspects of trying to provide instruction in a completely heterogeneous classroom group, some elementary school systems are testing a modified version of ability grouping referred to as *cluster grouping.* In situations where the number of pupils at any grade level is large enough to permit, at least three instructional groups are formed on the basis of the cluster principle. The attempt is not to develop homogeneous groups, but simply to shorten the range of differences, especially in the area of verbal ability, with which each teacher will be asked to work in the classroom. Each of the three classroom groups formed will still show a range in ability or achievement, but this will be considerably lessened by applying the cluster principle. One group will contain most of the fastest learners and about one-third of the average ones; another will contain the rest of the fast learners, a few more than one-third of the average group, and about one-third of the slow learners; the third will contain no fast learners, about one-third of the average, and the rest of the slow learners. Diagrammatically, such a division would look something like this:

Cluster Grouping with 100 Third Grade Students

Classes Formed	A	B	C
Number of fast learners	17	8	0
Number of average learners	15	20	15
Number of slow learners	0	6	19
Totals	32	34	34

It is to be hoped that elementary schools using this arrangement will take steps from the outset to evaluate it from many angles and will share their findings in the literature for all to study.

Uses of other schemes discussed. A recent survey and analysis, by one of the authors, of published reports of the attempts of various elementary schools to meet the problem of the gifted reveals the anticipated fact that all of the earlier discussed schemes for dealing with this problem are being used to some extent. In addition, these reports show that there are some efforts being made to identify young adults who it is known experienced one or the other of these arrangements in their elementary school experiences in an attempt to evaluate long-term effects

and feelings.[23] Undoubtedly, the most provocative of the studies reviewed was the one reported by Gallagher and Crowder. In an attempt to determine the degree of difficulty undergone by highly intelligent children in adjusting to a regular classroom situation academically, intellectually, socially, and emotionally, they found a great range of differences. In their conclusions they noted that acceleration, special classes, enrichment, or a traveling consultant who would instruct the child in the home would each have been either good or bad for particular children in their group. Their findings seem to verify the extreme complexity of this problem. The proper approach with any given child is a very individual thing, and any general administrative arrangement will be lacking accordingly as a solution.[24]

Partial Separation: A Pattern Worth Considering

In our view, superior learning children would profit from a partial kind of special class arrangement in the elementary school, at least from the third grade on, and we hope that school systems utilizing such an approach will share their experience with others. Such an arrangement brings gifted children, that is, children who are capable of a consistently high level of performance in one or more areas of human endeavor, together at least twice a week for special educational experiences. These groups would usually disregard grade and age lines and would bring together children with similar capacity to learn and a certain community of interest and aptitude.

Teachers would be assigned to work with the groups who had similar patterns of special interest and aptitude, and upon invitation by the school, selected community persons would be utilized for instructional purposes on a resource basis. In these groups there would be virtually no limits on learning. Active minds would be urged to question, to explore, to build, to express, to experiment in whatever area of human endeavor concerned. Membership in any one of these groups would have to be kept quite flexible, so that a bright child with a wide variety of interests could have an opportunity to explore more than one interest at school. Children would be encouraged to work on some of these special learning enterprises at home as well as at school. This encouragement

---

[23] See G. Wesley Sowards, ''Organization of the Curriculum,'' *The Educational Program: Early and Middle Childhood*, Review of Educational Research, April 1959, pp. 147–149. A publication of the American Educational Research Association, Washington, D.C.

[24] James J. Gallagher and Thora Crowder, ''The Ajustment of Gifted Children in the Regular Classroom,'' *Exceptional Children*, April 1957, pp. 306–312; May 1957, pp. 353–363, 396, 398.

not only could help to sustain interest, but also could help the family to recognize the ability of their child for what it really is.

The general purpose of these multiaged and multigraded groups would be to provide the kind of challenge that these young minds seem to seek, to provide for certain personal explorations on the part of the student concerning his ability and his interests, and to help the school in its efforts to identify real superiority in many different avenues of expression. At the same time, these children would work and play with the full range of pupils in the school for a great portion of the time, and thus retain some of the obvious benefits of enrichment, too. Such an approach is appropriate to the large or small elementary school, making it reasonable to consider on this basis, also.

STAFFING AND THE SELF-CONTAINED CLASSROOM

In the final analysis any curriculum plan is as effective as the teacher whose job it is to bring it to life in the classroom. The way in which elementary schools are staffed, then, has a great deal to do with the general effectiveness of the educational program. Over the years, elementary schools have been staffed in various ways. In the main, changes have centered on the question of whether one teacher or several specialists should be responsible for all of the learning experiences of a given group of children. The latter arrangement is referred to as *departmentalization,* and in it each teacher teaches only one or two subjects in which he is a specialist. The other scheme is most often referred to as the *self-contained classroom;* most elementary schools are staffed in this way at the present time. Interestingly, the development of the self-contained, or one-teacher-per-group, arrangement paralleled the growth of the graded elementary school. As the graded school concept spread after 1850 so did the single-teacher-per-class plan.[25] Along about 1900 some elementary school systems began to departmentalize the work of the upper grades again, and from that time until the 1930's there was a tendency for the practice of departmentalization to spread throughout the elementary school, sometimes even to the earliest grade levels.[26] About this time, however, the shift began to move in the other direction again. Increased insight into child growth and development, curriculum theories that placed great emphasis on the child, a different conception of the role of organized subject matter, and the development of learning schemes,

[25] Otto, *op. cit.,* p. 25.
[26] *Ibid.,* p. 26.

such as the unit of work, that envisioned a much different use of time available in school, all combined to cast grave doubts on the wisdom of departmentalized arrangements in the elementary school years. Thus, starting in the 1920's and on into the 1930's a great decrease in the use of departmentalization at this level was evident. Otto reported that by 1948 about a third of those districts still so organized said that it was definitely on the way out. Certainly the dominant pattern for staffing the elementary school in the 1940's and 1950's was the self-contained classroom.

The Self-Contained Classroom Concept

The rationale behind the self-contained classroom is based on the one hand on evidence concerning the growth and development of children, and on the other, on preferred pedagogical schemes for using time and for arranging learning experiences in the classroom.

First and foremost in the minds of the early proponents of a return to the self-contained unit was to find a classroom staffing arrangement that would be more in agreement with developing insights concerning human growth. The departmentalized set-up had tended to emphasize subject matter. What was sought was an arrangement that would emphasize children. It was felt important to begin to teach children first, and subject matter second, rather than vice versa. Here the self-contained classroom concept seems to fit. Teachers could be prepared as specialists who knew how to work with children; their subject matter preparation would be secondary. There was also considerable evidence from child development studies that suggested that children found it difficult to adjust to several different teachers over the course of a day's work. The information indicated that children fared best at school when they felt close to their teacher and when they felt that their teacher really knew and understood them. This evidence, coupled with the insights into the relation between a sense of personal security and released learning potential, helped to establish great support for the self-contained unit.

Also, following the ideas on curriculum that emerged in the early 1920's, the tendency was to endorse and develop ways of organizing learning units in the elementary school that extended over fairly large blocks of time daily and crossed over subject matter lines as appropriate and necessary. Certainly, such approaches to learning did not fit well into the departmentalized arrangement.

There can be little doubt that the self-contained classroom staffing plan has made a significant contribution to improved elementary school education, in our view. We feel sure that the education of children has been the better for it.

A tendency to re-examine this arrangement. At the present time, however, there are evidences of a feeling on the part of some elementary school educators that this concept should be re-examined. Human knowledge in all areas has greatly multiplied; best practices of many kinds in elementary education are extremely demanding of the teacher; and there is some point to the fact that today's children are themselves a different, better informed, intellectually more curious group. Together, these motivate some questions about the wisdom of using the self-contained classroom in the future.

The preparation of a teacher who can help children with learning in all areas of subject matter and skill is a most difficult task. Present patterns for teacher preparation require more general education as well as more opportunity for special study. To both of these requirements must be added professional course work. In this preparation, the individual differences that are dealt with ever more realistically in teaching children are being applied to teachers. The "peaks" and "valleys" in the profiles of interest and achievement of teachers are being weighed in terms of the kind of total learning experience they will permit for the child.

Attention is also being given to the demands that many "best practices" in elementary school education make on the time and the energy of the classroom teacher. These demands include such things as the preparation of instructional materials that "fit" certain children and particular learning problems in the group, the careful records that must be kept if evaluation is to be as comprehensive as it must be, and the way the teacher must bring to bear in the developing classroom situation the particular experience that is called for day by day without allowing the "fire" to go out through delay.

The matter of differences between today's children and yesterday's is hard to objectify. Certainly there are reasons to speculate that they might be different. Most of them have been able to live in a much richer and more stimulating environment than did their grandparents, owing in part to the easy access to printed materials and the widespread use of mass media of communication. In some ways their learning task is greater now. They must know and feel about and be able to do things that were not really "fundamentals" in an earlier day. Perhaps it is well that they are more "advanced," if indeed they are.

Continued support for the self-contained unit. That the self-contained classroom will continue to be used in the elementary school for a long time to come seems rather certain, partly because of the undeniable strengths inherent in the scheme. In part it will be continued out of fear that to do anything else is to go back to the highly subject-centered,

departmentalized elementary school of an earlier year.[27] But, there is increasing evidence that school systems are testing other approaches to the staffing question, approaches that seek to avoid the departmentalization of instruction and to retain the strengths found in the self-contained classroom idea. In addition, claims are made for these new arrangements that relate both to increased learning for children and to greater satisfactions for teachers. Let us consider what these arrangements constitute, in the main.

The Concept of Team Teaching

The central feature of the plans for staffing that are emerging in a few school systems is the concept of *team teaching*. By this is meant the assignment of a team of teachers to a group of perhaps one hundred third year students. Instead of dividing the children into four groups of twenty-five students each and assigning one teacher to each of these groups who is responsible for the program of that group, a team approach is taken. The four instructors constitute a team of teachers whose responsibility for the year is the development of the instructional program for all of these children. Thus their combined talents and skill are brought to bear on the curriculum provided. They plan the instructional program together, seeing it as a complete experience, and they evaluate the progress made by children jointly. Their knowledge of the children with whom they are working can be pooled to increase their individual effectiveness with them. Typically, one of the teachers is designated as the leader of the team, and as such, takes some extra responsibility for seeing to it that the best possible classroom program is arranged.

In order that children will not have to make adjustments to three or four new teachers each year, and to increase the effectiveness of the teaching team with their particular group, most of these plans call for the instructional team to work with the same group of children for two or three years. Thus, a teaching team might start with a group in the first year of school and work with them through the primary years. At that point another team would pick them up and work with them on through the intermediate grades of the elementary school. This arrangement makes possible a kind of longitudinal experience with the group, and should help to keep the focus of attention on the children as they progress through school. It also provides each child each year with some three or four "models," too, in the teachers with whom he works. A ques-

---

[27] See the article by Alice Miel, "The Self-Contained Classroom: An Assessment," *Teachers College Record*, February 1958, pp. 282–291.

tionable value system or peculiar cultural biases that might be possessed by one teacher are offset for the children by the experience of working with and getting to know the others. Thus, some of the concerns of educational anthropologists, such as Spindler, that focus on the teacher as an agent for cultural transmission are partially alleviated.[28]

One other advantage that may grow out of the team teaching concept relates to the induction of new teachers into the profession. At the present time they must accept in the first year of teaching the full responsibility for a grade group. In the team teaching approach, it should be possible to improve on the induction of the beginning teacher as he works alongside his experienced colleagues during the school year.

The cooperative group plan. The idea of team teaching is usually considered quite new in elementary education. However, in 1929, Hosic set about to devise a plan for organizing the elementary school that would help to expedite the kind of curriculum that seemed to be called for in the elementary school at that time. To this end, he developed eleven propositions to be used as guidelines in reorganizing the elementary school.[29] Certain of these propositions, as summarized and reported by Otto, were as follows:

1. A teacher can usually best assist in carrying out the purposes of an elementary school by undertaking not the whole but only a part of the educational stimulation and guidance of individual pupils and groups of pupils.
2. Each teacher in the elementary school should plan and carry on her work cooperatively as a member of a group of teachers who have the same pupils in charge.
3. Every group of teachers in the cooperative plan or organization should be led by one of their own number, designated chairman, or group leader.
4. Each group leader or chairman should bear a portion of the responsibility for the supervision of the teaching done by the other members of his or her group.
5. Even though five teachers, more or less, share the work of guiding the activities of a group of children, as proposed in the Cooperative Group Plan, nevertheless each of them should bear special responsibility for the welfare of one portion of the group, that is, for a "class."

Dr. Hosic's plan went on to include specially equipped rooms for each teacher in line with his or her specialty, referred to as laboratories, and

---

[28] See George D. Spindler, *The Transmission of American Culture*, Third Burton Lecture in Elementary Education, Graduate School of Education, Harvard University, 1959.

[29] James F. Hosic, *The Cooperative Group Plan: Working Principles for the Organization of Elementary Schools* (New York: Bureau of Publications, Teachers College, Columbia University, 1929).

the pupils were to move from place to place accordingly during the school day.[30]

These ideas were not followed to any great extent at that time, but within these particular propositions one finds an idea highly similar to the concept of team teaching described here and presently being explored in a few elementary school systems in the United States. Results to date, sparse and meager as they are, indicate satisfaction with the team approach sufficient to encourage these systems to explore it still further.

It may well be that out of these attempts to improve on the self-contained classroom arrangement will come a pedagogical scheme that can be used in conjunction with it in the years ahead. Perhaps we are entering a period of renewed creative effort in the area of school organization that will lead to improved school experiences for children. Certainly these experiments should be followed carefully by all elementary school educators. We end this discussion of school organization and staffing where we started, firmly believing that there is a close relationship between the kind of curriculum one is able to develop in an elementary school and the way in which the school is organized and staffed. We are certain that the plans for organization and staffing must follow from a selected curriculum plan, and not the reverse.

REFERENCES

Abraham, Willard. *Common Sense about Gifted Children.* New York: Harper & Brothers, 1958.

> A very readable statement concerned with many of the questions raised about the education of gifted children.

Adams, Joseph J. "Achievement and Social Adjustment of Pupils in Combination Classes Enrolling Pupils of More Than One Grade Level," *Journal of Educational Research* 47:151–155. October 1953.

> Some provocative data are presented here for the person who would give thought to grouping in the elementary school.

Association for Childhood Education International. *Grouping: Problems and Satisfactions.* Reprint Service Bulletin No. 26. Washington, D.C.: The Association, 1954.

> A good résumé of the choices faced in grouping children most effectively for learning.

Association for Supervision and Curriculum Development. *A Look at Continuity in the School Program* (1958 Yearbook). Washington, D.C.: The Association, 1958.

> Some of the more subtle aspects of a continuing school experience for children are treated in this yearbook.

---

[30] Otto, *op. cit.*, p. 149.

Caswell, Hollis L., and Arthur W. Foshay. *Education in the Elementary School* (Third edition). New York: American Book Company, 1957.
> Chapters 12 and 13 deal well with the matter of school organization and the regulation of pupil progress.

Cook, Walter W. *Grouping and Promotion in the Elementary School.* Series on Individualization of Instruction No. 2. Minneapolis: University of Minnesota Press, 1941.
> One of the outstanding efforts to bring together in one place and to interpret the evidence on grouping and promotion of elementary school children.

Elsbree, Willard S., and Harold J. McNally. *Elementary School Administration and Supervision.* New York: American Book Company, 1951.
> Parts II and III of this book develop some good ideas on grouping for instruction and on staffing the elementary school.

Goodlad, John, and Robert H. Anderson. *The Nongraded Elementary School.* New York: Harcourt, Brace and Company, 1959.
> Probably the best single statement developing the thinking basic to the idea of a nongraded elementary school.

Havighurst, Robert J., Eugene W. Stivers, and Robert F. DeHaan. *A Survey of the Education of Gifted Children.* Chicago: University of Chicago Press, 1956.
> An excellent report of a survey of the ways in which gifted children are being educated in a number of places in the United States.

Lobdell, Lawrence O. "Results of a Nonpromotion Policy in One School District," *The Elementary School Journal* 54:333–337. February 1954.
> The title suggests the contents of this report.

Otto, Henry J. *Elementary School Organization and Administration* (Third edition). New York: Appleton-Century-Crofts, 1954.
> Chapters 5, 6, and 7 are especially relevant to the matters discussed in this chapter.

Shane, Harold G. "The Promotion Policies Dilemma," *Journal of the National Education Association* 42:411–412. October 1953.
> Another provocative statement that draws attention to a basic dilemma in the matter of pupil progress in elementary schools.

PART 3

LEARNING AREAS IN THE ELEMENTARY CURRICULUM

9

SPECIFIC LEARNING
PROGRAMS:
AN INTRODUCTION

To this point, discussion of the elementary school curriculum has been focused on a consideration of general patterns for planning the instructional program, and on the varied and somewhat opposed points of view toward this task that are evident among identifiable approaches. In these next chapters attention is directed to the various programs of instruction that make up the whole of the elementary school curriculum. To this end, separate statements are presented dealing with the school's efforts to work with children in the areas of the language arts, arithmetic, social studies, science, health and physical education, and the arts. In each instance, the general area is defined and the objectives that guide and direct instruction in the area are discussed. Attention is given, too, to the generally accepted ways of planning and organizing for instruction in each area, with particular attention to what is considered "good" practice at the present time. Trends that are evident in each of these areas and actual innovations in practice are noted in terms of currently expressed ideas and aspirations as they suggest what the future may hold in each instance. Historical material is presented as appropriate and necessary in particular chapters.

There is a chance that, in discussing each of these instructional areas in this way, some will see this division as a commitment at this point to either the separate subjects or broad fields patterns. This is not the intent at all. Rather, we are using such a division because, no matter which of the various points of view toward curriculum planning predominates

in a given elementary school, there will be systematic efforts identifiable in that instructional program to provide learning experiences in each of these areas. It will be evident, as accepted "good" practices are discussed and as trends of particular kinds are outlined, that certain ideas for organizing these areas of learning into a general curriculum pattern at the school and classroom level enjoy more support at the present time than do others. It is hoped that, by bringing the material in the early chapters in this book to bear on each of these program-centered statements, reasons for these tendencies will become more clear.

EMERGING GENERALIZED IDEAS ABOUT ELEMENTARY SCHOOL EDUCATION

Perhaps it is not too much to hope for that at this point certain kinds of generalized ideas have begun to take form which enable one to view the present-day elementary school and curriculum with a kind of meaningful perspective. Among these would undoubtedly be such generalizations as the following.

A Product of History

The elementary school and curriculum, as we find them today, are in great part a product of past generations of elementary schools. The elementary school operates against the background of long years of experience, and the history of elementary school education is very much alive in today's schools and classrooms. As is true in most such processes, this educational "inheritance" is not all of one piece. Some of the traditions, and policies, and procedures that have come down through the years in elementary education are quite sound and today's elementary school is the better for them. Other aspects of this inheritance are questionable, however, and tend to work against the improvement of the elementary school program in certain instances. This educational inheritance has both its general and local dimensions, too. The elementary school as a social institution is influenced by the totality of its history. At the same time local elementary school systems are influenced additionally by specific local community educational history. Successes and satisfactions in elementary school education of one kind will cause a community to bring one sort of educational record to bear on its schools. Arguments, tensions, and suspected failures in the past in another community concerning its elementary schools will result in a different kind of pressure from the past. In any event the elementary school cannot escape its history to any great extent nor can it rid itself of its educational inheritance, good or bad, in any simple way. Change comes about

usually through evolution, and not through revolution in any such basic social institution as the school.

Working Amidst Contradictions

A forceful history, traditions, accustomed ways of operating, familiar methods, and so on, are cast for the elementary school against an ever-increasing amount of new evidence concerning learning and child growth and development on the one hand, and, on the other, the changing social scene and the changing values and aspirations of our society. This means that the elementary school is often an institution ''on the spot'' so to speak. The elementary school has always been close to the people, and the people are often reluctant to see it change. The profession, too, finds it difficult at times to respond quickly and easily to new evidence and new desires. This means, in most instances, that attempts are made to operate elementary schools and to ask elementary school teachers to work amidst a good many contradictions, which cause anxious moments for both teacher and pupils until these contradictions are resolved. Teachers are asked, for instance, to recognize individual differences but to use the same textbook in some area of the curriculum with all children. Or they are asked to think of satisfactory achievement in relationship to ability while given at the same time a comparative grading system to use. Or, they are urged by the public to be a progressing professional group at the same time that visitors to the classroom are openly skeptical of the fact that things aren't being done there in the way they were when they themselves were in elementary school. One needs to be sensitive to but not overly frustrated by this situation. True, not ridding ourselves of these contradictions does lessen our effectiveness with children. But, a look at elementary school education over a span of ten or more years does show progress in resolving these dilemmas. And careful consideration of some of them may indicate that they are often more imagined than real, that there are ways within reach of working around them quite often.

More Philosophy Than Know-How

It is evident that, in certain instances, we have more philosophy or theory in elementary school education than we have know-how and practice. This is, to some extent, a most distressing situation. The gap between what people say ought to be done and what they do reflects, to a degree, a bothersome lag in educational practice. And, of course, if elementary educators are doing one thing while identifying it as another, they are practicing an unforgivable kind of professional hypocrisy. The latter

circumstance is to be feared. The former may be bothersome, but may be related with some positiveness to the whole of elementary school education.

To a degree the ''reach'' of any social institution will outstrip its ''grasp'' in particular respects. This is to be expected and lived with. It may well be simply evidence of an existing ''frontier'' or ''growing edge'' in elementary school education, for instance. This may be the way in which goals can be advanced and ideals avowed well beyond those that can be realized at the moment. Security in such circumstances comes from the slow but steady progress which can be identified toward a more desirable kind of elementary school experience. Seen in this way, the ''lag'' may actually be involved in the dynamics of a situation that functions as a ''level of aspiration'' determiner for elementary educators.

Different Concepts of Function

All elementary schools hold to some concept of functions or purpose, and this concept differs somewhat from district to district, and in part from school to school. Some elementary schools follow a concept of function which holds that the elementary school's foremost and almost singular task is to develop reading, related language, and arithmetic skills in children. Where this is the case, total school programs and individual classroom programs will reflect it. Others see the job of the elementary school as largely one of citizenship development and everything that is done in the school is weighed against this ''good citizen'' backdrop. This concept of function will lead to efforts to help children with understandings and skills beyond those of literacy alone. Still other elementary schools may see their function as helping children with problems of personal and social adjustment in the main, and the whole program will reflect this bias in the sort of efforts that will be made to help children to move toward emotional maturity and social adequacy. Most elementary schools will actually be concerned about all of these responsibilities, of course, to some extent. The thing that tends to ''color'' a total program is the priority that will usually exist in relation to these areas of responsibility. And it is possible for some one priority to become so strong as to actually throw the total program out of balance to a questionable degree.

Labeling Schools Is Questionable

Spending time and effort in categorizing or labeling individual schools or teachers with tags such as modern, or traditional, or progressive, or conservative in any over-all way is of questionable utility. Schools and

teachers just don't fit in any one category. Any total elementary school program is likely to be forward-looking in certain areas and more traditional or conservative in other areas of its curriculum. The work of individual teachers also is characterized by this same sort of "unevenness." Conclusions with respect to progressive, or traditional, or any other types of practices must be drawn with specific aspects of a total program in mind. Most school programs and most teachers' efforts range over a continuum from traditional to modern, and from conservative to progressive. Observations may be made and defended that a particular school system, or individual school, or specific classroom teacher tends to be *more* of one thing and *less* of another, but it is probably unwise to go any farther in the use of such labels.

Such tentative generalized ideas concerning the program of the present-day elementary school may be helpful to keep in mind as these next chapters are read. It is hoped that other such generalized ideas concerning the elementary school curriculum will emerge from these program-centered statements.

REFERENCES

Benjamin, Harold. *Saber-Tooth Curriculum*. New York: McGraw-Hill Book Company, 1939.
> An entertaining and meaningful statement of the problems of lag and change in educational programs even in a "stone age" community. Chapter 3 is especially relevant to the focus in this chapter.

Caswell, Hollis L., and Arthur W. Foshay. *Education in the Elementary School* (Third edition). New York: American Book Company, 1957.
> Chapter 14 attempts a look to the future of elementary education.

Hunnicutt, Clarence W. (editor). *Education 2000 A.D.* Syracuse: Syracuse University Press, 1956.
> A collection of eighteen lectures that attempt an assessment of the present and probable direction for the future of elementary school education.

Ragan, William B. *Modern Elementary Curriculum* (Revised edition). New York: Henry Holt and Company, 1960.
> Chapter 1 deals with the changing curriculum of the elementary school in a helpful way.

Shane, Harold G. (editor). *The American Elementary School* (Thirteenth Yearbook of the John Dewey Society). New York: Harper & Brothers, 1953.
> A reminder of the way in which the future challenges the present in elementary education is found in Chapter 16.

Thomas, Murray. *Ways of Teaching*. New York: Longmans, Green and Company, 1955.
> Part I is especially helpful in calling attention to the variability in the ways that teachers and schools approach the task of helping children to learn.

10

LISTENING AND READING:
RECEPTIVE LANGUAGE ARTS

Communication—the exchange among people of thoughts, beliefs, information, and feelings—has gradually progressed, through the centuries, from primitive gestures and nonverbal sounds, through the development of spoken and written language based upon combinations of sounds and symbols, to the inventions of the printing press, the wireless, the telephone, the radio, and the television, which have made it possible for words to be reproduced or transmitted almost instantaneously. Language is not the only means of communication, for man also expresses ideas effectively through the media of music, dance, drama, and the graphic arts (see Chapter 15). Messages are communicated also by fire sirens, comic strips, advertisements, traffic signal lights, school bells, and numerous other sounds and symbols that have meaning for us. Their messages can evoke feelings of excitement or peace, tragedy or humor, love or hate. The term *communication* embraces *all* means of conveying ideas.

Communication Is Necessary to Mankind

Communication is a vital need of man. The ability to express oneself in the spoken and written forms so that others may understand is almost as essential to modern life as sleeping and eating. It is the basis for thinking, for sharing, for creativity, and for survival.

Communication has patterned and held social groups together: world groups that speak similar languages are closely identified; teen-agers, seeking social identity, develop their own ''language''; families, regional

groups, and occupational groups may be identified by their particular means of communication. A group develops its own language through specific meanings that reflect common experiences, common thinking, common purposes.

We transmit and preserve our way of life, our culture, through our language, which makes it possible to record experiences and ideas of men of the past. Our world has become smaller, and the problems of other peoples have become more closely related to ours, through modern means of communication. Language barriers present probably the simplest of problems. World communication involves understanding and accepting the fundamental thoughts, values, beliefs, and ideas of others. World peace is impossible without real communication skill.

The Communication Concept Is Changing

Communication is a two-way process that involves the expression and the reception of ideas. For many centuries, most communication was of the personally active kind only, in which two or more men involved themselves in talking together, writing letters by hand, and directing personal ideas to a specific individual or group. Today, with radio, television, and the many media for publication, a speaker or writer may be addressing an unknown, passive audience. The two-way process still exists, however, for the idea is not *communicated* unless the receiver in some way reacts to the message.

In our culture, literacy is necessary to this two-way process. In the past, *literacy* meant simply a minimal ability to read and write. The man of one hundred years ago was considered literate if he could read a little, write his name, phrase a simple note or letter, and add a column of figures. Today the literate man must be able to do more. He must know something of the historical background of present-day life, something of human relationships, something of the mechanical processes of the tools he uses constantly, something of scientific facts. Without this knowledge, he cannot understand the information presented in newspapers, television programs, or the conversation of the car-crazy kid who lives next door. The literate man of today must distinguish among various values, grasp the total idea of an argument, evaluate the constant avalanche of propaganda. Thayer summarizes by saying, "In short, literacy involves a minimum degree of facility in finding one's way around in a world where communication through plural media is a condition of intelligent living."[1]

---

[1] V. T. Thayer, *The Role of the School in American Society* (New York: Dodd, Mead and Company, 1960), p. 158.

Although literacy is important, it is not, by itself, enough to meet the demands of communication for modern living. The arts of communication are more than verbal skills. Communication requires skills with other media as well as with spoken and written language. Daily, one sees pictures, cartoons, illustrated charts that must be interpreted. Listening to radio and television requires skill in discrimination. Meeting and getting along with people with differing ways of living demands insights and understandings. Not only must teachers understand the meaning of "arts of communication," but they must constantly modify the curriculum so that these arts can be taught.

THE LANGUAGE ARTS PROGRAM

The demands of communication challenge the teacher to present a better and broader language program. Children need to learn to speak fluently and read well. Writing, with correct and effective use of vocabulary, spelling, and grammatical conventions, should be informative, interpretive, and creative.

The Four Related Language Processes

The language arts program of the modern elementary school comprises four language processes: the expressive (outgoing) processes, *speaking* and *writing;* and the receptive (incoming) processes, *listening* and *reading.* Among these processes there is constant interaction as indicated by the diagram. Each of the four language processes is involved in the whole of the communication process. Reading and writing contribute to each other, as do speaking and listening. Each of the areas contributes to understanding, and from the understanding proceeds the assimilation and action within the individual. This principle can be further illustrated by tracing the development of the four processes the young child initially learns about language.

First the infant *listens.* He listens to the sounds made by others, especially by his mother, who by means of words and arbitrary sounds communicates to him her love, her instructions, her anger. Through listening he begins to understand, and then to imitate, and soon to repeat the most common sounds. Thus listening appears to be the basis for oral language.

As the child practices imitating sounds, his speech becomes clear, his sentences longer, his vocabulary larger. His *speaking* ability grows steadily, stimulated by the many reasons he finds to communicate.

The child's next big step in the manipulation of language is learning to *read.* The reading program in school—based on oral vocabulary—is

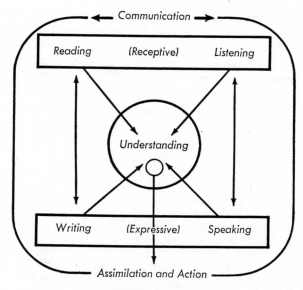

LANGUAGE ARTS

begun when children can handle the oral language with some fluency. The child associates abstract symbols with spoken words, and gradually achieves the ability to evoke meaning from printed symbols.

As a beginning is made in the reading process, the young child learns to *write* the same symbols he is learning to read. Skill in writing demands three kinds of learning: understanding of the formation of the symbols (penmanship), understanding of the formulation of the word (spelling), and understanding of the formulation of the sentence (grammar).

Complete discussion of principles, practices, trends, and issues in the four areas of the language arts program would take volumes; this chapter presents only some basic ideas related to the receptive processes of communication: listening and reading. Chapter 11 will present the expressive processes of communication: speaking and writing.

The Changing Language Arts Program

Schools have drawn the four processes of language arts together into a practical program; but because of the changing character of our schools, our recent knowledge from research about the relationship of children and learning, and our culture's changing quality and modes of communication, the language arts program of today is different from that of years past. A number of changes in curriculum procedure can be identified:

1. The term *grammar school* is no longer appropriate. Curriculum in the modern elementary school places proper emphasis upon reading and language, but its purposes go beyond instruction in grammar. Modern teachers try to avoid outdated procedures. Today, language experiences are provided that are closely related to practical problems in meaningful situations from daily life. David H. Russell describes this more meaningful approach when he speaks of reading and writing activities:

> ... Goals for reading and writing activities mean, of course, an increasing variety of good books in school libraries, classroom and daily activities, and increasing opportunities in writing for many purposes. It means planning in matching a boy and a book. But it means also a shift in group instruction from stress on the narrow mechanics of reading to emphasis on the place of reading materials in the life of the individual. It means the teacher asks questions not like, "What was the color of Bill's dog?", but "Was Bill the kind of boy you would like to have for a friend?" It means not hurrying to finish a story but stopping to savor what it tells us of courage or loyalty or justice or other lovely words of our language which we call values. If our children are to face the 1960's and 70's, they need some grasp of values for their personal living and for a "lacework of coherence" in our culture. Reading and writing can help give this.[2]

2. No longer is language approached through unrelated rote instruction; modern methods do not dictate and regulate learning by text or teacher prescription alone. Experiences in penmanship, for example, are not confined to copying meaningless phrases. Instruction based on repetition and recall is set in meaningful experiences that are varied, interesting, and challenging to children, and that stimulate action rather than passivity. Content materials for language come not only from basic texts but also from other subject matter areas as well as from the specific needs or weaknesses of the children. The interrelatedness of experience, content, and skills is recognized. Some skills may be useful for more than one area—skills such as the phonetic abilities that support and supplement both the reading and spelling programs.

3. Drill periods help only to develop and maintain skills, but language is made meaningful in practical situations. Usually drill periods are presented when a group of children have a special problem, or when special attention to one aspect of language will help individuals use skills more meaningfully in lifelike situations. It is from the practical situations that clues for drill periods are observed. Some continuing group experiences, devoted to skills such as reading, are part of the daily program.

---

[2] David H. Russell, ''The Issue in Instructional Improvement,'' *California Journal for Instructional Improvement*, October 1958, p. 5.

4. Throughout the school day the arts of language are practiced in relation to other subject matter considerations. Reading is necessary for research in social studies and science. Writing is utilized for record keeping, creative efforts, and many other tasks. Without attention to spelling, grammar, and vocabulary, learning activities would be ineffective. Practice of skills becomes most realistic when learning experiences are integrated in the curriculum unit, in holiday or seasonal preparations, or in special entertainments or programs. The teacher's concern is that the arts of language are not neglected in any aspect of the curriculum.

5. Larger blocks of time in the daily program provide for flexibility in the purpose, kind, and continuity of experiences. The small periods of time that were part of outdated curriculum methods (ten or fifteen minutes in an inflexible schedule) are now grouped together for an hour's work in general aspects of language. During this hour, the children may work in groups on common problems, or they may practice dramatization, creative writing, or other language activities. In the primary grades, the reading hour is usually kept intact for developmental activities, and the language period is scheduled in addition. In the intermediate or upper grades the organized reading program may become a part of an even larger block of time devoted to language.

The Purposes of Today's Language Arts Program

The major purpose of language arts in the modern program is to further personal and social development, to help the individual live a better life in the democratic society and scientific-industrial culture. In the elementary school the language arts program seeks to help children develop skills of communication for learning, for living with others, and for becoming self-sufficient, productive citizens. Literacy is of great significance in a world where it is ever more difficult for an illiterate person to find a job and to carry out the common details of everyday life, such as driving or shopping.

Another purpose of the language arts program—related to democratic living—is to develop the ability to respect and cooperate reasonably with others in solving common problems. In the modern world, without literacy and a means of exchanging ideas men cannot reason, cannot cooperate, cannot attack problems together, and cannot learn to value or live in peace. In a world tense with the fearful cold war of conflicting values, citizens need more than ever to be thoughtful, reasoning men. One reason for the emphasis on language arts is that language is necessary to thinking. Teachers are challenged to help children develop and recognize the power of thought and to guide them to conscious effort in thinking. Language is important to sound and effective thought for

several reasons: (1) language is necessary to communicate one's thoughts to others; (2) communication is meaningless unless it reflects thinking; (3) the ideas of others stimulate reaction and more careful individual thinking; (4) most thinking is done with words, or the mental action of translating feeling or experience into word-symbols; (5) the ability to translate into words, or language symbols, improves the quality of thought. Because of these relationships between language and thinking, some linguistic scientists consider language a conditioner of thought as well as a means of expressing thought.

Utilizing the foregoing basic principles, many school districts define the purposes of language arts in their courses of study. The City of New York states the general objectives of language arts as follows:

1. To help children communicate with maximum effectiveness in situations involving the organization, assimilation, and expression of ideas.
2. To help children acquire the specific language skills of listening, speaking, reading, writing, and studying.
3. To acquaint children with worth-while literature; to create and sustain an interest in reading it; to use literature to increase understanding of human behavior, ideals, and spiritual values.
4. To broaden children's experiences through the mass media and to teach the discriminating and effective use of these media.
5. To stimulate an interest in language and to extend children's appreciation of its development, beauty, function, power, and significance as a tool of learning as well as a medium of communication.
6. To help children acquire poise and self-confidence through using language and observing the amenities in a variety of situations.
7. To help children develop ethical standards, make sound judgments, and assume moral responsibility for their spoken and written language.[3]

LISTENING

The first communication skill developed and used by the very young is listening. The child must listen so that he may imitate the spoken sounds. He listens to learn. He continues to listen throughout his life until, as an adult, he listens more than he reads, speaks, or writes, for listening consumes the major portion of the time a man devotes to language each day. The use to which he puts his listening and the amount of skill he develops in it in part determine his ability to learn and to live with others. Indeed, most people of our world today are

[3] Board of Education of the City of New York, *Course of Study—Language Arts —Grades 1–6*, Curriculum Bulletin No. 4, 1954–55 Series, pp. 2–3.

influenced more by what they hear than by what they read. Russell points out:

> Children live in a world of sound. They are bombarded from morning to night not only with the sounds of the physical environment but with the words of peers and adults who want them to do something, or at least want to be heard. As Gerald Green puts it in *The Last Angry Man*, his novel of the television industry: "The most overwhelming fact of the twentieth century is the assault on the public ear and eye, the incessant, relentless avalanche of useless information."[4]

The child's ability to listen in school is also important to learning. Listening to instruction, to the ideas of others, to stories, reports, plays, conversations, and discussions becomes a means of gathering ideas and finding meaning in daily activities. Especially is this so in the primary grades when listening skills are more highly developed than reading skills.

The importance of listening as a skill is only now beginning to be understood. Because children come to school in a sense already able to listen, this skill has been taken for granted, and situations in which the listening skill may vary or need to be developed differently are sometimes ignored. It has been assumed until recently that because children have so much practice in listening, specific training is unnecessary. On the other hand, an emphasis on learning to read has been a natural one since the culture places great importance upon the reading skill, for which the child usually has no ability when he enters school. We cannot assume that children need to be taught only to read and do not need to be taught to listen.

The Nature of Listening

Listening is an ability that involves hearing—the auditory sensitivity needed to identify and "pick up" sound; auditory discrimination—the ability to recognize and distinguish various sounds; and auditory comprehension—the intellectual ability to enjoy the sound or understand the meaning of what is heard. Thus, listening is more than simple hearing; it is the conscious personal and mental reception of sound. (Certain educators and psychologists prefer using another term for the listening ability: *auding*. One finds this term in recent literature about mass communication of radio and television. It is a term with which teachers

---

[4] David H. Russell and Elizabeth F. Russell, *Listening Aids Through the Grades* (New York: Bureau of Publications, Teachers College, Columbia University, 1959), p. 1.

should be familiar since some authorities advocate using it with children. It usually refers to careful, attentive listening.)

In several ways, reading and listening, as receiving skills, are similar. First, like the art of reading, listening is used to gain information, to understand differences in situations, issues, and ideas, and to be entertained. Second, as compared to personal or concrete experience, the understandings gained from listening—and from reading—are secondhand and more abstract, since the knowledge comes from someone else. Third, listening *must involve action*. In some way the listener must accept, react, think, or in some way *feel* what he has heard.

Listening and reading also differ. Whereas the reader proceeds at his own rate and may reread or refer to other sections of reading matter, the listener must accommodate his pace to that of the sounds to which he is listening. The listener has no time for repetition or reflection. His pace in the listening process is that of the person speaking. Also, spoken material very often is not as well organized as written material. Thus listening demands greater alertness, perception, and critical thinking.

Factors Influencing Listening

Children demonstrate many individual differences in the kind and quality of their listening. As teachers constantly evaluate the learning process, they must also be conscious of the several factors that influence the listening of individuals in a group of children.

Physical conditions. Physical conditions influencing the manner in which an individual listens may be of two kinds. First, the physical conditions of the listener himself may have much to do with his ability to listen. If he is tired, ill, emotionally upset, hungry, or hard of hearing, his listening is affected. Sometimes a hearing loss may not be readily ascertained, and the teacher may think the child inattentive for some other reason. Second, the physical conditions of the environment may influence individual or group listening. Such conditions include matters of room temperature, the amount of air in the room, the comfort of the furniture, and distracting noises within or adjacent to the room. The speaker's voice quality, gestures, poise, type of speech, humor, or dramatics in presentation may be influential factors. If the communication source is other than a speaker, factors such as quality of sound, stage arrangement, and acoustics may affect the quality of listening.

Psychological conditions. Psychologically, a very different group of factors may influence listening. Attitudes, experiences, and personality traits will influence the interpretation of what is heard. For example, the Republican listens to a Democrat with a different mind set from that of a Democrat listening to the same speaker. A flute player listens to an

instrumental solo with a feeling different from that of the listener who does not play an instrument. Prejudice or lack of sympathy for the speaker or his cause will, of course, influence the ideas received and the interpretation of the words. Egocentricity, ethnocentrism, bigotry, humanitarianism will "tune out or in" certain aspects of verbal material being presented. Boredom, lack of interest in the subject, and the general attitude toward the speaker will make a difference in what is heard.

Conditions of experience. The experiential background of the listener is another cause of the presence or lack of emphasis, interest, and understanding of what is heard. People who are familiar with jazz will enjoy a jazz band more than will the listener who is familiar only with more conservative music. Meager experience with a topic being discussed influences the interest of the listener. An unhappy past experience might arouse antagonistic attitudes. Limitations of vocabulary influences the amount and kind of ideas assimilated. In other words, a listener receives from the listening situation the amount and quality of information in proportion to the experience he brings to the situation.

All of this implies that the teacher must know his pupils if he is to help them listen. He must be familiar with their over-all health and particularly with their physical limitations. He must be sensitive to unusual evidence of fatigue or other emotional or physical distress. He should understand something of each child's family background so that he may be cognizant of certain values that produce acceptance, prejudice, or other influencing attitudes in listening. Not only should the teacher be familiar with the experience background of his pupils, but he should make a concerted effort to develop common experiences on which learning to listen can more effectively be based.

Developing Skill in Different Kinds of Listening

The first prerequisite for a good listening program is the teacher's clear understanding of the various kinds of listening and how they may be developed in children. He must be able to bring attention to and explain different listening skills to children in specific situations that will bring meaning to the art of listening. Children need to think about various kinds of listening and evaluate their own.

Many experts in the field of language arts have developed classifications of the kinds of listening. Generally, they identify two categories: *marginal* or *casual* and *attentive* or *concentrated* listening. The casual type is exemplified by the very informal listening of a teen-ager as he studies near the playing radio. He is conscious of the music in the background, but listens to it attentively only when there is something of

special interest. Other examples of casual listening are to the music at a tea or in participation in social conversations.

Concentrated listening is of several varieties. There is the appreciative or entertaining kind in which one listens to a concert, drama, or poem. There is the more demanding kind in which one listens to directions, makes plans, or evaluates work or material. Much of this kind of listening may involve personal reaction so that questions may be asked or suggestions made. There is also the kind of concentrated listening that one does when specific points of view are presented, as in campaign speeches. Problem solving also is related to this kind of listening. One listens and reacts according to certain knowledge or experience. One thinks critically to be able to perceive weaknesses, lack of authenticity, or bias. This kind of listening requires the greatest effort.

In every phase of the child's life, demands are made upon him that involve listening. Such a demand may be the warning blast of an automobile horn on the street. It may be the frightened cry of a younger sibling. It may be the careful directions on how to prepare a booklet or solve an arithmetic problem. It may be the fun of listening to a joke, or the challenge of helping a fellow student solve a difficult situation. Children need help in deciding what amount of attention is needed and what kind of personal reaction is demanded by different situations. The environmental, psychological, and experiential factors determine the kinds of listening needed.

Creating the Environment for Good Listening

Developing skill in listening depends on the way the teacher organizes study habits and sets the physical and psychological environment for listening in all areas of the curriculum.

Teacher's voice and speech. The first consideration is the teacher's voice and speech. He must be sure that he is heard. That is, his voice must reach the children at the back and outer edges of the group, without being too loud. Most effective teachers use a soft, warm voice tone that can be heard by all, but does not have so much volume that the children have to tune out part of it. The teacher's voice should have life, warmth, energy, and enthusiasm.

The teacher's voice is used in a variety of ways. He does not put the children to sleep by using a monotonous drone, but he varies the tone and pitch of his voice as the situation demands. He is sure also that only the child who needs to hear him will hear; if he is speaking to a small study group he talks loud enough for that group only. He is not the one to do most of the talking, but seeks a fair balance of listening and speaking.

Manner in which the teacher gives instructions. A second consideration in setting the listening environment is the manner in which the teacher gives instructions. Frequently the young and inexperienced teacher will give the same directions in the same words and tone two or three times. The children learn quickly that it is not necessary to listen until the third time. The experienced and effective teacher is sure that all youngsters are ready to listen and then gives clear, concise directions only once to a fully listening audience. This kind of "listen once" study habit, developed carefully, will save much time and energy for both teacher and student.

Children's voices and manner of speaking. Another consideration is the children's voices and manner of speaking. Children must also be heard by the group, whether it be the total class or the small reading group. Each child must learn to change the volume or rate of his speaking to suit the situation, and to watch others to see that he is understood, as a matter of courtesy. The listening children must develop the same habit of listening once. Sometimes teachers hinder this development by repeating what each child says, to insure its being heard. Unintentionally the teacher risks changing the words and the meaning of the child's original idea. Such a risk is entirely unnecessary if the children speak to the whole group, and the group is "tuned in" for listening.

Physical environment. The physical environment is another consideration in the development of good listening habits. A quiet, comfortable classroom with children arranged as closely and compactly as possible is most effective for group listening. Children can converse much more easily within a small area than across a whole classroom, so planning and evaluating sessions should be held in a circle group at the front of the room, away from desks. Also, quiet discussions should be avoided when other children are playing noisily outside the windows of the classroom. When working with only part of the class, the teacher should arrange small groups so that talking within each group will not disturb the rest of the class.

Providing Listening Experiences

For the most effective listening program, the teacher should provide many kinds of listening experiences. Throughout the day opportunities for listening should be utilized, and children should be helped to sense the specific purposes of each situation. Even background music can be a pleasant and relaxing experience when used judiciously. Children should not be listening to the teacher all day. They must have experiences in which they talk and listen to each other, in which they can

learn to react to the ideas and problems of others and solve problems cooperatively. Making comments or asking questions in reaction to what is heard is an important part of the listening activity.

The teacher must also be conscious of the children's readiness for each listening experience. *Readiness* in this use does not mean an abstract attitude related to all listening situations. Rather, listening readiness requires an experience background for each particular situation, the development and clarification of vocabulary necessary to it, and guidance in the identification of major ideas. By recalling related understandings or materials, considering new words, and otherwise developing anticipation of the situation the teacher can prepare the children for the listening experience, usually by speaking only a sentence or two.

Habits and Attitudes of Listening

Important to the listening program is the development of certain habits and attitudes about listening. The first understanding is that listening and speaking are highly related activities with dual responsibilities for the people involved. Though the performer should make an attempt to be understood and appreciated, it is not his responsibility alone to make people listen.

Another understanding is that good listening qualities demand active participation. Reaction is reflected in posture, gesture, facial expression, speech, or other overt behavior. A good listener looks at the speaker, is alert, attentive, and responsive.

Certain mental processes are also part of the listening act: anticipating, or thinking ahead of what the speaker is saying; evaluating, or weighing what is being said; reconsidering or reviewing the ideas expressed; and searching within the listener's mind for meaning beyond the ideas being expressed.

Children also recognize that good listening habits must be consciously practiced to be developed. Difficult listening situations should not be avoided; real attention rather than simulation of an attentive attitude is necessary; outside distractions can usually be ignored. One learns to look for the good in what is being said, not just the manner in which it is presented. Too often when criticizing physical appearance or delivery of the speaker, immature listeners lose the good ideas he offers. The most effective listening involves grasping the meaning of large ideas and related items, rather than temporarily recalling single unrelated facts; retention is improved when relationships are understood. Too often young people "tune out" something because of premature evaluation. Listeners should give full opportunity for complete presentation before judging the content uninteresting or inapplicable.

Teachers should teach children to take notes. Inefficient note-taking can be laborious and detrimental to listening. Selective, intelligent note-taking can help the listener remember and make relationships that increase the effectiveness of the learning.

As part of the language arts program, the role of listening is assuming its proper importance. The necessity for a continuous program to develop skills of listening is more commonly understood. Opportunities to practice many kinds of listening are being provided, and through systematic evaluation children are becoming conscious of effective listening habits.

READING

Though our present civilization takes for granted that every child should learn to read, this communicative skill is a recent acquisition for the common man. Until the invention of the printing press in the middle of the fifteenth century made materials available to the ordinary individual, only a selected few acquired the skill of reading. Today, because of the phenomenal technological advances and their effect on our social and cultural life, the teaching of reading has received much attention from educators and a good deal of interest from lay people.

The Nature of Reading

Experts do not attempt to explain the reading process in a simple sentence or two because it is not a simple, single act or skill applicable to any printed material. Reading is a complex of abilities varying in importance in different kinds of reading situations. Basically, the act of reading is an individual's interpretation of certain printed symbols and an integration of the meaning within himself. *Reading is more than recognition and pronunciation of words.* It involves the total mental processes through which a person recalls concepts and meanings as a result of the recognition of printed symbols.

Three interpretations of the nature of reading indicate variation among authorities in the meaning of the word. In its broadest sense, *reading* has been defined as the intelligent response to all sensory stimuli. From this point of view it may be said that we read visual, aural, tactile, gustatory, olfactory, thermal, or kinesthetic stimulation. In other words, some sort of meaning is drawn from an experience by "reading" the experience. This definition is recognized as being synonymous with education, with learning, with experiencing.

A second point of view about reading is that which interprets it as the intelligent interpretation of all symbolic representations. This would

mean that a person interprets a picture, a graph, a map, as well as the printed symbols of language.

Dictionary definitions of reading emphasize the intelligent interpretation of the printed symbols of language or numbers. This definition, which refers to the process by which one looks at, recognizes, and draws meaning for himself from the printed symbols, is the definition that educators consider the most pertinent.

In describing the complexity of the reading act, Gray identifies four steps, or dimensions, in the total reading process:

1. *Perception,* or the ability of the individual to perceive a word and identify one word from another. This perception involves the understanding of the pronunciation of the word.
2. *Comprehension, or grasp of meaning of the symbol* involving two parts: the literal, or sense meaning that identifies what is there, and the supplementary meanings, or recall gained from the reader's experience and his ability to "read between the lines" and to recognize the thing left unsaid but intended or inferred.
3. Interpretative *reaction,* entailing appreciation of the meaning, and/ or a critical reaction to it. The ideas are evaluated in the reader's mind, fundamental assumptions examined and their validity tested.
4. *Integration* or fusion of the identified ideas with all our experience and knowledge. Such integration affects the individual through changed attitudes, different thinking, new insights of experience, changed personality.[5]

These four dimensions of reading demonstrate that what many consider to be a simple skill or act is in reality an involvement of physical and mental organs that may result in some change of the total person.

The Broad Reading Program of the Elementary School

In the past, reading as an elementary school subject has had a number of different emphases as the social and cultural problems of our nation have changed. Purposes for reading have ranged from the development of religious and patriotic values to the more utilitarian motives of today. Influenced by these changing emphases, and by the dominant role of reading in mass communication, reading in the modern elementary school is organized as a broad program in which everything a school does to promote growth in and through reading is considered an integral part.

Today, reading is taught as a practical, functional skill that extends into every part of the daily program. Reading is not considered a sepa-

---

[5] William S. Gray, *On Their Own in Reading* (Chicago: Scott, Foresman and Company, 1948), pp. 35–37.

rate subject, for every "subject" demands certain reading skills. The reading program is something more than a specific hour in which the children are grouped for purposes of instruction in reading. There is guidance not only in basic mechanical skills, but also in reading and research in content fields, reading for fuller personal development and recreation, and reading to appreciate good literature. When it is needed, remedial reading instruction is offered. Methods and materials are adjusted to abilities and interests of the individual child. This broad program ties the child's reading to his own experiences, emphasizes reading to supplement experience units and to develop skills of thinking, and gives the child understandings beyond the immediate environment to the outer regions of fact and fiction. Books are sought as teachers and sources of information; they are recognized as forces in shaping attitudes and enriching language and life.

The Stages in Reading

As children progress through school, several distinct levels of progress in reading can be identified.

Reading readiness. As a result of increased research concerning the ways children learn, the concept of reading readiness is widely accepted as the first level of development in reading. The readiness period is an actual stage of growth and preparation for the complex task of interpreting printed symbols, and includes all the reading development that precedes actual reading from a book. Readiness for reading involves within a child a combination of certain stages of physical, emotional, social, and mental maturity with certain understandings, skills, purposes, attitudes, and information.

Though several tests are available to help a teacher determine a child's readiness to read, the teacher's own judgment is usually considered valid. Readiness can be determined when the child shows the following developments:

1. The eyes should be developed to the point where the child is able to see well and focus exactly. He should be able to see a familiar object such as a chair at some distance and walk directly to it for identification. Every opportunity is taken to determine whether the child can see well or whether he squints, holds his head to one side, or uses any other unnatural means of observing things.

2. The ears should be developed to the point where the child can hear distinctly, and can relate certain sounds to symbols or understandings. He is able to enter conversations at the proper moment, answer questions, engage in games adequately with loud or soft voice, listen to stories easily and with interest.

3. The child should be able to speak correctly and accurately. No longer does he confuse a "w" with an "r" as in "wing" and "ring." Not only does he enunciate clearly, but he also uses language easily to share experiences, to discuss activities, to tell stories, and to plan or evaluate. His vocabulary has reached approximately 2,500 words and is constantly being enriched. This language facility is of great importance in reading readiness.

4. The child who is ready to read is socially a relatively happy child. He has developed to the point where he plays well in groups, is able to join interest groups and to adjust to the activity of the whole group. He shares materials and lives naturally and confidently with others in classroom play and work. He is successful much of the time in his manipulative efforts, and demonstrates emotional security in his relationships with others.

5. The mental development of the child who is ready to read indicates that he has a good understanding and use of concepts and word meanings, and the ability to organize and classify ideas. Concepts have been built through concrete experiences, and the child understands and is able to react to trips he has taken, things he has built, people he has listened to, and movies he has seen. He is able to talk about new and old words, and is constantly grasping new word meanings. He demonstrates the classifying of ideas as he gathers related pictures, tells jokes and stories, plays games that indicate what objects "go together"—paper and pencil, chair and table, and so on—and such activities. He has developed good work habits and attitudes: he is able to concentrate on the work at hand; he can follow simple directions; and he can discriminate between ideas and things.

6. To begin to learn to read, the child should have an adequate background of experience. He should know about or have a mental picture of a *merry-go-round* if he is to try to read that word. He should know also that the word *mother* is more than a name for his own young mother, that it names every woman who has a child.

7. Finally, the child who is ready to read must have a real interest in learning to read. He demonstrates this interest through his attitudes toward books and stories, through the manner in which he asks questions about the reading process or the information attained through reading, through his curiosity about pictures, letters, books, and other reading materials.

An adequate reading readiness program involves two major developments: First, the development of a wholesome classroom atmosphere and a secure and friendly rapport between teacher and children. In developing the psychological atmosphere of his class, the teacher does some purposeful thinking, much planning, and constant evaluation of his actions and the type of activities he provides for children. Second is the development of certain skills, mostly physical and mental, that are necessary foundations for reading.

Primary reading. The primary reading program, traditionally the

curricular emphasis of the primary grades, can be separated into two levels. The first is the initial period, or the very beginning situations during which the child learns to read. The second phase is that during which the children have some fundamental powers in reading and so a rather rapid progress in skills takes place.

The initial period is one in which the teacher strives to guide the child in positive reading interests and attitudes. An environment is arranged that encourages curiosity and the desire to read. The emphasis is on "reading for meaning," which necessitates adequate experience background. Materials contain a predominance of pictures so that the children can enjoy the stories in spite of limited sight vocabulary. The teacher's own insight, enthusiasm, and sense of humor in interpreting the pictures are very important in the development of attitudes and interests. Gradually the picture material is decreased as the child engages in continuous meaningful reading and relies more on the verbal content than on the pictorial material for meaning. The goal is the achievement of absorbed attention to the content and ease in interpretation of the printed symbols.

During this early stage of reading the teacher utilizes a number of methods based on sound research. The alphabet is not taught as an introduction to reading. The letter is no longer considered the unit of recognition and the ability to recognize and name the letter is of little importance in relation to the sounding of syllables. Sight vocabulary is built through constant repetition and use of words, and certain elemental and basic aspects of phonetics are utilized. For example, children are helped to recognize words that begin similarly, such as tree and toy, or sing, sister, and Sally.

The second level of the primary period is characterized by the children's increased power to understand and deal effectively with printed words. Reading has more varied purposes, and skill in reading as a thought-inducing process is becoming more effective. During this period, the child reads more frequently on his own; a rich variety of fairly simple materials are made available to intrigue him and answer questions for him. At this stage the materials are still related to things and events within the immediate environment or experience of the child. Speed in silent reading develops beyond that of oral reading. The word recognition program is strengthened so that independence is increased and reading experiences may be extended. At this time the teacher is careful to diagnose continuously the strengths and weaknesses of each individual, for this is the critical stage of development and reinforcement of the reading skills. The aim is to avoid failure and to correct bad reading habits.

During this period of rapid progress children read aloud after the

material has been read silently, especially when a real purpose has been found, such as to read the exact words answering a question, the parts spoken by the characters in the story, or a paragraph that expresses a specific idea. At these times it is important to help the children in the group to listen attentively to the reader.

Most teachers prefer to use one reading series as a flexible basis of the developmental reading program. Experts have written clever stories that develop vocabulary by the gradual introduction of new words and repetition of these words within material that is familiar and suitable to six-year-olds. The teachers' manuals accompanying the basal series are carefully developed and contain many fine suggestions for teacher-pupil activities centered around the reading.

Many other types of materials and activities are recognized as important to the broad reading program. In fact, many variations exist in procedural method and types of materials utilized, for not all teachers depend solely on the basal reading program. Experience charts illustrated by the children are used in various kinds of drills. Many reading games are prepared to provide independent reading activities and help in some of the specialized problems that need repetition. Activities children work on at their seats are selected carefully to insure real learning so that "busy work" is reduced to a minimum.

By the end of the third grade, a child should have a real anticipation for the reading period and means of procuring ideas through reading. He reads a variety of materials, uses a book easily, attains fluency in oral reading and interest in silent reading, and has the ability to work out for himself some of the unfamiliar words he encounters.

Intermediate-grade reading. In grades four, five, and six, the child enters a reading level of increased power and efficiency. The materials the child deals with carry him beyond the immediate environment to events and activities outside his own personal experience. The vocabulary and language of the material may be beyond the reader's own oral usage, but not beyond his level of comprehension.

Because of the different ideas, the unfamiliar words, and the many uses for reading, the child must learn a number of related skills. During these years the child learns to use the dictionary, the encyclopedia, and other reference books in the library. Use of more elaborate tables of contents and very detailed indexes are necessary to the research to be carried on. Understanding and ability to use the library card catalog becomes necessary. Ability to find specific parts in a book, to skim materials, and to take notes is developed. Phonetic skills are supplemented as children learn to use diacritical markings, to understand more complex rules of word construction, and to relate them to spelling.

In using reference materials, children need to understand that their

thinking is also shifting. Pupils are no longer dealing with familiar things and thinking reproductively. Now that they are reading about unfamiliar things the resultant thinking must be creative, imaginative. This is the time that reading beyond and between the lines becomes most important to the interpretation of the material. One must be able to use all he knows, all of his experience, to throw light on the meaning.

Frequently we find that teachers of fourth, fifth, or sixth grades have less formal group instruction in reading, but now, more than ever, group instruction must continue. Books for these children are much improved and can be a real delight to study. The teacher's manuals for these books are most helpful in giving the teacher suggestions for dealing with the material as well as for planning related activities.

Meeting Individual Differences in Reading

Not only do children vary in the verbal ability required for progress in reading, but they also grow at various rates in reading skill. The first grade teacher, who begins instruction in reading, will note differences among the very young children. Some will come to school with a high degree of readiness; in fact, some come with some reading ability already developed. The teacher will note that one individual may progress more rapidly in one area of reading than another. Then, as the children progress through the grades, their teachers will find that the range of differences grows even greater. Some children forge ahead of others in their ability to read, others lag behind because they grow so slowly in reading skill. Teachers are constantly attempting to make adequate adjustment to these variations; a number of procedures have been developed across the nation.

Grouping. Several kinds of grouping have been attempted to lessen the range of ability within a classroom. Homogeneous grouping, discussed in Chapter 8, is frequently determined on verbal ability, and is perhaps more helpful in reading than in other content areas. However, it has been found that no group can be truly homogeneous, and that even within a selected class, other methods of subgrouping must be employed.

Some types of semihomogeneous grouping have also been tried. Deliberate selection of classroom groups of heterogeneous nature but with three distinct reading groups within each class is termed "limited range grouping." In this way, a teacher may have any combination of three groups of low, average, or high readers. The range of abilities in reading for each class is in some measure limited in this arrangement.

Special reading classes of various sorts have been organized. In some schools children leave their own classroom during a specific hour in the day so that they may work in reading with another teacher and a group

of children more nearly at their own level of reading ability. This method has its problems, as pointed out by Bond and Wagner:

> It is unfortunate when the teacher who teaches skills and abilities of reading and who is acquainted with their developmental needs does not have the children during the remainder of the school day. . . . He must know what each child is achieving in basal reading in order to instruct him at other times. And, conversely, he locates the child's needs as he observes the child read throughout the day. . . . Furthermore, most school authorities have concluded that reshuffling the children for reading instruction is not so profitable because rates of growth in reading vary so dramatically. . . . Another problem in connection with assigning children to a different room to work upon reading with a different teacher and different classmates is that it is perplexing to decide which attribute of reading achievement to assign the children to the rooms.[6]

Probably the most popular and effective method of grouping is the organization of small, flexible working groups within one heterogeneous classroom. To do this, the teacher determines from as much data as possible the approximate reading level of each child. Then he groups together in three or perhaps four groups those who have achieved approximately equal ability in a number of reading skills. In the primary grades these groups are formed after the teacher determines the ability of a small group of children through their performance, certain tests attempted, and his observation of their reading skills and habits. In the intermediate grades information from previous records will help the formation of these groups. Also, with the older children, grouping for reading may be organized for other purposes than the development of mechanical skills.

One of the problems of subgrouping for reading arises from the necessity for careful planning to keep three or four groups busy with effective learning activities while the teacher works with one group at a time. Some schools have tried various program modifications to solve this problem. For example, with four reading groups organized, two groups arrive at school one hour before the others, and these reading groups work with the teacher between nine and ten o'clock. Then those children go home earlier in the afternoon while the children who arrived at ten work in reading the last hour of the day. A similar pattern has been tried in dismissing half the class early two or three days a week so that the teacher works the last hour of the day on reading with those that remain.

No matter the type of grouping utilized, there is a definite trend in

---

[6] Guy L. Bond and Eva B. Wagner, *Teaching the Child To Read* (Third edition; New York: The Macmillan Company, 1960), p. 357.

the direction of individualizing instruction. The teacher may take advantage of free reading periods and give guidance to individuals. Even within subgroups, questions asked pupils, materials distributed, modifications for slow or rapid learners, plans for and with individuals, and more individualized methods of evaluation support this trend.

Reading and failure in the primary grades. Teachers have always been concerned about what to do with the child who does not learn to read. Particularly there seems to be a problem about those children who do not learn to read at the primer (or some other standard) level, for traditionally it has been felt that children should learn to read in the first grade.

Educational and psychological research indicate that retaining a child in the primary grades does very little to improve his learning, and may injure the psyche of the ''failed'' child. Only when there has been an extended period of absence caused by illness or when a child is immature physically and socially does nonpromotion strengthen the child as a student and as a person. Because schools emphasize the well-rounded development of all aspects of the child's growth, promotional practices are now taking into consideration factors other than academic achievement.

When children are promoted regularly according to their chronological age, certain problems occur. Parents and teachers need to work together to guide the development of the child, with the parents aware of the lower academic achievement and of the variabilities in evaluation and grading. Special materials and instructional methods are utilized to help each child grow from his own academic level.

Slow learners need much concrete experience before the printed symbol will assume real meaning. They need the help of many illustrations, much repetition, and careful, deliberate explanations. Kinesthetic methods are frequently helpful in dealing with slower children. Careful presentation of word attack methods beginning with the most simple rules, the use of many cooperative stories in chart form, rewritten materials, and child-made dictionaries and word lists are all among the usual methods for teaching those who learn slowly.

One of the problems of the slow reader is his changing interests as he progresses through the grades and the availability of simple reading material to match those interests. Nothing is more embarrassing to the child or more conducive to poor interest and effort than to give a big boy a book prepared for a six-year-old. Though commercial groups have been helpful in making modified materials available, the burden of preparation of special materials falls upon the teacher.

Reading for the rapid learner. The verbally adept child, usually accelerated and identified as a rapid learner, needs special help and under-

standing so that his aptitude may be developed fully. For the best advantage of the child and the society, it is desirable to identify the rapid learner early in his school career. Roughly ten per cent of the school population will fall in this category; this distribution may mean that a teacher will have one or two in his class, or he may not have any really bright child. The child will be recognized by his exceptional verbal ability—a large vocabulary, use of unusual words, clear and well-established concepts, ability to understand abstract symbols, and usually an unquenchable curiosity and thirst for knowledge. Because of this highly developed verbal ability, the rapid learner is frequently adept in reading, the teacher must give the same careful help and guidance that he would give to any other exceptional child, except that the rapid learner can usually proceed on his own more easily.

Not only does the teacher capitalize on the child's special interests, he helps the child broaden and deepen interests through reading. In a formally organized class a bright child may easily hide his interests in dog breeding, magnetic motors, or rocket propulsion. The teacher is alert to clues and seeks to draw out the child. This child's special interests and his research skills and creative thinking ability will help to supplement the experience of the other children, making him a kind of "consultant." The opportunity to share his knowledge with others is most important to the learning of the accelerated child.

The rapid learner is helped to work with the rest of the class and also to proceed individually within the curriculum. He should not be held to rigid standards, for he needs to work beyond the ordinary curriculum plans. The rapid learner may be a member of a fast reading group, but his achievement should not be limited to the lesser abilities of others. He may not meet regularly with his group, and in this way time is made available to him to read independently, to explore materials that will challenge his ability and enrich his reading tastes. The teacher provides adequate materials for him and encourages him to find others. The teacher communicates with the child frequently, using various individual means of evaluating his progress and guiding his growth in the more mature reading skills of locating, assimilating, and organizing ideas, by the use of current materials. He helps the child to use varied forms of writing for recording, organizing, or thinking creatively about the information he has read. The assignments given this child in other curriculum areas may be more complex than the usual assignment. He is taught the use of reference sources early, so that he may work independently with a higher level of materials.

Because of, or perhaps in spite of, his exceptional intellectual ability, the rapid learner may have some very real problems with which the teacher must deal. In the kindergarten there is the problem of teaching

the rapid learner, who is ready and anxious to read, a skill that others have not begun. In kindergarten and also at other grade levels the teacher must be sure that the rapid learners have a well-balanced program of activities beyond the verbal experiences. Social skills and social acceptance are important to the very verbal child. Sometimes the bright child, thinking more rapidly than he can read, may present problems in developing reading skills because of impatience or lack of effort. Leadership ability that helps and pleases others, the demonstration of patience and concern for others, the hearty cooperative spirit are also characteristics that the teacher helps to develop in the rapid learner.

Special Aspects of the Elementary Reading Program

As research has given us more evidence upon which to plan programs and base methods, certain specialized ways of handling various aspects of reading have been formulated in the elementary school. Some have been issues about which there is difference of opinion among the authorities; some have been problems that still need more satisfactory solution; some have been creative instruments in the attempt to make the reading program more effective.

Word analysis. Educators have recently been most conscious of the amount and kind of work done in the word recognition program because of caustic criticisms of education. Though experts do not completely agree as to what, when, and how to teach phonics, a broad program of word attack has been for many years an integral part of the reading program that provides a basis for independent reading. Today the so-called "phonetic approach" is in reality one of *word analysis,* rather than of the synthesis of letters stressed in the traditional phonetic system. Modern methods involve more than "phonics" in that aspects of sight vocabulary, context clues, word form clues, and structural analysis are related to and supplement phonetic analysis. The six techniques that Gray describes so well are briefly outlined here.[7]

The first of Gray's techniques is the *mastery of sight vocabulary,* or the development of a fund of words the child recognizes easily in the printed form. Sight recognition of words is believed by some to be the most important single factor in good reading. In the beginning, sight vocabulary is built upon speaking vocabulary because sound and meaning are basic to word perception. As the sight vocabulary is developed the teacher insures instantaneous perception by giving the child opportunities to meet a single word in many kinds of situations. He presents controlled vocabularies so that the group of words is gradually and mean-

---

[7] Gray, *op. cit.,* Chapters 4 through 9.

ingfully developed. After the child has gained a fund of sight words, the words will become inadequate as the reading text grows, and the teacher may not be available to identify the new words for him. Thus other means of word recognition are necessary.

Gray's second technique in word attack is the skill of using *context* clues, or the ability to gain meaning from the text and pictures that will help identify the unknown word. As children read, and use the meaning of the text to help identify words, some limitations in this method are recognized because words that are closely related and look similar also have similar meanings, and the "guess" from context may not be correct.

A third technique in word attack is the use of *word-form clues* received by the child when he is able to distinguish the total form or the significant parts of a word to help him identify it. Basic to this technique is the skill of visual discrimination, or the ability to note likenesses, identify slight differences, and remember visual forms. An easy word for children to remember is automobile because the general form of the word is unique. On the other hand, was is different from has and book differs from books; to discriminate between these demands clear vision and real perception. However, word-form clues must be combined with other word attack techniques because the frequency of similarities in word forms, such as in *five* and *live,* may mislead the child.

The fourth technique of word attack is that of *structural analysis,* or the ability to look for meaningful units in words. Developing skill in word analysis involves ability to identify structural forms of root words, compound words, derived forms of words (adding prefixes and suffixes), and inflectional variants (adding *-s, -ed, -ing,* etc.) of words. Visual analysis must be checked with both sound and meaning, or pronunciation and understanding, of the individual words and the pronounceable units within them. The child must be thoroughly familiar with the spoken word before such analysis can take place. Structural analysis is not just "finding little words in big words," but looking for parts of words with a meaning or a pronounceable unit.

Phonetic analysis, the fifth of the word attack skills, has recently had much publicity, but, again, it is only one of several ways to identify a new word. By phonetic analysis is meant the association of proper sounds with the printed word form. Phonetic analysis is one of the most intricate of the word recognition skills, because of the complexity of the English language and the variability of pronunciation within it. Though we have only twenty-six letters in our alphabet, forty-three separate and distinct phonemes, or sound units, have been identified. One consonant or one vowel may have several sounds, according to its position and use in the word. To learn when a vowel is "long," or when a consonant is "silent,"

or how one letter influences the sound of another is generally taught over a period of years. Often a single phonetic clue, when combined with other clues, such as meaning, word form, or context clues, will tell the reader what the word is.

The last important technique in learning to find new words among known words is the development of *dictionary skills*. The use of a dictionary is necessary when the child can find no speaking-meaning counterpart for understanding the pronunciation and meaning of a word. The dictionary serves two functions: to check and to derive meaning and pronunciation.

Thus we see that word attack skills involve the development of a number of highly interrelated skills that are begun as early as first grade and developed throughout the elementary school. Though each technique has its limitations, every good reading program involves the use of the six skills, and every good teacher understands thoroughly the kinds and quality of skills necessary to the children of his age group.

Supplementary reading materials. Another area within the reading program that today causes much concern is the use of supplementary reading materials. These are the materials collected and prepared by the teacher for his classroom to supplement the regular work. Use of the basic reading series alone does not produce the rich reading program that is desired for children. The teaching manuals themselves suggest many kinds of activities and various kinds of materials to help children make more meaningful progress on the road to reading. The reading program is a necessary part of the whole curriculum, and therefore appropriate materials for various subjects sometimes become a problem.

Among the reading materials classified as supplementary reading are (1) the books selected as supplementary to the texts, (2) independent activities, (3) experience charts, and (4) rewritten material. Each of these deserves individual consideration here.

1. Every classroom has in it a library table and bookshelves for various kinds of supplementary reference material. In the upper grade levels the reading range of this material becomes more greatly varied in directions both below and above the grade level at which the children work. On hand is a large selection of "trade books," or literature other than textbooks, that represents a wide range of interests and reading levels suitable to a group of children. Books today are increasingly interesting, well-organized, and planned with effective format. The school librarian or the district or county librarian makes available the best on the market. Usually placed with the trade books are some of the texts of other series at a level of reading slightly lower than the books in which the children regularly work. Some basic series also have supplementary books designed to enrich the usual texts.

In addition to the trade books, the classroom is usually supplied with a number of reference books. Dictionaries adequate for the age group are on shelves or in desks. Encyclopedias are frequently found in upper-grade classrooms or are available in the school library. Books suitable for science, social studies, and other subject matter areas are also carefully selected in terms of interest and reading level.

2. Independent seatwork should be meaningful, purposeful, and related to learning goals and immediate plans. Materials in reading workbooks are frequently used with small groups and related to daily lessons. Workbook pages are not completed indiscriminately by children, for constant teacher supervision is important to effective use. It must be remembered that workbooks or other kinds of seatwork cannot be a substitute for the teacher. The use of many workbooks throughout the day is considered ineffective teaching.

Various activities are valuable for independent work during the reading period. Carefully prepared, semipermanent reading games are preferable to a half-dozen worksheets a day, and quiet activities related to the social studies are considered excellent when other assignments are completed. Reading activities related to scrapbooks, various forms of art, and drama and puppetry are useful in the enrichment of the reading program. Variety is essential because no one pattern of seatwork materials will fit the instructional needs of all children. These questions help to evaluate seatwork and other independent activities in the classroom:

a. Is each activity purposeful and educationally sound?
b. Does each activity challenge the child to vigorous effort?
c. Does each activity provide opportunities for satisfaction in accomplishment?
d. Are the activities sufficiently varied to provide for wide differences in ability, interests, and educational needs?
e. Do the activities strengthen the learnings being emphasized in the total program?
f. Do the activities relate to children's current interests and to other class activities?
g. Do the activities help to develop special interests and abilities?
h. Do the activities aid in the development of desirable work habits, such as independence, self-direction, self-control, coordination, neatness?

3. One of the best types of materials developed by both teacher and children as part of the reading program are *experience charts*. These charts are the simple stories worked out cooperatively by children and recorded by the teacher on oak-tagboard or similar material, and illustrated in various ways. The subject matter of experience charts may vary from the record of a field trip, or plans for one, to the description of a

child's new puppy, or just a delightful poem the children decided to write. The language structure also varies from the more common drill-type sentences similar to those in the textbook to the very picturesque language used informally by children. Complete sentences are not always necessary when children are expressing an idea creatively. Picture words, sound words, and feeling words should be encouraged as part of some experience charts.

Charts are also used to record many kinds of material for classroom living. Standards of procedure, plans, questions to be answered, outlines, records, and many other kinds of data are placed upon sheets of paper in chart style. Though experience charts can be used extensively in the primary grades, intermediate grade children should continue to use them only at a more sophisticated level.

Russell and Wulfing point out specific advantages of experience charts: (a) As an outgrowth of children's experiences, charts are of keen interest to the groups; (b) because the ideas or concepts expressed on the charts are usually clear, the reading process rightly emphasizes comprehension; (c) the charts may help in establishing good habits of reading such as left-to-right eye movements and phrase perception; (d) the building of a chart upon an experience may develop the children's abilities to work cooperatively in a group; (e) chart building encourages children to express themselves well in sentences or short paragraphs.[8]

The same two authorities also point out some disadvantages of experience charts, so to be sure the best use of them is made, the following suggestions are listed:

    a. Help children use a variety of good word recognition techniques to attack the wide range of vocabulary used.
    b. Encourage free oral expression and use as much of this as possible in the charts. Use positive words, action words, sound words.
    c. Do not try to use a great deal of repetition of vocabulary in charts; depend on other materials for this.

4. In every part of the country, and at every grade level, teachers find it difficult to procure informational material written at appropriate reading levels. This problem continues despite the fact that in recent years more publishers are producing a greater quantity and higher quality of simply-written supplementary informational material. Consequently, teachers must prepare information to be read in connection with social studies units, science experiments, mathematical problems,

---

[8] David H. Russell and Gretchen Wulfing, *Eight Controversial Issues in the Teaching of Reading* (Boston: Ginn and Company, Contributions in Reading No. 7, 1956), pp. 2–3.

and language activities. One type of supplementary material may be called *rewrites*. These booklets contain rewritten material from textbooks or other sources of information. For example, third graders studying Indians of the Southwest need material about the clothing of these Indians. When the teacher finds that some children cannot read the books available, he rewrites the information, using short sentences, simple words, and manuscript or primary typewriter, and limiting the ideas within one booklet. He dittos a few copies of the rewrite, lets the children bind and illustrate them, and as a result has a semipermanent addition to the library. The books rouse interest and give slower readers an opportunity to gain information through reading.

Individualized Instruction in Reading

Established authorities in reading have for years advocated "free reading" as a part of the broad reading program in the elementary school. Recently, however, a greater emphasis on free reading as a method of instruction developed around individualized guidance in reading has brought a good deal of discussion, experimentation, and controversy. A rash of articles in the professional literature since 1952, and especially since 1956, has brought to the attention of teachers a new means of organizing the reading program.

Because this method is still in the experimental and evolutionary stage, there are differences of opinion about the terminology, the procedures, and the effectiveness of the method. Some call it "free reading," "personal reading," "self-selected reading," "functional reading," "life-purpose reading," or "voluntary reading." Most commonly, the new method is termed "individualized reading," meaning that children individually select and read different materials at their own pace, and that the teacher gives guidance in reading on an individual basis. The movement represents a different attitude about reading for children and presents a difference in the curricular development of the learning area.

Basically, the trend toward individualized reading seems to be caused by dissension against a formal and rigid use of established methods of teaching that rely upon the basic reading series, the manual of suggestions, and commercially prepared supplementary materials. Doubts and questions have been raised about the kind of reading materials imposed upon children and their apathetic reaction to such materials. Educators are seeking to find a way to motivate greater child interest and wider taste in reading, and to find a way of getting at individual differences more effectively than by means of ability grouping. Reports indicate a large measure of success at all age levels in individualized reading.

Characteristics of the individualized reading program. Some generally

accepted characteristics of the individualized method of instruction in reading may be delineated:

1. A large assortment of books appealing to varied interests and written for a wide range of reading levels is made available to the pupils. Roughly from 175 to over 300 books may be collected for one class. The books consist of trade books, textbooks, subject matter reference books, and complete sets of basic reading series. The books are strategically placed in various parts of the room on racks or shelves accessible for browsing.

2. The children are free to browse among the books to select the one they wish to read. Some instruction is needed as to how to browse most effectively, how the child can determine whether or not he wishes to read the book. If the book seems interesting, the child takes it to his seat for more careful examination and the final decision to read it.

3. When books are read, a record of the books completed is made by the teacher or the child. In the child's record, author, title, and date of publication are noted, with a brief comment on the book. To teach children to comment effectively may require some patient instruction.

4. Usually a short story describing the contents of the book is written in the child's own words and filed in a folder made for this purpose. Sometimes the child keeps a list of interesting or difficult words encountered.

5. The focal point of the program is the teacher's individual conference with each child. These conferences occur frequently, according to the child's need for consultation. During the conference they talk informally about the book. The child reads both silently and orally for the teacher, who asks questions to determine the child's interest, comprehension, and progress in specific reading skills. This conference is also the best opportunity for the teacher to check and give guidance in the correct listing and annotation of the book, as well as in the child's writing about the contents. After the conference, the teacher notes an evaluation on an accumulative record sheet.

6. When weaknesses in a specific skill are noted among several children, a small group is formed for special instruction. The basis for this selection of a group is not reading achievement, but common instructional need. Such a group might work on beginning consonants, perhaps a phrase drill, or on skills such as outlining or skimming. The group might work together only one day, or for a number of days, as necessary.

7. Each child makes a decision about each book he reads as to whether he wishes to tell the class about it. He must decide whether the book is worthy of presentation, what form the presentation will take, and when he can be prepared to give it. Then he makes an appointment for time on one of the regularly scheduled presentation days. At this time, he tells

about the book, explains why he likes it, and tries to interest others in the book. Presentations are not formal ''book reports,'' but creative enterprises designed to give just enough information to challenge the interests of friends. Some oral reading, questions and answers, or discussions may facilitate the presentation. Pictures, puppetry, dramatization, realia, dioramas, and many other visual aids may be used in the presentations. Occasionally, two or more children having read the same book may make a presentation together. The work of preparing the presentation is done during the regular reading period, but the teacher is careful that the time and effort spent on the presentation is worthy of the learning situation.

Important factors in the program. Supporters of the individualized reading program recognize that certain factors are important to the success of the method. Crosby has presented such a list:

> —The teacher must have skill and know-how to enable her to draw upon many methods and resources to meet the reading needs of individual children.
> —The children must be supported and encouraged to learn to read in terms of their own individuality and their own unique pattern and pace of growth.
> —Motivation, the drive of the learner to achieve in reading, must be recognized by helping him seek for himself and choose those books for himself which will be satisfying to him. Expert guidance of teacher and librarian are essential.
> —A climate must be created in which reading becomes not only a necessity but irresistible. Rich collections of books in rooms and central libraries are essential.[9]

Problems that stem from such factors can be listed:

1. The teacher must recognize accurately each child's reading problems so that he can provide basic instruction in reading skills and abilities.

2. Instruction cannot be erratic when it deals with a complex process like reading. Some system must be followed so that more complex skills can be built upon the more simple ones. The program is not a laissez-faire situation.

3. The teacher must systematically keep in mind the reading needs of each child to a much greater extent than he does when he works with small ability groups, but the materials used in the individualized program are more conducive to constant evaluation and recognition of weaknesses.

4. Real and intense interest is necessary for the child to be motivated to work alone or with a minimum of supervision. The teacher may

---

[9] Muriel Crosby, ''Organizing for Reading Instruction,'' *Elementary English*, March 1960, pp. 169–173.

stimulate interest by careful exhibits, related trips, enriched curriculum units, and opportunities to listen to stories read and told by both teacher and children.

5. Without careful help, children may not choose books that will help them progress in reading. The child who chooses a book at too low a level is as much a problem as the child who chooses a book that is too difficult to read. Also, there is the child who may not want to choose at all.

6. The teacher needs some help in selecting the wide variety of books for his classroom. Lists of new titles in trade books, catalogs of reliable textbooks, and numerous other references and visual aids are needed.

7. This type of reading program can be effectively related to other subject matter areas. To isolate it entirely would be to defeat some of its purposes.

8. Children may spend too much time and energy on the preparation of presentations. The teacher must guide child activity so that learning is relative to the time spent, and so that irrelevant material is avoided.

Advantages of the individualized reading program. Some of the positive results achieved by the successful program of individualized reading instruction, at both primary and intermediate grade levels, are listed by Veatch:

1. The gifted child progresses at his own pace.
2. The slow reader is not publicly stigmatized.
3. Close personal interaction with the teacher serves the child's psychological needs.
4. Reading at one's own interest and ability level fosters development of skills.
5. Acquiring skills only as needed assures their normal development.
6. Oral reading is promoted by genuine audience situations.
7. Reading becomes its own reward.[10]

Other advantages are noted by Hildreth:

1. Learning takes place in a more permissive atmosphere than is possible when materials are invariably selected by the teacher and practice must conform to prescribed exercises and activities.
2. Giving the child a choice in selection establishes favorable and positive attitudes toward books. With this plan children begin to take an absorbing interest in books at once and become self-reliant in the selection and use of books.
3. The motivation and purposing from free choice of good story books holds the child's interest and helps him concentrate on the task.
4. Independent practice activities on an individual basis are always

---

[10] Jeannette Veatch, *Individualizing Your Reading Program* (New York: G. P. Putnam's Sons, 1959), pp. 28–33.

more economical of the pupil's practice time than taking turns and listening to other children read aloud.

5. The pupils cover more ground in continuous reading when they use story books than when they are confined to teacher selections.

6. The plan obviates the pressure slow children feel about getting into the "top group." No child is forced ahead at too rapid a pace, nor is any child held back by the slower progress of the rest of the group. The pupil receives specific help from the teacher at the time he most needs it.

7. Free-choice reading is a boon to the gifted child because it increases both the range and the quantity of his reading.

8. Children learn to use books of all types for study projects and school activities.

9. This program may actually be less expensive in terms of school book purchases because it does not require a dual set of basal readers and trade books in sufficient quantity for every child.[11]

REFERENCES

Following are recent general textbooks about language arts, written by established authorities in the field, for beginning and experienced teachers. They present all language processes, receptive and expressive, and they emphasize methodological procedures:

Applegate, Mauree. *Easy in English*. Evanston, Illinois: Row, Peterson and Company, 1960.

The Commission on the English Curriculum of the National Council of Teachers of English. *Language Arts for Today's Children*. New York: Appleton-Century-Crofts, Inc., 1954.

Dawson, Mildred A., and Frieda H. Dingee. *Children Learn the Language Arts*. Minneapolis: Burgess Publishing Company, 1959.

Dawson, Mildred A., and Marian Zollinger. *Guiding Language Learning*. Yonkers-on-Hudson: World Book Company, 1957.

Greene, Harry A., and Walter T. Petty. *Developing Language Skills in the Elementary School*. Boston: Allyn and Bacon, Inc., 1959.

Hatchett, Ethel L., and Donald H. Hughes. *Teaching Language Arts*. New York: The Ronald Press Company, 1956.

Herrick, Virgil E., and Leland B. Jacobs (editors). *Children and the Language Arts*. Englewood Cliffs, New Jersey: Prentice-Hall, Inc., 1955.

Strickland, Ruth G. *The Language Arts in the Elementary School* (Second edition). Boston: D. C. Heath and Company, 1957.

Tidyman, Willard F., and Marguerite Butterfield. *Teaching the Language Arts* (Second edition). New York: McGraw-Hill Book Company, 1959.

Language Arts books usually relate reading to the total language arts program, but they do not try to treat all procedures for a well-balanced reading program. Following are some of the many general textbooks presenting the nature of reading and accepted methods for teaching it:

---

[11] Gertrude Hildreth, *Teaching Reading* (New York: Holt, Rinehart and Winston, Inc., 1958), pp. 30–31.

Bond, Guy L., and Eva B. Wagner. *Teaching the Child To Read* (Third edition). New York: The Macmillan Company, 1960.

Dawson, Mildred A., and Henry A. Bamman. *Fundamentals of Basic Reading Instruction.* New York: Longmans, Green and Company, 1959.

DeBoer, John T., and Martha Dallman. *The Teaching of Reading.* New York: Henry Holt and Company, 1960.

Durrell, Donald. *Improving Reading Instruction* (Revised edition). Yonkers-on-Hudson: World Book Company, 1956.

Gray, Lillian, and Dora Reese. *Teaching Children To Read* (Second edition). New York: The Ronald Press, 1957.

Hildreth, Gertrude. *Teaching Reading: A Guide to Modern Principles and Practices.* New York: Henry Holt and Company, 1958.

McKim, Margaret G. *Guiding Growth in Reading.* New York: The Macmillan Company, 1955.

Yoakam, Gerald A. *Basal Reading Instruction.* New York: McGraw-Hill Book Company, 1955.

The following books will supplement the discussions of listening and specialized areas of reading:

Bond, Guy L., and Miles A. Tinker. *Reading Difficulties: Their Diagnosis and Correction.* New York: Appleton-Century-Crofts, Inc., 1957.
    Helpful for problems related to remedial reading.

Eakin, Mary A. (editor). *Good Books for Children.* Chicago: University of Chicago Press, 1959.
    One of the many publications helpful for selecting books for independent reading. Groups such as the Child Study Association of America, the Association for Childhood Education International, American Library Association, and others publish similar lists annually.

Hunnicutt, Clarence W., and William J. Iverson (editors). *Research in the Three R's.* New York: Harper & Brothers, 1958.
    A compilation of research related to reading and writing as well as arithmetic.

Miel, Alice (editor). *Individualizing Reading Practices.* New York: Bureau of Publications, Teachers College, Columbia University, 1958.
    Discussion of meaning and method for individualized reading by several authorities.

Nichols, Ralph G., and Leonard A. Stevens. *Are You Listening?* New York: McGraw-Hill Book Company, 1957.
    One of few books devoted entirely to listening skills and activities.

Pronovost, Wilbert. *The Teaching of Speaking and Listening.* New York: Longmans, Green and Company, 1959.
    Excellent descriptions for developing skills in speaking and listening.

Ruesch, Jurgen, and Weldon Kees. *Nonverbal Communication: Notes on the Visual Perception of Human Relations.* Berkeley: University of California Press, 1956.
    Many excellent pictures and careful discussion that will broaden the concept of human means of communication.

Russell, David H., and Elizabeth F. Russell. *Listening Aids Through the Grades*. New York: Bureau of Publications, Teachers College, Columbia University, 1959.

> A short overview of the nature and importance of listening followed by many effective suggestions for developing skill in listening.

Spache, George D. *Good Reading for Poor Readers*. Champaign, Illinois: The Garrard Press, Publishers, 1958.

> Helpful for teaching children with reading problems; includes excellent source lists for materials.

Tooze, Ruth. *Your Children Want To Read: A Guide for Teachers and Parents*. Englewood Cliffs, New Jersey: Prentice-Hall, Inc., 1957.

> A plea for making many worthy books available to children, in school and out.

Veatch, Jeannette. *Individualizing Your Reading Program*. New York: G. P. Putnam's Sons, 1959.

> An overview of individualized reading, its nature and presentation. Careful summary of recent literature about the topic.

Woolf, Maurice D., and Jeanne A. Woolf. *Remedial Reading: Teaching and Treatment*. New York: McGraw-Hill Book Company, 1957.

> A good psychological approach to the techniques of teaching remedial reading, with illustrative descriptions from case histories.

11

SPEAKING AND WRITING: EXPRESSIVE LANGUAGE ARTS

ORAL COMMUNICATION

As we listen today to TV, or talk across oceans on the telephone, it is difficult to realize the slow development of spoken language, which began with grunts, groans, and pantomime, but now involves highly complex language structure. The development of oral language as one means of communication differentiates men from lower animals and their simple cries. The barking of a dog may vary in tone, pace, and urgency, but the language of men is a more effective tool because of its complex innuendoes of sound and symbols. This development of intricate language-form was possible because of man's physical characteristics: intellectual ability, organs of speech, and muscular acuity of hands and arms. Man's ability to talk is a fundamental basis of civilization because he passed along collective learning by word of mouth long before written language was invented.

Today, the young child comes to school with some facility in speaking. He has listened and learned. At an early age he has established ability to communicate through "muted language," or the unsaid meanings conveyed by bodily movement, gestures, and facial expressions. He has progressed beyond this ability, and has developed enough vocabulary to communicate orally with other children and with his teacher. He can ask questions and give simple answers to queries about the things with which he is familiar. His use of language has helped him to reveal to

249

others his needs and desires: that he is hungry, that he is pleased, that he is angry. His speech enables him to become part of play groups. He has found that he can influence others in their actions and in their feelings by the things he says. Most of what he knows about his world has come through his experience and through oral exchange of ideas.

Not only does the child bring to school with him an ability to speak simply, but he brings with him a manner of speaking to which he is accustomed. His expressions, idioms, inflections, and mannerisms have been learned from his family, but he may or may not use accepted patterns of speech. Variations in diction, grammar, and colloquialisms may present problems in group situations.

The emphasis upon oral language is necessarily greater in the primary grades than in the intermediate grades. Until children can read fluently, oral communication is the basic medium of instruction. Much of their knowledge has been gained through the spoken word; they speak to demonstrate knowledge or seek information. Oral communication is important in today's school because children are encouraged to have something to say. By saying it, by accepting teacher guidance, and by developing self-evaluation, the child improves his speech, his vocabulary, and his effectiveness in oral communication. The teacher who "frees the child to talk" characterizes the oral language program throughout the day with informality and spontaneity, and by so doing lays a foundation for effective and creative written language skills.

Purposes of Oral Communication

Ours is a social world necessitating learning that will help to develop satisfactory human relationships with others. The aim of oral communication, for the most part social in nature, will include objectives such as enjoyment, exchange of ideas, giving of information and reaching conclusions for group action.

One of the most complete lists of goals for children's speaking experiences is given by Herrick and Jacobs:

1. Prizing thinking and feeling, or through experience to think and feel precisely and sensitively.
2. Valuing effectiveness, or the personal development of language manipulation which will be meaningful to the listener.
3. Aiming for acceptability, or the common use of language in a form which is expected of the educated American.
4. Increasing poise and assurance, or the development of ease, natural self-control in all speaking situations.
5. Developing word sensitiveness, or the development of discrimination in the selection of words from a broad vocabulary.

6. Improving voice qualities, or sensitiveness to varying kinds of voice tone and quality, and skill in the manipulation of one's own voice.
7. Extending language courtesies, or appropriate use of voice, manner and phrases to be courteous in a social situation.
8. Interrelating speaking and listening, or understanding of the dual relationship of speaking and listening.[1]

For purposes of instruction in school, oral communication experiences may be divided into two groups. First are those that involve face-to-face relationships in which the speaker is actually talking to others, or expressing ideas that result in immediate and personal reactions from the listener. These experiences may include such activities as conversing, reporting, telling stories, and giving directions. The second category includes situations in which the speaker is playing some sort of role, either to an audience or for the benefit of a fellow participant, as in dramatic play. Creative dramatics, puppetry, and verse-speaking choirs fall into this category.

Face-to-Face Speaking Relationships

Conversation. Though conversation is the most common type of oral communication for adults, it must be consciously planned and observed in schools. Children will converse among themselves in a free atmosphere. The development of conversation is informal, spontaneous, and preferably lively. Small talk and humor are encouraged. One person may express an idea and others may react to develop it; all have the fun of listening and reacting. Topics proposed at random are amplified, or there may be digressions. Children learn to be verbally courteous, to express interesting and appropriate ideas, to take turns speaking. Such informal and undirected conversations take place naturally on the playground, but in the classroom it must be encouraged at such times as milk or snack time, at the lunch table, before dismissal, or at other times during the day when voices will not disturb others.

Discussion. Discussion is a form of conversation wherein impromptu reactions take place among children, but usually some point of study or the solution of some problem is intended. Discussion is more carefully controlled than informal conversation; children develop the trend of thought to reach a specific end. Discussion helps to clarify thinking, gather new ideas, make reasonable judgments, accept various points of view. Children do not make speeches but comment briefly and succinctly. Questions are asked and answered. Teacher guidance is indirect and in-

---

[1] Virgil E. Herrick and Leland B. Jacobs (editors), *Children and the Language Arts* (Englewood Cliffs, New Jersey: Prentice-Hall, Inc., 1955). Adapted by permission.

conspicuous, for the children need opportunity to make the mental explorations and to give the consideration necessary to reach a conclusion. Discussion is essential to cooperative planning and evaluation periods.

Share-and-tell period. Closely allied to general discussions is the time during the day when children gather together to share their experiences and tell each other about items of news. This time is generally called the "share-and-tell period" in the primary grades and the "current events period" in the intermediate grades. Frequently a child acts as chairman, calling on those who wish to speak. The children bring artifacts, pictures, and other materials to make their presentations interesting. It is wise to make an opportunity for this sort of sharing every day, even if it may be very short at times. The first few minutes of the morning seem most appropriate, since children then get the news off their minds and the materials brought to class can be adequately exhibited for later leisurely examination.

Children are helped to achieve clarity of speech and a simple, easy manner of presenting worthwhile bits of information. Listeners are encouraged to respond with comments or questions, to develop a child discussion with little teacher intervention. The purposes of the share-and-tell period are defeated if child after child says his piece with no reaction from the class or with only an occasional comment or question from the teacher.

Taking part in meetings. Related to discussion, and similar to the presentations of share-and-tell, is the oral exchange during class or club meetings. Here children express opinions, relate experiences, and present ideas relevant to specific problems in a structured situation in which each child is individually recognized and comments are directed to a specific person. Such discussions involve records in the form of minutes and require leadership from a chairman and a secretary. Organization for such activities is very informal in the primary grades, but as children grow older they can conform to more formal rules of parliamentary procedure.

Giving directions, explanations, announcements. To give directions or explanations children must have the ability to think through a matter and arrange a sequence of ideas before speaking. The situation demands appearing before a group for a short period, talking clearly and succinctly, making sure that all items have been presented. The manner of the speaker must be direct, precise, and positive; the material must be well organized and presented with an air of confidence.

Reporting. Reporting usually demands a more involved presentation than does giving directions. Teaching the art of oral reporting is a real challenge because reporting by children may easily result in ineffective learning situations. The reporter must have a thorough understanding

of the topic, based upon adequate research, careful appraisal and selection of facts, and a planned presentation that stimulates the interest of the listeners. The report should seldom be read word for word, though well-prepared working notes are most useful. Well-selected vocabulary, simple and direct speech, and use of complete sentences should be encouraged. Some kind of audio-visual material to supplement the spoken words will help make the report more effective. Important to the giving of good reports is the period following the presentation in which the group discusses the ideas presented, clarifying and emphasizing the learning involved.

Interviewing. Teachers capitalize on the child's natural tendency to ask questions as a basis for interviewing techniques. A successful interview includes introductory remarks, questions, note-taking, and an expression of appreciation for the interview. For the intermediate grades, many opportunities for interviews can be found, such as interviewing staff members, resource people, and community workers. In the primary grades very simple interviews that involve no written record can be utilized.

Introductions. The rules for introductions should be taught to children as early as possible. Very young children can introduce parents in a simple and satisfactory manner. As the children grow older, more formal rules for introducing people may be practiced.

Telling stories. The activities in oral communication discussed so far have been those involving face-to-face situations in which the speaker says something and is then guided by the response of his listener. Storytelling definitely demands a response, but that response may not be verbal, for during the story, the listener reacts with facial expressions, laughter, or sighs. Questions, comments, or exclamations may come at the end of the story or rather infrequently during the story.

The storyteller learns many techniques that stimulate the interest and natural delight of the listener, such as variations of voice tone and quality, gestures, facial expressions, bodily movements, colorful words, and a modified form of dramatization. As a storyteller, the speaker must be thoroughly familiar with his theme, present it in correct sequence, and use words the listeners can clearly understand. Young children learn the beginnings of storytelling in their first years of school when they participate in share-and-tell activities and take advantage of other opportunities to tell a group something of interest. Riddles, jokes, and anecdotes, as well as original stories, are encouraged. As the child can handle more ideas and more complex relationships, his storytelling becomes more detailed.

Telephoning. Though one does not actually see the person he talks to while telephoning, the situation is virtually that of a face-to-face relation-

ship. Often children learn to speak over the telephone before they come to school, for the child of today accepts it as a normal part of life. In school, however, children can learn the many uses for the telephone, as well as the specific techniques for placing calls, giving and taking messages, and acting courteously.

Speaking To Play a Role

A second type of oral language activity is the dramatization or the kind of situation in which the child plays the role of some other being. Dramatization is valuable because children learn new words and ideas, improve enunciation, learn that their voices can be changed in tone and volume, and overcome self-consciousness in an audience situation.

Dramatization. The term *dramatization* is a general one that covers a number of dramatic activities in which children act out the parts of specific characters. The usual dramatics in some way represent a preconceived theme or story with rather formal directions or guides followed by the children. Such dramatization is found in the presentation of a formal play, an operetta, the reproduction of a story from a reader, or the dramatization of a funny experience, with rather formal planning and preparation. Variations include shadow plays, puppets, and pantomimes.

Teachers have found that some children can free themselves from their own personalities when playing the roles of others, and in this way learn to speak more freely and with greater clarity. Mentally retarded children who may have great difficulty expressing themselves in front of a group, for example, find comparative freedom in hiding themselves behind a puppet stage and using the little puppets to tell a story or take a part in a play. On the other hand, dramatic situations develop creativity and talents of more able children and thus supplement their learning.

Creative dramatics. Creative dramatics are the rather special type of dramatization in which the children re-enact a story or series of sequences and give their own creative interpretations of the roles. The action is impromptu and unrehearsed. For example, the child who demonstrates to the class the manner in which Jack Horner pulled out the plum does it according to his own idea about pulling plums. The first graders who act out the story of "The Three Billy Goats Gruff" also give their own creative twist to a familiar story. Thus the dramatic representation of a story or theme is creative according to the child's own interpretation.

Dramatic play. Another form of dramatization found effective for promoting learning is dramatic play, different from the usual dramatics in that no set story is followed, and there is no audience situation. The children utilize their natural tendencies to project themselves into the

roles of other people, usually people about whom they are studying and whose work-roles they wish to explore. For example, the third grade is studying the community. When children play the roles of the service station man, the policeman, the grocery clerk, they go through the activities of real people, using "props" they have themselves designed for the play. The situations are reproduced as authentically as possible, the children playing to the limit of their knowledge. The teacher makes sure misconcepts are corrected or that a little more information is available, perhaps through a story, a movie, or a field trip, or through interviewing a resource person. The dramatic play grows, develops, and is modified as the children gain insight into the roles of the individuals they are portraying. Dramatic play is frequently associated with the social studies, for it develops insights into the lives and relationships of people.

A variation of dramatic play is block play, usually provided for very young children in kindergarten and first grade. Here the materials facilitating the play are blocks or manufactured toys, rather than properties constructed by the children for dramatic play.

Verse-speaking choir. Another type of oral communication, performed in groups, is verse-speaking choir or choric speaking. In this, children speak poetry or poetic prose simultaneously in a manner that emphasizes the beauty of the words and ideas. It is performed before an audience only after satisfactory classroom experience. With young children the verses may be altered by spontaneous repetition in which the group chants a phrase or sentence. As the children become familiar with the medium, voices are arranged according to tonal quality, and solo parts are assigned.

Sociodrama and psychodrama. In another type of dramatization, more recently introduced to the elementary school curriculum, children are assigned roles and given some clue about the character so that they may try to behave as they think the character would. This dramatization is termed the sociodrama. The purpose is to explore with the pupils the solution of a social problem situation with which they are familiar. For example, a fight has occurred on the playground. The causes of the fight are re-enacted to determine if a solution other than fighting could have been achieved. Or the pupils may dramatize their actions toward a new foreign student who is expected to enroll in the class. One action is usually not enough. During the evaluation the children consider the effects of the solution, and then other children are assigned similar roles to see if a more effective solution can be worked out.

A variation of this kind of role-playing is the dramatization of the open-ended story. The children re-enact a story that the teacher has read them, and supply their own version of how the story ends. Again, this

is the kind of activity that necessitates several actions until a satisfactory solution is achieved.

The psychodrama is much like play therapy, and involves one person rather than a group of people in a social situation. A child is allowed to play through or dramatize a situation in order to help a technician diagnose a personal problem. This form of dramatization is not recommended for use in the classroom by teachers untrained in psychological procedure.

Special Skills in Oral Communication

Authorities in language arts differentiate between *expressional* lessons, which are provided primarily to give children experience and success in expressing themselves through language, and *training* lessons, which are organized to give children explicit guidance in language skills. The expressional lessons are more informal, concentrate on ideas or procedures, and emphasize fluency and creativity. The oral communication activities just described would most usually fall into the expressional category. From the expressional lessons, the teacher takes clues for the special abilities to be strengthened in the more formalized *training* lesson. Teaching oral language skills is one of the most important jobs of the teacher. The training lesson provides opportunity for careful instruction, practice, and practical evaluation. Though the major emphasis is on expressional oral communication in the primary grades, it is not to be neglected in the intermediate grades. Both expressional and training lessons are continued and developed in complexity as the children grow older.

Some of the skills in which the teacher observes progress during expressional lessons and provides instruction during training lessons are discussed here.

Speaking and listening. Speaking and listening are so closely related that the teacher needs to be aware of their interdependence. He helps children to understand the role of the listener; he points out the advantages of careful listening. He also helps the speaker learn his responsibilities in the listening process and the means by which he can motivate interested listening. (See Chapter 10.)

Articulation, enunciation, and pronunciation. The ability of the child to use acceptable language in a simple and direct manner involves something more than correct pronunciation. *Articulation* refers to the use of the vocal organs (the tongue, teeth, lips, and palate) and the breath in producing consonant and vowel sounds. *Enunciation* refers to the general clarity and distinctness of articulation. Both of these contribute to *pronunciation;* a word may be correctly pronounced but not articulated or enunciated distinctly. To learn to speak distinctly requires accurate

listening and good speaking examples. Also required are a sensitivity to good enunciation, an interest in good speech patterns, and a willingness to correct errors by speaking slowly and striving for clarity. The teacher can give much practical instruction to guide normal growth, but difficult speech problems may need the help of a specialist.

Voice and quality of expression. Use of the voice is related to volume and tonal quality. One of the first skills learned is achieving the volume necessary to be heard by a particular group. If the group is large, the voice should be louder; if it is only a small reading group, the voice must be heard by the group without being loud enough to disturb others. Children can learn to vary the pitch of their voice and the pacing of their speech to lend interest and emphasis to what they are saying. They can learn the difference between a sad tone and a happy one, and to avoid the uninteresting drone of monotony. Much of the expressional quality reflects the speaker's attitude toward what he is saying.

Poise. Effective speaking is greatly influenced by the speaker's poise. Children must learn to feel at ease when talking to others in either formal or informal situations. Confidence is built with experience, success, and careful guidance. Attention to details such as where to stand for the kind of speaking being done, at whom to look, when and where to move when speaking, and what kinds of gestures are appropriate will help to develop a poised manner and an effective delivery.

Courtesy. Because oral communication involves social situations, the social rules of courtesy are important. Children learn the polite forms of speech as well as the courtesy demonstrated while speaking. Taking turns and not interrupting are common social rules. Use of such phrases as "please" and "excuse me" are also easily learned. More difficult and more abstract courtesies while speaking can also be developed as children grow older. Regard for the feelings of others during an argument, ways of offering constructive criticism, or showing the patience necessary to reach a long-sought conclusion requires a more mature development of courtesy.

Organization of thought and content. Effective oral communication demonstrates clear thinking and careful, sequential organization. In the first grade children learn sequential development by telling stories or relating experiences, for even in the simplest of situations the telling necessitates the ability to "stick to the point." As children present more complex ideas and a greater accumulation of information, organization involves emphasis, relationship of ideas, balance of information, timing, supporting details, and other indications of preplanning.

Development of vocabulary. The child's speaking vocabulary is increased and enriched when he is helped to understand the meaning of words. Some words represent concrete objects: the word *rose* may bring

a mental picture of that flower. Other words are more abstract symbols: the word *truth* does not represent a concrete object and may be modified in meaning according to different values. Vocabulary can be developed through the children's activities and experiences, through consideration of the many meanings of some words, through sensitivity to the slight variation in meaning of similar words. Since words are best learned in context, the purpose is not merely to learn new words, but to learn to choose the words necessary to convey the intended meaning.

Grammatical usage. Frequently teachers feel that children should always use complete sentences and formally correct language. It is true that in some situations such language is necessary, but authorities today also approve the use of colloquial speech in appropriate situations. Frequently in discussions or conversations a word or phrase representing lower social form or an incomplete sentence is a complete and effective reaction. Children need to understand what a complete sentence is, and when the situation necessitates its use. Illiterate styles should be avoided.

Evaluation in Oral Language

Because much of oral language is spontaneous and must be maintained as such, evaluation needs some consideration. Three means of evaluation may be utilized.

Standards. Children learn to speak in great part by imitation. Thus an important part of the standard held for children is the teacher's own speech. His manner of speaking must be effective, his enunciation clear and distinct, his vocabulary appropriate.

The teacher also helps children set up cooperative standards. This does not mean that the class uses a multitude of chart-standards nor does it mean that lessons are interrupted to point out standards. After some weaknesses in a specific activity are noted, the teacher may provide a separate situation in which children can think through their purposes and arrive at a set of standards. Problems in the share-and-tell period, for example, may result in standards such as these:

> Speak so that all can hear.
> Don't talk too long.
> Ask for questions.

To help a sixth grade class give more effective reports, cooperative consideration may result in standards such as these:

> Know the material well.
> Use some aids to illustrate.
> Be sure all points are presented in logical order.
> Make opportunities for listeners to participate.

These standards are reviewed when preparations are made for the activity, or during a more formal evaluation period when their utilization is appropriate.

Teacher guidance. Teacher guidance, beyond the development of standards and the setting of a good example, is most easily provided through verbal correction, done incidentally and tactfully to avoid personal embarrassment. If possible, the correction is made so that only the speaker can hear the teacher's quiet voice. The correction is made at the moment the mistake is noted, and if the child does not react, no further effort is made at that time. Frequently the teacher can anticipate an individual's mistakes and help him to avoid them by a suggestion before he speaks. Favorable comments are most important in a positive approach to instruction. Also, teacher guidance includes kindly control of the aggressive talker and encouragement of the shy or retiring individual.

Group evaluation. Important to self-evaluation and to the total learning of the class is the use of group evaluation. After a discussion or a dramatization is over, the teacher can lead the children in an analysis that emphasizes the good accomplishments as well as notes the weaknesses that may need more attention. Children can sense a successful oral communication activity by evaluating their own interest and participation, by determining whether the ideas were well understood. Some teachers have improved both self- and group evaluation with the use of a magnetic recording tape that can be played back immediately or saved to compare with a similar situation.

WRITTEN COMMUNICATION

In modern civilizations, the ability to express oneself clearly in writing is almost as necessary as fluency in speaking. Writing effectively is much more difficult than speaking because the writer must anticipate ambiguities, differences of opinion, and questions, in order to produce exactly and clearly what he means. He cannot watch the faces of his listeners for clues that further explanation is needed, nor can he ask for questions. He cannot rely on tone of voice, facial expressions, gestures, or innuendoes to help him in expression. To communicate in writing a person must write legibly, spell correctly, and use acceptable language structure and a writing style that conveys ideas meaningfully.

Before children can learn to write accurately, an experiential background in other language arts is necessary. As children learn to recognize printed words, they can begin to reconstruct those words with pencil on paper. The ability to write requires a firm understanding of the symbols created to translate the spoken word to the written word.

Usually children begin to write in the latter part of the first grade,

but spelling is not presented formally until the latter part of the second or the third grade. The study of the alphabet is usually deferred until the third grade, when reading and writing are developed to the point of making dictionary work practicable. Correct grammatical usage is introduced with oral communication; when the child begins to write, the transition is made to written material.

As with reading, the proper maturity of the eye and the large and small muscles of the body, and the mental capacity to understand the meaning of words are necessary before children can be taught to write. In early development of the written word, its relationship to oral language development is very close and they are highly interdependent. The spoken word must be thoroughly understood before it can be read or written.

From Manuscript to Cursive

The handwriting program in today's elementary school is moving away from the formalized copying procedures utilized not many years ago. The trend has been established because educators have realized the many ways in which the formalized procedures were contrary to what we know about children and learning. Tidyman and Butterfield list several grounds upon which traditional formalism in handwriting is attacked:

1. The methods used—postures, copy, and drill exercises—are inappropriate for children.
2. The results are artificial and there is little carry-over into actual writing in school and in life.
3. Some scripts, in spite of pleasing appearance, are difficult to read.
4. Learning to write is unnecessarily complicated.
5. The extreme emphasis on drill takes all the joy out of learning to write.
6. Emphasis on formal drill disregards the natural stages in the neuromuscular development of children.
7. Individuality of style is unnecessarily sacrificed to the fetish of uniformity.
8. In spite of years of training, children fail to acquire a free, easy handwriting movement.[2]

As a result of such considerations, handwriting is now taught in a close relationship to the art of writing, as an integral part of the total language arts program. That is, a real purpose for handwriting is sought; instruction for legibility comes as the need is demonstrated. The develop-

---

[2] Willard F. Tidyman and Marguerite Butterfield, *Teaching the Language Arts* (New York: McGraw-Hill Book Company, Inc., 1951), p. 361.

mental program in handwriting begins with *manuscript writing,* then the transition to simple forms of cursive writing is made later.

The first day of first grade in school, the teacher may write on the blackboard at the small child's eye level a simple sentence, "We are in the first grade." He helps the group of children "read" this and at the end of that first day the children proudly go home to tell Mother that they can read! The children have been exposed to some written symbols, meaningful in thought to them. Though they simply memorized the idea and not the form of the symbols, they have, in fact, started on the long road to learning to read. In writing his simple sentence the teacher used a form of writing called manuscript writing, which is very similar to the printing in the preprimers and other texts. He used the exact letter formation and strokes that he will later guide the children in using. He will continue to use this type of writing for all the material he writes for classroom work, preparing children for later imitation, creating a readiness for writing. Children become familiar with the formation and character, as well as with the meaning, of the symbols.

Reasons for the use of manuscript. As manuscript writing has come into use, a few arguments against it have been pressed, most of them stemming from the fact that the form is not socially acceptable and that signatures in manuscript have not generally been legalized. Since children will have to learn cursive writing as the legally accepted handwriting, it has been felt that teaching another preliminary form is a waste of time. However, the arguments for the use of manuscript are so positive and strong that almost all schools now present it as the beginning form of handwriting.

There are several reasons for the wide acceptance of manuscript as the beginning step in learning to write. The first reason is a physiological fact: the small child's fine muscles of the hand, arm, and wrist joints are not yet developed. Cursive writing requires that a writer put his pencil on the paper and move his arm and hand rhythmically but without pause until the whole word is completed. In manuscript writing, each letter is made with one or more independent strokes; thus a child has an opportunity to pause or rest if necessary within a word or even within a letter. Second, since the letters are similar to the symbols of the printed texts, transition from reading to writing is not so difficult as it would be between cursive and the printed form. Children using manuscript tend to use larger vocabularies and write more fluently as beginners. The third reason relates to the legibility of manuscript. The forms of the letters (circles and straight lines) are so simple that children can easily copy them, learn to write them, and evaluate their own mistakes. The slant is always perpendicular; spacing is simple. Extra

strokes and flourishes are not necessary. Consequently, most children can achieve legible writing with a minimum of practice.

Beginning instruction. There are some variations in the forms of manuscript used throughout the nation. Though these variations are few, a teacher determines which system his school district is using, and never deviates from it. The primary teacher especially should be most competent in his format of manuscript, for he uses it constantly.

Usually children begin writing by learning to manuscript their own names. Then a word or two may be learned as the child needs to label a picture or some other work. The teacher is constantly alert to the situations that call for writing. Labels, cards to parents, stories, and letters provide a real purpose for writing.

As the children grow in their need to write, independent writing may be facilitated by providing a word box containing the words each individual may need. When the child asks for a word, it is written on paper of appropriate size. The child studies that word—several methods, mostly kinesthetic, are utilized—then writes it in his story. After he has used the word properly, he files the word according to its first letter in his box. If he has occasion to use the word again, he looks in his box and thus refreshes his memory.

Transition to cursive. The transition from manuscript writing to cursive writing is usually begun in the third grade. By this time the children have achieved proficiency in manuscript writing, and their muscles have developed. The change is made gradually, more slowly for some than for others. For cursive as for manuscript writing, the school should have a stated form and method used throughout the grade. Of the several writing systems available, each provides excellent manuals and evaluation scales, and gives explicit instructions for developing letter formation, spacing, slant, alignment, proportion of letters, and weight of line. Teaching children to form letters by writing them in the air or tracing them is no longer considered effective practice, though attention is given to rhythm and speed of the penmanship. Children who have a tendency to use the left hand should be encouraged to do so, and then correction made in the slant of their paper, pencil, and bodily position for left-handedness.

The quality of materials improves with new inventions. Ball-point pens have been adopted by many schools, eliminating some of the problems of the straight pen. Pencils are being used that are comfortable to the grasp of the small and poorly coordinated hands of young children. Paper of a size that encourages free movement and that has guidelines appropriately fixed is also helpful.

From the third grade throughout the elementary school, writing is an integral part of the total curriculum. There may be specific training

lessons for groups of children who have common difficulties, but encouragement and guidance of handwriting is given in all situations in which the child writes.

Use of the Typewriter

As long ago as the early 1930's research studies were made to determine the effectiveness of using typewriters with children in the elementary school. This growing body of research, some of it financed by typewriter companies, indicates first of all that educators are becoming more interested in the use of typewriters, and also that there is some educational value in their use. Some revolutionary predictions indicate that tomorrow's elementary school will teach two methods of writing: a legible handwriting and typewriting for speed. Surely the idea of using these machines cannot be a more revolutionary innovation than the current predictions for the use of teaching machines. (See Chapter 18.)

Experiments with typewriters have been made as early as the second grade to determine the feasibility of using the machine and the relation of its use to learning in various subjects and to handwriting. Though instruction in the use of the machine is necessarily involved, the major purpose has not been to train typists, although society well recognizes the value of an expert adult typist, but to increase learning through the use of this tool. Positive results have been achieved in regard to amount and quality of work, neatness and accuracy of written material. But, Capehart states, "reports of research and experiments do not agree on how much it (typing) improves learning, when it should be introduced, what materials are best, what methods are most effective, or who should teach it."[3] On the other hand, Capehart indicates some optimistic conclusions from research that would appear to be of importance to those who have a forward look in education:

The typewriter may aid in:

Spelling—It may create a need to spell more words, provide clearer word images, make corrections easier to find, and encourage more pleasurable practice activities.

Writing—Children write more on the typewriter with less fatigue. It is easier to hit a key than form a letter with a pencil. The actual presence of capitals on the machine, with other punctuation marks, probably helps to insure their use.

Social Studies—The typewriter makes possible a wider variety of

---

[3] Bertis E. Capehart, *Does the Portable Typewriter Stimulate Learning in the Elementary School Curriculum?* (New York: A publication of the Education Department, Hill and Knowlton, Inc., 1959), p. 13.

projects, such as individual and group booklets and written reports. It helps make attractive labels and descriptions for posters, maps, bulletin boards and displays; and stimulates other school activities such as newspapers, and magazines, and programs for assemblies.

Work Habits—Typing may help to develop habits of neatness and accuracy, wise use of time, checking work, concentration, attentiveness, following oral and written directions, caring for materials, cooperating with others, and working independently with self direction.

Neatness and Handwriting—The mechanical margins, even line spacings, and regular spacing between words, plus legibility of typing, appear to please pupils and encourage them. Achievements in typed work set standards which children try to imitate in all written work.

Morale—Typing may help make children more enthusiastic about learning and about school. Children are eager to type. They produce more work.

Finally, the economy of space, neatness of presentation, and saving in reading time made possible through typing would appear to be of real benefit in the teacher's task of reviewing and grading written assignments.[4]

It is obvious to observers that typewriters are increasing in popularity. Many elementary schools make them available in the classroom, and teachers are finding that as soon as the child can read with some proficiency, he can begin to learn to write with the typewriter.

Spelling

The spelling "list." To facilitate writing, pupils must learn to spell the words that they need in everyday writing activities; therefore, learning the meanings and usages of words must be closely related to the spelling process. Some schools use a spelling series with prepared workbook spellers, developed from research and based upon the spiral development of ability in spelling words.[5] In these lists, simple words are presented first, and more complex words with various kinds of spelling problems are listed in logical order. Though some experts today think the use of a list is important, many believe that the list should be supplemented by words growing out of the special activities of the children in the school and neighborhood environment. Words from the social studies, science, mathematics, art, and other subject matter areas are identified, recorded, defined, and studied as they arise. These words may be added to the basic list for testing, or they may be evaluated independently. Frequently children keep records of the supplementary words in dictionaries of their own making or in some other kind of word file.

---

[4] *Ibid.*, pp. 4–6.

[5] For a complete list of spelling textbooks and workbooks, see Walter A. Petty, *Improving Your Spelling Program* (San Francisco: Howard Chandler, Publisher, 1959), p. 72.

Instruction in spelling goes beyond memorization. The teaching of spelling is more than requiring of the pupil an independent, silent study of words. Nor is the aim memorization of the correct order of the letters. Rather, children are helped to study the words with increasing independence in terms of visual discrimination, clarity of hearing, pronunciation and enunciation, and meaningful use. Both teacher and child work to develop sensitivity to the form and structure of words and to the phonetic and structural principles involved, and to develop *spelling consciousness* on the part of the child.

Special aspects of spelling instruction. The most effective spelling program is highly related to reading and word recognition techniques, and is given attention throughout the school day. In spelling, as in other subjects, teachers modify methods to take care of the different ways in which children learn. A kinesthetic method may work well with one child, an oral method best with another.

One emphasis in spelling instruction is the development of spelling readiness. Such readiness involves not only the need to write and the desire to spell correctly, but preliminary skills in oral and written expression, reading, and ability to discriminate between forms of written symbols. These factors of readiness increase in complexity at the various levels of the child's development.

Some doubt exists about the effective use of spelling rules. The English language is a nonphonetic language, which makes the use of many rules unrealistic. There are too many exceptions. Mere memorization of spelling rules does not increase the child's ability to spell.

A growing trend is the use of various aids to spelling instruction. If a spelling workbook is used, it is considered the basic minimum, and in some cases its use is confined to slower learners. Teachers tend to add variety and interest to spelling instruction with such devices as spelling games, flannel boards, appropriate reference materials, puzzles, films and filmstrips, and mnemonic devices.

The problem of grouping for spelling is a common one. Many teachers seem to feel that children should all progress at the same rate in spelling even though they do not expect the same rate of progress in arithmetic or reading. Because of the basic differences in children, some children should be able to forge ahead faster and master many more words than is normally expected. Others may have to work at limited numbers of words in order to relieve the confusion and frustration of repeated failure that may lead to lack of effort.

Most suggestions for spelling instruction utilize five ways of becoming familiar with words in order to take advantage of all sensory stimulations. (1) The word must be seen, studied, looked at so that the child is familiar with the general shape of the whole word and context of the

letter symbols. One looks for the correct visual image, conscious of each distinctive letter in the word and also of the syllables. Analysis discloses parts of the word that may cause trouble in spelling. One notices the difference between *correspondence* and *correspondance*, between *familar* and *familiar*. (2) The word is spoken, pronounced, and enunciated clearly and accurately. The meaning and the visual image of the word are recalled as the vocal organs work to produce the exact sound. (3) The word is heard. The sound that is heard is related to the spoken word, the visual image, and the meaning, as one notices accurate and inaccurate pronunciation. Differences are recognized between *pospone* and *postpone*, *sophmore* and *sophomore*. Any confusion among letter sounds is clarified, as in *holaday* and *holiday*. (4) The word is written. When it is written legibly in context of a sentence, its meaning is made clear, and the shape of the word is demonstrated. Silent letters are identified; syllables and sounds are recognized in written symbols. (5) The word is carefully thought through. After having looked at, spoken, listened to, and written the word, the child then thinks about the meaning, sound, and written form. He can check inaccurate formation of derivatives, confusion of homonyms, and transposition of letters.

One author lists groups of questions asked of pupils to provide for phonetic, structural, and meaning analysis as well as usage practice in independent study of spelling words. Some of them are listed here:

For phonetic analysis:

    What other words can I write that sound like this word?
    What other words can I write that begin (end) like this word?
    What silent letters are contained in this word?
    Which syllable is accented?

For structural analysis:

    Is this a root word for formation of other words? If so, write the new words.
    What is the prefix, if any, in this word? Can other prefixes be added?
    Can this word be made plural?
    Can I write the syllables for this word?

For meaning:

    What is the dictionary definition of this word? Does the word have more than one meaning?
    What are some good synonyms for this word? Antonyms?
    Does the word have a homonym?
    Is this an action word?[6]

---

[6] Howard E. Blake, ''Studying Spelling Independently,'' *Elementary English,* January 1960, pp. 29–32.

The teaching of spelling can be one of the most challenging demands on a creative teacher. The development of positive attitudes, the encouragement of self-study and high motivation may be accomplished by any number of methods. Learning to spell is an individual matter. Though the teacher gives guidance, the major responsibility for learning to spell a word or a group of words lies with the individual child.

Language Usage

The teaching of formal English usage today is not merely instruction in *grammar;* it is not the teaching of isolated formal technical skills, principles, and rules in punctuation, capitalization, and sentence structure. All of these elements are present in modern language instruction, but *language usage* emphasizes the practical study of language that relates words and phrases to each other within the sentence structure. This kind of instruction employs an analytical, thoughtful approach that includes knowledge of correct form and understanding of the functions of words and their interrelationships in a sentence.

Usage has an oral basis. A background of correct spoken language is acquired long before the teacher begins to guide language structure in written composition. Children are helped to speak with complete sentences, use the proper verb or pronoun, and follow rules of grammatical construction. Most of the standards of English accepted in school are those of the upper middle-class society. Thus while children are learning one kind of usage at school, they may be learning a different kind at home. One of the problems of the teacher is to help the child understand why he needs to master a more formal English than the vulgar, and perhaps develop the use of double standards. Children need to understand that Americans use a variety of language forms, acceptable to specific situations.

In the primary grades the child is helped to understand that "I don't have" is more acceptable than "I ain't got." In the intermediate grades, children begin to learn some simple rules such as those for plurals and commas. Formal grammar, with diagramming and sentence analysis, is deferred to the seventh and eighth grades.

The need for correct usage comes from real situations. Effective guidance of correct grammatical usage by children is provided when they write for real purposes. "Real purposes" are not teacher-imposed purposes. If the teacher says, "Today we shall write about spring," some children may not want to write about spring, others may not have an impressional concept or a conscious idea about it. Nor should the teacher say, "Now we shall write. Do a composition about anything you wish."

There may not be many wishes. Motivation is the clue. The challenge is to create such a stimulating environment that the child has a desire to write about something upon which he has clear information or deep feelings. The aim is not to eliminate language errors, but to develop a desire to write at an acceptable standard and to build writing habits at that standard.

Training comes as a result of writing. Once writing has been motivated, excessive criticism of form during the writing can spoil interests or creativity. Natalie Cole, in her own creative style, suggests one method of teacher guidance, as related to punctuation:

> I remember when I was a child. With what joy the teacher jumped all over the paper, putting in punctuation marks! In this way she could vindicate herself ... it was her excuse for being. It kept before our minds constantly the fact that she was superior. No matter what we would write, she could always find something wrong. It kept us in our proper place. How kind that teacher would have been if once she had praised the content rather than correcting the form.... When we feel we must give attention to punctuation, why not take a bit from some child's story and put it on the board and stress its strength and beauty? Then say casually, "There are a few things we could do to this that would make it a little easier to read, but they are not the important things...."[7]

Thoughts and ideas are the first judged. Nevertheless, the ability to express ideas clearly and accurately is essential to the content of the ideas. A teacher cannot let a paper go home in poor form, or post it on a bulletin board in poor condition. Common errors, identified, are the clues to training lessons organized to clarify difficulties and give practice in correct application.

Determining content in language usage is a problem. What to teach in the area of language usage may be something of a problem if a teacher tries to provide experiences around the needs of children. The training experiences provided are determined by the varied means the teacher utilizes to identify the need: observation, demonstrated written errors, inventories. Emphasis is put upon the errors made by the majority of pupils, or at least by a group that can study one use together.

Language textbooks are available that offer basic understandings preliminary to grammar and a minimum of rules and definitions. Most authorities suggest that these be used judiciously, particularly in the lower grades, and that their best use might be for supplementary and enrichment activities of the program.

---

[7] Natalie R. Cole, *The Arts in the Classroom* (New York: The John Day Company, 1940), pp. 107–108.

Records and Reports

As children learn to write their thoughts clearly and interestingly, several different kinds of writing are studied. Letters and simple stories are probably most frequently used in the primary grades, whereas words and reports assume more importance in intermediate grades.

Younger children receive background for records and reports from the construction of experience charts and development of cooperative rules, plans, and standards. The ability to think the whole situation through, organize logically on paper, and illustrate in proper and interesting fashion is developed through practice in constructing the simple primary charts or oral reports.

As children write individual reports, they need the ability to synthesize ideas from different sources and write them in logical and effective style. The use of humor, illustrative stories, and interesting words and phrases is part of the skill inherent in writing an effective report. Ability to quote from references and other people's ideas can also be taught in a simple manner. Most of all, teachers need to encourage creativity, in assembling material and in presentation.

FOREIGN LANGUAGE

A current curriculum concern is the teaching of foreign languages in the elementary school. Within the last few years many schools have launched programs of foreign language that have raised questions as to their educational importance and effectiveness. That a second language broadens the education of an individual no one will deny. The issues arise in the appropriateness of such a program within the present organization of the elementary school.

Rationale for Foreign Language in the Elementary School

World understanding. The proponents of a foreign language program in the elementary school hold as a major aim the value of language study in human relationships of a world grown smaller by modern transportation and communication. They emphasize the role of a second language in understanding the people, the history, and the literature of another country. They hope to promote cooperation, mutual respect, and peaceful human relationships throughout the world.

Personality enrichment. Foreign language, it is felt, enriches the personality of the individual and becomes a tool in the pursuit of personal satisfaction in business, travel, and the observance of community and international affairs. Study in another tongue helps the individual better understand and appreciate his own language and use it more precisely.

Extending language study. Though there were some well-established foreign language programs in a few elementary schools in the early 1920's, the schools for the most part have deferred the teaching of foreign language to secondary and college levels. Recently, however, two years for learning a single language in high school has proved inadequate, and the program is now generally four years, with summer school in some cases extending the time. That the elementary school would or could teach a foreign language, it is felt, would extend and supplement the task of developing language competence.

Age. Another reason for teaching foreign language in the elementary school lies in the age at which individuals best learn a language. Ideally, the Foreign Language Association indicates, a language is best taught from birth, but because of the school's lack of control over these early years, the recommended time to begin such study was set from ages four to eight.[8] Also, some research has indicated that a child's development from ten to fourteen years in mental receptiveness to language and flexibility of tastes and attitudes, as well as in aptitude for pronunciation, would facilitate the teaching of foreign language at an early age. This is the age of "pig latin." Young children naturally imitate, use, and invent a variety of sounds, and this ability leads to ease in using the strange sounds of a foreign language without self-consciousness.

However, not all of these assumptions go unquestioned. The amount of language learned in an elementary school would contribute but a minimum to understanding of international affairs, and some feel this kind of appreciation can be taught in other ways. The age at which an individual most effectively learns a foreign language has not yet been satisfactorily determined by researchers or educators. Some feel that a real facility in English should be learned first.

The Trend in Foreign Language Instruction

A changing attitude. In spite of the controversy over the appropriateness of teaching foreign languages in the elementary school, new attitudes toward foreign languages have emerged since World War II. The common man is feeling the urgency of living at peace with the world; his ideas about learning a foreign language are less for personal gain and more greatly centered on group relationships. The ease of travel to foreign countries has also increased the desire to know something of other languages.

Greater offerings. As a result of changing attitudes, more languages

---

[8] Elizabeth E. Thompson and Arthur E. Hamalainen, *Foreign Language Teaching in Elementary Schools* (Washington, D.C.: Association for Supervision and Curriculum Development, National Education Association, 1958), p. 20.

are now being taught at more school levels than before. There are more course offerings and higher enrollments. Schools are increasing foreign language services by including classes in summer sessions, providing workshops for teachers, making available instructional guides, and hiring specialists in the field. Commercial producers have modified electronic equipment to make it suitable to classroom use, and school districts are making an effort to put this modern equipment and appropriate materials in the classroom. Many elementary schools are organizing new programs in spite of already heavy teacher loads and crowded curriculums.

Elementary programs are experimental. Many programs in the elementary school are experimental and exploratory. They are supported by studies and workshops on college and university levels, by foreign language conferences, and by the work of several associations such as the Foreign Language Association, and the professional education organizations such as the Association for Supervision and Curriculum Development. Funds made available by Title III of the National Defense Act have stimulated much activity in the field.

Characteristics of programs. It is difficult to outline general characteristics of the methods and procedures teachers utilize in teaching foreign language because each teacher does it according to his knowledge and understanding, and in line with the program set up in his district. Some general classroom teachers may teach a few words relevant to a social studies unit. Others may have a language background of their own that makes it possible to offer a detailed program as an integral part of the curriculum. When special teachers are available, the classroom teacher may work carefully with the specialist or he may leave the room and let the language teacher work independently of other classroom activities.

In general, however, most foreign language programs are capitalizing on the interest and intrigue of doing something different, and of the children's natural desire to show off a skill that others are not likely to have. The procedure is aural-oral; that is, the children listen, pronounce and imitate, first attaining an understanding of the language and a speaking acquaintance of about two years before learning to read and then to write it. During the fifteen to twenty minutes in the primary grades and the twenty-minute session in the intermediate grades, the teacher seldom speaks English. Vocabulary learned is the useful, practical kind that can be used in home and school activities. It is usually taught from the whole to the part; that is, first sentences and phrases, then a study of individual words. Sentences are associated with action or pictures. Learning is dependent on memory and oral repetition. Tapes are used as teaching devices, both for presenting language material and for recording the pronunciation of the children. Records and radio make it possible to listen to native speakers. Puppets and other

forms of dramatization are used to give the children practice in use of the language.

Problems and Questions Related to the Program

Age. The major problem seems to evolve around the best age at which to begin the teaching of foreign language. The advantage of teaching a foreign language in high school and college is that pupils have more sophisticated study habits and a knowledge of basic language structure in English. However, in the elementary schools, foreign language is being provided for some children as early as the third grade. Many schools begin their program with the fifth and sixth grades. We do not yet have enough evidence to determine which grade is most satisfactory.

Who will be the pupils? Related to the age of beginning is the problem of what children to teach. Should all children have such instruction? Some authorities do not recommend foreign languages for *all* children, yet many schools teach it to whole classes. In some schools only the very bright children are taught foreign languages.

What to teach? Another question arises when the decision is made as to what language to teach. Should the language be one of world-wide importance, such as Spanish or French? Should the language be that of the large minority group in the community? Or should the language be whatever the teacher happens to know? Should children and parents have a selection?

Who teaches? One of the greatest problems relates to the competence of personnel. The general classroom teacher has little facility with foreign languages unless he happens to have a foreign background. For this kind of instruction, thorough training seems to be necessary. We do not have enough specialists with elementary school experience to meet the demand for special teachers of foreign language. Some teachers trying to provide foreign language experiences unknowingly speak with a poor accent.

Continuity. Related to the difficulty of providing competence in personnel is the problem of continuity and regular progress in language instruction in the elementary program. Unless all teachers in a school are well trained in foreign languages or unless specialists are hired, a group of children may have excellent help one year and none for an undetermined number of years. In San Diego and Los Angeles, California, where the state has a Spanish background and Mexico is the neighboring country, a program in Spanish is fairly well established. In-service training for the teachers is provided, along with good materials, but even there, the continuity of the program is "spotty" for the children.

Spanish is the most frequently taught foreign language because of the proximity of Spanish-speaking countries. Geographical isolation is the major factor limiting the widespread use of foreign languages among Americans. Even immigrants soon lose speaking facility in their own languages because they have little use for them here. Americans, finding English increasingly understood abroad, have not needed other languages for business or travel. Consequently, acquiring language proficiency in this country is especially difficult.

Parental cooperation. One final problem deals with the parental cooperation with the program. Unless children are encouraged to study and use their new skills, the foreign language training in schools can be only minimally effective.

REFERENCES

Anderson, Paul S. *Resource Materials for Teachers of Spelling.* Minneapolis: Burgess Publishing Company, 1959.
> Presents the development, research, and methods of teaching spelling, with word lists and special activities.

Anderson, Theodore. *The Teaching of Foreign Languages in the Elementary School.* Boston: D. C. Heath and Company, 1956.
> How to develop and teach a foreign language program.

Applegate, Mauree. *Helping Children Write.* Evanston, Illinois: Row, Peterson and Company, 1954.
> A unique approach to children's creative writing.

Association for Supervision and Curriculum Development. *Reporting Is Communicating.* Washington, D.C.: National Education Association, 1956.
> Reporting in general is analyzed, and suggestions are made for both teachers and parents.

Burrows, Alvina T. *Teaching Composition: What Research Says to the Teacher.* Washington, D.C.: National Education Association, Department of Classroom Teachers, 1959.
> Research in the teaching of composition as a basis for method.

Cypreansen, Lucile, John H. Wiley, and Leroy T. Lasse. *Speech Development, Improvement and Correction: Methods and Materials for the Classroom Teacher and the Speech Therapist.* New York: The Ronald Press, 1959.
> Practical and comprehensive help for the classroom teacher.

Cole, Natalie R. *The Arts in the Classroom.* New York: The John Day Company, 1940.
> Although this is an old book, it is still useful, and in Chapter 5 offers an especially delightful account of children's experiences in writing.

Deighton, Lee C. *Vocabulary Development in the Classroom.* New York: Bureau of Publications, Teachers College, Columbia University, 1959.
> Helpful suggestions for developing children's vocabulary.

Durland, Frances C. *Creative Dramatics for Children.* Yellow Springs, Ohio: Antioch Press, 1952.
> A practical manual for guiding growth in creative dramatics.

Hildreth, Gertrude. *Teaching Spelling.* New York: Henry Holt and Company, 1955.

> Principles and practices for teaching spelling as an integrated part of the curriculum.

Horn, Ernest. *Teaching Spelling: What Research Says to the Teacher.* Washington, D.C.: National Education Association, 1954.

> Compilation of spelling research as a basis for teaching.

Mildenberger, Kenneth W. *Status of Foreign Language Study in American Elementary Schools, 1954.* Committee on Foreign Language Teaching, U.S. Department of Health, Education and Welfare, Office of Education, Washington, D.C.: Superintendent of Documents, Government Printing Office, 1955.

> A study.

Modern Language Association of America. *Childhood and Second Language Learning.* FL Bulletin No. 49. New York: The Association, August 1956.

> One of several publications of the Association in their efforts to improve and facilitate the teaching of foreign languages.

Mulgrave, Dorothy. *Speech for the Classroom Teacher* (Third edition). Englewood Cliffs, New Jersey: Prentice-Hall, Inc., 1955.

> For the classroom teacher's use in guiding the speaking development of children.

Petty, Walter T. *Improving Your Spelling Program.* San Francisco: Howard Chandler, Publisher, 1959.

> A manual of practical, direct, and simple guides for teaching spelling.

Scott, Louise B., and Jesse J. Thompson. *Talking Time.* St. Louis: Webster Publishing Company, 1951.

> A manual for primary teachers, presenting materials and methods for speaking and listening activities.

Shane, Harold G. *Research Helps in Teaching the Language Arts.* Washington, D.C.: Association for Supervision and Curriculum Development, National Education Association, 1958.

> Summarized research in language arts as related to teaching problems.

Thompson, Elizabeth E., and Arthur E. Hamalainen. *Foreign Language Teaching in Elementary Schools.* Washington, D.C.: Association for Supervision and Curriculum Development, National Education Association, 1958.

> Problems and issues clearly presented.

Van Riper, Charles, and Katherine G. Butler. *Speech in the Elementary Classroom.* New York: Harper & Brothers, 1955.

> Concrete suggestions for the improvement of speech habits in primary and intermediate grades.

12

USING THE NUMBER
SYSTEM: ARITHMETIC

PROMOTING ARITHMETIC LEARNINGS

Arithmetic—the study of our number system—has for many years been a fundamental part of the elementary school curriculum. It is deemed imperative that people understand this quantitative system, and that they be able to use it efficiently in the numerous and varied situations involving quantity that are met in their personal and professional lives. There is no indication that the future will demand any less in the way of understanding and skill with numbers. Rather, each bit of progress made seems generally to call for greater abilities to think about and to cope with problems involving quantity. The very recent development of highly complex computers or "electronic brains," the first explorations of outer space, the increasing application of mathematics to the social sciences and the field of communication, community development with its concomitant master planning for the wise use of natural space, a new interpretation of time in a world of instantaneous communication and jet-powered aircraft—all of these and more point to the central place of number and quantity in the "frontier" phases of life. Certainly, arithmetic will continue to hold an important place in the elementary school curriculum.

Changes in Arithmetic Teaching

The teaching of arithmetic—its purposes, subject matter, and methodology—has undergone great change in the last fifty to sixty years. Some educators have referred to this change as a revolution, others as natural

and continuing evolution. All agree that the arithmetic program of today's elementary school is vastly different from that found in 1900. In
the inaugural issue of *The Arithmetic Teacher*, a professional journal
focused on elementary school arithmetic, Brownell had this to say, in
part:

> The arithmetic of 1900 differed materially from the arithmetic we now
> include in the elementary curriculum.... Two of its characteristics
> stand out prominently: (a) it was hard, and (b) it was little related
> to practical living.... Children began the serious business of learning
> arithmetic as soon as they entered school. In the first two grades they
> memorized all the simple number facts. By the time they had finished
> grade three they were well embarked into computation with whole
> numbers. In grade four they performed operations with common
> fractions, many of which are now generally deferred to grade five or
> six, and others of which have been eliminated from school arithmetic. In
> the higher grades they studied square root and even cube root, worked
> long and difficult examples with decimal fractions, percentage, and ratio
> and proportion, and solved intricate "problems" involving many steps.
> Learning consisted largely in memorization. Teachers, relying pretty
> much upon what was in the textbook, showed pupils what to do and
> then relied upon abundant bodies of practice to produce mastery.
> Homework assignments were heavy, and many parents were called
> upon to revive, temporarily at least, skills that they had forgotten. The
> children who survived this demanding regimen, aided often by two
> one-hour periods for arithmetic a day, were capable of arithmetical
> feats far beyond the capabilities of eighth-graders today, whether or
> not they ever later put them to effective use.[1]

There are those, of course, who still feel that the kind of arithmetic
program described above is the kind that should be found in today's
elementary school. However, the vast majority of elementary school
educators, supported by a great deal of psychological and sociological
evidence, would not accept such an approach.

The change that has taken place in the arithmetic program can begin
to be understood if certain questions are kept in mind that have captured
the interest and efforts of curriculum workers and arithmetic specialists
since the early 1900's. Most important among these questions have been
the following:

1. What does it mean to be arithmetically educated?
2. What arithmetic should be taught in the elementary school?
3. How is the area of arithmetic best related to the total curriculum
   of the elementary school?
4. How does arithmetic learning best take place?

---

[1] William A. Brownell, "The Revolution in Arithmetic," *The Arithmetic Teacher,*
February 1954, pp. 1–5.

The discussion that follows should provide some understanding of these, and of related, important questions. They have not been answered finally for elementary school arithmetic, as this chapter will indicate. Rather, research and study continue; each decade brings progress in certain aspects of the total program. Today's program is different from yesterday's, and tomorrow's will undoubtedly differ from today's in some respects.

OUTCOMES SOUGHT IN ARITHMETIC

The initial question posed above makes reference to the sort of outcomes that should be sought in the arithmetic program. Certainly there has been a great deal of rethinking and redirection on this subject. In this century, the period from 1900 to about 1930 saw the elementary school arithmetic program oriented in the main to the single goal of computational skill. While other outcomes were sought to some extent, they were all subordinate to the aim of developing a high degree of efficiency with arithmetic skills. This preoccupation with computational skill colored the total arithmetic effort in the elementary school.

Since 1930 a significant shift has taken place. The phenomenon of "arithmetic feat" has given way to concern for "arithmetic thought." The modern elementary school curriculum seeks *meaningful* arithmetic development. The objective is to help the child to understand the structure of the number system and the logic of arithmetic processes, and to be able to apply this understanding with skill and efficiency in typical situations that involve quantity.

An Organized Statement of Outcomes

Writing in the Sixteenth Yearbook of the National Council of Teachers of Mathematics, Brownell presented the following statement related to a set of acceptable outcomes toward which the arithmetic program might well work. Subsequent study of this statement has evoked considerable agreement with it, and it is included here to indicate the sort of breadth of purpose of the arithmetic program at the present time. The list is organized as follows:

(1) Computational skill:
Facility and accuracy in operations with whole numbers, common fractions, decimals, and per cents. (This group of outcomes is here separated from the second and third groups because it *can* be isolated for measurement. In this separation much is lost, for computation without understanding *when* as well as *how* to com-

pute is a rather empty skill. Actually, computation is important only as it contributes to social ends.)

(2) Mathematical understandings:

   a. Meaningful conceptions of quantity, of the number system, of whole numbers, of common fractions, of decimals, of per cents, of measures, etc.

   b. A meaningful vocabulary of the useful technical terms of arithmetic which designate quantitative ideas and the relationships between them.

   c. Grasp of important arithmetic generalizations.

   d. Understanding of the meanings and mathematical functions of the fundamental operations.

   e. Understanding of the meanings of measures and of measurement as a process.

   f. Understanding of important arithmetical relationships, such as those which function in reasonably sound estimations and approximations, in accurate checking, and in ingenious and resourceful solutions.

   g. Some understanding of the rational principles which govern number relations and computational procedures.

(3) Sensitiveness to number in social situations and the habit of using number effectively in such situations:

   a. Vocabulary of selected quantitative terms of common usage (such as kilowatt hour, miles per hour, decrease and increase, and terms important in insurance, investments, business practices, etc.).

   b. Knowledge of selected business practices and other economic applications of number.

   c. Ability to use and interpret graphs, simple statistics, and tabular presentations of quantitative data (as in study in school and in practical activities outside of school).

   d. Awareness of the usefulness of quantity and number in dealing with many aspects of life. Here belongs some understanding of social institutions in which the quantitative aspect is prominent, as well as some understanding of the important contribution of number in their evolution.

   e. Tendency to sense the quantitative as part of normal experience, including vicarious experience, as in reading, in observation, and in projected activity and imaginative thinking.

   f. Ability to make (and the habit of making) sound judgments with respect to practical quantitative problems.

   g. Disposition to extend one's sensitiveness to the quantitative as this occurs socially and to improve and extend one's ability to deal effectively with the quantitative when so encountered or discovered.[2]

---

[2] The National Council of Teachers of Mathematics, *Arithmetic in General Education*, Sixteenth Yearbook (Washington, D.C.: The National Council of Teachers of Mathematics, 1941), pp. 231–232.

Clearly, this list includes but goes considerably beyond computational skill in describing what it means to be arithmetically educated. The outcomes listed are broad; the task is an extensive one.

Breadth of Present Arithmetic Program

A recent attempt to re-think the elementary school arithmetic program in a particular school district provides another point of view from which to examine the scope of present-day arithmetic. From this effort has come a new curriculum guide covering the work of the first eight years of the school experience. In it, three strands of development are noted, namely (1) science of number, (2) measurement, and (3) expressing mathematical relationships. Problem solving and vocabulary development permeate all of the work in each of the three strands; they are developed continuously throughout the total program, grades kindergarten through eight. The graphical representation of the Palo Alto, California, statement on scope, taken from the guide, is reproduced on page 280.[3]

This example is typical of the breadth of subject matter of the elementary school arithmetic program at the present time. As can be seen, the learning task for children is considerable. The scope of the program is broad, and the accomplishment of the required learnings calls for a wide variety of experiences with number and quantity.

SELECTING ARITHMETIC FOR STUDY

Implied, but not explicitly stated in the materials just presented and discussed, is the question of selecting particular arithmetic for study out of all of the possible arithmetic that might be studied. That is, it is one thing to say that children will be taught to divide; it is another thing to decide on the size of the divisors they should learn to handle. Or, it is only a partial decision to say that children will be taught to work with fractions; it must be decided also just what fractions they should be taught to work with. Put in slightly different terms, the question is: what subject matter in arithmetic is of most worth?

Early Concern over Content Selection

Along about the turn of the century, in the early 1900's, a good many educators close to the elementary school became increasingly concerned about the amount and kind of subject matter that was being selected from the broad field of mathematics to be taught in the elemen-

[3] Palo Alto Unified School District, *Arithmetic Guide—Kindergarten–Eighth Grade* (Palo Alto, California: Palo Alto Unified School District, 1957).

SCOPE OF THE ARITHMETIC PROBLEM

Science of Numbers	Measurement	Expressing Mathematical Relationships
Number System 15 XV	Linear	Percentage % % %
Addition $2 + 2 = 4$	Liquid and Dry	Tables
Subtraction $3 - 2 = 1$	Weight 1 lb.	Graphs
Multiplication $3 \times 4 = 12$	Time	Statistics
Division $3\overline{)18}\ 6$	Money \$ ¢	Scale
Decimal Fractions .001 .01	Temperature	Ratio and Proportion $\frac{1}{O} = \frac{F}{D}$
Common Fractions $\frac{1}{2}$ $\frac{21}{32}$	Area	Literals and Formulae $A = \pi R^2$
	Volume	Geometric Form and Position △ ● □

VOCABULARY DEVELOPMENT

tary school arithmetic program. On the one hand, it seemed that too much was being attempted in these first six or eight years of school. On the other hand, it seemed that what was being taught was often unrealistic and not necessary at all. A paper read by McMurry in 1904 before the Department of Superintendence of the National Education Association typifies this concern. McMurry's paper was entitled, "What Omissions Are Desirable in the Present Course of Study?"[4] He rooted his discussion in the proposition that the subject matter selected for the arithmetic program should be that which can "be shown to have a plain relation to some real need of life," and he presented a list of topics that he felt could be dropped from the arithmetic program at that time.

This sort of attention to the problem of the selection of subject matter in arithmetic gave rise to considerable discussion and argument at the time, and eventually provided motivation for the undertaking of particular kinds of research. Study was directed, in the main, toward two approaches to this central problem, namely (1) social usage, and (2) the science of numbers. Let us consider each approach briefly, bearing in mind that the major concern has been to ascertain which arithmetic should be taught in the elementary school, and when it should be taught.

The Social Usage Basis

Social usage, as a basis for selecting the proper subject matter for study in arithmetic, is oriented to the quantitative situations met by the so-called "average man" in his day-to-day life activities. The attempt is to identify that arithmetic which he actually needs and uses. Prodded by statements like McMurry's, elementary school educators found themselves considering the relationship between the number system and effective living.

A number of studies in the first two decades of the twentieth century agreed that the adult society was called upon to use only a small proportion of the arithmetic that was being taught in the schools.[5] The results of these studies were a tremendous challenge to the content of arithmetic that custom and tradition had tended to sustain. Later studies attempted to ascertain scientifically what, and how much, arithmetic should be taught. For example, one study concluded that halves, thirds, and

---

[4] F. M. McMurry, "What Omissions Are Desirable in the Present Course of Study?" *Yearbook* (Washington, D.C.: National Department of Superintendence, National Education Association, 1904), p. 104.

[5] Sarah E. Chase, "Waste in Arithmetic," *Teachers College Record*, 18:36–70, 1917; G. M. Wilson, *Survey of the Social and Business Usage of Arithmetic*, Contributions to Education No. 100 (New York: Bureau of Publications, Teachers College, Columbia University, 1919); C. T. Wise, "A Survey of Arithmetic Problems Arising in Various Occupations," *Elementary School Journal*, 20:118–136, 1919.

fourths were the fractions of common usage to the extent that they accounted for ninety per cent of adult usage. Beyond these, and in special cases, eighths and twelfths were needed and used by some, it was noted.[6] Other studies considered such matters as teaching decimals, memorizing tables, and using the fundamental processes with compound numbers.[7] Wilson wrote as follows in 1950:

> In summary, the various studies of usage indicate that the drill program in arithmetic should be restricted to the mastery of the four fundamental processes; fractions in halves, thirds, fourths; eighths in special situations and twelfths in other special situations; and reading of decimals. To date, the usage of percentages and interest has not been adequately investigated. Probably much of the work in percentage should be on a nondrill basis.[8]

This concern over social usage as a basis for the selection of appropriate subject matter for arithmetic undoubtedly reached its peak in the 1930's, though it continues to be studied and urged by a number of educators at the present time. That the cumulative effect of such studies has been for the good in the arithmetic program is well accepted. Singly, social usage is not a sufficient base upon which to plan this aspect of the curriculum; along with other bases it seems quite usable. The purposes for which arithmetic is taught in the elementary school are rooted in great part in the contribution that understanding and skill in arithmetic can make to more effective living. These early studies had a great deal to do with introducing a kind of reasonableness into the question of content selection in arithmetic for the elementary school. The now oft-quoted idea of arithmetic having a "social aim" is a contribution growing out of such concerns as these.

The Number System Basis

Much attention has been focused also on the number system itself—its various facts, processes, and procedures—as the question of most appropriate subject matter for arithmetic has been pondered. Arithmetic experts who favor this basis are likely to emphasize an analysis of the number system more than one of social usage. From this point of view

---

[6] G. M. Wilson and C. O. Dalrymple, "Useful Fractions," *Journal of Educational Research*, 30:341–347, 1937.

[7] J. E. Buckley, *The Uses of Decimals in Business*, Master's thesis, Boston University, 1935; Marion Dalrymple, *Decimals in Industries, Periodicals, and Textbooks*, Master's thesis, Boston University, 1933; Dorothy W. Wilson, "Teaching Denominate Numbers and Measures," *Educational Method*, 16:177–181, 1937.

[8] Guy Wilson, "Arithmetic," *Encyclopedia of Educational Research* (Revised edition; New York: The Macmillan Company, 1950), p. 46.

all possible types of number situations are identified, analyzed, and accounted for in arithmetic instruction.

This basis found ready application in the arithmetic of the 1920's and the early 1930's. This was a time when associationist points of view, variously known as connectionism, or the S-R bond theory, were the predominant psychology of learning; they held that each arithmetic situation had to be faced and learned in and of itself if it was to become the "habit" that was sought.[9] Thus, much time was expended in determining the least, but nonetheless comprehensive, number of unit skills, or types of processes, that were part and parcel of the various problems in arithmetic. For instance, in one such study Breuckner called attention to 178 unit skills for fractions—forty for addition, fifty-three for subtraction, forty-five for multiplication, and forty for division—as a basis for curriculum planning.[10] Other such studies can be found in the literature.[11]

Studies focused on the number system as a key to curriculum planning in arithmetic continue to be made. However, with the increasing use of field theories of learning, growing out of Gestalt or organismic psychology, from the middle of the 1930's to the present the general orientation of these studies has changed. In keeping with field theories of learning, the long lists of separate units and combinations to be taught have given way to studies that try to indicate the over-all unity, organization, and relationships within the number system. No longer is each combination seen as a learning task unto itself; rather, every effort is made to help children to generalize their number learnings to wider settings. A "family" approach to learning addition and subtraction, for instance, attempts to help the learner to see the relationships between $3 + 4$ and $4 + 3$ as approaches to the sum of 7, as well as the relatedness of the subtraction facts of $7 - 4$ and $7 - 3$ to these addition facts. Such a use of organization within the number system lends a great deal of security and support to the child who faces this large learning task.

The number system basis is largely responsible for the reference to a

---

[9] Edward S. Thorndike, *The Psychology of Arithmetic* (New York: The Macmillan Company, 1922). Note this statement from the Preface (page v) of that book: "We now understand that learning is essentially the formation of connections or bonds between situations and responses, that the satisfyingness of the result is the chief force that forms them, and that habit rules in the realm of thought as truly and as fully as in the realm of action."

[10] L. J. Breuckner and Fred Kelly, "A Critical Evaluation of Methods of Analyzing Practice in Fractions," *Twenty-ninth Yearbook*, National Society for the Study of Education, Part II, 1930, pp. 525–534.

[11] F. B. Knight and others, *Problems in the Teaching of Arithmetic* (Iowa City, Iowa: Iowa Supply Company, 1924); G. M. Ruch and others, *Schemata for the Analysis of Drill in Fractions*, University of Iowa Studies in Education, Vol. 10, No. 2, Educational Psychology Series, No. 3, 1936.

"mathematical aim" in arithmetic instruction that goes alongside the earlier mentioned "social aim." The discrepancy that some saw in these aims has largely disappeared. It is clearly understood that both aims are important, that there is a good deal of interaction between them, and that each relies heavily on the other for the realization of a comprehensive program in arithmetic.

THE GRADE PLACEMENT OF ARITHMETIC

The reasonableness indicated earlier with respect to the specifics in arithmetic that children are now asked to learn extends in great part to the grade placement of this subject matter. Although really definitive studies are not available, and many doubt that such studies will be forthcoming, the matter has received a good deal of attention, research, and careful thought. The result of these efforts is a placement of arithmetic subject matter by age and grade level that most educators would defend as superior to that found in the early 1900's, although there are still a great number of unsatisfactory answers.

Washburne's Committee of Seven

Undoubtedly the most extensive attempt to investigate the question of the grade placement of arithmetic topics was done by Washburne and his Committee of Seven.[12] The purpose of their study was to determine the mental age at which the various topics in arithmetic might be most profitably taught to children. Many thousands of pupils were included in the study, which culminated in a "table of placement" that was made available to curriculum workers. This table called attention to the minimum and the optimum mental age at which each arithmetic process, or large part of a process, could be taught to completion, that is, mastered by children. For example, the following data are taken from the study:

Topic	Minimum Mental Age	Optimum Mental Age
Addition facts — sums over ten	7 yrs. 4 mos.	7 yrs. 11 mos.
Like fractions (no borrowing) addition and subtraction	9 yrs. 10 mos.	11 yrs. 1 mo.
Long division (all types, complete)	12 yrs. 7 mos.	12 yrs. 7 mos.

---

12 C. W. Washburne, "Mental Age and the Arithmetic Curriculum," *Journal of Educational Research,* 23:210–231, 1931.

Using this information led to a consideration of the grade level at which certain items should be taught. In the case of the material quoted above, a child would be in the third grade before he learned to add sums over ten; he would be in the sixth grade before he learned to add and subtract like fractions; and he would be in the seventh grade before he learned to use long division.

The work of Washburne's committee seemed to spur people to action. The idea that it was unwise to attempt systematic instruction in a given arithmetic process until a child had reached the mental age to profit from it was persuasive. More people than ever before were willing to devote some time and study to this question of optimum grade placement. Specialists studied the work of this committee carefully and published their critiques of the study in professional journals.[13] The complexity of this problem was allied with the general developing literature on readiness. It became evident to most that, although mental age was an important factor in determining the grade placement of arithmetic content, it was only one of several factors to be considered. Along with the mental age factor must be weighed such factors as the general structural difficulty and complexity of particular arithmetic examples, the general social significance of the topic for children at various age and grade levels, the two matters of "can" learn and "should" learn, and the general methodology to be employed in teaching the particular arithmetic under consideration. Most of the investigations of grade placement have not dealt adequately with this complex of factors. Indeed, it is difficult to deal with them in a systematic, scientific way.

What has been done has affected the sequence of experiences in the arithmetic curriculum, however. To a much greater extent than in earlier years, readiness determines grade placement. There has also been a tendency to "teach for completion" over a period of more than one school year, rather than to spend a great deal of time in one year on one thing, then to shift to something else the next. There is considerable support now for starting a given process one year and continuing to work with it at intervals over the next two or three years. This tendency is evident from the examination of present arithmetic curricula; grade placement has its longitudinal dimension, too.

On the following pages is a chart that should help one to grasp the result of the combined impact of the social usage and number system criteria discussed earlier, and the concern over the matter of grade place-

---

[13] W. A. Brownell, "Critique of the Committee of Seven's Investigations on the Grade Placement of Arithmetic Topics," *Elementary School Journal*, February 1938, pp. 495–507; C. W. Washburne, "Reply to Brownell's Critique of the Committee of Seven Experiments," *Elementary School Journal*, February 1939, pp. 417–430.

GRADE PLACEMENT OF ARITHMETIC LEARNINGS

By End of Primary Grades	By End of Middle Grades	By End of Upper Grades
Science of Number	*Science of Number*	*Science of Number*
A. Number System Reads and writes numbers 1–1000 Rote counts to 500; by 2's, 5's and 10's to 100 Uses ordinals through tenth Reads and writes number names 1–10 Understands place value: 1's, 10's, 100's Understands 0 as a place-holder Understands Roman numerals through XII	A. Number System Reads and writes numbers to million Understands meaning of large numbers Understands place value to 1000's Reads and writes decimals through .001's Understands Roman numerals through D and M	A. Number System Completes understanding of place value—right and left Learns signed numbers (+2, −2, etc.) Develops understanding of unknowns
B. Whole Number Computation Knows basic addition and subtraction facts Adds and subtracts two- and three-place numbers, with carrying and borrowing Relates multiplication to addition and division to subtraction in meaning Begins to learn basic multiplication and division facts Computes simple multiplication and division problems	B. Whole Number Computation Extends skill with addition and subtraction Knows all basic multiplication and division facts Computes more difficult multiplication and division problems: two- and three-place multipliers and divisors (with and without quotient correction)	B. Whole Number Computation Extends mastery to adult level Learns square root
C. Common Fractions Uses and understands ½, ¼, ⅓, and ⅕ Adds and subtracts like fractions without reduction	C. Common Fractions Adds and subtracts fractions of all types Multiplies and divides fractions of all types Is learning cancellation	C. Common Fractions Extends mastery to adult level
D. Decimal fractions Reads and writes dollars and cents	D. Decimal Fractions Adds and subtracts decimal fractions Multiplies and divides with decimals	D. Decimal Fractions Extends mastery to adult level

Measurement	*Measurement*	*Measurement*
A. Linear: uses ruler to half-inch; knows $1' = 12''$; 1 yd. $= 36'' = 3'$	A. Linear: uses ruler to $\frac{1}{8}$ inch; knows rod and mile; uses four processes with denominate nos.	A. Linear:
B. Liquid: knows cup, pint, quart, gallon, half-pint, half-gallon	B. Liquid:	B. Liquid:
C. Dry: knows dozen, half-dozen, $\frac{1}{3}$ and $\frac{1}{4}$ dozen, pair	C. Dry:	C. Dry:
D. Weight: knows pounds and ounces	D. Weight: (B.–D.) Knows remaining common measures; converts measures; uses four processes with denominate numbers	D. Weight:
E. Time: uses clock to five-minute intervals; uses month, day, week on calendar.	E. Time: uses clock to second; knows time zones; AM and PM; uses four processes with denominate nos.	E. Time:
F. Money: knows all coins to dollar; makes change to 50¢	F. Money: knows and uses all money in typical situations	F. Money:
G. Temperature: uses thermometer; knows freezing and boiling points on Fahrenheit scale	G. Temperature: reads and uses the Fahrenheit thermometer; begins to use clinical thermometer	G. Temperature: (A.–G.) Completes learnings related to all of these aspects of measurement; maintains and extends understanding and skill, with emphasis on computation with denominate numbers
H. Area: estimates area in simple situations	H. Area: can find area of square and rectangle	H. Area: computes area of triangle, parallelogram, trapezoid, circle, prism, cylinder, etc.
I. Volume: experiences volume incidentally	I. Volume: continues to experience volume incidentally	I. Volume: computes volume of cone, cylinder, cube, prism, pyramid, and sphere
Mathematical Relationships	*Mathematical Relationships*	*Mathematical Relationships*
A. Scale drawing: works with simple maps	A. Scale drawing: works with maps and simple scale drawings	A. Scale drawing: reads and constructs scale drawings
B. Geometric form: defines and compares circle, square, triangle, rectangle	B. Geometric form: understands triangles, diamond, oval; readiness for cubic measurement	B. Geometric forms: understands angles, perpendiculars, parts of circle; constructs common figures; studies triangle in detail
C. Graphs: uses simple tables and bar graphs; can make pictograph	C. Graphs: uses tables, bar and line graphs; understands simple statistics	C. Graphs: constructs and uses all common types of graphs and tables
D. Literals and formulae: begins to see uses for formulae	D. Literals and formulae: uses simple formulae as: $L \times W = A$; $2L + 2W = P$	D. Literals and formulae: understands *pi;* begins algebra
	E. Percentages: knows % symbol; knows simple equivalents ($\frac{1}{2} = .5 = 50\%$)	E. Percentages: computes in various percent situations
Problem Solving	*Problem Solving*	*Problem Solving*
Solves quantitative problems identified in daily activities	Gives continued attention to methods of problem solving	Extends and refines all problem solving skills

ment of subject matter on the present arithmetic curriculum. The chart has been derived from an examination of a number of state and local district curriculum guides and arithmetic textbook series and indicates the learning tasks most often completed by the end of various years in the elementary school. Any particular school system may vary from this chart, but for the most part these are the things that children are asked to accomplish at various grade levels of the elementary school.[14]

PLACING ARITHMETIC IN THE CURRICULUM

The arithmetic program outlined here as being more or less typical of that which is currently found in the elementary school is an extensive one. That the learning task faced by the child is great cannot be denied. Considerable attention has been given to the most efficient way to relate arithmetic to the total elementary school curriculum, in light of both the importance and the extensiveness of the program. Historically, of course, arithmetic has taken its place separately in the instructional program; it has had a time and a place of its own. That this was fitting and proper was not questioned. However, the 1930's saw considerable effort exerted and a number of studies reported that challenged this historical approach to handling the arithmetic curriculum.

A number of people reported research to show the high incidence of arithmetic content in fields other than arithmetic in the elementary school curriculum.[15] Others published material calling attention to the difficulties that pupils had in managing the mathematical concepts they were meeting in various areas of study.[16] Coming at this particular time, with interest running high in the activity or experience curriculum, such studies were used to support the position that the placing of arithmetic as a separate subject for study in the elementary school was neither wise

---

[14] Chart material developed by one of the authors in 1959, based on an examination of selected curriculum guides for arithmetic in the elementary school. Related discussions with implications for content and sequence are found in the Fiftieth Yearbook, Part II, of the National Society for the Study of Education, *The Teaching of Arithmetic*, (Chicago: University of Chicago Press, 1951), Chapter 4, ''Arithmetic for Pre-school and Primary-Grade Children'' and Chapter 5, ''Arithmetic in the Middle Grades.''

[15] Agnes Gunderson, ''Nature and Amount of Arithmetic in Readers for Grades I and II,'' *Elementary School Journal*, March 1936, pp. 527–540; Clifford Woody, *Nature and Amount of Arithmetic in Types of Reading Material for the Elementary Schools*, Bureau of Educational Reference and Research, Bulletin No. 145 (Ann Arbor, Michigan: University of Michigan, 1932).

[16] Ernest Horn, *Methods of Instruction in the Social Studies* (New York: Charles Scribner's Sons, 1937), pp. 143, 189–193; Lucy Scott, ''A Study of Children's Understanding of Certain Statistical Concepts in Social Studies,'' unpublished doctoral dissertation, State University of Iowa, 1942.

nor efficient. The high incidence of arithmetic content in fields of study other than arithmetic was interpreted to show that if the arithmetical demands of these other fields were met adequately, in and of themselves, then children would indeed be learning a great deal of arithmetic. Studies on the difficulties that pupils showed in handling mathematical concepts and ideas in these settings were used against the usual practice of learning arithmetic in one place and applying it in another.

Formal Versus Incidental Teaching

Another argument over the best way of dealing with arithmetic in the curriculum stemmed from the dissatisfactions and doubts that many elementary school educators had developed over the then prevailing formal, or drill, approach to arithmetic teaching. They felt that this approach was not accomplishing the important outcomes in arithmetic learning, and they challenged this type of instruction. In the main, the intent of these educators was to show that formal arithmetic was being started too soon in the elementary school, and that a more informal, incidental approach, especially in the early years, would yield better results. To this end various experiments were carried out and provocative results were made available for others to study and analyze.[17] In almost every instance it was difficult to deny the persuasiveness of these reports. For example, Berman reported a study in which formal arithmetic was omitted from all grades through fifth, and compared the achievement of these children with others who had had formal instruction during these years. Scores on tests at the end of the fifth year in the fundamentals for the two groups were as follows:

Test	Informal Instruction	Formal Instruction
Addition	82	91
Subtraction	48	85
Multiplication	27	76
Short Division	18	73
Long Division	0	60

Students who had received formal instruction scored significantly higher in subtraction, multiplication, and short and long division. Scores in addition favored the formal group also. Nevertheless, at the end of one year of formal instruction in the sixth grade, the children in the ex-

---

[17] L. P. Benezet, ''Story of an Experiment,'' *National Education Association Journal,* November 1935, pp. 241–244; January 1936, pp. 7–8; Etta Berman, *The Result of Deferring Systematic Teaching of Arithmetic to Grade Six,* Master's thesis, Boston University, 1935.

perimental group were able to score almost equally on tests in the fundamentals with the children who had had six years of formal work in
arithmetic. Such evidence captured the interest of many elementary
school educators.

Arithmetic and the Activity Curriculum

A number of studies were made to test the effectiveness of arithmetic
learning in the activity curriculum in the 1930's and 40's. Such efforts
were motivated by a combination of the information from studies that
showed the high incidence of arithmetic content in other curriculum
areas and the growing dissatisfaction with the formal, or drill, approach
to arithmetic.

The arithmetic achievement of pupils in most of the investigations
compares quite favorably with achievement under the more traditional
forms of teaching.[18] However, some educators took the position that,
while much arithmetic learning took place by utilizing the activity curriculum approach, the functional experience of childhood is not adequate, in and of itself, to furnish the base for all of the arithmetic skill
that children need to develop.[19] Others questioned the evidence on different grounds. They felt that the units selected for experimentation
had been purposely taught because of the high incidence of need for
arithmetic in them. Still others felt that the record of some of these
experiments indicated that work of a more formal and systematic sort
had gone on in the classroom along with the instruction that had taken
place in relation to the unit.

Present Place of Arithmetic in the Curriculum

The best way of relating arithmetic to the total elementary school curriculum continues to capture the attention of many elementary school
educators. In 1951 the Committee on the Teaching of Arithmetic of the
National Society for the Study of Education took the following position:

> It is the unanimous opinion of the present committee, however, that,
> after a careful appraisal of such evidence as does exist, and after
> giving full credit to what has been or is likely to be accomplished

---

18 Henry Harap and Charlotte E. Mapes, ''The Learning of Fundamentals in an
Arithmetic Activity Program,'' *Elementary School Journal*, 34:515–525, 1934;
—————————, ''The Learning of Decimals in an Arithmetic Activity Program,''
Journal of Educational Research, 29:686–693, 1936.

19 Paul R. Hanna and others, ''Opportunities for the Use of Arithmetic in an Activity Program,'' *Tenth Yearbook*, (Washington, D.C.: National Council of Teachers of Mathematics, 1935), Chapter 5.

under integrated plans, such plans by themselves cannot be depended upon to develop arithmetical concepts and abilities to the level and scope required in life. An especially designed program should include not only provision for systematic and meaningful learning in the arithmetic class but also careful attention to the mathematical needs and contributions of other areas. . . .

Moreover, the acceptance of the proposal that arithmetic be taught systematically, with an important place in the weekly program, in no way implies a denial of the great potential contribution of other areas to arithmetic or a belittling of the importance and difficulty of the mathematical aspects of those areas. Nor does it underestimate the need of a careful plan for co-ordinating the meaningful development of arithmetical abilities in the arithmetic period with their motivation, development, and maintenance in the study of units in other fields. Maximum achievement cannot be obtained either in the arithmetic period alone or in integrated units alone. Both types of instruction are needed.[20]

The position taken by this committee is essentially the position we take here. This is evident in the statement on the use of time in the elementary school classroom, especially in the classroom programs referred to, and in the discussion on the unit of work as a way of organizing learning enterprises in the elementary school. We are of the opinion that the evidence, when put alongside the scope of the present-day arithmetic program, and when weighed in light of the outcomes sought, makes it necessary and wise to utilize both the arithmetic situations that develop in ongoing studies in other areas of the curriculum and a special time in which direct and systematic attention may be given to the study of arithmetic itself.

TEACHING ARITHMETIC TO CHILDREN

Great strides have been taken in dealing more effectively with the instructional or teaching task in arithmetic. The way in which arithmetic is learned is understood better now than ever before, and this understanding is reflected in the procedures and the materials now used in the classroom.[21] A great part of this change is due to the influence of field

---

[20] National Society for the Study of Education, Fiftieth Yearbook, Part II, *The Teaching of Arithmetic* (Chicago: University of Chicago Press, 1951), pp. 18, 21.

[21] Esther J. Swenson, ''Organization and Generalization as Factors in Learning, Transfer, and Retroactive Inhibition,'' and Lester G. Anderson, ''Quantitative Thinking as Developed under Connectionist and Field Theories of Learning,'' in *Learning Theory in School Situations*, University of Minnesota Studies in Education No. 2 (Minneapolis: University of Minnesota Press, 1949), pp. 9–39, 40–73; and Carl L. Thiele, *The Contribution of Generalization to the Learning of Addition Facts*, Teachers College Contributions to Education No. 763 (New York: Teachers College, Columbia University, 1938).

theories of learning on arithmetic teaching. The older explanation contained in the S-R bond theory, or connectionist theory, of learning, on the basis of which was developed a highly formal, drill-centered set of procedures for teaching arithmetic, has been altered significantly. In fact, this change has been great enough for the aforementioned Committee on Arithmetic Teaching to make the following statement in 1951:

> These arguments for the systematic teaching of arithmetic should not be taken as a defense for types of instruction, fairly prevalent, which consist mainly of formal, repetitive drill. As someone has said, "Systematic teaching is not synonymous with formal teaching." The members of this committee are as opposed to such methods as are the proponents of the experience curriculum. They favor the meaning theory, involving the active processes on the part of the pupils of discovering relationships, of utilizing concrete experiences, and of generalization. Indeed the meaning-and-discovery approach has been devised specifically to prevent formal teaching. As compared with formal methods, the discovery-and-meaning approach has been consistently shown to result in superior achievement as well as in greater interest on the part of both teachers and pupils.[22]

If one were to attempt to characterize the kind of teaching that goes on in elementary schools on the basis of this so-called ''meaning'' theory, the following would have to be included:

1. Present-day teaching makes every effort to help children to understand the subject matter of arithmetic. A great reliance is put on teaching the relationships within the number system and between the various arithmetic processes.
2. Present-day teaching tries to introduce the element of purpose into the work children are asked to do in arithmetic. It is clearly recognized that instruction in this area must include more than the ability to compute, and that in order to do this, number must become increasingly significant in the minds of pupils.
3. Related to the introduction of purpose into arithmetic teaching is the willingness and the desire in present-day teaching to start instruction at the level of the child. This approach requires the selection of quantitative situations that may be significant and interesting to children, and the acceptance of childlike approaches to the solution of arithmetic problems at the outset.
4. Present-day teaching attempts to rely less on telling and showing and demonstrating arithmetic for children and more on providing opportunities for children to try to figure things out for themselves as they meet situations that demand either the development of new arithmetic skills or workable proof of some already known. Children are active participants in their arithmetic experiences.

---

[22] National Society for the Study of Education, *op. cit.*, p. 21.

5. Present-day teaching utilizes a wide variety of instructional materials, including such things as counters and flannel boards, in an attempt to provide children with the sort of number equipment that is necessary to support the goals of discovery and meaning in arithmetic learning.
6. Present-day teaching recognizes and provides for the repetition and review of arithmetic experienced in the curriculum. Material once learned is met again in a planned way to help to counter the forgetting that is normal in this area.

EXAMPLES OF MEANINGFUL AND DISCOVERY-ORIENTED TEACHING

Perhaps it would be useful to include at this point two descriptions of classroom situations in arithmetic which embody the sort of thing being discussed here. The first is set in a second grade, the other in a fifth grade, class. Both have been adapted from actual classroom situations.

Addition in a Second Grade

A second grade class had been studying the supermarket in conjunction with a social studies unit of work focused on the neighborhood. The teacher saw a possibility of utilizing the small store that had been built in one corner of the room, for dramatic play purposes, to help her teach the class a generalization. The generalization related to a family of addition combinations that the children were to meet in their arithmetic program. It was the teacher's purpose to guide the pupils to the discovery of meanings that would lead them to add two numbers by regrouping them as "ten and so many more." She decided to have each child shop in the room store and buy two articles. One article was to come from a table of merchandise that sold for 9¢ each, and the other from a table of articles priced from 3¢ to 8¢. Pupils were given purses (envelopes) that contained play pennies and a few play dimes. As she planned for this lesson she knew certain things about her class. She knew that they had already formed a concept of addition; she knew that they could record numbers for purposes of addition; she knew that the class realized that objects could be grouped in tens; and she knew that the class could add numbers to 10.

As the children were ready to start shopping, she asked that only two articles be purchased by each shopper—one from the 9¢ table and one from the 3¢ to 8¢ table. As the first child finished shopping, the teacher asked the class to help him find out how much he owed. He had purchased

an apple for 9¢ and a bar of candy for 5¢. The teacher asked the children to write this on their papers. They wrote:

$$9¢$$
$$5¢$$

The teacher then asked them to lay out play pennies for each article the pupil had purchased. A check by the teacher showed that the pupils had placed 9 pennies in one row for the apple, and 5 pennies in another for the candy bar.

Before the children could count the pennies in the two rows to find the sum the teacher asked: "How many of you can pay for these things with a dime and some pennies, instead of only pennies? It takes so many of them." Some of the children solved the problem quickly, knowing how to count out the required number of pennies to make a dime. Some of the children moved one penny from the five row to the row with nine in it to make ten pennies, and then changed this row for a dime. Others counted the row of nine again, and then continued into the row of five to get a dime's worth of pennies. The teacher had to say to a few of the children, "I have some dimes I will give you for a dime's worth of pennies when you have them ready."

Soon the pupils were ready to show the teacher that the two articles would cost one dime and four pennies, or 14¢. The teacher suggested that the sum be written correctly on their papers as the answer to the problem that they had copied previously, with the 4 in the one's place and the 1 in the ten's place. The procedure as outlined here was continued as different children shopped, until the teacher thought that the majority of the pupils were ready to move to a higher level of thought. Thus, as the next purchase was made the teacher said, "I wonder how many people can find out how much the two articles cost this time without laying out pennies and changing some of them for a dime. If you think you can, just write your answer where it belongs on your paper. If you still want to lay out pennies and change ten of them for a dime you may do so, of course." The majority of the pupils simply worked the addition problem on their papers and were able to point to the figures and tell what they would have done if they had actually counted out the pennies and changed them for a dime. Those who had not discovered that they could do this regrouping "in their heads" were given special help by the teacher. This she did by referring to problems already done, asking how the dime had been made up, where the other penny had come from, and so on. Then she moved to a new problem, helping them to get to the point where they could discover for themselves and say, "You just take one of the _____ pennies and put it in with the nine and you have a dime and _____ pennies. That is _____ cents."

As the lesson drew to a close, the teacher used a set of problems like the following to check the children's progress:

$$\begin{array}{ccccccc} 9 & 9 & 9 & 9 & 9 & 9 & 9 \\ +7 & +4 & +6 & +2 & +9 & +3 & +5 \\ \hline \end{array}$$

The next day many children were able to tell orally how they would pay for articles that cost such amounts as 19¢ and 5¢; 29¢ and 4¢; and 39¢ and 6¢. Thus, they had begun to make for themselves an important generalization in addition. Essentially, this was "discovered" by the children themselves.

Fractions in a Fifth Grade

A fifth grade class had been doing some map work in conjunction with the Westward Movement study they were conducting. The teacher saw a way of utilizing a part of their map work to help pupils to discover a broad generalization that would help them to combine two unlike fractions, a learning task that was soon to be presented in the arithmetic program. She decided to focus the children's attention on a decision that had been made to increase the half-inch margin that they had been leaving around their maps by another quarter inch. This, they had decided, would give more space for information they wanted to include on their maps. Again, as she planned for this experience she knew certain things about her class: (1) they had already divided wholes and parts of wholes into different sized parts; (2) they had put like-sized parts together to make wholes and parts of wholes; (3) they were well acquainted with the meaning of fractions and the nomenclature of fractions. She had on hand, for the use of the children, many unlabeled cardboard fraction parts. These included halves, fourths, eighths, sixteenths, thirds, sixths, twelfths, fifths, tenths, and wholes. The teacher posed this question: "Do you think that you can show with these cardboard fraction parts, and on your papers with numbers, how wide you will make the new margin?" The pupils put half- and quarter-parts together on their desks, and wrote ½ + ¼ on their papers with the correct answer of ¾. The teacher agreed that this was the correct answer, but asked if they could show her why by using their fraction parts. Most of the pupils readily placed two fourths over the ½ and accounted for the three fourths that they had in their answers. The teacher then posed a problem that asked the pupils to add ½ and ⅛. They recorded the problem, placed the appropriate fraction part with each, but were not just sure how large the two fractions were when they were added together. The teacher called their attention to the problem just finished, the one in which they added ½ and ¼. The class noted that in that problem they had changed the ½ to fourths, the size of the smaller fraction.

The teacher asked if that didn't help them with this new problem. Pupils began covering the ½ part with parts ⅛ in size, and soon had the correct sum of ⅝. At this point the teacher showed the class the customary way of writing the numbers in a problem like this:

$$\begin{aligned} \tfrac{1}{2} &= \tfrac{4}{8} \\ +\tfrac{1}{8} &= \tfrac{1}{8} \\ \hline &\ \ \tfrac{5}{8} \end{aligned}$$

Next, the class was given a number of similar problems to compute, such as ⅛ plus ⅟₁₆ ; ⅓ plus ⅙ ; ⅓ plus ⅟₁₂ ; and so on. The teacher kept a close eye on the manipulations of the pupils, and when she felt that the majority had grasped the idea she suggested that as many as possible omit the step of using the cardboard fraction parts themselves and instead to try to make the manipulation "in their heads." As answers were computed, the teacher asked them to tell how they might have solved the problems if they had employed the learning aids.

As the lesson drew to a close the teacher helped the class see that whenever a problem contained unlike fractions, and the larger fraction could be changed into parts the size of the smaller fraction, they could make this change and then simply count (or add) all of the parts.

These are two descriptions of teachers and classes at work "discovering" arithmetic principles. Obviously, this approach to arithmetic learning calls for a resourceful, skillful teacher. The results obtained are gratifying to learner and teacher alike.

Readiness Applied to Arithmetic

Over the years a more valid concept of readiness as applied to work with arithmetic has developed. The application of this dynamic concept to arithmetic has been done with respect to both the general advisability of attempting to teach arithmetic to young children and the concern for teaching particular children certain arithmetic at various points along the way in the elementary school.[23] Increased insight into the phenomenon of readiness has rather well destroyed the notion of searching for a point in time on one side of which a child is not ready for arithmetic instruction and on the other side of which he is. Rather, elementary school educators are more likely to speak in terms of children being "more ready" or "less ready" for arithmetic. They will quickly become

---

[23] William A. Brownell, *The Development of Children's Number Ideas in the Primary Grades*, Supplementary Educational Monographs No. 35 (Chicago: University of Chicago Press, 1928); —————, "Readiness and the Arithmetic Curriculum," *Elementary School Journal*, 38:344–354, January 1938.

specific about the arithmetic they have in mind, too, since readiness is to be seen in relation to particular arithmetic to be learned, not to arithmetic in general.

The present understanding of readiness has carried the elementary school past the question of whether there should be arithmetic instruction in the first years of the elementary school. It is generally agreed now that it is a great mistake not to provide arithmetic instruction from the very first contacts the child has with the school. But, the nature of the arithmetic experience provided in these early years has changed a great deal on the basis of evidence presented by such people as Brownell. It is accepted that the instruction must be systematic, in the sense that it is not haphazard and unorganized, and it is accepted that it must be "formal" in the sense that it must not be left to chance. But, beyond these considerations, arithmetic instruction differs a great deal from that of former years.

While it is clear that the teacher must plan for learning activities in arithmetic from the very beginning of the child's schooling, it is equally clear that these learning activities must be within the experience, the interest, the general mental maturity and the more specific "arithmetic" maturity of the children involved. We know that some children will come to the school with a much greater number background and therefore a greater readiness for arithmetic than will others, and this difference will be reflected in the way arithmetic experiences are differentiated for children.

A great deal of the number work can be and is derived from the daily activities of the children and the quantitative situations that develop therein. Pupils are counted, chairs are counted, charts are numbered, and so on. The teacher exploits these situations directly, "picking up the experience," so to speak. She works with forthrightness to help children develop an awareness of numbers, basic number meanings, quantitative vocabulary, positive attitude toward numbers, and sufficient skill with numbers to have confidence in meeting quantitative situations. The experiences in arithmetic are planned for, the teacher anticipates accomplishing certain arithmetic learnings, but the situations utilized are rooted in the environment close to the children and are as concrete and realistic as possible. The teacher, even at these beginning levels, employs procedures that make a place for discovery, generalization, and frequent application of numbers, while holding work with abstract symbols and drill to a reasonable minimum. The teacher tells and shows only when absolutely necessary.

The same basic ideas about readiness are kept in mind as each bit of progress is made in arithmetic, and as each new step in the total curriculum is anticipated. This concept is applicable not only to kindergarten or first grade; it has great relevance to the work of each year

in the elementary school. It is as important for the teacher of the fifth grade to assess the readiness of his class group to meet and deal with a new learning as it is for the teacher of the second grade to do the same under similar circumstances.

Providing for Understanding

In this chapter the idea of understood, or meaningful, arithmetic has been mentioned several times. Arithmetic understanding is a clearly established aim of the curriculum. The total arithmetic program moves toward this goal, and the work of each individual teacher contributes to it. Again, we have developed insights into number learning that guide our instructional efforts effectively in reaching this goal.

An awareness of place value. An example of the way in which the elementary school educator can utilize the over-all form and structure of the number system as an aid to reaching arithmetic understanding is found in helping children to cope with place value. Increasingly, the importance of knowing place value has been grasped by elementary educators. The child who understands that our number system is a positional or place value system is on his way to an understanding of many important arithmetic concepts and operations. Realizing that our number system is based on tens, that the value of each digit in a multidigit number is ten times that of the digit to its right, or one-tenth that of the digit to its left, unlocks many meanings in general. Obviously, it gives meaning to multidigit numbers. It leads to the understanding that 10 of one order may be exchanged for 1 of the next higher order; or inversely that 1 of any order may be exchanged for 10 of the next lower order. The relationship of such understanding to carrying in addition or in multiplication and to re-grouping in subtraction is clear. An extension of place value understanding to the right of one's place provides the key to understanding decimals. The concept of zero as a "place holder" adds significance to its use and clarifies many number situations. The use of the place value concept has made a great contribution to understood arithmetic.

A rationale for the fundamental processes. The approach to the four fundamental processes that recognizes their relationship to counting and the fact that they are fundamentally processes of regrouping is another evidence of improved approaches to understood arithmetic. Children have grasped an important insight into these processes when they realize that any problem that can be solved by adding, subtracting, multiplying, or dividing can also be solved by counting. Opportunities to solve particular problems by the appropriate fundamental process and by the process of counting can do much to sensitize children to the

efficiency and the economy of the four fundamental processes in arithmetic work.

Similarly, the teacher who helps children to see these fundamental operations as processes of regrouping is contributing to their understanding of arithmetic. Children who see addition as the process of "putting together" and subtraction as the opposite process of "taking apart," and who sense that multiplication is simply a more efficient approach to "putting together" and division a more efficient approach to "taking apart" in many number situations are on their way toward meaningful arithmetic. Such approaches to learning help the child to combine an understanding of these processes per se with an awareness of their basic efficiency as arithmetic procedures.

Stages in Concept Development

The way in which concepts in arithmetic develop is more clearly understood now than before, and has led to certain definite provisions in the instruction provided for children. The abstractness of arithmetic concepts and the symbolic nature of the number system are now seen in truer perspective as they relate to the learning tasks of pupils. Curriculum specialists now speak of three levels or stages in the development of arithmetic concepts. These are (1) the presymbolic stage, (2) the modified or semisymbolic stage, and (3) the abstract stage. Recognition of these stages has had a great deal to do with determining a number of important innovations in arithmetic teaching in recent years.

Using daily experiences. The already mentioned concern to root early arithmetic experiences in situations close to the child is related to the recognition of the presymbolic stage in concept development in arithmetic. This is the stage at which teachers and pupils deal with specific things, with concrete materials and objects, and with daily quantitative situations. The children may help count the straws needed for milk, help distribute the proper number of books for their reading group, or assist the teacher in determining the daily attendance. Such involvement contributes to a general awareness of number in daily living as well as to arithmetic skill itself.

Using manipulative materials. The use of counters, discs, and tallies is directly related to the stage of modified symbolism noted above.[24] Children are helped to depict and to reconstruct quantitative situations by the use of these manipulative materials. They are no longer dealing with the actual objects themselves; they are using something to represent

---

24 Foster E. Grossnickle, "The Use of Multi-Sensory Aids in Developing Arithmetical Meanings," *Arithmetic,* Supplementary Educational Monographs No. 66 (Chicago: University of Chicago Press, 1948), pp. 1–14.

these objects. However, they use representative materials that are not as abstract as the number symbol itself. They use materials that can be handled, grouped, regrouped and so on.

Using symbolization. Finally, efforts are made to move children to an awareness and use of the abstract symbols of the number system itself. Five counters become *5;* three tallies become *3*. It is clearly recognized that understanding and skill at this abstract level is most necessary and desirable. It is also recognized that it takes time to arrive at this stage of development, with different children reaching this level at different times. And, it is accepted that some children will be capable of much better thinking and working in the abstract than will others. However, the awareness and use of abstract number symbols in dealing with quantitative situations is a goal that the school helps each child to realize within the limits of his potential.

From this sort of insight into concept development comes a sequence of experience in arithmetic learning, especially with young children, that starts with the real and the concrete, moves to a form of modified reality, and culminates in work with abstract number symbols. Depending on the specific situation this sequence may be utilized in one period of instruction or over several days of instruction. For purposes of "proof" and testing for adequacy in learning, this sequence may be traveled in reverse, with children proving with counters what they have done with symbols.

Teaching for Discovery in Arithmetic

Closely related to concept development is the present-day commitment to the necessary role of *discovery*, if children are to learn arithmetic meaningfully.[25] That is, children must have an opportunity to discover facts and principles of the number system for themselves. To some this course of action appears to be unwise. They would still replace time and attention to discovery with repetition and rote learning. But, the great majority of elementary educators realize that this seemingly efficient way actually holds false promise only; therefore they are committed to an approach to teaching and learning that embraces the role of discovery. Swenson wrote as follows in a recent statement on arithmetic in the primary grades:

> Enough research studies have been done on the comparative results of different methods of arithmetic instruction in the primary grades

---

[25] T. R. McConnell, *Discovery Versus Authoritative Identification in the Learning of Children,* University of Iowa Studies in Education, Vol. IX, No. 5, September 15, 1934.

to support the statement that methods which lead the children themselves to discover relationships and note generalizations yield superior learning results.[26]

And, in a similar vein, Thiele worked from the following assumption, among others, in a statement in the same publication with respect to arithmetic in the middle grades:

> Psychologically, teachers cannot give children meanings. They must be discovered by children themselves. Teachers can do no more than guide, stimulate, create situations, bring about conditions, and generally speaking, help children gain meaning.[27]

Now, there is one possible misconception about this matter that should be cleared up at the outset, concerning the role of the teacher, which suggests that the discovery approach assigns the teacher to a passive, apathetic role. The quotation from Thiele suggests the error in such a conclusion. Certainly the teacher wants the children to discover facts and principles for themselves, but he actively participates in the process, and the children's success is in great part related to the teacher's skill. He does hold his telling and his explaining to a minimum, and he illustrates and demonstrates sparingly. However, the teacher does try continuously to *lead* pupils to discovery. This he does for the most part by proper selection of problem situations and by careful and insightful questioning during the arithmetic experience that follows. He draws the discovery out of the children, moving from the known to the unknown. He provides, also, a wide range of materials for children to use which are well suited to exploration in quantitative situations. That is, he will have counters, abacus, flannel board, measuring instruments, and the like readily available in the environment so that children may meet the problem situation at the level of abstraction at which they are ready to work. It is known that the ability to discover in arithmetic differs widely among children, and the teacher reflects this difference in the manipulative materials used.

Also, the teacher knows that children cannot discover everything for themselves about an arithmetic process or principle. For instance, children cannot discover the standard algorism, or way of recording a given type of problem, without direct help from the teacher. Similarly, much of the vocabulary of arithmetic will have to be supplied to students as they move along. There is a large area for active participation by the teacher, then, in the discovery approach to arithmetic learning. The classroom situations described earlier in this chapter shows this clearly.

---

[26] National Society for the Study of Education, *op. cit.*, p. 74.
[27] *Ibid.*, p. 80.

Drill and Practice in Arithmetic

There has been some confusion as to whether the newer approaches to learning in arithmetic found it necessary to make a place for drill and repetitive practice. This sort of activity is still most essential in the arithmetic curriculum, but considerable change has come about in providing for it. The fact that some educators are reluctant to discuss the question of drill experiences is indicative of their negative reaction to the time when the whole arithmetic program was built on a drill theory of learning. In that earlier period drill and rote memorization were the very heart of the curriculum. As mentioned before, the predominant psychology of the time, namely association psychology, with its connectionist theory, described learning in terms of S-R bond development. Many connections needed to be developed between given stimuli and appropriate responses if the mind was to develop its arithmetic power and potential. Drill on arithmetic facts and processes was deemed the most appropriate methodology for this development. Thus, instruction started and ended with drill experiences.

Repetitive practice. When association psychology was questioned, persons interested in arithmetic began to provide information on drill, perhaps better referred to as repetitive practice. This information began to throw some real light on the contribution of such experiences to arithmetic learning. It is now known that drill can come too soon, can be pursued too vigorously, and may work as an obstacle to the very things it is supposed to achieve unless it is carefully considered.[28]

It is equally well known that repetitive practice is a necessary aspect of the total curriculum in arithmetic. While we want to achieve learning in arithmetic that embodies understanding and meaning, we want, too, the ability for immediate and automatic recall. Children need to be able to see and respond at once with a sum, or a difference, if they are to be as proficient with arithmetic facts and processes as many situations will demand. Thus, the challenge is to provide the proper amount of repetitive practice and provide it at the proper time to insure such learning. Attention should be directed to a number of things that help to make this decision.[29]

First of all, repetitive practice must follow the development of understanding of a given arithmetic fact or computational process. It must come after discovery. The beginning of such meaningful practice may follow very closely the discovery act itself, serving as a check on the in-

---

[28] W. A. Brownell and C. B. Chazal, ''The Effects of Premature Drill in Third Grade Arithmetic,'' *Journal of Educational Research*, 29:17–28, September 1935.

[29] B. R. Buckingham, ''What Becomes of Drill?'', National Council of Mathematics Teachers, *op. cit.*, pp. 196–224.

sight developed by the children as well as providing some immediate practice with the type of example involved. The second and fifth grade teaching situations described earlier both terminated in simple practice situations. But, these were short practice situations, providing for repetition and extending understanding of the lesson. Varied drill situations were continued in the days and weeks that followed.

Practice should always, of course, be geared to the level of understanding evident in the pupils. Drill can increase the speed and accuracy of recall, but it cannot furnish a better or more efficient way of doing a given thing. Formal drill is of little value until meaning has been well established; then the provision of opportunities for practice is quite necessary to move the handling of computational processes to the level of automatic response.

Mastery and drill in arithmetic. The matter of mastery, as a goal in a skill area, is always a source of concern to the elementary educator. While the term is easy to use, it is difficult to define, especially in operational terms. That is, it is difficult to say when a student has or has not achieved mastery of an arithmetic process or procedure. Some would relate mastery to the scores made on practice or drill lessons. This enables one to speak of "100% mastery," citing as evidence a perfect score in such a lesson. If drill is to come after understanding, as has been suggested here, there is something to think about in this proposition. It would thus follow that less than perfect scores are accepted as less than complete understanding, and therefore less than mastery. However, this simple sort of logic is quickly clouded by some other considerations. Perhaps the practice lesson was not designed in such a way as to make a perfect score a reasonable expectation. The lesson may have been too long, introducing elements of boredom and fatigue; or the time allotted for completion may have been too short, introducing elements of tension and strain. Thus, the definition of mastery is pushed back to some subjective judgment as to the number of examples children at various ages should be expected to complete correctly in a given period of time. Too, if the practice load is to be reduced, the most useful examples should be retained and the less useful eliminated. Some criteria for usefulness must then be employed, and these criteria generally focus on "usefulness in life." Thus, the practice load takes on certain characteristics that limit the development of mastery only to those computational situations most likely to be met in living.

One other factor must be considered: the individual learner himself. He may well be establishing his own definition of mastery in terms of either (1) the degree to which the skill he has developed enables him to meet successfully whatever quantitative situations he encounters in the natural course of events, or (2) the relationship that he identifies be-

tween the level of skill he has reached and the level of skill of those around him. Either of these definitions, separately or in combination, can lead a given child to the conclusion, often mistaken, that he has or has not achieved mastery in arithmetic.

Thus, an acceptable definition of mastery must of necessity be somewhat complex. It seems profitable to conceive of mastery in arithmetic as being that level of control and response reached by students that enables them to meet quantitative situations with security and accuracy, within whatever time limit particular situations typically demand.

Problem Solving in the Arithmetic Curriculum

In a very real sense, all that has been discussed thus far in this chapter suggests that the total approach to arithmetic is one of problem solving. Note again the way in which the arithmetic scope chart on page 280 in this chapter for the Palo Alto, California, schools sets the whole program in a problem solving context. However, let us focus directly on the matter and call attention to some of the things that the curriculum developer must keep in mind about problem solving proficiency—the ability to meet and solve quantitative problems in typical situations of use.

Problem solving and child experience. To an adult, problem solving is a fairly logical and systematic procedure; but the evidence on children's problem solving in arithmetic seems to contradict this assumption. Often, the child's attack on a problem seems to be a rather random one, especially if the situation is simply a "thought problem" composed for "thought" purposes. Children do not reason in such situations, typically, in the way that we would perhaps hope that they would. They do better on problems that are set in familiar situations, expressed in familiar terminology. Such problems evoke a more mature reasoning process from the children, and more of them are met and solved successfully. This evidence has led to two significant developments in the selection of problems to be included in the arithmetic program.

First, there is an increased tendency to rely on problem situations that grow out of the child's experience at school, or situations that he meets outside the school. Such an approach to problem selection helps to keep the situation within the child's experience, thus helping him to visualize the quantitative problem to be met. The teacher may call attention to arithmetic problems that occur in the classroom from time to time, especially in the early grades. Later both teacher and pupils may collect problems from the environment that will have meaning for the group. Thus, it is hoped that the setting will be kept close to the children, and that the problems will carry personal and social significance for them. Second, writers of textbooks in arithmetic are doing their best to

improve the quality of the word problems included for solution. They attempt to describe problem situations that will be within and related to the experience of the majority of children. They try to compose problem situations that can be readily visualized by children, knowing that such visualizing is the best substitute for actual experience.

Procedures for problem solving. Since the children do tend to attack arithmetic problems in a somewhat random manner, they need help in the development of more systematic procedures for problem solving. Thus, the methodology in arithmetic calls for direct attention to procedures. Much effort is directed to helping children see the relationship between the question or questions to be answered and the known facts in the problem situation, to helping them to develop ways of interpreting problem situations, ways of visualizing the arithmetic that must be done. Such efforts usually include a number of sequential steps:

1. Reading the description
2. Recognizing the problem situation
3. Identifying the facts; noting relationships involved
4. Determining the process or processes to be used
5. Estimating the answer
6. Performing the computation
7. Checking the answer for reasonableness and accuracy

The results that accrue from direct attention to problem solving show gains for the learners. While they may not use the step-by-step procedure provided as a model, they do develop a somewhat more systematic approach to problem solving that they can use. The evidence indicates that the school is better off to utilize fewer problems, focusing carefully on interpretation, meaning, and procedure in problem solving, than it is to try to cover a problem load that is heavy and causes the teacher to pass lightly over the important aspect of problem solving.

There is also a growing tendency to spend time in class with mental problem solving experiences. These problems are solved without the use of paper and pencil. The situation is discussed, important elements in the situation are noted, and the computation called for is handled "in the head." Evidence indicates that mental problem solving is a very profitable use of time. So many of the quantitative situations met in living must be solved in this way. This problem solving skill must be developed in the arithmetic curriculum.

Problem solving and reading skill. Authorities also suggest that certain special reading skills are involved in the solution of descriptive, situational problems. The over-all reading skill of a child, the extent to which his arithmetic vocabulary has been developed, and the ease with

which he can read and interpret the style of expression used in word problems are related to problem solving ability. These skills must be considered as curricula are developed and as teachers work with classes. Reading instruction can, at times, utilize arithmetic content, and the teacher can become sensitive to the fact that she is extending a child's over-all facility with reading when she spends time helping him to "read" situational problems in arithmetic.

Sensitivity to Individual Differences

Throughout this chapter recognition has been given to the matter of individual differences among pupils as related to concept development, to readiness, and to mastery. Here at the end of the discussion this matter of individual differences is singled out for special consideration in order to call attention to its importance. We may set general expectancies and goals for accomplishment for the arithmetic curriculum that become real goals in relation to pupil capacity. Statements of purpose provide a sort of "arithmetic norm," or a picture of the condition as it "ought to" exist. Schools and teachers must approach these objectives in and through the human material with which they are working. Many of the improvements discussed in this chapter are directly attributable to the understanding of concept formation, to the application of the readiness idea to arithmetic, and to other such concerns stemming in great part from information on individual differences.

One thing that is increasingly understood by elementary educators is the important role a child's feelings play in his efforts to learn. This is no less true in arithmetic than in any other learning task. The role of the emotions, the attitudes, the likes and the dislikes that children develop must be dealt with in curriculum planning and must be of concern to the teacher as she works with her class. It seems clear that if children are going to form positive feelings toward arithmetic they must experience a good deal more success than failure with it. Goals that they are asked to achieve must, in the main, be attainable goals. They must be successful participants in the arithmetic learning enterprise in their classroom, or they may begin to "close the door" on arithmetic and mathematics at a very early age. Therefore the arithmetic program must adjust itself to differences in achievement, and the teacher must accept differences in arithmetic learning in her class group. The psychology of individual differences has amply demonstrated the fact that all children do not possess the same ability and potential for learning arithmetic. Some children, no matter how hard they may try or how much they may want to learn, will be limited in their achievement. Goals for them must be set with this in mind. On the other hand, attainable goals for certain bright

children will go way beyond those that are reasonable even for the majority of the group.

The problem posed is that of providing procedurally for these individual differences in the instructional program. The two most frequently utilized approaches to this problem are (1) the division of a classroom group into two or more subgroups for arithmetic instruction, or (2) the provision for different levels of learning and thinking as any given concept is dealt with. The two are not mutually exclusive arrangements, obviously. Each has some of the characteristics of the other.

In the first scheme, the teacher makes rather definite subgroups within her class, reducing the range of ability and achievement in each to the point that she is able to manage the learning enterprise more efficiently. All groups may be dealing with the same arithmetic content, or each group may have a different assignment. If the first plan is followed, the teacher is more likely to have concluded that "complete learning" will simply take more time for some than for others, but that all can gain some skill and insight into any given arithmetic learning task. If the latter plan is followed, she is more likely to have decided that certain children will simply have to "stay with" some learning jobs for an extended period of time, for to attempt to move on in the program without rather "complete learning" at any given point is not wise.

In the second scheme, that of organizing for differentiated levels of learning within the class, it is accepted that for the most part the whole class can and should deal with the same arithmetic content at the same time. However, it is clearly recognized that some students will deal with certain of the assigned learning tasks at an immature level, perhaps a manipulative level at best. Others may be ready to move to a semisymbolic experience with the subject matter; and still others will move quickly to the most abstract level of work and will be dealing with the conventional algorisms with skill and understanding. At times, for purposes of efficiency, the teacher may bring together certain pupils as a group to help them at whatever level of learning they are working, by using a modified and temporary scheme of classroom subgroups. However, the groups are more flexible and are less permanent than in the other scheme. This "levels of learning" approach to the problem of individual differences is growing in acceptance. It calls for a resourceful and sensitive teacher at any given grade level, and for a well-conceived over-all arithmetic curriculum that has been thought through by the entire faculty. Teachers must understand the whole of the program as well as their particular part.

Efforts such as those described here, skillfully handled, can do much to insure that children form a positive attitude toward arithmetic and mathematics. Realizing that learning tasks that appear extremely simple

to adults do not appear the same way to all children, and providing curricular experiences accordingly, makes good sense. Adjusting arithmetic instruction to the individuals partaking of it helps to insure that all children are challenged by the learning provided.

The Future of Elementary School Arithmetic

In closing, it should be noted that there is a great deal of study and activity going on at the present time in the field of mathematics and arithmetic. As mentioned earlier, our developing civilization demands more in the way of mathematical understanding and skill than ever before. Experts in mathematics and education are developing new approaches to the more advanced levels of the field. Special projects, aimed at fundamentally revising the content and method of secondary school and college mathematics, have been and continue to be carried out in some of our major universities. Just what the impact of this activity will be on the elementary school curriculum is difficult to say at the present time. It does seem inevitable that these developments will operate as a force to alter the arithmetic program in the elementary school ultimately in some ways. Some experimental efforts are underway in elementary school classrooms. Such proposals for change must be weighed thoughtfully and carefully in the light of the sort of evidence and experience that has been cited in this chapter. Steps taken must be consistent with the best that we know about helping children to understand and to use the number system. On the whole, these experimental efforts are exciting and provocative and hold the promise of even greater improvements in the teaching of arithmetic.

REFERENCES

Boehm, George A. *The New World of Math.* New York: The Dial Press, 1959. This paperback book can help the teacher to know something about modern mathematics and to anticipate to some extent the probable future direction of elementary arithmetic.

Brueckner, Leo J. *Improving the Arithmetic Program.* New York: Appleton-Century-Crofts, Inc., 1957.
    A monograph containing many helpful and tested procedures applicable to sound arithmetic teaching.

Clark, John, and Laura Eads. *Guiding Arithmetic Learnings.* Yonkers-on-Hudson: World Book Company, 1954.
    A very meaningful statement on the newer approaches to curriculum planning for arithmetic.

Grossnickle, Foster E., and Leo J. Brueckner. *Discovering Meanings in Arithmetic.* Philadelphia: The John C. Winston Company, 1959.
    A comprehensive statement on the place of arithmetic in the ele-

mentary school, with procedures for developing understanding and skill with the number system.

Hollister, George E., and Agnes G. Gunderson. *Teaching Arithmetic in Grades 1 and 2.* Boston: D. C. Heath and Company, 1956.

A statement aimed at helping the reader to understand the teaching of arithmetic in the early grades.

Hunnicutt, Clarence W., and William J. Iverson (editors). *Research in the Three R's.* New York: Harper & Brothers, 1958.

In Chapters 12, 13, and 14 are reviewed almost all of the significant research studies in the area of arithmetic, with the conclusions pointed up for the use of the classroom teacher.

McSwain, Eldridge T., and Ralph J. Cooke. *Understanding and Teaching Arithmetic in the Elementary School.* New York: Henry Holt and Company, 1958.

This methods textbook for elementary teachers puts the meaningful teaching of arithmetic central in its point of view.

Spitzer, Herbert F. *The Teaching of Arithmetic* (Second edition). New York: Houghton Mifflin Company, 1957.

A very useful edition of an informative book.

——————. *Practical Classroom Procedures for Enriching Arithmetic.* St. Louis, Missouri: Webster Publishing Company, 1956.

The teacher will find a wealth of ideas for new and improved teaching devices in arithmetic in this volume.

13

EXPLORING THE SOCIAL ENVIRONMENT: THE SOCIAL STUDIES

To elementary school educators, and to most of the public, the knowledge and understandings, the values and attitudes, and the skills and abilities sought through the learning experiences that focus on the social environment demand a top priority in the elementary school curriculum. Similarly, studies of children's interests and questions indicate that children are concerned about the origins of early man, the development of nations and governments, the causes and effects of war, the search for peace and other social matters.[1] To study the social environment is to study man in all of his manifest interactions with other men, with the natural environment in which he lives, and even with himself. It is in this network of human relationships that man's personal and social needs must find satisfaction.

Thus, study of the social environment includes attention (a) to the ways that men have devised for living and working together, (b) to the extent to which men have found ways of utilizing the natural environment to meet their needs, (c) to the ways in which man adapts to the natural environment when he can neither use nor control it, and (d) to the customs, institutions, and value systems developed by man as an aid in helping him to live the "good life." Society looks to the elementary school to help insure that each succeeding generation will be able to understand, value, and be competent in democratic ways, so that they

---

[1] Emily V. Baker, *Children's Questions and Their Implications for Planning the Curriculum* (New York: Bureau of Publications, Teachers College, Columbia University, 1945); Edythe E. Clark, *What Children Want To Know About Their World,* unpublished Master's thesis, Boston University, 1952; Herbert C. Rudman, "The Informational Needs and Reading Interests of Children in Grades Four Through Eight," *Elementary School Journal* 55:505–512, May 1955.

can realize ever more fully the good life for themselves in whatever social circumstances may arise. This social competence we often refer to under the general term *citizenship education* and it has been a central responsibility in public education for many years.

THE CHALLENGE OF OUR TIME

The elementary school has never faced a greater challenge than it does at the present time to contribute effectively to the development of this composite of social competence that we call democratic citizenship. A reconsideration of the material presented in the earlier chapter dealing with society, culture, and values as guides to curriculum planning will make this challenge very clear. Ours is a time that puts heavy demands on the citizen. The present calls for many momentous, courageous, and creative decisions; the future will call for no less.

The basic commitment of our society is, of course, to democracy as a way of life. It is within democracy that learnings in the social area find their greatest sense of direction. As a social, economic and political philosophy, democracy presents us with an ideological yardstick by which we can measure progress or lack of progress, need or lack of need, achievement or lack of achievement in almost all aspects of life. It provides direction for an examination of both national and international circumstances. It sketches out a "human behavior" profile toward which both individual and group development may be oriented.

Some characterize the present period as the "age of science"; no one can deny that the setting out of which many of society's most pressing problems emerge, and in which they must be solved, has been and will continue to be affected dramatically and fundamentally by science. In fact, there is a tendency to feel at times that a grasp of science in its fullest meaning will best prepare one to meet his obligation of citizenship. The importance of science in the modern world does not alter the fact that many of man's most urgent problems are social problems, demanding social awareness and sensitivity, and social "engineering" for solution. So important are these problems that many educators speak of the studies that deal with the social area as constituting the very heart or core of the elementary school curriculum.

Childhood is the time to begin to develop meaningful social concepts and generalizations, wholesome social attitudes and values, and efficient social skills and abilities. In fact, the consensus is that unless such learnings are started in childhood they are not likely to be accomplished with the depth and breadth of understanding and efficiency demanded by the emerging social scene. Neither is our population as likely to reflect basic

personality characteristics that are consistent with democracy if the period of childhood is overlooked.

PURPOSES OF THE SOCIAL STUDIES

The fact that school learning is goal-oriented learning has been discussed already. Thus, one would expect to find clearly stated lists of purposes published and disseminated within school systems to give direction to the work in the social studies. Many excellent statements from individual school systems could be included here, but perhaps the most efficiently stated summary of major purposes for the social studies is the one reported by Michaelis. Studying recent programs of social studies, he concludes that their major purposes are to help each child to:

1. Become a democratic person whose behavior is guided by democratic values, who is loyal to the American way of life, and who appreciates the sacrifices and contributions made to promote democratic living here and throughout the world.
2. Develop modes of behavior consistent with democratic values, such as responsibility, concern for others, open-mindedness, creativeness, and cooperation, and to use them in relationships with others.
3. Develop group-action skills and social competency in inter-group relations, recognizing the value of group decision making, showing respect for differences of opinion, and exhibiting high regard for rights of minorities yet abiding by majority decisions.
4. Develop the ability to think critically and creatively and use problem solving skills in situations involving human relationships; use dependable sources of information; locate, evaluate, select, organize, and present information effectively; and base action on sound conclusions.
5. Appreciate and respect other persons, cultural similarities and differences among peoples, and the contributions of others to our ways of living, realizing that human dignity and personality are of first importance in human relationships regardless of race, color, or class.
6. Acquire and use functional information, concepts, and understandings of: basic social functions of human living such as production of goods and services, transportation and communication, conservation of resources, aesthetic and religious expression, education, recreation, and government; the impact of scientific advance and education upon ways of living; the effect of moral and spiritual values upon human behavior; ways to improve family life, community living, and national-international welfare; and the increasing interdependence characteristic of modern living.
7. Become responsive to needs and problems of others and act courageously and with integrity to bring about changes consistent with democratic ideals and processes.[2]

---

[2] John U. Michaelis, *Social Studies for Children in a Democracy* (Second edition; Englewood Cliffs, New Jersey: Prentice-Hall, Inc., 1956), p. 12.

If these be accepted as the general objectives of the social studies program, the breadth of the task becomes readily apparent. They range over understandings, attitudes, values, and skills. Some are predominantly content goals, in that their achievement is related in great part to the quality of the subject matter with which children are brought into contact. Others are primarily process goals, and their achievement is related directly to the kind of learning experience provided for children, and to the role that children are allowed to play in the learning enterprise. But, it must be noted here, the breadth of purpose evident in Michaelis' summary has had even greater ramifications in educators' thought about the social studies.

CHANGING DEFINITIONS AND POINTS OF VIEW

The broad task the elementary school is asked to assume toward learnings in the social area, coupled with increased insight as to how these learnings take place, has led to some revisions in meaning of terms, to the use of some new terms, and to a generally more comprehensive point of view toward the social studies.

Typical Definition of the Social Studies

The most typical definitions suggest that the social studies are those portions of the social sciences selected for instructional purposes in the school, usually embracing subject matter from history, human geography, political science, economics, sociology, and anthropology.[3] As the goals toward which the social studies program is directed became more explicitly and clearly stated, and as it became evident that *process,* or the way of learning the social studies, needed to be seen as *content,* too, such additional meaning was added to the above definition.

The Broader Concept of Social Education

Further consideration of a definition of the social studies that accepted not only subject matter but also the way of learning that subject matter as appropriate social studies content led to the conclusion that there was still something to be desired. Considerable support developed, born of experience in elementary schools, for the idea that a real contribution could be made to promote these desired citizenship objectives if certain aspects of the general life of the school were consciously utilized. Thus, organized service projects in and around the school, such as a lost and

---

[3] E. B. Wesley, ''The Social Studies,'' *Encyclopedia of Educational Research,* W. S. Monroe, ed. (New York: The Macmillan Company, 1950), p. 1214.

found service or a school store, were seen as fertile activities for exploitation. Also, the operation of appropriate forms of classroom and schoolwide student government groups, the support of periodic social service drives such as the Junior Red Cross program, and participation in school playground and safety patrols were viewed in a new and more instructive light. The term *social education* has now come to be used for all school activities that contribute to and can be utilized for the accomplishment of the goals formerly associated only with the social studies program. As such, the term is broader than *social studies,* and is used by most educators in this broader sense.

The Broadest Concept: Social Learnings

Along with this tendency to think more comprehensively of the efforts of the elementary school to educate in the social sphere has come an ever-increasing stream of information and arguments addressed to the total social learnings task that the child faces in our culture. These writings have directed attention both to the great amount of social learning that has taken place before the child comes to school, and to the many persons and agencies, both in school and out, who continue to provide social learning experiences to children after they begin to attend school. Such information, coming from cultural anthropologists, sociologists, psychiatrists, psychologists, and pediatricians, as well as from professional educators, has been both provocative and confusing. Although elementary school educators have been attracted to this information, they have not always known how seriously to take it or just what to do about it. Nonetheless, insights from this material are slowly finding their way into the general stream of affairs concerning the social development of children and the efforts of the elementary school in the area of social education are resting on a broader, more inclusive base than ever before.[4]

In light of these developments, this chapter is organized with particular attention to the organized social studies program found in the elementary school, but with attention also to those efforts typically made to utilize other ongoing activities of the school for the accomplishment of the broad purposes of social education, and to the use of evidence concerning the more subtle aspects of social education that our maturing social sciences are uncovering. To an extent this sort of separation is artificial, but it is used for purposes of convenience in the discussion. Especially is this true with respect to the isolation of some of the more

---

[4] Edna Ambrose and Alice Miel, *Children's Social Learning: Implications of Research and Expert Study* (Washington, D.C.: Association for Supervision and Curriculum Development, 1958); Alice Miel and Peggy Brogan, *More Than Social Studies* (Englewood Cliffs, New Jersey: Prentice-Hall, Inc., 1957).

recent insights concerning personality development and child socialization referred to above. This newer literature on social learnings indicates that a good deal of "teaching" is taking place within the give-and-take of the organized social studies program and planned social education activities. It goes even further, of course, to call attention to the "social teaching" that is going on all day long at school within the setting of teacher-pupil, pupil-pupil, and even teacher-teacher relationships. This interrelatedness must be kept in mind as this chapter is read.

THE PLANNED SOCIAL STUDIES PROGRAM

An examination of the summary of purposes quoted above makes it very clear that there is a place and a need for a planned and systematic social studies program as the major strand in the school's total efforts toward social education. Let us turn our attention to the ways in which elementary schools organize for work in the social studies.

The various organizational plans that have been put forth have all had to develop defensible rationales to answer the whole range of curriculum questions posed in Chapter 7, which dealt with general patterns of organization for the elementary school curriculum. Such matters as the most appropriate organizing centers for instruction, the proper grade placement of subject matter, a valid plan for determining the sequence of learnings, a commitment to certain methodological principles have all been considered. Undoubtedly in the area of the social studies more than in any other curriculum area have all of the general points of view toward curriculum planning been tried in an attempt to find an improved way for the social studies to contribute to citizenship education. To some extent all of these general patterns are still evident in today's elementary schools, although certain general tendencies do predominate in both theory and practice.

Two General Approaches to
Planning the Social Studies

In general there have been two different approaches used in planning for the social studies, utilizing two different points of departure. One of these approaches takes the subject matter of the various social studies as the principal point of departure for planning the program. The other focuses on the social problems met by man in society and tries to develop a social studies program that would be in harmony with man's continuing efforts to meet and solve social problems effectively. The first approach has been more sympathetic to and influenced by the various tenets of the separate subject and broad fields points of view toward cur-

riculum planning, while the latter approach has found the activity and the core points of view more attractive.

Planning from Subjects

The earliest programs in the social studies were developed around the separate social subjects themselves. History, geography, and civics found their way into the curriculum about the time of the American Revolution and continued to be taught separately well into the twentieth century. During this early period the social studies program reflected rather completely the characteristics of the separate subject curriculum pattern. The program was committed almost exclusively to informational purposes in these early years, with the evident belief that good citizenship stemmed in the main from knowledge of history, geography, and the organization of government.

Modifications toward a broad field plan. Since about 1920 those who are still committed to a subject matter point of departure for developing the social studies program have modified their planning in the direction of the broad field point of view. One reason for this change is that it became ever more apparent that content from fields such as economics and sociology had to be dealt with in the social studies program, and there was a limit on the number of separate subjects that could be introduced into the curriculum. Too, there was a growing acceptance of the fact that the relatedness among the various social studies should be made more evident to pupils, and that by developing a social studies broad field this relatedness was more likely to be dealt with in the classroom. Awareness of this relatedness has led, in those schools following such a plan, to the assignment of one larger block of time each day to the social studies; teachers are urged to use subject matter from all of the social studies in carrying out the instructional task. The label *subject matter units of work* in the social studies is a reflection of this broad field development. To a considerable extent this way of organizing the social studies program is still used in the elementary school curriculum, and its influence is obvious in almost all planned programs.

Planning from Problems

The greatest challenges to the idea of planning the social studies program directly from the social subjects have come from the activity and integrative-core points of view in curriculum planning. Both of these positions have sought a more challenging and more dynamic approach to the social studies, a kind of program that would relate more intimately to school and life around the school. Both are committed to the use of organized subject matter as a resource for learning and for solving prob-

lems, and both are committed to problem solving processes as a basis for the teacher's methodology. Finally, both have said that the social studies program is best planned around social problems of importance, but in the implementation of this planning the two points of view differ quite markedly.

Problems in the activity curriculum. Those educators following the activity curriculum base for planning the social studies program are committed to select problems for study that are consistent with the expressed interests and concerns of children. These become the organizing centers for the social studies program; such interests and concerns are seen as emerging over the school year as children continue to live in and to probe their culture. Thus, there is very little predetermination in this approach to the social studies. Problems and questions keep coming to the fore in the classroom during the school year; they are discussed, criticized, and selections for study are made. The planning of the program emerges over the school year. The general impact of this point of view was greatest from about 1920 until the early 1930's, and it still influences practice in some very obvious ways.

The predominance of integrative-core ideas. Most of the criticisms of the activity curriculum noted earlier generally have been directed against its use as the base for planning the social studies program. While accepting problem solving as a basis for method, and while supporting the idea of using something other than subjects as the initial point of departure in planning the social studies program, the majority of elementary school educators have not supported the use of children's interests and concerns to the extent that the activity point of view calls for, and they have not accepted the idea of the emergent curriculum. There is some indication that many have felt that process goals are likely to be given undue emphasis at the expense of content goals in the social studies unless the activity point of view is tempered.

This feeling has resulted in a turning away from children's interests as organizing centers for the social studies, to an acceptance of the anthropologically identified list of basic human activities as being uniquely fitting for use in the social studies. (See Chapter 7.) The use of these basic human activities as the scope of the social studies has seemed to insure that the program will have the necessary breadth of study. Furthermore, it is held that life is lived actually by means of these activities, that social problems and questions take form in terms of these activities, and that their use in curriculum planning should result in a closeness between study in school and life outside of school.

An examination of city, county, and state curriculum guides in the social studies attests to the acceptance and usefulness of this scheme as a curriculum tool. For example, the scope of the present elementary

school social studies program in San Francisco, California, uses the
following list of basic social activities as the centers around which
the work is planned:

Protecting Life and Health	Understanding the Role of Education
Conserving and Utilizing Resources	Providing for Aesthetic Expression
Understanding the Relationship between the Individual and Government	Providing for Religious Expression[5]

In Missouri, the curriculum guide for elementary education utilized
the following statement of social functions in establishing the scope of
the social studies–science program:

> Protecting life and health. Conserving and utilizing the physical
> environment. Understanding the relationships among people. Under-
> standing the role of growth in education. Cultivating and nurturing
> moral and spiritual growth. Stimulating aesthetic interest and ex-
> pression.[6]

The question of curricular sequence in the social studies has come to
be answered in different terms, too. The earlier subject-structured
programs had found their response to sequence within the subjects themselves. The activity program found its answer to sequence in the continuous teacher-pupil planning procedures that were basic to an emerging
sequence of classroom experiences. Influenced heavily by core thinking,
a way of handling the sequence matter has developed that, it is felt,
can be defended on both psychological and sociological grounds. This set
of ideas has come to be referred to as the *expanding environment* plan.
Following this plan, children first study the very immediate in time
and place, and gradually move out into places more removed in distance
and more remote in time. Such a program typically focuses on the family
and the school in the kindergarten and first grade, moves into the neighborhood, the local community, and the extended local community in the
second and third grades, on to the state and the nation in the next two
grades, and finally to the world for the work of grade six.

Such a sequence is defended as being sound psychologically because the
child focuses first on what he knows and experiences in his day-to-day
living, a setting out of which he is more likely to develop accurate beginning awareness and understandings of the operations of the basic human

---

[5] Teaching Guide, *Social Studies, Kindergarten Through Grade Six*, Curriculum
Bulletin No. 300, San Francisco Public Schools, pp. 26–30.

[6] *Missouri's Elementary Curriculum Guide, Grades One–Six*, Publication No. 100
(Jefferson City, Missouri: State Board of Education, 1955), p. 48.

activities in his own life. The more vicarious learning experiences are reserved for the later grades, when children have more chance of handling these learnings successfully on the basis of increased personal development, wider experiences, and a background in careful study of the local situation.

Hanna refines this idea even more and argues the sequence question additionally on the basis of a concept of "communities of men."[7] He calls attention to the many "communities" in which we must all exercise successful citizenship roles in today's world. These run the full gamut from home and family, through school, neighborhood, and local community, to state, regions of states, nation, hemispheres, and on to the world scene itself. He sees in this ever-expanding arena for community participation and citizenship a very persuasive argument for a solution to the problem of sequence in the social studies. This is in great part a sociological analysis that takes its place alongside the psychological rationale mentioned above.

This expanding environment plan for sequence in the social studies has been accepted rather wholeheartedly by elementary school systems. Almost every social studies curriculum today utilizes this principle to a great degree. Hodgson reported on a survey of city school systems in which an "overwhelming preference" for this approach to sequence was found.[8] Fraser, writing recently in a yearbook devoted to social studies in the elementary school, comments that "Every recent curriculum bulletin or guide for elementary-school social studies examined by the present writer utilizes to some extent this plan (of expanding environments) for establishing sequence. . . ."[9]

A Resulting Framework for the Social Studies

On the basis of these accepted ideas, the tendency now is for the elementary school to plan an over-all framework to serve as a guiding structure in the social studies program. Most typically its scope is determined by some use of the lists of basic human activities; its sequence is determined by the expanding environments or communities of men ideas. These two dimensions come together at each grade level in a way that focuses the work of that year accordingly. Typically, teachers are also

---

[7] Paul R. Hanna, "Society—Child—Curriculum," in *Education 2000 A.D.*, Clarence W. Hunnicutt, ed. (Syracuse, New York: Syracuse University Press, 1956).

[8] Frank M. Hodgson, "Organization and Content of the Social Studies Curriculum," Unpublished doctoral dissertation, University of Southern California, 1953, p. 169.

[9] Dorothy M. Fraser, "The Organization of the Elementary School Social Studies Curriculum," in *Social Studies in the Elementary School, Fifty-sixth Yearbook*, Part II (Washington, D.C.: National Society for the Study of Education, 1957).

given lists of suggested problems for exploration and study during the year that are appropriate in terms of this over-all framework.

Preston reports the following as the commonest subject matter in elementary school social studies programs as a result of the application of the above ideas.[10]

Commonest Subject Matter in Elementary Social-Studies Programs

Commonest Offerings	As found by both Preston and Hodgson	As found by Preston only	As found by Hodgson only
Grade I	Home, School, Pets	Farm Life	
Grade II	Community Helpers	Transportation	Farm Life, Pets
Grade III	Food, Clothing, Shelter	Community, other communities, Transportation, Communication, Indians	
Grade IV	Type regions of world, U.S. history, Community	State	Indians, Eskimos
Grade V	U.S. geography, U.S. history	Latin America, Canada	
Grade VI	Latin America, Canada, Asia, Europe	World geography, Old World backgrounds, Transportation, Communication	

Following from such an over-all determination of subject matter one might find any of the following in a present-day social studies curriculum guide for further teacher guidance:

Possible Foci for Units of Work

Grade I   Living at Home and in School (grade level theme)

How does a family work together?
Who are the helpers in our school?
How can we be safe and well at home and school?
Etc.

---

[10] Ralph C. Preston, *Teaching Social Studies in the Elementary School* (New York: Rinehart and Company, 1958), Chapter 3.

Grade III   Living Together in Our Community (grade level theme)
What kinds of homes do we provide for ourselves?
How do foods get to our tables?
Has our community changed over the years?
Etc.

Grade V   Living in Our Nation (grade level theme)
Who are the people living in our nation?
How did our nation begin?
How has life changed in our nation since the early days?
What is meant by "the Westward Movement"?
Etc.

It is generally felt that such planning as this is wise to insure that the social studies program actually begins at some point and moves increasingly toward some more distant point. Such a framework, it is generally felt, gives a kind of stability to the total program, lends security to the classroom teacher, and still leaves room for a great deal of teacher-pupil planning within the broad outline of the plan.

A Closer Look at Commonest Subject Matter

A closer look at many present-day elementary school social studies programs in action makes possible the following observations with respect to developments in the curriculum.

First of all, it is obvious that there is far greater agreement as to the communities from which units of work are appropriately drawn for the primary grades than for the middle grades. While some schools do treat the local community in the middle grades, the study of living at the local level is most often restricted to the primary grades. The themes of home-school-neighborhood and local community are almost universally used as foci for the social studies in kindergarten and grades one and two. Within this general limitation there is some tendency to spread the study of "community helpers" over all of these years instead of concentrating this study in grade two, and to consider a wider group of "helpers" than was formerly the case. This tendency seems to go along with a change in these studies to focus on the *services*, broadly conceived, that people need, rather than focusing on a small stereotyped group of "helpers." Thus we find various professional people and tradesmen being studied in addition to the mailman and the fireman.

Holidays, studying the flag as a national symbol, learning the pledge of allegiance, and giving attention to the stories and to the birthdays of famous Americans, past and present, all continue to be included as important social studies content over these years.

The study of the local community extends quite regularly into grade

three. While the basic human activities of procuring food, clothing, and shelter are the ones most commonly included within these local community studies, there is evidence to suggest that other activities like re-creating and educating are being given some attention. When "other communities" are studied in grade three, they may be contemporary ones in the United States, or the orientation may be to a community in another time and place. The latter may include an historical study of the local community, or the focus may be on a so-called primitive or "simple" culture in an attempt to see how basic human needs were met in such a setting. The study of Indians may well find its way into the third grade on either of these last two bases.

The difference in meaning between *local community* and *extended community* as used in this grade is increasingly important. Extended communities, such as the Bay Area in and around San Francisco, or the North Shore or the South Side of Chicago, or the Greater New York area, become increasingly important areas to understand as our population concentrates itself in and around large metropolitan centers, extending over county and even state lines.

The state, as a community, is given added attention in the social studies program, to point out the similarity and the relatedness of problems of living at the local and state levels. Typically, the study of the state is undertaken in grade four. This does not mean that the long familiar study of type regions, world around, such as "hot-wet," "hot-dry," and so on, has disappeared from the elementary school. This geographic orientation continues to be the dominant theme in many schools, while in others study of the state is combined in the same year with some study of type regions.

The study of the United States in some manner or form is almost universal as a focus for grade five. If there is any lack of agreement here, it is concerned with deciding whether to take an "historical periods" or "geographic regions" approach to the year's work. Some schools will include attention to our national neighbors—Canada, Mexico, Latin America—as a part of this year's work.

There is probably more variation in content at the sixth grade level than at any other in the elementary school. In great part this variation stems from the trend of the last several years to terminate the elementary school at the sixth grade, and in this light to search for a most appropriate final experience for the elementary school social studies program. Though it is clearly recognized that the social studies program will continue through the remaining years of school there is some tendency to try to "round out" the experience of the first years. Some elementary school educators, influenced by this idea, would center the grade six experience in a kind of world setting, usually a world geography approach with an

emphasis on human and economic geography, generally. Such advocates feel that the child born into today's world should not leave elementary school without some effort being made to help him to comprehend the world as a community of people. Within such an approach, selected culture units on such countries as India, or Japan, or Russia may be developed, pointed toward increased intercultural and international understanding.

More typically one finds either of two content orientations in grade six. One of these extends the study of the Western hemisphere, which would have started with a study of the United States in grade five, into grade six with the focus on Canada, Mexico, and Central and South America. The other focuses on the Eastern hemisphere and deals in the main with Europe, past and present. Still others, searching for a selection of content that would make sense in grades six and seven, would develop the work in grade six around the Atlantic Community, and the work in grade seven around the Pacific community. They reason that life, for many reasons, will be lived in the future around this very natural geographic as well as political division. Such a plan anticipates a return in the eighth grade to a reconsideration of American history in light of considerable world understanding.

No matter which of these approaches is used as the predominant one in the school, selected technology units on such broad themes as transportation or communication are likely to be interspersed for study. In the development of such units of work, insight is developed into these particular areas of activity in terms of advanced technology; considerable attention is also given to the general social impact of these developments, to their role in causing the world to "shrink," and to the task man faces in insuring that all such advances are used to make for a better life.

Thus, while there is definitely a most common subject matter in the social studies at the present time, there is some change noticeable and there are some continuing attempts to improve on the general focus of the program in light of changing social circumstances at home and abroad.

A Closer Look at Accepted Bases for Planning

There is, as noted earlier, great agreement that a social studies program organized around either the expanding environment principle, or the "expanding communities of men" rationale, is superior to a sequence based on chronology or on some other internal characteristic of one of the separate social studies subjects. However, within this wide area of agreement there are questions raised by elementary school educators con-

cerning the application of these principles to program planning in the social studies. Let us consider two of the most often expressed concerns here.

Cautions against too mechanical an application of principles. There are some who caution against too mechanical a use of such principles for program planning. They question whether children and their experiences really "square" with these principles as much as we might conclude. They suggest that children really don't move just from home to school to neighborhood, and so on, as they push out in their social experiences. They wonder whether present expanding environment principles restrict the social growth of children when school experiences are limited accordingly. They point to such things as the improved mass media of today's world, especially television and motion pictures, to the increased mobility of the family with respect both to vacations and to changes in residence, and to our expanded fund of children's literature, and they wonder just what the impact of these modern changes is on the children coming along in our elementary schools. They wonder whether we are planning the social studies program to take sufficient advantage of the experiential background of today's children.

Strong proponents of the use of these principles indicate that there is something to the arguments put forth by these educators. They indicate, however, that there is room for certain other kinds of explorations into the social environment in any given year as well as for giving major attention to the systematic study of a community of men or an expanded social environment. It is held that focusing on a given aspect of the social environment as a first priority item is akin to lighting a stage with a spotlight. Although one's attention is first caught by the actor or actors in the spotlight, the spotlight does not black out the whole stage from one's view. Similarly, they say that focusing on a given community of men does not blot out all other such communities and does not keep them from being considered appropriate for a given group of children.

In fact, many elementary schools are planning their social studies work so that a teacher has time to develop some shorter studies in her classroom during the year as well as to carry on the prearranged large studies. These shorter studies may or may not be in keeping with the emphasis called for in the over-all social studies program. They may be selected from a long list of appropriate problems for study, or they may be derived from current happenings on the state, national, or world scene. Or they may arise out of events in the local community, even in the school community itself. The important idea to grasp is that the prearranged program of work in the social studies may be planned to allow some time for the development of learning experiences that go beyond

the emphasis for the given grade level. A teacher would place first priority on the prearranged emphasis for the year's work and would direct a main effort to the cumulative development of social understanding and sensitivity in line with the preplanned sequence of experiences; beyond this priority there would be some time for the identification and study of social situations determined by the teacher and the class to be important to them.

Desires for an early effort toward intercultural and international understanding. Some elementary school educators are concerned because the application of the expanding environments principle to the development of the social studies program tends to restrict the study of any culture other than our own until the sixth grade. As they view today's world with its great need for improved intercultural and international understanding they question seriously the advisability of waiting so many years to help children in some systematic way to begin to comprehend and accept the differences among groups of people. In this connection, they sense a real limitation in the type region studies of faraway places that are still often the focus of work in the fourth grade. It is felt that too often such studies dwell on physical geography alone, rather than taking a human geography approach that might contribute greatly to intercultural understanding.

The use of culture units in the elementary school program is an issue of long standing in and of itself. The worth of such units has been seriously questioned by some.[11] Those who have observed the development of such studies in years past cannot support the stereotyped treatment of other peoples and their way of life, or the general sentimental and "tolerant" way in which these studies were usually carried out. They question whether such efforts lead to increased intercultural understanding or detract from it.

The authors tend to support those who argue on the one hand that today's world makes experimentation concerning ways of increasing this sort of study in the elementary school vitally necessary, and on the other that the impact of the modern world on children, coupled with improved instructional tools and procedures, may make it possible to study other cultures and peoples at an earlier age than has heretofore been thought possible. It seems imperative that children must be given opportunities early and often to develop understandings and insights into the lives of people other than our own. There is evidence to suggest that the failures of earlier years were due to the poor quality of the learning

---

[11] Wanda Robertson, *An Evaluation of the Culture Unit Method for Social Education* (New York: Bureau of Publications, Teachers College, Columbia University, 1950).

enterprise in the classroom, and that teachers, armed with certain improved procedures and with proper instructional materials, have demonstrated the possibilities of culture studies for children. There will undoubtedly be increased attempts to introduce the comprehensive study of foreign cultures into the middle grades of the elementary school. Carefully selected foreign cultures will be studied; the choice of these cultures will be based on considerations both of children and of today's world.

There will also most likely be some attempts in the early grades at cross-cultural study in conjunction with studies of family and local community life in the United States. In these attempts great care will have to be taken to avoid the misunderstandings that may occur if the culture is not seen as a comprehensive whole, wherein each part, such as family life, is influenced by and in turn influences many other parts.

Some Conclusions on Planning

There is food for thought in all of these concerns about improving the social studies curriculum. Certainly continued experimentation is needed with children to indicate ever more clearly the possibilities for sound social education at these ages. Carefully gathered data are needed to help in evaluating the degree to which purposes sought through the social studies are realized in one or another type of curriculum organization. Experience to date indicates a rather general acceptance of the idea that some definite framework for a sequence of grade-by-grade emphases in the social studies must be established in the elementary school. At the present time all indications are that the expanding environments and communities of men plans for this framework are the most satisfactory. At the same time there is continuous effort and study to improve upon these principles in light of the demands of today's world on the social studies program, and of the possibilities for social education that may be inherent in today's children.

In the hands of a skillful teacher, a great deal of sound learning can be implemented within this typical framework. A carelessly interpreted program for the primary grades can be restrictive, repetitious and unstimulating. Also, the jump from the ''here and now'' of the primary grades to the wider settings of the middle grades, if it is to be effective, must be done by treating these wider social environments appropriately in terms of the particular school and children with whom a teacher is working. Without the application of sound teaching skill these vicarious experiences can be void of meaning and fleeting in the memory of the student.

A preference for the unit of work. A sound effort in the social studies

demands, too, a sound methodology. That is, an effective way must be used to organize for learning in the classroom the social understandings, the values and attitudes, and the skills that are sought. Concept formation and the development of generalizations in the social sphere must be approached with a scheme for learning that is consistent with our evidence on learning and on child development. To date, the most effective way of organizing for learning in the social studies is the pedagogical scheme referred to as the unit of work. This way of working relates process and content in a mutually supporting way in the classroom. A variety of instructional materials, resources, and procedures can be utilized in unit teaching. This scheme also makes a place for total group, small group, and individual learning experiences—important in their own right as social learnings. There is not sufficient space here to discuss the unit of work in detail, nor is this scheme used only in the social studies. A much more complete discussion follows in the chapter dealing with the teacher's use of time in the classroom. (See Chapter 19.) At this point let us conclude that in the best of unit teaching one finds the dynamic kind of learning experience that is demanded for proper learning in the social studies. Additionally, within the unit approach there is more likelihood that activities such as (a) viewing films and filmstrips, (b) taking trips into the community, (c) acting out plays, (d) keeping records and listening to reports, (e) drawing pictures and murals related to the unit, (f) working in committees on projects and study assignments, (g) preparing exhibits, and the like—all activities that studies have shown to be valued by children—will be utilized by the teacher.[12]

The present learning load in the social studies. A final word is called for here with respect to the learning load of the "typical" social studies program described here. The tendency is, in the eagerness to do a quality job in an area of great concern, to include more content and to cover more material than can reasonably be expected. Teachers find it very difficult to find time for all of the things that they are supposed to teach, especially in the middle grades. The insights we have into the ways children develop meaningful social concepts and generalizations indicate that any attempt to hurry such learning in the interests of getting over the course of study is unwise.

It would seem that a great deal more careful attention to this problem of load in elementary school social studies would be worth while. The ease with which the curriculum may call for the study of a complete continent, or of the vast Pacific Basin area, must be viewed in light of the sort of classroom experience that is necessary if such efforts are not

---

[12] Linnwood W. Chase, "Individual Differences in Classroom Learning," National Society for the Study of Education Yearbook, *op. cit.*, pp. 168–170.

to be wasted. Selecting representative countries, for instance, rather than attempting a "Cook's tour" of a whole continent, may be called for. Reasonableness in terms of all of the "Old World backgrounds" in which selections are made that indicate through the study of one old, contributing culture the way in which the present is related to the past may make more sense for the period of childhood. The authors are of the opinion that to allow time for a more comprehensive, even leisurely, learning experience within a more restricted range of subject matter may be wiser than to attempt too much in the classroom. Children can then transfer their learnings, both content and process, to further learning tasks in the social studies both within and outside of school.

ADDING NEW DIMENSIONS
TO THE SOCIAL STUDIES

So far in this chapter attention has been given solely to the planned social studies program operating in the elementary school. It was indicated at the outset that the basic concern to develop persons who will exhibit the characteristics and personal disciplines and skills demanded by democracy suggests that in addition to this planned social studies program there is a broader social education task to be done. Opportunities for positive social education exist beyond the social studies per se, and are in fact crucial for the fulfillment of the purposes. It goes without saying that much of this opportunity exists even apart from the school itself; in the give-and-take of family life and peer group living children experience social education. Still there is a very strategic role that the elementary school experience can play in child socialization. The planned social studies program, with its systematic opportunities to understand, to value, and to become skillful with the social arrangements in our own society, and to study others, has been discussed as one part of the school's contribution. Let us look beyond this now to some of the more provocative and persuasive aspects of an expanded approach to social education.

An Earlier Challenge

In a lecture delivered in 1940 and later published in a small pamphlet entitled *Culture and Personality,* Mary Shattuck Fisher commented on the bringing up of children in the modern world. In part she had this to say:

> For purposes of this discussion, there are only two likenesses or basic personality structures into which children of the world today are being formed by the adults who care for them—the likeness of free and responsible men or the likeness of dominated and irresponsible men.

And a bit later in the same writing:

> The unescapable fact still remains, however, that understanding the development of democratic personalities lies at the heart of our common problem and our common responsibility.

And still further:

> We cannot hope to create a democracy, let alone defend democracy, until we who are educators—that is, who are parents and teachers—know how to bring up children who behave democratically because that is the kind of persons they are. We cannot conserve democratic values until we are clear and honest and intelligent about how "democracy" gets into the personality.[13]

There has been emerging since 1940 a considerable body of literature that can be used to help in differentiating the democratic personality we seek from the undemocratic one we want to avoid. Also, this accumulating evidence contains strong suggestions for the kind of general living experience and school experience that support personality development in the direction of democracy and away from authoritarianism and autocracy. It is this evidence that elementary school educators, interested in the social education of children, try increasingly to understand and apply in the classroom and school situation.

The Democratic and Authoritarian Personalities

Let us consider briefly here what it is we seek in the person when we speak of the democratic personality, and for purposes of comparison let us refer also to that which we do not willingly seek to develop, the authoritarian personality.

The democratic personality. In a somewhat idealistic vein, Flowerman describes the democratic personality in the following statement:

> The extremely democratic personality is a man with a mind of his own; he is a flexible individual, adjusting readily to new situations. He is sensitive to the part he plays in conflicting situations, and he is ready to take responsibility for his own behavior.... He is without prejudice against religious or racial minorities. He regards persons as individuals and not types.... It is easy for him to see some good in the world and hope for its future. Most important, he refuses to surrender his individuality to a "big shot" although he may submit to authority when he believes such authority is based upon equality, superior ability and cooperation, and that the authority is subject to dismissal for a job badly done.[14]

---

[13] Ralph Linton, Mary Shattuck Fisher, and W. Carson Ryan, *Culture and Personality* (Washington, D.C.: American Council on Education, 1941), pp. 20, 25, 27.

[14] Samuel W. Flowerman, "Portrait of the Authoritarian Man," *The New York Times Magazine*, April 25, 1950. Quoted in Ambrose and Miel, *op. cit.*, p. 44.

The person described here is the person the elementary school is expected to help to develop. Reference to an earlier chapter dealing in part with democratic values, beliefs, and assumptions suggests that the profile found in this descriptive statement is consistent with what one might anticipate from an understanding of democracy. The goal we seek is clarified even more by a description of that which we do not seek.

The authoritarian personality. A descriptive statement of the authoritarian personality that seems to arise from the material available at the present time is presented by Miel and Ambrose. They describe this type in the following terms:

> The extreme authoritarian (true totalitarian) has a world outlook which determines his behavior in a variety of arenas, including self-other relationships, in-group–out-group relationships, international views, religious sentiments, social and political philosophy. Conventionality, rigidity in thinking, fear and dependency, characterize his behavior in all areas of living. He clings desperately to whatever appears to be strong and rejects disdainfully whatever is relegated to the bottom. He thinks in black and white terms. He sees the leader and the led; the strong and the weak; the right and the wrong; the "ins" and the "outs"; we and they; our nation and other nations. He is inclined to have narrow, ethnocentric attitudes; outside his own group he sees not individuals but masses; he thinks in superpatriotic terms and is inclined to view other nations as hostile and untrustworthy. He feels that everyone needs a strong leader to ensure that right is done and to protect against the enemies who are all about. He cannot tolerate differences, cannot face alternative solutions, cannot attempt the unconventional. In short, he lives in a narrow, restricted world where he feels threatened by the evil around him—not recognizing that most of the evil he sees lies within himself. His superpatriotism, his seeking for a strong leader, his dichotomous thinking, his distrust of others are but outward manifestations of the hostility and insecurity which lie buried within.[15]

To an American, this is not a pretty picture. This kind of personal and social behavior is the very antithesis of that which we seek in our democracy. To avoid any support for this kind of personality development, and to throw resources solidly behind the nurturing of the democratic personality, is the goal of the elementary school. It is desired that children build socially useful concepts and generalizations, a meaningful set of values, and adequate social skills. All of this must be done with respect to our own society and at the same time attention must be given to an ever enlarging life-space as children are helped to become aware of times and places, and institutions and processes other than our own. At base is a person who feels good about himself, seemingly a prime

---

[15] Ambrose and Miel, *op. cit.*, p. 38.

prerequisite for feeling good about others. There is no substitute for sound and healthy personality development—in this case described as the democratic personality.

BEYOND THE SOCIAL STUDIES

There is a great opportunity for the elementary school to be effective in the social education of children in ways that are beyond the social studies. This opportunity lies in the fact that the classroom and the school provide, actually, a society of their own in which the very stuff of day-to-day living together provides a reality setting in which social education takes place. Here is firsthand contact with people and with things. Here space, and time, and materials are used jointly by many children and adults. Social education is bound to take place in such a setting. The responsibility of the elementary school educator is to be able to exploit this setting fully in the interests of improved social learnings. Children should undergo, in their relationships to each other and to adults at school, a living experience grounded in the basic tenets of democracy.

A Strategic Role for the Teacher

While teachers cannot control the nature of the relationships that will operate between children, they can have a very great deal to do with making one kind of relationship more likely to develop than another. They can determine with considerable certainty the nature of the relationship that will exist between teacher and pupil. Teachers, in their work with children, must attempt to show the face of democracy in a consistent and persuasive way. Providing a proper model for children as they live close to and interact with adults in the school situation is very important.

According to Miel and Ambrose:

> Of all the environing conditions, the *human environment* comprises the most pervasive and most decisive factors. It is through people—what they do to, for, and with him—that a child learns who and what he is, what he can do, what he should strive for. It is through people and their responses to his strivings that the child gains his basic orientation to life.[16]

Rasey and Menge comment directly on this point, too. In discussing the cruciality of the human environment they contend that "the philoso-

---

[16] *Ibid.*, p. 28.

phies [people] operate upon, the constellation of values that trigger their actions'' are most important. And they go on to say that ''The teacher's role is influential because his choices and preferences are themselves contagious and ways of life of young humans have a considerable admixture of the choices and preferences of those in their environment.''[17] The findings of studies that have dealt with this matter are in agreement with the statements quoted here.[18] The impact of human environment, and of the teacher especially, on the social learnings of children puts a considerable responsibility on those who would teach children.

Some Implications for Practice from Parent-Child Studies

As elementary school educators try to exploit more fully the total school living experience for the ends of social education there is information that comes from studies focused on the parent-child setting that seem to hold suggestions for the teacher-child setting, too.

For instance, in a study that attempted to gain certain insights into the parent-child relationship with respect to general personality development, the following factors seemed to contribute to developing friendly children who were constructive group members and who were relatively free from anxieties:

1. *There was acceptance:* children were listened to; they were permitted to engage in rough play; school reports were accepted without punishment or rebuff.
2. *There was freedom:* parents encouraged children to make friends outside the family, to play with the peer group.
3. *There was support:* parents gave time and thought to the child and endeavored to meet his needs.
4. *There was comradeship:* children saw family members as doing things for and with each other. Parents laughed and joked and told stories to children.[19]

After examining a great many studies similar to the one above, Miel and Ambrose commented that among the practices of adults toward children which encourage self-acceptance and openness toward others are:

---

[17] Marie I. Rasey and J. W. Menge, *What We Learn from Children* (New York: Harper & Brothers, 1956), pp. 23, 39.

[18] Helen Trager and Marie Radke-Yarrow, *They Learn What They Live* (New York: Harper & Brothers, 1952); Kenneth Wann and Arthur W. Foshay, *Children's Social Values* (New York: Bureau of Publications, Teachers College, Columbia University, 1954).

[19] A. R. Martin, ''A Study of Parental Attitudes and Their Influence on Personality Development,'' reprinted from the June 1943 issue of *Education*, pp. 596–608, by special permission of The Bobbs-Merrill Company, Inc., Indianapolis, Indiana.

1. Recognizing the individuality of each child.
2. Listening to, respecting and using children's opinions.
3. Accepting their feelings.
4. Accepting the aggressive, rough and tumble play of exuberant youngsters.
5. Planning work and play so they can use their abilities.
6. Giving time and thought to them and their needs; endeavoring to meet their needs.
7. Allowing opportunities for them to be with their friends.
8. Using power with them. Exercising the type of control they need to learn to exercise with others.
9. Participating with them in pleasurable activities.
10. Having a sense of humor, laughing and joking with them.[20]

If these kinds of practices characterize the human environment that supports the development of feelings of adequacy within children, teachers need to give them some thought as they establish a working relationship with their classes.

It is well, in this connection, to bear in mind that, along with a planned social studies program, and along with the celebration of national holidays and the recognition of national symbols in relationship to citizenship education, emotional needs must be recognized. The report of the five-year citizenship education project in the Detroit Public Schools had this to say in part:

> As data about children were gathered, as ideas from others were examined, and as other educational and sociological theories were studied, the idea (that citizenship depends upon emotional adjustment) became a conviction. . . . Regardless of the approach, they (the teachers) sooner or later focussed attention on the emotional needs of children.[21]

Utilizing Classroom Living for Social Education

There are many social decisions to be made in the operation of any elementary school classroom and they can be approached in such a way as to take advantage of many of the insights noted in the preceding discussion. Let us consider some of these decisions at this time.

Standards for behavior, for instance, must be arrived at, understood, and enforced in every classroom. This can be done with a great deal of child participation if the teacher so chooses. Naturally, the extent and kind of participation will depend to a degree on the age of the children, and also on the past experiences of children both at home and at school

---

[20] Ambrose and Miel, *op. cit.*, p. 47.
[21] Elmer Pflieger and Grace Weston, *Emotional Adjustment: A Key to Good Citizenship* (Detroit: Wayne University Press, 1953), pp. 10, 131.

with such matters. The teacher who is willing to utilize this opportunity has a good chance to approach some significant social learnings concerning authority and social control. Children can be allowed to feel the consequence of living up to or not living up to group-derived decisions that are important to the well-being of the life of the group.

Also, there are many tasks to be done in a classroom to insure that the life of the group will run smoothly. To the degree that these tasks can be shared, they can be used to sensitize children to the necessity of allocating responsibility and authority to some in the group in the best interests of all. And children can become more aware of the way responsibility and authority in society are delegated to and shifted from one person to another from time to time. Thus, being classroom librarian for awhile, or ball monitor, or being in charge of the classroom pet, or being the room representative to the school student council give the delegated and the delegators opportunities for democratic learnings.

It is obvious, too, that the opportunities a teacher gives children to participate in planning for the use of class time, or space, or materials, and the criticizing together of the adequacy of such planning, helps in the development of skills and attitudes demanded by democratic living. Such shared decision-making will involve conflicting ideas about the way things should be done; in fact, disagreement will be evident over the value of the activities themselves from time to time. Such situations provide a dynamic setting in which the participants, in this case the teacher and his class, are called upon to solve common group dilemmas and to make sound group decisions.

A concomitant of this experience in shared living should, in light of the research reviewed earlier, be the development of stronger individual personalities along the lines of democracy.

Utilizing School Living for Social Education

Everything that has been said about the possibilities for utilizing the classroom living experience for social education purposes is present at the school level in just a little different way. That is, a schoolwide activity or an all-school experience in decision-making involves more people, with more likelihood of varied interests and concerns, and a greater chance for conflicting opinions concerning a most sound course of action. Contacts between children, and between children and adults in the corridors, on the playground, in the lunchroom, or in the gymnasium all carry some potential for social education.

In this larger social setting there is again the necessity for understood and accepted standards for personal and group conduct, and an opportunity for child participation in this "social control" decision. Similarly,

there are schoolwide opportunities and demands for social service if the living experience at school is to be as safe and as happy as it should be. A school safety patrol will usually be stationed at busy intersections near the school in an attempt to safeguard the children as they come and go to school. Boys and girls in the upper elementary grades can often be found assisting young children on the playground. Selected children can be operating a schoolwide lost and found service for the convenience of all. There can be participation by a delegated group of children in many schoolwide decisions that relate to the use of time, or space, or materials. While the final responsibility for many such decisions rests with the adults in the situation, children can participate in an advisory capacity, and as members of a deliberative body, to the benefit of all.

Here again, conflicting ideas, alternative choices, and varied possible courses of action will become evident. The necessity for choice, and the process by which such choices are made in a democracy can be learned as such situations are faced. Especially, children should not be denied the opportunity to assist in the solution of a social problem at school when the "social machinery" breaks down. In this way can real social understanding and sensitivity be helped to develop. These situations can be used to nurture our young "social engineers."

A great deal of meaningful cultural transmission can take place in the way the school experience is "lived." The values that govern human relationships and guide human action, the things and the way the teacher and the school rewards and punishes, the role that is extended to or denied children all determine in a very significant way the kind of social education that takes place. A stronger program in citizenship education results from the combination of a well-conceived program of social studies and the insightful and conscious use of the total school living experience itself in the direction of desired social behaviors and strong individual democratic personalities.

THE SOCIAL STUDIES AND SCIENCE EDUCATION

At the present time there is considerable controversy over the proper relationship between the social studies and science education in the elementary school. Over the past years much of the science has been taught in conjunction with the broad units of work developed in the social studies program. A little reflection will indicate the many possibilities for finding science content to be taught in conjunction with such studies. Units of work on the Air Age, on Modern Transportation, on Improved Communication, and so on have a heavy ingredient of learnings about science and technology for their complete understanding.

General sentiment has been that the learning in both science and social studies is improved by preserving this relationship in the learning situation. In the past few years, however, there have been many science specialists taking the position that until science has a time and place of its own in the curriculum, the program in science will be subordinated to the social studies and will suffer accordingly. This is a complex and important problem for the elementary school educator to face. It is discussed more completely in the chapter that deals with science, but mentioning it here will serve notice that this is a curricular problem that will have to solved.

FOREIGN LANGUAGES AND THE SOCIAL STUDIES

Although this is not the place to discuss the ability of children to learn foreign languages, or to debate methodological advantages, it is appropriate to give some attention to foreign language in this chapter because so much of the argument for including foreign language instruction in the general education of all children grows out of the contribution that such learning can and will make to general intercultural and international understanding. In this connection the answers do not come easily.

We do have examples within the United States of the importance of foreign language instruction in the improvement of relationships between particular groups of people. In many areas of the Southwest the teaching of Spanish in the elementary schools has for many years been considered an effective approach to the intergroup human relations problems between the Spanish-American peoples and other residents. By studying the Spanish language, avenues of communication, both linguistic and emotional, have been strengthened. Improved understanding and more positive intergroup feelings are believed to follow from the schools' readiness to find time to study the Spanish language. To some extent New York City has faced a similar problem in recent years with the great influx of persons from Puerto Rico, and the efforts to solve this problem appear to be strengthened when some time and attention is given to the problem of communication. The attempts to help New York City teachers, for instance, to learn the language of the Puerto Rican children sufficiently well to aid them in their initial adjustment to school life have been well received by all concerned. Such experiences as these lead one to conclude that where an immediate problem of intergroup relations exists that is partially based on language differences, it is well to devote attention to language along with other efforts to arrive at some mutually satisfying understandings.

This kind of thinking can be carried to the level of international

understanding, too. It can be reasoned that where problems of under-standing and good feeling exist between national groups who speak different languages, a contribution to their resolution may be made by giving some attention to the matter of communication. The necessity of communication to the smooth proceedings of the direct relations main-tained in matters of government and trade is obvious. Contacts of this kind will usually be improved if the persons involved can talk directly with each other, can read the current periodicals produced in each other's countries, and can even make some headway in the literature of the country as an aid to developing general perspective and as a way of increasing mutual empathy.

It is more difficult to arrive at a clear line of action when attention is turned to the problem of general education. In this setting the focus is on the child who will most likely become the adult with indirect and remote, but nonetheless important and crucial, relations with foreign peoples. He may, owing to improved transportation facilities and the growing internationalism in social, political, and economic affairs, see more foreign people in his own country and he may even tour one or two times among foreign peoples. But, in all probability, most of his "foreign experience" will be limited to trying to understand the world scene, to trying to develop empathy for foreign peoples by vicarious means, and to making efforts to maintain a defensible position as an active citizen when he uses his ballot to influence national policies in the area of foreign relations. At this point the social studies program may look for support from the introduction of foreign language instruction into the elementary school. And it is precisely at this point that, in the view of the authors, much more experience is needed with foreign lan-guage programs before firm conclusions can be drawn.

Generally speaking, there are two approaches that a school system might take. One approach would commit the school to a long-term experience with some foreign language for most, and perhaps all, stu-dents. This program might well be started in about the third year of the elementary school and would continue on through the high school, with language skill increasing steadily over the years. At graduation the student should have a good command of a foreign language, and, on the basis of this developing skill, should have developed sound under-standings of the people and the culture associated with the language. It would be anticipated that the impact of the total experience would contribute significantly to the student's ability and willingness to face general problems of intercultural and international understanding.

The other approach would make some sacrifices with respect to lan-guage proficiency in the beginning years, and would give children an opportunity to explore the language environment of selected foreign

cultures as a part of their general study in school. In such a program a child might study two or three foreign languages for about one year each in close relationship to the social studies. The hope would be that he would learn, among other things, that language is a very meaningful difference among people, that other languages serve other people efficiently for communication, and that language differences do create a formidable barrier to intercultural and international understanding. Commitment to a serious, long-term study of one foreign language would follow this kind of experience with foreign languages, starting in the junior high school and continuing through the senior high school. The final outcome would be the same as for the first alternative—a person able and willing to face and to help resolve the knotty problems of intercultural and international understanding.

Neither of these types of programs operate in our elementary schools today. Although some schools are starting foreign language instruction in the elementary school, the programs are not designed to continue through the junior and senior high school. The authors know of no elementary school systems experimenting with the latter approach in any organized way. The extent to which the citizen of the future will and should be bilingual is a question still to be answered. Unknown, too, is the seriousness with which international agreements may some day be reached concerning a world-wide "second" language. In the meantime, experimental efforts in this area are to be encouraged; there is a need to know the possibilities ever more clearly to help in shaping a proper answer to the question. The social studies program has a stake in these developments that elementary school educators need to exercise. The decision whether to develop foreign language instruction in the elementary school is in great part a social education decision.

REFERENCES

Ambrose, Edna V., and Alice M. Miel. *Children's Social Learnings: Implications of Research and Expert Study.* Washington, D.C.: Association for Supervision and Curriculum Development, National Education Association, 1958.
>   This monograph is a report of the findings in the literature concerning children's social learnings and how they are acquired.

Association for Childhood Education International. *Social Studies for Children.* Washington, D.C.: The Association, 1956.
>   This is a revision of a bulletin on the social studies which teachers have found to be helpful.

Estvan, Frank J., and Elizabeth W. Estvan. *The Child's World: His Social Perception.* G. P. Putnam's Sons, 1959.
>   A report of studies intended to show the varieties of children's perceptions of significant aspects and circumstances of their social world. Rural-urban, sex, social class, and age differences are discussed.

Jarolimek, John. *Social Studies in Elementary Education.* New York: The Macmillan Company, 1959.
> A comprehensive statement focused on current instructional practice in the social studies.

Kenworthy, Leonard. *Introducing Children to the World.* New York: Harper & Brothers, 1956.
> A guide describing a variety of ways of increasing international interest and understanding among children.

Merritt, Edith. *Working With Children in Social Studies.* San Francisco: Wadsworth Publishing Company, Inc., 1961.
> Provides a practical guide to the achievement of course objectives in social studies through specific teaching techniques.

Michaelis, John U. *Social Studies for Children in a Democracy* (Second edition). Englewood Cliffs, New Jersey: Prentice-Hall, Inc., 1956.
> This comprehensive book continues to command the respect of elementary educators.

Miel, Alice, and Peggy Brogan. *More Than Social Studies.* Englewood Cliffs, New Jersey: Prentice-Hall, Inc., 1957.
> An excellent and provocative statement on the processes of social education, with emphasis on the often-missed opportunities for it in the general living in the classroom and school.

Otto, Henry J. *Social Education in Elementary Schools.* New York: Rinehart and Company, Inc., 1956.
> Attempts a clarification of the meaning of social education, using examples from various schools adjudged to be carrying it out.

Preston, Ralph C. *Teaching Social Studies in the Elementary School* (Revised edition). New York: Rinehart and Company, 1958.
> This book attempts to weave together material from child development, learning theory, and the social studies to point the way to an improved social studies program in the elementary school.

——————— (editor). *Social Studies in the Elementary School.* Fifty-sixth Yearbook of the National Society for the Study of Education. Chicago: University of Chicago Press, 1957.
> An attempt to define the role of the social studies in the present elementary school curriculum, drawing on new information from the psychological and social foundations of education.

14

EXPLORING THE NATURAL ENVIRONMENT: SCIENCE

The improvement of science programs in elementary schools is a matter receiving much attention at the present time. Science is increasingly accepted as a basic and fundamental force in the lives of people. The research laboratory is coming to be recognized as the twentieth century "frontier." The application, the engineering task, of the discoveries of science to the day-by-day affairs of men continues to improve and expand an already amazing technology. Atomic energy as a power source, automation and the development of the automatic factory, antibiotics for the control and treatment of disease, jet propulsion applied to aircraft, rockets for the exploration of outer space, increased understanding of mental illness—all of these are but a few of the contributions of science that make life both more pleasant and more complex in our time. Few would question the importance of science for the continuing improvement of living. In fact, in a troubled and tense world, our very survival depends on the quality of our science. Any attempt to provide an answer to the question of what it means to be educated in our time must inevitably concern itself with science.

Children have a great deal of understanding to develop as they try to build meanings about their natural environment. A part of the security of *knowing* when one is a child has long included some understanding of such phenomena as the day and night cycle, the causes of the seasons, the growth of plants, electricity and magnetism, or the origin of and differences in rocks. Added to this need for knowing now is the concern for such things as why a jet airplane flies, or where the

television picture comes from, or what it really would be like on the moon.

At the present time science seems to be assured of a lasting and important place in the elementary school curriculum. Typical statements in recent curriculum guides for elementary schools are quite positive in tone. For instance, one comments as follows:

> The need for science as a definite part of the elementary program is no longer a matter of debate. Its need is predicated upon a world requiring an abundance of scientific knowledge.[1]

Another states:

> Science is a regular part of the school curriculum. A planned science program is the only way our elementary school pupils can be assured the understandings necessary to intelligent living in a modern democracy.[2]

A great deal of the general sentiment over the improvement of elementary school science is reflected in the following statement from another recent guide:

> No text has been adopted; no specific time requirement has been established. The important thing is that a beginning be made with a program that is planned and structured rather than one that is incidental or perhaps even accidental.[3]

There are those spokesmen for elementary school science who, in order to make their point with force, say that science is the only subject in the elementary school program that does not have to justify its being there in today's world. There is evidence of wide and growing acceptance of the science program in the elementary school.

EARLY SCIENCE PROGRAMS

It should not be concluded from these opening paragraphs that there has been no science in elementary schools over the years. There is, in fact, evidence of science programs in our elementary schools for the past hundred years. Some have characterized the earliest programs as "walks and talks with nature." Children would be helped to identify

---

[1] Lakewood Public Schools, *Science in the Elementary Schools—Upper Grades* (Lakewood, Ohio: Lakewood Public Schools, 1956–57).

[2] San Bernardino City Schools, *Science Guides—Elementary Grades* (San Bernardino, California: San Bernardino City Schools).

[3] Marion, Ohio Public Schools, *Science in Marion, Ohio Elementary Schools, Grades One–Six*, Curriculum Bulletin (Marion, Ohio: Marion, Ohio Public Schools, 1956).

things in the natural environment; that is, they would make up lists of names of trees, of flowers, and so on. Instruction would pretty much start and end with the making of such lists. Sometimes objects in the environment—rocks, or nests, or insects—might be carefully scrutinized, but again, the learning would stop with this careful look. That which was accepted as the "end" of science learnings in these early programs would now be seen as a most vital link, or means to more worthwhile ends. Present thinking would indicate that the learning in these early programs simply stopped too soon.

Most of the early science programs restricted themselves, also, to plant and animal life. Little was done with the physical sciences. While this imbalance persists still to a degree in elementary school programs, it is recognized and efforts are being made to correct it. The present state of development of science makes it imperative that the physical sciences be included.

One characteristic of much of the early elementary school science should be noted. Reference is made to the fact that almost all of the science that was taught, limited though it may have been, utilized firsthand experiences with the natural environment. Children actually looked at trees growing, or at wild flowers in the woods and fields. Or they searched out nests in trees, or rocks along the banks of streams. We realize the importance of this firsthand contact with the natural environment, and the boost that modern science textbooks gave to science instruction has fallen short of expectations to the degree that children have been held to a "reading about" experience in the classroom.

Slow Development of Science Programs

It is true, however, that concern over science in the elementary school has fluctuated over the years. Most of this fluctuation can be attributed to three sets of circumstances.

First, there have been some uncertainties over the years as to the readiness of young children for science, and the necessity for science at these ages. A conception of the scientist, busy with complicated equipment and formulae in the laboratory, tended to cause many to doubt the readiness of children for such an experience. Science learning did not seem to be an activity that would be appealing to children. Also, it was doubted that the experience was necessary for children of elementary school age. Science was something they could study and experience later, when it would make more sense to them. The feeling was that there were more important and desirable things to do for and with children.

As we have studied children over the years, one of the most encouraging considerations in planning a science program for the elementary school is the nature of childhood itself. Out of this information some

have concluded that children are more naturally scientists than they are anything else. Certainly they are curious; they seek explanations; they want to know why things happen. They enjoy the security of prediction, that is, of being able to say that a given thing will happen under certain conditions. Children tend to be imaginative and creative in much that they do. They are innovators of the first order; they are continuously trying, making, doing—all to the end of satisfying an insatiable curiosity. This trait is certainly suggestive of the "profile" of the scientist.

Research of various kinds has been conducted, too, to try to identify some of the strong interests and concerns of children—the things they are interested in, the things that capture their attention, and what they would like to know more about. In all such studies, there is a great number of questions raised about science and technology. Children ask many questions in this area, and they indicate strong interests in things scientific. For instance, a study a few years ago asked children to indicate the things they would most like to be able to ask somebody about, or to look up in a book; first priority was given to science. That is, more children had more concerns that fell into the category of science and technology than anything else.[4] Other studies focused on this matter have come up with similar results. As a group, they indicate strong science interests in children; and they tend to show a pattern of wide interests ranging over the various fields of science. Thus, the nature of childhood complements the strategic nature of science in the modern world. Children are reflecting the fact that they are growing up in an age of science. Interests are learned, and children are learning well. Pupils in the elementary school are ready to accept science learnings. It is up to the school to make available a provocative and informative program.

Second, teachers have not always felt secure in handling science study in the classroom. Typically, their own science backgrounds have been meager, and this shortcoming has led to ambivalence about the science they would make available to children in their classroom programs. Too, some teachers who had studied science as a part of their own general education were at a loss to devise ways of bringing science to children. The gap between their adult learnings and the beginning learnings of children was too great for them to bridge procedurally. It must be remembered, too, that as persistent areas of interest develop at the adult level it is rather obvious that science is more often a male interest than

[4] Herbert C. Rudman, "The Informational Needs and Reading Interests of Children in Grades Four Through Eight," *Elementary School Journal* 55:502–512, May 1955.

a female one. With our elementary schools staffed so heavily with women teachers, there has not been as much group interest in science within the teaching corps itself.

The problem of teacher readiness persists today and must be dealt with if science is to flourish in the elementary school. Happily, certain changes are being made that will work to the advantage of elementary school science. Most colleges and universities now require considerably more science as a part of the fixed general education experience of all candidates for undergraduate degrees. Over the years, this requirement will mean that teachers will be better informed and more skillful generally in the area of science. Also, departments of education are increasingly offering course work in methods for teaching science in the elementary school, which will help us to meet the general problem. In a recent study by Berryessa, which focused on outstanding teachers generally, but differentiated between those with superior science programs and those with only mediocre ones, it was found that the methods used in science differed significantly between these two groups.[5]

Third is the fact that the curriculum in the elementary school has always been "crowded"; that is, there has been much more to do than time to do it. Thus, certain priorities have operated and science has been "in" at times and "out" at other times. A statement in an elementary school science course of study some years ago called attention to this situation in the history of a particular school system:

> No subject in our school program has undergone such mutations as elementary school science. This subject in the form of natural history was taught in upper grades of certain of our public schools from their organization, and in all by 1850, but was dropped from the course in 1853. Elementary school science was reintroduced in 1857 in the form of object lessons for the lower grades. The science work was broadened in 1870 and physics was added for the sixth and seventh grades. This was, however, omitted from the new course of study of 1880. Effort was again put forth in 1895 to give science instruction an important place in the schools. This course was carried forward for ten years, when in 1903 the instruction in the upper grades was eliminated and that for the lower simplified and joined with language ... with no separate place upon the program.... [F]rom 1903 to 1926, there was little elementary science taught in Cleveland. In 1926, however, a committee prepared a tentative outline in elementary science.
>
> With the establishment of the curriculum center for elementary science at Doan School in February, 1928, the subject was given a definite place in the program of the schools.[6]

---

[5] Max Berryessa, unpublished doctoral dissertation, Stanford University, 1959.

[6] Cleveland Public Schools, *Science Course of Study: Sixth Grade, Cleveland Public Schools* (Cleveland, Ohio: Cleveland Board of Education, 1948), p. 9.

Statements cited earlier in this chapter from recent curriculum guides in certain school districts indicated that this "on-again–off-again" approach to science is coming to an end. Its importance is realized, and efforts are being made to develop significant programs for children. The matter of time for science is a problem. Supporters of the program feel that until science has its own time in the instructional schedule it will really never prosper as an area of learning. Others take the position that science is best taught in the elementary school in relation to the social studies, and perhaps to health and safety. They feel that such an approach is not only more economical in terms of time in an already overcrowded schedule, but they feel that more significant and meaningful learning, which puts science and technology in its proper social context, results from such an approach.

Making Progress in Science

The demands on the elementary school and on the individual teacher if there is to be a dynamic, meaningful program in science in the elementary school become more obvious at this point.

Some clear conception of what science really is, and of what the job of the scientist is, is clearly called for. Needed, too, is agreement as to just what such instruction should try to accomplish with children; in other words, clarity of purposes is necessary for a program in science at this level. It means, in addition, that one must possess insight into the possibilities and the limitations of childhood; developmental levels and stages of maturity are guides to the development of a science program.

A great deal of thought must be directed to the kind of experience that should be provided for children if purposes are to be realized. Questions concerning the place of experimentation, the role of demonstration, the nature of needed equipment, and the like must be answered. Certainly, too, the question of evaluation is a central one; what procedures can be used? What data can be collected in the classroom to shed light on the development of science learnings?

A DEFINITION OF SCIENCE

Perhaps it would be well, at this point, to venture some attempt to understand what we mean when we say *science,* some attempt to show what science is. A number of facts can be stated that together give a rather meaningful definition of science.

What Is Science?

First, science is a study of the environment, more particularly of the natural environment. It includes both the *physical* (earth, sky, energy, matter) and the *biological* (plants, animals, life, growth) aspects of the natural environment. It concerns itself with trying to understand this natural environment, with trying to help man to adjust to it in comfortable, efficient, and safe ways; and with trying to control it and use it to the advantage of man.

Second, science is a method of solving problems. In the problem solving methods of science man possesses an intellectual tool of the highest order. The systematic way in which the scientist identifies and defines problems, projects hypotheses or hunches as to their explanation and solution, gathers data to support or to negate them, and analyzes and describes his findings has provided man with a model for seeking the truth in science, and in solving a great many of life's problems generally.

Third, science is an attitude. Science demands objectivity; there is no place for personal bias or prejudice. The explanation for something is in the findings, not in the mind or the desire of the scientist. It is an attitude that calls for open-mindedness and a readiness to change one's mind in light of the evidence. Things are as they are, there is no place for superstition, for mysticism, or for witchcraft. The truth of the matter is in the phenomenon itself; it is there to be checked and verified by others.

What Is the Job of the Scientist?

The fundamental job of the scientist, then, is to search out facts about the natural environment. His major tool is observation; he may use intricate apparatus and equipment to make his observations more accurate, or to observe phenomenon otherwise unobservable. Thus, his laboratory will include microscopes, telescopes, cameras, x-ray machines, and the like. In the facts he discovers he may perceive relationships that lead to generalizations, or to laws of science. Just what the worth of any given fact or relationship will be, once discovered, is difficult to say. However, one does not have to look very far to be aware of the major changes that have been wrought in our lives as a result of the searchings of the scientist.

The application of the facts and generalizations discovered by the scientist to the practical affairs of life is more accurately referred to as *engineering* than as *science*. It is engineering that develops the various technological improvements that are part and parcel of present day living. It is engineering that develops rockets, and satellites, and atomic-

driven submarines and ships. It is science that makes available the fundamental knowledge upon which such engineering feats are based.

PURPOSES OF SCIENCE IN THE ELEMENTARY SCHOOL

Out of such information as this emerges, then, the purposes for which we teach science in the elementary school. The following goals seem to be acceptable and defensible:

1. Children should be helped to know and to understand some science facts, and some science generalizations and principles that they can use in their attempts to understand the natural environment.
2. Children should be helped to develop the ability to solve effectively problems that relate to the natural environment, and to become aware of and skillful with the scientific method.
3. Children should be helped to develop a scientific attitude, to become objective, open-minded individuals, dedicated to truth.
4. Children should be helped to develop an ever deeper interest in and appreciation for the world in which they live, especially with respect to its natural and technological aspects.

These broad and general goals are suggestive of the sort of program that should be developed in an elementary school. They indicate experience with a process or method, namely the scientific method; and they indicate the necessity for contact with the content of science in such an experience, too. That is, they make a place for both the product and the process of science. The nature of the experiences that will be provided for children from the kindergarten through the sixth or eighth grade is the curriculum building task. These experiences, cumulative over the years, must add up to the accomplishment of the objectives stated above.

PLANNING FOR SCIENCE LEARNINGS

As the inclusion of science in every grade of the elementary school becomes a goal sought actively by elementary educators, many complex questions must be answered. Most important among these are the following:

1. How can we be assured that in each year the program will be broad and balanced over all of the various fields?
2. How can we select out of the all of science that content which children should meet in school? Which facts, concepts, and generalizations should they be helped to learn?

3. How can we determine the sequential placement, year by year and grade by grade, of the science content selected for inclusion in the elementary school program?

Let us consider each of these concerns here, in turn, for a more complete grasp of both the questions and the most typical answers.

Maintaining Breadth and Balance

The science taught in the elementary school is actually general science. Little or no effort is made to develop course work restricted to any one of the separate fields of science; that is, there are no courses in chemistry, biology, and the like as such. Although some special interest groups, or clubs, may operate in an elementary school with the work organized around a special area of science like geology or astronomy, the common pattern is to develop general science programs. In developing this general program, educators must arrive at a defensible balance over the years between the biological and the physical sciences, as well as an equitable distribution of the areas within these two broad subdivisions.

To illustrate this point, the 1947 Yearbook of the National Society for the Study of Education, focused on science education, stated as follows:

> By the end of each year the children should have experienced some growth in the broader areas of the physical and biological environment, such as the following:
>
> *The Universe.* Here provision is made for the study of the stars, the sun, the moon, the planets, and their interrelationships. Pertinent materials would include those essential to an understanding of the causes of day and night, seasonal changes, tides, eclipses, and (less commonly) the vastness of the Milky Way galaxy and galactic systems beyond our own.
>
> *The Earth.* Among the pertinent topics in this phase of the environment are such problems as the origin of the earth, the formation of mountains, weathering of rock into soil, erosion, volcanism, prehistoric life, and the forces which have changed and are still changing the surface of the earth.
>
> *Conditions Necessary for Life.* What living things need in order to exist, how they are affected by changes in the environment, and the struggle for the conditions necessary to life are suggested materials in the development of this aspect of the environment.
>
> *Living Things.* Suitable materials include the variety of living things, the social life of animals, adaptations for protection, life cycles of plants and animals, how living things obtain their food, the economic importance of living things, and man's influence upon nature.
>
> *Physical and Chemical Phenomena.* Such chemical phenomena as rusting are considered in this phase of the environment. Physical phenomena which may be appropriate include: light, sound, gravity,

magnetism, and electricity, changes in the state of matter, and the phenomena associated with radiant energy and atmospheric changes.

Man's Attempt to Control His Environment. In this aspect of science the child may study man's control in gardens, on farms, in orchards; his inventions and discoveries; his use of power, of minerals; his control over living things; his study of places he cannot reach directly; and other topics.

In addition to the areas of the physical and biological environment, the curriculum maker and the teacher should consider the areas growing out of living and social needs, such as health, safety, conservation, economics. It is evident that these areas of living will utilize content described in the areas of the physical and biological environment and will form the basis for the development of desirable knowledge, attitudes, and appreciations.[7]

This statement suggests, certainly, a broad program in any one year of the elementary school. Content from all of the major branches of science must be studied if this breadth is to be achieved. As particular facts, concepts, and generalizations are selected for learning this test of overall balance must be met acceptably.

Organizing Science Learnings

Persons who have concerned themselves at length with the questions of content selection and grade placement in science have usually taken one of three positions. One group believes that the expressed interests of children should determine content selection and grade placement. A second group believes that the cues to these two concerns reside in the important concepts and generalizations in science itself. A third group believes that the personal and societal needs of the individual should determine the selection and arrangement of content. It should be obvious that these positions are directly related to the earlier general discussion (Chapter 7) of curriculum theory for the elementary school. A look again at that material would be helpful at this point. Let us here take a closer look at each position.

The children's interest approach to planning science experiences rests heavily on the idea that children are deeply interested in and fascinated by the natural environment. Children are accepted as being more naturally scientists than anything else. This line of reasoning concludes that children are constantly probing this natural environment in many ways, and that they develop interests and curiosities as a result. Such basic

[7] National Society for the Study of Education, *Science Education in American Schools, Forty-sixth Yearbook,* Part I (Chicago: University of Chicago Press, 1947), pp. 75–76.

motivation to learning should not be dismissed lightly, so the argument goes, but rather should be capitalized on directly for the development of the science program in any given classroom, and collectively for an entire school. The decisions as to what should be taught and when it should be taught are a result of teacher-pupil planning. It is believed that a most adequate scope in science would develop if the interests of children were allowed to operate freely; evidence is cited that, when given the chance, children raise questions that range over the whole of the sciences. Coverage of particular science content is not viewed with as much concern as is the matter of supporting and nurturing the science interests of children. It is incumbent upon the teacher to find out about the science interests and concerns of her pupils, and it is incumbent upon teacher and pupil alike to be critical of their expressed interests, selecting for study those interests that show promise of leading to both depth and breadth experiences in science for individual class members, as well as for the grade group as a whole.

Our developing insights into learning, and into child development generally, tell us that the interests of children cannot be ignored in planning science programs. Similarly, we are well aware that interests are *learned;* that is, we know that what we are interested in at any given time is in great part a result of our experience. Thus, despite the provocative nature of the set of ideas inherent in the "interest approach," most schools do not make children's interests the major determiners of the experience in the science program. Our knowledge of children, and of the role of interest in motivation for learning, does cause us to make a place for this approach in the planning of science experiences. Any set of criteria posed for the selection of science content in the elementary school will include the consideration of child interest and concern. However, child interest will be just one of several considerations that relate to such curriculum planning.

The science concepts approach is a set of ideas that, together, constitute a design for developing science programs based on an analysis of most important science concepts and generalizations. Originally, this system was developed by Craig, sometimes referred to as the "father" of elementary school science. In his early work in elementary science he described the approach he felt would be most effective in settling the questions of subject matter selection and grade placement in science. He suggested:

    a. Setting up criteria for the selection of science objectives.
    b. Obtaining science objectives satisfying these criteria.
    c. Evaluations of these objectives by educators, laymen, and children for their importance.

    d. Examining treatises on science to determine how these objectives can be analyzed into their constituent elements.

    e. Assigning these subordinate concepts as specific objectives to various grade levels on the basis of logical development.[8]

This approach, obviously, puts a high priority on the value of certain science content in contrast to other science content. It is assumed that informed people can determine the important science generalizations and principles that children should be helped to know. It is assumed, also, that a critical analysis of these generalizations will indicate the concepts to be developed and the facts to be learned if the generalizations are to be meaningful. This approach assumes also that a logical sequence will be evident that will enable one to assign these concepts and facts to various grade levels in a defensible and teachable order. It is held that, with children being so obviously interested in science, the teacher will meet no great difficulty in enlisting their efforts to learn whatever has been assigned to their grade. In fact, with the interests of children in science being so broad and inclusive it is felt that the relationship between current interests and assigned content will be easily established.

    This set of ideas has operated to produce science programs described as "spiralling" science curricula. That is, this approach quite methodically plans for some experience each year in all of the major branches of science, returning to teach in turn in succeeding years, with the assigned content building on but extending the experience of the year or years before.

    This is the approach that has been used, and continues to be used, in the development of most science programs in elementary schools. The series of textbooks developed for use in the elementary school science program are built on this spiral notion. One can trace the development of a given generalization through the books in these series as it is extended and refined each year. Or, a given school district may plan its own science program, utilizing these ideas. That is, the important science understandings to be developed by the completion of the elementary school are identified, then parts of this total job are assigned to particular grade levels. For instance, consider this material from the Los Angeles, California, City Schools as an illustration. Included here are some samples of grade-by-grade learning on plant life and on earth. Note the cumulative nature of the learning over the six years of the elementary school.

---

[8] Gerald S. Craig, *Certain Techniques Used in Developing a Course of Study in Science for the Horace Mann Elementary School*, Contributions to Education No. 276 (New York: Bureau of Publications, Teachers College, Columbia University, 1927).

Some Concepts Relating to Plant Life

Kdg.—Grade 1

Plants are living things.
Some plants are big.
Some plants are little.
Some plants live for a long time.
Some plants live for a short time.

Grade 2

Each kind of plant is different from any other kind of plant.
Each kind of plant has its own way of growing.
Some plants have roots, stems, leaves, and flowers.
Some plants produce seeds.

Grade 3

There are different kinds of plants, such as trees, bushes, vines.
Seeds are moved about in many ways; by water, by wind, by animals, and by man.
Plants use minerals that are dissolved in water that is in the soil.
Some plants grow on land; . . . in water; . . . ocean water; . . . in marshes.

Grade 4

Some plants live a short time and some plants live to be very old.
Some plants grow best in one kind of climate and some in another.
Some plants reproduce by bulbs, stems, roots, or leaves.

Grade 5

Different kinds of plants live in different parts of the world and in different environments.
Some plants are protected by a tough outer layer, or bark.
Some plants rest during the winter months.

Grade 6

Some plants live in water; some plants live on land, in soil, upon host, or on decaying organic matter.
Mold and bacteria are non-green plants.
Non-green plants may reproduce by spores, or grow and divide.

Some Concepts Relating to Earth

Kdg.—Grade 1

The earth is made of land, water, and air.
The earth has mountains and hills.
The earth has rivers and oceans.

Grade 2

The earth is round like a ball.
The earth is very large.
Each time the earth makes a full turn there is one day and one night.

Grade 3

The earth is round or almost round.
The earth is very old.

Land, rocks, water, and air are part of the earth.
There is more water than land on the earth.

Grade 4

The earth spins once on its axis every 24 hours.
The earth moves around the sun once in about every 365 days or one year.
The position of the earth in its relation to the sun and its movement around the sun causes seasons.

Grade 5

The earth has magnetic poles.
The earth's gravity pulls everything toward the earth.
The pull of gravity decreases as the distance from the earth increases.
Air pressure is greater near the earth than high above it.

Grade 6

The speed of the earth's turning at the equator is over 1000 mph.
Seasons are different in different parts of the earth.
Running water, glaciers, and wind wear away rock and cause erosion.
Geological periods of the earth are revealed through erosion.[9]

The logic of this approach becomes readily apparent. One can insure both breadth and balance in the science curriculum. With well informed people selecting most important science subject matter, and arranging it on a more or less "simple to complex" continuum, the matter of content selection and grade placement is readily resolved.

In spite of the rather universal appeal of the ideas presented in this approach to curriculum planning, it has been appraised rather critically by many, too. It was inevitable that such an approach would motivate studies that would attempt to ascertain the "most important" science content and to indicate the most "natural" sequence inherent in the content selected to be dealt with. And, it was natural that some would take a careful, analytical look at ongoing science programs and at available instructional materials for whatever cues they might yield in this matter. For instance, some years ago Pella analyzed the five most widely used science textbooks series, for the purpose of identifying areas of science included, topics discussed, and concepts presented in each area.[10] He found a fair degree of agreement in the content of the five series when the areas (such as plant life, electricity, animals) included were used as an index. When he examined the topics discussed in each area he found a relatively small degree of agreement, and an extremely small degree of agreement when he used the concepts presented as an index for

---

[9] Los Angeles City Schools, *Elementary Science Guide* (Los Angeles, California: Los Angeles City Schools, Division of Instructional Services, 1956).

[10] M. O. Pella, "Development of Concepts in Elementary Science," *Science Education* 33:269–272, October 1949.

similarity. He found an even greater variation in the grade placement of the concepts than in the actual concepts presented for study. He concluded that there was little or no agreement among the authors of elementary science textbooks concerning what or how much science should be included in the curriculum of the elementary school or the grade levels at which it should be taught. About this same time, Michals[11] reported a study in which he compared the content of a basic science series published in 1932 with the content of the same series published in 1946 (both by the same author). He found changes in the grade placement of certain content, and in the amount of content included from other areas such as geology or astronomy. Michals felt that the changes resulted from broader concepts of child development and learning that had become available.

The fact that little uniformity in subject matter selection and in grade placement has been found has led to two kinds of activity. Some have simply "looked" all the harder for the agreement that they felt could be achieved. In fact, extensive studies are presently being conducted by very learned science groups, in an attempt to reach some agreement on the most important science content to be learned and the best order or sequence in which to learn it. Others, chiefly those who would encourage more attention to the interests of children, have held that as much uniformity results from their more dynamic and spontaneous approach to curriculum planning as from this logical approach. They cite the results of studies like those mentioned above to support their notion that the specific content covered in the science program is secondary in the accomplishment of the purposes toward which the program is directed. Priority, for these people, goes to the nature of the experience with science, whatever it may be.

The personal-social problems approach is the third used to provide for science in the elementary school. It is built around an idea of the child in society. It accepts the notion that children growing up in our present-day society have many problems of a personal-social nature, which they need to be helped to understand and to solve. Some of these problems to be considered in school will be determined in terms of their general significance to the child and to the wider society. For the school to do less, say those who support this approach, is to shirk a great part of its responsibility to the children who come to it.

These problems may or may not be restricted to the content of science for their understanding or their solution. It is assumed that, if other

---

[11] Bernard E. Michals, "Content Changes in One Elementary Science Series," *Science Education* 34:248–250, October 1950.

assumptions about the basic importance of science in today's world are correct, a goodly number of such social problems will be heavily weighed with science and technology learnings. In fact, it is assumed that some of them would be dealt with successfully as science studies, or science units of work. Other problems would make it necessary to include content from fields other than science for the development of full understanding. That is, many of these studies would be social studies–science oriented, or health-science oriented, and so on. One of the curriculum guides cited earlier on science has this statement in it:

> *Integration with other curriculum areas.* Most social studies units are excellent in providing many possibilities for first-hand experiences with science materials. A large portion of health and safety practices are based upon scientific information.[12]

Another takes the following position on this point:

> At the present time it is not planned that science be taught as a separate subject; this does not mean, however, that time should not be provided in the weekly schedule for science activities. . . . For these reasons it is recommended that elementary science be introduced through an integrated approach. . . . It is obvious that social studies (especially geography), health, and arithmetic have many rich opportunities for integrative science activities.[13]

If this kind of integrative study is to be successful it must be planned for. That is, teachers must think ahead and anticipate the possibilities for dealing with subject matter from both the social studies and the natural sciences as they contemplate the development of a given unit of work. Some school districts have taken steps, as a way of encouraging the inclusion of science material in ongoing units of work, to assist teachers in developing sensitivity to the way in which science learnings may be developed alongside social studies learnings. For instance, the San Francisco City School System has prepared a supplementary teaching aid to show teachers how the relationships may be shown.[14] This aid was prepared in response to expressed need from teachers for some help on how they might develop more effective science instruction in the social studies. The material following shows in part how this aid has been organized and gives an idea as to the relatedness found in various large grade themes.

---

[12] San Bernardino City Schools, *op. cit.*

[13] Marion, Ohio Public Schools, *op. cit.*

[14] San Francisco Unified School District, *Science in the Social Studies: A Supplementary Teaching Aid* (San Francisco, California: San Francisco Unified School District, 1958).

SOCIAL FUNCTION

Conserving and Utilizing the Physical Environment of Home, School, and Neighborhood

PROBLEM AREAS	POSSIBLE SOCIAL CONCEPTS	POSSIBLE SCIENCE CONCEPTS
1. What kind of homes are in our neighborhood.	1. A home is where a family lives.	1. Wood, iron, glass, and stone are used in making buildings.
	1. Homes in the same community are often alike in many ways.	1. Wood comes from trees.
	1. Some homes differ within the same community.	1. Iron comes from the ground.
	1. Homes in our neighborhood are often like homes in other neighborhoods.	1. Glass is made from sand and other things. The mixture is melted by a hot fire into glass.
	1. Homes in our neighborhood may be different from homes in other neighborhoods.	1. Heat often makes things look different.
	1. Homes help protect us from the weather.	1. Concrete is man-made stone.
	1. Homes help protect us from strangers.	1. Artificial stone for buildings can be made by mixing sand, water and other things together
	1. Many homes are in a neighborhood.	1. Stone comes from the ground.
	1. Many homes may be in one building.	1. Wood is easier to cut and nail than stone or iron.
	1. Some people own their homes while other people rent their homes.	1. Iron rusts unless protected by a coat of paint.
		1. Some things let more light come through them than other things do.
		1. Different materials are suited to different purposes.
		1. The pipes in our house are connected with pipes in the street.
		1. A water pipe brings water from the main pipe in the street to the faucets in our house.
		1. A gas pipe brings cooking gas into the house from larger pipes from gas tanks.
		1. Electric wires bring electricity to and from the house from the power station.
		1. There are different kinds of soil.
		1. Most plants grow better in good garden soil than in sandy soil.
		1. Plants need water and light.
		1. Seeds grow up to be plants that make more seeds.
		1. Seeds are carried in many ways.
2. How many workers help to build our homes. A. Carpenters B. Plumbers C. Electricians D. Masons E. Painters F. Ironworkers G. Plasters H. Glaziers.	2. Many different workers help to build our homes.	2. When we move things from one place to another, work is done.
	2. Workers have to know many things to build part of a home.	2. When men move things without aid, they use their muscles.
	2. Since most workers can not do all the jobs needed to build a home, workers learn to do fewer things and do them well.	2. Sliding or rolling things is easier than carrying them.
	2. It often takes a long time to learn to do different jobs well.	2. It is easier to pull or push a heavy load when wheels are used than it is to drag or push it along the ground.
	2. Workers use different machines to help them work faster or easier.	2. It is easier to push or pull a load up or down a ramp than it is to lift it up or lower it down.
	2. Workers must learn to follow plans and directions.	2. Wheels and ramps are used to make work easier.
	2. Someone has to make the plans workers follow.	2. Many different trucks are used to carry building materials.
	2. Workers must learn to work together well.	2. Some trucks are made to carry particular materials.
	2. Workers must practice safety.	2. Workers use many machines to make work easier.
	2. Workers must keep healthy.	2. Workers need to protect themselves from becoming overheated.
	2. Workers earn their living from their work.	2. Workers need time for work and time for rest.
	2. Workers often learn new ways of doing things.	2. The earth pulls things toward itself.
	2. Many workers live in different neighborhoods.	

SOCIAL FUNCTION

Conserving and Utilizing the Physical Environment of the World Today

PROBLEM AREAS	POSSIBLE SOCIAL CONCEPTS	POSSIBLE SCIENCE CONCEPTS
How inventions and scientific discoveries have added to man's ability to utilize, to conserve, and to control natural resources.	Because of scientific inventions and discoveries, man has been able to better control his environment than at any time in his history.	1. Alkalies can be tested by red litmus paper. Red litmus is turned blue by alkalies.
1. Improved methods of agriculture.	1. With modern machinery and practices, today's farmer can produce more food than at any other time.	1. Starch will turn blue or violet when iodine is added.
A. Farm machinery		1. All food is made with the energy from the sun.
B. Fertilization	1. Farmers add to the soil to replace the minerals and other substances that have been absorbed by the crops.	1. Plants can make food out of water and minerals from the soil and a gas from the air.
C. Irrigation	1. Farmers can test their soils by means of litmus paper.	
D. Soil conservation		1. Root hairs absorb water and dissolved minerals through their thin walls.
E. Plant culture	1. Farmers can apply scientific knowledge to increase their production.	1. Plants get carbon dioxide from the air through tiny openings in the leaves.
F. Animal culture		
G. Reclamation	1. Farmers of many nations depend upon nitrate supplies from other nations.	1. When light shines on chlorophyll, chlorophyll causes carbon dioxide to combine with water and produce a sugar.
H. Weather study		
I. Insect control.	1. Formerly primitive countries are increasing their production and national economy through development of irrigation projects.	1. Every living cell contains protein.
		1. Vaccination and antitoxins help fight disease.
	1. Dams even out the flow of water from season to season and help prevent floods.	1. Vitamins are needed for good health.
		1. A kernel of grain contains a tiny baby plant and a large supply of food materials.
	1. Wrong methods of farming and lumbering have sped the erosion of soil.	
	1. Soil is one of the most valuable resources of a nation.	1. Food contains minerals.
	1. Many governments have conservation bureaus.	1. When bacteria and fungi feed on a plant or animal substance, they break them apart into its minerals and other raw materials.
	1. Soil must be saved and used wisely.	
	1. Grains are one of the world's most important food crops.	1. Soil has been built up gradually by the accumulation of grains and the crumbling materials of dead plants and animals.
	1. Rice is the chief food of many Oriental countries.	
	1. Grains are nearly complete in food value; they are more economical to grow; therefore they become the staple crop of highly populated areas.	1. The farmer can apply group tests for acids, alkalies or nutritional substances to determine the condition of soil.
	1. Milk and foods made from milk are among the most complete foods for people; many pastoral cultures are based on this food supply.	1. Contour plowing, planting cover crops, building check dams, and proper lumbering all help to protect the soil from washing away.
	1. Holland has reclaimed land from the sea by constructing dikes and pumping salt water from the land.	
	1. Weather study is enabling man to understand and eventually control weather.	
	1. World insect control will probably be one of the major problems of agriculture.	
2. Improved methods of forestry.	2. Conservation means "wise use," not merely "saving."	2. Disturbing one area of nature often disturbs other areas of nature by upsetting the "balance of nature."
	2. The world's natural resources must so be managed as to insure continued use by future generations.	2. There are two classes of trees: evergreen and deciduous.
	2. Forests must so be managed that new growth will insure supply and replace trees harvested.	2. Evergreen trees do not lose most of their leaves at the same time.
	2. Fire, disease, and man are the chief destroyers of world's forest resources.	2. Most broad leafed trees are deciduous; they lose most of their leaves at the same time.
		2. Forests help store ground water.
		2. Forests help protect soil from erosion.
		2. Forests help reduce floods.
		2. Trees are the oldest living things.
		2. Coal deposits are the remains of ancient forests.

This third approach to organizing science learnings tends to utilize science content more as a resource for the understanding and solution of problems rather than as an end in itself. Such joint, or integrative, studies attempt, too, to reflect the reciprocal nature of the science–social welfare relationship. That is, an attempt is made to develop awareness and appreciation of the efforts put forth by science for the welfare of society, as well as to call attention to the social impact of the further development of science. Educators are well aware of this close relationship. The 1957 Yearbook issued by the National Council for the Social Studies was entitled *Science and the Social Studies;* and similar interests have been reflected in the publications of science-oriented groups, too.

It would be accurate to say that most of the science taught in this approach is taught through and in relationship to social studies units of work. In many instances the scheme of handling social studies and science together is so much the normal pattern that many units in social studies, when carefully examined, are actually science units with very little social studies material at all. However, some misunderstanding and some concern inevitably arise. On the one hand, the elementary school may be dealing with more science and technology than is typically realized. On the other, the science specialist becomes concerned for the identity and definition of the field of science, and urges a more careful labeling of the studies and units that are undertaken in the classroom, resisting the all-encompassing way in which the term *social studies* is used. Too, the science specialist is concerned lest such an approach really restricts itself to a consideration of technological and engineering achievements, with children missing the opportunity for an experience with science itself. He calls attention to the fact that to the degree that such would be the case, all of the purposes stated for the science program would not be accomplished.

These concerns are to be taken seriously. Without a doubt there are some good educational reasons for relating these studies whenever it is wise and reasonable to do so. The interlocking nature of development and progress in the scientific and social spheres is obvious to all. And such an approach does help the learner to sense this relationship and to accomplish the task of integration for himself. This relationship must not be pursued, however, to the detriment of learning in either or both areas. Whenever such a joint handling obscures some important learnings, or limits the breadth of experience needed to accomplish all of the goals held important for the science program, it should be questioned.

No doubt many schools and teachers have moved in this direction because the social studies are already well entrenched in the curriculum and offer a time and place where some science may well be included. Science specialists call attention to the fact that this situation could be

revised. That is, why not have a time and place for science, moving to a consideration of social studies concerns as appropriate? Present trends indicate that time must be found for both, with neither flourishing at the expense of the other. In fact, a strong program in one of these areas complements and supports the work in the other. The discussion on the unit of work (Chapter 19) deals in detail with some of the questions suggested here that relate to planning a balanced educational program.

OTHER IMPORTANT CONSIDERATIONS IN SCIENCE INSTRUCTION

Experimentation and Demonstration

The accomplishment of the purposes set down for the science program calls for an experience with science itself, that is, for a *personal* experience with the processes and procedures of science as an area of human endeavor. This experience should include opportunities for *experimentation* in the classroom by individuals and groups, as well as *demonstrations* of known scientific principles and phenomena. Both kinds of *experience* make a contribution to science learnings. The difference between these two types of experience, however, is not always kept in mind, and the labels are interchanged a bit too freely for most efficient instruction in the science area. Let us try to contrast the two for the sake of clarity. Experimentation suggests a situation in which something is unknown or very much in doubt; where a conclusion can, at best, be held only as a hunch or an "educated guess" until certain actions are actually taken to verify or to nullify it. Typically this demands an experimental situation, such as the following:

a. Two young animals of the same kind are fed different diets to see which diet results in the more rapid and greater weight gain.
b. Two young animals of different kinds are weighed and measured and observed each day to ascertain which one develops more rapidly.
c. Certain weather data are collected for a month during winter and compared with long-term averages to see if impressions of colder, wetter, or snowier (or the reverse) than usual are verifiable.
d. Rain is "caught" on a local school site in order to compare the amount of rainfall there with the amount announced for the area in a given 24-hour period as a check on the evenness with which rainfall is distributed over a town or city.

Such situations approximate an experience with science itself. Problems or questions have to be discussed and understood clearly before the experimentation gets under way. Certain manipulations of equipment or

subjects is involved; observations must be carefully and regularly made; data must be systematically gathered and recorded; conclusions accepted must be found in the data, readily verifiable by others who follow a similar pattern of experimentation. While one may know certain things closely related to the particular experimental situation, he does not know what the results of the experiment will be until it is over and done.

In a demonstration the situation is somewhat different. Here something is known by the demonstrator (usually the teacher) and is to be shown to the class. This knowledge can be shared with the class at the outset in the form of a careful explanation, and followed by a demonstration proving the explanation; or a scientific principle can be simply stated to the class and followed by a demonstration, slow and deliberate, in which the principle is demonstrated for all to see and accept. All of the manipulations may be performed by the demonstrator only, while the class watches, or multiple sets of material and equipment demanded by the demonstration may be made available, with small groups of students demonstrating to themselves along with the teacher-demonstrator. The conclusion, then, in a demonstration is typically shared with the class prior to the experience, and that which follows is to give the class confidence in accepting the conclusion or principle originally stated.

There is a place for both types of experiences in an elementary school science program. Their differences must be clearly understood, however, so that their individual use will accomplish certain important purposes and not others. That is, as techniques they must be used with insight and deliberateness. Teachers need to have a clear conception of both, and skill and security to use both. Individual teacher differences inevitably come into the picture. Some teachers are uncomfortable with the experimental situation since they are not sure just what it is that the class will learn. These teachers need to keep the processes of science clearly in mind as content to be learned along with the end products of these processes. Others, in contrast, are quite comfortable with the experimental situation but are concerned lest something go wrong with the demonstration, where content to be learned is known, that will obscure what they are trying to demonstrate. In the great majority of instances both situations will go according to plan, and their use will make it more likely that both the content and the process of science will be learned by children. Often the rechecking of equipment, the audible utterances in which the demonstrator reviews steps already taken in an attempt to see where the situation "went off the tracks" actually causes the demonstration to take on added meaning for the observers. Certainly teachers should be encouraged and helped to include quality experimental situations and demonstrations in their classroom programs.

Materials for Science Teaching

The question of materials and equipment for teaching science is important to every classroom teacher. Such supplies run the gamut from equipment to support experiments, demonstrations, and science activity generally to the use of printed materials in the science program. Without an adequate supply of proper materials for teaching, the science venture will not flourish.

The use of low-cost, homemade equipment has been encouraged in the elementary school science program. Most of the reasons for using this equipment are commendable and acceptable. If one can use familiar materials out of the kitchen and the garage or the local hardware or dime store for science experiences it associates a kind of comfort and security with an experience that may have seemed remote and even mysterious. The use of such simple equipment contributes to the concept of simplicity in science as an endeavor. It means also that children, as well as teacher, can participate in bringing together equipment for the science program. It demands a kind of resourcefulness and ingenuity on the part of teacher and class that is not completely foreign to the scientist at work in the laboratory. Thus, screwdrivers, glass jars, measuring spoons and cups, blotters, baking soda, flower pots, pie pans, and the like find their way to school and into the classroom science program. Also, brushes, bags of corks, dry cell batteries, medicine droppers, wire, and the like can be purchased economically at local stores, and adapted for use as science equipment.

However, the complete realization of the purposes and values of science for children calls for accessibility to certain moderately expensive and complex equipment. Microscopes must be available if microscopic life is to be opened up for examination and thought by children. Telescopes are needed if space is to be an object of concern in the modern world. Balances and weights are important for certain weighing and measuring tasks. A galvanometer, hygrometer, magnetic compasses, barometer, electric motors, a microphone, certain chemicals, and so on have their place in an elementary school science program. To rely too completely on the kitchen cupboard and the local dime store is to thwart the fullest development of science learnings.

Certainly, each classroom does not have to be equipped with these more expensive and complicated pieces of equipment. Schemes establishing "science closets" in local elementary schools, and science resource centers at the central office level have proved effective means for sharing such equipment among teachers and schools. In particular instances, equipment may be loaned by the high school science department. County level centers may be established that parallel in science the services often

found for audio-visual aids to instruction. The local situation will determine the best arrangement for purchase and distribution of such equipment, but it must be available for classroom use.

The use of books and other printed material has been an object of concern in the development of elementary school science instruction, too. This concern stems from the urgency to make certain that the science experience is something more than reading about science. In the process of taking a firm position on this matter some have been in doubt as to the place of books and related printed material in the science program. It seems rather clear that there is a real place and need for printed material in science instruction.

The scientist—and this term includes the classroom scientist—finds it necessary and efficient to check on already available information pertinent to a given problem before undertaking activity designed to resolve the problem. Making the known a matter of public property for other scientists to use has been a great boon to the development of science. Children in the classroom should early develop the habit of consulting books and similar resources for assistance in science. The overuse of books to the exclusion of other necessary experiences must be guarded against for the development of a well-rounded science effort. As students use printed resources, checking one reference against another, and resolving authority issues when references used do not agree on given points, they are having a science experience of real value.

There are a number of types of printed materials that may be used in the classroom. First are the textbooks made available through various elementary school science series. The textbook is the major instructional tool made available to teachers; in some instances it is the only one. If teachers *use* the textbook to help them to develop a sound science program, and not have the textbook *use* them, these printed materials can be very useful in the science program. They are well written, well illustrated, and organized efficiently. Their use offers security to some teachers and helps them to anticipate and perceive a program for the classroom. So long as this security stops short of settling for simply "reading the books" their use will support and not conflict with the aims of the science program. Variety and flexibility may be enhanced by using several copies of textbooks from more than one series in a classroom rather than restricting one's resource to one series only. Zim, an outstanding science educator, puts it this way:

> Perhaps an ideal situation might be something like the following—
> for a fourth grade of 25 pupils. This fortunate teacher would have
> three copies of each of the fourth-grade science texts from five different
> elementary science series. Then, in addition, one copy each of third-

and of the fifth-grade texts of the same series. Such a selection of 25 books would be of greater service to the class than 25 copies of one fourth-grade text. It would better allow for individual differences and would provide information for a wider and freer science program.[15]

A great boon to science teaching at the present time is found in the rapidly increasing quality of trade books available for use in the classroom. These kinds of books are found in the library and in the bookstore, written not only for school use, but rather as highly reliable informational books on science topics. They address themselves to quite specific topics (such as stars, or whales, or snakes) and are thorough but concise in style. They supply a maximum amount of information in a minimum of pages and are a wonderful supplement to the textbook. The style of writing and the excellent illustrations combine to hold children's interest. Teachers need to know about and to use these books.

Additionally, there are other types of printed materials that have a place in the science program. Sets of children's reference books, material from magazines, free and inexpensive materials produced by industry, national nonprofit organizations, state and national governmental agencies, and so on are all available.

Certainly the printed page has its place in the fullest development of an elementary school science program.

Utilizing Community Resources

The utilization of community resources as an adjunct to instruction is particularly useful and helpful in the area of science. Taking the class into the community, and bringing the community into the classroom, can do much to vitalize and give added meaning to learning experiences in science. Community exploration may at times be the source of problems and questions for consideration and study. A visit to a local industry, a walk to a nearby housing development, a classroom visit by a person recently abroad may all suggest areas of concern for further exploration, or lend additional meaning and vitality to work presently under way. Certainly the community, as a source of essential data, can play a fundamental role in support of the science projects undertaken in the classroom. As observations are made, and as persons are consulted, additional information over and above that which reading and experimentation yield becomes available. Too, the contact with the community helps children to see and to become more aware of the varied applications of science to day-to-day living.

Some schools, desiring to strengthen their science programs, but

---

[15] Herbert S. Zim, *Science for Children and Teachers* (Washington, D.C.: Association for Childhood Education International, 1953).

realizing the inadequacy of science skill and understanding possessed by the faculty, have utilized science personnel in the community to advantage. In part, such persons have been willing to give time and assistance to teachers who were attempting to build up their own backgrounds in science. Also, many of these scientists have been willing to do much more than simply visit a classroom for a single presentation. Some have actually assumed responsibilities for meeting regularly with small groups of interested children on a sort of science club basis, thus helping the school to identify and to nurture science potential beyond that which the classroom teacher might be able to do.

To do what is suggested here calls for a certain flexibility in the school program, and a willingness on the part of the teacher to "go that extra mile" in planning and arranging such community experiences. But, the results are typically gratifying beyond the expenditure of time and energy. As mentioned elsewhere, there is skill to be developed in the use of community resources, and teachers continually learn better and more efficient ways to use the community. Properly used, the community can make considerable contributions to the science program.

EVALUATION IN THE SCIENCE PROGRAM

The task of evaluation in the science program is difficult and exacting, but it is fundamental to the vitality and continued well-being of the program. In Chapter 20 the problem of evaluation is discussed more completely as one of the chief areas of responsibility for the classroom teacher. What is said here is prefatory to this more extensive consideration of the problem.

Behavioral Statement of Purposes

A great deal of clarity and direction is introduced into the job of evaluation if the statement of purposes against which such evaluation is taking place are so stated as to give real direction to the instructional efforts for a particular area of study, in this instance science. It follows then, that the degree to which the general kind of statement of goals mentioned earlier in this chapter can be reduced to "statements of desired behaviors" will have a great deal to do not only with guiding instruction but also with furnishing cues for evaluation. That is, such a behavioral statement is suggestive of the kinds and sources of data a teacher will need to evaluate the learning taking place in the science program. You will remember that the general statement of purposes cited earlier here embraced:

1. Information—about and concerning science
2. Method—specifically the process of science; the scientific method
3. Attitude—the objectivity and openmindedness of science
4. Appreciation—for science, technology, and the natural environment

The analysis of any one of these general goals in the direction of "behaviors sought" obviously bares clues for an approach to evaluation. For instance, a listing of behaviors that might openly be pursued in instruction related to the "development of a scientific attitude" could include:

a. Holds a conclusion as tentative while he seeks information supporting it
b. Changes his mind easily in the face of new information
c. Refuses to accept superstitions as explanations for happenings in the natural environment
d. Shows evidence of an emerging set of criteria to judge an authoritative source
e. Listens willingly to others who have information relevant to his concern

Such a statement not only gives more helpful direction to the teacher anticipating the instructional situation, but it is immediately suggestive of approaches to the evaluation task.

Approaches to Evaluation

It is readily apparent that the teacher has only certain ways of collecting information for assessing the learning taking place in any program. That is, he can use certain paper and pencil approaches to this job, or he can converse with pupils seeking insight into accomplishment, or he can observe pupils systematically for similar data. The particular evaluation job at hand typically suggests the technique or approach most profitable to use.

The selected behaviors listed above that relate to the development of a scientific attitude suggest more use of conversation and observation techniques for evaluation than the use of paper and pencil tests. As one contemplates the total range of purposes in the science program, it is evident that these techniques plus paper and pencil instruments could be designed and would be useful in assessing the effectiveness of the instruction taking place. The job of evaluation in science is broad enough to embrace all of the typical approaches to evaluation in terms of style or form, and to include instruments ranging from teacher-made ones to various standardized tests available for science. The skill of the teacher must be broad for the task itself is a broad one.

That science must and will flourish in the elementary school is evi-

dent. It is a "fundamental" for today's children as surely as is anything else that the schools might aspire to do for them. An understanding of science is basic to general citizenship, and the scientific endeavor calls for personnel especially skilled in research and in engineering to participate in it. The elementary school years can contribute to both of these ends; the future for elementary school science looms bright.

REFERENCES

Blough, Glenn O. *It's Time for Better Elementary School Science.* Washington, D.C.: National Science Teachers Association, National Education Association, 1958.
> This is the report of an exploratory conference on the elementary school science program, covering such matters as proper objectives, desirable curriculum plans, needed equipment, and so on.

Blough, Glenn O., Julius Schwartz, and Albert J. Huggett. *Elementary School Science and How To Teach It* (Revised edition). New York: The Dryden Press, 1958.
> Prepared as a textbook for elementary teachers, this volume includes both science content as such and suggestions as to how to teach it most effectively.

Craig, Gerald S. *Science for the Elementary School Teacher* (Second edition). Boston: Ginn and Company, 1958.
> A book written by the man often referred to as "the father of elementary school science"; contains both science content judged appropriate for children and suggestions for teaching.

Dunfee, Maxine, and Julian Greenlee. *Elementary School Science: Research, Theory and Practice.* Washington, D.C.: Association for Supervision and Curriculum Development, National Education Association, 1957.
> An excellent summary of the research findings and the general literature on the teaching of science in elementary schools.

Freeman, Kenneth, and others. *Helping Children Understand Science* (Revised edition). Philadelphia: The John C. Winston Company, 1959.
> Describes desirable teaching practices and points to the implications for science learning in the general developmental characteristics of children.

Hubler, Clark. *Working with Children in Science.* Boston: Houghton Mifflin Company, 1957.
> The title suggests the content of this book.

National Society for the Study of Education. *Rethinking Science Education* (Fifty-ninth Yearbook, Part I). Chicago: University of Chicago Press, 1960.
> This important statement sponsored by a group that is influential in policy formation contains in Chapters 1–8 provocative material for the elementary educator.

Sheckles, Mary. *Building Children's Science Concepts* (Practical Suggestions for Teaching No. 15). New York: Bureau of Publications, Teachers College, Columbia University, 1958.
> Reviews the development of concepts in science and outlines experiences for children that should help to develop concepts about rocks, soil, air, and water.

15

ESTHETICS AND
CREATIVITY: THE ARTS

THE ESTHETIC PROGRAM

Throughout history, man has endeavored to think creatively and to express in word, picture, music, or dance some of his innermost feelings, some of the joys, fears, and important ideas that he has felt. Every cultural group has produced rituals of song and dance, crafts relating to a mode of living, and other means of expressions through the manipulation of raw materials, sound, and bodily movement. These are forms of communication that utilize as media not only the language of words, but the language of music, movement, line, color, and form. These "languages" are identified as the fine arts.

As man has sought to express himself creatively through the materials he has found in his environment, so he has constantly endeavored to bring esthetic pleasure to every phase of his life. The development of dyes for textiles, the creation of unique and characteristic architecture, the use of practical but esthetic lines on a boat, the cultivation of flowers and shrubs to make his home beautiful—these are the results of man's desire to have beauty around him, the result of creativity in finding and producing means of esthetic enjoyment.

Such is the heritage of America's children today. Theirs is a world of esthetic desire, of fine creation, of creative potential that should be nurtured as their natural right.

The Nature of Creativity

Creativity has several dimensions. Creativity implies the ability to create, but generally speaking, it refers to human response that has in-

herent in it qualities of spontaneity or uniqueness. It is a manner of expressing ideas and thoughts in a truly original way as opposed to the imitative process of production, or the less purposeful, free thinking of reverie. Spontaneity, flexibility, insight, imagination, interpretation, fluency, and inspiration are all involved, but do not alone produce creativity. In the area of fine arts, creativity involves a personal, imaginative, or feeling response resulting in a concrete product. This concept has many implications for education.

The most common interpretation of creativity involves the artist who paints a picture to express his experience, the musician who composes a lovely bit of harmony as an expression of his inner feeling, or the poet who selects appropriate words and puts them together to express a thought in most pleasing fashion. These are the people who have developed skills in the manipulation of their medium, who have found ways to produce something a little different, or characteristic of an individual way of thinking or feeling. The creative act within the fine arts setting is the most typical, however limited, concept of creativity.

Creativity can be of another kind. Einstein, who developed the theory of relativity, is an example of a creative mind that utilizes all known facts in a manner that goes beyond those facts. This kind of creativity is the production of ideas or things projected beyond present knowledge or products to a development that is an improvement of the old. Other examples of this kind of creativity might be the toolmaker who develops a new technique for using the lathe, the teacher who creates a different method of vocabulary drill, or the tanner who changes successfully the chemical formula for processing leather.

In the studio, the research laboratory, and the shop, the creative process is essentially the same. The creator manipulates materials or ideas according to his experience and knowledge, seeking the result that will become the creative product. The product may not necessarily be one of esthetic reaction, but a highly practical creation. In this process, then, a similarity is recognized between high level problem solving and the creative act.

Though the relationship of creativity to problem solving is recognized, they are not entirely identical. Russell indicates this difference when he says:

> The difference between problem solving, or "reasoning," and creative thinking is that problem solving is more objective, more directed toward some goal, which is usually external. Problem solving must be more consonant with the facts. Creative thinking is more personal, less fixed. It achieves something new rather than coinciding with previously de-

termined conditions. It also tends to involve more intuition and imagination. . . .[1]

There is in the creativity of the poet and the researcher a common factor: ingenuity, originality, or something different from that which has gone before. Quality of creativity in the picture, the poem, the theory, or the tanning formula may vary as to the amount of difference, originality, uniqueness. While almost every individual act has an element of uniqueness because of the difference in personal experiences brought to the new activity, the level of creativeness is usually measured by the degree of originality, difference, or ingenuity expressed.

To demonstrate creativity, a child need not produce something that has never been done before, or something that must always be esthetically expressive. Rather, he should demonstrate an ability to produce or express in an individual way, to progress beyond the facts, to communicate feelings and ideas from a different point of view or with some amount of unique modification arising from his own personal reaction.

Creative thinking. The term *creative thinking* can embrace this whole process of creative production. Indeed, some authorities use *creative thinking* synonymously with *creativity.* Creative thinking is the process of deriving new meaning, new interpretation, new relationships, or developing new combinations and new patterns from experience and known facts. The process of consideration, of mental exploration, of some ingenious and imaginative reasoning is the method whereby the new emerges from the old through thought.

Consideration of the concept of creativity in terms of creative thinking, which is a purposeful and orderly process, indicates that the creative act must be guided by some *conscious purpose.* Creativity is "not an affair of idle moments."[2] No creative product can be the result of completely planless endeavor because it is an attempt to express an idea or feeling. There has been a motive or stimulus of some kind. Though the stimulus could be emotional in origin, the changing of the abstract feeling to concrete form necessitates active and rational behavior. Dewey states this idea aptly when he says,

> What most of us lack in order to be artists is not inceptive emotion nor yet merely technical skill in execution. It is the capacity to work a vague idea and emotion over into terms of some definite medium.[3]

---

[1] David H. Russell, *Children's Thinking* (Boston: Ginn and Company, 1956), p. 306.
[2] Italo L. De Francesco, *Art Education: Its Means and Ends* (New York: Harper & Brothers, 1958), p. 46.
[3] John Dewey, *Art as Experience* (New York: Minton, Balch and Company, Inc., 1934).

A child experiments with or explores a medium that is new to him, but the noisy pounding and energetic manipulation of a ball of clay ceases shortly when the child wants to fashion some object. Thus his actions are guided by the kind of product he wishes to create. The more mature the child and the more skilled he becomes with a material, the greater the conscious purpose involved. Because of this conscious direction of effort, the child should be able to express in words something about his creative product.

If the creative act does seem to demonstrate unconscious purpose, that is, the symbolization of feeling in concrete form, it may be merely the expression of impressions or memories. The ''feelings'' become conscious expression of subconscious experience as they are reproduced in artistic form.

Process and product. Some writers express concern about the importance of the creative process as opposed to the importance of the creative product. Which is more important, the process or the product? Lowenfeld emphasizes the creative factor as being a mode of expression, not content; the *how*, not the *what* of a product.[4] Surely we would agree that if creative thinking is important to the education of children, the creative process assumes much value. This process involves the identification of a feeling or an idea that needs to be expressed through some medium. Also involved is the direction of activity toward the completion of the product; decisions, manipulation, and ongoing evaluation become part of the process. All of the maneuvering an individual experiences, alone or in a group, in the act of creation becomes a part of the person and influences the development of his creative potential. The delineation of the problem, the sharing of ideas, the development of a concrete expression of an abstract feeling, is a process through which growth takes place and character is formed. Even if the product is entirely unsuccessful, the creator may sense satisfaction from the procedure and involvement that produced the end result. Children who create a song that may be technically inferior have learned much about the process of creating.

On the other hand, the product created may sometimes assume more importance than the process developing it. The playwright, for example, is especially concerned about his creative product and its effect upon theater patrons. The process that the author goes through assumes less importance than the message held within the finished product. Perhaps a group of children who develop a rhythm pattern may also receive more value from the performance of the final activity than from the experiences in developing it.

---

[4] Viktor Lowenfeld, *Creative and Mental Growth* (Revised edition; New York: The Macmillan Company, 1952), p. 4.

So we cannot indicate that either the process or the product will assume greater importance. Both are necessary in an esthetic program. Generally, a balance may be found, though different media may demand different emphases. The challenge to the teacher is to help children achieve ever more effective processes of creation and higher levels of production.

Social importance of creativity. As we consider the importance of process and product, another concern becomes apparent: the question of the social importance of the creative product. Should the creative act be assessed for its social worth? Must a creative product be accepted by others before it is deemed of creative value? Must it evoke others' emotional reactions, intellectual or emotional curiosity?

Some feel that creativity can be important because of the individual satisfactions of the creator, because the product created satisfies the personal purposes of the creator. The young child who models a pot of clay may produce a result of little social worth or esthetic value. Only the child and his mother are delighted by the crude work. Even adults engaging in various arts as leisure time activities seldom produce something that will arouse the intellect or emotions of others. But the mere act of creating, of producing something that is one's own creation, is important to developing the creative potential of all men.

Who possesses creativity? One of the problems related to the school's program for esthetic development lies in the lack of understanding about who possesses the creative potential. Authorities agree that there is creative potential in all individuals; the difference lies in degree. Even within one individual, differences occur in the degree to which he may be creative in various fields. Most children in school possess more latent creative ability than most teachers suspect.

Creativeness is apparently dependent upon both hereditary characteristics and environmental factors. That some inherited ability influences creativity is suggested by the life of Mozart, who composed at the age of four years. On the other hand, studies have shown that artistic ability can be influenced by experience, for environmental factors may promote or delay the development of creative ability. It is generally agreed that with encouragement, creativeness within an individual may be improved.

Very young children seem to demonstrate greater freedom of expression than older people. As children grow older, social pressures—especially group standards and social criticism—discourage originality or individuality. Children who make up their own songs or who dance "senselessly" meet adult ridicule, part of the stern reality of life. Imaginative stories may be met with derision. Schools themselves insist upon social conformity. Even television and advertisements influence child behavior and its natural spontaneity by demanding some kind of conformity. It is understandable that as the child grows older his behavior falls in line

with socially acceptable attitudes and ideas. We cannot assume, however, that younger children will be the most creative; in spite of social pressures, many individuals make important creative contributions at mature ages. Such men as Victor Hugo and Beethoven produced original, lasting material when they were over fifty years of age.

The task of the teacher is to develop and encourage a psychological atmosphere within the classroom that accepts spontaneity, individuality, freedom of expression, creativity. A fine balance must be achieved between the creative behaviors and social conformity. The teacher must also remember that while creative potential is inherent in the individual, it is not a characteristic that can easily be turned on and off, as water in a faucet. Esthetic expression is the result of all experience. A teacher cannot conduct a rigid and directive program most of the day and then expect to be successful in a nondirective art lesson. Creativity must be nourished—fed by many esthetic experiences, cultivated by many opportunities to create, and fostered in a consistent atmosphere of flexibility and constructive teacher guidance.

Upon that ability common to problem solving and creative thinking, civilization has been developed, and man has changed his manner of living throughout history. It is this creativity, this expertness, that produces new ways of doing things that advance a culture; without it, the culture would stagnate. Our democracy in particular is dependent upon creative minds and the flow of new ideas that bring desirable change.

Issues in the Modern Creative and Esthetic Program

The fine arts program in every school and classroom encounters a number of problems specific to the fine arts program that need consideration here.

Should the arts be taught by specialists? The majority of the children in the nation are provided esthetic experiences by the regular classroom teacher for two reasons. In the first place, elementary schools have been traditionally organized around one teacher for one group of children. Almost all elementary teachers are prepared and receive credentials to teach every subject in the curriculum. Second, some school districts have had much difficulty in procuring adequately prepared teachers in the ratio of one to a group. There is neither money nor personnel available to provide specialists to teach the various arts in all schools.

For a number of reasons, it is well that the regular teacher be responsible for the esthetic program. He is more likely to know the interests and needs peculiar to his own group than a teacher who teaches a single subject to a number of groups. He can more adequately integrate various esthetic and creative experiences into the over-all program, for creativity

should be a part of all activity rather than limited to a special time and place. He can make special emphases when the situation calls for it. He can provide instruction to small groups at the moment they need it rather than wait for a special lesson when the whole group expects guidance.

On the other hand, it seems rather unrealistic to expect that every classroom teacher can be highly skilled in all areas or have the training and expertness demanded for some instructional situations. Special teachers with talent and ability can in many ways bring greater richness to the esthetic and creative program. Because administrators recognize the need for some specialists, many schools are finding the means to provide them, particularly for instrumental and vocal music, and for general arts and crafts.

Special teachers may operate in many ways. Some teach the regular classroom lessons at designated hours. These lessons may be enrichment lessons entirely unrelated to other activities. In this case the regular teacher must assume responsibility for other types of creative experiences. Some specialists work closely with the teacher in planning experiences and teaching lessons that not only enrich creative experiences but also are suggested by other curriculum areas or previous experiences of children. Many special teachers act as consultants to the regular teachers, giving them ideas and instructions to help them enrich their program. When special teachers work with the regular teacher, or act as consultants, it is important that the teacher not leave the room when the specialist conducts a lesson. Some special teachers conduct classes like band, dance, or dramatic activities, which include selected children from a number of rooms.

The problem of special help is solved in some schools by providing services of special supervisors or consultants. Such consultants may conduct workshops to extend the skills of the teachers, prepare written materials for teacher and child reference, or gather materials for use in the classroom. They may visit classrooms regularly to find ways in which they may help improve instruction, or they may encourage teachers to call upon them when specific help is needed. Experts are very helpful in enriching esthetic and creative experiences for children.

Patterns of teacher education also help to alleviate this problem. Some institutions give minors in special subjects, others help young teachers develop "strength" in a particular area. In this way, teachers may teach their regular classes and act as consultant in a special area to other teachers.

The time and place of esthetic experiences. Questions of concern to young teachers about teaching esthetic and creative activities are: When should they be taught? How can they be related to the over-all program? How much time should be allotted to each activity?

Usually courses of study or other school district bulletins will help teachers arrive at a reasonable distribution of time. Definite allotments are commonly made for music and art; some musical activities such as rhythm and dance may be part of the physical education period; poetry and literature may be included with language arts. These time allotments are usually flexible and should be used with discretion.

Several methods of allocating time can be utilized. If twenty minutes a day are allotted for art, it may be wise to lump the twenty minutes of two or three days together in order that adequate time is available for an activity. If the creation of a cooperatively composed song runs over the usual time for music, the next period is simply cut short or the time is made up the next day. Another way of adjusting time is to use flexibly the time for certain subjects. Work on choric verse is a justified use of the language arts hour. Practicing a folk dance or painting a mural may well be part of the social studies hour, if the activity is related to the major topic being studied. This kind of flexibility is easily worked out in the self-contained classroom of the elementary school.

The teacher needs to recognize the amount of time necessary to complete the activity. Some activities may well be extended over a number of days; others necessitate completion in one day. To develop a lesson well, time must be made available to prepare, to do, to clean up, and to evaluate. The introduction, motivation, or planning periods may vary in length according to the previous experiences of the children. The time for the activity period must be predetermined and understood by all children. Preferably, the teacher warns the class a few minutes before the closing of the work period. The time for evaluation may also vary in length. If children do not complete the work they have undertaken in the period allotted, additional time should be scheduled so that the satisfaction of completion may be realized.

Another problem of time and place is how the esthetic activities are to be made a part of the over-all program. Some feel that all activities should be integrated as part of the unit. Others feel that all esthetic experiences should be presented regularly as special lessons and unrelated to other curriculum areas. The type of curriculum planning that utilizes both of these ideas is becoming increasingly popular.

Within the unit all types of esthetic activities are used, and apparently for two purposes. First, they allow the children to express their own ideas about the central topic in pictures, murals, creative songs or stories. Second, some activities help the children better understand the cultural group being studied. Authentic songs and dances, study and use of authentic realia, designs, and literature help the children understand the creative expression of others. Such activities are frequently made an integral part of unit study.

Since esthetic activities provided only in the context of the unit may not give the variety of experiences deemed valuable for children, teachers also arrange some special lessons that are unrelated to the units. Activities associated with holidays, special auditorium programs, or other events such as unusual thunderstorms, the first spring flowers, or frost on the windows might well be motivation for special experiences. Or a teacher might plan a delightful hour of work with aluminum wire sculpture just to add variety of media, to provide another kind of creative experience for children.

Another way to bring esthetic activities into the over-all program is to make them part of the regular ongoing daily program. Opening exercises bring an opportunity to sing. Rest periods give an opportunity to listen to music played quietly. Many teachers find that some of the art experiences become excellent independent activities when children have completed other assignments. Easel painting, clay modeling, weaving, or finishing other uncompleted projects related to unit work may be continued quietly and individually with a minimum of teacher supervision.

What comes first, technique or experience? A constant controversy exists around teaching basic techniques versus providing basic experience, or freedom of uninhibited expression. Should children be provided with materials and allowed to manipulate them in their own way or should they first be given some guidance in the basic techniques for the use of the medium?

Educators today rather widely agree that persistent and formalized drill on the use of a paint brush, the mixing of colors, or any other technique usually should *not* precede more informal experiences with a medium. Teachers recognize the fact that children and adults need to experience a period of exploratory manipulation before creation takes place or before specialized techniques may be understood. For example, the child who first uses calcimine paint will play with the brush on the paper just to see what happens to the paint. The child who handles clay for the first time will pound and push and pull experimentally before producing a definite shape. All individuals seem to go through this exploratory phase to some degree, though the length of the period may differ among individuals or according to the material involved. This characteristic gives teachers a clue to allow some time for free manipulation of some materials before much guidance in technique is given.

Generally speaking, educators agree that children should first be provided with many kinds of experiences in many kinds of creative expression. Then as the child himself expresses a desire for technical help, or as the teacher helps him to discover a need for it, the basic techniques are taught to help him gain greater satisfaction from the medium. This

consciousness and insight will give children greater benefit from the formal teaching of skills.

Part of the rationale that suggests some manipulation prior to training in technique is the expectation that the child will be creative, that he will express some ideas in his own way. Ideas emerge from experience, and the experience may be the manipulation of a material or some other activity that develops and clarifies ideas so that they may be expressed in concrete form. For example, if children dramatize pioneer family life, they need much information gleaned from reading, talking, studying relics, and looking at pictures. For a dramatic production, this kind of knowledge is much more logical than instruction in the use of gestures, voice control, or how to move on the stage. If children are writing poetry, they may need to try out many phrases to see how they sound before the structure of the poem will develop.

The general rule of experience before technique cannot always be followed. In the case of some craft activities, instruction is necessary before the child can participate. Before asking children to weave a basket, for example, the teacher will need to explain the procedure for weaving. Or if children are to do some paper sculpture, they might first need some techniques in how to "sculpture" the paper. In these cases the teacher makes sure he demonstrates only technique and does not present materials in such a way that the children's creativity with the technique is influenced.

The presentation of techniques is not to be confused with a teacher's method of organizing the experience. When he helps children arrange the paper for finger painting and guides the distribution of the paint, he uses good common sense to avoid confusion and disorder. Once plans are made and material distributed, the children are free to use the medium as they wish.

What about evaluating the arts? Another problem of the esthetic and creative program of the elementary school is evaluation. Instructional guidance which moves forward in terms of growth necessitates evaluation. However, work in the esthetic area can be neither right nor wrong, as it is in arithmetic; nor can it be labeled good, satisfactory, or poor as it is in handwriting. Evaluation in the esthetic area must be flexible, must be designed to inspire children to freedom of expression and ever finer levels of creativity. Therefore all levels of creativity must be accepted in a way that will preserve the dignity of the individual and the intrinsic worth of the product.

Every opportunity should be taken to help children find satisfaction in the expression of their own ideas in widely varied responses. Satisfaction is the major criterion in both individual and group activities. Because satisfaction is a part of growth, evaluation helps children reach

for ever more satisfactory levels of production. Arbitrary standards are generally avoided.

Evaluation for esthetic activities takes several forms. It may be asking the simple question after a song is sung, "Did you like it?" After a child has painted a picture the evaluation may consist merely of his telling the story about the picture. A little more mature evaluation of this type involves answering questions from children and teacher about the picture. With very young children part of the evaluation process is to encourage verbalization, or talking about the idea that has been concretely expressed. The teacher develops the atmosphere of acceptance without ridicule or judgment. As children become more sophisticated in their creative efforts, the teacher probes to provide stronger guidance. Such questions as "Why do you like it?" and "What part do you like best?" are asked.

For projects that take some time, ongoing evaluation is important. The group painting a mural is constantly studying it to be sure that all ideas are included, that the various parts hang together well, that color, proportion, and size are consistent. Self-evaluation as well as cooperative evaluation is encouraged.

Young children seem to use naturally and unconsciously some of the principles of art. For example, they create large centers of interest, subordinate lesser details, and produce effective contrasts. When this is done well, the teacher may wish to point out such effects to the whole group. Other principles, such as depicting movement or filling the whole page with content, only a few may achieve, but a compliment from the teacher may encourage others to try something similar.

Teachers who know the sensitivity of the individuals in their groups will be careful about the evaluation given publicly. Frequently a private word or two will help a youngster without the embarrassment that might be caused by a group evaluation.

Content and Purposes of the Esthetic Program

Teaching in the fine arts area has gone through a cycle of different approaches, beginning with the traditional method of exposing children to the products of experts and encouraging them to copy the work. Later, as the appreciation-imitation approach was modified, children were stimulated to free expression in the arts without much direction or guidance. Today the program seeking to achieve creativity and appreciation offers a variety of experiences. Some of these experiences deal with music, dance, and rhythms; some are concerned with arts and crafts; and others apply to poetry, literature, and creative writing. Each of these areas has its characteristic activities.

Content. The content of the program in most schools is an outgrowth of curriculum units, other subject matter, various holidays and seasons, and other specific needs for art activities. The kinds of experiences that teachers provide are determined by the curriculum and the esthetic needs and desires of the children as they live and work in the school and community. However, the *scope* of the art program must be determined by the perspective that is placed on the content—the depth to which the content is explored. Children should have the opportunity to deal with various kinds of content activities within a frame of reference including these elements: *observation,* or looking and seeing things with sensitivity; *exploration,* in which the natural curiosity of children is satisfied by going beyond the routine path of life to find out about things; *experimentation,* or the opportunity to discover or test an idea or material; *appreciation,* or the awareness and perception that give one the ability to understand the worth of a thing; *correlation,* or the ability to determine the relationship or systematic connection between two things or two parts of one thing; *evaluation,* or the direction to learning given in an ongoing, cooperative situation by an individual or a group; *sharing,* the form of communication in which there is give and take about an object, idea or performance; *enjoying,* the means by which more than mere satisfaction is felt in achievement or production; *designing,* or the production or creation of something with a scheme or plan in mind; *organizing,* or bringing together several parts into a meaningful whole; *arranging,* or the adjustment which comes through the determination of proper order, position, plan; *constructing,* or the fashioning or making of a three-dimensional piece. These elements are closely related and in certain situations may be difficult to distinguish. However, it is important that children have the opportunity to operate in all these approaches to art.[5]

Two directions of communication. Esthetic ideas necessitate a two-way communication just as language does; one must be able to express himself, but he must also be able and willing to receive, appreciate, and understand the expressions of others. Therefore the broad program that develops esthetic responsiveness in children will emphasize two directions. One direction—expressive—seeks to develop within each individual his own creative potential and the ability to recognize and use that potential. This direction involves experiences encouraging creativity, the self-assigned creative enterprise, and the development of skills (lessons in techniques and esthetic principles) promoting greater satisfaction in creation. Also part of this direction are skills like musical and dramatic reproduction that enable individuals to recreate the creative product

---

[5] From *Teaching Elementary School Subjects,* edited by Kenneth L. Husbands. To be published by The Ronald Press Company, 1961.

of another. Both skilled technique and creativity are essential for interpretation, meaning, and artistic reproduction.

The second direction—receptive—seeks to help children appreciate and enjoy esthetic qualities around them. Its purpose is to develop sensitivity and appreciation for the beauty of nature, for efforts of other cultures, for the esthetic heritage of our society, and for current artistic contributions.

The purposes of the program are built around these two dimensions, and might include the following ideas:

1. To develop the individual creative potential, the unique personal expression in both intellectual and manipulative abilities, by
   —providing experiences for self-expression with many media
   —developing skills and abilities in the manipulation of various media
   —promoting satisfaction and fulfillment in creation
   —encouraging emotional release through communication of feelings and ideas, and through freedom of expression
   —providing recognition for individual achievement
   —fostering interests for recreation and leisure time activities
   —encouraging creative thinking and willingness to modify and adjust to social arrangements in a democracy
2. To develop an esthetic sensitivity and response to beauty and creativity, an appreciation for the creative efforts of others, by
   —developing a capacity for esthetic response on the feeling and verbal levels
   —developing understanding of the esthetic heritage of our society
   —developing sensitivity to beauty in all facets of life
   —encouraging participation in esthetic social activities as group singing, dancing, symphony
   —fostering understanding and enjoyment of the esthetic efforts of peoples of other cultures
   —understanding principles of good taste which make for more efficient consumers of manufactured products

MUSIC, DANCE, AND RHYTHM

Music can and must be a part of the mind and heart of every child, in this day of radio, television, and rapid transportation that brings opera, symphony, and ballet within personal-appearance or hearing distance of most Americans. Today we may enjoy music in many forms. Not only do we have the classical performances of symphony, solo, and small instrumental groups, but we have frequent and accessible performances of operetta, ballet, marching bands, popular dance bands, and television entertainers. One enjoys the pleasant effects of background music as one shops in suburban shopping centers. Many meetings involve participants in community singing. Dancing to folk music has become so popular that neighborhoods organize their own groups.

Since our modern society produces music and rhythm and dance in many kinds of situations, in many modifications of form, the young child must be provided school experiences that will help him develop appreciation, discrimination, and ability to participate in these many musical activities. Children differ in musical interests and abilities just as in any other life activity; the teacher must be sensitive to each aspect of music that stimulates the interests of individual children. Some may enjoy most a single melody, others may delight in rhythm or bodily movement, still others may prefer to listen passively, some may receive greatest satisfaction from instrumental participation.

Listening

Music, as well as language, demands that each individual develop skill in listening. Children should understand that music may demand various kinds of listening. The background music in the market may be appreciated with less conscious effort than the formal performance of the chamber music group. And as with language, musical performances involve "sending" and "receiving"; the receiver is an important part of the operation. In live programs of music, dance, or drama, the appreciation of the audience is a strong influence on the effectiveness of the performance. To an enthusiastic audience a player plays better, but enthusiasm on the part of the listener can only be generated through appreciation and understanding of the skills of production.

Learning to listen, for the child, comes through developmental experiences in listening. Today's teacher provides many situations for listening to music of various kinds. Children listen to the simple songs they learn to sing. They listen to the familiar tunes they hear in family and neighborhood life. Melodies are introduced which are part of the historical life of the American people and their world neighbors. Popular tunes, classical themes, and descriptive melodies are all a part of the musical listening program.

As children develop their own manipulative skill in music, they will also enrich their appreciation of music as they listen. When musical instruments are identified, they can be recognized in instrumental numbers. Interrelationships of instruments to the melodic parts and to the total production are understood. When children learn to sing the various parts of a choral melody, they can then distinguish the elements of harmony.

As early as the kindergarten, children learn to recognize the differences in rhythm and to move to the music. As they listen, kindergarten children soon learn that music will tell them to skip or walk. Later, they

learn whether music is a waltz or a march, and the fun is not only in the listening, but in the bodily movements the music evokes. When children grow older and are able to understand more complex music, they move in more complicated rhythms, and their appreciation of the technical aspects of music increases.

Songs

Some children come to school with the ability to sing simple tunes. The others will soon attain this ability, for the singing of very simple little tunes is an important part of the kindergarten and first grade program. Fortunately, the simple songs for young children, much improved over the years, are really singable, with interesting stories behind the words. And as the songs for the various grade levels develop in complexity, they continue to be of interest to children at each developmental level.

Most kindergarten teachers have a piano available for teaching singing, but the most successful kindergarten teachers do not rely on the piano entirely. If over-used, the piano can be a crutch for the youngsters; their own singing comes a fraction of a second after the piano note sounds, and they do not use their own memory or ability to remember the continuity of a tune. To use the piano for pitching the song is fine when the song is first introduced and studied. But teachers often find that children will gain more confidence and strength in singing when the song is led often only by the teacher's light voice. If no piano is available, as so frequently happens in upper grades, a teacher must be sure to use a pitch pipe, for most of us cannot pitch a song accurately. It is discouraging for children to have a song pitched too low or too high for their voices. Sometimes a teacher will have a child start a song, and pitch must especially be kept in mind then. Let the child use the pitch pipe or find the opening note on the piano before starting the song.

Some children will learn their songs by rote. As the children gain ability to sing and understand music, and when they can read words, they will look at the music written in their books. Then they can follow the notes and sing up or down as the notes indicate. And as they learn more of the mechanics of music, they will be able to sing the song from the notes without much previous listening or study of the song.

More and more, teachers are finding that most children can sing. and that the monotone is rare. The ability to carry a tune comes from the opportunity to listen to simple tunes and from a little effort in trying to sing it. Children who do seem to have difficulty finding the pitch and singing the tune accurately need time and patient encouragement and

sometimes just the physical nearness of the teacher's or another strong singer's voice. Frequently the teacher will make a game of tone drill, or the exercise in which she sings a simple question on one pitch, and expects a simple answer from the child in the same tone. For each child, the pitch is varied. With older children, the exercise may contain two or three closely related tones in a simple phrase.

Usually, part singing is taught in the intermediate grades. By fourth grade the children are ready for two-part singing; three parts may be introduced as boys' voices begin to change at the end of the sixth grade. The background for this technical kind of part singing is built by helping children sing rounds of simple songs even in the first grade. Before formal part singing is attempted, the descant, or singing of two melodies that work together in harmony, is also developed.

Frequently children will be introduced to singing games, but the action of these games should be limited. That is, children sit in their seats or stand quietly, and any movement does not necessitate great activity. Too much movement will affect the quality of the singing.

Another problem is related to the tone of voice the children use. Their natural voices are light and clear. To urge them to sing loudly and strongly may damage the singing voice as well as make the tonal quality of the group crude and harsh. Teachers must encourage children to sing in sweet, unstrained tones. The aim is to develop true voices that are clear and flexible.

Records

Most schools maintain a good library of records for musical instruction. The teacher who does not play the piano or who lacks talent for singing can procure records that will be of great help. For appreciation, almost all the classical and semiclassical numbers are recorded. New music texts now have supplementary records that play the songs of the books. Records for dancing and rhythms are produced. Records are available for identifying individual instruments and later, for recognizing their voices in instrumental groups. Tapes are also a valuable aid in teaching music. To listen to new productions of stereophonic sound is a splendid esthetic experience for children. Although good records are so easily used and so accessible, teachers should not always sing to record accompaniment.

Techniques of Music

Music educators question the importance of teaching staff structure, music reading, and theoretical principles of music at the elementary

school level. How many pupils will need and use such skills? How many gain real satisfaction from their use? How many thoroughly understand the theoretical principles of music when taught within a heterogeneous group? Questions such as these indicate that some educators feel the techniques of music are inappropriate for elementary school children. On the other hand, some music educators feel that elementary children should develop literacy in the language of music just as they do in the mother tongue. Since many children have no contact with music in high school, the fundamentals of reading and writing music must be accomplished by the end of the eighth grade.

In light of these considerations, the teaching of mechanical techniques of music is usually delayed. Since children cannot read with ease in the primary grades, the use of music books is easily postponed until the late third or fourth grade. Very little formal drill is used to teach techniques. Rather, the children first use books and "read" the music of songs they know well. Then gradually as individuals can comprehend, they learn to find the key of a song, distinguish the time values of notes, and gain insight into the other technical knowledge that in the past has been presented in formal drill periods.

Instruments

Children learn early that music is produced by instruments as well as by the voice. As early as kindergarten, children learn to use rhythm instruments to accompany marked rhythmical music or bodily movements of other children. As a rule, only in the intermediate and upper grades are children taught to recognize the individual instruments in size, shape, and tonal quality.

Throughout the elementary school children have opportunities to participate in instrumental groups, and learn that music sounds different when produced by such a group. Typically, kindergarten and first grade children learn to use rhythm instruments to emphasize the pulse of a melody in a rhythm band. Later, pitch producing instruments are added to develop a rhythm orchestra. Frequently musical groups are formed in second and third grades to teach use of harmonicas or other simple musical pipes.

More and more elementary schools are providing instruments so that older children can become participants in bands or orchestras as an enrichment activity. There is a real satisfaction in becoming part of a cooperative group that follows a leader and that produces a delightful harmony to be enjoyed by others. Usually this takes the time of a special music teacher, and some arrangement must be made to excuse these special students from their regular classrooms.

Rhythms and Dancing

Since the human body naturally functions in a rhythmical fashion, the kinesthetic response to music is easily guided. Children have a natural desire to imitate others, to dance or move their bodies to reflect a musical tempo. The baby who is barely able to walk may dance for delighted parents, and the young child can easily imitate a zooming airplane.

In the kindergarten rhythm activities begin through utilization of this desire to imitate. To the teacher's music, children can imitate the movement of animals they know. Also, elemental clapping develops into the varied rhythms of jumping and skipping to music, for development in rhythms becomes closely related to muscular coordination. As children develop in bodily grace and knowledge of the outside world, they produce rhythmical movements that represent other activities of living: the movements of machines, work patterns, and sports.

Very early in the elementary program, usually the second grade, children enjoy group dancing. Young children enjoy the opportunity to dance together in organized patterns of the square dance that are related to the history of our country. As the children grow older, and more interested in people of other countries, they enjoy learning folk dances of other cultures. Children of intermediate and upper grades also enjoy dancing and recognizing the music of the gavotte, schottische, waltz.

The use of creative dance is another opportunity for children to communicate their ideas through bodily movements. Little children may listen to music and rather naturally interpret it in slow or fast movement, in the bending and swaying of their bodies, in the gesturing movements of arms and legs. As children grow older, communication through dance assumes deeper meaning, more complexity in movement, and more variety in interpretation. The selection of music for this kind of activity necessitates some careful consideration.

Creative Music

An important part of the esthetic program in the elementary school is the way in which the teacher helps the children to be creative about producing music. First graders receive much satisfaction from the composition of a simple song that comes out of the experiences of their classroom situation. Once children learn the skill of emphasizing the rhythm of a musical number with rhythm instruments, they can make the emphases in their own way, and thus be creative about the rhythms.

Creativity comes through much experience and real enjoyment. After the children have sung many songs, they may indicate the desire to com-

pose their own, hence the teacher must be sensitive to this need when it arises. His attitude must be free and flexible so that he may help the children record their creative efforts. His task is to help children learn to communicate through the language medium of music.

ARTS AND CRAFTS

The art program of the elementary school today seeks to achieve the general objectives of the over-all esthetic program through its emphasis on the manipulation of and appreciation for many kinds of materials. Today's art program no longer follows an inflexible pattern of activities. Nor are children merely allowed to indulge in free expression that has no guidance or evaluation. Rather, today's program is one in which a great variety of activities are provided and all clues from the children's work are utilized to plan these experiences. The art program has far more depth and variety than the opportunity to paint or experiment with other two-dimensional drawing materials. Teachers are finding that painting or drawing alone does not satisfy all children or all esthetic desires. Therefore the craft activities, which involve many kinds of materials and three-dimensional products other than pencil, crayon, and paper, are introduced into the program.

In the primary grades, the art activities are provided as a means of expression, free from restraint or a great deal of criticism. Children evaluate their art work in terms of the stories they tell or the purposes for which the project was made. They share reasons why they like a product, and point out the particularly pleasant aspects of the art work. The teacher helps the children to use the art work to decorate the classrooms. As the children grow older, teachers help them to understand some of the basic principles of art. They begin to identify the reasons why certain pictures or three-dimensional pieces are more pleasing than others. As a need of curiosity is aroused in dealing with the art activities, teachers explain and help children identify such points as line, center of interest, mass, unity, subordination, variety, color. The teaching of these principles comes as a part of a well-thought-through plan to help children understand our cultural ideas of beauty.

The Materials of Art

Some of the most popular materials for painting and drawing are crayons, calcimine paints, chalk, charcoal, and pastel crayons. The use of pencil is not encouraged in primary grades for drawing, and water colors as a single medium are introduced only in the upper grades. Variations

with these materials are achieved through the use of different textures and colors of papers, wet or dry papers, and combinations of media.

Craft materials are as endless and varied as the imaginations of the children and their teacher. Clay, textiles, wood, and paper may be used in many kinds of craft projects and modeling. Scraps, such as bits of yarn, wire, metal, rubber, glass, shells, and colored paper, can be used for making baskets, dioramas, mobiles, and collages. The imaginative child can utilize many of the materials we have in the home—the plastic berry baskets, cardboard boxes, and used Christmas wrappings—to make numerous three-dimensional pieces.

Printing and lettering are important parts of a well-balanced art program. Since children learn manuscript writing in the first grade, if this skill is maintained throughout the grades, the matter of lettering is not difficult. Teachers help children to use Speedball pens, felt brushes, crayon, pencil, charcoal, and chalk for various kinds of labels and charts. Printing is worked out when children use potato stencils, silk screens, and linoleum blocks to make booklets, posters, and decorative papers.

Art in the Classroom

The environment of the classroom reflects the art activities of the children. When one enters a room where a rich art program is in progress, one sees attractive displays of paintings and drawings, child-planned bulletin boards, exhibits related to other studies, and a beauty spot or two.

Children who have developed a sensitivity to beauty, and who are proud of their classroom, are more than eager to make it a pleasant place to live. They will bring flowers, knickknacks, bits of scrap, which may be arranged into spots of color and beauty. They will bring articles and pictures illustrating their studies, which they can arrange attractively as exhibits or on bulletin boards. They are eager to have their art work displayed and will help to make frames for paintings or arrange the necessary space for a mural or illustrated timeline.

The classroom that demonstrates the orderliness and the effective learning of its occupants has places for every tool and material, and these are always maintained in order. In the primary rooms the places for things may be labeled. In intermediate classrooms the places for things are not necessarily labeled but have been arranged cooperatively after careful thought about traffic lanes and the use of the material.

The classroom is the place where the children live with their teacher. Every part of it should be a part of them, their effort, their pride in maintaining it. A rich stimulating environment is the most important basis for the development of creative expression.

The Relation of Art to the Curriculum

The development of creativity cannot be achieved in one or a series of so-called "art lessons" that are unrelated to anything else in the classroom. Creativity must be encouraged in every aspect of daily activity, and over extended periods of time. The form, shape, color, and texture of all things children experience are not limited to art lessons. All beautiful objects must be considered and appreciated at the time and place and in the context in which they are found. Thus art is an integral part of the curriculum. Just as we cannot logically isolate a people's art from their religion, leisure time activities, technology, and other elements of their culture, we cannot separate the art program in school from other subject areas that contribute to esthetic and creative development.

POETRY AND LITERATURE

The elementary school places a good deal of importance on experiences with fine literature and poetry by providing time and materials for children to explore, enjoy, and develop appreciation for the creative writing of others. The challenge to the teacher in this situation is that love of literature cannot be taught, but becomes something that the spirit catches. Experiences with literature and poetry must be delightful, happy, and stimulating. Therefore the teacher must present the material with an adequate understanding of the children, and with a deep and abiding love and appreciation for literature.

The Definition of Literature and Poetry

Both literature and poetry result from the author's desire to present ideas on life and living. His interpretation may be through humor, fantasy, or realism, and the literature may vary in structure, tone, and appeal. The form of the writing is artistic in that it is pleasing and in accordance with cultural standards that determine choice of words, phrases, and sentence structure. The structure exudes charm through the mental picture it evokes. Not only the ideas but the style reflect the creativity, personality, and thinking of the author. Actually there is little difference between prose and poetry, and the experts in the field themselves have a hard time defining them.

Child Needs Satisfied Through Literature

Reading stories and poems about people and things provides vicarious experiences for children. Through experiences of living with the charac-

ters of literature, children may meet a number of their emotional needs. They may experience emotional and spiritual security, belongingness, the feeling of loving and being loved. They can attain a sense of satisfaction through knowing about various people and the things that make their lives different from ours. They find an appreciation for change, for change in the products of civilization and style of living. They find esthetic satisfaction in realizing that other people enjoy products of creativity. Such feelings, motivated by the understanding of other people's problems and ways of living, may well give guidance to children as they develop into mature and well-adjusted individuals.

Literature can develop within the reader an appreciation for moral and spiritual values, a desire for beauty, as well as provide an avenue of escape from the monotony of daily life. These means of appreciating literature are good for children in their proper proportions, but effective teachers watch to avoid letting children lose touch with reality by overdoing the dream world of literature.

The Characteristics of Good Literature

One of the first things a teacher or a child notices about a book is the physical make-up. If the jacket is colorful and eye-catching, well designed, the book will be more appealing. The binding should be durable, yet flexible and practical. The format, or arrangement of the print and pictures on the page, is important to the readability of the book. The type of print and the kind and quality of the pictures are also important to the appeal of the physical make-up.

The content of the literature should first of all have emotional appeal. Except for fantasy tales, there should also be a quality of being true to life. Good literature also demands ideas and activities as well as moral implications that are socially acceptable.

A good style makes the material readable, so in the selection of good literature for children we must consider style as well as content which stimulates the interest of the child.

One type of material now available, which long has been under controversy, is the comic book. The very popularity of the material has proved that it contains appeal, and there has been much to suggest that it has great influence on the young mind. Educators now are fairly united on the kind that has value for children in and out of school. This is the comic book that satisfies the usual criteria for literature: that is, the material has socially acceptable language, action, and theme; the format is of a quality that can be appreciated by children.

Literature available for children today is of great quantity. Stories include folk tales, fables, myths, epics, modern fanciful tales. Stories of

the here and now, stories of other times and places, animal stories, and biographies related to almost every corner of the world are available. Poetry can be found about everything: nature, fantasy, adventure, and all sorts of people.

Poetry in Particular

Arbuthnot gives a most interesting summary of various people's definitions of poetry through the ages. In summary, she says, "If you will examine these definitions and others you will discover certain ideas recurring: poetry surprises and delights; it sings like music; it makes you feel intensely; poetry gives you an arresting thought in rhythmic words, plus a shiver up your backbone."[6] And these are the things that good teaching of poetry will do for children.

The teacher who can be familiar enough with poetry to relate it to many classroom activities can indeed surprise and delight children. Poetry is presented in today's program for the exquisite feel of listening to it, for the joy of hearing the singing quality, the beautiful sequence of words. No longer is poetry a problem to children because of forced memorization. The appreciation of poetry comes in the appreciation of vigorous and colorful words, the singing quality rather than formal analysis of meter and related structural elements. Children look for the appealing ideas and the humor and beauty of a poem, rather than for the moral lessons it teaches. The successful teacher whose children really love poetry has created a mood each time children experience a poem. His introduction is simple and to the point. He waits for reactions of the children rather than asks formal and pointed questions.

Creative Writing

Creative writing is similar to all other means of creative expression in that writing is a vehicle for the expression of ideas and feelings. From the wells of experience and original thought comes expression, using words as a medium rather than sound, movement, or the materials of art. Creative writing was one of the first means of creative expression developed in the elementary school, and much has been learned from long experience and significant research in this area that intimates what children can do. Development of ability in the writing of creative stories, plays, poems, and other types of original composition is now frequently related to other programs in the curriculum.

In its initial stages, the basis for creative writing is oral, but ability

---

[6] May Hill Arbuthnot, *Children and Books* (Chicago: Scott, Foresman and Company, 1947), p. 159.

in creative writing is developed through listening and reading as well as speaking. In the kindergarten and first grade, children may compose delightful oral prose or poetry by dictating to the teacher. From this beginning, creative oral expression later becomes written expression. As children listen to well-phrased poetry and well-written stories or read children's books, they learn to express themselves orally with greater originality, clarity, and precision. The child who speaks with colorful words, apt phrases, a dash of humor or pathos, does so to a great extent because he has been exposed to such language, understands the subtleties of words, and is encouraged to experiment with literary expression.

Creative writing is usually the result of wide and varied experience. Time and opportunity should be provided for the preliminary experiences as well as for the actual creative act. Creative writing is not produced from a vacuum. Experiences about a circus might include viewing films, posters and other pictures of a circus, visiting a zoo, imitating the movements of circus animals, hearing stories and poems and singing songs about the circus, and discussing activities within a circus. Rich personal experiences such as these are both practical and literary, and constitute a basis for thought. Free and original thinking precedes the adequate expression of ideas in both oral and written form. Children need time to think, sometimes in silent, introspective meditation. Children also need to develop sensitivity, receptiveness to new ideas, and the habit of thinking independently. In order to encourage original thought the teacher sometimes withholds judgments, and he frequently needs to help children think through nebulous ideas or clarify vague impressions. A permissive, friendly atmosphere in a classroom stimulates the expression of spontaneous, inventive ideas, for children then do not fear criticism, rebuke, or ridicule from the teacher or their classmates.

The sharing of ideas stimulates the development of more fluent oral expression upon which written compositions depend. As children talk together, the teacher encourages the use of new words, the study of word meanings, and the choice of unusual, colorful, and dramatic words, neatly turned phrases and pleasing word illustrations. Oral communication among children, guided but not dominated by the teacher, helps to provide the background needed for effective writing.

With greater maturity and skillful guidance, children become increasingly proficient in writing. They become conscious of the differences among words and the variance in meaning between two very similar words. They appreciate the pleasant sound of certain words used in combination and the ease with which some sentences or phrases can be understood, consciously appreciated, and evaluated. Children enjoy trying to express an old idea in an entirely new manner, in trying to be completely original

in style and phraseology. The written expression of fantasy or ideas in relation to very practical situations is easily encouraged.

The teacher's sensitivity to individual differences influences his guidance of the writing situation. Inner motivation and feelings, special interests, and individual mannerisms in writing are understood to be encouraged. Burrows (and others) point out variation rather dramatically when they say:

> The infinite variety of human nature is nowhere more apparent than in the strange and sometimes devious ways that children follow in putting thoughts on paper. Some can write in the midst of swirling activity while others find the presence of even one other person a deterrent. Some love notebooks and the smugness of pages between covers; others choose the freeness of single sheets. Some think out all of a story in advance; others work from the most trivial starting point and know only what is going to happen next. Some write best in solitude; others like to write occasionally with a partner.[7]

Lee and Lee discuss three major handicaps that often deter children from writing creatively. First, children may lack experience in original thought, second, they may have had limited opportunities for developing oral expression, and third, they may encounter mechanical difficulties in putting words on paper. An analysis of these handicaps gives a number of clues for the development of creative writing.[8]

Skilled written expression requires a knowledge of correct grammatical usage, accurate spelling, and legible penmanship. Creative writing is both a craft and an art. It is sometimes said that any person of average intelligence can be taught the craft, the mechanics of writing. Certainly teaching the art of writing, the development of an individualistic style and original expression, is a more complex task. Mastering the craft is a prerequisite to achieving the art. Nevertheless, much creativeness has undoubtedly been stifled by teachers who interrupt the flow of ideas by insisting upon mechanical perfection. The better course of action is to defer instruction in these areas until later when carefully planned lessons emerge from demonstrated weaknesses.

REFERENCES

Barham, Manuel. *Through Art to Creativity.* Boston: Allyn and Bacon, 1960. General discussions of theory and practice of teaching art. Many pictures.

---

[7] Alvina T. Burrows and others, *They All Want To Write* (Englewood Cliffs, New Jersey: Prentice-Hall, Inc., 1952), pp. 109–110.

[8] J. Murray Lee and Dorris May Lee, *The Child and His Curriculum* (New York: Appleton-Century-Crofts, Inc., 1950), p. 625.

Boyden, David D. *An Introduction to Music.* New York: Alfred A. Knopf, 1956.

    A basis for teaching music appreciation.

Conant, Howard, and Arne Randall. *Art in Education.* Peoria, Illinois: Charles A. Bennett Company, Inc., 1959.

    An overview of art in the public schools, including method, philosophy, evaluation, and materials.

De Francesco, Italo L. *Art Education: Its Means and Ends.* New York: Harper & Brothers, 1958.

    Presents art in the total school program, with complete summary of literature in the field.

Ellison, Alfred. *Music with Children.* New York: McGraw-Hill Book Company, 1959.

    How the classroom teacher can teach music with the help of consultants.

Gaitskell, Charles D. *Children and Their Art: Methods for Elementary Schools.* New York: Harcourt, Brace and Company, Inc., 1958.

    Art related to the total curriculum with emphasis upon relating art to historical and esthetic foundations.

Henry, Nelson B. (editor). *Basic Concepts in Music Education* (Fifty-seventh Yearbook, Part I, National Society for the Study of Education). Chicago: University of Chicago Press, 1958.

    Interpretation of the implications for music from major disciplines and a description of the features of good music programs.

Jefferson, Blanche. *Teaching Art to Children.* Boston: Allyn and Bacon, 1959.

    A general text in the teaching of art with good discussion of creativity and the importance of creative learning.

Kagan, Pauline W. *From Adventure to Experience Through Art.* San Francisco: Howard Chandler, Publisher, 1959.

    How to handle art materials effectively and meaningfully in relation to a consistent philosophy of art education.

Lindstrom, Miriam. *Children's Art.* Berkeley: University of California Press, 1957.

    A fine discussion of art related to individual differences by one who knows children. Emphasis on visual imagery and visual development.

Lowenfeld, Viktor. *Your Child and His Art.* New York: The Macmillan Company, 1954.

    A thoughtful presentation of children's art activities for teachers and parents.

————. *Creative and Mental Growth* (Third edition). New York: The Macmillan Company, 1957.

    An intellectual approach to creativity.

McFee, June King. *Preparation for Art.* San Francisco: Wadsworth Publishing Company, Inc., 1961.

    Relates the foundations and objectives of art education to actual classroom practice. Applies psychological, sociological, and anthropological findings to art instruction.

McMillan, L. Aileen. *Guiding Children's Growth Through Music.* Boston: Ginn and Company, 1959.

    Means of providing rich musical experiences for children.

Mearns, Hughes. *Creative Power* (Second edition). New York: Dover Publications, 1958.

An exciting presentation of the development of creativity.

Mendelowitz, Daniel M. *Children Are Artists*. Stanford: Stanford University Press, 1953.

Written to help adults understand children's art. Excellent pictures.

Mursell, James L. *Music Education*. Morristown, New Jersey: Silver Burdett Company, 1956.

A general text for teaching music.

Myers, Louise K. *Teaching Children Music in the Elementary School* (Second edition). Englewood Cliffs, New Jersey: Prentice-Hall, Inc., 1956.

How to help children make and enjoy music.

National Art Education Association. *Research in Art Education*. Ninth Yearbook. Washington, D.C.: the Association, National Education Association, 1959.

A careful summary of research in art and art education in well-organized sections.

Nye, Robert E., and Vernice T. Nye. *Music in the Elementary School*. Englewood Cliffs, New Jersey: Prentice-Hall, Inc., 1957.

Presents the importance of music in the curriculum and suggests possible activities.

Pace, Robert. *Music Essentials for Classroom Teachers*. San Francisco: Wadsworth Publishing Company, Inc., 1961.

Music fundamentals for the teacher who has had little experience with music, or who needs more, for teaching it to children.

Pierce, Anne. *Teaching Music in the Elementary School*. New York: Henry Holt and Company, 1959.

What and how to teach music in grade sequence or integrated with other subjects.

Russell, David. *Children's Thinking*. Boston: Ginn and Company, 1956.

Chapter 11 gives an especially good discussion of children's creative thinking.

Seiberling, Frank. *Looking into Art*. New York: Henry Holt and Company, 1959.

An introduction to visual arts.

Sheehy, Emma D. *Children Discover Music and Dance*. New York: Henry Holt and Company, 1959.

Many pictures help discuss methods and procedures for fostering music and dance.

Snyder, Alice M. *Creating Music with Children*. New York: Mills Music, Inc., 1957.

Well-illustrated suggestions for the teaching of creative music.

Swanson, Bessie R. *Music in the Education of Children*. San Francisco: Wadsworth Publishing Company, Inc., 1961.

Unique, exploratory, and creative presentation of music for children. The simple approach compares old and new practices and refers to up-to-date materials.

Wickiser, Ralph L. *An Introduction to Art Education*. Yonkers-on-Hudson: The World Book Company, 1957.

A general text for classroom teachers.

16

HEALTHFUL LIVING:
PHYSICAL AND HEALTH
EDUCATION

PROVIDING FOR HEALTH
AND PHYSICAL EDUCATION

Today's elementary school increasingly accepts health and physical fitness as important objectives of education. In fact, the entire school system is called upon to develop programs of health and physical education.

In the 1938 statement of the Educational Policies Commission, entitled *The Purposes of Education in American Democracy,* the position is taken that the educated person ''understands the basic facts concerning health and disease . . . protects his own health and that of his dependents . . . works to improve the health of the community . . . and is participant and spectator in many sports (and other pastimes).''[1] The more recent study of objectives for elementary education, carried on by Kearney and others for the Russell Sage Foundation in 1953, was quite explicit as to the responsibilities the elementary school was typically accepting in these two areas of the curriculum. Noted were responsibilities to physical development, health, and body care—including individual health, elementary aspects of public health, safety, physical education, grooming, and understanding of growth.[2]

---

[1] Educational Policies Commission, *The Purposes of Education in American Democracy* (Washington, D.C.: National Education Association, 1938), p. 50.

[2] Nolan Kearney and others, *Elementary School Objectives* (New York: Russell Sage Foundation, 1953), p. 52.

These, and other statements, make it quite clear that the elementary school does have responsibilities in the areas of health and physical education. The extent of these programs, and the effectiveness of the effort expended, varies from school system to school system. In increasing numbers of school systems, a very well-conceived set of experiences is guided by clearly stated and well-understood purposes. In others, purposes are less clear and the school's efforts in health and physical education are vague and correspondingly less effective. The nature of a complete effort in the areas of health and physical education is increasingly understood, and the elementary school moves ever closer to the development of programs that accept a full share of responsibility to contribute to the health and physical well-being of children.

Factors Affecting Program Development

As the elementary school has moved to strengthen its efforts in health and physical education, several fundamental matters have had to be considered and resolved. Most important among these have been the following.

The shared nature of the health responsibility. In the area of health, it has taken considerable study and discussion to clarify the way in which the school might and should share in the maintenance and improvement of children's health. The primary obligation of the family to look after the health of its members has been and continues to be unquestioned. The responsibility for the health of children rests, in the main, with parents. At the same time, society has taken steps to protect itself, and the local, state, and national communities have accepted certain responsibilities in the area of public health. For example, doctors are required to report contagious diseases, communities exercise the right of quarantine, and various community health agencies provide both education and service to the general public. The particular way and extent to which the school, as a specialized social institution, could and should participate in the area of health has been of concern. This matter is clarified considerably when the school is asked to take on major responsibilities consistent with its basic purposes as a social institution—that is, to provide for health instruction. While family and community both instruct to some extent, the school is looked to for the greatest part of this burden. That other responsibilities for the total health effort are shared is clearly recognized.

A clear rationale for physical education. By the end of the American Revolution in 1783, it was generally agreed that the schools should help to insure that each generation would be physically fit and possessed of physical strength. This was of special importance insofar as the males

in the population were concerned, with the motivation arising from the demands of military service. A soldier needed to be strong and to have considerable powers of endurance; physical education was almost synonymous with military education. This idea is still with us to the extent that students at the college level may be exempt from required physical education experiences if they are taking military training.

From this sort of beginning, it has taken time for people to recognize the basic importance of physical fitness in all aspects of life—in one's personal, family, and vocational-professional activities—and to want a varied program of physical education, accordingly. With recognition of the way in which physical fitness conditions success in all undertakings, personal and social, have come extensively developed physical education programs. Along with this general development in physical education has come a more specific demand for the elementary educator: to state clearly and precisely how a planned physical education program in school should make a contribution to a child's physical development distinct from that made naturally by engaging in play and work experiences outside the school. In other words, was there really a need for a formal physical education program in the elementary school? This question has been answered affirmatively by the allocation to the elementary school of certain responsibilities for which it is peculiarly fitted. Here is a social institution that can be provided with adequate space, both indoors and outdoors, and with necessary equipment and personnel to carry on the kinds of experiences that are basic to physical fitness in childhood. The reciprocal relationship between in-school and out-of-school activities has become rather obvious. Skills and abilities learned in school have a wide application in the child's life away from school. And, of course, out-of-school experiences provide considerable reason and motivation to participate in the organized program of the school. Well-conceived programs of physical education in the elementary school are actively sought, and their distinct contribution to the over-all objectives of education is increasingly recognized.

A more adequate definition of health. The fact that a much different definition for "being healthy" has recently emerged has also had an effect on the development of elementary school programs in health and physical education. The older definition described the healthy person as one who was without sickness and disease. This has given way to a more dynamic and inclusive definition that speaks of being healthy as a state of general physical and mental well-being, with energy and zest for approaching life in all of its many manifestations with security and confidence. In the words of the World Health Organization, "Health is a state of complete physical, mental, and social well-being, and not merely

the absence of disease.''[3] Such definitions do not deny the importance of being without sickness and disease; they do go beyond these considerations in important ways. It becomes a goal not only to keep children free from sickness and disease, but also to provide them with the knowledge, the attitudes, and the habits that will help them to maintain a continuing state of well-being. They must ''feel good'' physically and they must ''feel good'' about themselves.

Increased insight into the conditions that contribute to this well-being has called attention to the general way in which the school environment itself instructs and educates. The human element, especially the teacher, and the school plant combine with the intellectual and emotional elements in the school situation to provide both the setting for health education and health education itself. Thus, to realize the purposes of the program calls for an all-out effort at school that differentiates between the formal and the less formal aspects of the health curriculum, and recognizes the general comprehensiveness of the health effort.

Thus, the modern elementary school realizes the basic importance of its efforts in health and physical education. It accepts as its major responsibility the provision of sound and effective instruction in health and physical education. Armed with increased insight into human development and more dynamic concepts of health and physical fitness, it strives to provide healthful school living conditions for their contribution to children's well-being. In addition, the school provides a program of health services that recognizes health education as a cooperative effort and is conceived to operate in agreement with and in support of this shared responsibility.

PROVIDING FOR HEALTH INSTRUCTION

The instructional phase of the health education program seeks to develop lasting health interests, wholesome attitudes toward health, and adequate health information. Most importantly, the program aims at the development of proper health habits and practices on the part of children. Unless the health interests, attitudes, and information developed culminate in sound health practices, the school will have fallen short of its intended objective. The curriculum is designed on the assumption that it will be primarily the regular classroom teacher's responsibility to develop the learning experiences necessary in health instruction. He may call on certain specialized personnel employed by the school, such as a school nurse or a school physician, or he may utilize similar community

---

[3] From a publication of the World Health Organization, a special organ of the United Nations.

people as resource persons on special occasions to increase the effectiveness of his efforts.

Basis for Selecting Health Experiences

Health education experiences for the elementary school are determined chiefly by the basic health needs of children. These health needs are, of course, not too different from those for any other age group. The fact that the years from five to twelve are "growing and developing" years of great importance does add elements of special concern for health in childhood. Children's basic health needs, insofar as physical health is concerned, center around proper nutrition, adequate rest and sleep, opportunities for physical activity, protection from disease and accidents, and the understanding and appreciation that lead to proper care of the body. In the area of mental health, the basic needs of children for acceptance, security, love, success, recognition, intellectual stimulation, and a basic sense of personal worth must be recognized and dealt with. These basic health needs give direction to the selection of appropriate subject matter for the curriculum in health. At the same time they furnish the basic information that influences the way in which the school plant is designed, the school day is organized, and the teacher-pupil relationship is established.

The Scope of Health Education

The scope of the health instruction program, following as it does from the basic health needs of children, is broad. It provides for learning experiences focused around broad areas of concern that are directly related to the manifold needs of children's health. An examination of typical elementary school curriculum guides prepared for use in the health education program reveals a list of topics such as:

> Maintenance of personal health
> Care of the eyes, ears, and nose
> Care of the teeth
> Developing proper posture
> Foods and nutrition
> Personal appearance; cleanliness and grooming
> Rest and exercise
> Bodily growth and maturation
> Functions of the human body
> Prevention and control of disease
> Prevention and control of accidents
> Personal adjustment and mental health
> Community health problems

All of these are important if the individual is to protect and conserve his own health and, in the larger setting, that of his fellows in the community. While it is not too difficult to reach agreement on the fact that the scope of the health education curriculum must be broad, it is somewhat more difficult to gain agreement on certain other related questions.

The relative value of various areas to total health instruction. All areas of health education are not equally vital in the elementary school program, and therefore each must take its proper place, demanding and getting time and attention commensurate with its importance to health education. This calls for careful study and deliberation as the curriculum is planned. Most school systems find it helpful to obtain the assistance of medical personnel and health education experts as they make such decisions.

Byrd, an authority in the field of health education, called attention to this point recently by commenting on "good grooming" as a topic in health education. He wrote as follows:

> Virtually every physician has rendered medical service at one time or another to unkempt, poorly groomed, untidy and even dirty patients who possessed the vigor and vitality to give them a long life at the high level of energy. Such physicians have also treated neat, well-groomed, fastidious, clean and attractive persons who were suffering from tuberculosis, mental illness and a host of other serious diseases. Grooming does not make a fundamental contribution to high levels of vitality, endurance and length of life. There *are* certain relationships to health in the field of good grooming, but these should not be overemphasized. A person can learn to wash his hands as a part of his training in cleanliness, food sanitation and control of communicable diseases. This may also be a part of the process of good grooming. It is likewise true that to be well groomed is to give a person an added measure of confidence and self-respect. These factors have mild relationships to mental health. It is only when teachers and those who develop a health curriculum have the misconception that "good grooming" makes a major contribution to health education that the total development of the school health curriculum suffers.[4]

Implicit in this quotation is the kind of studied and enlightened choice which must be made again and again as health instruction is planned for in the elementary school. All of the earlier listed topics are of some value; but some are considerably more important than others.

Selection of subject matter. Another difficult question met in planning the health curriculum has to do with the selection of subject matter to

---

[4] Reprinted by permission of the Association for Childhood Education International, 3615 Wisconsin Avenue, N.W., Washington 16, D.C. "School Health," by Oliver E. Byrd, M.D., from *Childhood Education*, May 1959, Vol. 35, No. 9, pp. 394–397.

be taught in relation to each of these general areas. Content selected for study must be appropriate content; it must meet certain criteria for selection. Information that the school attempts to provide for children should be in keeping with the specific purposes for which health education is offered and the ends toward which the health education effort is directed. This is undoubtedly the best, and often the most difficult, criterion to apply to this question. Proper learning situations are more likely to be provided and appropriate subject matter is most likely to be selected when the elementary school is very clear as to the objectives of the program. This point is well illustrated by Byrd in the same recent statement on health education:

> Many health textbooks and health courses have been constructed under the mistaken concept that learning about the structure and function of the human body is health education. Anatomy and physiology are long-established sciences, predating hygiene and health education by many years, but the content of these fields is different and should not be confused with health education. To illustrate this distinction among anatomy, physiology and health education, we may postulate that a classroom teacher falls to the floor in a classroom, breaks the humerus and severs the brachial artery. A person well versed in anatomy might view this unfortunate teacher and observe accurately: "This teacher has broken her humerus and has severed the brachial artery." A second observer, well versed in the field of physiology, might observe: "This teacher will empty the circulatory system within a few minutes if the bleeding is not stopped." A person qualified in first aid or health education, without knowing the name of the bone that has been shattered or the name of the blood vessel that has been severed, might conclude: "I must apply a compress to stop this bleeding if this person's life is to be saved." The latter might then proceed to save the life of the patient without knowing anything about the patient's anatomy or physiology.[5]

Now, obviously, this is not to say that there is no place or need for providing information to children concerning the anatomy and the physiology of the human body. In the illustration above some knowledge of physiology is necessary in order to know where to apply the vital compress. But, the need to make choices as to "how much" and "what" subject matter to include in the health education curriculum becomes clear. The way in which these choices are influenced by the purposes for which the instruction is being provided is pointed up. Generally speaking, the health curriculum aims at healthful living. That such living is dependent to a great degree on adequate health knowledge is undeniable. But the knowledge the school attempts to develop, as well as the

---

[5] *Ibid.*

way in which it attempts to develop it, must meet the fundamental test of its contribution to enlightened and effective health practices.

Together, these two quotations vividly call attention to the preparation an elementary school system must make if effective health instruction is to be offered. It will not suffice to operate in the classroom at the level of "hold up your handkerchiefs, and now let me see your nails." Rather, the elementary school must be continuously alert lest its program be out of balance and it fall behind the best ways of improving and maintaining health.

Placing Health Education in the Curriculum

If the health education program is to be effective, it must find its proper place in the total elementary school curriculum. Time, a most precious thing in the classroom, must be found for health instruction. Generally, instruction in health is carried out in the elementary school in three ways.

Relating health instruction to other curriculum areas. A good deal of the instruction in health is related to or developed in conjunction with broad studies that are pursued in the social studies or the science areas of the curriculum. In the social studies, for instance, attention to family and local community living can effectively deal with matters of health. Things that families do or do not do in order to live healthfully can be noted. Studies of local community living can direct attention to the persons and the facilities in the community that are there to safeguard the health of all concerned. Field trips can be made to the local public health office; a doctor may visit a class and describe the work of a local health clinic. In these, and many other ways, health education may find a meaningful place in a social studies unit of work.

Similarly, work in science may be related to health education. Studies of living things, of plant and animal life, of bacteria, or of basic food content may furnish the setting in which to call attention to the human need for fresh air and sunshine, to practices that help to control the spread of communicable diseases, or to the desirability of a balanced diet.

Some classroom studies, as noted elsewhere, are so broad as to become social studies–science–health units of work at one and the same time. For instance, a comprehensive study of the way in which a community is supplied with fresh, safe drinking water will deal with local government, municipal and private services, minerals, bacteria, chemical processes, bodily functions, human uses of water, and so on. The "related study" setting is one in which much health instruction is accomplished.

Direct instruction in health education. It is necessary to provide certain opportunities for direct instruction in health matters, too. All of the

things that must be considered in the health program cannot be treated in relation to other ongoing studies, or cannot be as profitably treated in such a setting. At times it is better to start with a direct effort in health education. This effort may be an attempt to understand communicable diseases and the sorts of living habits that are basic to their control. Or, the school's and the teacher's objectives may suggest a direct study of accident prevention in all of its ramifications. Or again, to accomplish the necessary understandings about the rest-exercise-sleep relationship, the way in which the body expends and recovers energy may well be treated in a direct instructional setting. In each of these instances related social studies or science learnings may be accomplished, but the relatedness would be *from* health education *to* science or social studies learnings, rather than the reverse.

A functional setting for health instruction. The school has another sort of opportunity that it can and does utilize for health education: the broad school living experience, in and of itself. With the ultimate ends of the program being healthful practices based on adequate understanding and positive health attitudes, the idea of using the ongoingness of the school living experience *in toto* as a setting for health instruction is sound. Understandings can be developed and practices can be strengthened by utilizing the lunch period in relation to instruction about foods and nutrition; certain playground activities or planning for field trips can be seen in relation to efforts to educate for safety and accident prevention; regular weighing and measuring schedules can be seen in relation to understanding growth and development; vision screening tests can be related to proper education for care of the eyes; and so on. Once the possibilities for health instruction in such situations as these are grasped by the elementary school and the teacher, some very meaningful health education takes place.

Guarding Against Fears and Anxieties

Enthusiasm for a commitment to the provision of sound and adequate health education in the elementary school must be tempered with great sensitivity for and understanding of the children with whom the school is working. It is possible, and usual, for the results of instruction in health to make quite positive contributions to children's learning. It is not unknown, however, for such teaching to lead in some instances to the development of fears and anxieties on the part of some children. Instruction in this area must be offered with a great deal of awareness of the situation in which particular children find it necessary to try to live healthfully. If goals are put forth absolutely, with certain "or else" implications, and children realize that these goals are beyond their reach

at the present time, the negative results in terms of mental health may overshadow any gains that might come from the instructional effort. A way of living that calls, for instance, for a bath each day is simply not realistic in certain situations. A fixed number of glasses of milk or particular balanced formats for meals are daily goals that some children cannot meet. Other illustrations come quickly to mind. Now, to be aware of this possible harm is not to suggest that the school provide either false or incomplete information. It is intended to call attention to the range of healthful living practices that must be accepted. Information about bodily cleanliness may indicate that a daily bath is most desirable; it may also indicate that something less than this is acceptable and not to be feared. Similar information may indicate that meals balanced in particular ways with respect to food content are most desirable; but it may also show that eating in these ways is to be done as often as possible and that "bad things" are not going to happen immediately to one who does not have such a diet regularly. Often, children are simply powerless to control certain aspects of their living experience, such as the place in which they live, the adequacy of facilities to be shared among a number of people, or the long-established eating habits of parents. They may be helped to live as healthfully as possible in their present situation, and they may form attitudes about healthful living which will cause them to want to live differently as the situation permits. This is a far more acceptable result of the instruction provided than is the development of fears and anxieties based on wondering "what will happen to me since I don't live that way." Sometimes, a family may recognize the soundness of some health knowledge or practice brought home by a child and try to revise some aspect of their living accordingly. Often patterns of living cannot be altered until a person is independent enough to be establishing his own way of life.

PROVIDING FOR PHYSICAL EDUCATION

Directly related to the instructional program in health education in the elementary school is the program in physical education. These two aspects of the curriculum act in direct support of each other. Clearly, a definition of *healthy* as "a total state of well-being" calls for a person that is physically strong, possessed of sufficient stamina and strength to carry on both work and recreational activities without undue fatigue. Too, a certain degree of physical skill and dexterity is demanded by many aspects of daily living. Control over and coordination of one's physical self is important.

From what has been said earlier in this chapter, it is clear, too, that it is just as important for children to learn how to "play" properly as it

is to "work" properly. The need for a person to have ways of relaxing and recreating is well accepted. Many will find a source of relaxation in the area of physical activity.

Actually, a very basic developmental task for children in our culture is to be able to handle the body efficiently. This most often means that girls and boys must be able to handle themselves with a high degree of poise and coordination as they participate in various individual and group activities appropriate to their sex. It means they must be able to run, jump, throw, and so on, with speed, agility, and accuracy. Such skills are combined into many individual and team sports in our society, and we expect great numbers of our people to participate in them. This "norm" is so clear for boys that the pressure to develop physical skill to some degree is quite strong; for a boy, to be a successful athlete is to be admired and approved by the majority of our people.[6]

Additionally, the possibilities that physical education activities hold for the accomplishment of certain general objectives of education should be noted. Many of the dual and team activities in which children participate in the physical education program make a certain contribution to the development of such personal traits as loyalty, responsibility, and fair play. They help a child to sense what it means to be a good team member and what teamwork is all about; they make their contribution in helping a child become a good winner and a good loser. All of these characteristics are admired and sought in our society, and the setting that much of the physical education program provides for their development should not be overlooked.

For all of these reasons, physical education is an integral part of the curriculum of the elementary school. Its purposes include:

1. *Physical development*—the building of physical power
2. *Motor development*—the performance of physical movement
3. *Mental development*—knowledge of the physical, and of physical activities
4. *Personal development*—the development of the self
5. *Social development*—participation with others in physical activities

The Distribution of Time and Effort

Physical education is to be provided, then, as a daily experience for all children. It is felt that all students need this experience, and most states require it as a part of their state legislation pertaining to education. Almost all children will be able to participate in whatever regular program of physical education is provided. Some children will need to

---

[6] See Robert J. Havighurst, *Human Development and Education* (New York: Longmans, Green and Company, 1953), p. 28.

participate in a modified program. These children, handicapped in some way and to some extent, must be identified and the program adapted accordingly for them. As far as possible, the regular curriculum is modified for them so that they can participate with their classmates in it. But at times a very special program is necessary to meet the needs of certain pupils.

Physical Education as Instruction

It is important to make one thing quite clear early in this discussion: that physical education is an instructional program, first and foremost. The major goals and objectives of this aspect of the curriculum, no less than of others, can be realized only by perceiving the activities provided as guided experiences, or as teaching-learning situations. It *is not* physical education simply to release children from their classrooms to spend a fixed period of time on the playground, with certain basic equipment and apparatus at their disposal. It *is* physical education to instruct children, or to guide and assist them in some specific physical education activity, with the purposes for which the experience is provided clearly in the teacher's mind. It is this latter perception of physical education that makes a place for it in the elementary school curriculum. It is this perception that helps us to differentiate between physical education and playing on the vacant lot after school hours. It is this sort of planning, which attempts to remove the chance factor from physical development, that brings the physical education program into the mainstream of formal education.

Physical education and school recreation. As with any other area of learning in the elementary school, it is necessary to provide recurring opportunities for use if physical skills, once developed, are to be maintained and refined. And, if these skills are to be used in the ways intended by the purposes of the program, it is important to provide typical situations in which to practice them. The elementary school tries to do this in a number of ways in addition to the physical education period. There may be noon-hour intramural sports programs; or there may be noon-hour folk dancing opportunities. Day-long "play days" may be organized to bring larger groups of children together for recreation and fun; or the school may join hands with the community in operating an after-school recreation program centered in the elementary school plant and grounds.

These enterprises are all a part of the physical education program, but they are not the heart of it. This lies, as noted above, in the instruction that is provided in the daily, guided physical education experience.

Physical education and recess. Recess periods, usually required for

about ten minutes out of every hour, are related to the health and physical education effort in its broadest sense. These short periods of time provide a few minutes of relaxation and exercise, fresh air, a chance for toileting, and an opportunity for conversation. They make their contribution to the physical and mental health of pupils, without a doubt. But, these are not to be confused with the program of physical education, either. They are just what their name implies, periods of recess from the major tasks at hand.

The bulk of the total time and effort devoted to physical education in the elementary school is divided between the physical education class and the school recreation program. Some elementary schools will have teams competing in interscholastic sports, and in these instances some additional time and effort must go to this aspect of the program. The distribution of time, effort, and pupil involvement can be shown in the diagram.

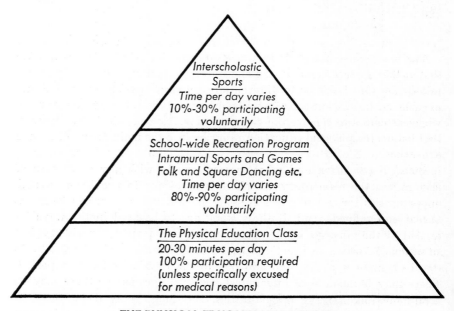

Interscholastic
Sports
Time per day varies
10%-30% participating
voluntarily

School-wide Recreation Program
Intramural Sports and Games
Folk and Square Dancing etc.
Time per day varies
80%-90% participating
voluntarily

The Physical Education Class
20-30 minutes per day
100% participation required
(unless specifically excused
for medical reasons)

THE PHYSICAL EDUCATION PROGRAM

The physical education class, as noted earlier, tries to include all children as participants. It is usually scheduled for about twenty minutes daily in the primary grades, and for from twenty to thirty minutes daily in the intermediate and upper grades.

The recreational program of the school, including intramural sports and games, folk dancing, and the like, is usually scheduled for noon

times, or for the last part of the school day on certain occasions. It is hoped that from 80 to 90 per cent of the students will participate voluntarily in these activities, and the program is designed to involve such numbers.

Some elementary schools have an organized interscholastic sports program, too. This is especially true in those instances where the elementary school is organized to include grades seven and eight. Certain communities develop such an intensive interscholastic sports program at the secondary school level that the elementary school begins to loom as a potential "feeder" for these high school teams, and efforts are made to identify and develop the athletic potential that might be found in elementary school age children. Where such an interscholastic sports program is found in the elementary school, some 10 to 30 per cent of the children are expected to be participating voluntarily in it. More is said later in this chapter as to the advisability of such interscholastic ventures in the elementary school.

The Scope of Physical Education

The broad purposes of the physical education program call for a broad and varied scope of activities. The following paragraphs give a more detailed picture of this breadth, and some insight into the nature of the experiences that each aspect of the program is expected to provide.

Coordination and control activities. These experiences are provided to help children to develop proper use of the body. In the main, these uses are concerned with locomotion and playing skills. The experiences in locomotion are focused on learning to move the body in various positions and at various speeds appropriate to particular activities. The experiences with playing skills are focused on helping children to learn to throw, catch, jump, and the like, with the idea that these skills will be applied, singly and in combinations, in various work and play activities in which children engage.

Quickly organized activities. These activities are simple in organization, and do not demand highly refined skills for participation. In the main, these are games and relays, and they operate from simple line, circle, or scatter formations. They are adaptable to almost any number of participants, to almost any available play area, and to almost any block of time. Such activities are designed to include everyone in a class or group, providing vigorous activity, use of physical skills, and some feeling for team effort in a situation that is relatively simple to learn and to conduct.

Rhythmic activities. Experiences in this area of activity are related to the basic impulse of human beings to move to rhythm. A variety of situ-

ations are made available for children, extending from opportunities for individual self-expression to music and rhythm, to more organized and systematic responses such as are found in folk and square dancing. Provision is made for creative expression, and for increased efficiency and control in bodily movement. A by-product is the gain for children in social grace and social experience.

Individual and dual activities. This area of activity consists of games that pit one person against another, or two people against two others. These experiences contribute heavily not only to the general goals of the physical education program, but especially to the recreational aims of the program. Such activities as tetherball, foursquare, and shuffleboard fall into this general category, setting the stage for eventual participation in such games as handball, bowling, tennis, and golf.

Self-testing activities. These are experiences that have as their purpose the development of the individual child's strength, coordination, balance, and endurance. They are typically organized and administered in such a way as to help a child to gain insight into his ability at a certain time in the school year, and to check on his improvement at a later date. Such activities as balancing, chinning, simple tumbling, and stunts are typical of those used for these self-testing purposes. It is hoped that such experiences will make a worthwhile contribution to the physical development of the child, and that personal insight may be gained that will be helpful in interpreting an emerging self to the individual youngster.

Athletic team games. This is an area of experience in which children come into contact with more highly organized games, usually seasonal in nature, and traditional in our culture. The age and the general development level of particular children have a great deal to do with the degree to which and the manner in which such games are presented in the elementary school. Games like kickball, catchball, modified volleyball, modified soccer, and touch football are played in prelude to regulation football, basketball, baseball, volleyball, and soccer as played later by youths and adults.

That these games provide an opportunity to develop physical skill and endurance, to have fun and enjoyment in playing, and to develop some of the desirable personal and social traits mentioned earlier is undoubtedly true. That they must be used with discretion and reason in the elementary school is equally true. This is especially clear when the matter of interscholastic team games is considered.

Almost every study that has ever been made, by separate or combined groups of elementary educators, physical education specialists, and medical doctors, has recommended against the participation of ele-

mentary school age children in interscholastic sports competition.[7] They suggest that such contests, if held at all, be held infrequently and under very informal auspices. The length of the contest, the rules under which it is played, and the spectator situation should be arranged with the age level and the maturity of the participants clearly in mind. Reports such as these point out the dangers inherent in highly organized interscholastic team sports for both the physical and the mental health of children. With the strong cultural value placed on athletic prowess in our country, this is not always a popular or easy position for the elementary school to try to take. However, the impact of such evidence is increasingly persuasive as manifest in the small amount of such sports competition found in a six-year elementary school, and the fairly reasonable approach to such contests in the eight-year elementary school. Of course, much of this sort of activity has of late become a community-wide enterprise, subject to control and regulation from groups other than school.

This, then, is the scope of the program. It is broad and varied, and must be so if it is to accomplish the goals set for physical education in the elementary school.

Sequence in the Physical Education Program

The matter of sequence in the physical education program is based primarily on the rate at which, and the ways in which, the child grows and develops. Readiness is a concept that is particularly applicable to this aspect of the curriculum. Children are not able to profit from certain kinds of instruction in physical education until they have matured physically in certain ways. While instruction in physical education is committed to the development of physical skills and coordinations, effort is not expended wisely until the body has developed to the point that it will respond efficiently to such instructional effort. Some of the earliest basic studies in readiness were focused on physical and motor development. An educational psychologist summed this matter up recently as follows: "Both observation of children's learning of such complex skills as ball playing, skating, swimming, or writing and an experimental investigation of the hypothesis indicates that for complex skills, training makes a relatively greater contribution to improvement than for simple skills. But for complex skills, neither uninstructed practice nor teacher-guided training can make up for limitations in maturity...."[8]

---

[7] American Association for Health, Physical Education, and Recreation, Joint Committee Report, *Desirable Athletic Competition for Children* (Washington, D.C.: the Association, 1952).

[8] Arden N. Frandsen, *How Children Learn* (New York: McGraw-Hill Book Company, 1957), pp. 72–73.

Sequences within the physical education curriculum are also based on the ultimate setting in which physical skills are to be used. Young children are taught to run properly, to hop and to skip, to jump and to throw, for instance. Certain ''lead up'' activities precede attempts to combine these various physical skills into an organized game. Throwing, and catching, and running games, for example, precede attempts to play organized softball or baseball. Similarly, touch football as an organized game is preceded by chances to learn to throw, catch, and kick a football. Simple folk and square dances that contain most of the basic steps are learned before the more intricate and involved dances are attempted.

Thus, a cut across the physical education curriculum at any particular point should reveal activities and experiences designed with both the readiness of the child to profit from the instruction and the ultimate ends of the program clearly in mind.

Mastery and the Development of Physical Skill

As with other areas of the curriculum that demand high skill, so in physical education does the concept of mastery have to be dealt with. The school must answer the question of how much physical skill it should try to exact from each child. A number of facts must be kept in mind as this question is answered.

Individual differences. The fact of individual differences is probably more obvious in the physical education area than in any of the other strands of the curriculum. We can easily see the differences in height, strength, weight, and so on, and can predict with considerable effectiveness which children will run faster, jump higher, and throw farther than others. The natural endowment with which children have to work is more highly visible in the physical area than in the areas of activity more highly related to mental ability.

Personal choice and motivation. More difficult to appraise, and certainly more difficult to reflect in our practices, are the differences that are based on personal choice and motivation in the area of physical accomplishment. A child may obviously possess the physique to accomplish more or perform better in certain areas of physical activity. But both his choice of areas in which he desires to participate and the level of skill development acceptable to him in those areas are highly personal things. In the elementary school, where physical ability and outlets for physical prowess are being explored for the first time in any systematic way, the school will do well not to mistake timidity, lack of personal security, or lack of information concerning certain physical activities for a considered choice to be a nonparticipant. Without undue pressure, children should be helped to meet and accomplish certain physically oriented develop-

mental tasks while they are young, at the ages where the culture tends to expect this of them. However, as children move on through the intermediate grades and into the upper grades, and the school can be relatively sure that a child is choosing to pursue or not to pursue physical activities as an area of interest on the basis of some personal experience with them, this preference must be recognized and respected. And, with evidence that the acceptance of a level of skill in any such activity is made as a personal considered choice, the school will do well to allow for a very flexible and individualized definition of mastery in this area. Some children will be motivated to develop a level of skill beyond their physical endowment, and they will need to be counseled and guided sensitively. Others will be highly motivated and possessed of a high degree of physical skill. This they should be helped to appraise and exploit to their best interests, too. Surely no precise or rigid definition of mastery will do.

Sex differences. Lastly, the level of skill which the elementary school will seek to develop in children is related to sex differences, both organismic and cultural. Differences in rate of physical development between girls and boys make for some differences in accepted levels of achievement and skill at various age and grade levels. Although boys tend to develop in height and weight a bit more rapidly than girls in the earliest years, this gap tends to close by the end of elementary school. At the same time, the physical strength of boys continues to be greater. While we may expect girls to compete on fairly even terms with boys during most of the early elementary school years, this ceases to be the case in the last years of the intermediate grades and in the upper grades of schools that include the seventh and eighth years. Though many girls may be taller and heavier than boys at that time, they will not be as strong physically. Accepted levels of skill development at given ages will, then, be somewhat specific to the sex of the child concerned.[9]

Culturally, too, there are different expectancies set in this area for boys and for girls. These expectancies influence the acceptance of particular levels of skill development as satisfactory. The female role does not require or demand as much physical strength, endurance, and skill as does the male role. In fact, girls with high levels of interest and potential in physical activities sometimes find it extremely difficult to reconcile these with the expected female role. Boys find the opposite to be the case, with the cultural expectancy being set for high interest and skill in physical things, and certain levels of achievement more or less expected of them. The work of Havighurst on the developmental tasks of middle childhood puts it this way:

---

[9] L. Cole and J. B. Morgan, *Psychology of Childhood and Adolescence* (New York: Rinehart and Company, 1947), pp. 4–5.

Boys are expected to learn these [physical] skills to a higher degree than girls. A girl can do rather poorly on them and still hold status in the peer group, while a boy who does poorly is called a "sissy" and loses status. Boys of all social classes are expected to acquire physical skills.[10]

Thus, attention to the idea of mastery in physical education must include consideration for physical endowment, personal choice and motivation, and sex differences both physically and culturally based.

Staffing for Physical Education

In most elementary schools, the regular classroom teacher is expected to handle the instruction in physical education, as in all other areas of the classroom program. Some elementary schools will provide a special consultant in this area to work with classroom teachers as they strive to grow in ability to handle physical education. Some few schools will actually be staffed with a special physical education instructor, assigned probably to the intermediate grades, who will do the teaching in this area. Most of the physical education at the seventh and eighth grade levels is handled by special teachers.

HEALTH AND PHYSICAL EDUCATION AND THE SCHOOL ENVIRONMENT

In agreement with the evidence in the field of physical and mental health concerning the importance of the total environment in which a person spends his time, the elementary school gives considerable attention to the provision of a healthful and safe school environment for children. If the school experience is to contribute as completely as it might to a total state of well-being this provision is quite necessary. The school plant and the school grounds, the provision of certain special facilities therein, the general way in which the school day is organized, and the relationship the teacher tries to establish with his class and among the children in his charge all come to be seen as parts of the school's effort to provide for the health of children. Let us consider each of these briefly here, to grasp the sense in which the total environment provides for and helps to insure effective health education.

The School Plant and Grounds

The whole matter of site selection and school building design is carried out now with a direct concern for providing a safe and healthful place for

---

[10] Havighurst, *op. cit.*, p. 28.

children. The school is located in the community with these things in mind. Every effort is made to place the school in a safe place, safe in the sense that children can come to and from the school without undue fear for their personal safety. Also, a site is sought on which to locate the school building that will be large enough so that several hundred children can live healthfully on it, without undue crowding and limitations on physical activity. Most states now have recommended minimum standards for the size of an elementary school site, and communities strive to procure ground accordingly.

The building itself is designed with children in mind, and the sort of living that should go on in an elementary school is reflected in the way in which space is arranged and ordered. Most new elementary schools are built as one-story buildings, so that children do not have to climb up and down stairs all day long. Such a building simplifies living for individual children, and especially increases the safety of the large groups of children that must move from one part of the building to another at particular times. The building is designed not only to be functionally adequate, but also to be attractive. The general outside appearance of the building is pleasant, and the grounds are usually landscaped to add to the beauty of it. Colors used to decorate both the outside and inside of the modern elementary school are selected to add to the general pleasantness of the school environment. Proper lighting, heating, and ventilating systems are provided, which make their contribution to a healthful school environment. Classrooms are equipped with running water and drinking fountains to make it easier to practice certain desirable health habits day by day.

School furniture has undergone drastic change in the past ten years. The result is that the comfort, as well as the esthetic qualities, of the classroom furniture has improved. Attractive designs and the use of color in school furniture have been welcome additions in the classroom. The changes that have come about all contribute to the physical and mental health of students.

Special Equipment and Facilities

Providing ample play space. Outdoor play space, divided with the safety of children in mind so that young children and older children can participate with satisfaction in games appropriate to their ages, continues to improve. Also, the kinds of special equipment and apparatus placed at the disposal of children on the playground are increasingly designed and selected with greater sensitivity to the kind of play in which different age groups want to participate. Even the general surfacing of playground space, and the special surfacing that is provided under cer-

tain kinds of equipment, more often is selected with the health and safety of children clearly in mind. It is encouraging to see, too, the more frequent provision of an adequately covered play area for elementary schools. If the physical education program is to operate successfully the year around, such a facility is badly needed.

Providing adequate lunch facilities. Elementary schools give attention, also, to the provision of suitable noon lunching facilities for children who find it necessary to have their lunch at school. In some instances all that is necessary is to arrange for a proper place for eating for those children who bring their lunch to school from time to time. Many elementary schools, however, must have a lunching facility for practically their complete student body. In such situations the elementary school is increasingly equipped with kitchens, serving facilities, and ample eating space to prepare and serve a hot lunch at school at a very nominal price. The direct contribution which such a service can make to sound nutrition is obvious. Additionally, the indirect educational benefits which accrue from such a facility must be noted. The opportunity to impress upon children the necessity for taking enough time to eat a relaxed lunch, the advisability of eating a balanced meal, and the satisfaction which comes from eating varied lunches can be exploited. The chance for children to participate in the preparation and serving of the lunch again adds to the significance of this special facility for the over-all goals of the health education program.

Providing healthful toilet facilities. A word is in order, too, as to some of the most recent developments in providing toilet facilities in the elementary school. If the ends of the health program are to be realized, children must be able to live healthfully at school. This means that children must be able to take care of their toilet in an efficient and sanitary way. For many, many years the only way in which such facilities were ever designed was to provide one large room for girls, and another for boys. Usually these were very poorly placed, so that reaching them from inside or outside the school building or both was difficult. The task of keeping such facilities clean, and of controlling some of the things that took place inside was very great. Recently, there has been a move to provide toilet facilities adjoining each separate classroom, to be used by a single classroom group, or perhaps to be shared between the classrooms on either side of it. Such an arrangement has proved to be a great improvement. The hesitancy that some teachers and parents have had about the use of such facilities has disappeared after they have had a chance to see them in use. In addition to avoiding the interruption that comes of having children make the long trek to the "bathroom" is the infinitely more normal approach to toileting habits that can be established and maintained under such arrangements. The school environment reinforces

habits that the home is trying to establish with children. Since most classrooms are designed now with a sink and running water for hand-washing, a very normal set of practices can be carried out by children. Some elementary school buildings are designed with additional toilet facilities for use when children are on the playground.

New schools are usually built and furnished with the things described here kept in mind from the outset; older schools are continually re-modeled and refurnished, if they are to continue to be used, to bring them more into line with these advances.

Organizing the School Day

In present-day elementary schools teachers organize the school day with the physical and mental health of children in mind. Of course, the length of the school day itself is adjusted in the elementary school with an eye to the well-being of children of various ages. Five-year-olds usually attend kindergarten for a half-day session of about two and one-half hours. Children in the primary grades complete a school day that is con-siderably shorter than the day put in by children in the intermediate grades. For instance, a first grade child will be in school for about five and one-half to six hours each day, exclusive of the lunch hour. Home-work assignments are made sparingly during the elementary school years. Such decisions as to the length of the school day and the amount of work to be done away from the school are made with the intent to help children to live healthfully. They try to take into account the twenty-four-hour day of the child, with attention to time for work, play, rest and relaxa-tion, personal interests and hobbies, and family experiences.

Within any one of these school days we find teachers planning their program to provide a proper balance among work experiences, play and physical exercise, rest and relaxation. Every effort is made to instill variety into the school day and to dispel feelings of boredom and fatigue. Teachers speak often of ''pacing'' activities in the school day. They are indicating that they plan the work of the day so that a quiet activity, such as a sitting and listening experience, is followed by some more lively ac-tivity in which the children may participate in a different way. Recesses which come each hour are a part of this same attempt to pace the school day. Then, too, the length of time children are asked to concentrate and work on certain tasks varies with the nature of the task itself. An at-tempt is made to guard against nervousness, daydreaming, and tension, and to keep children at given tasks for periods of time commensurate with their ''staying powers.'' Pacing, then, is a very important aspect of a teacher's daily and weekly planning. Thus, health education is served by the way in which the school day is organized.

The Teacher-Pupil Relationship

The nature of the relationship a teacher establishes with his pupils, individually and collectively, makes its contribution, good or bad, to the total well-being of children. A wealth of testimony from pupils indicates the positive contribution that comes from working with a teacher who is kind, friendly, firm but consistent, fair and impartial, understanding and patient in his dealings with them. Abundant testimony is available, too, as to what happens when the opposite sort of circumstances prevails. Teachers know this, and they do their best to create the sort of psychological climate in their classrooms that will support, and not thwart, the emotional well-being of their pupils. There are times, of course, when it is difficult for a teacher to find something about every child in his classroom that he can honestly admire. But, this is the goal that he must work toward to help to bridge the distance that otherwise might stand between teacher and pupils. The reverse is equally true, of course; children come to school wanting to like their teacher, and there are times when they have to look hard for the link that can join them in a satisfying working relationship.

As teachers work with their class group they keep a number of things in mind. They know that children must see themselves as one of the group. They know that children must all find a way of participating in the activities of the group. Further, they know that this participation must be reasonably successful, and that children must be given recognition for this successful participation. Finally, they know the security that comes to children from knowing that their future is secure in the group, too. These concerns suggest the efforts the teacher must make for the mental health of his pupils. This is a large task, but one of fundamental importance.

Teachers are aware, too, of the natural competition found among children when they are associated together in any close way. This is accepted and used as positively as possible for motivation to learning. But every effort is made to do away with intensive, "manufactured" competition that leads to tension and anxiety of an unwholesome sort. Every effort is made to insure "fair" competition for the children in the class. Grouping, rotating class-wide responsibilities, balancing committee memberships, and the like, are all a part of the work of the teacher who would guard and strengthen the mental health of children.

HEALTH SERVICES AND HEALTH EDUCATION

Health Services in the Elementary School

The health program of the elementary school extends into the area of health services. The services offered by the school are related to very

specific purposes. Certain health services are provided by the elementary school so that the welfare of the pupils in attendance may be protected. Others are designed to enable the school to work cooperatively with parents, community medical personnel, and community health agencies to help insure the physical and mental well-being of the children of the school community. Now, it is clear that elementary school teachers are not expected to practice medicine in any sense of the term. In fact, most states have very explicit legislation stating the limits on the activities of school teachers in the area of health services. Many elementary schools have a nurse as a regular staff member, and some have a school doctor and dentist who work in the district full-time, making regular visits to individual elementary schools, or otherwise providing service to children. Others use public health nurses on a part-time basis, and contract similarly for the services of a doctor who will spend some agreed upon amount of time in the school district. Classroom teachers do assist in certain ways as the service program operates, but the total effort is guided by persons qualified to do so. Let us consider in some detail the exact nature of this health service responsibility, and the service activities that are provided.

Determining Health Needs

Encouraging periodic health examinations. Clearly, the "health status," so to speak, of the child is of concern to many people. It is to the benefit of each child that his developing health "profile" be determined as completely as possible. Such health data as are needed to determine this profile must come from a number of sources. Information comes from parents and from children themselves, from examinations made by private or school medical personnel, from the daily observations of classroom teachers as they work intimately with children, and from the regular screening and recording programs related to height, weight, vision, and hearing that the school typically carries on. Clearly, only a part of this evidence is appropriately collected by the school itself. But, as a community institution, it can act as a strong protagonist with individual families and with community groups to encourage the development of a broad program for determining the health needs of children. For instance, school and community may join together in developing a plan for periodic health examinations, medical, dental, and psychological, for all children. Often such programs provide that examinations are to be held at school and on school time. Parents are not forced to use this service, but its convenience is difficult to resist and the result is usually that more children receive regular health examinations than would normally be the case. The school is also in a position to urge parents to have children examined when the day-to-day contact at school seems to reveal some deviation

from the normal that should be investigated and explained. Referral routines and channels can be established that make it easy for parents to follow through on such suggestions, and the realization of the ends of the school's health program are helped accordingly.

Maintaining a health record system. A part of a continuing assessment of the health status of the child is to make data available to concerned persons. When information is recorded systematically and housed in a convenient place it is much more likely to be referred to and used. To some extent, the elementary school can provide another needed service in this regard. Information on the health status of each child can be brought together on a cumulative health record form, and can readily be made available to appropriate school personnel, parents, and family physician. All of these persons need access to this information and an interpretation of it at different times for different purposes. Parents and children, obviously, need to become increasingly aware of the pattern of development that is unfolding in these data. Teachers need to be well informed, too, on this matter, if they are to understand certain aspects of the pupil's performance properly, and are to adapt the classroom experience realistically to specific health conditions. The family physician may find these school-centered data a useful supplement to whatever health records he maintains on a given child. School and community health personnel can work together to develop a valuable health record service.

Assisting in Disease Prevention and Control

The elementary school is also given certain responsibilities to meet in the area of the prevention and control of disease. Part of the responsibility is related to the protection the school must extend to the children in attendance. Operating as it does on an "in the place of the parent" basis in matters such as this, the elementary school must have an ongoing service program designed to identify and isolate the sick child. Children who exhibit symptoms of illness must be immediately separated from the larger group until the illness can be properly diagnosed. While teachers are expected to be alert to such warning signs, they are also expected to call for assistance from school or community medical personnel for a final determination of the child's condition. The school's responsibility for action is greatest when the illness is diagnosed as a contagious disease. In such instances its responsibility extends beyond the ill child. Parents of other children who may have been exposed need to be informed of this. Such immediate notification may enable parents to procure preventive treatment for their children, and will make them alert to symptoms of the disease that may develop.

In discharging these responsibilities the school does have an opportunity for certain health service instruction activities, too. Contacts with parents provide an occasion for encouraging the use of effective preventive health measures with children. An effort can be made, for instance, to help parents to see the wisdom of providing for regular immunizations for their children. In fact, this effort may provide the motivation for a community-wide immunization program, co-sponsored by the school, community medical personnel, and community health agencies, that will operate in and through the school system.

It also provides an opportunity for the school to develop a more realistic position for all concerned on the matter of regular school attendance. Some parents, and even some schools, seem to feel that a child should be in school, no matter what. Records of "perfect attendance" are valued out of all reasonable proportions. Undue emphasis on this sort of thing can often work to the detriment of the child who is ill but comes to school anyway, and to the rest of the children in his class and school who are thus unnecessarily exposed to disease. A realistic policy on attendance urges the parent to keep the sick child at home, with the decision usually in favor of a day of absence to "make sure" rather than of attendance until "the last moment."

Caring for Emergencies at School

The elementary school must have, also, a planned program for the care of emergencies that occur at school. This, again, is rooted in the charge to the schools to act in the place of the parent. These health emergencies will sometimes be of sickness, as mentioned earlier. At other times they will be personal injury incidents. The school is charged with the responsibility for providing immediate care or first aid in all such situations. A sick child must be moved to a safe place and made as comfortable as possible. An injured child must be administered proper first aid. Teachers, in conjunction with school health personnel, are expected to be able to handle such occurrences safely and wisely. Parents are to be notified immediately of such happenings, and guidance is to be given to them as to the extent of the injury and what action would seem to be necessary. That is, a child might obviously need the immediate attention of a physician. Perhaps he should be taken to a physician's office; perhaps the doctor should be summoned to the school because it may appear unwise to move the child. The aim is to get the proper care for the child, at the proper place, at the proper time. Anticipating occasions when parents cannot be contacted, the elementary school must take the initiative in working out procedures for meeting sickness or injury in the absence of direct parent contact. Thus, names of physicians to be called, of neighbors

to be notified, and the like, are kept on file at the school to insure that the service program will be able to meet emergencies efficiently under any and all conditions.

Thus, through these various programs of service, the elementary school rounds out its total program in health and physical education.

REFERENCES

Bucher, Charles A., and Evelyn M. Reads. *Physical Education in the Modern Elementary School.* New York: The Macmillan Company, 1958.
>   An excellent overview of health and physical education in the elementary school, with descriptions of activities recommended for inclusion.

Fraser, Ellen D., John Bransford, and Mamie Hastings. *The Child and Physical Education.* Englewood Cliffs, New Jersey: Prentice-Hall, Inc., 1956.
>   A statement on the teaching of physical education in the elementary school that attempts to be consistent with child development and accepted educational philosophy.

Haag, Jessie H. *School Health Program.* New York: Henry Holt and Company, 1958.
>   Presents health education in the setting of teamwork between school and community personnel in activating some eight related areas of a complete health program.

Halsey, Elizabeth, and Lorena R. Porter. *Physical Education for Children: A Developmental Approach.* New York: Henry Holt and Company, 1958.
>   The developmental approach to physical education; contains many illustrative lessons.

Irwin, Leslie W., James H. Humphrey, and Warren R. Johnson. *Methods and Materials in School Health Education.* St. Louis: C. V. Mosby Company, 1956.
>   A presentation of many techniques designed to make health instruction in the elementary school more effective with children.

Larson, Leonard, and Lucille Hill. *Physical Education in the Elementary School.* New York: Henry Holt and Company, 1957.
>   Deals comprehensively with the theoretical foundations of physical education and describes appropriate activities.

Miller, Arthur G., and Virginia Whitcomb. *Physical Education in the Elementary School Curriculum.* Englewood Cliffs, New Jersey: Prentice-Hall, Inc., 1957.
>   Treats class organization for physical education; offers helpful suggestions for the teaching of physical education activities and for relating physical education to other areas of the curriculum in appropriate ways.

Neilson, N. P. E., and Winifred Van Hagen. *Physical Education for Elementary Schools* (Revised edition). New York: The Ronald Press Company, 1957.
>   This book has consistently been one of the most used and helpful texts in this area of the curriculum.

Schneider, Robert E. *Methods and Materials of Health Education.* Philadelphia: W. B. Saunders Company, 1958.

A good presentation of valuable guides and ideas for educating children in the ways of healthful living.

Smith, Helen N., and Mary E. Wolverton. *Health Education in the Elementary School*. New York: The Ronald Press Company, 1959.

This book deals with the organization of the school health program and includes a great deal of information on the instructional aspect of that program.

Wheatley, George M., and Grace T. Hallock. *Health Observation of School Children* (New edition). New York: McGraw-Hill Book Company, 1956.

In a readable style this book outlines a usable approach to understanding and working with children in the observation of the state of their health.

Willgoose, Carl E. *Health Education in the Elementary School*. Philadelphia: W. B. Saunders Company, 1959.

A complete overview of the school health program with particular attention to its instructional aspects; practical suggestions for development are included.

Vannier, Mary H., and Mildred Foster. *Teaching Physical Education in Elementary Schools* (Second edition). Philadelphia: W. B. Saunders Company, 1958.

A statement dealing with the teaching of activities recommended for inclusion in the elementary school physical education program; a useful guide for teachers.

PART 4

CURRICULUM IMPLEMENTATION IN THE CLASSROOM

17

THE CLASSROOM
TEACHER: IMPLEMENTOR
OF CURRICULUM

The understandings and the professional skill of classroom teachers are the means by which the realization of desires for educational experiences, the development of general curricular ideas accepted as basic guidelines for providing those experiences, and the specific involvement provided for children with language, number, science are achieved. The teacher is the central agent in the whole educational process.

To order certain experiences that will result in learning for another person is a complex art.

> [Teaching] is a profession that demands a human touch and an ability to inspire young people to achieve great things.... No one should teach who is not a bit awed by the importance of the profession.[1]

Teaching is a personal action, implicating the very personal human qualities of thinking, communicating, experiencing. It involves interaction with and the influence of personal motives, desires, abilities. The effectiveness of teaching depends in great part upon the teacher's concept of the teaching role as reflected in his personal behavior, the understanding and sympathy he imparts, the way he organizes the tools and materials of learning, and the way he works with human beings. The teacher must be an expert, scientific, insightful individual.

---

[1] George W. Fraser, *An Introduction to the Study of Education* (New York: Harper & Brothers, 1951), p. 18.

TEACHING AND HUMAN RELATIONSHIPS

That teaching is a role involved in an extensive network of human relationships is evident. Teachers work with people first and foremost, as they work with ideas, materials, space, and time. Evaluation takes place in terms of modified human behavior. Let us consider the extent of this human relations involvement.

Relationships with Children

The most important human relationship that must be satisfactorily established is that between the teacher and children. Elementary teachers work with children first, last, and always. They must understand them and feel empathy toward them. They must be able to view the world through the eyes of both an adult and a child. The teacher-pupil relationship is central in all of elementary school education.

Relationships with Parents

Beyond children, the most important set of relationships to be established effectively is undoubtedly with parents. Parents send their most precious possession to the elementary school, and they want to assure themselves that it is in good hands. Therefore, they are very much interested in elementary school teachers. At the same time, teachers find it important and necessary to get to know parents as much as possible if they are really to understand the children with whom they work. The tendency in elementary school education is to find teachers and parents working together and talking together more frequently than in former years. This is a relationship that teachers will want to establish well.

Relationships with the Community

The teacher inevitably has a certain kind of professional relationship to establish and maintain with the wider adult community. While one may participate to a degree in social and civic organization just as any other person, he also participates as a teacher. As such, he is supposed to be interested in and well informed on a variety of local, state, and national educational problems. It is important to the teacher singly, and to the total system of which he is a part, to establish this kind of extended adult relationship effectively. Some might call this the public relations role for teachers.

Relationships within the Profession

Professional responsibilities. Within the profession itself is found another set of human relationships that needs to be established in ways that

will be both personally and professionally satisfying. More than teaching his own class, the teacher must meet other professional responsibilities with (1) conscious personal behavior as an ethical teacher, (2) effort toward professional growth, (3) service in professional organizations, and (4) services to the profession in general.

The teacher's conduct reflects the moral principles to which the profession as a whole subscribes. He is familiar with and practices his code of ethics in his relationship with children, community, and colleagues. In addition, he is conscious of the standards that govern the quality of his teaching. He helps to define these standards, enforce them, and contribute to their improvement.

Professional growth is another responsibility of the successful teacher. The manner in which the salary schedule is organized is a reflection of the district's emphasis on continuous growth. Increments are usually dependent upon course work completed or degrees attained as well as accumulated experience in the classroom. Professional growth means more than college credits, however. It involves practical understanding of current trends that directly influence classroom procedures. It means modification of techniques that prevent a teacher from "standing still" in his method of operation. He gains this growth not only from the informal chats and organized meetings he attends but also through the professional literature and special brochures he reads. The teacher's job of broadening his own educational and professional insight is never finished.

A responsible member of the profession is also active in his professional organizations. In almost every part of the country both local and state teachers' organizations work with the National Education Association. In some areas, teachers' unions are also organized to work for the best interests of teachers. The teacher who is a contributing member helps to strengthen himself and the profession.

Of the other means by which a teacher can contribute to the profession, recruitment is a particularly important element at the present time of teacher shortage. Teachers may recruit informally as they work with young people, contact community residents, or live the normal, busy life of a teacher. Consciousness of the need for more and better teachers will help individuals say the right thing at the right time when another may be influenced to enter the profession. Work with student teachers, requiring extra effort and very little recompense, is another means of strengthening the profession. Some teachers write for professional bulletins or give talks to public groups. In all, the teacher must be happy and effective in his work, able to maintain high levels of scholarship and professional ideals, conscious of what is expected of a teacher, and willing to work toward the improvement of teaching.

Relationships with immediate colleagues. A most important relationship to establish centers on the work that one will do as a member of an elementary school faculty. It is important to make a satisfactory place for oneself, not only in the more formal aspects of the work that may be done in faculty meetings, study groups, and the like, but also in the informal contacts with one's associates in the lunch room, in the work room, on the playground. It is important to "take one's place" in the faculty group and to show total school responsibility. In so doing, one's own professional integrity must be preserved in the face of what may well be a wide range of ideas concerning sound elementary school education. To find oneself in professional agreement with some and in disagreement with others, but to maintain wholesome personal relations with all, can be a challenging responsibility.

Relationships with the building principal. The relationship established with the building principal becomes a special sort of thing. The principal is the teacher's immediate superior in the hierarchy of school system management; the teacher will feel certain responsibilities and allegiances toward the principal, will want to respect him as an educational leader and understand his role as an administrator. The principal, in turn, will have a special relationship to establish with his faculty, collectively and individually. Typically, today's elementary school principal will try hard to establish this relationship in a democratic way. He will try to respect and honor an individual teacher's professional judgments along with his own, and he will try to share decisions with his teachers that are appropriate for such participation. At the same time, he will be called upon to evaluate the work of each of his teachers, to make recommendations on tenure appointments, and to do other things in keeping with his responsibilities. Properly established, this particular relationship can be an inspiring one.

Relationships with supervisors and consultants. In addition to working with the building principal, most teachers are asked to work with one or more supervisors or consultants who have special responsibilities for curriculum improvement in the school district. This again can be a most profitable and satisfying working relationship if the individuals involved, that is, the teacher and the consultant, can be insightful about and secure in their respective roles. The point of view that prevails most widely in elementary school education today perceives the supervisor's role as one that helps the individual teacher do a better job. It is not an inspectorial role, nor is it a prescriptive one; rather it is supportive and cooperative. In many districts, consultants work on an "on call" basis in order that teachers will more readily perceive the consultants' role as the consultants see it and will use them accordingly.

Relations with special teachers. The working relationship that a class-

room teacher must establish with special teachers, such as speech therapists, instrumental music teachers, and the like, is sometimes a difficult
one. Most often the difficulties arise from a lack of communication between the individuals involved. A classroom teacher may question the
fact that children are being taken out of class continuously for various
reasons when he is trying to help them to accomplish a heavy learning
load. The specialist sometimes forgets this, and in the light of his heavy
schedule he tends to rush in and rush out from class to class and from
child to child. The classroom teacher must know why Billy or Mary
will be out of class and must have some idea as to how often this will
be necessary. The specialist must be aware that his work is disruptive, as
viewed by the classroom teacher, must try to schedule his program in
such a way as to keep interruptions to a minimum, and make sure that
his schedule is known to teachers. None of this will happen unless a good
working relationship is established between the classroom teacher and the
corps of specialists that operate in any given school district.

Relations with the wider faculty group. Increasingly teachers are
called upon to work with a faculty group that extends beyond their own
immediate building staff. These groups will include other elementary
school teachers and administrators, personnel from the secondary schools,
and central office staff. The important thing is to be an active, participating member of whatever curriculum study group, teacher welfare
committee, or the like, one is asked to serve with, preserving one's
professional integrity in the process. In return for an opportunity to
express ideas and a point of view, one must be ready to listen to and consider the ideas and views of others. Out of such district-wide group experiences can come a great deal of professional stimulation, and a great
deal of personal satisfaction.

Relationships with Non-certificated Personnel

Each school employs a nucleus of nonteaching staff essential to the
maintenance and operation of the school. The working relationship between the teacher and these employees is important because they offer
not only special services, but they see children in situations different
from that of the classroom. Though they do not teach in the formal sense
of the word, they may have great influence on child behavior. Also they
are school representatives within the community; they are from and
of the community as well as the school.

The school secretary, who is aware of all school activities, is the first
contact with the public; she answers the telephone and greets all who
enter the school. She does the "million things" that keep the school operating smoothly, and the teacher values her services as he works closely

with her. The custodian takes care of the building and grounds, and does many little tasks to help others. It is to the teacher's best interests to work out a cooperative relationship with the custodian, to be sensitive to his strengths and interests. Like the custodian, the cafeteria worker meets children informally and contributes to their routine behavior, as well as to their happiness in school. She may also supply the teacher with information, tools, and materials related to food and diet. The bus driver meets the children the first thing in the morning and the last thing in the afternoon. He is likely to know what unhappiness has occurred in a family, what child has missed breakfast, what pals are chosen, and other important facts that influence child behavior. Though the teacher may seldom see the bus driver, he might well be advised to cultivate a speaking acquaintance with him and use him as a source of information.

THE TEACHER'S SELF-CONCEPT

The teacher assumes a number of roles as he performs his responsibilities. He may be a citizen, a leader, a counselor, a friend.

> He is a technician who arranges materials, plans schedules, and uses a variety of methods in working with groups. He is a social engineer— one who joins with his teammates in selecting out of the cultural heritage those ideas which are of greatest value to transmit to the young. He is an artist who is sensitive to human feelings and able to evoke creativity in others.[2]

In all of these roles he must know himself, his strengths and weaknesses, his desires and aspirations for himself and ultimately for the children he is teaching. The teacher can recognize both possibilities and limitations for action in the way he perceives himself in general, and as a teacher in particular.

The Self-Concept

Definition of self. The understanding of one's own purposes and behavior is called the *self-concept.* Jersild gives a comprehensive definition of *self* in one statement that includes the ideas of a number of authorities:

> The self is a composite of thoughts and feelings which constitute a person's awareness of his individual existence, his conception of who and what he is. A person's self is the "sum total of all that he can call

---

[2] Association for Supervision and Curriculum Development, *Creating a Good Environment for Learning* (Washington, D.C.: The Association, a department of the National Education Association, 1954), p. 151.

his." The self includes, among other things, a system of ideas, attitudes, values and commitments. The self is a person's total subjective environment. It is a distinctive "center of experience and significance." The self constitutes a person's inner world as distinguished from the "outer world" consisting of all other people and things.

The self is "the individual as known to the individual." It is "that to which we refer when we say 'I.'" It is the "custodian of awareness"; it is the thing about a person which has awareness and alertness, "which notices what goes on, and ... notices what goes on in its own field."

The self has also been described as the nucleus of personality.

The self is both constant and changeable. It includes the ". . . constant nature of an individual plus all that is conditioned by time and space and that is changeable." It provides a "nucleus on which, and in which, and around which, experiences are integrated into the uniqueness of the individual." In the process of experience, the healthy self adds, assimilates, and integrates within its own system that which is essential and authentic, while renouncing what is "unessential, strange, and harmful."[3]

Jersild's definition pictures the self as a subjective, complex being or image, a composite of experience, reaction, integration. The self-concept is the consciousness of this composite being, the awareness and interpretation of one's own powers, ideas, behavior. Succinctly, "an individual's self-concept is the set of inferences drawn from self-observation in many different situations. These inferences are descriptions of his characteristic behavior patterns."[4]

The self-concept may be influenced by several factors: (1) one's own desire or willingness to observe and examine himself; (2) the sum total of one's experience; (3) one's perception of the judgment of others and one's acceptance by society; (4) the balance of homeostasis, or how one maintains himself inwardly; and (5) the differentiation one perceives, or the recognition of differences between one's own purposes and the intentions of others.

Willingness to examine oneself. A self-concept grows, matures, and changes just as any other concept develops through knowledge and understanding over a period of time. However, one cannot have an accurate self-concept unless one consciously and willingly studies himself. Too many people take experiences of life for granted, are blind to themselves just as they may be blind to the beauties, joys, and sorrows of the world about them. Some people consciously or unconsciously avoid an intro-

---

[3] Arthur T. Jersild, *In Search of Self* (New York: Bureau of Publications, Teachers College, Columbia University, 1952), pp. 9–10.

[4] Frederick J. McDonald, *Educational Psychology* (San Francisco: Wadsworth Publishing Company, Inc., 1959), p. 464.

spective examination of the causes for their own behavior. Some may attempt to conceal their real natures either inwardly, to themselves, or outwardly, to others. Most of us learn about ourselves a little at a time, building and developing self-concept gradually.

> . . . [the teacher] will again and again find himself in a process of self-examination. To a person who is insecure such self-examination can be painful and threatening. The more insecure a person is, the more desperately he will feel a need to remain rigidly set in his ways. But to one who is secure enough within himself to face his thoughts and feelings when the opportunity arises, the process is challenging and rewarding.[5]

Experience. Every person is a product of his experience. His family, his childhood, his own school experience, his friends past and present, all make him what he is. His thoughts and ideas on life and living and his feelings about people and things are a result of his accumulated life experience. Many teachers need to broaden their experience, their liberal education, and their contact with different kinds of people, for the breadth of the self-concept will reflect that experience.

Judgment of others. Part of one's feeling about himself is how he thinks others are judging him. Man needs the moral and physical support of other people in all types of life activities. So many of our individual behaviors, such as manners, fashion of dress, and habits of speech, are developed because of what others may think about us. The teacher who feels the acceptance of his students works more easily with them. Methods of teaching, selection of curriculum content, management of classroom activities are also influenced by what the teacher thinks the principal, the parents, and other teachers may think.

Traditionally, teachers have been "put on a pedestal" by society. That is, people have felt that to be a "good" teacher a person must be almost perfect. The good teacher did not drink or smoke; his was the "right" religion; he had no unpopular prejudices; he was always in good mental and emotional health. Only recently have people allowed themselves to think of teachers as normal human beings, with joys and sorrows, with problems, and with the strengths and weaknesses of other people. Teachers can now understand more clearly that they may be "models" of a kind to the children but that they are also human. Their self-concept is strengthened in the knowledge that the community is more understanding and more accepting of the humanness of each teacher.

Homeostasis. Usually, the normal, well-balanced self maintains an internal balance, or constancy, an equilibrium termed "psychological homeostasis." Because of this, the individual "seeks to preserve the self

---

[5] Jersild, *op. cit.*, p. 119.

of which he is aware.''[6] In other words, human beings may tend to resist change unless a sound self-concept can justify and condone change. One may not wish to do something different unless he is sure he is capable of successfully accomplishing the task. An idea may not be accepted easily if it is in conflict with the self-concept.

Differentiation. Any individual's behavior, influenced by what he thinks and feels about himself, will be the same as or different from the behavior of those about him. In some situations the individual is expected to act the same as others, but in other situations to act the same would be entirely unacceptable. For example, a mother may come to school in a pair of slacks, but a female teacher would not do so. The self-concept is influenced by the degree to which the individual recognizes the differentiation between his own purposes and those of others interacting in the same specific situations. That is, a teacher decides upon the appropriate role in various situations through his understanding of himself as a teacher.

The Self-Concept and Teaching

Jersild makes three points in support of his thesis that teachers must know themselves:

1. An essential function of good education is to help the growing child to know himself and to grow in healthy attitudes of self-acceptance.
2. A teacher cannot make much headway in understanding others or in helping others to understand themselves unless he is endeavoring to understand himself. If he is not engaged in this endeavor, he will continue to see those whom he teaches through the bias and distortion of his own recognized needs, fears, desires, anxieties, hostile impulses, and so on.
3. The process of gaining knowledge of self and the struggle for self-fulfillment and self-acceptance is not something an instructor *teaches* others. It is not something he does *to* or *for* them. It is something in which he himself must be involved.[7]

The teacher who is secure within himself, who knows himself and feels no consistent inadequacy, is most likely to be a well-balanced, stable teacher. If he knows that he is doing his best, and that his best brings positive results, he will teach with more ease and efficiency. If he feels he ''belongs'' he can accept and work more readily with differing motives and characteristics of others. He can help children to help themselves.

Because of his self-concept, each teacher's interpretation of the teach-

---

[6] Donald Snygg and Arthur W. Combs, *Individual Behavior* (New York: Harper & Brothers, 1949), p. 56.

[7] Arthur T. Jersild, *When Teachers Face Themselves* (New York: Bureau of Publications, Teachers College, Columbia University, 1955), pp. 13–14.

ing role varies. The manner in which he guides children will be reflected in his concept of himself as a teacher, of what he thinks a teacher should be, and of the behavior expected of a teacher. One may consider himself to be kind and gentle when in reality he is rigidly impersonal. If a teacher feels he will gain better discipline by being overly friendly with children, he will behave accordingly. On the other hand, if he feels a teacher's role necessitates autocratic discipline, he will picture himself as most successful in that role.

Self-examination requires consciousness of one's own behavior in all the varying situations of teaching. On the playground, within a small study group, during total class discussion, in the activity period, throughout the quiet work-study period, the teacher needs to be conscious of his interaction with children. He determines why he asks a certain series of questions, why he speaks to a child in a special manner, why he ignores the behavior of another. And during these situations what are his feelings: depression, exhilaration, confusion, satisfaction, success?

> Self-understanding requires something quite different from the methods, study-plans, and skills of a "know-how" sort that are usually emphasized in education. . . . What is needed is a more personal kind of searching, which will enable the teacher to identify his own concerns and to share the concerns of his students.[8]

A teacher needs to relate the acts of teaching to his own notions of meaning, anxiety, loneliness, emotion, conformity, sex, hostility, and compassion.[9] He needs to examine his ideas of the meaning of existence, of life and living, of the work he is doing. He needs to understand his inner problems, realize his own limits. What in life "counts" for him? He needs to define his anxieties, to realize that anxiety is shared by all mankind, and that anxiety may cause one to be industrious, impulsive, competitive, or a perfectionist. He needs to identify his own limits of loneliness, and know that this may be a barrier, a real cause of acceptance, rejection, or fear of others. He needs to understand that emotion is frequently present and that people need freedom of emotional expression. He should know of the burden of conformity. He needs to comprehend that the sex roles, as prescribed by society, change, and that one's own interpretation of the sex role greatly influences purposes. He needs to know the pain of anger and the inner causes and effects of hostility. And he especially needs to understand that true compassion is a mature feeling and a quality among mankind that is not to be avoided or ignored.

---

[8] *Ibid.*, p. 3.

[9] *Ibid.* These ideas are listed and described in detail in several chapters of the book, and modified here.

The Self-Concept and a Philosophy of Education

Too often teachers work with children without a real understanding of the reason why certain actions are taken. They have never carefully thought through their educational goals or the basic philosophy upon which their teaching is planned.

> The techniques are important, but in the last analysis the techniques used by a teacher will be determined by his concept of himself, of his duties, and of his students.... No matter how thorough his training in skills and techniques of teaching, those skills and techniques will not be used if they do not conform to his personal philosophy of life and serve his immediate ends. If the results he wishes to secure are not those which can be secured by the approved methods, the methods will be distorted or abandoned.[10]

The following questions may help in an attempt to define a philosophy of education:

1. Do you want to help each child become a truly effective individual, behaving according to democratic standards? What does democracy mean to you? What democratic standards should children achieve?

2. Do you feel you should help children in their adjustment to and participation in our technological culture? Do you understand (and help children understand) the relationship between our own way of life and the various aspects of the curriculum you teach, such as arithmetic, physical education, science, and the cultures of other people?

3. Are you thoroughly accepting of the facts of individual differences? Do you teach children from the point at which learning will take place? Do you understand and use several methods in dealing with individual interests and abilities? Do you help children develop self-direction and use self-evaluation? Do your relationships with children convince each child that he is important to you as an individual?

4. Are your purposes also influenced by the principles which define a good learning experience? Do you understand the importance of stimulating favorable working conditions? Are you convinced of the necessity for learners and teacher to plan and develop work cooperatively? Are you aware of the continuity of experience? Do the children's learning experiences emerge in basic understandings, fundamental concepts, or generalizations? Do you provide for balanced development? Do you believe in variety of experience as an aid to learning?

Concise answers to questions such as these provide a basis for sound teaching practices. A teacher with convictions clearly thought through should have no fears of parental criticism or community condemnation.

---

[10] Snygg and Combs, *op. cit.*, p. 243.

CREATIVE TEACHING

The teacher who develops effective interpersonal relationships, a balanced, secure self-concept, a sound philosophy of education, and an open and flexible mind has the fundamental bases for the finest quality of creative teaching. With an insightful, self-directed educational perspective, the teacher can implement the curriculum through mature and well-balanced creativity.

Definition of Creative Teaching

Creative teaching is that kind of dynamic guidance a teacher gives to the learning situation that ever increases its effectiveness and stimulates children's intellectual and social growth. Involved in creative teaching are creative perception and professional competence: sensitive, imaginative leadership based on a solid foundation of what has in the past proved effective. Creative teaching is *not* uncontrolled or purposeless caprice of the teacher's imagination. Nor does it necessarily represent marked talent. Any individual has the capacity for creativeness, but the development of it emerges from constructive thinking, concentrated effort, and manipulation of basic principles.

The development of creative teaching involves not only the way in which material is presented to the children but also the kinds of reactions it elicits from children. It is finding another way to look at a topic, to motivate, to involve participation, or a better way to care for individual differences. Zirbes lists a number of contrasting characteristics as dichotomies that represent extremes in choices for teaching situations.

Uncreative	*Creative*
stereotyped conformity ⟶	free expression
passive compliance ⟶	active identification
imposed direction ⟶	cooperative planning
coercive requirements ⟶	voluntary commitments
mass handling ⟶	individuated guidance
extrinsic motivation ⟶	intrinsic value concerns
submissive acquiescence ⟶	wholehearted involvement
restrictive domination ⟶	responsible self-direction
stultifying repression ⟶	spontaneity
fixing of habits and skills ⟶	cultivation of flexible, adaptive responses to life-related situations[11]

---

[11] Modified from Laura Zirbes, *Spurs to Creative Teaching* (New York: G. P. Putnam's Sons, 1959), pp. 26–27.

Guiding Principles for Creative Teaching

Specific and pat suggestions for creative teaching are impossible to list. Each teacher operates from his own experience, with his own talents, and within his own philosophy of education. Creativity in one situation will be different from creativity in another. However, an attempt is made here to discuss some basic principles that may give the individual teacher some clues for more creative approaches to teaching.

An attitude toward teaching. Probably most important in the desire to teach creatively is the teacher's attitude about teaching. He cannot be content with what he knows. He understands that man has not yet learned everything there is to be learned and that presently accepted methods can and will be improved. He is constantly looking for new ways to understand, interpret, and teach. His mind is open to new ideas. His attitude is one of constant re-evaluation of approaches and concepts of knowledge and teaching.

Thoughtful action. Creative teaching results from reasonable and purposeful action. This kind of creativity emerges from careful thinking through and beyond known circumstances. Rarely is an unplanned, spur-of-the-moment action effective. What appear to be spontaneous, creative ideas about teaching can usually be traced to some previous consideration or incubation, hatched suddenly within an appropriate situation. In general, creative teaching is based upon well-evaluated perceptions, upon considerations made that are related to specific procedures or problems. For this a teacher needs time to "mull it over."

Treating children as individuals. When a teacher treats all children as individuals and devises means for respecting individual differences, teaching assumes greater creativity. The planned program is flexible and encourages differences in ideas and actions, differences in pace and progress. The natural growth processes in children are fostered and guided so that progress is the maximum for each. Conditions are favorable for active pupil participation in selecting and initiating activities, planning experiences, and evaluating.

Taking advantage of every opportunity for variety. The creative teacher is alert to the many ways our modern civilization can lend variety and interest to the learning situation. Clues can be taken from the community and the environment, from the cultural background of the children, from the unique regional characteristics, from current world-wide affairs, from the teacher's own experience and those of his colleagues. Variety in organization, materials, kinds of activities, and teaching procedures strengthens and enriches creative teaching. The teacher's only concern is that the variety be reasonable and appropriate, rather than a conglomerate of unrelated or confused situations. Children

like something new. But they also gain a measure of security from a familiar basis of routine.

Providing opportunity to enjoy creativity of others. One dimension of creative teaching is the means by which the teacher provides the children with opportunities to meet and recognize creativity. (See Chapter 15.) Children need to appreciate not only their own creative acts and products, but those of others. That members of a class see, hear, and in other ways consciously experience delightfully creative products, ideas, and acts contributes in important ways to their own ability to create and to offer suggestions that will also make the learning situation more creative.

Enjoying and making the profession more attractive. A final consideration for the development of creative teaching is the teacher's own enjoyment of the role. Problems occur, and not all teaching experiences are truly enjoyable, but among the routines and the difficulties are the moments of light, the times when teacher and children are delighted by observable results. The more creative the teaching, the more often appear the really satisfactory moments when teaching is worthwhile. When teachers and children are happy with accomplishment, parents also are usually happy. In these days of increasing criticism of schools and teacher shortages, the teacher who is happy in his work raises the status of the profession and makes teaching attractive to young people choosing a profession. To be a creative teacher is to be a successful teacher.

ORGANIZING THE CLASSROOM

To fulfill the obligations of a teacher in today's schools calls for considerable knowledge of society, of children, of learning processes, of the school as a social institution, of the specific responsibilities of the elementary school years, and of curriculum both generally and in terms of particular learning programs. The greatest portion of this book has been given over to these various elements. In these closing chapters we would like to focus directly on the classroom and the teacher in the classroom. If, indeed, this is where elementary school education is "made," this would appear to be a fitting focus for these final pages.

In the following chapters there are extended discussions of the teacher's use of instructional materials, space, and time in a developing classroom situation. Elementary school education is not only goal-directed education, it is also goal-evaluated education. Teachers use educational ideas and combine materials, space, and time into a defensible classroom program in order to accomplish particular objectives. It is against these same ideas that the teacher must evaluate from day to day, week to week, and report period to report period.

In this whole process the teacher is to a great extent a free agent. At

the same time, any classroom teacher is a part of a total school system, and is more intimately a member of a given elementary school faculty. Some aspects of the decisions as to which ideas will be used, what materials of instruction are to be made available, what sort of space is to be provided, and how much time will be involved will be made for the teacher, so to speak, by the central school office and the local board of education. Other aspects of these same decisions will have been made in participation with other elementary school teachers, and especially in work with one's own building principal and faculty. Any classroom teacher must expect to work with these kinds of "realities." And, in most instances such realities work to the individual teacher's benefit, not against it. There is still a great deal of room left for the teacher to exercise creative professional skill in combining and recombining these various elements into an ever more efficient classroom program. In fact, were it not for the discussion that takes place and the decisions that are made at both the system level and the individual school level concerning the total educational program which children are to experience, classrooms would operate as so many individual "schools" simply housed under one roof. Such an approach to elementary school education would take away a great deal of the effectiveness that resides potentially in a coordinate effort. Thus, our efforts to focus this discussion on the teacher are set in the framework of the teacher as a member of a school system and of a given elementary school faculty.

REFERENCES

Association for Supervision and Curriculum Development. *Discipline for Today's Children and Youth.* Washington, D.C.: The Association, National Education Association, 1956.
> Presents sound principles of democratic discipline.

Beauchamp, George A. *Basic Dimensions of Elementary Method.* Boston: Allyn and Bacon, Inc., 1959.
> Helpful suggestions about knowing children, organizing materials, and planning a good teaching-learning situation.

Bush, Robert N. *The Teacher-Pupil Relationship.* Englewood Cliffs, New Jersey: Prentice-Hall, Inc., 1954.
> A report on an exploratory study of human relationships in school life.

Commission on Teacher Education, California Teachers Association. *Teacher Competence: Its Nature and Scope.* San Francisco: The Association, 1957.
> A clear listing of the competencies demanded of the teacher.

Garrison, Noble Lee. *The Improvement of Teaching: A Two-fold Approach.* New York: The Dryden Press, 1955.
> A different presentation of teaching, involving problems in guiding academic achievement in relation to the problems of group functioning in the classroom situation.

Harrison, Raymond H., and Lawrence E. Gowin. *The Elementary Teacher in Action.* San Francisco: Wadsworth Publishing Company, Inc., 1958.
Presents the scope and character of good teaching by looking at the job and the profession.

Heffernan, Helen. *The Kindergarten Teacher.* Boston: D. C. Heath and Company, 1960.
Presents the unique problems and responsibilities of the kindergarten teacher.

Haskew, Laurence D. *This Is Teaching.* Chicago: Scott, Foresman and Company, 1956.
A personalized textbook explaining principles, processes, and situations of teaching.

Johnson, Earl A., and R. Eldon Michael. *Principles of Teaching.* Boston: Allyn and Bacon, Inc., 1958.
A modern concept of teaching as extending beyond the classroom to community and extracurricular activities. Practical suggestions for working with children.

Kelner, Bernard C. *How To Teach in the Elementary School.* New York: McGraw-Hill Book Company, 1958.
Specifically a "how-to-do" book with practical suggestions for establishing basic skills.

Lane, Howard, and Mary Beauchamp. *Human Relations in Teaching.* Englewood Cliffs, New Jersey: Prentice-Hall, Inc., 1955.
Develops concepts about the dynamics of human relations in school.

Wiles, Kimball. *Teaching for Better Schools.* Englewood Cliffs, New Jersey: Prentice-Hall, Inc., 1952.
Chapters 1, 2, 3, and 4 are especially helpful for understanding teaching responsibilities.

Wynn, Richard. *Careers in Education.* New York: McGraw-Hill Book Company, 1960.
An overview of the many responsibilities of professional educators.

18

UTILIZING MATERIALS AND SPACE: ORGANIZING THE ENVIRONMENT

As we turn to the ways in which the teacher organizes the environment for learning we think first of the physical structure of the classroom. Architecturally the room has been designed so that light, air, furniture, chalkboards, books, and other materials may be stored, displayed, or used with the greatest possible ease. When the teacher enters his room shortly before the opening of the school year he finds a standard variety of equipment. From the supply room of the school he procures other materials. He adds to the collection from his own personal accumulation of good teaching materials. Throughout the school year he gathers more materials, stores some, replaces others.

What the teacher selects as important aids to learning and the considerations he makes as he plans their use are the center of discussion for this chapter. We will consider the variety of materials that are used to raise questions, facilitate problem solving, allow practice in skills, effect experimentation, permit observation. We will consider the selection of these materials, their sources, and the relationship between them as the teacher allots and organizes classroom space for learning.

DEVELOPING INSIGHT INTO INSTRUCTIONAL MATERIALS

Instructional materials facilitate communication. They make new ideas alive and meaningful. Their use helps the teacher illustrate the spoken

word, provide variation in the repetition of facts, and practice in the skills. They bring to the sight and the mind of the children wonders of far-off places and past eras. They help to teach effectively our rapidly accumulating new knowledge. Instructional materials make teaching more effective; they help to raise the level of learning from verbalism and out of the rigid structure of the textbook.

Differentiation Between Kinds
of Materials and Techniques

It would appear to be a simple matter to define the term "instructional materials." In reality it is not. It is easy to form a vague idea as to what one has in mind when this term is used, but such vagueness at the outset compounds the confusion that may develop later. Differentiating between a textbook, a chalkboard, a pair of scissors, and a motion picture becomes important to the teacher who selects and uses them, to the child who learns from them, and to the administrator who must order them. Authorities try to differentiate among terms, but there seems to be little agreement, and many of the terms are used synonymously. The following definitions are outlined to clarify this differentiation, and will be used consistently in this chapter.

Instructional materials is the broadest term, a general category to indicate all material that will facilitate or help the teaching-learning process. Thus, instructional materials may include a piece of chalk, a chalkboard, or a film.

Audio-visual materials is a term best defined as encompassing those multisensory materials specifically provided by an audio-visual center. Originally conceived, "audio-visual" was limited to films, slides, filmstrips, and recordings, and was typified by audio-visual "gadgeteers." The term in educational usage has become increasingly broader, and at present it includes materials and services that are integrated with all areas of learning. Authorities frequently use terms like "sensory devices" and "perceptual experiences" when referring to audio-visual procedures. One definition exemplifies the broad meaning and relates techniques integrally to materials:

> [*Audio-visual*] is a generic term referring to experiences, equipment, and materials used for communication in instruction. [It] implies techniques based upon practices utilized in education and training.[1]

The term audio-visual materials, then, is an inclusive term and represents items ranging from magnets for bulletin boards to sound filmstrips.

---

[1] James W. Brown, Richard B. Lewis, and Fred F. Harcleroad, *A-V Instruction: Materials and Methods* (New York: McGraw-Hill Book Company, Inc., 1959), p. 527.

Instructional supplies limits the materials to those used in the educative process that are expendable, used up within a short period of time, constantly needing reordering. Such items are chalk, pencils and paper, scissors, art materials, and workbooks. These are the "raw materials," and usually facilitate the activity, give practice in skills, and in this way contribute to meaning of the learning.

Instructional equipment, the term most generally standardized in meaning and use among authorities, refers to permanent or nonexpendable materials, which usually require a capital outlay such as the apparatus or furnishings in a school. Frequently these materials are mechanically operated, but not always, for under the category of equipment are listed chalkboards, bulletin boards, and screens as well as projectors, mimeographs, and other machines. Equipment facilitates the presentation of information.

Source materials, resource materials, and instructional resources are terms that may be used synonymously. For purposes of definition we will use the single term *source materials*. This includes objects, people, and places that supply information. Here are the study materials that facilitate the learning situation. Included among them are textbooks, documents, realia, people, films, and community settings that help children answer questions, clarify and broaden concepts, organize thinking, and solve problems.

Instructional devices imply materials that are devised or especially constructed for assistance with specific tasks. In the elementary school we think of a device as primarily teacher-constructed or school-constructed rather than exclusively commercially prepared material. Examples are charts, flannel boards, pocket charts, mock-ups, arithmetic counters. Such devices are another means of furthering understanding or imparting knowledge.

Instructional aids are not synonymous with materials. The term *aid* implies something supplementary, something that is a help and furthers the teaching act. To some it implies something added, not necessarily complementary or integral to the learning. Some persons think of an aid as a gadget or crutch. Because of this confusing connotation, the term is not used in this book.

Instructional techniques are the methods the teacher utilizes with the children for the most efficient use of the materials. They require knowledge about the content and manipulation of the material demonstrated at the time the materials are experienced by learners. Techniques involve broad skill in planning, organizing, and timing that will relate one material to another and the material to the experiences of the children. For example, pictures may need the supporting evidence of books or

maps. Transcriptions may need the supplementary information provided by pictures, resource people, or documents. Such materials are not effectively provided at random or in unrelated situations. Nor is children's experience with them unstructured.

The table below demonstrates the relationship between materials and techniques as well as the differentiation between them. In this representative listing, we see in the first column the special group of instructional materials that are the sources of information. The second column indicates the particular places where the materials are produced, collected, and made available to the schools. The broad techniques of presentation are in the third column, and the fourth column lists the kinds of activities demanded of the children for participation.

Materials	Found in	Organized for use through	Learning accomplished by
People	Community	Interviews	Listening
Places	Libraries	Research	Reading
Realia	Catalogs, bulletins	Exhibits	Observing
Books, documents,	Museums	Field trips	Talking
periodicals	Organizations,	Programs	Creating
Maps, graphs	agencies, as-	Demonstrations	
Films, pictures	sociations, in-	Dramatic play	
Radio, television	dustry	Experiments	
Records, tran-			
scriptions			

Categorizing Instructional Materials

Instructional materials are the "tools of the trade." As such, they must be known well, from their inherent possibilities to their limitations. A teacher must be clear as to what certain "tools" can do for children, and what they cannot do. Clear insights into instructional materials should lead to a more precise use of them, based on a more enlightened rationale and conscious justification. By analogy, a carpenter will be less likely to select a screw driver to chisel wood when a wood chisel is available if he understands the unique characteristics of each of the two tools and the sorts of jobs they are designed to do. If circumstances force him to use the screw driver, he will recognize the limitations that use of the wrong tool may put upon the finished product, and his expectancy will be more realistic because of it. Similarly, the teacher, knowing the capabilities of one instructional tool as opposed to another, is more likely to choose a certain one when it is available, or will adjust his expectancies for success in the learning situation in the light of the material with which he has to work. The experienced technician, either

THE CONE OF EXPERIENCE[2]

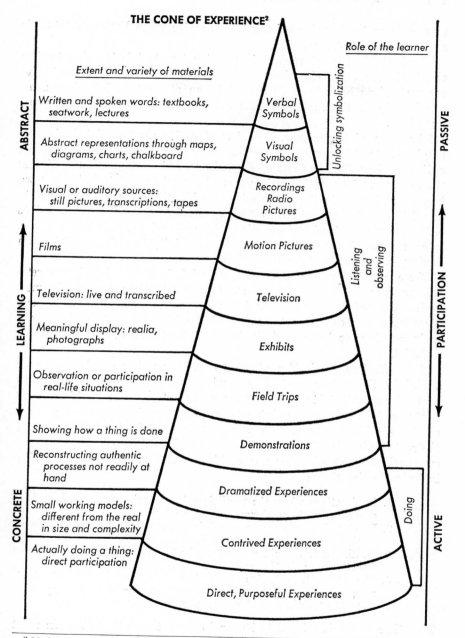

Role of the learner

ABSTRACT

Extent and variety of materials

Written and spoken words: textbooks, seatwork, lectures — Verbal Symbols

Abstract representations through maps, diagrams, charts, chalkboard — Visual Symbols

Visual or auditory sources: still pictures, transcriptions, tapes — Recordings Radio Pictures

Films — Motion Pictures

Television: live and transcribed — Television

Meaningful display: realia, photographs — Exhibits

Observation or participation in real-life situations — Field Trips

Showing how a thing is done — Demonstrations

Reconstructing authentic processes not readily at hand — Dramatized Experiences

Small working models: different from the real in size and complexity — Contrived Experiences

Actually doing a thing: direct participation — Direct, Purposeful Experiences

CONCRETE

LEARNING

Unlocking symbolization

Listening and observing

Doing

PASSIVE

PARTICIPATION

ACTIVE

[2] Modified from Edgar Dale, *Audio-Visual Methods in Teaching* (Revised edition; New York: Dryden Press, 1954), pp. 42–56.

carpenter or teacher, knows any job is easier when the correct tool is available and skillfully used.

The individuality of various instructional materials is evident when one begins to categorize those that are available. Several meaningful categorizations have been developed in an attempt to introduce some relationship to the materials that are available. Two are commented upon here.

The Cone of Experience. Dale has offered a most useful device for helping us to obtain some perspective on instructional materials through a diagram he calls *The Cone of Experience.* This configuration indicates the extent, variety, and relationships of materials and techniques. Two important factors in the relationship are identified. One of these has to do with the relative position that each material holds between the points of "concreteness" and "abstraction." The other indicates the role of the learner as ranging from rather complete passivity to active participation during the use of the various materials.

The cone enables us to categorize materials in terms of their concreteness or their abstractness. It helps us to reflect on the role of the learner, noting the points at which and the degree to which he experiences directly, and when he must resort to skill with some system of symbols, as in reading, or in map work, in order to derive meaning from the material.

A longitudinal projection of categories. Barnes has provided us with a slightly different concept of categories for instructional materials; he uses a longitudinal idea, rather than a vertical one. Again this concept relates materials between points of concreteness and abstractness. Barnes carries his ideas further to indicate the way this developing line of abstractness is related to learning theory itself. He lists four operational assumptions concerning the use of his model that will guide learning in desirable directions:

1. In situations where the pupil is naive, learning proceeds best from concrete, direct experiences and materials.
2. In situations where the pupil is mature, learning proceeds most efficiently from symbolic materials.
3. Continuity in school learning may be found in the pupil's directional growth from naiveté to maturity.
4. The continuity factor is of prime importance both in relatively short-range, specific learning situations and also in general, long-range maturing toward adult levels of performance.[3]

One other factor is related to Barnes' assumptions: that children must be helped to relate abstract ideas to concrete situations.

---

[3] Fred P. Barnes, "Materials of Learning—and Learning," *Educational Leadership* 9:402–408, April 1952.

MODEL FOR MATERIALS SELECTION AND USE[4]

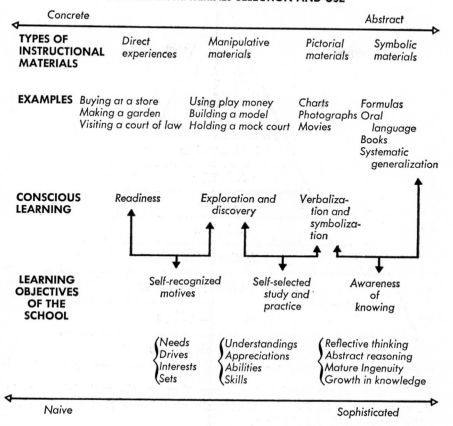

Concrete

Abstract

TYPES OF INSTRUCTIONAL MATERIALS	Direct experiences	Manipulative materials	Pictorial materials	Symbolic materials
EXAMPLES	Buying at a store Making a garden Visiting a court of law	Using play money Building a model Holding a mock court	Charts Photographs Movies	Formulas Oral language Books Systematic generalization
CONSCIOUS LEARNING	Readiness	Exploration and discovery	Verbalization and symbolization	
LEARNING OBJECTIVES OF THE SCHOOL	Self-recognized motives	Self-selected study and practice	Awareness of knowing	
	Needs Drives Interests Sets	Understandings Appreciations Abilities Skills	Reflective thinking Abstract reasoning Mature Ingenuity Growth in knowledge	

Naive

Sophisticated

Reflections on Today's Typical Practice

Knowledge of the elementary school classroom indicates that teachers rely most heavily on verbal symbols in books, workbooks, seatwork, and spoken words. Next most frequently used are visual symbols as found in maps, charts, and diagrams. Both are at the far reaches of Dale's cone in terms of abstractness, and to the far right of Barnes' outline in the same way. Today's most common practice would be more accurately shown by inverting Dale's cone to indicate the most commonly used materials at the base and the amount of use of each medium represented by the widest part of the cone. Note that the verbal and visual materials, used more today than the others listed, are shown on the pyramid as

---

[4] Modified from Barnes, *op. cit.*

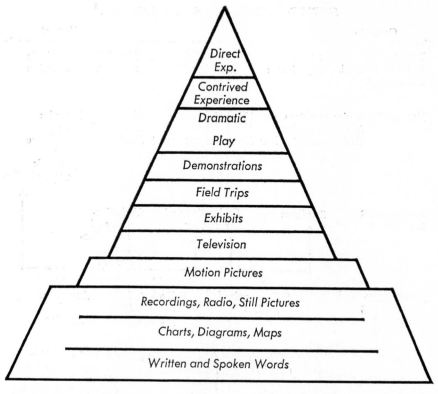

diminishing only a partial step. From then on, the materials seem to decrease in use to the direct, concrete experiences that are the most difficult to provide for children.

Barnes' model, showing the same diagrammatic scheme for today's common practice, would invert symbolic materials to the left:

ABSTRACT   **CONCRETE**

←——→

| Symbolic | Pictorial | Manipulative | Direct |
| Materials | Materials | Materials | Experiences |

←——→

SOPHISTICATED   **NAIVE**

If present teaching procedures were more in agreement with research in learning, teachers would provide more experiences with instruction materials that are closer to the concrete end of the continuum, and not concentrate so heavily on abstract situations to facilitate learning. If children could receive more of their educative experience from actual experience the effectiveness of much of what we do would undoubtedly

be improved. Especially would this be true for young children and for children who are limited in the kind of ability that we refer to as "intelligence," since intelligence is focused on verbal ability in great part. Unfortunately, we cannot always provide as much concrete experience as we would like and still meet the goals that we are asked to achieve in the classroom. On the other hand, one of the greatest achievements of human beings is the ability to learn from the experience of others and the development of symbol systems so that we may deal with things in the abstract. Thus, for children not to be proficient with our symbol systems is for them to be deprived of a great human invention. There does not seem to be any real reason, however, why we could not change the shape of "typical practice" in the way shown, using Dale's cone as an example.

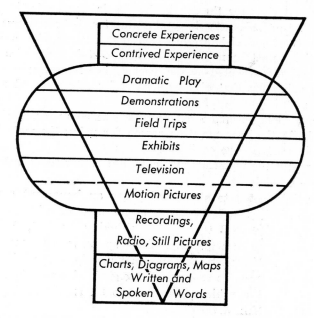

From this bulging, "lantern-type" diagram we can see that modified practice might include less of concrete and contrived experiences and more of recordings, charts, maps and written symbols so that each type of experience is offered equally. Balancing these activities at either end of the concrete-abstract continuum, we would provide greater numbers of experiences in the center, represented by techniques that organize several materials for the learning process.

Throughout elementary school years, however, the shape of this "learning lantern" may need modification because of the characteristics of the children and the purposes of the educative experiences provided. In the

first grade, for example, more concrete experiences are necessary because of the limited verbal skills of the children and the fact that in their preschool years direct experience has been the vehicle for almost all their learning. At the other extreme of development, pupils in sixth, seventh, and eighth grades may require more abstract experiences to bring the necessary sophistication to their education.

Selecting and Evaluating Instructional Materials

Why select? The foregoing section has pointed out the great variety of materials available to teachers and something of the difference in their possibilities and limitations. Because he cannot ignore these materials, or even use them all, the teacher is faced with the task of selecting the proper materials for the job he has to do. Such selection includes evaluation that precedes selection and evaluation that follows use.

How select? If materials are to be selected with consciousness of purpose, selections must be made in line with certain principles that can be understood and accepted by the teacher. The following are examples of guiding principles that give us a basis for selection and evaluation of materials.

1. The materials selected must be those needed in terms of the purposes sought in the program. The *reason* for using the materials must be found, in part, in the established goals. One does not organize the program around the materials available, but rather seeks materials appropriate to the goals set.

2. Materials selected to aid learning are an important part of the means to the desired end. They are means used to raise questions, to provide information, and to stimulate thinking. In fact, the use of a given material, such as a textbook or a map, serves as a means to two ends when we realize that the children not only are gaining content, but are also learning to do research and to gather information. Thus, the material selected is a vehicle to carry two kinds of learning: content gained from it and skill in the use of it.

3. The materials selected should be appropriate to the specific learning situation. To enrich the learning situation these considerations become important: Does it provide new and important information, or does it extend existing knowledge? Is it related directly to the unit, lesson, or problem? Is it worth the time and expense involved? How well does it perform its intended function? Is the teacher's guide helpful? Does it work well with other instructional materials to achieve the desired learning purposes?

4. Materials selected must provide genuine, real, and valid learning. The best are accurate, truthful, authoritative. That is, the content pre-

sents information that is authentic for the time and place represented; the ideas are presented with integrity and contribute to the study topic in a realistic, meaningful manner. If the teacher cannot determine the accuracy of the material, he must depend on authorities that do. Many materials are authenticated by educators in the field who endorse them.

5. The materials selected should be appropriate to the individual differences of the learners. The intellectual or verbal ability of the group influences the selection as to vocabulary, abstractness, pace, and general understandability; materials need to challenge mental powers but not go beyond them. Prior experience will influence understanding, motivation, acceptance, and interest. What has gone before determines in great part the kind of learning the material will produce.

6. Materials selected should represent variety in kind and function. Differences in interests and abilities demand a variety of approaches to learning, hence materials should provide numerous kinds of interrelated experiences for children—the use of all the senses, active and passive participation, concrete and abstract ideas, black and white or color, sound or silent, moving or still, real or represented. One does not use the motion picture, for example, to the exclusion of other materials. The best use of materials is made when more than one kind are used to supplement and reinforce each other.

7. Selected materials should make possible either overt or covert participation on the part of the learner. This kind of participation may be physical, mental, or emotional, whether the child is doing, listening, watching, or making interpretation from language symbols. Every learning experience is proportionately effective to the amount of involvement for the learner.

8. Materials selected should promote cooperative learning, improve human relationships, help children recognize and accept both individual and group research, and develop problem solving skills. As children work with materials to assess and organize, they provide ideas for sharing and questioning or defending. The ideas from interrelated materials are woven together to form a generalization or to broaden a concept.

9. Materials selected should approach a high standard of mechanical excellence. Organization, format, length, sound, photography, color, and vocabulary should be technically satisfactory.

Who selects? Interestingly, evaluation of materials exists at the national, regional, state, and local levels, and is a kind of screening process carried on by a variety of groups. On the national and state levels, various professional associations such as the National Educational Association, and its affiliated groups such as the National Council of Teachers of Mathematics, or Social Studies, select and review materials in their

journals. Magazines such as *The Instructor* and *The Grade Teacher* devote regular columns to the evaluation and use of new materials. Audiovisual journals are an excellent source for evaluation and current listing of materials. Also, other periodicals such as *The Saturday Review* provide critical evaluation of books, films, and other materials. Commercially prepared catalogs contain evaluated listings of audio-visual materials. Several universities issue similar bulletins. All of these have some influence on the selection of materials at the local level.

Within the school district, selection responsibilities are frequently divided. The school board, as a policy-forming group, recognizes the importance of instructional materials by providing the budget for purchase. The superintendent, working with the board, assures recognition of the need and provides means by which teachers know about materials and their availability and use. This may be accomplished by the addition to the staff of a Director of Curriculum or a Materials Coordinator, either one with the responsibility of leadership in the materials area. He may, while doing other types of in-service training activities, publish appropriate bulletins, establish a Selections Committee, and procure adequate supplies, equipment, and source materials for classroom and district use.

Teachers, administrators, technical personnel such as the librarian or materials coordinator, and sometimes parents or community representatives, are members of the local Selection and Evaluation Committee. This committee examines the materials and the guidebooks accompanying them, relates materials to established school objectives, considers the manner in which various materials supplement each other, and relates material to the school's curriculum outline. Selections are made and recommendations forwarded. Teachers involved in this kind of responsibility are well informed about new materials and can pass this information along to others in their buildings.

Faculties in individual buildings normally arrange discussions about materials. This sharing of ideas and information helps individual teachers become familiar with exactly the materials and services available, and how to procure them. Development of policies and techniques for classroom use also result from these discussions. Thus the teacher keeps up to date and gains information and understandings that will help him and the children of his group make the final selection of materials used in the learning situation.

SOURCES OF INSTRUCTIONAL MATERIALS

There are a number of sources of instructional materials to become acquainted with, and a number of things to be considered about them.

All of this bears, in the final analysis, upon the choices that must be made in the procurement of instructional materials for use in the elementary school curriculum.

Four types of instructional materials are often referred to in the effort to indicate sources of supply. These are:

1. Materials from educational publishers.
2. Free and inexpensive materials.
3. Community resources.
4. Teacher-made materials.

Let us consider each of these groups of materials, remembering that instructional materials overlap any classification of this sort since some commercially produced materials may also be teacher-made, and some free and inexpensive materials are also available from the immediate community. Our discussion will enter these items in the most appropriate classification, and only mention their use elsewhere.

Materials from Educational Publishers

A great many of the materials used in the elementary schools are the "ready-made" items that are commercially produced and purchased by schools. The kinds of thing available from this source include an infinite variety of supplies, precisely constructed equipment, and carefully prepared, authoritative source materials. In the matter of supplies, though quality of materials may vary, the selection and procurement is usually accomplished in the school district at the administrative level. The teacher has only to choose among the supplies available. We need say very little about them. Equipment, too, is usually screened and purchased by a staff member with technical knowledge. The teacher's responsibility lies in knowledgeable operation and use. Some ideas about this will be presented in this chapter as we discuss space utilization. Of source materials and instructional devices, the teacher makes more complete selection. A few comments on trends and problems concerning these should be helpful here.

Commercial materials are improving. It is not difficult to understand, even for the most unsophisticated observer, that materials the schools use today are much better than those of just a few years ago. Commercial houses are utilizing improved techniques in printing, use of color, and binding. Paper, ink, illustrations, and other materials are of increasingly finer quality. The raw materials of industrial production are being organized into an artistic design and a dramatic format with clarity and practical function.

Producers are also acquiring professional help for the planning of

materials. Not only specialists in education, but experts in such areas as cartography, science, photography, history, and engineering are being consulted. Studies of teacher use to get at curriculum needs are also influencing the planning and sale of materials. In all, producers are making every effort to use technical progress and professional help to produce materials that are effective and appropriate to differing elementary curriculum patterns. Brown refers to the efforts of producers to increase effectiveness of materials when he says:

> Commercial producers of ready-made instructional materials must always meet the needs of many people to be sure of selling their products. They usually obtain the best advice possible from members of the educational profession and from specialists in the field to be portrayed or discussed. In some cases—such as for films, maps, or globes—commercial companies often have been far ahead of teachers. They have pioneered in providing new materials and in suggesting how they should be used most effectively. But with all types of ready-made materials, content coverage, organization, form, and treatment have been preselected, leaving to the teacher only the decisions of whether to use them and how to use them with a particular class.[5]

Books: text and reference. The use of books as instructional materials has been historically important to the school and probably will continue to be. Reports covering 93 per cent of the commercial textbook business alone indicated that the total volume of sales in 1956 was $277,000,000.[6] High competition in the use of other kinds of materials has brought about improved quality of textbooks and a trend by publishers to supplement them with materials such as workbooks, tests, films and filmstrips, and transcriptions, as well as teacher's guides. Greater numbers of related books are also being published to supplement the textbook series.

The advantages of textbooks are rather obvious. They may be used and reused and are therefore economical. They present a logical arrangement of subject matter that is carefully organized, arranged in graded sequence, and supplemented with teaching suggestions. These very advantages have long been the subject of heated debate, however. Some educators feel that preselected material is limiting, that added supplementary materials may further influence rigid teaching according to prearranged plans. It is also felt that use of textbooks fosters learning centered about recall. Content is considered to be too highly compressed in one book. Who can understand the Civil War after three pages of reading? Also, texts are criticized because they may be quickly out-

---

[5] Brown, Lewis, and Harcleroad, *op. cit.*, p. 60.

[6] B. R. Buckingham, "Textbooks," *Encyclopedia of Educational Research,* Chester Harris, editor (New York: The Macmillan Company, 1960), p. 1521.

dated. The methodological trend has been to a differentiated use of the textbook plus the use of other materials to facilitate learning.

In an article discussing the textbook, Barnes points out the three common uses of textbooks that are highly related to curriculum development and methodological procedure.[7] First is the use of the single textbook, followed rather rigidly as it is planned by the authors. The effect of such use is dependent upon the teacher, tends to be rather formal, and may have limited adaptability. The textbook outlines what to teach and the sequence in which it is to be taught with little adjustment for the individual differences of children or local conditions. The second is the multiple textbook method in which books are used by different groups of pupils in the classroom. This method provides wider adjustment to individual needs but may introduce problems concerning different sequence and vocabulary among the various textbooks. The third method is to use textbooks as references only. Problems with this method occur in the questions of whether a special subject is adaptable to other organizational patterns and whether a topic out of sequence has sufficient details to stand alone. Its strength lies in the flexibility and adaptability to individual needs. Barnes further indicates that very little research is available on the best use of textbooks, and implies that educational leaders have provided little information as to the best use of textbooks as instructional material.

Our textbook dilemma, according to Barnes, is the result of two opposing ''camps,'' one claiming textbooks as a panacea, the other as a cause of pedagogical problems.

> On the one hand, the publisher and his authors defend the textbook, while being constantly alert for necessities to modify or replace it. Implicitly, this group recognizes specific flaws in the product and the developing threats to its continued dominance. The publisher also has a set of values and ideals concerning the educative process. Without doubt he is much closer to his market intellectually than are most other industrialists to consumers of their products. Finally, the publisher may be expected to act in terms of enlightened self-interest. The role of printed materials in school learning has been altered greatly since the time of the McGuffey brothers. Their books did not compete with sound-films, radio, television, and attractive trade books. The *Eclectic Readers* were not used during a period of profound change in pedagogical theory.

> On the other hand, protagonist educators have denounced the textbook in terms of frontier educational concepts and philosophies. Professional pressures force educational leaders to live on the cutting edge of the

---

[7] Fred P. Barnes, ''The Textbook Dilemma,'' *Teachers College Record* 55:369–383, April 1954.

culture. From this elevation the textbook has appeared far distant and obsolescent. Considered in relation to changing culture patterns and new knowledge of what the best-conceived schools can do, these educators' views appear quite logical. But even horizon-pushing professional educators admit, quietly, that most schools and most teachers in practical situations would have to close up shop were they suddenly to be deprived of the textbook. The admission has to be made that the textbook, as it is, has a logic in most circumstances.[8]

Trade books are those that are not designated as textbooks and that are sold in bookstores to the general public. They include such types as fiction, biography, travel, and science books. In the classroom, they are frequently used as supplementary reference books and recreational reading books. They are helpful because they are colorful and intriguing, get at various points of view, usually are less condensed, and are suitable to different interests and reading levels.

Reference books play a definite role in the elementary school curriculum as sources of information on particular topics that may not be adequately handled in textbooks. These include the student encyclopedias that are written in simple language and with a multiplicity of illustrations. Dictionaries are also published for use by children at various levels of ability. Adult references such as almanacs and atlases are also useful in the classroom. All of these materials demand special skills of research and interpretation to facilitate their use.

Current reading materials such as newspapers and magazines have been especially produced for children, and some strictly for school use. *Reader's Digest,* for example, publishes a special school edition. Such papers as *My Weekly Reader* and *Current Events* are commonly used so that children may read about current human affairs.[9] Other materials frequently utilized by children are the ''fugitive'' sources of pamphlets and brochures.

The use of another type of commercially published material, the comic book, has been highly controversial. Because of the pictorial type of communication, these booklets intrigue youngsters and tell a vivid story with few words. Criticisms have been directed at questionable moral standards, language, art, and emotional appeal. Many of the comic books have proved their worth in all these aspects and are now accepted in schools.

Michaelis presents a checklist for evaluating social studies textbooks that is helpful for the consideration of texts and references:

---

[8] *Ibid.,* pp. 382–383.

[9] For a complete list of magazines and newspapers, see George D. Spache, *Good Reading for Poor Readers* (Champaign, Illinois: The Garrard Press, Publishers, 1958), pp. 92 ff.

As an instructional resource:

Is it related to the content of the program?

Is it accurate and up to date?

Can concepts and understandings be grasped by children who will use it?

Is level of reading difficulty—vocabulary, style of presentation, sentence structure—appropriate for children who will use it?

Will it contribute to problem-solving skills?

Do illustrative materials—maps, pictures, drawings—contribute to the meaningfulness of the content?

Are study aids, suggested activities, and related references adequate?

Physical features:

Is it attractive and appealing to children?

Are margins and page arrangements adequate?

Are size, spacing, and type size adequate?

Major emphases:

Does the book inspire loyalty to American ideals and institutions?

Does it contain material that can be used to develop positive attitudes?

Are generalizations supported by facts?

Are controversial issues handled fairly and objectively?

Are movements and trends emphasized rather than isolated events?

Does it stimulate interests that lead to further study?[10]

Maps and globes. Teachers and children construct maps as one way of organizing information, but because most of the maps used in the elementary school are prepared commercially, we include them in this section. Next to books, maps are perhaps the most used instructional materials. Recent social and cultural changes, development of a mobile population, and space age transportation have placed a greater emphasis upon maps.

Although maps are historically tied to geographic study, their modern use is not limited to any one curriculum area. Classroom situations call for constant references to maps. No longer are maps used only to locate places or facilitate the memorization of a list of names. Today the map is considered a vehicle for making relationships and for understanding the contemporary affairs of people and their cultures. Systematic development of skill in using maps occurs only as the need arises, so only tentative grade placement of skills is made.

Reading a map involves interpretation of such abstractions as color, shading, outline, and scale. One must be able to find and follow the map legend, or information data, and understand the semipictorial form symbolically indicating items as rivers and mountains. To gain an ade-

---

quate concept of the map's representation, one must also understand the various types of projections used to construct maps.[11]

Producers have helped to adjust maps to maturity in the interpretation of symbols by making available maps at three levels: a simple map for beginners, a more advanced map for intermediate grade pupils, and maps of standard complexity for advanced students. Another help to the teacher is that maps are produced in a multiplicity of types. Content is available from physical or topographical maps, economic maps showing products, resources, or industry; political maps with location of cities and countries; cultural maps that present information about population or war. Forms of maps vary as to outline, wall maps, atlases, decorative maps, globes, three-dimensional maps, and some slides for projection.

Dale lists some standards that may be used in selecting maps:

1. *Visibility*—can the map be seen by all?
2. *Detail*—is there too much for the maturity of the children?
3. *Scale*—are the markings clear and easily interpreted?
4. *Symbols*—are they easily recognizable and few enough to understand?
5. *Color*—does it help to clarify information? Color use on maps is standardized only as the International Color Plan on some maps indicate elevations and water. Color should not interfere with legibility and should show relationships and emphasize contrasts.
6. *Accuracy*—is the map accurate for its specific purpose?
7. *Grade level*—is the detail and amount of material appropriate?
8. *Point of view*—does the map increase the child's point of view beyond his own?
9. *Durability*—can the map survive constant classroom use?[12]

Filmstrips, photographs, and photographic slides. These materials are increasingly available as free and inexpensive materials, and can be teacher-made, but their greatest use is from the commercial source.

Filmstrips, photographs, and photographic slides are the attention-focusing still pictures studied by prints or projection. They have their limitations because they are a still form, but they can suggest motion. Their advantages lie in the ease with which they can be manipulated, their adaptability to all areas of the curriculum, their use in overcoming problems of space and time, and the way in which they reproduce reality.

Skill is required to "read" or interpret the picture. The child's maturity, ability to notice details, or previous experience may influence the depth and validity of the clues received from the picture. The teacher's

---

[11] For an excellent description of map projections, see Brown and others, *op. cit.*, pp. 132–133.

[12] Dale, *op. cit.*, pp. 341–342.

responsibility lies in selecting pictures appropriate to the children and helping them gain the skills of interpretation.

Flat pictures are naturally a medium to which children respond. Personal identification, too, is easily made with a well-photographed picture. The greatest advantage of photographic flat pictures lies in the flexibility of use for individual study and display. They can introduce subjects, provide information, motivate learning, correct impressions, or review subject matter. One picture may be used for a number of learning situations. Some of the problems in their use lie in mounting, display, appropriateness to time, and the possibility of ambiguous presentation.

Types of pictures are greatly varied. There are originals or reproductions of photographs, line drawings, paintings, and posters. Their function varies from those that demonstrate or explain a structure or operation to those that are documentary, that candidly present information about ways of life or phenomena. Also, there are the esthetic interpretations of artists that serve more than informational functions.

Dale's standards for judging still pictures are helpful:

1. Will it achieve my teaching purpose?
2. Does the picture convey a generally true impression?
3. Does the picture give an accurate impression of relative size?
4. Will the picture add to the student's fund of knowledge?
5. Will the picture stimulate the imagination?
6. Is this a good picture technically and artistically?
7. Does the picture focus attention upon one main idea?
8. Does the picture have a proper amount of detail?[13]

A *filmstrip* is a group of pictures organized in a related sequence on a transparency for projection. When accompanied by a transcription, they are termed *sound filmstrips*. These materials are helpful because they are easily projected, require little storage space, may be observed on the screen for as short or as long a time as necessary, need only a semi-darkened room, and present information in a logical sequence. Some teachers feel this orderly sequence is not flexible and is something of a limitation. Also, these long strips of film are easily damaged and rather difficult to repair. In evaluating a filmstrip one notes the suitability of the captions, the effectiveness of the sequential organization and relevance, the currency, the ways in which photographs, drawings, and diagrams are effectively related, and the ways in which discussion and other activities will result.

Transparent slides are usually in $2'' \times 2''$ and $4'' \times 4''$ dimensions. Slides can be shown in any order, and present many kinds of graphic representations: cartoons, graphs, diagrams, tables. Though they are slightly

---

[13] *Ibid.*, pp. 269–274.

more costly and require a more fully darkened room, they have great usefulness in the classroom.

Several other types of equipment are designed to project materials. The opaque projector will project any nonopaque picture. The overhead transparency projector is designed so that the teacher may face the class rather than the screen as he draws or inserts pictures for projection. The stereographic projector contains twin lenses so that a three-dimensional projection results. The tachistoscope is used for a timed exposure so that recognition of words, phrases, or pictures may be controlled. Microprojection is the projection of material from a microscope. Microfilm is a transparent picture in reduced size that may be projected. Each of these types of projection have advantages for particular situations.

Motion picture films. ''Movies'' bring both reality and imagination into the classroom. Their advantages are great in that they depict motion and sound, contain a minimum of titles to be read, and present a continuity of action. Films available today pertain to any area of the curriculum and may be presented at the convenience of the teacher and the children. Their production utilizes techniques so that real things may be reduced in size for an over-all view, or things usually unseen by the human eye may be enlarged for studying. Microphotography, telescopic photography, X-ray photography, slow motion or fast motion, and animation help to overcome ordinary problems of time, size, and distance that would occur if the real things were observed. Movies have become invaluable records of actual events, and techniques of production facilitate documentation that is dramatic and authentic. Other types include fictional drama, religious information, travelogues, and training films. Innumerable films of increasingly high quality are being produced by governmental agencies, educational organizations, and commercial producers.

Though films are becoming more and more popular with teachers, a few limitations are discernible. When time and size are reduced or enlarged, children may form incorrect concepts. Films are being adapted to various age levels, but they may not always be adequate to the maturity of a special group. They are utilized for group instruction; individual use is difficult to arrange. Frequently mechanical difficulties occur in projection. Because films are so expensive, schools arrange to borrow them from a central source, and this makes more difficult the ordering and length of time they may be kept. Gradually teachers are understanding that films are not merely for entertainment, and that careful study, involving preparation and follow-up, is necessary to film utilization. Generally speaking, however, the educational value of films outweighs their limitations, so that their use is encouraged. In evaluating films, teachers use three criteria. First, the information presented is con-

sidered in terms of the age of the children, the direct interest appeal, the authenticity, and the direct relationship to the topic being studied. Second, the technical characteristics are important. One notices the color, sound, photography, organization, and good taste of the production. Third, the teacher is concerned with the educational quality, that is, the amount and kind of learning that it produces for the children.

Exhibits, objects, specimens. The "real things," such as objects, models, specimens, and samples that are three-dimensional, are commonly termed *realia.* Produced in greater abundance, and with the modern improvements of packaging, plastic-embedding, and the engineering accomplishments of mock-ups, cutaways, and models, some splendid materials are available. Their advantages stem from the fact that children can handle, sense, manipulate these materials; they are working with the things, not just studying *about* them. Children can become familiar with the unfamiliar or extend understandings of the familiar. Children can assemble and disassemble, care for, organize, classify, mount, and display these realia.

Samples may be living or preserved, in kits, in prepared exhibits, and either natural or man-made. Models may be enlarged or reduced from the original size to be made more useful for study. They may display working parts, or merely authentic structure and design, as ship models. They may be stationary, mechanical, or power driven.

The use of realia is most helpful, but, like some "busy" window displays or pictures, too many such things can detract rather than add to a learning situation. Realia must be convenient in size, durable, simple, easy to find, inexpensive, and safe to have in the classroom.

Children and teacher find many means for displaying realia, but the primary method is the exhibit, or a specially arranged room environment. Social studies and science activities frequently call for arrangements of materials, and particular ideas in language arts or arithmetic often need emphasis through a carefully arranged display that includes a number of related source materials. Dale lists several standards for exhibits that are worthy of note: An exhibit should (1) have one central idea, emphasizing simplicity; (2) be placed where it is certain to be seen; (3) be seen and not read—the message is received at a glance; (4) contain labels that are short and simple; (5) utilize labels that are uniform and legible, with careful lettering; (6) sometimes use motion to attract attention, such as a turning vase or waving flags; (7) be well lighted; (8) add *interest and attractiveness* with color; (9) add sound for emphasis as music or speech; (10) be worth looking at.[14]

---

[14] *Ibid.*, pp. 184–186.

Free and Inexpensive Materials

More and more public and private agencies, profit and nonprofit organizations whose business is not primarily education, are making available materials and services for the teacher's use. Among these free and inexpensive materials so well used in the classroom are books, pamphlets, cartoons, charts, comic books, samples and specimens, charts, diagrams, pictures, maps, exhibits, films, and recordings.

Problems concerning use. The use of free and inexpensive materials has in some instances been questioned, and the major issue has apparently been concerned with the amount and quality of advertising accompanying the materials. Several years ago a number of materials were used that seemed poorly organized from an educational point of view. Too many ideas were displayed on one chart; materials were issued on the adult level and so had little meaning for some children; only one short sequence in a film would be relevant to the children's problem. Some school boards, in an attempt to screen materials that contained too much advertising and were educationally poor, set up strict policies concerning the use of free and inexpensive materials. Because of the criticism, organizations producing them have in recent years made an appreciable attempt to produce acceptable materials.

Sources. Business and industry and other types of organizations have found that it is good business to inform teachers, children, and parents about their products. Airline companies, oil companies, lumber and paper companies, and almost all large industries now have educational departments organized as part of their public relations programs. Excellent films, exhibits and loan materials are commonly available, and in some situations personnel will be sent to talk with children and demonstrate materials.

Some industries have developed cooperative organizations that place education as one of their major purposes. The National Dairy Council and the American Association of Railroads are two examples of these. Governmental organizations also plan materials for school use. The United States Printing Office makes available for small sums many informational bulletins. Chambers of commerce, consuls, tourist bureaus, and other groups will send either free or for small sums many kinds of descriptive publications.

Criteria for selecting free and inexpensive materials. As teachers evaluate these free and inexpensive materials preliminary to selecting them, they will consider several factors. Grambs has developed a check list for selection of current materials that will serve as standards for evaluation.

1. Is the agency that produced the materials clearly stated?
2. Are sources given for quoted facts? If so, are the sources reputable and authoritative?
3. Is the date of publication given? Is the material recent, when usefulness of the data depends upon recency?
4. Are any particular groups or individuals singled out for derogatory portrayal that is likely to give offense?
5. Is the cost, if any, commensurate with the educational value of the material?
6. Can materials be filed for future use?
7. Are the films and filmstrips reviewed in standard guides to films? If so, is the review favorable for the use contemplated?
8. Do commercial aspects of the material outweigh the educational contribution?
9. Does the material support a special-interest point of view without due regard to objectivity?
10. Does use of the material obligate the school in any way?
11. Is the material in accordance with school policy regarding the use of textbook material?
12. Are the reading level and the idea content within the range of ability of the class?
13. Would any of the community mores be offended by use of the materials?[15]

Community Resources

The community in which the school operates, in which the children live, is one of the most valuable sources of instructional materials.

The community-school concept. In Chapter 1 of this book we acknowledged the elementary school as a community or neighborhood institution. In Chapter 5 were mentioned the kinds of influences the community has upon the school. There can be no doubt that the close interrelationship of school and community makes the school a more effective social institution. The community-school concept, an emerging idea in the administration of a school, places primary importance upon viewing the school as a part of the human affairs that surround it, in knowing the community, serving it, and using it as a source for learning. Michaelis states well the importance of the community-school relationship:

> The community is the setting in which the child lives and learns; in it he develops the meanings and concepts essential as an understanding of group living; in it he experiences life in a democracy. The experience he has in churches, stores, theaters, home, neighborhood, and school become his background of meanings for study, thought, and expression.

---

[15] Jean D. Grambs, *Using Current Materials To Study Current Problems* (Stanford, California: Stanford University Press, 1952), p. 27.

Out of all these experiences in the community come the backgrounds for developing an understanding of human relationships and processes of living.[16]

The teacher who knows the community utilizes it as a rich source for instructional material. He finds people, places, and things to bring to the classroom and to take the children to. He uses the community as a laboratory that furnishes at all levels of participation both concrete direct experiences and the means of exploring social functions. He finds in the community a source for service to which he and the children can contribute.

The contributions of the community resources to classroom learning involve the practical features of life itself. Through observing, listening and talking to people, visiting places, reading, looking at and studying things, children are learning more about the world about them. They understand about work and the interdependencies of many jobs. They find out something of people's recreation and esthetic enjoyment; they learn of the problems facing men and the solutions partially or completely made. The community can bring to the classroom historical and current facts about all areas of life and living.

In the process of borrowing, visiting, or accepting materials and services from the community the teacher is careful to maintain accepted social amenities. Letters of invitation and thanks are sent. Common courtesy is demonstrated in every situation. Preplanning facilitates orderly conduct of children and orderly thinking in the act of learning. No material should be collected without permission, even from a vacant lot. All materials should be carefully labeled so that they may be promptly and accurately returned to the owners. Children learn to handle and use the materials carefully to avoid damage.

Kinds of resources available. Among the places and community activities usable as sources of learning are the city and county libraries, in some of the larger urban areas private libraries and those of other schools and colleges, local and state museums, private museums, historical museums, factories and places of business such as newspaper publishers, an oil refinery or airport, governmental agencies such as the courthouse and post office, parks, lighthouses, service agencies or organizations such as hospitals, chambers of commerce, labor unions, Red Cross, and community festivals and celebrations such as May Day and Columbus Day.

From these places and through various organizations come the *people* used as consultants: teachers, "old timers," the postman, the fireman,

---

[16] Michaelis, *op. cit.*, p. 204.

businessmen, travel agents, and government officials such as the county agricultural agent.

Within the community—in industry, libraries, or governmental offices —are found valuable *published materials,* census reports, courthouse records, telephone books, city directory, weather reports, industrial and other organizational reports, advertising, brochures and pamphlets, pictures, films. Samples, specimens, and other realia available from community services have already been discussed under free and inexpensive materials.

One question arises in the consideration of gathering sources of information. How does the teacher find them? He, of course, utilizes the usual references—the district source files and published catalogs. (See list at the end of this chapter.) Also the wise teacher consults the children. Thirty sets of eyes, ears, and questions are more effective than one. Also children who help to gather materials have a greater interest in classroom activities, higher motivation for learning, and a stronger feeling of belonging, having made a contribution to the group.

Field trips. Field trips are becoming a widely used method of instruction. Entering kindergarteners and first graders are often oriented to the school and its immediate neighborhood by actually visiting the community. Little walks to see the kinds of houses, the busy street, the shopping center, or the fire station will help children appreciate their community and the activity within it. Field trips to factories, museums, zoos, government agencies, and other community institutions are well established in most schools as important to understanding the local area and to the enrichment of curricular content at all levels of development.

Taking the children out of the school on a trip involves administrative procedure that varies with each school district. More and more community organizations are cooperating with the schools as they seek to build good public understanding of their functions. Most frequently the teacher arranges for an expert to guide the children and make explanations during the trip. The teacher first ascertains if the factory or business is willing to cooperate, what facilities they will exhibit, how the tour will be conducted, and to what extent the information gained will contribute to the purpose of the trip. The date and time are carefully prearranged. In some districts, school buses are readily made available; in others, parents or other means must be used for transportation. Usually the trip is preceded by careful study and a formulation of questions to be answered. Follow-up includes evaluating the information received in answers to prestated questions as well as recording information and pursuing emerging activities.

Consultants. Another method of bringing the school and the community closer together is to ask members of the community to contribute

to the school program. A most valuable source of information is the direct contact with people who are ''experts'' about the topic under study. The policeman, the judge, and other community helpers are frequently invited to the classroom to tell the children about their services. A pilot from the nearby airport, the grocery man, the ticket agent, and other businessmen can serve as consultants at every school level. Children can help to find the aunt or the neighbor who can make Mexican tortillas, the friend who has traveled in Canada and taken pictures, or the engineer who worked on the big dam and has personal experiences to tell about it. Many large businesses employ men who deal with public relations and educational services; they are happy to talk to the children and bring materials for them to use.

Preparing for a consultant involves more than inviting him according to the accepted social custom. Arrangements are made with careful timing and planning. Michaelis lists the following guidelines for use with consultants:

1. Through group discussion determine whether or not the use of the visitor is the best way to secure required information on existing needs and problems.
2. Clarify and list the specific needs and questions on which help is desired.
3. Select a resource person who can make a rich contribution.
4. Plan with the visitor, giving attention to needs and questions, timing, interests and age level of the group. Give special attention to vocabulary and illustrative materials that may be used.
5. Both the teacher and children should be ready to raise questions and state problems.
6. The teacher should guide the discussion and stimulate group thinking as needed.
7. Use the information to solve problems and to further expression through reporting, art, writing, dramatization, and so forth.
8. Evaluate the effectiveness of the use made of the information secured.
9. Write a letter of appreciation including (if possible) material showing how the contribution was used.
10. Continue the unit, moving on to new needs and problems that have arisen.[17]

Radio and television. Mass media provided by community enterprises cannot be ignored as an instructional material. We have already said a little about newspapers and magazines; radio and television are growing in importance and have a number of characteristics in common. Both are

---

[17] Michaelis, *op. cit.*, pp. 223–224, as cited from Edward G. Olsen and others, *School and Community* (Second edition; Englewood Cliffs, New Jersey: Prentice-Hall, Inc., 1949), pp. 128–136.

utilized within the home more often than at school. These media have a great influence upon the opinions and ideas of the people of our country; children come to school expressing these opinions and behaving accordingly. The tunes they hum, the advertisements facetiously quoted, the programs discussed that have been heard or viewed at home become part of the school life. Both radio and television produce planned programs that are arranged according to public demand and sponsor need. It is difficult to know how much the programs influence what people want and how much what people want influences the programs presented.

Both radio and television can broadcast events at the time of origin and can record these events for later presentation. Sports, political meetings, world activities and special events such as election returns are listened to and viewed by millions, some of whom could not read about these events in the newspapers. One hundred years ago this kind of news would have taken months to reach the far corners of the world. In spite of these advantages, the rigid program scheduling and one-way communication of these media are problems that must be met in school.

Radio is the older of the two media, and since the advent of television it has decreased the kinds of presentations it offers for the public and in the schools. Radio programs have been helpful to teachers because children can listen in some cases more easily than they can read. The uniqueness of the medium is in itself an influence upon learning. One disadvantage stems from scheduling. The science or music program must be heard when it is scheduled, whether at recess time or arithmetic time. Also, some excellent programs worth using for school purposes are scheduled during out-of-school hours, and the teacher must accordingly make modifications in the teaching procedure. Another disadvantage is the limitation of one-way communication. The teacher on the radio can only "tell" his audience. Questions and discussions are only possible with the local teacher after the broadcast. Some programs have attempted to overcome this problem by preparing in advance materials that are sent to participating schools, and by receiving questions that may be discussed in later broadcast lessons.

Television is a new and constantly improving medium, and its advantages for education seem to be mounting. Some good research is now in progress but we still need to know more about its effectiveness. We do know that children spend many out-of-school hours watching television, and that television has greatly broadened experiences for today's children. Their vocabulary and ideas reflect these experiences. Interest and reading in various curriculum areas have been stimulated because of television. The elementary school teacher needs to watch the children's programs once in a while just to understand their language and their ideas. It is well to remember that the programs designed for the general

public are produced by showmen, not educators. Some of Walt Disney's programs, for example, have much educational worth, but their primary purpose is entertainment. It is no wonder that youngsters are more interested in subjects like "Beaver Valley" than in subjects found in the basic textbook. The problem of content and who determines it in television programs, especially those used in classrooms, is of great concern to educators.

Several kinds of television programs are emerging that can be helpful to the teacher. More and more educational channels are being established that present both national and local programs of educational interest. Most programs now are on the adult level, but a number are especially designed for children. The *kinescope*, or photographically recorded transcription of TV programs, is being increasingly used. Special events and other appropriate programs that have been recorded are available for school use. *Videotape* (television recording on magnetic tape) is used similarly. *Closed circuit television* is gaining such acceptance that some schools are purchasing the expensive equipment necessary for it. In the closed circuit, a broadcast is made not to the general public, but only to the sets that are connected directly.

The consensus is that television can teach. The training of instructors for television is not complicated, and the teaching is good because careful preparation is made. Teaching done over television is not "off the cuff" as it sometimes is in the classroom. Part of the good teaching is that many kinds of instructional materials are used on television, such as pictures and charts, chalkboard illustrations, and demonstrations serving to point out carefully and relate the small details of a topic. Such techniques have been worked out because of the limitations in time and scope of the picture. Some feel that oversimplification could result, at the cost of effectiveness. Television techniques must be understood by the classroom teacher so that the classroom teaching used for preparation and follow-up may be modified to make the best use of the medium.

The disadvantage of one-way communication has been identified and some steps are being taken to overcome it. These steps are taken in the classroom follow-up. Though television can bring specialists to the children, the teacher is a necessary factor for following through the ideas and providing some participation for the children other than listening and watching.

Teacher-Made Materials

Finally, we discuss the kinds of materials that are prepared by the teacher or, under his guidance, by the children themselves. Though this section is titled "teacher-made materials," the term here will include those materials produced either by cooperative effort of children and teacher, or by the teacher himself.

The need for teacher-made materials. Not all materials necessary to teaching are available from outside sources. Schools make every effort to procure adequate and varied materials of instruction, but it is well understood that financially and educationally the prepared materials must be supplemented by the teacher. Often the only means of individualizing instruction is the preparation of materials to facilitate classroom activities. Because of special needs, very special materials are demanded. They provide reading material for slow readers, they provide obscure information, they extend to the most varied of interests. They increase or reestablish content, they provide for children experiences in organizing information, producing, and creating. They provide means of recording classroom activities in such materials as tapes, booklets, charts, and photographs, that serve as a basis for evaluation or further study.

Kinds of teacher-made materials. Almost all the materials discussed previously under commercially prepared, free and inexpensive, or community resource materials may also be designed and prepared in the classroom. Models, maps, posters, cartoons, booklets, charts and graphs, transcriptions, realia, pictures, slides, and puppet theaters may be organized, collected, or produced by teacher and children.

One of the first things a young teacher-in-training does is to start collecting and organizing his picture file. During his first year in the profession he probably will make a number of devices for teaching various subjects. The flannel board has a number of uses, among them to help to make illustrations and to build sequence. Pocket charts, number fact-finders, fractions charts are a few materials for teaching arithmetic. In language arts, experience charts, scrapbooks, "rewrites," puppets, and magnetic tapes are all useful. For science activities teacher-made devices such as barometers, electric switches, or charts of growing plants are readily constructed.

Skills needed for teacher-made materials. The production and use of teacher-made materials requires something beyond the usual ability to select the material and plan its use. Certain kinds of skills in design and construction are required for motivating, planning, and guiding the production activities of children. Familiarity with layout and lettering, knowledge in the use of such tools as lettering pens, simple carpenter's hand tools, measuring and cutting tools, and an understanding of the techniques of mounting, scoring, and spatter and spray painting—all will help the teacher achieve more excellent teacher-made materials.

MATERIALS FOR INDEPENDENT STUDY: A SPECIAL PROBLEM

When the teacher is working with the children on specific subjects such as reading, spelling, and arithmetic activities, and to a lesser degree in

other curriculum areas, he finds it necessary to organize the class so that he can work with some children while others are independently occupied. This necessitates decisions as to the kind of work that can be designed and assigned for independent study. Such work is sometimes referred to as *seatwork*.

Criteria for Independent Work

So that children may work quietly and independently at their seats, on material that is more than just "busy work," the following criteria are helpful:

1. The material should be in a form that can be easily carried from the storage space to the individual's work place.
2. The material must be simple enough to complete with a minimum of guidance.
3. The work should involve a minimum of supplies.
4. The material should be interesting or challenging enough to stimulate growth or reinforce learning, and should be varied from day to day.
5. The material should be carefully related to other classroom activities.
6. The material should be such that results are easily evaluated by the child and the teacher.

Problems Related to Independent Study

Both children and teacher need to develop techniques and habits that will facilitate the kind of independent study that is meaningful and conducive to learning.

The teacher's consideration. The preparation and use of independent study materials demand some skill on the part of the teacher, especially in the assignment of materials. Successful completion of a written assignment is directly related to the instructions given by the teacher when the assignment is made. Since a teacher must work with many children, he must make sure that each individual can follow both oral and written directions. He develops this "tool of learning" as early as possible and maintains it through consistent reference and instruction. He guides the children into doing exactly what the directions tell, in the proper sequence, and complete within each part. No worksheet or workbook page is assigned without instructions that include the page number, the special directions, the particular problems or expected outcomes, and an opportunity for children to ask questions. Frequently the teacher will make assignments when the children are in small groups, as they are at the end of the reading period, so that he is sure each individual understands the task. Children should also understand what they are to do

after the work is completed. In this, the teacher considers the length of time each assignment should require.

Correcting workbook pages or dittoed sheets may become a problem if assignments are made indiscriminately. No teacher likes to spend his free time correcting mountains of papers. Probably the most effective time for correcting papers is during the arithmetic, spelling, or reading lesson, when the children are in small groups. Frequently teachers will correct the papers just before assigning the new material, or just before the major portion of the lesson, if the assignment is related to it. In this way children and teacher can see reasons for mistakes and understand the means of making corrections. Such evaluation must be well organized so that the work is done with no loss of time or interest.

The teacher must also consider the shortage of independent work materials and the availability of supplies. The children must know where to find work materials and supplies such as paper and crayons. They cannot disturb the teacher. Therefore they must listen carefully, remember the directions, begin work without waste of time, assert self-direction in solving problems that may arise, and work alone without disturbing other children. They must develop work habits that make independent work successful.

An important skill when working independently in a group situation is concentration. A child's ability to concentrate when listening and to concentrate when working quietly alone increases as he grows. He has to "tune out" and "tune in" the sounds that effect his work. In this age of television, radio, and jukeboxes, this ability to "tune out" extraneous sounds is easily established.

Variety in Independent Work Activities

Some teachers feel that most of the independent work activities have to be written work of the drill type. Sometimes children are burdened with one workbook after another all day long, or they are given a sheaf of papers intended to keep them busy at their seats all morning. A little of this kind of seatwork can be very helpful, but the material must be effective and the completed work evaluated. A variety of materials and activities is the most satisfactory for learning, and a thoughtful and creative teacher utilizes many kinds of supplies, source materials, and devices.

One of the finest sources for suggestions about independent activities is the teacher's manual of the textbook used. Reading manuals suggest many supplementary activities, and similar suggestions are found in manuals for arithmetic, spelling, and handwriting. Textbooks in science and social studies list questions to be answered and activities to pursue that supplement the information written in the text.

One material that can be substituted for written work is the kind of semipermanent "game" that makes drill more digestible and maintains skills already taught. It is particularly applicable to reading, arithmetic, and spelling. The games are similar to bingo, matching games, combination drills, mazes, jigsaw puzzles, and "find-what-is-missing" games. They are organized so that individuals, couples, or small groups may participate with a minimum of noise.

Other materials are also helpful. One teacher framed a mirror in a corner and labeled it, "Can you draw a picture of yourself?" Picture files, flash cards, experience charts, old magazines, scrapbooks are also sources of independent activity for primary grade children. Quiet activities related to the curriculum unit or other studies in progress are interesting and productive. Library books, art and science materials, and exhibits also lend themselves to browsing and manipulation that becomes thoughtful learning as part of independent work activities. The creative teacher develops many possibilities in which children select and pursue their own independent work activities.

Teaching Machines

The recent introduction of "teaching machines" has created great interest and some concern in educational circles. Such terms as *automatic teaching, mechanical learning,* and *jukebox teaching* have attracted some and repelled others as the wheels of technology move closer to the confines of the classroom. Just as some educational leaders look upon television with suspicion, they also doubt the value of teaching machines. As with television, the issue evolves around the extent to which the use of electronic machines will increase the quality of the educational experience.

First suggestions and designs for a machine that would "teach" came from Sidney L. Pressey in 1926,[18] but Pressey's machines involved primarily a method of testing information or arriving at a correct response through repeated choices. The "father" of the present machine is B. F. Skinner of Harvard University, who, improving upon Pressey's ideas, in 1958 produced a more versatile machine.[19] At present, automatic teaching machines, with films, tapes, and other electronic equipment, are being used on an experimental basis for instruction in many subjects throughout the country. Even at this point it seems apparent that some subjects are more adaptable to machine use than others.

The general operation of the teaching machine involves the presenta-

---

[18] For details of his ideas, see Sidney L. Pressey, "A Simple Device Which Gives Tests and Scores and Teaches," *School and Society* 23:373–376.

[19] See B. F. Skinner, "Teaching Machines," *Science*, October 1958, pp. 969–977.

tion of material to which the pupil makes an active response. Responses require some understanding of the problem and a thoughtful composition rather than a selection of possible choices. Recall rather than recognition is emphasized. In arithmetic, a numerical answer may be written; in Spanish, a phrase is verbally repeated. Immediately the machine indicates a correct or incorrect answer for the numbers or plays back the language response enabling the student to compare his own accent with that of the expert. The learning continues step by step through a pre-designed program. That is, each step is explained or illustrated, then requires an immediate and active response from the student. Only when the response is satisfactory, as indicated by the machine, does the learning proceed to the next level of instruction.

Advantages. A number of advantages are pointed out by the proponents of teaching machines. One lies in the individual work done at the student's own pace. The child goes as fast or as slowly as necessary to assure satisfactory responses. This is individual self-study, requiring active participation and sustained activity. Some authorities liken it to the tutorial situation in which the instructor gives guidance by probing with questions and stimulating thinking of the student in a one-to-one relationship.

The machine immediately reinforces correct responses or immediately corrects or indicates wrong answers, and thus prevents habits of error. Progress also assures "mastery" at every level. Experimental results have shown that some topics are covered in half the time taken by ordinary teaching.

An enticing claim is that the equipment will relieve teachers of much dull, repetitive teaching, objective testing, and evaluating and correcting of many papers. Consequently, the teacher will have more time for the creative details of teaching, for more inspiring tasks, and for the "personal touch" that machines cannot perform. In fact, some observers believe that the use of the machines will drastically change the role of the teacher and of present teaching methods.

Related problems. Despite the advantages of teaching machines, some questions arise concerning their use. Probably the most important is that of the design and development of the "program," or the material used by the machine to outline and direct the learning. The teaching effectiveness is dependent upon the logical steps through which the learner progresses. Independent machine study is said to be self-contained, complete within itself. Preparing the lessons then requires selected skills including both scientific technology and the artistry of teaching. One asks: Who determines the design? Where do we start? What do we include? What are the levels between steps? Will the machine manufacturers prepare the programs? Will publishers make them as supplements to

textbooks? Will school districts include them in their curriculum services, or will this be the responsibility of the teacher? How is increasing vocabulary, difficulty in reading level, and subject complexity to be controlled? What differences are made for regional groups? How can we be sure that the program is not too hard or too easy? How can clarity of presentation be determined? Can mastery at every step be assured and maintained?

Another problem exists in regard to how the teacher uses the machine. The children will no doubt be stimulated initially by the mechanical aspects and novelty of using a machine, but maintaining motivation and interest will ultimately rest with the teacher. The machine material, used independently of teaching guidance, cannot be as easily supplemented or clarified as a textbook. The possibility is always present that the machine may become the basis of a rigid curriculum that emphasizes stereotyped and rote learning.

We have the machines. They are currently being used for college entrance examinations, remedial reading work, and foreign language teaching. Whether or not teaching machines disappear as a fad or gain in effectiveness depends upon continuing experimentation and modifications by educators and technicians in an effort to adapt them to the best interests of the school. At present the greater part of experimentation with machines has been at the college and secondary level; a good deal more must be known about their use with children. It is possible that in time the proper equipment will bring radical change in present methods of teaching at all levels of instruction, especially in certain subject fields.

The advent of teaching machines has instigated a flurry of interest among businesses that deal in school equipment. Manufacturers of machines and related equipment are working to produce machines that can be purchased cheaply enough to make them useful in mass education. Publishers are trying to determine the effect of machines on already prepared materials. Furniture companies are making detailed surveys to be ready for the changes that may occur if machines attain widespread use. Possibilities are conceived that teaching machines, in changing teacher role and method, will also change the way rooms are used and will require different kinds of furniture and architectural modifications of school plants. These predictions may be exaggerated, but businessmen must consider these possibilities and be prepared to design and develop equipment for delivery years in advance of when it is needed.

UTILIZATION OF CLASSROOM SPACE

The character of the classroom differs according to the ideas of the teacher and the group of children who work there. Rooms differ in ar-

rangement and atmosphere. Each teacher, with the help of children, consciously makes his classroom a reflection of his philosophy and his personality and strives to make it the most pleasant, the most efficient, and the most effective for the learning that goes on there.

Children and their teacher live from two and one-half to six hours each day in their classroom. This amount of time and the character of the modern curriculum necessitate the utilization of classroom space for many kinds of activities. The whole classroom or parts of it may at different times in one day perform the function of a committee meeting room, a laboratory, a library, a workshop, a recreation room, an art and music studio, and a lecture room. This kind of diversified utilization calls for careful yet flexible and functional utilization of space.

Functional Arrangement of Furniture

Most teachers have little to say about the selection of the basic furniture in their rooms, but sometimes have freedom in the placement of tables, chairs, and desks. The ways in which children move about the room, work in groups, and proceed individually at tasks can be one of the most important contributions in learning. It may be noted that in more and more classrooms, furniture is no longer arranged in the long rows of immovable, individual desks. The modern movable furniture popularly purchased allows for much flexibility in its use, and is helpful to the teacher in his utilization of space. Desks or tables, adequately suited to the size of individual children, are grouped so that the work under way is best accomplished. Such grouping depends on the size and shape of the classroom, the number of children, the kind of furniture, and the curricular and methodological emphasis of the teacher. Flexibility of movable furniture also means modifications in arrangements may be made during the day and during the year.

Further consideration of environmental factors include temperature of the room, ventilation, and lighting. Adjustment of windows, shades, and lights is a constant procedure. Though tables and desks are placed in circles or other informal arrangement, children should not directly face glare from the outside for too long a period.

Areas for Learning Experiences

A classroom organized with *centers of interest* facilitates work in various curriculum areas. This system of arrangement of furniture and materials means that each area of activity has its "spot" where the children find space to work and all the tools needed for working there. The location of the specific centers of interest depends on their necessity for bulletin board space, exhibit shelves, or display tables, and on the origi-

nal plan and design of the fixed equipment in the room. The kinds of centers the teacher prepares will depend on the curriculum emphasis he wishes to make.

At the reading center, or teaching area, will be found the reading table and the small chairs for accommodating the reading group. Nearby are shelves with needed textbooks, flash cards, workbooks, and other reading materials. A chart rack is in this area, and a chalkboard is right behind and within arm's reach of the teacher.

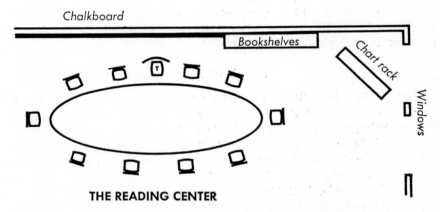

THE READING CENTER

In the art center are the easels, with brushes, mixed paints, paper, scissors, crayons, clay and clay boards, and other art materials that the children might use. Nearby is a sink with appropriate accessories and space to place completed projects.

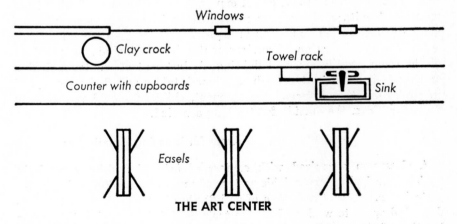

THE ART CENTER

A library table for recreational reading, research, or just browsing is located in a quiet corner of the room. Attractively displayed books of all

levels and all types of interest encourage children to do quiet reading. Here also are scrapbooks, teacher-written material, and trade books displayed and stored.

A most interesting library center was a Christmas-time arrangement. Against the wall was placed a replica of a fireplace, covered with paper printed to resemble bricks over a lath frame. In the fireplace opening was a grate and red paper hiding a small light that was plugged to a nearby electrical outlet. On the mantel were two candleholders with candles in them. At one side of the fireplace was a rocking chair, and behind it an old floor lamp. At the other end of the fireplace stood the bookshelves with the library table in front of them. In the shelves and on the table were arranged a number of books, many of them related to Christmas; some were held open by racks that displayed colorful pictures. When it was time for the teacher to read to the group, the classroom lights were turned off, the fire turned on, the candles lit; the teacher sat in the rocker with the children gathered around her. When storytelling time was not in session the children browsed in the corner, rocked in the chair, and utilized the materials as they pleased.

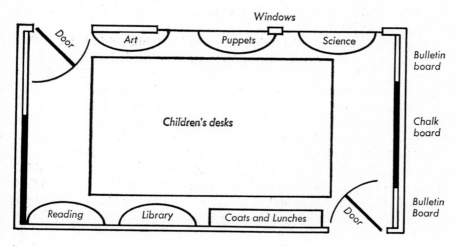

A science corner may contain the table with the current science exhibits, books about them, and probably a bulletin board behind with appropriate materials to interest and supplement the materials exhibited. An aquarium may be a permanent part of the science area. The duties involved with the temporary care of pets caged in the science area and the wonder of observing them at free moments during the day are worthwhile activities. When pets are in the classroom, health department regulations about this should be understood. Besides the pets, other specimens, pictures, and devices may be exhibited or stored.

Some teachers maintain puppet stages, where children can quietly entertain each other with dramatic presentations. Primary classrooms frequently have a block play or dramatic play area. Others have construction areas where tools, sawhorses, and wood are available. A major consideration in planning the work areas of the classroom is to remove the more active or noisy activities from the quieter ones. Block play, for example, is not placed near the reading table.

Facilitating the Use and Care of Space

Part of the organization of the environment involves the establishment of routine and regulations among the children in the care and use of materials. Closely related to management and control are the development of work habits and standards of behavior. Each school and each class needs some planned structure that influences orderly behavior. Such standards are not set up autocratically by the teacher, but through democratic, cooperative planning and constant guidance of procedure. The reason for each standard is well understood and frequently reviewed, for both teacher and children mutually understand the conditions and limits under which they work. Freedom of choice is governed by the standards set.

The act of entering and leaving the room is established in habit so that traffic areas are utilized to best advantage, no time is lost, and orderly procedure is followed. Though many schools are now avoiding formal lines, certain standards include the amount of noise and talking, loitering in the halls or on the playground, the place to store lunches, and the manner in which wraps are hung. The signals for entering or leaving the room may be a friendly and quiet word or signal from the teacher or the dismissal monitor. Fire drill routine is especially well defined.

Care and handling of the various materials in the classroom are guided by common standards. Frequently teachers plan a monitor system so that responsibilities like opening windows, passing paper, taking messages, preparing for snack time can be assumed by the children. Also, children must understand the rules about the use and cleanliness of the sink, floor, and other areas of the room, and about the housekeeping of their desks. They must understand when to use the pencil sharpener and when to use the centers of interest. Each item has its place, and each child is expected to maintain that orderly placement.

Habits related to the individual work done at the seats are also consciously formed. Because of the expectations of the daily schedule and specific assignments made by the teacher, the children know what kind of work is expected of them. Thus immediately after a recess the intermediate child may set to work upon his arithmetic. A primary child will

understand that he is to put his head down and rest, without loitering or disturbing others, until he receives further directions from the teacher. Children also know whether or not they should take out books, paper, and pencil in readiness for the lesson, or wait until the teacher asks them to do so. The business of undertaning what is to be done, and then proceeding to do it without delay or disturbance, is achieved not only by established routines, but by the amount of interest the child has in the kind of work to be accomplished.

SOURCES OF MATERIALS

For lists of sources of textbooks, periodicals, films, recordings, equipment, three-dimensional materials, maps and globes, pictures and graphics, free and inexpensive materials, see the appendices of the following books:

> Brown, James W., Richard B. Lewis, and Fred F. Harcleroad. *A-V Instruction: Materials and Methods.* New York: McGraw-Hill Book Company, 1959. p. 554.
>
> Dale, Edgar. *Audio-Visual Methods in Teaching* (Revised edition). New York: The Dryden Press, 1954. p. 534.
>
> Eboch, Sidney C. *Operating Audio-Visual Equipment.* San Francisco: Howard Chandler, Publisher, 1960. p. 73.
>
> Kinder, James S. *Audio-Visual Materials and Techniques* (Second edition). New York: American Book Company, 1959. p. 592.
>
> Murray, Thomas R., and Sherwin G. Swartout. *Integrated Teaching Materials.* New York: Longmans, Green and Company, 1960. p. 545.
>
> Sands, Lester B. *Audio-Visual Procedures in Teaching.* New York: The Ronald Press Company, 1956. p. 670.
>
> Wittich, Walter A., and Charles F. Schuller. *Audio-Visual Materials: Their Nature and Use* (Second edition). New York: Harper & Brothers, 1957. p. 570.

Commercial materials are varied and many, but finding them is made easy by the numerous catalogs that list free and inexpensive materials. Following is a list of the most popular of these catalogs:

> Educators Progress Service. *Elementary Teachers Guide to Free Curriculum Materials.* Randolph, Wisconsin.
>
> Field Enterprises, Inc. *Sources of Free and Inexpensive Educational Materials.* Merchandise Mart Plaza, Chicago 54, Illinois. (Patricia H. Suttles, Ed.)
>
> George Peabody College for Teachers. *Free and Inexpensive Learning Materials.* Division of Surveys and Field Services, Nashville 5, Tennessee.
>
> Kenworthy, Leonard S. *Free and Inexpensive Materials on World Affairs.* Public Affairs Press, 2153 Florida Avenue, Washington 8, D.C., 1954.

Miller, Bruce. *Sources of Free Pictures. Sources of Free and Inexpensive Teaching Aids. Sources of Free and Inexpensive Pictures.* Box 368, Riverside, California.

National Education Association, Association for Supervision and Curriculum Development. *Using Free Materials in the Classroom.* 1201 16th Street N.W., Washington 6, D.C.

Salisbury, Gordon, and Robert Sheridan. *Catalog of Free Teaching Aids.* P.O. Box 943, Riverside, California.

REFERENCES

Association for Supervision and Curriculum Development. *Creating a Good Environment for Learning.* Washington, D.C.: The Association, National Education Association, 1954.

How to create the atmosphere, morale, and conditions for effective learning.

Barnouw, Erik. *Mass Communication.* New York: Rinehart and Company, 1956.

The media of television, radio, film, and press and their use in the United States.

Barnes, Fred P. "The Textbook Dilemma," *Teachers College Record* 55:369–383. April 1954.

An objective presentation of an old but prominent issue.

Brown, James W., Richard B. Lewis, and Fred F. Harcleroad. *A-V Instruction: Materials and Methods.* New York: McGraw-Hill Book Company, 1959.

Dale, Edgar. *Audio-Visual Methods in Teaching* (Revised edition). New York: The Dryden Press, 1954.

Eboch, Sidney C. *Operating Audio-Visual Equipment.* San Francisco: Howard Chandler, Publisher, 1960.

A manual with diagrams for operating machines.

McDonald, Blanche, and Leslie Nelson. *Methods That Teach.* Dubuque, Iowa: William C. Brown Company, 1958.

Suggestions and procedures for teaching.

Sands, Lester B. *Audio-Visual Procedures in Teaching.* New York: The Ronald Press Company, 1956.

Thomas, R. Murray, and Sherwin G. Swartout. *Integrated Teaching Materials.* New York: Longmans, Green and Company, 1960.

Wittich, Walter, and Charles Schuller. *Audio-Visual Materials: Their Nature and Use.* New York: Harper & Brothers, 1957.

19

UTILIZING TEACHING TIME: ORGANIZING THE ENVIRONMENT

Time is, without a doubt, one of the most precious aspects of elementary school education. There are so many things to be done, and a limited time in which to do them. This book has called attention to the very extensive educational responsibilities the elementary school is asked to accept. A most compelling question is "how do we get it all in?" Considerable energy and ingenuity have been applied to this question, and planning at the school and classroom level has moved toward greater efficiency over the years. It is the purpose of this chapter to discuss this time phenomenon from a number of angles, with the intent to develop a wide range of awareness concerning it, and to point to what we feel are some sound approaches to the utilization of time.

Fixed Times Within Which the School Works

There are fixed time limits within which the elementary school and teacher must work. First, the length of the school year is determined by state law. The usual practice is to set the length of the school year at about 180 days. Local school districts may exceed this limit, but they may not operate their school system for fewer days out of the year and still receive their expected financial aid from the state.

Second, the school week in the United States is a five-day affair. Children are in school from Monday through Friday in almost every instance; Saturday and Sunday they are free.

Third, the length of the school day is itself typically fixed by law.

Again, local school districts may exceed this required period of time, but they cannot adopt a policy of shorter school days. The length of the day is different for the primary grades than for the intermediate grades. Usually the primary grades are in session for about 240 to 270 minutes per day; the intermediate grades from 330 to 360 minutes. Or, expressed differently, primary teachers usually work with their classes for about 4½ hours each day, while intermediate grade teachers work with their groups from 5½ to 6 hours per day. In each instance these figures include all recess periods except the noon lunch period. Translated into "hour week" terms, the primary child "works" about a 20 to 22½ hour week; the intermediate grade child a 27½ to 30 hour week. The extension of this time factor into hours away from the school, through a policy of assigned homework, is used sparingly in the elementary school in the United States. Almost all school work is done at school.

The "Time for What?" Question

The answer to the question "time for what?" has been dealt with both explicitly and implicitly throughout this book. One aspect of this is readily grasped. That deals with the need for finding time for instruction in the various areas of the curriculum such as the language arts, arithmetic, social studies, science, and so on. The other aspect is not so apparent, or is seldom seen in "time" terms. It is, nonetheless, of the utmost importance. This aspect is the necessity for finding time for such experiences as thinking, reasoning, creating, experimenting, and the like. These provide the second dimension to the "time for what?" question. The good school year, week, or day comes from a skillful and efficient weaving together of these two dimensions. There is much to be planned for, and time is to be used with purpose and direction. One sometimes hears questions raised concerning the necessity for planning, that is, for making actual week-by-week and day-by-day plans, on the part of the teacher. It is hoped that the preceding portions of this book have made obvious our thinking on this. Sound planning is central to the total school effort if it is really to accomplish the manifold tasks it is asked to accomplish. Let us consider this briefly here.

Planning at the System Level

One kind of planning must, of course, take place at the school system level. Decisions are called for with respect to clarity of goals, general curriculum organization, preferences in the area of methodology and materials, procedures in evaluation, policies for reporting progress, and so on. The extent of planning that will take place at the system level with respect to such matters as these has varied in education over the years.

At one time, and still to some extent, these decisions were made completely and fully at the system level and in the central office of the school district. Plans that were most complete were passed on to individual elementary schools and teachers. All of the time decisions had been made, along with almost all other sorts of decisions, and the teacher was simply to follow the course of study which had been prepared for him. Increased insight into the way in which a social structure like the school system actually operates, and greater acceptance of the idea that one elementary school unit in a system might be serving a socially very different group of parents and children in a much different setting than another began to throw doubt on the merits of such a highly centralized approach to planning. Two other points of view have developed in opposition to this one.

One takes the position that the individual elementary school is the preferred unit for planning. Thus, almost complete autonomy should be extended to each attendance center. The principal of any elementary school in the system and his faculty should make all of the decisions noted above in ways that seem most relevant and realistic in their particular school. The central office unit, from this point of view, should assume largely the role of helping each school to realize as fully as possible the plans that it has developed.

The other point of view takes the position that there are some plans that have to be made at the district level. For instance, district-wide decisions on materials and supplies and district-wide purchasing and distribution procedures seem to be wise. Similarly, the goals toward which the total school effort is directed, it is felt, ought to be district-wide goals. Additionally, certain aspects of the decisions about curriculum organization, methodology, reporting periods, and reporting processes are felt to be legitimate planning tasks at the system level. In these tasks the system involves central office staff, principals, and classroom teacher representatives. From this planning, broad outlines, often published in the form of curriculum guides, are made available to all schools and teachers. These guides call attention to agreed-upon common purposes, to preferred types and kinds of learning experiences for the classroom, to resources available in the system for the use of teachers, to approaches to evaluation deemed most appropriate, and so on. Such materials set the broad base from which the individual teacher is to begin his planning. In most school systems, the teacher is rather free to plan beyond this point in the way that he feels is most efficient for the children with whom he is working and most appropriate for himself as a teacher.[1]

---

[1] See National Society for the Study of Education, *In-service Education*, Fifty-sixth Yearbook, 1957, pp. 199–218, for a report on the approaches to curriculum development in use in school systems in the United States.

This last point of view operates today in the majority of elementary school systems. Teachers, individually and as faculty members, have both the privilege and the responsibility of planning their work in the school and classroom to a very great extent. Thus, all teachers need some conception of a "best day" for children in the elementary school, an understanding of the various elements in such a day, and skill to actually realize their plans for children. The remainder of this chapter will focus on the planning of the teacher, and the best utilization, in our view, of the time available for instruction in the classroom. The school system, as such, will be dealt with only as it bears on this matter directly.

THE TEACHER PLANS HIS WORK

Time Use and Longitudinal Planning

It is wise, in our view, for the classroom teacher to consider at least three longitudinal dimensions in planning for the most efficient use of time. One of these is the school year itself, another is a complete learning unit or enterprise in itself, and the third is the school week. The school day is seen as a vertical time dimension, and not a longitudinal one, in the general scheme of things, and will be discussed in connection with this third point.

Planning over the school year. The teacher is wise to lay out at the beginning of the year a tentative "time plan" for dealing with the complete range of responsibilities for teaching that he is expected to encompass. In such a plan, the weeks and months that school will be in session would be tentatively allotted to the various broad topics or units of work, to the kinds of skill extension and refinement, to desired esthetic experiences, and so on that are considered to be legitimate expectancies. Clearly, once the work of the year actually gets under way and the teacher begins to be more intimately acquainted with his class, adjustments will need to be made in this long range time plan. There is a great deal of truth in the idea that "plans are made to be departed from." However, when departures are made on the basis of an anticipated use of the school year, the teacher is clearer in his mind as to just what it is that he is extending, or cutting down, or omitting entirely from the original plan.

Planning for learning units or enterprises. Within this year-long time plan the teacher needs to make other anticipated longitudinal choices. He must estimate how long a given learning enterprise, such as a unit of work in social studies or science, or an initial experience with long division, or a unit on liquid measurement, is likely to continue in the classroom. Sometimes such choices are made wholly or partially at the system

level. A teacher may be required to spend nine weeks on each of four social studies units suggested for his grade and six weeks on each of six science units. Or, the system may simply suggest what are considered to be most appropriate time spans for various learning units at different age and grade levels. In other areas, the time may be tentatively divided in terms of the various art media a teacher wants his class to experience, or in terms of the seasonal cycle and games that are appropriate on an almost seasonal basis. Of course, any such decisions must be held as tentative ones, for once the actual classroom experience is under way any one of a number of things may cause the teacher to shorten or to lengthen the anticipated block of time. Child motivation may be extremely high or low in relation to particular enterprises, and adjustments in time will have to be made accordingly. Unforeseen developments on the social scene may make it wise to carry certain experiences to points not originally called for at all. Again, the plans may often be departed from, but the choice involved is more likely to be seen as the choice that it really is when such a tentative kind of time division among learning units in all areas has been made.

Planning for the school week. Within the kind of planning discussed thus far here, the school week is the most useful and realistic time span for the teacher to deal with in a great many instances. The activities and learnings at school can very readily be seen as ''Monday-to-Friday'' accomplishments. The school day may seem the most logical unit for planning, and certainly it is a time unit the teacher must deal with, but we see this more as a vertical experience within the space of one week. It is more efficient to think of balancing the ''educational diet'' for children over the span of a week than of a day. Some things should undoubtedly occur daily in the classroom program, but all things need not and cannot. The chart presented in the beginning of this chapter should make this idea clearer; however, in most instances, children should have a chance to experience all or the vast majority of the activities listed each week. Thus, while the teacher may plan for a daily experience in social studies, the work may focus on construction on one day, research on another, and discussion on still another. And, while the teacher may feel that some esthetic experience is important daily, it may be one of personal creation one day, and appreciation another, and it may be with music at one time and with art media at another. Each teacher is faced at the close of the day on Monday with decisions as to ''what shall we do tomorrow?'' and at the end of the following day specific plans must have begun to emerge for the next. These decisions are most realistically seen as the kind of day-to-day planning that is necessary to accomplish the total job anticipated for that particular week. Balance is developed in the educational experience of children over these wider spans of time. Too heavy

a commitment to daily planning may work against the very thing which the teacher wants most to accomplish in the long run.

Time Plans and Unanticipated Teaching Opportunities

Questions are often raised with respect to the teacher's exploiting unanticipated teaching opportunities that arise during the school year. Obviously, this is not a simple question of time, but a more involved matter related to curriculum planning generally. If the reader has learned his lesson well from the earlier chapters in this book, he will realize that a commitment to one point of view in curriculum suggests one answer to this situation, while allegiance to another suggests a different approach. This becomes a time question when it is interpreted in time terms. That is, does a teacher have time to lay aside previously made plans when such unanticipated opportunities arise? Needed immediately, of course, is some interpretation of the phrase *lay aside*. Does this mean to lay aside for a day, or for a few days—or does it mean to drop some ongoing study completely in favor of this more important opportunity for teaching? This matter calls for sound professional judgment on the part of the teacher. No doubt certain "golden opportunities" will develop; teachable moments arise almost every day. In each instance there will be several avenues for action open to the teacher, ranging from completely "ignoring" the opportunity to using it to launch a major learning enterprise.

It is difficult to set down general criteria to use in making such decisions. We can agree that no teacher should be so saddled with prior plans that he must let all such teachable moments pass by. At the same time, it may be unwise to cast aside certain well-thought-out but only partially developed learning situations too readily. Some things that must be kept in mind can be pointed out. Small projects that arise can often be worked into the time plan for a few days without really dropping anything when the class is highly motivated to pursue the matter. Time allotments may simply be cut back here and there to make room for this venture. Also, a teacher must be careful in the assessment that is made concerning the extent of pupil interest in certain unanticipated developments. Often only a few students are really concerned about the happening or could profit from the additional learning opportunity. In such cases, time can usually be found for these students to pursue the matter without again altering too drastically the ongoing program of the total class group. Another consideration that teachers might well apply in such decisions relates to the need for children to have opportunities for carrying on a learning enterprise "all the way" at times, starting with the unexpected but nonetheless wholehearted identification of an

area of concern to them. We would hate to see such opportunities withheld from pupils completely. There is a certain kind of enthusiasm and satisfaction that comes from identifying something that ought to be done, even studied, and making successful plans for carrying through with it. A good many school systems recognize this need at the present time and try to plan for it accordingly. Thus, the learning load assigned to a given grade makes a place for certain selections to be made by the teacher and the class, usually in the area of social studies or science. In such situations, a certain number of "standard" units of work are to be developed each year, with others coming either from a long list of optional units suggested by the district, or from the on-the-spot emergence of a completely unanticipated but highly valuable learning possibility that ought to be exploited.

GUIDELINES FOR DEVELOPING A BEST SCHOOL DAY AND WEEK

There are certain elements that should be planned for in a "best" school day or week. These elements grow out of the commitment the elementary school has to the education of children and must be combined into a teachable classroom program. There are many ways to develop a teaching schedule, and it would appear that all of these various approaches to programming result in some learning on the part of children. At the same time, the kinds of insights and understandings that have developed in elementary education in the past several decades and that have been dealt with in this book seem to indicate a preference for certain approaches to designing a good day or week. What is sought, of course, is a general plan for the very broad task that the child and the teacher face that will make the very best use of the time available. This "best use" criterion includes both a concern for quality and significance in the content of learning experiences selected, and a concern over implementing these experiences in ways that are in agreement with the best that is known of the educative process itself.

Elements To Be Planned for in a Classroom Program

At least the following sorts of experiences must be planned for in a balanced classroom program; that is, time must be found weekly or daily, depending on the particular circumstances at hand, for these elements:

> 1. Time for a comprehensive and somewhat "leisurely" experience centered on some significant aspect of the social, natural, or technological environment.

2. Time for direct and systematic help in the extension and refinement of language and arithmetic skills.
3. Time for esthetic experiences, both creative and appreciative, and very broadly defined to include music, art, poetry, literature, and the dance.
4. Time for recreation and for rest and relaxation.
5. Time intermittently to participate in school-wide activities.

Following are two examples of classroom programs developed with these five points in mind, for primary and intermediate grade groups.

A Possible Plan for a Primary Group

9:00–9:15	Getting the day started (sharing and planning)
9:15–10:15	Developing the unit of work (exploring some aspect of the social, natural, or technological environment)
10:15–10:30	Recess
10:30–11:50	Time for work with language and arithmetic understanding and skill; in groups and individually (A recess period would come from about 11:15–11:25)
11:50–12:00	Preparing for lunch (some will eat at school; some will go home)
12:00–1:00	Noon hour (lunch, recreation)
1:00–1:30	Esthetic experiences of various kinds
1:30–1:50	Physical education
1:50–2:00	Preparing for dismissal (including an informal look back at the day's work in anticipation of tomorrow)
2:00	Dismissal

A Possible Plan for an Intermediate Group

9:00–9:15	Getting the day started (sharing and planning)
9:15–11:00	Developing the unit of work (exploring some aspect of the social, natural, or technological environment). A recess period would come from 10:00–10:15
11:00–11:10	Recess
11:10–11:50	Flexible time for work with language and arithmetic understanding and skill (in groups and individually)
11:50–12:00	Preparing for lunch (some will eat at school; others will go home)
12:00–1:00	Noon hour (lunch and recreation)
1:00–2:00	Additional time for work with language and arithmetic
2:00–2:30	Combined recess and physical education time
2:30–3:20	Esthetic experiences of various kinds (perhaps a class club one day a week)
3:20–3:30	Preparing for dismissal (including an informal look back at the day's work in anticipation of tomorrow)
3:30	Dismissal

Obviously, any such attempt to indicate a possible schedule for using time obscures the dynamics that are so much a part of the classroom

situation. It is impossible to call attention to all of the shifts and changes a teacher and a class may decide to make in any given week or any particular day in such an arrangement in light of the situation at hand. Periods of time normally allotted to certain kinds of experiences may become much longer or shorter during certain weeks or on given days in order to get particular jobs started or completed. Unit of work experiences, which usually come in the early part of the day, may shift to the afternoon in order to take advantage of a particular resource visitor (Mr. Brown, the city recreation leader, can leave his office at 1:30 to talk with us about plans for the new park), or a field trip (the postmaster suggests that we come about 2:00 in order to see the big pile of mail that arrives at the post office for distribution the next day). The time for esthetic experiences may shift according to the availability of facilities (we can get the all-purpose room at 11:00 this morning for our dancing), the weather (there are such beautiful clouds to sketch this morning), or the general mood of the class (let's sing for awhile; it may make us all feel a little brighter). It is our intention that this kind of flexibility be "read into" these schedules.

Maintaining balance in a changing program. It does follow that a shift in any one part of the weekly or daily anticipated work plan calls for shifts in other parts of that same day's program or in a general rearrangement of work expected to be done over the week. In our view, the teacher has a continuing responsibility to insure balance and comprehensiveness in the child's learning experience at school. Therefore, shifts and changes are made with this responsibility in mind. For instance, no matter how exciting and crucial the unit of work experience may become, it is hard to defend taking more than a given amount of time each day for it, except under very unusual conditions. When such occasions present themselves, as they will intermittently, and it seems to be important to stay with some situation for a period of time extending over several days, the teacher has a responsibility to help the class to sense what is happening to the rest of their educational diet and to project some plans beyond these immediate crucial days for bringing a semblance of balance back into the program. It must be remembered that balance is not something that must or will occur on a daily or even a weekly basis. Balance will usually emerge over a longer period of time than that. What is important is that the teacher and the class can look back over a balanced and comprehensive classroom program from time to time during the year.

Time for school-wide activities. The time that we feel is wisely invested in intermittent school-wide activities, such as programs, assemblies, school safety drives, and the like must inevitably come "out of the schedule" so to speak. Knowing ahead of time that such an activity is to

take place enables a teacher and class to plan their work accordingly. These kinds of experiences are usually rather well spaced throughout the year, and the time they take away from classroom activities brings growth dividends of a kind which justify the time involved.

But, let us take a close look at these various elements suggested for a teacher's classroom program. There is much more to them than just an allotment of time.

THE UNIT OF WORK IN THE CLASSROOM

The unit of work as a scheme for exploring problems and developing understanding in some significant aspect of the social or scientific-technological environment makes available to the classroom teacher a very useful teaching tool. Properly understood and efficiently managed, it is a most rewarding teaching experience. It makes great demands on the classroom teacher, calling for a broad general informational background, an awareness of developments on the current social scene, an understanding of and empathy for children, and broad teaching skill. But the results that follow from a well-developed unit of work are most satisfying.

In the elementary school, the units of work developed at various grade levels assume a strategic importance in the over-all scheme of things. Some refer to these unit experiences as the *core* of the elementary school program. Conceived from the point of view expressed here, they do play a central role in much that happens in a given classroom program. The sample schedules included in this chapter provide a large block of time, in both instances, for a unit of work. Some elementary school systems and some individual teachers would budget even more time for this experience.

Various Labels for Units

As a label, the phrase *unit of work* has been put on a variety of things in elementary education. Some use the phrase as a term synonymous with a given block of subject matter, and many textbooks are no longer made up of chapters but contain a list of units. Another use of the label stems from the earlier days of project teaching in connection with a learning activity that is, in the main, child originated and child consummated. Units of work have also been categorized as being *subject matter* and *experience* or *activity units,* or have been referred to as *content units* or *process units.* This first "either-or" division attempts to differentiate between units that may be highly subject-matter-centered or experience-centered in the classroom; the latter attempts a similar differentiation between the content with which the unit deals and the

learning process itself around and through which the unit takes form.[2] However, these labels are only partially meaningful and useful. In our view, all well-developed units of work are concerned with subject matter and with experiences and activities of many kinds. Similarly, the teacher is concerned about both the content and the process aspects of the developing learning enterprise. The use of such seemingly contrasting labels has grown up in attempts to call attention to matters of emphasis, or of degree, rather than of kind. It is in this sense that they may be useful as points of reference.

Defining the Unit of Work

Growing out of what has been said here, the unit of work can be defined as a series of highly related learning experiences of various kinds, all focused on some significant aspect of the social or scientific-technological environment, and having as its purpose the development of understandings, attitudes, values, appreciations, and skills that lead to modifications of behavior that are important to the children involved and to the wider society.

Selecting Units of Work for Development

Most often the elementary school teacher is able to exercise some choice over the selection of specific units to be developed in the classroom. While some school systems may still stipulate this completely, the more general tendency is to include a place for teacher determination to play its part.

School districts that follow the practice of developing a broad, general framework for the total curriculum of the elementary school usually expect the teacher to make the final determination of specific units to be developed over the year. Thus, if the general theme for the year is one of "exploring the local community" in a primary grade, the teacher is free to approach this theme in whatever way seems to make most sense to him and to his class. Specific units may eventually be developed on "supplying our community with water," or on "working in our community," and so on. Similarly, if the general theme at an intermediate grade level is one of "becoming acquainted with the development of the United States," the teacher is free to do what he will with Colonial America, the Westward Movement, and so on.

Particular school systems will not only develop a broad curriculum

---

[2] See William H. Burton, "Implications for Organization of Instruction and Instructional Adjuncts," *Learning and Instruction*, Forty-ninth Yearbook, National Society for the Study of Education (Chicago: University of Chicago Press, 1950), p. 218, for a discussion relevant to this matter.

framework, but will also develop rather extensive lists of units of work that are related to the theme at each grade level and that stand the test of general significance. In such situations the teacher may be asked to select units from the list prepared for his grade, but still there is some element of choice involved.

Selecting when there is no predetermined framework. Should a teacher find himself working in a school where there is no predetermined framework at all for the curriculum, he will need some criteria by which units of work will be selected, and some guidelines to help him in the planning that he may do by himself and with his class. In this connection a number of things readily come to mind. Such a teacher will need:

1. To make himself aware of units of work already experienced at school by the pupils with whom he will be working.
2. To know something of the general nature of the group of children that will be in his class.
3. To assure himself of the social significance of any units of work he might contemplate developing over the year.
4. To assure himself that the pupils in his class will find the units suitable to their abilities and maturational level.
5. To know something of the local community in which the school is situated and the kind of life that children there generally lead, because it might bear on the unit to be selected.
6. To consider his own background of knowledge, skill, and experience, and satisfy himself that he can now handle the contemplated unit successfully or can prepare himself to handle it.
7. To assure himself that there are sufficient material resources, such as reading materials, audio-visual aids, construction materials, and the like, in the school district and community resources to be utilized to make it possible to develop the contemplated unit efficiently and comprehensively.

Developing "supports" for unit teaching. The importance of the seven points listed immediately above and the time that it takes to follow through on them have had considerable influence on the decisions of school systems to develop both over-all framework in curriculum and lists of possible units for development within the framework.

It is important that individual units selected are appropriate for particular age levels of children involved. Along with this comes the concern for trying to insure that children experience a cumulative series of socially significant unit studies over the elementary school years. The day of the grandiose circus unit is, we hope, past, and in its place we find a real effort to select more worthwhile topics and problems for such enterprises. These are considerations that cause many school systems to develop broad curriculum designs for their total elementary school program.

Along with these concerns come some others that are quite close to the classroom teacher, and that are of great importance to the particular children involved. Earlier it was mentioned that unit teaching is demanding. This scheme calls for the use of a variety of approaches to learning, fed by a variety of instructional materials and resources. Many school systems have found that teachers, if they are to do a good job of unit teaching, need help in locating materials, in having materials made available to them, in knowing what to utilize in the community in the way of learning resources, and so on. Such assistance extends to the matter of helping teachers to broaden their own backgrounds of knowledge, skill, and experience to make possible the kind of unit teaching envisioned here.

It is out of this general "need" setting that the concept of the "resource unit" has developed. Many school districts not only list a great many possible units of work that might be brought to life in the classroom, but they furnish the teacher with a catalog, literally, of ideas for the unit, of materials found in the district and in the community that are useful in the unit, of suggestions for broadening their own backgrounds, and so on. This catalog gives the busy classroom teacher a kind of support and security in approaching the development of a new unit of work. It enables him to anticipate some of the problems that may eventually develop in the unit; it directs him to materials and resources, and to techniques and procedures for solving these problems when they do develop.

Such supporting arrangements are commendable, in our view. They are best limited, of course, to the role of source materials for possible experiences. Teachers should never be made to feel that they must actually do all, or for that matter any, of the things set down in a resource unit. But, if it can be there for the use of those teachers who want to use it as a valuable aid to teaching, it may make a significant contribution to the developing unit of work.

THE UNIT OF WORK AND THE EDUCATIVE PROCESS

As a way of organizing classroom activities, the unit of work method is more consistent with what we know about children and the learning process. Let us take a look at some of the characteristics of the unit that lead to this conclusion.

Teacher-Pupil Planning

The unit of work makes a place for a great deal of teacher-pupil planning. Children will be involved from the outset, often as a part of

the unit selection itself, as active, participating partners in developing the learning enterprise. Thus, the teacher utilizes the psychological information that describes the child as an active, goal-seeking individual who will be more likely to understand and accept learning tasks and to carry through on them with enthusiasm if he has helped to select and plan them. By doing a great deal of planning with the class the teacher is much more likely to keep the unit experience "close to the children." Although original unit selections are made with an eye to child maturity levels, they must be constantly assessed in terms of the particular children with whom the teacher is working. Some years ago, Jersild commented on the social studies curriculum thus, ". . . the problem becomes one of scaling to size the ideas and concepts that go into the social studies curriculum and of harnessing these to projects that have meaning in the everyday lives of children."[3] The task of making these ideas meaningful to children is a perennial concern, not only in the social studies but in other areas of the curriculum as well. The use of teacher-pupil planning techniques can do much to keep this concern before the classroom teacher. The teacher still preplans, of course, but all such planning has a kind of anticipatory focus and is subject to change.

Planning between teacher and pupils covers a wide variety of things related to the unit, with the teacher quite active as a guide and participant in these sessions. Theman does a good job of helping teachers to sense some aspects of their role in these sessions. She suggests that the teacher help children to remember such factors as:

> *Balance.* What else do we need to do?
> *Sequence.* What ought we do first?
> *Time.* Will we have time to do all these things today?
> *Consideration for others.* Will a work period at that time bother others?
> *Permission.* We need to have our parents' written permission to take a trip. How can that be done?
> *Course of study.* This is a topic we are required to study. . . . How and when can we include this topic in our plans?
> *Sharing opportunities.* Should we always select the boys who can do the best work with tools or should the girls be given a chance?[4]

Other questions come readily to mind. Some would be attempts to satisfy the teacher that material covered up to a certain point in the unit has been understood by the children. Thus, these planning sessions make their contribution to the teacher's effort to evaluate what has been hap-

---

[3] Arthur T. Jersild, *Child Development and the Curriculum* (New York: Bureau of Publications, Teachers College, Columbia University, 1946), p. 115.

[4] Viola Theman, *A Good School Day* (New York: Bureau of Publications, Teachers College, Columbia University, 1950), pp. 38–39.

pening. As teachers grow in skill and security with teacher-pupil planning, unit teaching improves.

No Subject Matter Barriers

Since the focus in a unit of work is on some significant aspect of the social or scientific-technological environment, the teacher's job becomes that of exploring and investigating the area as completely as possible with his class, with no restrictions as to subject matter boundaries. The advantages that are related to this are readily apparent. Whatever the unit may be—the study of a foreign culture, an analysis of the air age, or a systematic look at local community life—the teacher and the class are free to make their way through the unit in terms of the questions and concerns that come to light, utilizing organized subject matter as appropriate and necessary. This brings a kind of comprehensiveness to the learning enterprise and makes possible the sort of relatedness among the various subjects that is sought in present-day curriculum plans. Perhaps an illustration will make this advantage even clearer.

Suppose that a third grade group is developing a unit of work focused on studying the supply of water to their local community. In the process the teacher and class take a field trip to the local water purification plant to increase their understanding of the unit. Once back in the classroom, the teacher will try to exploit the experience in the interests of additional insights into the general matter under study. In a planning session, the group asks questions such as the following:

1. What is in the water that makes purification necessary before the water can be used in the community?
2. What is put into the water to make it safe for use in the community?
3. Who owns that big plant that we visited?

A little reflection, in terms of organized subject matter, will indicate that answers to the first two questions will lead the class into the natural sciences, while the third question demands attention to matters that are the province of the social sciences. Any reading done, any pictures viewed, any resource visitors utilized would of necessity be influenced by this. An approach other than the unit of work would cause the teacher and class to sort these questions out so that they would be treated in that part of the day set aside for either social studies or science and health. By using the unit of work idea, however, the class is free to follow these questions through to the answers, with no cause for concern as to the subjects that are actually being studied. This does present the teacher with an opportunity to help the class to begin to sense the differences in their questions and to increase their awareness of

and skill in using organized subject matter. Children can begin to see what natural science as a large learning area encompasses and to contrast the social studies with this. And certain specific areas within these large divisions, such as bacteriology, chemistry, economics, and civics, can begin to take on meaningful definitions, too.

One last point should be made about subject matter limitations. There would be advantages in using fewer subject matter labels for units of work, in light of the above discussion. We are prone in the elementary school to speak of social studies units and science units. Usually these labels are attached to units at the outset, in anticipation of the experiences that will follow. Often the label fits as the unit is actually developed. But, to go back to the illustration above, a label of either social studies or science would fit the unit on community water supply only on given days when particular kinds of questions and problems are being dealt with. On other days both labels would have to be used. Undoubtedly some clarity would come from simply referring to these enterprises as units of work, without the subject matter label. Then, as the experience develops in the classroom, and as the questions and problems emerge and are dealt with, a *look back* at intervals would indicate the degree to which the unit has been either a social studies experience, a science experience, or both. This might work to sensitize the teacher to certain long-term elements of balance in this aspect of his classroom program, too. Certain units may be primarily science units, others rather singly social studies experiences, while still others will deal proportionately with both. In any given school year children must be assured such a balanced experience, and "looking back" may help to insure this.[5]

A Dynamic Concept of Method

It is in the area of method that the unit of work is both most demanding on the teacher and most rewarding in terms of results. The central focus is on problem solving, with most of the dynamics that carry the unit forward coming from the children themselves. The teacher plays a decisive role in all of this, of course. Let us consider this directly here.

Related to drives present in children. The basic methodology that is part and parcel of unit teaching relies heavily on the drives exhibited by children for much of its form. From psychology we know that children have strong inclinations to find things out, to create, to experiment, to build, to dramatize, and to feel the security that comes from knowing.

---

[5] For other comments on this see G. Wesley Sowards, "Units of Work in Elementary Schools: Observations and Comments," *Teachers College Record*, May, 1955, pp. 435–439.

All of these can be used directly in the approach that the teacher takes to develop the unit of work, step by step, with his class.

Focused on problem solving. The central focus in developing the learning sequence in the unit is on problem solving. The teacher's role is that of helping the class to be explicit about concerns they have that should be resolved and questions they have that need to be answered in relation to the general theme of the unit at hand. And, of course, the teacher's role extends to making available to the class or arranging with the class the particular learning experiences that are necessary to follow through on these identified interests, concerns, and questions. It is anticipated that as particular interests, concerns and questions are dealt with in the classroom they will lead to the identification of still others and that this process will repeat itself until the area of the social or natural environment on which the unit is focused has been completely explored. The process can be illustrated with the following diagram:

Needs and desires	*Experiences Involved*
The expression of interest, the presence of concerns, the asking of questions, the identification of problems.	Those experiences in which the class will be involved to further the interest, resolve the concern, answer the question, or solve the problem,
which in turn develop additional interests, concerns, questions, and problems,	for which other experiences must be made available to the class.
And so on	And so on

Or, if one could image a second grade class studying the postal system in their community, the following sequence might develop in the form suggested above as a part of the unit:

Desires, Questions, Concerns, Problems	*Experiences Provided*
To find out about the job of the postman	Reading an informational story that tells about the work of the postman
	Interviewing the postman who comes to the school
	Getting permission for the class to sort and deliver the mail received at the school
	Deciding to write letters to friends in other grades

To know how to write a letter and address an envelope	Studying a model letter that the teacher has prepared on a chart
	Studying a model addressed envelope that the teacher has prepared
	Discussing the importance of accurate addresses on envelopes
	Learning about the "dead letter" office
To know something about postal rates	Reading about first class, second class, air mail, etc.
	Examining samples of these different types of mail
	Establishing the relationship between the weight of a letter and the cost of mailing it
	Relating stamps to classes of mail; reading about regular and special issue stamps
To know more about special types of mail service	Listening to or reading teacher prepared stories about registered letters, parcel post, special delivery, C.O.D., money orders
	Discussing the use of these various types of mail service and situations in which they would probably be used
To know more about special jobs in the post office	Discussing jobs that they know about in the post office
	Viewing a film that calls attention to a variety of jobs in a city post office
	Visiting the local post office to find out about special jobs there

Or, perhaps a sixth grade class studying something of the air age and the impact of air travel in the world today might spend a portion of their unit time as follows:

Desires, Questions, Concerns, Problems	*Experiences Provided*
To find out why the newest airplanes do not need propellers	Discussing the use of engines in airplanes
	Determining the properties of air that make aviation possible
	Looking at a wing diagram showing how the shape of the wing affects the passage of air over it
	Looking at a chart that shows the four forces acting on a plane
	Reading an informational story: *Airflight,* which discusses the function of the propeller, among other things
	Looking at a diagram of a jet engine, showing the lines of thrust exerted by it
	Viewing a film that discusses jet propulsion
	Discussing their findings in relation to their questions

To know more about man's early attempts to fly	Reading certain mythological tales of man's early attempts to fly
	Painting pictures of what they think those early attempts may have looked like
	Viewing pictures of some of the earliest successful heavier-than-air craft
	Learning the difference between lighter-than-air and heavier-than-air craft
	Becoming aware of man's early attempt to fly with balloons
To make a timeline of the history of man's successes with flying	Reading to find accounts of famous flights of the past
	Writing reports (each student one flight) of these most famous flights
	Deciding to make both a timeline and a world flight map showing certain historical achievements
	Viewing a bulletin board, prepared by the teacher, of pictures of early famous planes and flyers
	Reading about and discussing the Wright brothers
	Planning to visit a nearby museum where an old plane is exhibited

At times, of course, the next general area of concern in the unit will not readily emerge simply from the dynamics of the situation. The class will reach a "dead end" in the questions and concerns they can express. At these times the teacher must make a careful assessment of the development of the unit of work up to this time, determining whether or not there are still significant areas within it that ought to be made known to the class. If there are, the teacher will make plans for a kind of "priming" experience that may provide the momentum needed to help the class to take this next step. This might be a special field trip, a carefully chosen resource visitor, some printed material that the teacher shares with the class, or an exhibit of pictures and artifacts. It will be carefully chosen with an eye to the kinds of questions the teacher would like the class to raise concerning the undeveloped portions of the unit at hand. If it is deemed important enough, and the questions do not come from the class, the teacher will suggest some key questions himself in an attempt to move the unit along.

The teacher's assessment of the situation, as the process begins to be sluggish and mechanical, may lead to the conclusion that the unit had best be terminated. It may indicate that the class has really become aware of most of the significant aspects of the area and that to force it beyond this point is neither wise nor efficient. If this be the case, steps will be

taken to plan for the culmination[6] of the unit, and the teacher will begin to anticipate the next unit that will be treated in the program.

Structured around four types of activities. An analysis of the experiences that take place in the classroom during the course of the development of a unit of work will indicate that the teacher tries to provide time and opportunity for four types of activities:

1. The development of *research skills*—opportunities to consult a wide range of materials, such as books, maps, charts, graphs, motion pictures, encyclopedias, people, places, and so on to gather the information needed to handle the questions and concerns that arise in the unit of work. Along with this, of course, comes attention to the development of skills and techniques for using these various sources, for organizing material from them, for making judgments concerning the accuracy and authoritativeness of the material, and so on.

2. The development of *problem solving skills*—opportunities to come face to face with problems that are real and important to the children in the class and that are significant in terms of the unit being developed. The intent is not only to realize some gain in the unit from the end product of the problem solving undertaken but also to grow in the ability to sense a problem, to bring past experiences to bear on it, to gather and apply new evidence to it, to test various satisfactory solutions to the problem in the process, and finally to select the most appropriate solution or response that leaves the children ready to face a new problem situation.

3. Opportunities to *dramatize*—Play is a serious business to children, seldom recognized as such by adults. But, teachers use a technique most often referred to as *dramatic play* in developing units of work, which gives children an opportunity to explore an area of human experience by reliving a past happening or simply re-creating a current situation. Under teacher guidance they bring to bear the understanding and insights they have as they dramatize the situation. They may use costumes and props to make their dramatic play more realistic, but their actions are improvised out of their fund of information related to the situation, and they are limited accordingly in what they are able to do. Dissatisfaction with dramatic play can lead, obviously, to discussion, research, and so on in the unit. Too few teachers sense the value of this technique.

4. Opportunities to *construct and to process*—Capitalizing again on the desire of children to construct, and to process raw materials into various finished products, the teacher will provide opportunities for children to make and build things that are needed in the unit as it is developing. Not only do the children gain things for use in the unit; they also gain in opportunities for problem solving, for making plans, for following through on them, for evaluating along the way

---

[6] In discussing units of work, the terms *initiation, development,* and *culmination* are usually used to refer to the beginning, the major portion, and the termination of the unit respectively.

as well as at the point of completion. Too, they gain in general insight and understanding of the ways in which man processes raw materials of many kinds in the satisfaction of his basic needs.[7]

Together these four types of activities indicate the large areas into which the many experiences and approaches to learning in the unit group themselves.

Related to democratic group living. There are two virtues of the unit of work approach to learning that make it a desirable experience in relation to the larger concern to provide experiences at school in democratic group living. One of these is that the unit of work is a cooperative venture in learning, with both individual and group achievements contributing to the final success of the unit. The other is that individual differences among children can be used to promote the success of the venture, helping children to assess this phenomenon in society more realistically.

The unit of work is adaptable to both individual and small group work. Opportunity to observe the development of the unit of work experience in a classroom over a period of a few weeks would show the way in which this learning enterprise is, first and foremost, a total group experience. This is something that the class is experiencing, contributing to, and learning from. This same opportunity to observe would show also, however, that the large group finds it necessary and wise to delegate certain tasks from time to time to either small work groups or to individuals. Responsibilities of various kinds are assumed, in the interests of the total group enterprise, by these small work groups or by individual children, and the fruits of their labors then contribute to the progress of the total unit of work. Thus, in the classroom the children can participate in a learning experience that reflects many of the dynamics of democratic living. The tenet of democracy related to ''the cooperative solution of common problems'' becomes a reality in this learning venture. Democratic insights and skills of important kinds can be developed in the process.

The unit of work is adaptable to individual differences. Related to the above point is the possibility the unit of work presents to turn the matter of individual differences in the group into a valuable asset rather than a classroom liability. With the utilization of so many avenues to learning in the unit, differences in aptitude and interest become a valuable resource for the full development of the unit. Children who have interests and strengths of particular kinds can usually find a place and a way of contributing to the progress of the enterprise. Things must be

---

[7] See Lavone A. Hanna, Gladys L. Potter, and Neva Hagaman, *Unit Teaching in the Elementary School* (New York: Rinehart and Company, Inc., 1955), chapters 7, 8, 9, and 10, for excellent detailed discussions of these four types of activities.

built, reports must be prepared, murals must be designed and completed, discussions must be led, and so on. In each instance there are children who are able to do these things with ease and security.

At the same time, of course, the teacher is anxious that all have a chance to construct, and to dramatize, and to read and report, and to participate in other ways in the enterprise. For this reason, he will make sure (1) that his shelves hold a wide range of reading materials, all useful in the unit but some more simply written than others, (2) that construction tasks range from simple to complex so that all may find an opportunity to participate at the level their skill will allow, and (3) that roles in dramatic play are assigned thoughtfully and in the best interests of the children participating as well as in the interests of the success of the play session.

A child is more likely to be realistic about the variations in his ability and aptitude, and more willing to work to strengthen areas where progress might reasonably be made if he has at the same time areas in which he realizes that his contribution to the unit's success is an important and vital one. Similarly, the group will assess its "differences" in a somewhat different light. This is not unlike the elements of "individual worth and mutual respect" that are found, again, in democracy. Thus, the teacher who can see the positive side to the individual differences factor will find in the unit approach a challenging but rewarding opportunity to deal with it.

Protecting the Integrity of the Unit

Finally, some comments are in order with respect to protecting the integrity of the unit of work in the classroom. While some would contend that the unit, properly conceived, can encompass the full day of teaching and learning at school, we tend to doubt the wisdom of attaching quite so much comprehensiveness to it. We do feel that the unit must have a considerable block of time assigned to it out of the classroom program. The learning that takes place within it needs to be developed as thoroughly as possible, and, as mentioned earlier, may profitably be characterized as "leisurely" learning. That is, there must be time to think, to reason, to contemplate, to experiment, to plan, to evaluate, and so on. Too, we have noted that good unit teaching knows no subject matter barriers in its emergence in the classroom. The questions and problems that will develop in the unit, and the nature of the learning experiences that will appropriately follow from them, will cut across the whole of the school experience. As a scheme for learning, the unit approach truly puts organized subject matter in a resource role in the classroom. Language and arithmetic skills of various kinds will inevi-

tably need to be used in the experiences developing within the unit. Attempts to express one's thoughts and feelings concerning the unit, or to appreciate fully some aspects of it, will call for the utilization of art and music of various kinds in various ways. But, it is to be remembered that all of this takes place within a sharply focused unit of work and as direct means of making that particular learning venture more successful.

Thus, a part of the teacher's responsibility, as we see it, is to protect the integrity of the unit experience by not trying to make it the carrier of all learnings that are vital and important for children at school. True situations of use will emerge all of the time in the unit in which language will function as the strategic individual and social tool that it is. Quantitative situations will be met from time to time in the unit, and out of these children will have a chance to use much of the arithmetic they are being asked to learn and to see the number system as an important social invention. For the teacher to decide to teach all of his language and arithmetic within the unit of work is too often to destroy the setting that provides the dynamics of good unit teaching. The unit becomes strained and artificial as attempts are made to get this or that into it, and many of the values of unit teaching are lost. In fact, the teacher will have his hands full keeping the unit focused as it is. Such an experience will usually cause children to think of many interesting things and to raise a variety of provocative questions. The teacher will do well to keep the class from being led down too many byways in the process. Again, Burton, in writing on the introduction of certain subject matter into the unit on logical grounds or activities only superficially related to the real purposes of the unit, comments as follows:

> The point here is that, regardless of whether the local emphasis is upon subject matter or upon the experiences of the learner, only subject matter and experiences should be included with an instructional organization which relate to and support the central purpose, thus enhancing the integration within the learner.[8]

The classroom programs presented in this chapter, then, reserve time for other sorts of learning experiences, too.

TIME FOR TEACHING THE SKILLS

To develop understanding and proficiency in the areas of language and arithmetic skill remain as primary goals for the elementary school years. Classroom teachers will need to reserve time in their weekly and daily programs for this. Time so reserved will make possible direct and

---

[8] Burton, *op. cit.*, p. 222.

systematic attention to the progress that children are making in these areas and to the provision of needed learning experiences to further extend and refine their developing skills. We have already committed ourselves to the proposition that the unit experience, in and of itself, will not provide sufficient opportunity to do this, even though it will provide a very functional setting in which these skills may be used and practiced. Perhaps an additional word on the relationship between the time set aside for work on language and arithmetic skills and the unit experience is in order.

There will be many occasions, as mentioned above, to use language and arithmetic skills in the unit of work setting. Most often this will be a matter of "practicing" skills already developed to some point. At other times attempts to use the various language skills and arithmetic skill will cause individual children or the class to become aware of their deficiencies in the skills that they need to be able to use. For instance, a unit of work centered on the postal service in the second grade can be developed so as to provide many opportunities to practice simple addition and subtraction in relation to the sale and use of various kinds of stamps. Or, in settings ranging from the development of simple experience reading charts in the first grade to the preparation of research reports in the sixth grade, the unit experience will provide motivation and situations in which developing language skills can be used. In the process more meaningful reasons for working on these skills in the first place emerge in children's minds.

When attempts to use supposedly already learned skills show weaknesses, the teacher may move in a number of directions. It may be that he will decide to devote a day or more of the "skills" period to review and further work on some language or arithmetic skill. If the weakness appears to be a class-wide one, he may involve the whole class in the work. If only some of the class need the review and practice it will be limited to them, with the others doing something else. The teacher may decide to devote some of the unit of work time to a review of the skill, seeing the ability to apply this skill in a particular "situation of use" as being of central importance to the developing unit itself. Thus the skill may best be reviewed in that setting. At a time in a unit when the class will be involved with maps for a period of time, and the teacher finds necessary a review on the use of the ruler in measuring map distances, he may decide to take time in the unit for this review. Or, if in the sort of unit mentioned earlier on investigating the supplying of water to the community, it becomes important to add numbers consisting of several digits in conjunction with the consumption of water, with perhaps a review of carrying involved, the teacher may decide to do this within the structure of the unit.

Finally, the unit experience may develop to a point where language or arithmetic skill is needed of a kind which the teacher decides is not appropriate for teaching to the class at this time. In such a case, he may explain the matter to a degree, demonstrate it before the class, and then do the job himself that has to be done to move the unit along. The skill involved would be met later by the class in a different context for the actual teaching and learning of it. Again, this can be illustrated in relation to the community water supply study. A part of the work of the class that is concerned with the consumption of water may call for the reading of very large numbers. This may be something that the teacher decides is not really appropriate for his class to spend much time on right now. Therefore, he will read the large numbers to the class, and will discuss them with the class sufficiently to help them to grasp the general meaning and significance that must be derived from the information. Other more systematic attention to numbers into the hundreds of thousands or millions will come at a later time, perhaps at another grade level.

In the meantime, in our view, the teacher will be developing rather separate and distinct instructional programs in these skill areas apart from the unit of work completely. All children will be seen as having an "advancing front" in these skill areas, along which there will be a place and need for direct, systematic help. In certain instances this "front" will be such that the teacher can work with the class as a unit. Often, however, this will necessitate the teacher's working with individuals or small groups of children who have particular needs or are ready for certain more advanced instruction in reading, written expression, or arithmetic. In this connection, there will be times when the particular learning task developing within the skills period will coincide with a need to do something in the unit of work. In these instances, an aspect of the unit experience will be "highlighted" to enable the teacher to exploit this situation as much as possible. It is not assumed that this will happen in any consistent or continuing way, but when it does, it should be used. Note that this is a matter of spotlighting a particular point in the unit in the interests of the skill learning that is going on in the classroom, rather than the other way around.

TIME FOR ESTHETIC EXPERIENCES

In much the same fashion, we feel that it is important for the teacher to provide time for esthetic experiences that are completely removed from the unit of work experience. Again, we have noted that the arts, broadly defined, are to be used by teacher and children to enhance the study tak-

ing place in the unit in whatever manner or means appears to be appropriate. But, we would not like to see the use of the arts restricted to this role. This has been made clear in an earlier chapter that dealt with esthetic experiences in the curriculum. (See Chapter 15.) To implement the policy endorsed here calls for time in the daily and weekly program for such opportunities. We want children to read and enjoy poetry at times for the values that may come purely from the experience, not because it will help them to understand the unit. We want children to be invited to sketch clouds on a beautiful day apart from a unit focused on weather. We want children to sing and dance apart from using these activities to help them to understand some given period in American history. Esthetic experiences, both creative and appreciative, can be justified on many counts that relate to the direct contribution that they make to the developing child in addition to the use that may be made of them in a unit of work. This calls for time, and we would commit time to it.

Teachers will get some cues for the type of esthetic experience that may be most appropriate at given times from the unit. If the unit experience has been such as to motivate the class to do a great deal of drawing and painting, it may well be that a poetry reading session is in order for that week. Or, if the unit has utilized songs and dances to help children to "feel" a given culture, or a past happening, it may be a good time to work with some art media during the week. As in other matters, the teacher's professional judgment will be most important here. What is sought is obvious—ample time and opportunity for children to have esthetic experiences in light of their direct contribution to human development.

TIME FOR REST, RELAXATION, AND RECREATION

Little need be said about the provision for opportunities for rest, relaxation, and recreation during the school day. This is time that must be taken, and it is time well invested. There is one thing related to this that might be mentioned here, however. Our arrangements for operating elementary schools cause these periods of time to fall at very regular, predetermined time intervals. This regularity is often necessary to assure the proper sharing of playground and other facilities around the school, and in most instances this kind of schedule takes care of the time need being discussed here very well. There are occasions, however, when the need for rest and relaxation does not appear "by the clock." To the degree that the local situation permits, it is often wise to commit time to this need at points other than those that the fixed time schedule would allow. In some instances this will constitute an extra use of time in a

given day over and above these scheduled breaks, in others it may mean taking time for rest and relaxation when it is needed and ignoring one or more of the other scheduled periods during the day. This kind of flexibility is not always possible, but sometimes it is, and it should be used.

SUMMER SCHOOLS: AN EXTENSION OF TIME

One of the fastest growing new developments in elementary schools in the past few years is the establishment of summer school programs for children. This is an extension of time, beyond the earlier noted 180 days of schooling, to help the elementary school meet better the educational needs of all children. In some communities the summer school has been common for a number of years, with programs usually designed for children needing remedial help of some kind in their school work. But the practice of conducting summer schools on such a wide scale is something new, and the programs themselves are being broadened to offer educational opportunities for a wide range of children. In some instances the major effort is focused on providing enriching experiences for superior children, along with continuing remedial classes, but in many communities the programs are being opened up to any child desiring to avail himself of the opportunity.

These summer school programs run for varying numbers of weeks, with few operating for less than four weeks and some extending to as long as ten weeks. The daily schedule is usually something less than the typical full school day. Most often children attend in the morning or afternoon only, and two different groups of children are able to register accordingly in some districts. In many of the communities that sponsor them, these summer school programs are not yet a recognized part of public school education in the financial sense. Many charge tuition for the privilege of enrolling, while others assess a minimal registration fee to help defray certain costs in the program.

We see this as a significant development in elementary school education. In contrast to the usual cartoon approach to children's use of time in the summer vacation period, a great many children are actually bored very soon from the lack of intellectual stimulation and personal associations that they enjoy at school. It seems unwise literally to lock up the school buildings and grounds that the community has at its disposal for the total summer period. While children undoubtedly need and deserve a "vacation" from the regular routine of school for a part of the year, and should have an opportunity to enjoy the out-of-doors in the summer and to participate in the kinds of activities that only sum-

mer weather allows, some sort of experience at school for a part of the long summer months would in all probability prove to be welcome and beneficial.

As this growth of summer school programs becomes a more general thing in elementary school education it will bring with it, obviously, an extension of time for learning. As a development it seems to us to be inevitable, and it behooves elementary school educators everywhere to begin to anticipate this, to consider the possibilities in it, to weigh the experiences of others with such programs, and to be ready to move in their community when the possibility presents itself.[9]

REFERENCES

Almy, Millie. "Are They Too Young for Problem Solving?" *Progressive Education* 27:143–148. March 1950.
>An excellent statement on the general concern for improving the class... The ideas expressed here have implications for the unit of work approach to organizing for learning.

Association for Supervision and Curriculum Development. *Creating a Good Environment for Learning.* Washington, D.C.: National Education Association, 1954.
>An excellent statement on the general concern for improving the classroom environment as an aid to learning.

——————. *Toward Better Teaching.* Washington, D.C.: National Education Association, 1949.
>Chapters 3 and 4 are especially relevant to the matter of allotment of time.

Baxter, Bernice, Gertrude Lewis, and Gertrude Cross. *The Role of Elementary Education.* Boston: D. C. Heath and Company, 1952.
>Part Four describes different programs at various levels of childhood education, pointing up the ways time is used at each level.

Department of Supervisors and Directors of Instruction. *Newer Instructional Practices of Promise* (Twelfth Yearbook). Washington, D.C.: National Education Association, 1939.
>Chapter 7 discusses the use of time for such activities as dramatic play and dramatizations in the classroom.

Department of Supervision and Curriculum Development. *Group Planning in Education.* Washington, D.C.: The Department, 1945.
>Relates group planning to the general development of democratic social behavior.

Hanna, Lavone A., Gladys L. Potter, and Neva Hagaman. *Unit Teaching in the Elementary School.* New York: Rinehart and Company, 1955.
>A most comprehensive discussion of the unit of work in the use of time in the elementary school classroom.

---

[9] For some information on summer schools, see National Education Association, Research Division and American Association of School Administrators, *Summer School Programs in Urban School Districts,* Educational Research Service Circular No. 7 (Washington, D.C.: The Association, 1959).

Horn, Ernest. *Methods of Instruction in the Social Studies.* New York: Charles Scribner's Sons, 1937.

> Pages 413–440 provide an excellent discussion of the use to which time for construction activities can be put.

Kyte, George C. *The Elementary School Teacher at Work.* New York: Henry Holt and Company, 1957.

> Chapter 13 discusses the planning of classroom procedures, including the initial planning made by the teacher and the cooperative planning for the use of time between teacher and pupils.

20

UTILIZING EVALUATION: DETERMINING PROGRESS TOWARD GOALS

The effective teacher knows organized subject matter and the means by which content is utilized in attaining educational objectives; he understands children; he maintains rapport with his colleagues and parents; he plans and organizes his work well. But teaching is incomplete without a conscious and objective evaluation that demonstrates the extent to which goals have been achieved. Responsibility for continuous evaluation is therefore a final consideration of the teaching role.

THE FUNCTION OF EVALUATION

Defining Evaluation

Evaluation, in modern education, is a term that carries the broadest meaning. General agreement exists in the matter of breadth, but different authorities place different emphases upon certain aspects of evaluation and their definitions of the term differ accordingly. A review of some definitions found in the literature on evaluation will help us understand the broad significance of the term.

Shane and McSwain point out five interpretations of the word *evaluation,* concluding that

> ... evaluation is not limited to the application of value to a problem. Neither is it merely a synonym for measurement, a means of gauging

good teaching, a way of appraising curricular practices, or a procedure in studying human behavior. Rather, evaluation is a comprehensive process of which any or all of these variations may be components.[1]

Ahmann and Glock, on the other hand, emphasize the value connotation in evaluation when they define it as:

> ...not only measuring or in some way identifying the degree to which a pupil possesses a trait or the degree to which a pupil's behavior may have been modified as a result of an educational experience, but also judging the desirability and adequacy of these findings.[2]

Morgan implies continuous involvement when he says:

> [Evaluation] includes the close scrutiny of present adequacies and possibilities for the future as well as shortcomings, and involves the continuing consideration of where a student is, what he is like and why, where he is trying to go, and how education can serve him.[3]

Among teachers, too, we may find variation in definition and emphasis. To some teachers, the periodic testing program carried on in the school is the major evaluating activity. To other teachers, evaluation is more than testing; it includes other means of collecting data, interpretation, and reporting pupil progress to parents. To a supervisor or administrator, evaluation may include the examination of school curriculum, and the means of determining the most effective methods of "teaching" it, as well as the appraisal of individual teacher competency.

For the purposes of this book, *we shall consider evaluation in elementary school education as a broad, continuous program involving a carefully ordered inquiry to determine effectiveness of educational content and process, in the light of goals that are clearly defined and that are used as a basis for appraisal.* The evaluation principles implicit in this definition are applicable to all levels of school effort. At the state level, the district level, and the single elementary school level, evaluation is as important as it is at the individual classroom level. Even for the classroom, levels may be delineated to the learner's level, the parents' level, and the community level. Direct references in this chapter may be made to evaluations in the total school or in the school system, but our major emphasis is upon the work of the teacher as he evaluates the effectiveness of the classroom program.

---

[1] Harold G. Shane and E. T. McSwain, *Evaluation and the Elementary Curriculum* (New York: Holt, Rinehart and Winston, Inc., 1958), p. 60.

[2] Stanley J. Ahmann and Marvin D. Glock, *Evaluating Pupil Growth* (Boston: Allyn and Bacon, 1958), p. 6.

[3] H. Gerthon Morgan, "What Is Effective Evaluation?" *National Education Association Journal* 48:15–17, November 1959.

In this need to evaluate activities, teachers are no different from any other group of workers. Both machinists and businessmen, for example, have devised means for determining whether or not their work is effective. The machinist measures to minute dimensions the accuracy of his product as it is formed and checks the final performance against earlier agreed-upon specifications. The business executive checks costs, sales, stock markets, and public opinion to appraise and judge the work of his company. So schools and teachers seek means appropriate to their work that will help them to evaluate their products in terms of accepted educational purposes.

Characteristics of Evaluation

The various connotations of evaluation and the flexibility of our definition suggest the following characteristics for the classroom evaluation program in the elementary school.

1. *Evaluation is a complex process.* Evaluation takes place for all aspects of the individual child's personality and academic achievement, as considered in relation to himself and to group progress, to personal and social expectations, and to the many varieties of situations that arise in the classroom and the school environment. Complexity exists in these diverse relationships. Many intangibles are involved in the learnings considered important for the child today, especially those that go beyond the strict confines of subject matter. Furthermore, the many interpretations that can be made of a single type of behavior add to the complexity of the task.

2. *Evaluation is an integral part of all educational activity.* Education is a continuous life activity, and evaluation is accepted as an essential and interrelated aspect of the teaching-learning process. Effective evaluation is ongoing, constant, and continuous. It is not a terminal activity, and it is more than sporadic testing at nine- or twelve-week intervals. As an integral portion of teaching and learning, all means of evaluation become helpful, supportive instruments for determining change of behavior or growth, and for lending direction to future experiences. In this light it is especially helpful to evaluate early in the learning activities.

3. *Teaching effectiveness is best determined by appraisal of growth as related to goals set in the individual situation.* Clearly defined goals formulated for each group and in each learning situation help the evaluator determine the progress made toward achieving them, and indicate improvement, strengths, and weaknesses, and next steps in the learning process. New goals may be indicated through evaluation, and daily lessons as well as long-term plans are also influenced. Learner, teacher,

parents, and school staff are all related to the situation directly or indirectly and are involved in formulating the goals, interpreting them,
and accepting them. A national norm, unrelated to a specific situation,
is not alone an adequate goal for evaluation, nor are judgments that
indicate status or interpersonal comparisons enough to determine growth.

4. *The total personality and all aspects of individual development and
behavior are evaluated.* Not only mental or verbal progress, but social,
physical, and emotional growth are important in the broad and complex
evaluative process. Achievement in creative thinking, personal talents
and interests, readiness, social competence, and esthetic development need
to be judged in terms of growth and acceptable performance. Individuality and integrity are encouraged and preserved; optimum development
of all potentials is considered.

5. *Many tools and procedures and many types of evidence are utilized
in the evaluative process.* Standardized and teacher-made tests, self-rat-
ing scales and inventories, sociometric techniques, cumulative records,
anecdotal records, conferences, written work, check lists, oral performances, informal conversations, observation techniques, questionnaires, and
similar tools are the data-collecting devices. Evidence of all kinds and
appropriate to all phases of learning are necessary. For this, testing
instruments are increasingly valid and reliable, but other standardized
and teacher-produced instruments are being used with professional care
that makes them practical and increasingly helpful. Some devices, like
anecdotal records or observations, yield descriptive evidence; others,
like standardized tests, yield quantitative results. Real understanding
of the limitations and advantages of both are essential to intelligent
evaluation.

6. *Evaluation means not only appraising, judging, diagnosing, but
also determining whether the results are adequate and desirable.* Because
"adequate" and "desirable" are value judgments, the terms may mean
different things to different societies, regions, teachers, and individuals
of a classroom. Growth, development, adjustment, or any other behavioral
change is "good" or "bad" in terms of individual ability and social
acceptability, or whether it coincides with the aspirations and desires of
the teacher, the child, the parents, the community. Effective evaluation
will determine not only the quantity of change, but also the quality.

7. *After individual accomplishment or the effectiveness of content and
progress is determined, something more follows.* Evaluation is not an
end in itself. Follow-up is an evolving and contributory factor that makes
evaluation complete and instruction constantly improving. Collected
data may become the basis for reports to parents, remedial procedures,
or new experiences. Information gleaned from evaluative efforts influences teachers to continue or to modify their personal behavior, their

use of methods, their use of materials, and their selection of content. Evaluation is the fundamental tool for estimating effectiveness and for indicating needed and appropriate changes. In such a program, teacher attitudes can be neither fearful, blind, nor overconfident. Evaluation is perceived as a means of gathering supplementary evidence that will support and reaffirm, give direction to, or help to make more effective the teacher's own knowledge of curriculum, methods, and the needs of the children as individuals and as members of a group.

8. *The evaluation process is not completed by the teacher alone; cooperative efforts by many participants are indicated.* Primary responsibility for evaluation of teaching-learning activities lies with teachers, children, and parents. The teacher, as director of learning, guides the setting of goals and provides opportunities for assessing the measure of their achievement. Children assume responsibility for conscious definition of their own goals and self-evaluation of their work. Parents are also involved in cooperative goal-setting and the sharing of evaluative information. Others such as the principal and special teachers may contribute to the evaluation process.

Educational Goals as the Basis for Evaluation

Goals need interpretation. When setting up objectives against which behavior can be evaluated, elementary educators are constantly challenged by interpretation of the over-all goals of American education. (See Chapter 3.) An objective such as "to develop democratic behavior" is too broad, too abstract to be used for appraisal. One must interpret "democratic," define the kinds of behavior, and estimate the level of development. McKim, Hansen, and Carter outline this three-fold function of goal interpretation when they say:

> ...to evaluate the progress of your pupils with some feeling of security, you must be able to combine, on a practical level, your best insights from three major areas: what you understand to be the over-all objectives of education in general and of your school system in particular; what you understand these objectives to mean for pupils of the maturity levels of those whom you are teaching; and what you believe to be appropriate adjustments of your general standards in the light of strengths and weaknesses of individuals.[4]

Broad, general educational goals need to be specifically translated or defined in respect to behavioral expectations. Once a teacher understands his own philosophical commitment in education, then appropriate interpretation and translations of goals emerge naturally.

---

[4] Margaret G. McKim, Carl W. Hansen, and William L. Carter, *Learning to Teach in the Elementary School* (New York: The Macmillan Company, 1959), pp. 422–423.

As the teacher seeks to satisfy his responsibilities to children, parents, and the community, his interpretation of educational goals will include three kinds of learning: knowledge and understandings, attitudes and values, and skills and abilities, all three of which are interrelated with the intellectual maturity, social competence, emotional stability, and physical well-being of individual pupils and of the classroom group.

Goals are expressed in behavioral terms. How can a teacher effectively evaluate the interrelationships that are necessary to everyday life? Intangibles such as open-mindedness, ability to meet quantitative situations, and getting along with age-mates can be appraised when demonstrations of attitudes, habits, and appreciations, or a child's behavior, are specifically defined. Such objective definition takes time and involves careful consideration and clear thinking to include knowledge, skills, and attitudes in the light of intellectual, social, emotional, and physical development.

Michaelis lists some objectives for social attitudes that contain aspects of physical, emotional, and intellectual knowledge and skills.

> Individuals who are open-minded in group work:
> 1. Entertain and think about, explore, and use new ideas.
> 2. Sense and state genuine problems or needs.
> 3. Accept help and suggestions and use improved ways of doing things.
> 4. Have confidence in their own abilities, yet recognize their own shortcomings.
> 5. Base judgment on all pertinent facts and test validity of conclusions.
> 6. Investigate all sources of information and withhold conclusions until sufficient facts are available.
> 7. Hold conclusions tentatively, always keeping an open mind.
> 8. Have courage to attack new problems and to begin again if they fail.
> 9. Gain insight into emotion as a factor in making decisions and forming opinions.
> 10. Evaluate group and individual action in order to improve group processes.[5]

A group of objectives helping a teacher to evaluate the child's understanding and use of the number system and to meet quantitative situations in a primary unit on the home and neighborhood might be the ability to:

> 1. Make simple change.
> 2. Add prices together.
> 3. Know the relations between pints and quarts, half-pints, foot, yard.
> 4. Know such terms as *buy, sell.*

---

[5] John U. Michaelis, *Social Studies for Children in a Democracy* (Englewood Cliffs, New Jersey: Prentice-Hall, Inc., 1950), p. 197.

5. Weigh and measure and to write price tags.
6. Read the calendar.
7. Calculate certain number concepts of size such as *longer, longest, high, low, smaller, larger.*
8. Know arrangements such as *up, down, over, under, right, left.*
9. Know such concepts as *square, triangle, circle, rectangle.*[6]

Behavioral expectations related to *getting along with age-mates* might well be stated in this way:

1. Acting independently yet with respect for the independent action of others.
2. Assuming a dynamic role in the group, sometimes as a leader, sometimes as a follower.
3. Demonstrating courtesy in his relationships with others.
4. Accepting cooperative rules as well as those made by one in authority.
5. Accepting graciously status situations for himself and others.
6. Commending and praising others when appropriate.
7. Working harmoniously and cooperatively in groups that have different purposes.
8. Conscientiously accepting the suggestions of others.

Problems in Evaluation

Methods of evaluation are limited. To make effective evaluation of achievement from goals, teachers may utilize one of three procedures: (1) the paper and pencil instruments or devices that reveal written evidence, (2) observational techniques through which teachers watch children, and (3) the conversational or discussion techniques in which teachers talk with and listen to children by asking questions and exploring ideas that yield verbal demonstration of growth.

Note the objectives related to arithmetic. How does a teacher determine a child's achievement toward the goals? He listens to the child use terms like *buy* or *sell* in conversational situations; he notes on written work the use of squares and circles; he watches the ability to compute; he may watch and listen to the child make simple change.

The three procedures for collecting evaluative data may be used in various combinations for one situation. For example, before assigning a written composition, the teacher may talk with a group to draw out knowledge and determine the important points to be written. During the discussion he notes the understanding of the subject exhibited by the individuals. As the children write, he may observe confusions, concentration, skill in putting down a flow of ideas, and handwriting techniques. Later, an examination of the completed written work reveals the chil-

---

[6] Modified from J. Murray Lee and Dorris May Lee, *The Child and His Curriculum* (Second edition; New York: Appleton-Century-Crofts, Inc., 1950), p. 451.

dren's ability to organize ideas and to handle knowledge in a practical and meaningful manner.

Though teachers have worked out helpful techniques for evaluating the various areas of the curriculum, they find that many objectives are not accessible, and also that it is difficult to objectify some of the behaviors that need evaluation. Educators are realizing these limitations and are joining forces to work in the direction of refining evaluation techniques and devising ever more effective means of gaining concrete evidence.

Objective versus subjective judgment. An objective evaluation requires a minimum of personal judgment on the part of the evaluator, that is, the data themselves reveal the quality of the behavior. A spelling test, for example, indicates what words the child can spell correctly and what words he cannot spell. The person scoring the test need make no judgment because the words are either "right" or "wrong." Usually, an objective evaluation device includes clear and simple instructions for use, a scoring key that indicates the correct answers, and a system for recording and translating scores.

Subjective evaluation, on the other hand, requires the evaluator to make an interpretation of the data. Though evaluation involving objective evidence is clearly the most acceptable, a careful look at methods in common use reveals that many techniques are, in fact, subjective. When a teacher determines the quality of a contribution to "share-and-tell," the kinds of questions a child asks, the depth of knowledge demonstrated when a question is answered, or the originality of an art product, the evaluation is dependent upon the personal opinion of the teacher.

Though much appraisal includes subjective analysis, educators are finding ways that help to objectify the judgment. When specific goals are formulated, such as those on open-mindedness, the teacher uses each of the goals as an objective guideline for making evaluation. He notes the frequency with which a child thinks about or uses new ideas, accepts suggestions, attacks new problems, evaluates group action. He determines the quality of action and growth the child demonstrates as he defines problems, recognizes his own abilities and limitations, and makes conclusions. Even though most of these are subjective decisions, the accumulated judgments covering all facets of open-mindedness help the teacher to make an over-all evaluation that is more objective than a decision based on impressions or a general "feeling" about the child.

A teacher's evaluation of a written report can be made more objective if he will first list the number and kind of ideas he expects, and other factors that may influence the quality of the work such as length, handwriting, spelling, and sentence structure. In reality, such guidelines are expected goals of the report; the degree to which they are achieved

determine the evaluation of the paper. Similar guidelines can be set up for almost any kind of a learning activity, from swinging a bat or dancing a folk dance, to singing a song, calculating an arithmetic problem, producing a skit, or exhibiting democratic behavior.

Evaluation involves a subjective decision in regard to follow-up. The teacher must decide, for example, if the number of words incorrectly spelled in the test indicates growth or lack of achievement for that particular student. Even on a carefully standardized test, the achievement profile stated in national norms must be subjectively evaluated by the teacher in order to determine individual growth, teaching effectiveness, and the next steps in the educative process.

In spite of the fact that classroom evaluation demands subjective decisions in many areas, it is encouraging to realize that a teacher is a professional person. The judgments he makes are the result of careful training, practical experience, and the insight of an informed person. Professional judgments are not uncontrolled, careless, or unreasonable. The teacher's evaluations are made in the light of all the data collected, all his knowledge and experience in the teaching-learning process, and his personal dedication to the professional guidance of each child.

THE INSTRUMENTS AND TECHNIQUES OF ASSESSING PUPIL GROWTH

Available for use in the elementary school evaluation program is a great variety of valid instruments and techniques. The program today probably includes more standardized tests than ever before, simply because more and better tests are available. Researchers are producing more explicit data upon which materials can be modified or produced. Commercial organizations are making available carefully prepared instruments in greater variety and of higher quality. Teachers are developing greater sophistication in the use of standardized materials and more creativity in devising effective means to evaluate classroom situations.

To distinguish between those materials made available commercially and those the teacher prepares, we will consider the two categories separately. Evaluation materials that a school may purchase through established publishing houses will be termed *commercially prepared materials*. The term *teacher-devised instruments* will refer to all the informal devices the teacher prepares specifically for local use in his own classroom.

Commercially Prepared Materials

Commercial materials include nationally standardized tests, rating scales, check lists, inventories, and various other instruments. Not all commercial materials are standardized.

Standardization. The process of standardizing an instrument of evaluation is structuring the content, administration, scoring and interpretation in such a way that the results can be compared. Standardized tests are the most familiar of the standardized instruments. These tests are prepared with empirical selection of content to assure validity and reliability. For example, after experimentally giving a test to a representative group of children, the makers of the test exclude the ambiguous questions and those questions that do not differentiate between high and low scoring individuals. Establishment of norms that provide a basis for effective comparison are then developed from median scores of the test as given to hundreds of children. Fixed procedures are also defined relative to testing instructions, time limits, and objective scoring keys that help to maintain uniformity of results.

To understand standardization even more, a few terms need definition:

Tests are tools that measure "samples of behavior and traits of individual pupils that indicate quickly and with reasonable accuracy their status at a particular time and their potential."[7]

Validity indicates whether or not a test actually measures what it intends to measure. For example, does a test of achievement in arithmetic yield an effective measure of the child's ability to compute? Validity is determined by an examination of the content, either by relating individual items to the whole content, or by relating the test score to other means of evaluation, such as specific performance. The numerical expression of validity is the correlation coefficient.

Reliability refers to the degree, accuracy, or consistency with which the test measures. In other words, would a pupil make relatively the same score if he took the test again? Reliability is determined by several methods: by comparing results of alternate forms, split halves, by retesting, or by examining all items to determine whether they measure the same thing. The numerical estimate of reliability is called the coefficient of reliability.

Norms are the arbitrary units into which the raw scores of a test are translated for practical comparison and analysis. The term is a derivative of "normal performance" and indicates the typical performance of the selected group that is used as a sample for a particular test. Because size and nature of the sample group influence the norm, publishers select as representative a group as possible of all grade or age levels. However, the norm indicates *what is,* in terms of the selected group. The norm is not a standard or *what should be* for any other group. Norms are most frequently stated in tables of grade norms, age norms, or percentile

---

[7] Denis Baron and Harold W. Bernard, *Evaluation Techniques for Classroom Teachers* (New York: McGraw-Hill Book Company, Inc., 1958), p. 1.

norms. Grade norms indicate median performance or achievement of a defined grade level. Age norms refer to typical performance of a specific chronological age group. Percentile norms refer to the percentage of cases below a point on a scale. A sixth grader's score translated as the 60 percentile means the pupil's score is higher than 60 per cent of all sixth graders taking the test.

Carefully prepared manuals of instructions are available for the tests administered by the teacher. In them will be found descriptions of the content of the test, statements of validity and reliability, information for interpreting test scores, and specific directions for giving the test. The directions must be followed to the letter, because variation will invalidate the standardized scores.

Group mental maturity tests, reading and other readiness tests, and subject matter achievement batteries are those that the regular classroom teacher is most likely to administer. Other tests used less frequently are individual diagnostic tests of various types. Most of these require a carefully trained specialist for both administration and interpretation of results.

Achievement tests. The type of test with which the elementary school teacher is most familiar is the standardized test of subject matter skill and achievement. One authority has this to say about the planning of an achievement test program:

> Standardized tests should be selected for the purpose of measuring pupil achievement towards the day-to-day objectives of classroom instruction. These objectives would not be compromised to meet the contents of a published test.... A common mistake is to utilize too many tests, to administer them sporadically during the year, and to have no specific plans for using the test results.... To enable teachers to make the best use of the test results, standardized achievement tests should be given early in the school year. This gives the instructor time to benefit from the test information in determining instructional procedures, in selecting materials, and diagnosing individual and group needs.[8]

One may select an achievement test from a great variety on the basis of purpose, emphasis, or form. Some achievement tests may emphasize skills such as reading comprehension or arithmetic computation. Other tests may emphasize knowledge as related to subject matter achievement. *Diagnostic tests*[9] are constructed to identify strengths and weaknesses

---

[8] California State Department of Education, *Evaluating Pupil Progress*, Bulletin Vol. XXI, No. 6 (Sacramento: The Department, April 1952), pp. 31–32.

[9] Definitions of specific instruments used throughout this chapter are adapted from Harry A. Greene, Albert N. Jorgensen, and J. Raymond Gerberich, *Measurement and Evaluation in the Elementary School* (New York: Longmans, Green and Company, 1953), pp. 38–60.

in the highly related abilities that underlie achievement in subjects. A promising trend is the use of more diagnostic tests in place of survey tests. *Analytic tests* are similar. *Prognostic tests* predict future success in a subject.

The achievement test commonly used in the elementary school is the *survey test*, which measures general achievement in a general subject or field. Survey batteries test several fields, such as reading, arithmetic, social studies, nature study, and language arts. One survey battery, the Iowa Tests of Basic Skills, tests five major areas: vocabulary, reading comprehension, language skills (spelling, capitalization, punctuation, usage), work-study skills (map reading, reading graphs and tables, knowledge and use of reference materials), and arithmetic skills (arithmetic concepts and arithmetic problem solving). This kind of survey produces a profile of achievement when the individual's subject matter strengths and weaknesses are plotted.

Another type of achievement test commonly used is the *readiness test*, which is constructed to determine whether or not the child has reached the maturity necessary for success in a certain subject or skill. Reading readiness or arithmetic readiness tests are frequently administered in the primary grades.

Other instruments, also commercially available, help to determine subject matter achievement. Among these are the *rating scales*, or a series of objective samples or products of differing difficulty or quality. The samples are equally spaced on a scale of values, difficulty, or quality so that children's work may be compared and the level of quality identified. Examples are in the areas of handwriting, lettering, and the arts.

It is well to remember that standardized achievement-test results for a given school become a comparison with the group upon which the norms for that test are made. This means that results in one school may be high or low depending upon the segment of population represented in that school. If the school's population differs from the "normal" group, results will be different. Rural children, bilingual children, or children from underprivileged homes may achieve poor scores merely because their experiential background is different from that of the "normal" group. A good suburban school populated by children of well-educated parents can expect to achieve higher than the norm. In other words, test results are not necessarily an indication of good or poor teaching or learning.

Intelligence tests. Another kind of standardized test commonly used in the elementary school is the intelligence test, or scholastic aptitude test, usually designed to test abstract reasoning ability. These psychological examinations have as their purpose the measurement of pupil aptitudes

by assigned tasks that are supposedly unrelated to what the pupil has learned either in or out of school. One list of abilities presumably measured by an intelligence test includes the following:

1. Memory: immediate or delayed, meaningful or rote
2. Ability to deal with verbal materials (vocabulary)
3. Ability to deal with spatial relationships or to orient the self in space
4. Ability to deal with verbal relationships (analogies, opposites)
5. Ability to deal with numerical materials either as sheer facility with numbers or as ability to reason numerically or quantitatively
6. Ability to find the guiding principle involved in tasks which may be verbal, numerical, spatial, or pictorial in nature
7. Ability to perceive essential details, make fine distinctions, and notice similarities[10]

Most intelligence tests translate raw scores into M.A., or mental age, then into I.Q., which is the ratio of M.A. to C.A. (chronological age) times 100.

Though the term *intelligence tests* implies the measurement of general intelligence, the items have not sampled the complete range of human intelligence. In truth, we are not really sure what total intelligence is; definition of the term incites controversy and many points of view. The science of psychology is still maturing, and the various factors contributing to intelligence have not yet been specifically identified. It is unfortunate that our present tests are called "intelligence tests" because, for the most part, they measure one factor: abstract verbal ability.

Intelligence tests are produced in a number of forms to better measure children with different experience backgrounds. Most of the tests are *verbal tests*, or the paper and pencil type that use words for meaning or response. Some are *nonverbal tests*, but these too may be pencil and paper tests using figures, pictures, and diagrams rather than words. *Performance tests* are nonverbal tests in which the pupil manipulates objects. *Aptitude tests* differ from general intelligence tests in that they measure "intelligence" specifically for certain areas of performance. They attempt to measure the natural traits necessary for proficiency in areas such as art, mechanics, or mathematics.

Intelligence tests are prepared for both group administration and for individual administration. Some of the individual intelligence tests such as the Stanford-Binet Scale need special skills for administering, which limit their use for teachers. When special cases occur, a teacher may arrange to have a trained person give such tests and interpret the results. Some intelligence tests are projective techniques, or unstructured tests,

---

[10] Baron and Bernard, *op. cit.*, p. 70.

utilizing a unique stimulus to produce an uninhibited "whole person-ality" response. The administration and interpretation of projective tests, such as the Rorschach Inkblot Test and the Thematic Apperception Test, are so complex that they are used only by clinical psychologists.

Though intelligence tests give fairly good predictions of academic potential, their limitations are to be seriously considered. Intelligence test scores indicate the verbal ability of a child in terms of the English language, and these tests favor children from the American, urban, mid-dle-class culture. As with achievement tests, children from rural areas, bilingual families, or underprivileged urban groups may produce low scores that reflect only their limited experience. Furthermore, mental tests do not measure motivation. Consequently, the usefulness of I.Q. scores in predicting academic success is often overemphasized. It is also im-portant that teachers remember that the I.Q. is not a measure of personal worth. In the primary grades particularly the results of an intelligence test are not as reliable as later results in a child's schooling. For these reasons, I.Q. should be used only as a guide, not as a final judgment of ability.

Personality, interest, and attitude instruments. Personality tests at-tempt to measure such intangible aspects of behavior as attitudes, inter-ests, and emotional adjustment.

Another term for personality tests is *adjustment inventories*—instru-ments that probe behavior, likes and dislikes, environment, and aspects of life in an attempt to get at emotional adjustments. *Attitudes scales* are usually two-, three-, or five-point scales stating critical issues or items upon which there are differences of opinion, and among which the pupil makes a choice. *Interest inventories* attempt to get at the degree of interest in such items as occupations, activities, reading, recreation.

In most elementary schools, teachers do not administer personality tests, but in secondary schools counselors sometimes use interest inven-tories and attitudes scales. Because these tests are still in the develop-mental and research stage, and are often of doubtful validity and re-liability, they should be used with caution.

Teacher-Devised Instruments

To make the minimum formal testing program more complete by de-vising his own means of evaluation is part of the teacher's professional responsibility. The evaluation that goes on in the classroom between the teacher and the pupils in the everyday situation is an effective, practical factor in the teaching-learning process.

Teacher-made tests. Limitations in the standardized tests lie not only in the type of norms that they yield, but in the content of the tests them-

selves. Teacher-made tests are not only flexible and readily adapted to local conditions, but they can be given more frequently, cover more limited areas of content, and serve as a diagnostic as well as a learning tool. Written tests of this sort are seldom appropriate in the primary grades, but from grades four through eight the formal teacher-made test is sometimes needed.

One point should be made about the construction of teacher-made tests. A *good* test is not easy to develop; it takes considerable time, effort, scholarship, and creativity to produce a test that will adequately measure learning beyond mere recall.

> A good test will take account of factual information; in addition, it should challenge pupils to apply these facts to new situations, to interpret data, and to perceive relationships.[11]

The so-called "objective tests" are those that involve "one correct answer" and may be scored objectively. They include test items cast as true-false, multiple choice, one word or short phrase fill-in answers, and matching format. Some of the criticisms of these tests are that chances of guessing the correct answer or of finding an answer by the process of elimination produce spurious scores. It is difficult to phrase a true-false item that is not either too obvious or misinterpreted. The fill-in type is also difficult to construct with such clear meaning that only one word or phrase is appropriate.

On the other hand, objective tests are preferred because they are scored quickly and accurately, and because many facts may be sampled. Improvement in items has resulted from the use of diagrams, charts, and other figures in multiple choice or items that require pupils to use critical thinking and develop functional relationships as they find the right answers.

Essay tests in the primary grades have not proved practical because of the children's lack of skill in written language. For older children, the essay test is encouraged by some because it permits freedom of response, and provides opportunity to organize, analyze and synthesize information. However, these skills can also be developed outside a testing situation. The major problem with the essay test occurs in the subjective judgments that must be made for scoring it.

Observation. Each new classroom group necessitates additional gathering of data, observation, study and analysis, and insights on the part of the teacher as he becomes acquainted with each individual and pervading

---

[11] Grace Graham, "Teachers Can Construct Better Achievement Tests," *Curriculum Bulletin* No. 170, Vol. 12, December 1956 (Eugene, Oregon: School of Education, University of Oregon).

"character" of the group as a whole. Though the teacher can anticipate his group from his general knowledge of children, he must cope with uniqueness of individual and group behavior that he cannot foresee. Teacher observation of child action, thought, written and oral expression, use of factual content, and development of special skills is the basis upon which insights are gained and day-to-day instruction makes progress.

Part of knowing children is watching their eyes, their expressions, their reactions to things and to people, and while watching, trying to understand their feelings. The teacher is sensitive to child behavior in every sort of situation: playing on the playground, reading in the group, listening to directions, working alone, seeking choices, expressing ideas, reacting to others, being under stress, and relaxing.

He notes immediate and sudden changes, such as the child who begins crying in school, the boy who seems ravenous at lunch, or the girl who must leave the room more often than usual during the day. He watches to see what especially pleases youngsters, or particularly absorbs them, makes them indifferent, or angers them. He observes who is friendly with whom; he notes evidence of those who assert strong leadership and those who follow in a supportive role. Every movement, sound, or expression is observed that will indicate an attitude, a feeling, or an evolving concept.

The teacher's observation gives clues to the child's personal motivation, his interests, his approach to thinking and reasoning, his individual purposes, problems, and concerns. Though observation may not at the moment include complete understanding of the situation, the recognition of deviations in behavior warns the teacher that something is amiss. For example, the child who has been making normal improvement develops a problem in reading; no other changes are immediately discernible. Haskew points out the teacher's use of such clues when he says:

> [The teacher] treats behavior as a symptom which gives a clue to background causes. He accepts and loves a child regardless of the child's actions right now. He may encourage or he may curb a child's present behavior, but he is always aware of two facts: first that it is (often) more important to find out why a child acts as he does than to control him right now; and second, that what he does to a child right now— and for that matter all the experiences a child has today—will become part of the set of causes influencing the child's behavior tomorrow. The experienced teacher knows that a child's reactions—as well as his own actions—are the end product of a complex host of causes. Behavior is caused.[12]

---

[12] Laurence D. Haskew, *This Is Teaching* (Chicago: Scott, Foresman and Company, 1956), pp. 55–56.

Because teacher evaluation and judgment may differ with every teacher and classroom, a number of considerations are reflected in professional judgments based on observation. First are the teacher's knowledge of children and learning, his experience in evaluative procedures, and his skill in observational perception. Second is his awareness of the effects of fatigue, emotion, and indifference to informal observational and judgmental techniques. Third is his frame of reference as an adult or teacher-authority, for this status situation influences what one sees. Fourth is the teacher's awareness of the fact that he may be conscious of only part of the total action of an incident in behavior, or not understand the total effort or experience behind a behavior. Fifth, in an observational situation it is important that the teacher do more listening and watching than talking.

Class response. Further evidences of growth can be found through observation and evaluation of children's interpersonal reactions and responses to the total class situation. Children may attract, reject, or neglect each other, though with young children the relationships are not always consistent. Increasing maturity is reflected in the way children respond in class discussions, in group evaluations, and in informal play.

A part of "good" class response is the ability of the individual to work effectively both alone and with others. The teacher recognizes increasing ability to follow directions, begin work with little waste of time, solve problems independently, work without disturbing others, complete a task efficiently, help others when necessary, and recognize the need to seek help of others.

While noting each individual's responses in the group situation, the teacher is asking himself questions that will help determine the guidance of child growth. Is the child using an increasingly larger vocabulary? Is his oral expression constantly clearer, more meaningful to the situation, more insightful? Are bodily poise, facial expressions, and gestures more mature and expressive? Are questions asked indicative of intelligent and reasonable reaction? Are questions appropriate, clearly related to the idea being considered? Are the children able to stay on the topic, and through questions, answers, and reactions develop the thesis of the subject at hand? Is leadership evidenced, and if so, is it shared? Do varying situations provide leadership roles for different persons? Is the class participation increasingly harmonious, supportive, accepting of all ideas? Collecting valid answers to these ideas, categorizing them, and filing them for future use are difficult tasks. Some bits of information are filed mentally by the teacher, but an ever-present little notebook is a helpful aid for recording important observations.

Written assignments. The evaluation of daily work done with pencil and paper develops for both pupil and teacher an insight into the effec-

tiveness of teaching and learning. Appraisal of this work is accomplished in two ways: the immediate day-to-day evaluation of each piece of work completed, and the evaluation of accumulated samples of work that gives clues to progressive development. Within the broad evaluation program some trends are apparent that make written assignments more useful as evaluation tools.

One trend exists in the kind of work being assigned. Instead of the repetitious tasks of spelling, handwriting, or arithmetic, that have in the past served drill purposes only, more purposeful and intriguing tasks with unique goals are being assigned. For example, a group of arithmetic problems gives practice in using zero as a place-holder; a report is made to present committee research to the whole class; a letter is written to thank the pilot for his talk to the group. Also, more creative kinds of projects are developed. Long compositions or essays, tedious oral reports and multiple sets of seatwork are avoided. Rather, practical maps and graphs, panels, booklets, or other means are devised for presenting information and for maintaining and developing skills. In other words, "written assignments" tend to be new, different, challenging projects.

Another trend is that the giving of grades or other symbols as a mark of evaluation on completed work is less frequent. Pupil-teacher conferences and cooperative evaluation of work achieve mutual insight into strengths and weaknesses. Also when the teacher evaluates, a brief comment written on the paper is helpful to the pupil when it can cite obvious errors, positive constructive suggestions and complimentary remarks.

As teachers evaluate written work they look for evidences of growth and progress. Is the work adequate to accomplish the purpose? Is the organization clear and concise? Is the handwriting or printing increasingly more legible? Are the ideas presented succinctly and in proper sequence?

Group Evaluation

Because the school has a responsibility to help children learn the values, skills, and social arrangements concerned with working together, and because group work facilitates the learning situation (see Chapter 8), two specific responsibilities lie with the teacher: helping children cooperatively evaluate their group work, and evaluating the growth and learning accomplished by the group as a whole.

In kindergarten and first grade children have many opportunities to work together and evaluate the work cooperatively accomplished. After a work period, for example, the whole group looks around to check the efficiency of the "clean-up" activities. These primary children are given

evaluative experiences almost from the first day of school and as a conclusion to every lesson. As children progress through school the group
evaluation becomes more insightful and more adaptable to mature, democratic group effectiveness.

To guide group activity and foster careful evaluation, the teacher's
first responsibility is to help children plan adequately. Just as his own
evaluative techniques stem from clear-cut goals, so must those of the
children. For primary children the over-all plan may be very general,
and the specifics are worked out day by day. For example, a first grade
group may plan to prepare a garden in the patio. The over-all plan is,
simply, to make a garden. As the project develops, however, the teacher
helps the group think through specific details such as what tools to
gather, how to prepare the soil, the kinds of seeds to procure, how to
plant the seeds, how to care for the growing plants. Each day the group
decides what the task for the day will be; each day the evaluation considers the accomplishment of the task and makes projections for the next
day's activity.

A group of fourth or fifth graders, planning the same type of activity,
will spend more time in the development of over-all plans. These may
include the measurement of the space, development of a planting
design, careful consideration of the materials to be planted. The plans
are probably in writing, and include all decisions: materials to be pro-
cured, responsibilities to be assumed, and a time schedule as a guideline. Daily evaluation of this plan is less specific, for the children are
familiar with the expected sequence of activities.

The organization of plans for group activity requires teacher guidance
at all developmental levels. The teacher helps children consider the ideas
of all members, utilizes the special capabilities of each individual, explores all facets of the problem, keeps the activities at a level that
stretches the abilities of each child but that is also within reach of successful attainment. After plans have been made, and during group activity, the teacher helps the children appraise their work at various
stages. Consideration is made of the ways in which the plans are being
completed or of any modifications of them that are necessary, of the
efficiency of the workers, and of the manner in which responsibility is
assumed.

Another method of guiding group behavior is establishing standards
for behavior. Little children soon learn the skills of thinking together and
producing cooperatively as they develop experience charts in the first
grade. The building of cooperative standards for sharing tools, speaking
before a group, or working in committees is a natural outcome of the experience charts. Some standards may be important enough to record on
charts or in the individual's own record book. Other standards for work-

ing are not recorded but understood by all and discussed only when evaluation of a certain standard is necessary. Standards for group work might be these:

> Understand the task
> Recognize and assume responsibility
> Work quietly and efficiently without disturbing others
> Share information
> Seek help and give help when necessary
> Complete the job

The teacher who has carefully guided the group plans and has built a common understanding with the children about expected behavior has little trouble evaluating group activities. He simply keeps in mind the established goals as he observes or works with the groups. His own evaluation of the level of work must, of course, precede the guidance he gives children in their own group evaluation, therefore he must formulate clearly in his own mind the plans, the procedures, the standards of behavior that he expects of the children. This does not mean that he arbitrarily forces his plans upon the children. He is flexible, but he does have a clearly-thought-through idea of what the goals are to be.

Some factors are evaluated that may not have been discussed with the children. One is the concept of leadership and participation. In groups, several kinds of leadership are manifest, but the leadership often shifts and changes as the activities of the group change. Groups should challenge all individuals to their best thinking and their best work, to performing group roles to the best of their ability, and to "pulling their own weight." Even the slow pupil can be assigned a task in which he is successful or makes some contribution to the efforts of others. The more able student should be challenged and encouraged to do his very best rather than held to a mediocre group level.

The teacher helps children settle conflicts, make decisions, and solve problems in a constructive manner. The ideal interaction of the members is one of cooperative efficiency. With younger children in particular, the teacher's constant evaluation and subsequent guidance are important to the development of more mature dynamics.

Working with groups takes much teacher time, because the teacher confers with groups frequently, strengthens and encourages their action, and helps them to evaluate. He supports them by giving each group adequate recognition and opportunity to communicate with other groups in the class.

Sociometric techniques. Sociometry is a method of appraising the social relationship within a group. By using various sociometric techniques, a teacher can identify leadership, popularity, rejections, friendships, and

cliques within his classroom. Sociometry produces more reliable evidence than informal observation and teacher judgment, because it gets at true peer relationships without the authority role of the teacher as an intermediary.

The most common of the sociometric techniques is the sociogram, the map or chart on which children's preferences are plotted. First the teacher asks a question, such as, "Who would you like to sit next to on the bus?" The children answer by listing three choices of preference. The sociogram is drawn to show first, second, and third choices of each student, and in so doing, the stars, isolates, and near-isolates are determined. Different questions will produce somewhat different patterns of relationships. Generally, younger children's responses will be less stable and change more frequently than will adolescents', but the choices in all groups will change over a period of time.

A second sociometric technique is the social distance scale. With this instrument, the teacher can determine the degree to which a child accepts or rejects all children in the group, and conversely, the degree to which each child is accepted or rejected. The names of all children are listed, then with a social situation in mind, such as "I would like to invite him to my party" or "I'd choose him for my ball team," each child checks names. The number of times one child's name is checked indicates the strength of his acceptance.

A third sociometric technique is the "guess who" questionnaire. In this, the children match their peers with a list of behavioral characteristics, such as, "a big talker," "best thinker." Not only does this identify the way children feel about each other, but it may also shed light on how the child feels about himself in behavioral situations.

Pupil Self-evaluation

The most mature and desirable expression of evaluation, of course, is self-evaluation.

> The child ought to have a positive consciousness of what he is about, and to be able to judge and criticise his respective acts from the standpoint of their reference to the work which he has to do. Only in this way does he have a normal and healthy standard, enabling him properly to appreciate his failures and to estimate them at their right value.[13]

One of the first evidences that children are developing self-evaluation is that they recognize their own problems and seek help from others. In the primary grades, children learn this early. For example, Jim is hav-

---

[13] John Dewey, "Ethical Principles Underlying Education," *Educational Essays* (London: Blackie and Son Limited), p. 36.

ing trouble sawing a piece of wood for the engine of his truck. During the evaluation period he is encouraged to bring his work to the front of the circle. After some discussion, someone suggests to Jim that he use a miter box to help him cut the wood square. Later, he is given the opportunity to show the group the fine square engine that has been nailed to the chassis of the truck. Not only is this a problem solving situation, but Jim is learning to recognize his own problems, solve them with help, and later receive the satisfaction of group approval. As children grow older, the ability to identify a problem is balanced with skills that will help the individual solve the problem more independently. One of the first steps in self-evaluation is the ability to determine what obstacles are in the way of achieving goals.

A technique that encourages self-evaluation is the use of locally prepared rating scales and progress records to evaluate tangible and concrete learning. For example, a handwriting scale is one of the most simple of all self-evaluation tools. The teacher helps children recognize the criteria for good handwriting such as size, spacing, slant, and letter formation in order that individuals may judge their own work according to the scale. A folder containing samples of handwriting taken throughout the year is a satisfying record of achievement. Other types of rating scales may be devised from group standards. For example, children may set up criteria for more effective "share-and-tell" situations. If the scale is entered in the child's notebook, he could at times evaluate himself and through accumulated ratings determine his progress.

Rating Scale for Group Standards

Date	Topic	Speaks clearly?	Watches group?	Answers question?	Comments
October 15	Family picnic	Yes	No	No	Funny
October 29	New book	Yes	Yes		Passed it around

The use of progress records will help to determine an individual's accuracy and rate of progress. For example, when spelling lists are supplemented with words from social studies and other curriculum areas, the development of growth graphs will indicate the number of words tested each week and the number correct. This kind of record-keeping is especially important for more able students who can master more spelling words than usual, and also for less able pupils who study a limited number of words each week. The record will indicate growth and suggest when the list may be lengthened.

Records of books read that are recorded by the child and talked over quietly and privately with the teacher encourage more frequent and more comprehensive recreational reading. Children learn the reasons for noting the title, author, publisher and date included on the record. A good deal of guidance is needed to help children make valid and unique comments about a book, but such comments increase their ability to evaluate the book, and make apparent to the children their own progress in reading.

Progress Record for Reading

Title	Author	Publisher	Date	Comments

Progress Record for Classroom Responsibilities

Job	Dates	Comments
Milk monitor	September 2–7	————
School chorus	Fall semester	Alto part, Christmas program
Read to kinder-garten	May 14	Miss Jones was called out. Fun!

A third evaluative procedure is the pupil-teacher conference, probably the most effective means of helping children evaluate their own behavior and interpret their own progress in learning. The teacher tries to schedule a little time each day when he can sit down with a child or two in a relaxed situation for the purpose of chatting informally in a give-and-take manner about the child's interests, work, and reactions to other aspects of school life. In the intermediate grades, when children can work independently over longer periods of time, conferences are more easily scheduled. However, primary children need the encouragement and support that a private conversation with the teacher can give.

Conferences may cover a myriad of topics, but the teacher makes sure that only one or two topics are discussed at any given conference. The teacher's role in this conference is to help the child understand himself, gain insight into his own academic progress and into his relationships with other children. The teacher helps the child see himself as

others see him; the teacher points out strengths and inadequacies in such a way that there is a realization that progress is taking place.

Other types of self-evaluation may be as varied as the children and the teacher wish. The writing of an autobiography, for example, can be an introspective evaluation. Writing one's own characteristics as others may see him, self-report inventories, and even letters written to parents develop insight into one's behavior and beliefs.

Though many methods of strengthening self-evaluation may be devised some limitations should be recognized. Since children are young and inexperienced, self-evaluation is difficult for them. They need much guidance if self-evaluation is to be objective and helpful rather than frustrating. Self-evaluation may have a negative rather than a positive effect. Some people can become too introspective for their best mental health. It is also wise to remember that most children are likely to be either too critical or too lenient when making judgments about themselves or their peers.

Cumulative Records

The elementary school collects a wide variety of information on each child enrolled. This information is filed in a *cumulative record* to be used by the teachers to better understand the child. The folder form is usually preferred for the cumulative record because of its flexibility of use. Begun when the kindergartener first enters school, the record usually contains not only factual information about the child and his family, but health records, test scores, anecdotes, subject matter progress records, unit experiences, and activity lists. The nature and amount of material filed reflects the value placed upon the record. Some folders are frequently used and others are not. "To be of maximum value, they should be transferred with the student as he progresses from grade to grade and from school to school."[14]

Identifying data. Almost all folders include identifying data completed when the child enters school. Name, address, date and place of birth, age at entrance, school and district from which transferred (if applicable) are some of the items used. Now that the practice of taking pictures in school is so prevalent, many schools provide spaces for individual pictures that are added from time to time as the child grows older.

Home and family background. Supplementing the identifying data is a section in the folder related to home and family background. Here are entered the names of the mother and father, occupations of each, names and ages of siblings, with additional spaces provided so that changes in

---

[14] California State Department of Education, *op. cit.*, p. 158.

family status may be entered. Also included are data related to socio-economic background and religious or national background.

Health record. Frequently filed with the cumulative record, but on a separate card for the convenience of the nurse or doctor, is the health record. These data include height and weight changes, results of vision and hearing tests, posture tests, and other special examinations. Also there is a record of illnesses, physical disabilities, or other health problems.

Anecdotal records. Anecdotes become a most valuable means of appraising child behavior and objectifying observation. These are the purely factual, unjudged descriptions of critical incidents that occur during the years at school. Because of time limitations, teachers cannot collect anecdotes on all children, but only on a few "hard to handle" children.

To make anecdotes useful, teachers need to write up the incident immediately after it occurs, date it, and place it in the folder. If other incidents relating to the first follow, they are also recorded and filed. Important to the use of this evaluative tool is the ability of the teacher to determine what incidents are significant in the child's development and to write them accurately and factually.

An example of an anecdote might be: "Jimmy for the first time led the rhythm orchestra today." Or, "During committee work this afternoon John and Tom had a quarrel. Other members of the committee reported that John had made a suggestion for the map, but that Tom would not let him work it out." These anecdotes, together with others, may point to characteristics of Jimmy's shyness, or Tom's aggressiveness. On the other hand, if these anecdotes are not related to others in an accumulated group, the characteristics indicated may not be of great importance.

Anecdotes should be both positive and negative. That is, not only unacceptable behavior is described, but also unusually good behavior. All anecdotes should be descriptions of out-of-the-ordinary behavior or of most typical behavior. Cumulative series of anecdotes reveal a child's pattern of behavior, and may give the teacher cues for further child guidance.

Activity records. Also useful over a period of time are records of individual children's activities. It seems useful to list carefully all the basic reading books a child has completed. The social studies or science units completed by children are also helpful in determining the over-all experiences of a group. Special school activities such as participation in a choral group or orchestra, the Christmas play, or special sport activities will add to the general picture of interests and abilities of an individual that a cumulative record builds.

Work samples. Carefully selected samples of work that show growth

or particular strengths or weaknesses are sometimes included in the folder. Teachers must be very careful that the samples filed will be of real value in a developmental picture.

Records of parent-teacher conferences. Schools that schedule regular parent-teacher conferences frequently have an outline to direct the discussion. Copies of these outlines placed in the cumulative folder will reveal not only the progress of the learner but the developmental relationship of parent to teacher and the cooperation of the family with the school.

The school's use of the cumulative folder. The cumulative folder is a professional record, and should be treated as such. Folders filed in the classroom where they are easily accessible encourage more frequent and more practical use. Care is taken that the records are kept up-to-date. Teachers or others may make pertinent entries during the year, but at the end of the year one of the teacher's final responsibilities is to make the entries necessary so that next year's teacher will have a complete record of each child.

Familiarity with all the records of a group of children will give many clues to a teacher. He will gain insights into the background, experience, and strengths and weaknesses of the group as a whole. He will note special interests, abilities, and problems of individual children. He will find clues as to what books he may use, how to group children for both achievement and interest. He will find guides for expectations, the learning level at which to begin, and special notes about individuals that will give greater insight into their behavior. Only one caution is necessary, and this is that one does not let the past record influence too rigidly one's attitude toward a child. However, just as a physician refers to a patient's past medical record, so the teacher can make technical use of the child's past educational record.

REPORTING PUPIL PROGRESS

Perhaps the most important part of the evaluation program in terms of school and community relationships is the manner in which parents are informed about school activities and individual progress. Communication with parents becomes a vital part of the public relations program, because the parents themselves can be one of the most influential community pressure groups. Satisfied parents are necessary to a successful school.

Reporting to parents is not as simple as sending home a report card or telephoning a mother once in a while. The school wages a constant campaign to educate parents so that they really understand the school's purposes. How activities contribute to over-all goals, why special emphases

are made, what school symbols such as marks mean, and other educational concepts that may be unfamiliar to parents need to be demonstrated and explained.

There are a number of reasons why parents may not understand school methods and procedures. Today we have a mobile population; parents may be living in a community far different from the one in which they went to school. We have learned much about child development and the process of learning that has changed the atmosphere and environment of a school. Because the school environment is different from that of their own experience, parents may not understand it.

Families may also hold dear traditions and beliefs that are different from those emphasized in schools.

Teachers usually are middle class in status, and they tend to teach middle-class values. On the other hand, they work with children and parents from all socioeconomic levels who hold varying values. Parental attitudes in regard to honesty, cleanliness, "book-learning," and a host of other matters complicate the teacher's task. The kinds of discipline the parents administer, the educational advantages they provide, and the expectations they hold for their children have an effect on the learning that takes place in school. Familial behavior patterns such as the use of speech and gestures are brought to school by children and increase their differences in the classroom. When parents use less accepted forms of speech, children employ these practices and learn correct usage with great difficulty.

The school is an agency of the community, and its responsibility is to provide education that will best prepare children for their life now and in the future. Therefore the school must not only inform the community of its plans and procedures, but it must also be sensitive to the changes taking place in the community that will influence the goals and curriculum of the school. The program for reporting to or, rather, communicating with the parents may in part serve the function of finding out about social and cultural changes, as well as about the desires and aspirations of the community members for their children.

Reporting to parents, then, should be a give-and-take proposition in which child accomplishment is assimilated and considered by members of the school staff and the people it serves. Careful examination of such devices as marks, report cards, parent-teacher conferences, and other methods of home-school communication will make the reporting of evaluation more effective.

Grading and Marks

Marks, grades, or other single symbols of appraisal have long been recognized as ineffective. Grades are in reality a superficial, impractical

assignment of status or reward. What machinist is graded ''C'' on the tool he turns out with his lathe? What doctor tells you you are in ''B'' health after a physical examination? What secretary gets 72 per cent for a letter typed? The point is, can a secretary produce a neat, accurate letter in a minimum amount of time? Does a child actually know how to spell the words he needs, or subtract the amount of the check from the bank balance?

What does a ''B'' mean? What is the difference between a ''B'' and a ''C''? Does a ''B'' mean the same thing to a business executive father as it does to a plumber father? How does a ''B'' differentiate between a superior, average, or slow student? What is the difference between 72 per cent as passing and 69 per cent that does not pass? Do these numerical figures indicate quality or amount of learning that has taken place? What *is* satisfactory achievement? Because the answers to these questions are nebulous, there has been a good deal of concern about marks used as evaluation symbols in the elementary school.

In order to understand educational growth, any changes in progress as well as strengths and weaknesses of child achievement need to be understood. Also an arbitrary starting point serving as a basis for ''growth'' needs to be defined. The points at which the child needs improvement, and the next steps assuring that improvement, should be described. A ''B'' or any other single score gives only a partial picture, does not make the distinctions mentioned above. Also, any symbol such as ''C,'' ''S,'' or ''✔,'' may mean different things in different schools, among different teachers, or indeed, among different children and their parents. Because of these inadequacies of the traditional marking system, modifications in the format of report cards and the recent prominence of teacher-parent conferences are promising trends.

Report Cards

Report cards have been the traditional vehicle for reporting academic progress to parents. Even now many parents resist abolishing the formal card with numerical or letter grades because it is a familiar way of reporting. Disagreement on form has caused many school districts to reexamine their cards. Many modifications have been made so that today the organization and content of report cards differs greatly among districts.

Most report cards are attempting to report a more comprehensive analysis of total growth. Items have been added to describe more than academic achievement. Differentiation between skills and ability, analysis of performance, effort, and work habits have been attempted in various ways. Types of multiple evaluation on some cards give marks according to comparative achievement as well as the pupil's own growth. Single

checks under headings as superior, good, fair, and poor attempt to report progress in personal-social behaviors. Frequently the report card
is "personalized" by providing space for narrative comments by the
teacher.

In spite of the many efforts to improve report cards, some basic problems remain. The new symbols still tend to compare achievement with
that of others on a two-point to five-point scale. Items varying
from subject matter areas, such as courtesy, industry, and cooperation,
are new to parents and need careful definition. It is difficult to indicate
on formal report cards an individual's differing potentialities in the
various fields of learning. Cards cannot provide enough space for the
descriptive reporting that seems to be most desirable.

The promising trend is that report cards are gradually being replaced
by other forms of reporting. It will probably be a long time before they
are entirely eliminated, but if more effective types of descriptive analysis
can be given parents, the formal report card will then be used to support
understandings about their child's education that have been gained
from the other methods.

Parent-Teacher Conferences

Conferences with parents are perhaps the most effective means of reporting pupil progress. Frequently, conferences are scheduled to supplement the formal report card, for the conference enables the teacher
to talk about growth and show tangible evidences of it. Here is the opportunity to present to parents data from many kinds of evaluation
devices and to discuss the total growth of the child, rather than a
limited segment of school activities. In this face-to-face situation, tone
of voice, expression, choice of words, and over-all attitude help both
teacher and parent understand each other. The informal situation encourages comments and questions by both teacher and parent, and thus
assures mutual understanding, cooperation, personal interchange of
ideas, work toward sharing responsibility for accomplishment, and the
solution of problems in the education of the child.

Preliminary to the individual parent-teacher conferences in some
schools, group conferences are arranged shortly after the new school
year begins in the fall. All parents are invited to meet the teacher in the
classroom where the children work, and during the meeting parents and
teacher become acquainted. The teacher points out the objectives of the
school, his particular interpretation of those objectives for this class of
children, as well as a description of the behaviors that would demonstrate the achievement of objectives. In describing these expectations,
the teacher may also show and talk about the materials to be used, the

kinds of activities to be provided, and something of his classroom routine and homework policies. Also he discusses the methods he plans to use in appraising the learning that takes place. Informal group discussion at this meeting serves to clarify over-all expectations for the school year and clears the way for the teacher conferences.

The trend has been to schedule more than one individual conference with parents during the school year. In some cases, when formal report cards are also used, two conferences are adequate. The ideal situation is one where both parents meet the teacher at the same time, and some schools include the child in a three-way conference. In any event, the conferences are scheduled with all parents so that the positive approach will be understood.

The planning for parent-teacher conferences varies widely. When the parents find the teacher in the classroom at the appointed time, the teacher usually has a plan to follow. Sometimes an outline of the plans is worked out cooperatively by the school faculty so that some uniformity takes place in the conferences. Also the plan helps the teacher cover all the basic points, because frequently an informal conversation can wander from the basic purpose of the conference. The teacher has decided upon a few basic ideas that focus upon the child, and has gathered together samples of work, test data, anecdotes, and the results of all other evaluation devices to illustrate to the parent the direction of the child's growth. He and the parents talk together to gain further insight into the child's various potentialities, limitations, and progress. During the conference the parents have an opportunity to raise questions and present problems. As the discussion progresses, the teacher will gain better understanding of the home relations, the parental aspirations for the child.

The conference is concluded by the teacher with a short summary of the evaluation that has been made. In some cases, when the teacher has followed a preplanned outline, the teacher and parent review it together, then both sign the dated statement so that it may go into the cumulative folder.

Though the parent-teacher conference is one of the most promising methods of reporting comprehensively and accurately to parents, some problems about it remain to be solved. One is that teachers need some training to maintain good rapport with parents, interpret satisfactorily the evaluation data for the parents, and determine the most appropriate aspects of learning to cover at one conference. Schools working to develop an effective parent-teacher conference program work cooperatively in faculty meetings, workshops, and with supervisors to accomplish this training.

Another very real problem exists in the amount of time necessary for conferences. In order to facilitate the scheduling of conferences, some schools arrange minimum school days or hire substitutes so that the teacher may have the time necessary to prepare for and execute them.

It has been found that most parents are eager to meet appointments for these conferences; the problem of getting the parents to school is not too great. The time selected to make the appointments varies according to the work responsibilities of the parents. Some teachers schedule early morning or evening appointments for working parents. In other schools where the time schedules of parents are more flexible, afternoon appointments can be arranged.

Other Means of Communication with Parents

Report cards and parent-teacher conferences do not represent the sole means of communication between the school and the family. To report best the continuous progress of the child, his accomplishments and his problems, his activities in school and his relationships with others in the school, the periodic issue of cards or schedule of conferences is not enough. Telephone calls, bulletins, letters, and home and school visits are also ways in which the teacher communicates upon occasion with the parents. These devices become part of the teacher's planning and part of the ongoing evaluation of his program.

Letters and bulletins. Written bulletins, handbooks, letters, and notices from the school staff to the parents seek to develop the best working relationships. Parents are informed in simple and friendly terms on matters of policy, routine, and special events. Information is included about individuals and special groups. Parents welcome and enjoy such bulletins when they are carefully prepared, contain real and vital information, and are not received too frequently. Involving some parents in the production of the bulletins may also increase the parent interest.

Individual teachers may supplement the formal school bulletins with written papers, pictures, and notebooks, and in this way help parents understand what is being accomplished. The teacher makes sure, however, that any papers taken home show evidence of careful supervision and guidance, such as correction of spelling and grammar, teacher notes of encouragement, and helpful comments for improvement.

Visiting schools. Part of successful communication is observation in schools by parents and other community residents. Parents of all children are urged to visit, with and without formal invitations. Usually teachers are available for designated periods before and after school, and parents should be informed that these are the best times to talk

with them; visits during the day will then be observational visits. Classroom visits do not have to be long or formally arranged. A mother who sometimes brings a lunch to school for her child will thereby accumulate an impression by the occasional glimpses of classroom procedure she notices. The point is to get the parent to the school when there is not a problem, when the program progresses normally, when an honest picture of school life can be observed.

Parent-Teacher Associations and parent groups that meet at the school help to bring people to the center of educational activity. Here teachers may meet parents and talk not only about child progress but about educational topics of common interest. An organized Public Schools Week usually encourages large numbers of visitors. Care is taken that such an annual affair does not become an exhibit of the year's art materials rather than the normal presentation of school activities.

Home visits. The busy life of the schoolteacher does not allow much time for visits to the home. Home visits can, however, facilitate the reporting of pupil progress and give the teacher the best insight into the personal side of the child's life. Though regularly scheduled home visits are not the rule, their usefulness cannot be denied, and occasional visits about important matters may be planned. Teachers of primary children feel them so helpful that many, particularly kindergarten teachers, make the effort to visit as many homes as possible.

The happy child. Probably the most important factor to successful home-school relationships is the happy child. Impressions of the school and the education it is providing are first formed by the remarks made at the dinner table, by the snatches of conversation overheard by parents, by the eagerness about school that the child exhibits. The child who is growing and learning according to his own powers and who goes home with happy tales of productive activity gives many clues to his own progress.

Very young children in the kindergarten or first grade are likely to develop an affection for the teacher that may be misunderstood at home if parents do not know and understand the teacher. This is another reason why the teacher should seek to become acquainted with the parents so that he may assure them that the school relationship is not a substitute for the home relationship.

REFERENCES

Ahmann, J. Stanley, and Marvin D. Glock. *Evaluating Pupil Growth.* Boston: Allyn and Bacon, Inc., 1959.
  Careful analysis of evaluation problems in both elementary and secondary schools, including testing and nontesting procedures.

Ahmann, J. Stanley, Marvin D. Glock, and Helen Wardeberg. *Evaluating Elementary School Pupils*. Boston: Allyn and Bacon, Inc., 1960.
>   A new textbook on elementary school evaluation, including grading and marks.

Baron, Denis, and Harold W. Bernard. *Evaluation Techniques for Classroom Teachers*. New York: McGraw-Hill Book Company, 1958.
>   A general text on measurement and evaluation.

California State Department of Education. *Evaluating Pupil Progress*. Bulletin Volume 21 No. 6. Sacramento: California State Department of Education, April 1952.
>   Simple and explicit presentation of all aspects of evaluation in the elementary school.

Cunningham, Ruth, and others. *Understanding Group Behavior of Boys and Girls*. New York: Bureau of Publications, Teachers College, Columbia University, 1951.
>   Still a well-reputed book that discusses how children behave in groups.

Furst, Edward J. *Constructing Evaluation Instruments*. New York: Longmans, Green and Company, 1958.
>   General text presenting evaluation as an integral part of instruction. Gives good details for constructing tests.

Horace-Mann–Lincoln School Institute of Experimentation. *How to Construct a Sociogram*. New York: Bureau of Publications, Teachers College, Columbia University, 1948.
>   Careful directions for constructing a sociogram.

Jennings, Helen H. *Sociometry in Group Relations*. Washington, D.C.: American Council on Education, 1948.
>   A unique presentation of child relationships as revealed through sociometry.

Langford, Louise. *Guidance of the Young Child*. New York: John Wiley and Sons, Inc., 1960.
>   A new book with helpful suggestions for teachers of young children.

Noll, Victor H. *Introduction to Educational Measurement*. Boston: Houghton Mifflin Company, 1959.
>   A general textbook on educational tests and measurement.

Sarason, Seymour B., and others. *Anxiety in Elementary School Children: A Report of Research*. New York: John Wiley and Sons, Inc., 1960.
>   Another approach to the study of children.

Shane, Harold G., and Eldridge T. McSwain. *Evaluation and the Elementary Curriculum* (Revised edition). New York: Henry Holt and Company, 1958.
>   Emphasizes the appraisal of curriculum and educational opportunities for children.

Thomas, R. Murray. *Judging Student Progress* (Second edition). New York: Longmans, Green and Company, 1960.
>   A comprehensive overview of tests and measurements.

White, Verna. *Studying the Individual Pupil*. New York: Harper & Brothers, 1958.
>   Helpful suggestions for methods of gathering and interpreting data, as well as cautions against misinterpretations.

INDEX